THE OXFORD HISTORY OF

WESTERN MUSIC

THE OXFORD HISTORY OF WESTERN MUSIC

THE OXFORD HISTORY OF

WESTERN

MUSIC

Richard Taruskin

Volume 3

THE NINETEENTH CENTURY

OXFORD
UNIVERSITY PRESS
2005

OXFORD
UNIVERSITY PRESS

Oxford   New York

Auckland   Bangkok   Buenos Aires   Cape Town   Chennai
Dar es Salaam   Delhi   Hong Kong   Istanbul   Karachi   Kolkata
Kuala Lumpur   Madrid   Melbourne   Mexico City   Mumbai   Nairobi
São Paulo   Shanghai   Taipei   Tokyo   Toronto

Copyright © 2005 by Oxford University Press, Inc.

Published by Oxford University Press, Inc.

198 Madison Avenue, New York, New York 10016

http://www.oup.com/us

Oxford is a registered trademark of Oxford University Press

Library of Congress Cataloging-in-Publication Data

Taruskin, Richard.

The Oxford history of western music / by Richard Taruskin.

p. cm.

Includes bibliographical references and index.

ISBN 0-19-516979-4

1. Music — History and criticism. I. Title.

ML160.T18 2004

780'.9 — dc22

2004017897

ISBN Vol. 1   0-19-522270-9
ISBN Vol. 2   0-19-522271-7
ISBN Vol. 3   0-19-522272-5
ISBN Vol. 4   0-19-522273-3
ISBN Vol. 5   0-19-522274-1
ISBN Vol. 6   0-19-522275-X

1   3   5   7   9   8   6   4   2

Printed in the United States of America

Contents of Volume 3

THE OXFORD HISTORY OF

WESTERN MUSIC

Real Worlds, and Better Ones

BEETHOVEN VS. ROSSINI; BEL CANTO ROMANTICISM

DEEDS OF MUSIC

In only one area did Beethoven fail to exert a transforming influence on the music of his time, and that was opera. *Fidelio*, his single operatic venture, initially a flop, was revised so often and so extensively that three distinct versions and no fewer than four overtures for it survive. As if recognizing that his talent suffered a limitation where the theater was concerned, Beethoven concentrated thereafter on composing "incidental music" for dramatic plays.

The overture to *Coriolan* (Ex. 32-4), meant to be performed before the curtain went up on Collin's tragedy, was his first essay of this kind. The complete performance of the play no doubt included more music by other composers in the form of entr'actes (music to fill up the time it took to change the scenery), music to accompany silent stage action (chiefly fights and duels), "melodramas" (lofty declamation to musical accompaniment) for the main characters, and perhaps some little songs and choruses for minor characters.

In 1810 Goethe's historical tragedy *Egmont*, about a Flemish general and statesman whose political martyrdom sparked the revolt of the Low Countries against Spain, was performed with a complete incidental score by Beethoven. The Overture is in F minor, which with Beethoven was a kind of intensified C minor — compare his Piano Sonata, op. 57 (called the "Appassionata"), the String Quartet, op. 95 (called the "Serioso"), and so on. One of Beethoven's most characteristically heroic orchestral works, the *Egmont* Overture plays out the *Kampf-und-Sieg* scenario to the very hilt. The brief but boisterous F-major coda in military style seems to compress the whole effect of the Fifth Symphony finale into a couple of coruscating minutes; it was reprised at the end of the play as the "Siegessymphonie" — the Victory Symphony.

Two years later, two plays by August von Kotzebue (1761–1819), the most popular dramatist of the time and a notoriously reactionary politician, were staged with incidental scores by Beethoven to inaugurate the National Theater in Pest, the administrative seat of the Hungarian provinces. One was an exercise in exoticism: *Die Ruinen von Athen* ("The ruins of athens"), from which a "Turkish March" and a chorus of whirling dervishes became great concert favorites. The other was a somewhat ambiguous exercise in nationalism: *König Stephan* ("King Stephen"), about the semilegendary founder of the Hungarian nation, who formed Hungary's first alliance with the German-speaking

F I G. 33-I   Beethoven's *Fidelio*, lunette by Moritz von Schwind (1804–1871) in the foyer of the Vienna State Opera.

lands. It, too, features victory music, but the victory it celebrated was a thinly veiled celebration of Hungary's submission to Germany.

The ill-favored opera, toward salvaging which Beethoven labored all through the period of his incidental music, started out as *Leonore, oder Der Triumph der ehelichen Liebe* ("Leonora, or the triumph of conjugal love"), on words translated and adapted by the court librettist Joseph von Sonnleithner, assisted by a whole committee of Beethoven's friends, from a famous libretto by Jean-Nicolas Bouilly dating from 1798. The libretto exemplified a genre that became something of a craze after the French revolution. Modern scholars have christened it the "rescue opera," a loose, anachronistic term that covers many situations. In general, though, French *opéras comiques* (operas with spoken dialogue and happy endings) in the decades surrounding the Revolution symbolized the theme of social emancipation in stories that portrayed an unjust abduction or imprisonment (usually at the hands of a tyrant) and a liberation, usually as the result of sacrifice — by lover, spouse, or servant, but in any case by a "common person" whose virtue is contrasted with the depravity of the tyrant.

The chief composers of rescue operas on their native soil were André Grétry (1741–1813), whose *Richard Coeur-de-Lion* ("Richard the Lionhearted," 1782) launched the genre and provided an early example of a motto melody that returned at significant points throughout the drama; Étienne-Nicolas Méhul (1763–1817) with *Euphrosine, ou Le Tyran corrigé* ("Euphrosine, or the Tyrant Rebuked," 1790); Rodolphe Kreutzer (1766–1831), with *Lodoïska* (1791), which combined the liberation motif with Polish patriotism; and especially the transplanted Italian Luigi Cherubini (1760–1842), with another *Lodoïska* in the same year, and with many more rescue operas to follow. The first composer to set Bouilly's *Léonore, ou L'amour conjugal* was the otherwise unimportant Pierre Gaveaux (1760–1825), for performance in Paris in 1798. Thereafter it was set twice in Italian by composers well known to Beethoven: Ferdinando Paer (as *Leonora, ossia L'amore conjugale*; Dresden, 1804) and Simon Mayr (as *L'amor coniugale*; Padua, 1805). Paer's score was in Beethoven's library at the time of his death, and contains some conspicuous parallels with Beethoven's setting.

The basic story line of this much-traveled and much-translated libretto, set in a fictionalized Spain, was a virtual paradigm of the rescue formula. Here it is, as summarized by the opera historian Scott Balthazar, with the names of the characters, and their voice ranges, adapted to Beethoven's setting:

> Leonore (soprano), disguised as the boy Fidelio, has apprenticed herself to the jailer Rocco (bass), hoping to free her husband Don Florestan (tenor), who has been unjustly imprisoned for two years by his enemy Don Pizarro (bass-baritone). Pizarro learns that his superior, Don Fernando (bass), who is unaware of his treachery, will arrive the next day. Fearing a reprisal, Pizarro orders Rocco to arrange for Florestan's murder by a masked man (to be Pizarro himself) and permits Leonore to be present at the scene. Before Pizarro can kill Florestan, Leonore intervenes, long enough for Fernando to arrive and rescue her husband. Rocco is pardoned and Pizarro imprisoned.[1]

Sonnleithner's adaptation of this simple plot for Beethoven complicated and extended it with subplots for minor characters (such as Marzelline, Rocco's daughter, who has fallen in love with "Fidelio"), so that Bouilly's swift two-act play became a slow-moving and fairly shapeless three-acter, which probably accounts for its initial failure. *Leonore* closed after three unenthusiastically received performances in November 1805 (ironically enough, during Napoleon's occupation of Vienna; the audience consisted largely of French officers). A slightly shortened revision failed again in 1806, whereupon Beethoven radically scaled the work back and replaced several of the remaining items with shorter, more forceful alternatives. Leonore's large aria — "Komm, Hoffnung," or "Come to me, O Hope" — near the end of act I, for example, was furnished with a very intense accompanied recitative addressed to Pizarro: "Abscheulicher! Wo eilst du hin?" ("Despicable man! Where are you rushing off to?").

The new version, now titled *Fidelio* to distinguish it from its predecessors, has been a repertory item ever since its premiere at the Vienna Kärntnertor Theater on 23 May 1814. One of the reasons for its staying power is surely the fact that it at last allowed Beethoven to play to his strengths. The short second act, beginning with the imprisoned Florestan's recitative and aria (his first appearance) and ending with a jubilant choral finale in praise of Leonore's steadfastness, embodies yet another permutation of the basic dark-to-light scenario we have already traced from Haydn's *Creation* into several of Beethoven's instrumental works. Here it could be made more explicit than ever, not only by the presence of words, but by the use of actual stage lighting and scenery.

Beethoven recognized the congruence between the reshaped libretto and his trusty heroic trajectory, and took steps to abet it. The only second-act items in the 1806 version of the opera that were significantly revised for the 1814 performance were the first and the last, and both were revised to make more vivid the contrast of dark and light as emancipatory metaphor. Florestan's recitative and aria, "Gott! welch dunkel hier!" ("O God, what darkness here!"), is preceded by an orchestral introduction containing some of the "darkest" music Beethoven ever wrote. It resembles the beginning of the *Coriolan* Overture, except that the unisons are played softly (as if emanating from a remote place) and, as already mentioned, it is plunged one degree deeper into the dark flat region of the circle of fifths, to F minor. In pointed contrast, the C-major Finale begins with the chorus of townsfolk and prisoners praising the day ("Heil sei dem Tag!") in bright colors intensified, as in the Fifth Symphony and the *Egmont* Overture, by the addition of a piccolo to the orchestra.

The darkness and harshness of the introduction to Florestan's aria are underscored by a number of well-understood conventions, including the hoary *passus duriusculus*, the chromatically descending bass with a history that extends back to the passacaglias and ciacconas of the sixteenth century. A more modern, indeed almost prophetic touch is the tuning of the timpani to a tritone, E♭ and A, on which discordant notes the drums beat out a jarring tattoo during long-sustained diminished seventh chords. The stabbing woodwind phrases that follow have an uncanny vocal quality — cries in the dark (Ex. 33-1a). They are answered, as it were, by Florestan's own opening cry — "Gott! welch dunkel hier!" ("Oh God, what darkness here!") — one of the truly bloodcurdling moments in opera (Ex. 33-1b).

EX. 33-1A   Ludwig van Beethoven, *Fidelio* in vocal score, no. 11 (Florestan, introduction and aria, mm. 14–20)

Just as the musical artifices in the introduction are Janus-faced, linking past and future, so the aria has two stanzas that play on the same dramatic contrast. The first, in A♭ (the relative major), is a reminiscence of the past, in which youthful freedom is contrasted with present slavery by the use of a sudden modulation to the pathetically fraught key of the flat mediant (C♭). The second, in F (the parallel major), was added to the aria for the 1814 revival. It foreshadows the metaphorical coming of day, as much by the use of the concertante solo oboe in its highest register as by the words that predict as a dream of heavenly immortality the events that are about to unfold in real life.

The Finale testifies to the opera's descent, for all its seriousness and its high ethical tone, from the comic operas of the eighteenth century, with their complicated "chain finales" in which continuous music underscores and reflects the dramatic action. It is constructed very much like a symphonic movement, with significant departures from and returns to stable tonalities. An opening march and chorus are followed by Don Fernando's accompanied recitative, which maintains the C-major tonality as the words explicitly evoke the "stripping off of night." Then, while Florestan is brought up from the dungeon out into the sun, the tonality begins to modulate flatward, as if Florestan's dark key were accompanying him, only to be dispelled as Don Fernando recognizes the prisoner.

The reuniting of Florestan and Leonore takes place in the warmly gleaming key of A major, which darkens momentarily into its relative minor as the crowd vents its wrath on Pizarro. The moment in which Leonore, at Don Fernando's behest, actually unlocks her husband's chains is set, as if in fulfillment of Florestan's dream, in the dream key of F major, approached as a deceptive cadence from the dominant of A. All that

EX. 33-1B   Ludwig van Beethoven, *Fidelio* in vocal score, mm. 33–41

remains now is for the assembled characters and chorus to celebrate the reuniting of the pair, and Leonore's steadfastness, in a concluding blast of C major that reaches its peak of energy (Presto molto) in a veritable *Siegessymphonie*, colored every now and then with a little dab of B♭ harmony just so that it can be dispelled again and the modulation into the bright clarity of C major reenacted (Ex. 33-2).

So powerful is the tonal trajectory of the second act of *Fidelio*, and so practiced and surefooted Beethoven's enactment of it, that one can fairly regard it as the "nub and kernel, preceding all form,"[2] to quote Schopenhauer, the reality that underlies the

EX. 33-2   Ludwig van Beethoven, *Fidelio*, Act II finale

dramatic action and gives it life. This is what Richard Wagner, who saw himself equally as Beethoven's heir and Schopenhauer's, would later try to summarize in his famous definition of "music drama" — *deeds of music made visible*.[3]

Is the music in an opera a supplement to — or metaphor for — the action and emotion portrayed? Or are the action and emotion portrayed a metaphor for the underlying life force in which we all participate, of which music is the most direct and palpable embodiment we can ever know on earth, hence prior to all reason and representation? The latter, of course, is the true romantic (or at least the true German) answer — the answer that boggled the nineteenth-century mind and crowned instrumental music, of which Beethoven remained the preeminent master even when writing opera, as the supreme artistic medium.

THE DIALECTICAL ANTITHESIS

All these heady considerations notwithstanding, *Fidelio* had a negligible impact on the operatic culture of its time, nor did Beethoven loom very large in the consciousness of the theater-going public. Within that world, within that consciousness, and within Beethoven's own career, the work was something of an aberration. Its pedigree was decidedly off the main operatic line, which remained Italian or at least Italianate. So it would remain, arguably, for another hundred years, or as long as opera retained its cultural potency. In this sense, at least, Beethoven did not come anywhere near "receiving Mozart's spirit." To claim, as many (beginning with Wagner) have done, that Beethoven's impact on opera came belatedly, through Wagner, is to regard Wagner as in some sense Beethoven's direct or ordained successor. As we shall see, there were many claimants to that title.

The man who did inherit the Mozartean operatic legacy (albeit not "from the hands of Haydn") was cast immediately — and in terms that resonated far beyond the confines of the opera house — as Beethoven's opponent, his rival, or (to use the language of German philosophy), his dialectical antithesis. In Gioacchino Rossini, the hardy pre-romantic temper survived into the romantic age, and thrived to the point where even Raphael Georg Kiesewetter (1773–1850), an Austrian nobleman who in 1834 published the first scholarly history of music in German (thus becoming the first "musicologist" in the present-day sense of the term), found he had to title his concluding chapter not "The Age of Beethoven," as national pride might have prompted him to do, but (somewhat grudgingly) "The Age of Beethoven and Rossini." This is well worth pointing out because a century and a half later, in 1982, the eighth

FIG. 33-2   Gioacchino Rossini, in a photograph taken long after his retirement.

volume of the authoritative and impeccably scholarly *New Oxford History of Music* was issued, its title page emblazoned "The Age of Beethoven, 1790–1830." The only apology came in the form of an editorial introduction, which began, "The title of no other volume of the *New Oxford History of Music* includes the name of a composer. But no other period of musical history is so completely dominated by one composer."[4] Nobody during the period in question would have agreed with that statement. The word "history" in the second sentence should obviously have been replaced by "modern historiography." A historiography of early nineteenth-century music that allows itself to be completely dominated by Beethoven is one that has deliberately read his antithesis out of the canon.

Kiesewetter's recognition of Rossini as a counterweight to Beethoven is first of all an acknowledgment of opera's continuing importance, indeed its dominance, among musical genres, which accounts for Rossini's dominance among composers. As the Rossini scholar Philip Gossett has emphatically stated, "no composer in the first half of the nineteenth century enjoyed the measure of prestige, wealth, popular acclaim or artistic influence that belonged to Rossini."[5] But Kiesewetter's recognition of Rossini can also be taken as an indication that German nationalism had not yet reached its most aggressive and intolerant phase. (For one of the dogmas of German nationalism, as we have already seen, was that "prestige, wealth, and popular acclaim" are inimical to true artistic values, which lie entirely within the artist and are vouchsafed to every artist by his national patrimony.)

Nationalism, in the modern sense, was as much, and as importantly, a creation of the nineteenth century as was historiography. Indeed, neither concept can be understood except in terms of the other. Modern historiography was the product of nationalism, and modern nationalism was crucially supported by modern historiography. This nexus will be an important subtext to all the nineteenth-century chapters that follow, not only those that deal with it overtly. Hence this little digression. Like anything else when viewed historically, Kiesewetter's title tells us more than it told its contemporaries.

At the time Kiesewetter wrote, Beethoven had been dead for several years, but Rossini was still very much alive. And yet, as Kiesewetter may have known, both their careers were over, even though Rossini still had more than thirty years of life ahead of him.

Rossini was born on 29 February 1792 in the central Italian town of Pesaro on the Adriatic, then part of what were known as the Roman or Papal States, ruled directly by the Holy See. His father was a professional horn player in local bands, his mother a soprano. By the age of thirteen, the future composer was already appearing as a boy singer in operatic performances. He was sent the next year to the Liceo Musicale in Bologna for as well-rounded a traditional musical education as could then be had anywhere in the world. He wrote his first opera the year after that.

A lucky break in 1810 landed the eighteen-year-old Rossini a contract with the Teatro San Moisè in Venice, and during the next eighteen years he would compose under contract some thirty-eight operas for houses all over Italy and eventually abroad, for a career average of better than two a year. Naturally, the frequency was at its greatest at the beginning, and became sparser near the end, when the composer commanded greater compensation and was no longer so driven by material need. Many of the early operas were composed in a month or less. The contract for *Il barbiere di Siviglia* ("The barber of Seville"), perhaps Rossini's masterpiece and surely his most famous work both then and now, was signed on 15 December 1815. The first performance took place on 20 February 1816. Composition could not have begun immediately after signing, since another opera of Rossini's (a now-forgotten rescue opera called *Torvaldo e Dorliska*) was nearing its hectic premiere, which took place on 26 December. During the eight weeks that remained the new opera had not only to be composed, but also copied, designed, and rehearsed. The actual writing probably occupied three weeks at most.

These facts and figures bear eloquent testimony to the conditions under which Rossini, like all composers for the Italian commercial stage, then worked. Italian operatic life was a maelstrom of commissions, revivals, revisions, triumphs, fiascos, and pastiches, in which composers worked as part of a team with a theater impresario, a librettist, and a performing staff. His product, like any commercial product, was subject to all kinds of exigencies and prerogatives once it left his hands, with the result that, as Gossett puts it, "an Italian opera in the first half of the nineteenth century," and no matter how distinguished the composer, "was treated as a collection of individual units that could be rearranged, substituted or omitted depending on local conditions of performance, local taste or, on many occasions, whim."[6] Nor did only impresarios and singers so treat it. Composers' attitudes were no different. Rossini reused a duet from his first opera in five subsequent works. The very famous overture to *Il barbiere* was borrowed wholesale from a previous opera that had flopped.

It was a kind of factory system, the economy in which Rossini flourished — music's industrial revolution. It was centered not on scores but on performances, and so the central figures in the musical economy were the performers, and among performers the *prima donna* (leading lady) above all — which is how the term acquired the meaning it now has, applied to persons of either sex who expect others to cater to their every whim.

Needless to say, no composer could afford to act like a prima donna. Nobody was about to treat a mere hired hand with that sort of deference. His was essentially a service role. Like the librettist's, his primary aim was to please — the impresario, the singers, and (finally and most importantly) the paying public. He regarded his activity as a career, not a calling. Often enough he did not even get to choose his subject, and only rarely did he choose his librettist. Up to the very raising of the curtain on opening night he was busy with last-minute alterations at the request of all and sundry, and thereafter would be compelled to make endless revisions, at top speed, if the opera's reception fell short of a triumph. The vocal lines had to be written in such as way as to accommodate the singers' personalized ornaments (unless he was required to write the ornaments himself, as Rossini was compelled to do for at least one famous singer).

Never did composers enjoy — if that is the word — a more practical, hands-on involvement with the rest of the musical economy. At the same time, rarely was there a musical economy that offered novice composers so many opportunities. And while any commercial undertaking will throw up its share of duds, by no means did it preclude "quality," by whatever standard one measures. More than eighty years after its premiere, Giuseppe Verdi, Rossini's undisputed successor as Italian opera king, looked back on *Il barbiere di Siviglia*, that three-week wonder of 1816, as "the most beautiful *opera buffa* there is."[7]

Mozart would have understood this life, these activities, these exigencies and these aims (as, more recently, would a composer of Broadway musicals). Once he moved to Vienna, Mozart lived a life not unlike Rossini's, though a less successfully adapted one since commercial prospects were fewer and he had to act as his own impresario (which is why he produced more piano concertos than operas). Indeed, Mozart was Rossini's chosen role model: "the admiration of my youth, the desperation of my maturity, and the consolation of my old age,"[8] as he put it, famously, in retirement. The reclusive Beethoven, by the end of his life, for reasons both within his control and very much outside of it, had become wholly estranged from the practical world of music. Thus the dialectical relationship in which Beethoven and Rossini have been cast is fully warranted.

Every facet of Rossini's musical life and activity thus far described stands in the maximum possible contrast to Beethoven's—beginning with the contrast between a career average of two operas a season and an output consisting of a single opera thrice revised over a period of a dozen years. It is the latter that is now regarded of course as "great composer behavior," with Beethoven's sketchbooks, a living record of agonizing labor, providing the ethical yardstick by which the work of all composers now tends to be measured.

The score produced by such exacting toil is now regarded (or if the composer is great enough, venerated) as a definitive text embodying the "work," of which performances can only be imperfect representations. Rossini—who did not leave a single sketch behind (which of course does not mean that he never made them), and who once boasted that, composing (as usual) in bed, he started a new overture rather than get out from under the blankets to retrieve one that the wind had blown away—represented

a completely different value system, in which little importance was attached to the score as a document. All the score was, to a composer like Rossini, as to the impresario and the cast, was part of the equipment that made an opera performance possible.

Within his own world, of course, Rossini was recognized as a great figure indeed. During his lifetime he achieved a prestige and authority that easily rivaled Beethoven's. His first international successes came in

FIG. 33-3   Title page of the first edition of the vocal score of Rossini's *L'Italiana in Algeri* (Mainz: Schott, 1819).

1813, when he was twenty-one: *Tancredi*, an *opera seria* (or *melodramma eroico*, in the newer language of the time) based on Voltaire, and *L'Italiana in Algeri* ("The Italian girl in Algiers"), the frothiest of farces. To write in direct (and, of course, lightning-swift) succession two masterpieces at opposite ends of the stylistic spectrum marked Rossini as by far the most "universal" master of his highly specific craft.

A signal triumph was his appointment in 1815 (aged twenty-three) as director of all the opera theaters in Naples, then still the operatic capital of the world. He still answered to the impresario, but now had a say in the hiring of librettists and the casting of roles, both for his own operas and for those of other composers. That was real power, such as composers rarely enjoyed. During the seven years of his Neapolitan reign Rossini composed nine operas for the theaters under his jurisdiction, and another nine for other cities ranging as far afield as Lisbon. All but one of the Neapolitan operas were large tragic works, quite belying Rossini's posthumous reputation as a jester. That reputation was in part the result of the survival patterns of early nineteenth-century opera generally, in part the result of the composer's own later life in retirement (when his reputation as a "character" began to rival his reputation as composer), but also the result of insistent "northern" propaganda that continues to this day, inhibiting the revival of Rossini's serious operas.

After 1822, Rossini, by now (aged thirty) an international celebrity, worked mainly abroad. His last five operas were written for the theaters of Paris, the wealthiest in Europe. For one year (1824–25), Rossini served as director of the Théâtre-Italien, where operas were given in Italian. There he produced a single opera (*Il viaggio a Reims*, "The Journey to Rheims") to celebrate the coronation of King Charles X, the surviving grandson of Louis XV, who succeeded his brother Louis XVIII on the restored Bourbon throne. Thereafter Rossini transferred his allegiance to the main Paris opera house, the Académie Royale de Musique.

His first two productions there were adaptations of works from his Neapolitan period to French librettos, and to the incredibly lavish production values of what the French called *grand opéra*, a term that has gone virtually untranslated (as "grand opera") into English to denote opera as extravagant or downright excessive spectacle. These operas certainly lived up to that billing, but all were cast into the shade by Rossini's last opera, the vast historical epic *Guillaume Tell* ("William Tell"), after a play by Schiller.

This was a work of unprecedented scale. The arias were of a newly expanded scope, composed according to a formula that

FIG. 33-4 "Oath of the Three Cantons," illustration by Celestin Deshayes for Rossini's opera *Guillaume Tell*.

Rossini had perfected in Italy. And yet the musical texture is dominated not by them but by the ensembles, many of them including the chorus for a truly huge frescolike effect. There are also two ballet episodes and several grand processions of a kind the French had been using for some time, making the opera an eclectic summary, a kind of operatic "state of the art" as of the third decade of the nineteenth century.

Guillaume Tell had its premiere performance on 3 August 1829. Rossini, aged a mere thirty-seven, then retired from the operatic stage; so that although he lived (luxuriously, in the Paris suburb of Passy) until 13 November 1868, when he died at the age of seventy-six, his actual career was of a downright Mozartean precocity, intensity, and brevity. And yet, it appears that Rossini regarded it, even at the peak of inspiration and innovation, as a job; having made his fortune — not only from the fruits of his pen but also from investments, one of them in a gambling casino — he could reward himself with a life of leisure.

While it would not be fair to repeat without qualification the old jape that Rossini gave up composing for eating (for all that he was indeed a famous amateur chef and gourmet, albeit frequently impeded in these activities by bad health), his early retirement does confirm the essentially commercial nature of his career, one completely out of joint with the new romantic temper — possibly another reason for Rossini's decision to quit. In 1854, in a letter to an admirer, Rossini referred to himself in retrospect as "the last of the classics."[9] On one level, of course, this was just an ironic comment on his inactivity; on another it was a boast that his art had weathered a quarter of a century of change in style and fashion and still remained viable in the repertory.

On perhaps the most profound level, Rossini's comment was an affirmation of the artist's status as a social animal in solidarity with his audience, in opposition to the romantic cult of the lonely, alienated hero. On the most spurious level, the one Rossini meant to mock, it signaled the spread of the anachronistic notion, associated in the last chapter with the critic Amadeus Wendt and other writers of the 1830s, that there had been a "classical period" in music that had ended with Beethoven. To claim in the 1850s to have been a part of that was to acknowledge that one was indeed a walking anachronism.

Rossini did not give up composing altogether during the last forty years of his life. But he did it increasingly as a sort of hobby — to amuse himself and the friends who attended his exclusive Paris salon at a time when to amuse or "please" was no longer considered a worthy aspiration for a self-respecting artist in the public arena. Most characteristic of all were the 150 or so little songs and piano pieces, composed between 1857 and 1868 but never published during his lifetime, to which Rossini gave the nickname *Péchés de vieillesse* — Sins of Old Age (a takeoff on the cliché *péchés de jeunesse*, sins of youth).

A few of these elegantly silly pieces found their way into print in an album called *Quelques riens* ("A few nothings"), published in Paris in the 1880s. They immediately acquired a cult following among connoisseurs, and were finally orchestrated in 1919 (by the Italian composer Ottorino Respighi) for a popular ballet called *La boutique fantasque* ("The magic toy shop"). Later the *Péchés de vieillesse* became the basis of another ballet — or rather two ballet suites, *Soirées musicales* (1936) and *Matinées musicales* (1941), by the English composer Benjamin Britten. These arrangements take their place alongside the writings of Edward Dent and the repartee of Igor Stravinsky, quoted in the last chapter, in the anti-Beethoven discourse of the cynical and disillusioned period between the two World Wars. Rossini, though no longer given recognition as such, was still Beethoven's dialectical antagonist.

The only large-scale works Rossini attempted during his retirement were religious ones: an oratoriolike setting of the thirteenth-century hymn *Stabat mater* ("The mother stood by the cross") for soloists, chorus, and orchestra, composed at a snail's pace between 1831 and 1841, and a thoroughly idiosyncratic *Petite messe solennelle* ("Little solemn mass"), for soloists, chorus, two pianos, and harmonium, composed a few years before his death. (Almost his last work was an orchestration of the Mass, done in order to foil "pirates" in an age that did not yet provide international copyright protection to composers.)

Unlike Beethoven (but again, quite like Mozart), Rossini did not make any substantial alteration in his style when writing sacred music. The immensely popular *Stabat mater*, in particular (and especially the aria "Cujus animam," belted out by a *tenore di forza*), became an emblem of "secularized" or "operatic" — that is, sensuously appealing — sacred music, and a frequent target of abuse from the clergy (though a favorite with choirs). It was finally banned in the wake of a *motu proprio* or personal pronouncement by Pope Pius X, promulgated in 1903, famous (and popular) among music historians for its restoration of the Gregorian chant to active church use and its discouragement of polyphonic music (a battle the Church hierarchy had been fighting with composers and singers since the fourteenth century).

The *motu proprio* contained the warning that

> since modern music has risen mainly to serve profane uses, greater care must be taken with regard to it, in order that the musical compositions of modern style which are admitted in the Church may contain nothing profane, be free from reminiscences of motifs adopted in the theaters, and be not fashioned even in their external forms after the manner of profane pieces.[10]

Accordingly, a convention of the Society of St. Gregory of America, meeting in Rochester, New York, in 1922, drew up an index of "disapproved music," in which Rossini's name headed all the rest. A whole paragraph was devoted to the *Stabat mater*, in which it was directed that "all of Rossini's compositions should be excluded from the Catholic choir. These works are unchurchly, to say the least. The *Stabat mater* is most objectionable from a liturgical standpoint."[11]

So yet again it appears that Rossini and Beethoven stood as dialectical antagonists: the one as a composer of secularized church music, the other as a composer of sacralized secular music. And the Vatican's objections to Rossini's "profanity" are (as we shall see) directly comparable to romantic objections to his sensuality — his *Sinnlichkeit*, to use E. T. A. Hoffmann's language, as against the *Geist* or spirituality of Beethoven. And yet the fact that Rossini's *Stabat mater* still needed banning more than eighty years after its first performance is only another indication of Rossini's equal, if opposite, rank with Beethoven in the active repertory, if no longer in the official "canon" of great art. His fame surpassed that of any previous composer, and so, for a long time, did the popularity of his works. Audiences took to his music as if to an intoxicating drug — or, to put it decorously, to champagne, with which Rossini's bubbly music was constantly compared.

We have already had an inkling of his unbelievable vogue in chapter 31, when (as we then saw) it almost drove the 1822 premiere of Beethoven's Ninth Symphony out of Vienna, a city Rossini had then just conquered. And we have seen how reaction to the Rossini craze cemented the association of Beethoven's art with spirituality on the one hand and with Germanness on the other, thus forging a fateful nexus between idealism and nationalism. Another choice indication of Rossini's wingspread came from far-off St. Petersburg, the capital of Imperial Russia, where between 1828 and 1831 eighteen different Rossini operas were performed, eleven in 1829 alone. (*Semiramide*, the last and largest of Rossini's serious Italian operas, first performed in Venice, came to St. Petersburg in 1836, and launched a period of absolute Italian operatic hegemony in the Russian capital, with severe consequences for the development of indigenous opera there.) The Rossini craze has been associated with the spirit of imperial restoration; indeed, Prince Metternich, the arbiter supreme of post-Napoleonic Europe and the very apostle of political reaction, personally commissioned a pair of cantatas from Rossini for performance at the Congress of Verona (a sequel to the more famous Congress of Vienna) in 1822. The Rossini craze in Imperial Russia, and in the Paris of the Bourbon Restoration, would seem to give credence to this association. And yet, as we already know, this was one sphere — perhaps *the* one sphere — in which Rossini and Beethoven were not dialectical antagonists but comrades. Beethoven also supplied music for Metternich's consumption, and was also especially popular in Imperial St. Petersburg (where the *Missa solemnis* actually had its premiere). Beethoven's heightened, somewhat archaic spirituality (as exemplified by his fugal style) and Rossini's flighty nonchalance — or at least their reception by European society — were thus responses to a common antiheroic or pessimistic stimulus. Both stances, as the music historian Carl Dahlhaus wisely pointed out, signaled a resigned detachment.[12]

THE CODE ROSSINI

Perhaps the greatest difference between the romantic sensibility, as represented by Beethoven, and the pre-romantic one, as exemplified by Rossini, lay in their respective attitudes toward forms and genres. As early as his op. 1, as we have seen, Beethoven was strongly inclined to "push the envelope" with respect to genre, transgressing generic and stylistic boundaries in a way that made Haydn uneasy. As his career went on, Beethoven's attitude toward form became increasingly — and deliberately — idiosyncratic, with the result that it was always with him (and with us, contemplating him) an important esthetic issue.

Or perhaps it would be more appropriate to call Beethoven's formal procedures not so much idiosyncratic as *syncretic*, a word that emphasizes the recombination into new wholes of elements (symphonic and chamber styles, for example, or sonata and fugue) formerly regarded as disparate or even opposing. The familiarity or traditionalness of the elements recombined insures a degree of intelligibility, but the need for novelty and constant modification reflects the romantic emphasis on individuality and peculiarity, which became over the course of the nineteenth century an ever more pressing demand for originality, the more fundamental (radical, profound) the better.

Rossini, by contrast, was very respectful of genres, as a composer whose works were assembled out of interchangeable parts had to be, to say nothing of a composer who staked his livelihood on pleasing an audience that, like all entertainment audiences, was fickle and conservative and knew what it liked. His idea was not to experiment radically with form in every piece, but rather to hit on a winning formula (ideally one that he could turn out better than any competitor) and, having created a demand for his product, stay with it and, if possible, keep on improving it. (Only a proven recipe, with a known purpose and a tested mechanism, can be improved or perfected in the strict sense, rather than merely changed or departed from.) So successful was Rossini in standardizing and improving his wares in accordance with public taste that his formulas eventually became everybody's formulas. The history of Italian opera in the *primo ottocento* or early nineteenth century became the story of their continual growth and expansion at the hands of Rossini himself and his many followers.

The opera historian Julian Budden very wittily called this set of formulas and conventions the Code Rossini.[13] It is a marvelous term because of the way it parodies the so-called *Code Napoléon* — the French emperor's revision of the time-honored Roman Law, an extremely rationalized and systematic civil code that spread over Europe in the wake of Napoleon's conquering armies. Despite its imposition by force of arms, it was considered a model of enlightened efficiency and liberality, and remained in force long after Napoleon himself had passed from the scene. (It is still the basis of the French civil code, and its influence survives in all the countries of the European continent and their former colonies.) The *Code Napoléon* achieved its standardizing purpose in the short run by force of Napoleon's authority, but in the long run because it worked, and provided a basis for further elaboration. That is what makes it such an apt analogy to the "Code Rossini."

The Code Rossini, like its Napoleonic namesake, was the basis for an extraordinarily detailed modus operandi. Its full measure is something only specialists can take. (One specialist, Richard Osborne, has constructed a "prototype" for the first act of a Rossinian comic opera, for example, consisting of nine standard sections, some of them with several equally standardized constituent parts.)[14] Here it will suffice to describe a few of the typical components — overture, aria, ensemble — and show how they operated. All of them were based on models inherited from past practice; none was Rossini's wholly original invention ("wholly original invention" being after all contrary to the whole point and purpose of the Code). Nor did he complete the process of standardization that modern musicologists have described. But he revised and renewed all components and turned them into proven recipes — which is only a more casual and businesslike, less "mystified" way of saying that he turned them into classics.

Mozart was of course one of Rossini's antecedents. More direct ones were Giovanni Paisiello (1740–1816), Rossini's predecessor as opera czar in Naples, serving there for almost half a century (1766–1815), with a few years out for duty at the court of Catherine the Great in St. Petersburg (1776–84); and Domenico Cimarosa (1749–1801), another Neapolitan whose exceptionally peripatetic career also included a lucrative St. Petersburg stint (1787–91). There is nothing in Rossini that does not derive ultimately from the work of these three; but there is also nothing in Rossini that does not have "New! Improved!" stamped all over it.

Take the overture to begin with. As we may remember from Mozart, the Italian opera *sinfonia* by the end of the eighteenth century was essentially a short "first movement" (or "sonata-allegro"). As a reminder we can take a brief look at the overture from Paisiello's *The Barber of Seville*, first performed at St. Petersburg in 1782, based on the very same play—and partly on the very same libretto—as Rossini's smash hit of 1816. The play, incidentally, was the first in Beaumarchais's famous trilogy of which *The Marriage of Figaro*, musicked by Mozart and Da Ponte as *Le nozze di Figaro*, was the second. It concerns the madcap courtship of the young Count and Countess whose midlife marital woes form the premise of the second play. (In both plays the barber Figaro acts as the invincible comic accomplice—in the first to the Count, in the second to the Countess.) Paisiello's setting was also a great and famous success; so much so that Rossini took a big risk in competing with it.

Paisiello's overture (like Mozart's to *Figaro*) starts off with a busy, scurrying theme that sets an antic mood from the very start. Like many such themes, it stirs anticipatory excitement in the audience by proceeding through a rising sequence and a crescendo. Ex. 33-3 shows the beginning of Paisiello's overture up to the elided cadence that sends the harmony off in search of the dominant key. When that key is reached, there will of course be a new theme group and a cadence. Then, according to the binary model, we expect a modulatory passage leading, through a far-out point (FOP), to a double return (first theme in original key), and a replay of the opening section with all themes in the tonic, concluding with a reinforced cadential flourish by way of coda.

What Paisiello actually supplies is a streamlined or compacted version of the usual procedure, one regularly employed in *opera buffa* overtures. Instead of happening at the end of a modulatory passage and a FOP, the double return follows immediately after the dominant cadence, as if the opening section were being repeated. But where there had originally been a quick move to the dominant, now we get the modulatory section, replete with FOP, which, when it circles back to the tonic key, hooks up not with another "double return" but with the second theme group, now in the tonic. In standard "sonata form" lingo we could say that the development section, instead of coming between the exposition and the recapitulation, has been miniaturized and shoehorned into the recap.

Now compare the overture to Rossini's *Barbiere*. It is at once fancier and more streamlined. It has an extended slow introduction of the kind we have encountered in Haydn's London symphonies, or Mozart's *Don Giovanni*, but it is far more elaborate than either. In fact, it is a bigger introduction, and more important to the impression the piece makes, than in any but the most elaborately prefaced symphonies (among Beethoven's, only the Fourth and the Seventh). It makes the customary functional

EX. 33-3   Giovanni Paisiello, *Il barbiere di Siviglia,* Overture (beginning)

EX. 33-3 *(continued)*

progression from a strong tonic opening to an expectant dominant finish, but it is cast very decoratively in a miniature ternary or ABA form of its own: the midsection, consisting of a flowery cantabile melody reminiscent of an aria, is sandwiched or showcased between two segments that feature a pliant, harmonically malleable motive (four repeated thirty-second notes as upbeat to an eighth) from which a melodic fabric is constructed to support the necessary modulation from tonic to dominant (Ex. 33-4a). (It is a technique closely related, in fact, to the one by which the first movement of Beethoven's Fifth is so famously constructed.)

The quick main section of the overture is "binary," cast in two parallel but not quite equivalent halves. The first, as in Paisiello, is similar in content to a symphonic exposition: a theme in the tonic, a more lyrical theme in the dominant (or, as here, in the relative major because the tonic is minor), with a headlong, noisily orchestrated dash of a transition to connect them and a codetta to confirm arrival at the secondary key. What is unlike the usual symphonic binary movement is the full-blown structure of both themes. Especially striking is the second, cast in the form of elaborate woodwind solos (including a juicy solo turn for the horn, Rossini's father's instrument).

The codetta (Ex. 33-4b) is Rossini's special trademark, something without which no Rossini overture (except the self-consciously "Parisian" one for *Guillaume Tell*) is ever complete: a series of ostinatos over a regular tonic-dominant seesaw in the harmony, sustaining a gradual, inexorable, magnificently orchestrated crescendo to a blazing fanfare of a *tutti* in which the bass instruments carry the melodic ball. This orchestral juggernaut — the "Rossini crescendo" — was the moment people waited for. Its implied emphasis on sensuous values — volume, color, texture — stands in the baldest possible contrast (or so it seems) to the spirituality of the German romantics.

The exposition having come to its brilliant conclusion, the most perfunctory four-bar transition imaginable leads into what sounds like its repetition, but turns out to be a truncated recapitulation, with both themes in the tonic, and the transition between them virtually eliminated. The crescendo is not omitted, however: in the tonic it makes a bigger splash than ever. In fact, the way the recapitulation is abbreviated to

EX. 33-4A   Gioacchino Rossini, *Il barbiere di Siviglia*, Overture, slow introduction

EX. 33-4B   Gioacchino Rossini, *Il barbiere di Siviglia*, Overture, Allegro, Codetta ("Rossini crescendo")

speed its arrival makes the repetition of the rollicking crescendo seem like the overture's very raison d'être. Its point and purpose has been to create a mood of festivity — or, to put it another way, to mark the occasion of its performance as festive.

The mood of festivity is a generic one, unrelated to the content of the particular opera that follows. "Opera," not *this* opera, is what is being marked as festive, and that ritualized sense of occasion — that sense of social ritual — will bring back to mind a great deal of what was observed in chapter 23 about the nature and function of the old *opera seria*, that most festive and social of all "pre-Enlightened" genres. In fact — and this may seem surprising in light of the romantic notions we have lately become acquainted with — overtures like this prefaced Rossini's tragic operas as well as farcical ones like *Il barbiere*, for they were festive social occasions, too.

Indeed, the overture we have just examined *was*, originally, the preface to a serious opera, the forgotten *Aureliano in Palmira* (1813), the one flop in the otherwise golden year that produced *Tancredi* and *L'Italiana in Algeri*. Dissatisfied with the overture that prefaced *Il barbiere* at its unsuccessful premiere (or perhaps acting in response to the audience's dissatisfaction), Rossini salvaged the earlier overture and tacked it on to the new opera, of which it now seems such a perfect encapsulation. That will show just how interchangeable Rossinian parts were meant to be. Even individual themes could be shifted and recycled from overture to overture.

From this it follows that the generic description of one Rossini overture, such as the one to *Il barbiere*, can serve as generic description of them all. They all have the same tripartite slow introduction; they all have the same bithematic exposition (in which the second theme is always a woodwind solo); they all have the same "headlong, noisily orchestrated dash of a transition"; they all have the same crescendo-coda; they all have the same truncated recapitulation. Does this mean that "when you've heard one you've heard them all?" Not at all! What differs inexhaustibly are the details — "the divine details,"[15] as the novelist Vladimir Nabokov used to say of novels, another form in which generic similarities can blind a naive or unsympathetic reader to what connoisseurs rejoice in.

FIG. 33-5   Costume designs for Rosina, Don Basilio, and Figaro from the first production in Paris of *Il barbiere di Siviglia* (Théâtre Italien, 1819).

Rossini's orchestration, for one thing, is more varied, more minutely crafted, and (at the climaxes) more richly sonorous than that of any other composer we have met thus far. The great nineteenth-century flowering of virtuoso orchestration starts with him. His woodwind writing, above all, was epoch-making. And so was his use of percussion or "pseudo-percussion" like the beating out of rhythms by violin bows on candlesticks (nowadays on music stands) in the overture to *Il signor Bruschino*, another opera from the amazing year 1813 (Rossini's twenty-first). Every Rossini crescendo may produce a similar frisson, but the specific means of production (the gimmicks, to use a current insider's term) are endlessly variable.

For another thing, Rossini's melodic invention is the most fertile we have encountered since Mozart's. Those cantabile themes in his introductions, and those full-blown woodwind solos in the expositions may be interchangeable in function, but that function was to be catchy. They each retain a distinct profile in the aural memory. The combination of generic uniformity with distinction in particulars was the Rossini secret — seemingly anyone's secret, but inimitable. Most memorable of all are the true virtuoso solos found in some overtures, which simulate with instruments all the appurtenances of a vocal scene. In *Il Turco in Italia* ("The Turk in Italy," 1814) the florid cantabile, replete with roulades and trills, is played, improbably but all the more memorably, by the French horn. One of the most difficult horn solos in the repertory even now, with the benefit of the modern valve mechanism that revolutionized brass instrument design beginning around 1820, it must have been all but unplayable in Rossini's time — the ultimate tribute to the composer's father. The successful player must have earned the same kind of spontaneous ovation enjoyed by the singers — behavior increasingly disallowed under the new romantic etiquette.

That is not the only aspect of Rossini to antagonize the romantic temper. Most conspicuous by its absence in his work is any hint of thematic "development." Rossini overtures are often described, rather lamely, as sonata forms without development sections; but as we have seen as recently as the overture to Paisiello's *Barbiere*, one can have development in other places, too. Rossini seemingly shuns it everywhere; nor is there any real FOP in his tonal design. The place where Paisiello had them (between the first and second themes in the recapitulation) is the place where Rossini dispenses with transition altogether.

It is doubtful whether Rossini shunned development by design; more likely he merely found it unnecessary to his very direct and sensuously appealing purpose. Dispensing with it was a matter of business efficiency. But the avoidance in his music, on the one hand, of rigorous motivic unfolding, and, on the other, of symbolic harmonic drama was something German musicians and their colonial adherents found infuriating, for these (along with the spirituality that was assumed to result from them) were the very terms on which they staked their claim to universality. Music that could do without them, and yet succeed with many audiences, undermined the claim.

And once Germans had pronounced their anathema on Rossini, his music was turned into a high esthetic cause by resisters. The lack or avoidance of thematic development became a matter of principle. Or rather, what was a lack in Rossini was turned by later generations of "Latinate" composers into an avoidance, and touted. The best illustration is a quip supposedly made by Claude Debussy, thought by many to be the greatest French composer at the tail end of the nineteenth century, while listening to a symphony by Johannes Brahms, thought by just as many to be the greatest German composer at the time: "Ah, the development section! Good, I can go out for a cigarette." The century-long war of *Geist* vs. *Sinnlichkeit* — "spirit" vs. "sensuality" — was reaching a head.

Yet, as is always the case with culture wars, this one was founded on an absolutely needless polarization of values. And as always, the polarization breaks down under scrutiny. Nothing in Rossini was so offensive to idealistic romantic taste as those infernal crescendos that appealed to an audience's basest, grossest instincts. But as we have already observed, one of the greatest of all "Rossini crescendos" is the one that informs the coda to the first movement of Beethoven's Third Symphony, the towering *Eroica*, which (as any romantic idealist will tell you) is the loftiest expression of absolute musical values — spiritual values — achieved as of its date (or, at any rate, as soon as that silly dedication to Napoleon was removed). What makes the one crescendo brutish and the other sublime? Context alone, as always — including the context of interpretive discourse and polemic.

IMBROGLIO

The comic ensemble is another area in which comparison with Paisiello will help us take the measure of the Code Rossini. As we may recall from Mozart's operas, the comic ensemble finale was the site where composers began to experiment with ways of suffusing fully composed music, formerly the province of the static or "freeze-time" aria, with real dramatic action, the more frenetic the better. Audiences loved the effect, and librettists began seeking opportunities to contrive dramatically active ensembles, often based on slapstick gimmicks, in other spots besides finales. As the *opera buffa* became more musically antic, it reverted once again to purely comic type, reversing the trend toward mixing dramatic genres that we observed in Mozart's "Da Ponte" operas, with their occasional serious characters and their attendant vocal genres. The Countess in Mozart's *Figaro* is a *seria* character, despite the nature of the opera as a whole. Rosina, the same character (albeit not yet a countess) in *Il barbiere*, is a pure *buffa* ingenue (or, if more knowingly played, a "soubrette").

We can sample the pure-comic style pre-Rossini in the *trio buffo* from the second act of Paisiello's *Il barbiere di Siviglia* (Ex. 33-5). The action revolves around a plot, masterminded by Figaro, to bring Count Almaviva and his beloved Rosina together, thus thwarting the designs of Dr. Bartolo, Rosina's jealous guardian, who is planning to marry her himself. The first act ends with Figaro smuggling the disguised Count into Dr. Bartolo's house. At the beginning of the second act, a frantically suspicious Dr. Bartolo is trying to find out who had visited the night before. He interrogates his two servants, Giovinetto ("Youngster," i.e., an old man) and Lo Svegliato ("Mr. Wide-awake," i.e., a simpleton), but to no avail. Figaro had taken the precaution of slipping drugs to each of them: Lo Svegliato has received a sleeping draught and can only yawn; Giovinetto, having taken a powder, can only sneeze.

The musical trick here is constructing the whole interrogation out of typical pairs of balanced ("question-and-answer") phrases, and endless melodic sequences derived from them: musical clichés given renewed freshness by their unexpected appositeness to the inane dramatic situation. Familiar from Mozart (especially the role of Leporello in Don Giovanni, the quintessential *basso buffo* servant role) is the rapid patter — even declamation at a note value shorter than a beat — to which Dr. Bartolo's part in the trio is largely confined, with all three parts joining in at the end.

Paisiello's trio is a little masterpiece, and Rossini, when it came his turn to set *Il barbiere*, wisely refrained from competing with it. He left the episode with the yawning and sneezing servants in recitative, and nowadays it is almost always dropped in performance. Nevertheless, he did surpass his predecessor — indeed all predecessors — in the new level of zany virtuosity to which, hiding his sophisticated craftsmanship behind a smokescreen of ludicrous situations and effects, he brought all their techniques and devices. He loaded his operas with more ensemble pieces than ever, meanwhile extending the finales to a previously unheard-of scale, both in length and in what old Da Ponte, Mozart's comic librettist, called *strepitoso-strepitosissimo*, "tumult upon uproar," which required fantastic virtuosity from all concerned, resourceful composer and rapidly enunciating performers alike.

As far as rapid *buffo* patter is concerned, Rossini's *Barbiere* contains the two absolute classics of the genre: "Largo al factotum" ("Make way for the jack-of-all-trades!"), Figaro's bumptious cavatina or entrance aria in act I; and "La calunnia è un venticello" ("Slander is a gentle breeze"), the caustically brilliant aria in which Don Basilio, Rosina's music teacher who doubles as a marriage broker, concocts a word-of-mouth campaign to disgrace Count Almaviva and thwart his designs. Figaro's cavatina begins like a typical da capo aria: its "A" section and "B" section are easily spotted. But the return to A is hilariously preempted by a frenzy of patter, as Figaro is overwhelmed with thoughts of all the demands everybody makes of him, uniquely gifted as he is. The final

EX. 33-5   Giovanni Paisiello, *Il barbiere di Siviglia*, Act II, *Terzetto buffo* (yawning and sneezing)

section ("Ah bravo, Figaro . . . ," Ex. 33-6) is traditionally taken as fast as the singer can manage it (and often a lot faster than that).

Don Basilio's aria does not quite hit such a peak of vocal virtuosity; the virtuosity this time is the composer's. For the whole dramatic point of this seemingly traditional "simile aria" rests on the crescendo idea: a little breeze of slander gathering force and becoming a hurricane of scandalous babble. And so all of Rossini's skills as an orchestral illustrator are called into play, including such *recherché* effects as violins bowed *al ponticello* — "right on the bridge" — producing a strangled whisper to start the breeze on its way; or, at the storm's acme, tongued tremolos in the woodwinds.

The *buffa* style can only be exhibited at fullest strength, of course, in a finale; and there is no *buffa* finale in all of Rossini — which is to say, in all of opera — that can equal

EX. 33-6   Gioacchino Rossini, *Il barbiere di Siviglia*, "Largo al factotum," coda

the first-act finale from *L'Italiana in Algeri*, one of the big hits of 1813, as an exhibitor of what it was that made Rossini the great counterweight to Beethoven in the eyes even of his German contemporaries. Running through almost a hundred pages of vocal score in record time, it is the most concentrated single dose of Rossini that there is.

A first-act finale, we remember, portrays the height of imbroglio—the moment of greatest, seemingly hopeless, tangle in the plot line. So here is what has happened:

Mustafà, the Bey of Algiers, has grown tired of his wife Elvira and decides to marry her off to his Italian slave Lindoro. He sends his pirate commander out to find him an Italian girl. The pirates sink a ship, on which Isabella, the Italian girl of the title, is cruising in search of her fiancé (Lindoro, of course), and bring the survivors to the Bey's court as captives. The commander announces her capture, and the Bey tells Lindoro he can go home if he takes Elvira with him.

That is the setup. Things come to a head as the captive Isabella, on her way into the throne room, catches sight of Lindoro, on his way out. (Here is where the first-act finale begins.) The moment of recognition has a very conspicuous Mozartean resonance. Like the moment of recognition in the ballroom finale to the first act of *Don Giovanni*, it takes place over the strains of an unusually slow minuet—the trio (*andantino*) in which Lindoro, Elvira, and Zulma (Elvira's slave) had been singing their farewells to Mustafà. A Rossini finale always takes to extremes the tempo trajectory of which Da Ponte had written. The Andantino is, so to speak, the launching pad.

The lovers' emotion is reflected in a wrenching flatward turn in the harmony, but just as the expected cadence to E♭ is about to happen (and a love duet seems imminent), Mustafà chimes in with a typically bouncing, satirically florid mood-shattering *buffo* aside to express his befuddlement. The threatened duet turns into a septet, set against the continuing strains of the Andantino, in which all the assembled characters take part, Lindoro and Mustafà (as it were competing in confusion) in the lead.

This moment of frozen perplexity having passed, the quick-witted Isabella confronts the Bey in a fast tempo that from here on will only get faster. With what we are now apt to recognize as the "arrogance of Enlightenment" (arguably the butt of Rossini's humor, depending on how it is played), she berates the cowering Mustafà for his barbarian transgressions against universal human norms. How can he expect her to love a man who treats his wife so cruelly? How can he simply order Lindoro to marry a woman he does not love? Then, immediately contradicting herself, she insists that Lindoro, a fellow Italian, be made her retainer forthwith. A hopeless impasse has been reached: as the assembled singers declare, "Va sossopra il mio cervello, sbalordito in tanti imbrogli!" ("My little head is topsy-turvy, dumbfounded at such imbroglios!"). It is time for metaphors.

The first metaphor, expressed *allegro vivace*, is the time-honored shipwreck, familiar to us since the days of Farinelli (chapter 23). Then, in a *stretta* marked *più mosso*, everybody goes into an onomatopoetical tizzy. This is Rossini's favorite comic device, the idea (as Budden puts it) of "human beings transformed by emotion into puppets,"[16] and this ensemble set a benchmark of mechanical grotesquery never to be surpassed (Ex. 33-7). The ladies compare their mental agitation to a little bell a-ringing ("din din");

Lindoro compares his to a little clock a-ticking ("tic tic"); Taddeo, Isabella's chaperone, compares his to a little crow a-cawing ("cra cra"); the pirate commander Ali to a hammer pounding ("tac tac"); and Mustafà to a cannon firing ("bum bum").

For twenty or so pages of vocal score they continue shouting and gesticulating in this vein, the chorus of Algerian harem girls and Italian sailors finally joining in to

EX. 33-7   Gioacchino Rossini, *L'Italiana in Algeri,* from the Act I Finale

raise the hubbub to an even higher pitch of furious futility. And then the masterstroke: contrary to all reasonable expectation, the whole *stretta, din-din, bum-bum*, and all, is replayed *ancora più mosso*—yet faster! In a good performance the audience will not believe its ears. Rossini has taken bootless delirium, the jewel in the *buffa* crown, about as far as it can go. (Just in case anyone is worrying, though, the opera ends with Isabella and Lindoro in each others' arms, and Mustafà and Elvira reconciled.)

We have been familiar with the device of comparing human emotion to mechanical or animal noises ever since our first exposure to operatic comedy: recall the closing duet in Pergolesi's intermezzo *La serva padrona* from chapter 27, an item that produced a sensation comparable to Rossini's about eighty years earlier. Over that span the *opera buffa* had traced a fairly straight trajectory of expanding technical resources (but not harmonic ones—that was German terrain!) and mounting, fairly coldhearted hilarity. Rossini stands unquestionably at its pinnacle. The *buffa* had reached the end of the line.

HEART THROBS

Not so the *seria*. Under the impact of romanticism, serious opera flowered anew, and again Rossini was at the forefront, although this aspect of his historical contribution is less evident in the context of today's performing repertoire. It may be argued, in fact, that the most fertile articles in the Code Rossini were those that pertained to the serious aria (or more precisely and to the point, the *scena ed aria* that replaced the recitative-plus-aria unit of old) and those that pertained to the dramatic ensemble, imported from the *opera buffa* to serve serious or tragic aims. These were crucial renovations. They gave serious opera a new lease on life, transforming it into opera as we know it today.

Once again it should be emphasized that neither these nor any Rossinian novelties were his wholly original invention. They were newly standardized and redeployed adaptations from previous practice. One can find them foreshadowed in the work of many composers, including Mozart. But beginning with Rossini, opera became unthinkable without them.

The Rossinian serious aria (or duet) consisted of two main sections in contrasting tempos—the *cantabile*, or lyric effusion, and the *cabaletta*, or brilliant conclusion. The etymology of *cabaletta*, a term first encountered around 1820, is uncertain. It may be a corruption of the Iberian *cobla*, meaning stanza, for it usually consisted of a short stanza strophically repeated either in whole or in part, with an orchestral ritornello in between the repetitions and a brilliant coda, all of which amounted to an eager invitation to the singer to embroider away. Indeed, the double-aria conception is a quintessentially singerly one. It allowed the virtuoso to show off everything from beauty of tone and breath control (in the cantabile) to euphoric fireworks (in the cabaletta).

For Italian opera, especially serious opera, remained a singers' showcase. The new style of aria did serve new dramaturgical purposes and meet new dramaturgical criteria by allowing, through its new emphasis on contrast, for more action to be accommodated within what had formerly been static "aria time." When preceded by an orchestral introduction and an accompanied recitative, when fitted out with a turn of plot (often involving the chorus) between the cantabile and the cabaletta to motivate the latter's incandescence, or when enhanced by what were called *pertichini* (brief interventions by other characters in dialogue with the soloist), the aria could be built up into a whole *scena*, or dramatic scene, with a self-contained dramatic trajectory. But it served old purposes, too, and better than ever, since every aria became a varied demonstration of traditional vocal prowess, giving the audience that much more of what they had come to bask in.

The item that put this new style of aria permanently on the map and made it de rigueur for perhaps fifty years to come was "Di tanti palpiti" ("So many heart throbs"), the hero's cavatina (entrance aria) from *Tancredi*, the other colossal hit of the miraculous year 1813, and the most famous aria Rossini ever wrote. (As was often the case, the piece is named after its cabaletta, the most memorable part.) Years later, looking back on his career and feigning shame at his success (all the better to mock the pretensions of the great), Rossini thanked his publisher for a gift by abasing himself as the "author of the too-famous cavatina 'Di tanti palpiti.'"[17] Too famous, indeed. So completely had it come to symbolize Italian opera and all its values that, as long as it remained current on the recital stage, parodies of it were a universally recognized code among German composers and their audiences for triviality, flightiness, and inanity. As late as 1868, Wagner quoted it (and surely expected his audience to notice it) in the bleating Tailors' Chorus from *Die Meistersinger* (Ex. 33-8). What could better recommend it to our attention?

Tancredi, a "heroic musical drama," is in its externals a quasi-historical opera of the old school, even down to the casting of the title role, a valiant knight-crusader, for a so-called *musico*—a contralto "in trousers." (See Fig. 33-6; a generation or two earlier, the role would have been composed for a castrato.) In other ways, the libretto substantiates the frequent claim (or complaint) that romantic opera amounts in essence to a constant rehash of the myth of *Romeo and Juliet*: "star-cross'd lovers." The title character, the exiled heir to the throne of Syracuse, and his beloved Amenaide are the children of warring clans. In Voltaire's drama, on which the libretto was based, mutual suspicion prevents their union, and the drama ends with the hero's death on the battlefield. In the first version of the opera, a happy ending was substituted. Later, Rossini retrofitted the last act with a tragic finale closer to the original (but also with a love duet, otherwise lacking in the opera). Nineteenth-century audiences preferred the first version; twentieth-century revivals, mainly instigated by scholars, have favored the more serious tragic ending.[18]

Tancredi's cavatina (act I, scene 5) marks his first appearance in the opera that bears his name. He has just returned to Syracuse in disguise, torn between his love for Amenaide and his duty to his father, whose rule is threatened by Amenaide's father. The orchestral Andante that opens the scene (Ex. 33-9a) is one of Rossini's characteristic tone-paintings, full of nature sounds that conjure up the beautiful landscape to which

EX. 33-8 Richard Wagner, *Die Meistersinger*, Act III, Tailors' Chorus ("*mit Bockstriller*")

Schnei - der, ein Schnei - der, ein
tail - or, a tail - or, a

Str. dazu.

*Die Triller (*tr*) sind von den Sängren als sogenannte Bockstriller ausuzführen.
ˣ*These trills must imitate the bleating of goats.*

Schnei - der zur Hand,—— der viel Mut hatt'
tail - or ap - pear, wise and good, who

und Ver - stand.
knew no fear.

FIG. 33-6   Marietta Alboni (with moustache) in the trousers role of Arsace and Giulia Grisi as the title character in a revival of Rossini's *Semiramide* (St. Petersburg, 1844).

Tancredi addresses his first words of accompanied recitative: "O sweet, ungrateful native land, at last I return to you!" The accompaniment to the recitative is full of orchestral and harmonic color, both of which change subtly to register the hero's fugitive moods. A switch, first to the relative minor and then to the subdominant, accompanies thoughts of Amenaide, at first painful, then sweet, finally resolute.

The cantabile section, "Tu che accendi questo core" ("You who set this heart of mine afire," Ex. 33-9b), ends with multiple cues for embellishment: the markings *a piacere* ("at pleasure," i.e., do whatever you want) in the vocal part and *colla parte* ("stay with the soloist") in the accompaniment. The fermata means "cadenza, please," just as it did in the days of the da capo aria. If the notes on the page are recognizable at this point, the singer is not doing her job. The same goes double, of course, for the repeated strains in the cabaletta.

What made this particular cabaletta such a favorite? One thing must have been the surprising modulation to the flat mediant (A♭ major) just where the first stanza seemed about to make its cadence (Ex. 33-9c). Not only did the little jolt give the audience a pleasurable frisson, it also functioned as a sort of FOP, requiring a modulation (via

EX. 33-9A   Gioacchino Rossini, *Tancredi*, Act II, "Tu che accendi/Di tanti palpiti," orchestral introduction

EX. 33-9B   Gioacchino Rossini, *Tancredi*, Act II, "Tu che accendi/Di tanti palpiti," cantabile

EX. 33-9C   Gioacchino Rossini, *Tancredi*, Act II, "Tu che accendi/Di tanti palpiti," cabaletta

EX. 33-9C (*continued*)

F minor) back to the tonic for the repetition of the opening line. The last dominant chord carries another fermata, requiring another cadenza: the harmonic structure and the vocal virtuosity work in tandem here to increase the satisfaction of return. And of course, the effect also plays upon — and plays out — the meaning of the words in the context of the action: the whole aria is about returning, and the very words that had launched the harmonic digression were "mi rivedrai, ti rivedrò," "you will see me again, and I will see you." The quick *passaggii* on the last page (Ex. 33-9d) were, as always, only a springboard for improvised delirium.

But such explanations are rationalized reflections and, to the extent of their rationalization, false to an experience whose essence is sensuous immediacy, a sense that the music is playing directly on the nerves and calling up the listener's own memories of the emotions portrayed. As the French novelist Stendhal put it in his *Life of Rossini* (1824), "without the experience, or the memory of the experience, of the madness of love, as love is known in the happy countries of the South, it is quite impossible to interpret the phrase *mi rivedrai, ti rivedrò*." Stendhal's *Life* is far more than a biography. (As a biography it is quite useless in fact, being full of errors and fabrications.) It is a great work of music criticism, as crucial in its way, and within its Franco-Italian milieu, as Hoffmann's writings on Beethoven for an understanding of what — and how much! — the music of the early nineteenth century meant to its hearers. What Rossini's contagious heart throbs meant to Stendhal, or stimulated in him, was a great liberating impetuosity of soul that contrasted utterly with the (as he saw it) pompous and vapid spirituality touted in the Protestant north, where manners were restrained and souls unmusical. Pitting Stendhal against Hoffmann is perhaps the best way of encompassing the increasingly split world of music in the early romantic era, with its nation-based esthetics and its hardened antagonisms.

As the quotation about "Di tanti palpiti" already shows, Stendhal used Rossini (just as Hoffmann used Beethoven, just as Rousseau had used Pergolesi) as a springboard for national stereotyping. The passage continues, even more pointedly:

> The nations of the North might devour twenty *Treatises on the Art of Poetry* as learned as that of La Harpe [Jean-François de La Harpe (1739–1803), French literary authority and theorist of "classicism"], and still have no understanding why the words *mi rivedrai* precede the words *ti rivedrò*. If any of our fashionable critics could understand Italian, they would surely detect a *lack of breeding*, if not indeed a *total contempt for the delicacies of social intercourse* in Tancredi's behavior towards Amenaide![19]

Beyond that, Rossini's inimitable talent is said to reside in his plainness and clarity, in the indescribable rightness of his portrayal of things as they are, a rightness that silences criticism. Nowhere is this rightness better exemplified than in "Di tanti palpiti." "What is there to be said about this superb *cantilena*?" Stendhal asks, using the fancy Italian word for song. "Talking about it to those who already know it would seem to me to be as absurd as talking about it to those who have never heard it — if indeed, in the whole of Europe there may still *be* people who have never heard it!" And in a footnote that drips with sarcasm, seemingly pointed directly at writers like Hoffmann who wax endlessly about the transcendent and the ineffable, he adds, "O happy lands,

EX. 33-9D   Gioacchino Rossini, *Tancredi*, Act II, "Tu che accendi/Di tanti palpiti," coda

within whose boundaries there is known no stronger guarantee of a reputation for sublime profundity than a talent for being obscure and incomprehensible!" Behind this there lurks once again the figure of Beethoven, still alive at the time of writing, and already cast as the antipode to Rossini. In another passage, Stendhal removes all doubt that, compared with his idol, Beethoven and all that he stands for, is . . . well, limited. "Human emotions," he declares, "tend to remain obstinately tepid when their reactions are interrupted by the necessity of choosing between two different categories of pleasure, each of a different quality." And he illustrates his assertion with a remarkable comparison:

> If I were to feel the urge to listen to a resplendent display of pure harmony, I should go and hear a symphony by Haydn, Mozart or Beethoven; but if I were to desire melody, I should turn to *Il matrimonio segreto* or to *Il re Teodoro* [*The Secret Marriage* and *King Theodore*, operas by Cimarosa and Paisiello respectively]. If I wanted to enjoy both these pleasures simultaneously (insofar as it is physically possible to do so) I should pay a visit to La Scala [the Milan opera house] for a performance of *Don Giovanni* or *Tancredi*. But I confess that, if I were to plunge any deeper than this into the black night of harmony, music would soon lose the overwhelming charm which it holds for me.[20]

How might Hoffmann have answered this? It would be easy enough to guess, but as it happens we can do better. Hoffmann himself never issued any comparable pronouncement about Rossini; but a writer known as "the Russian Hoffmann" did, and did it with specific reference to "Di tanti palpiti." He was Vladimir Odoyevsky, a Moscow aristocrat who published novellas and fantastic sketches very much like Hoffmann's, and who (again like Hoffmann) was an enthusiastic musical dilettante with some decent compositions to his credit.

In 1823, aged nineteen, Odoyevsky published a satirical novella that contained a scene at the opera drawn pretty much from life. A troupe of Italian singers had come to town under the direction of Luigi Zamboni, a famous *basso buffo* who had "created" (that is, sung the first performance of) the role of Figaro in Rossini's *Barbiere*. A Count Gluposilin (the name means "Strong-and-stupid") is holding forth to young Arist ("The Best"), the first-person narrator, on the merits of Rossini during a performance of *Tancredi*. (They listen to the arias, converse during the recitatives.) "Di tanti palpiti," the moment everyone has been waiting for, proves too much for Arist:

— "What!" I shouted, "Tancredi is singing an écossaise, and a pretty poor one at that! And everyone is delighted with it??"
— "Calm down," Gluposilin remonstrated, on the verge of anger, "you want to quarrel with the whole world. Don't you know, kind sir, this aria is so good that every gondolier in Italy is singing it!"
— "I quite agree," I answered him coolly. "This is a fine aria for a gondolier; but for Tancredi it won't do at all. Do Mozart and Méhul write their operas like that? With what simplicity and strength they depict the slightest tinge of character! You won't find Tancredi expressing his joys and sorrows like any old gondolier with them!"

— "Enough already! Forgive me," Gluposilin insisted, "but this aria is first-rate! It's beyond argument, beyond argument!" . . . I had my revenge on Gluposilin. For the whole duration of the performance I tormented him with my doubts. When, for example, he went into ecstasies at roulades and trills, I stopped him cold with the remark that they were being done to the words *Io tremo* ("I tremble"), *i miei tormenti* ("my torments"), *il mio dolente cor* ("my grieving heart"). Another time I pointed out to him that Argirio really shouldn't be using a dance tune to tell Amenaide *Non ti son più genitor* ("I'm no longer a father to you"); and so on. I spent the evening angry at myself for understanding Italian, angry at the singers for their distinct enunciation; it took away half my pleasure.[21]

"REALISM"

Even as he denounces the cabaletta, Arist makes an important point about it when he notes its (to him) offensive dance rhythm. An *écossaise* (in German *schottische*, "Scottish") was the early nineteenth-century version of the contredanse, by 1813 a ballroom favorite. So was the polonaise ("Polish"), a strutting processional dance in triple meter and another characteristic cabaletta rhythm. The use of ballroom dances as aria models had a considerable history; we took note of it especially in connection with Mozart. But it was in Mozart's comic operas that we encountered the practice, not his serious ones. The infiltration of serious opera by the rhythms of the ballroom was only one of the ways in which by Rossini's time the serious had adopted — and adapted to its purposes — the resources of the comic.

To say this is by no means to imply that serious opera had become comic, or in any way less serious. It had, however, become more "realistic" within the admittedly unrealistic terms of romanticism. (And from the perspective of a Hoffmann or an Odoyevsky, of course, that made it less "spiritual.") It was more concerned, to recall Wye J. Allanbrook's keen formulation, to "move audiences through representations of their own humanity," and playing subliminally on their memories of social dancing was a potent way of achieving that. The other all-important resource that serious opera borrowed from the comic in the nineteenth century was the ensemble piece — at first in finales, then in introductions and finales, and finally wherever the plot reached a crux.

This, too, had nothing to do with comedy, but with "realism": the possibility of integrating full-blown lyricism with interaction among characters, which is to say with dramatic action. In the nineteenth century, then, serious or tragic opera achieved what the comic opera had achieved in the eighteenth: the reconciliation of dramatic and musical values, so that they could be integrated in a single continuity rather than spotlit in an "artificial" alternation.

But of course words like "realism" and "artificial" have to be put in quotes in discussions like this because opera (like any medium of artistic representation) is artificial and conventional by definition. What appears realistic is merely whatever artifice or convention happens to be accepted as that by a given audience. Dancelike arias and ensembles no more resemble real-life behavior than do alternations of continuo recitative and da capo aria. The most that can be said in favor of "true realism" is that the newer techniques enabled a somewhat more evenly unfolding action, so that operatic events took place in something more nearly resembling "real time" than before.

Another change that to us may signal greater realism is the gradual abandonment in the 1830s of the heroic role *en travesti*. Men played men and women women; but the soprano lead was usually given a confidante sung by a lower-voiced woman — a contralto or a "mezzo-soprano" (to use a term coined in connection with the change) so that audiences could continue as before to enjoy virtuoso female duet singing, the brilliant cadenzas in thirds now representing devoted friendship rather than erotic love. But all of these modifications are matters of degree, not kind; and the degree, while crucial enough to matter (and to be in its time an object of controversy and acrimony), is rather small.

The idea that "men are men and women women" might seem to have come late to opera, but in fact (as some recent cultural historians have argued) it arrived there no later than in many other areas of nineteenth-century thinking and doing. Gender identities, as categories incorporating and regulating both biological and social roles, seem to have hardened around the same time that national identities, and many other forms of personal identity, took on their modern definitions. In fact, the development of modern voice categories in nineteenth-century opera is an excellent illustration of the process described by Michel Foucault (1926–84), a French historian of ideas, whereby *ars erotica*, erotic art (or sexual artifice), was replaced by *scientia sexualis*, the science (or true knowledge) of sex.[22]

Only since the nineteenth century, in this view, have gender roles and their attendant behaviors been as well defined, as standardized, and (consequently) as well policed as they are today. Another symptom of the change was the coining of the terms "homosexual" and "heterosexual" — terms that radically dichotomized, and set in opposition, modes of sexual behavior that had formerly coexisted and mixed more freely, especially among the aristocracy. Matters that had formerly been regarded as varieties of social behavior were redefined as matters of natural endowment or identity. As Foucault put it, it was nineteenth-century society, and no earlier one, that "set out to formulate the uniform truth of sex."[23]

This development, abetted as much by the nineteenth-century scientific revolution (which envisioned the possibility of a single, all-encompassingly "true" representation of nature) as it was by the rise of "Victorian" morality (whereby the behavior of the middle class was accepted as a social norm for all classes), made it harder for nineteenth-century audiences to accept soprano voices in heroic roles. The voice range could no longer be separated from the rest of the "female" constitution, nor could it credibly represent a character type that did not accord with Victorian notions of femininity, firmly identified with an ideal of bourgeois domesticity that would not be effectively challenged until past the middle of the twentieth century.

BEL CANTO

To see the new serious opera in its fullest flower, we can turn to Rossini's successors: Vincenzo Bellini (1801–35), who was to the early 1830s what Rossini had been to the

1820s, and the somewhat late-blooming Gaetano Donizetti (1797–1848), who enjoyed a like preeminence in the decade 1835–45. In viewing their works we will see the coming of a truly romantic temper to the *opera seria*, and (partly for that reason) we will be dealing with operas that survive in active repertory, unlike those of Rossini, who is represented on today's operatic stage by his comic operas alone. More specifically, we will see how the cantabile-cabaletta format was continually expanded until it could encompass long scenes packed with highly diversified action.

Bellini, the son and grandson of composers, received intensive musical instruction from the Mozartean age of four, but did not write his first opera until his twenty-fifth year. He made up rapidly for lost time,

FIG. 33-7   Vincenzo Bellini, anonymous portrait at the Museo Teatrale alla Scala, Milan.

even if he never quite developed Rossinian facility. By the time of his death, two months before his thirty-fourth birthday (more shades of Mozart), he had completed ten operas. At least four—*I Capuleti e i Montecchi* ("The Capulets and Montagues," 1830), *La sonnambula* ("The maiden sleepwalker," 1831), *Norma* (1831), and *I puritani* ("The Puritans," 1835)—have entered the permanent Italian repertory, while the two 1831 operas are international standards.

Eight of Bellini's operas were written in collaboration with Felice Romani (1788–1865), the leading librettist of the period, whose eighty-odd scripts were set by dozens of composers from Rossini in 1813 to the Austrian piano virtuoso Sigismond Thalberg in 1855, some of them many times over. With Bellini, though, Romani formed the closest working relationship of his career; their partnership merits remembrance on a par with Lully/Quinault, Gluck/Calzabigi, and Mozart/Da Ponte. Like the others, the Bellini/Romani partnership created a type that defined a phase of operatic history.

That type is sometimes rather vaguely called *bel canto*. All that the term means is "fine singing," and it has been applied to many things, starting as far back as the Venetian opera of the 1630s. The application is always retrospective, however; bel canto is always something that has been lost—a golden age. The application to the operas of Bellini's time, the one that has remained current in loose common parlance, was made by none other than the sixty-five-year-old Rossini, in a conversation that supposedly took place after dinner at his Paris residence one evening in 1858.

"Alas for us, we have lost our native bel canto," Rossini's interlocutor, a wealthy amateur, reported him as saying. The loss consists "of three elements: first, the Instrument—the voice—the Stradivarius, if you like; second, Technique—that is to say, the means of using it; and third, Style, the ingredients of which are taste and feeling." Such a loss can only portend debasement of all culture. The first symptom, as always, was contempt for honest labor.

The "Stradivarius," Rossini remarked (continuing the analogy with a priceless violin), used to be manufactured (he was referring, of course, to castrati), but now had to be cultivated—a task that began by assigning to the pupil, a child of no more than twelve, a strict regime of "guttural contractions," soundless throat exercises, and this

EX. 33-10A   Vincenzo Bellini, *Norma*, Scene e cavatina (Act I, scene 5), *Parlante*: "In pagine di morte"

"purely aphonic gymnastic," he noted, "could go on for months and months." What was sought next was "equality of timbre over the whole range of the organ, equalization of the registers." This took years, and no music was involved, only scales.

Technique was acquired by singing exercises. Every voice teacher had his "page" — a set of studies or *vocalises* that imparted correct vowel placement and agility, leading to

EX. 33-10B   Vincenzo Bellini, *Norma*, Scene e cavatina (Act I, scene 5), Cavatina con coro ("Casta diva," beginning)

facility in *gruppetti* (fast ornaments), *roulades* (fast scales and arpeggios), trills, and the like. Typically, a student worked on the "page" for three years, and then another three were spent in "putting into practice as a whole," or in combinations, "everything that had been studied in detail." "Then," according to Rossini, "at the end of a final year, the teacher could say proudly to that student (who had scarcely tried out a cavatina in class): 'Go now, get on with you. You can sing whatever you wish.'"

But not even then was training over. Style had to be acquired before a singer dared perform before a paying audience. It meant listening to great singers and imitating them. For "style is traditions, and the secrets of those traditions could be surprised by the young novice only among great singers, the perfect models consecrated by fame." Traditions, Rossini continued,

> elude scholastic instruction. Only the performing model, taken from life, can inculcate and transmit them. So that if those who possess the great, true traditions disappear without leaving disciples on their level, their art vanishes, dies.

And of course, that is precisely what had happened. "Today there is no such school, there are neither models nor interpreters, for which reason not a single voice of the new generation is capable of rendering in *bel canto* the aria 'Casta diva.'"[24]

Inevitably, Rossini had named Bellini's greatest and most famous aria, Norma's cavatina in the opera that bears her name. And what was most telling was the fact that he referred to it not by the opening words of the cabaletta, but by those of the cantabile, for that was precisely the difference between the *opera seria* of Rossini's generation and the romantic *melodramma* of Bellini's. The great music now was the slow music, a music rarefied into fantastic *melodie lunghe, lunghe, lunghe* ("long, long, long melodies," as an admiring Verdi called them),[25] for composing which Bellini had an unparalleled gift. There was nothing like them in Rossini. The Bellinian cantabile was music that, like romantic music anywhere, sought to plumb subjective depths and scale transcendent heights.

FIG. 33-8 Poster for a revival of Bellini's *Norma* at the Teatro alla Scala, Milan.

It also partook of a romanticism that, as spoofed by W. S. Gilbert in *The Mikado*, "praises with enthusiastic tone/Every century but this and every country but [its] own." Long long ago and far far away remained the preferred operatic locale, so that time could unfold in a leisurely mythological or epic manner. In the case of *Norma*, the place was ancient Gaul (the Celtic provinces of northwestern France) standing in for Britain — land of misty islands and the romantic locale par excellence for continental artists — and the time was that of the Druids as described by Julius Caesar in his history of the Gallic campaigns.

The premise, as usual, was forbidden love. Norma, the Druid high priestess, is torn between her public duties and her guilty love for Pollione, the Roman proconsul, against whose occupying forces the Druids are planning to revolt. Her love has lately been aggravated by jealousy; for, although she has borne Pollione two children in violation of her oath of chastity, he has forsaken her in favor of Adalgisa, a temple "virgin." In the end, Norma and Pollione, his love for her rekindled, perish on a sacrificial pyre in the Druid temple in voluntary expiation of their sin.

"Casta diva," Norma's cavatina, provides the framework for a scene of grandiose

FIG. 33-9 Giuditta Pasta (1797–1865) in the title role of Bellini's *Norma*.

proportions, involving the participation of another soloist, her father Oroveso, the Archdruid (bass), and the full chorus, with the orchestra supplemented by what was known as the *banda*, a brass ensemble played on stage by musicians in costume. Almost all of its components have their counterparts or prototypes in the scene from Rossini's *Tancredi* that culminates in "Di tanti palpiti." But the growth in dimensions, the infusion of spectacle, and especially the enormous influx of stage action into what had formerly been an exclusively reflective domain can be interpreted as either a new romanticism or a new realism, and shows the ultimate futility of trying to distinguish between the two.

The scene depicts a ritual: a sacrifice to the moon goddess and an augury in which the Druids hope to learn from the goddess whether the time is ripe for revolt. First, in an accompanied recitative, Norma haughtily addresses the populace and counsels patience. Her father objects, supported by stormy tremolando strings and seconded by the chorus, but she silences one and all by claiming divine inspiration. In a sort of speech-song called *parlante* (Ex. 33-10a), in which a repeated orchestral motif lends a momentary march-time regularity to the rhythm as if to underscore her words, Norma assures them that Rome will perish — but through decadence, not military defeat. She then leads the assembled congregation in a prayer. This is the famous cantabile, in which the priestess, entranced, cuts the sacred mistletoe from the holy oak and, responsively with the chorus, begs the goddess to calm the hearts of her compatriots.

The long, long, long melody is heard three times in all. It sounds first as a flute solo, the new key prefigured by a sudden excursion into its Neapolitan region, as if graphically to portray the advent of Norma's altered state of consciousness. The first two phrases of the ecstatically embellished melody, balanced four-bar periods, are played complete, but the third phrase is cut off after three measures and followed by a fermata — a favorite device for heightening expectation before a big lyric moment. Norma then sings the first stanza complete (Ex. 33-10b).

The miraculous coherence of the melody despite its inordinate length is achieved by a paradoxical trick. It is deliberately irregular in phrase structure, so that it cannot be parsed all the way down by successive binary divisions. The first two phrases, foreshadowed by the flute, have "classical" regularity. The eight-bar whole comprises two equal and parallel four-bar phrases, and each of these in turn comprises a pair of two-bar phrases set off by caesuras. Then follows a pair of parallel phrases (or rather a single phrase of one measure's duration and its embellished repetition) that veer off toward the relative minor.

But instead of being answered in kind, they are followed by a phrase of five bars' duration without any caesuras or internal repetitions at all. This last, longest, and least regular phrase, moreover, encompasses a thrilling contour. It arches quickly up to the melody's highest note, preceded by a whole measure that does nothing but "stall" a half step below, its momentary inability to move forward emphasized by the unstable diminished-seventh harmony and the syncopated rhythm of its repetitions. And then, over two luxuriant measures, the tension relaxes by degrees, with every beat sung to the same rhythm, and the harmony zeroing in on the tonic along the circle of fifths. As the dynamics subside from the passionate *fortissimo* at the melodic peak to the *pianissimo* on which the chorus will enter, the melody sums up its entire range, finally touching down on the low tonic G that has not been heard since the middle of the first phrase.

But there is another stratagem at work as well to keep this melody afloat, one that can be probed by taking note of how many beats begin with the melody sounding dissonances against the accompanying harmony. At first they are sparse. After the downbeat of the second measure, no such dissonance occurs until the functionally equivalent downbeat of the sixth. But then the tide of dissonance suddenly surges. Every beat of the seventh bar emphasizes the dissonant seventh (or the more dissonant ninth) of the dominant harmony, and the resolution to the tonic takes place against a chromatic appoggiatura to the third of the chord that clashes against its neighbor in the accompaniment as if G minor were vying with G major. The two one-measure phrases that provide the bridge to the climax are similarly riddled with accented dissonances; but the prize goes to the last two ostensibly relaxing measures, in which every single beat sounds a momentary discord, whether accented neighbor, appoggiatura, or suspension.

These purely melodic dissonances are smoothly approached and quit. None stands out as a jagged stab. One is conscious only of peaceful lyricism, but one's ear is kept perpetually on edge by an insistent undercurrent of harmonic tension in which practically every beat, crying out softly for resolution, maintains an understated but powerful undertow. When this great wave, this surge of melodic and harmonic electricity, has at last subsided, one feels that one has been transported and deposited in a different place. One's own consciousness has been altered. That is romanticism.

The two stanzas of the cantabile are separated by the choral response, to which the enraptured Norma adds the kind of roulades that Rossini, in 1858, already said no one could sing properly anymore. (We'll never know; and we'll never know what we're missing). On repetition, the cantabile is enhanced by the continued participation of the chorus and a short coda + cadenza. To provide a transition to the cabaletta, which requires a change of mood, something must snap Norma out of her trance. This the *banda* does quite handily, signaling the completion of the service.

Norma renews her promise that when the goddess commands, she will be ready to lead the attack. Oroveso and the chorus demand that Pollione be the first to die, and this of course sets Norma's heart afire. She promises to punish him, but her inner voice of conscience confesses her inability to harm the man she loves. The whole cabaletta ("Ah! bello a me ritorna," "Ah, come back to me, my beloved") is sung as an extended agitated aside (that is, an expression of unspoken thoughts), cast in a military march rhythm that emphasizes the war that rages within Norma's breast (Ex. 33-10c).

Like virtually all cabalettas of the period, it is cast in a very regular form with a pedigree that goes all the way back to the middle ages (see chapter 4): a (four bars) a' (four bars) b (2+2 bars), a" (freely extended). Despite its rigidly conventional structure, however, it is the most personal music Norma gets to sing. "Heard" only by the audience, she addresses private words of love to Pollione, at complete variance with her public stance. This time the choral interjections between her phrases (and especially right before the coda + cadenza), in which the people wish ardently for a day that Norma hopes will never come, underscore not their community in prayer, but their secret irreconcilable opposition.

EX. 33-10C Vincenzo Bellini, *Norma*, Scene e cavatina (Act I, scene 5), Cabaletta ("Ah! bello a me ritorna," beginning)

EX. 33-IOC (*continued*)

Thus between them the cantabile and the cabaletta encapsulate the heroine's fatal dilemma. The musical form has managed to embody the dramatic crux; or rather, the librettist has managed to cast the dramatic crux in terms that the musical form can embody. That is the high, if oft-maligned, art of libretto-writing, of which Romani, on the evidence of this scene (to say nothing of the contemporary demand for his work), was a proven master. Finding musically motivated ways of constructing—or, in the case of preexisting plots, of radically reconstructing—dramatic scenarios required the exercise of considerable imagination and a highly specialized skill. It required the ability to imagine any dramatic situation in specifically musical terms.

Why, then, have the efforts of professional theatrical poets been so frequently maligned? The reasons have principally to do with a generalized antipathy to conventions that was part and parcel of nineteenth-century esthetics, especially in the second half of the century when standardized musical forms themselves came under increasing suspicion. This, too, is something that could be ascribed either to romanticism or to realism. It also has to do with increasing reverence for canonical authors and texts — a feature of romanticism that often masqueraded as "classicism." Thus adaptations of Shakespeare (as in Romani's *Capuleti e Montecchi*, set by Bellini but not only by him), or of Victor Hugo (as in Romani's *Lucrezia Borgia*, set by Donizetti), are presumed to be debasements rather than legitimate transpositions to an equally — or, for Italians, a far more — effective dramatic medium. Ironically enough, the more skill a librettist showed in redeploying the contents of a novel or drama for musical effect, the more artistically suspect his efforts were often held to be.

The matter becomes especially ironic when one considers that, as demonstrated by the music historian Michael Collins as recently as 1982, *I Capuleti e i Montecchi* was based on Shakespeare's *Romeo and Juliet* only indirectly if at all. Its actual sources were the same sixteenth-century Italian novellas that had originally served Shakespeare, as filtered through more recent Italian plays, librettos, and ballets. This other tradition enabled Romani, as Collins put it, "to transform Giulietta and Romeo into nineteenth-century ideal types, the languishing heroine and the ardent hero, thus furnishing Bellini with the occasion to rise to great heights of Romantic expressiveness in his music."[26] To put it that way is to put the cart and the horse in the right order. It was the music that had to be served. Otherwise, why write operas?

This may seem obvious enough, but there has always been a vein of opera criticism that implicitly prefers spoken plays to musical ones, remaining blind or deaf to the way in which conventional musical forms expertly deployed (and beautiful voices expertly employed) can serve to channel and intensify emotion, often beyond the means of the "legitimate" stage. The primary target of such criticism has always been the cantabile/cabaletta combination, the libretto's supreme artifice. Thus Joseph Kerman, one of the most influential opera critics of the mid-twentieth century, could denounce the cabaletta ("one of the worst lyric conventions of early nineteenth-century opera") as inherently antidramatic:

> This cabaletta was a fast, vehement aria or duet of extremely crude form and sentiment; it always came after a slower, quieter piece for the same singer or singers, and served to provide a rousing curtain. The form was strophic, and of the simplest pattern; the accompaniment consisted of a mechanically repeated polonaise or fast march rhythm. Between the slower aria and its cabaletta, a passage of recitative or *parlante* served to present some sort of excuse for the singer to change his mind.[27]

But notice that everything is mentioned in this critique except the chief thing — the singing, for the sake of which the crude form and sentiment, the repeated rhythms, and the artificially contrived situation existed. Rossini might have ascribed this indifference to the vocal and sensuous aspects of opera to the critic's impoverished experience.

A hundred years earlier, after all, Rossini had already proclaimed the death of "fine singing." But there was something else at work, too. Antipathy to Italian opera, quite the norm among mid-twentieth-century critics, was further testimony to the unquestioned dominance of the Hoffmannesque brand of German romanticism, with its strong preference for the "absolute" values of instrumental music and its idealist (Protestant and puritanical) contempt for all sensuality. Kerman's critique might as well have been written a hundred years earlier by Odoyevsky.

UTOPIA

Even more adjustment became necessary when the object of "librettization" was a narrative rather than a dramatic work. As novels became increasingly popular, they furnished an ever greater proportion of operatic plots, which then had to be turned into scenarios, and finally into poetry for singing, with all the exacting formal and metrical requirements that implied. One of the most successful early nineteenth-century novel-operas was Donizetti's *Lucia di Lammermoor* ("Lucy of Lammermoor," 1835), to a libretto by Salvadore Cammarano, a staff poet and stage director at the royal theaters of Naples with whom many composers collaborated. Their opera was in fact the sixth one to be based on *The Bride of Lammermoor* (1819) by Sir Walter Scott, then the most popular writer in all of Europe, whose novels and poems were the source for more than fifty operas. But there would never be a seventh. In its way, *Lucia* was the romantic opera to end all romantic operas.

FIG. 33-10   Fanny Tecchinardi-Persiani (1812–1867) as the title character in the first London production of Donizetti's *Lucia di Lammermoor* (lithograph by Edward Morton, 1839).

Living a good deal longer than Bellini, and working throughout his quarter-century career at a Rossinian pace, Donizetti amassed a lifetime total of sixty-six operas. Like Rossini, he excelled in all genres. At least three of his comic operas — *L'elisir d'amore* ("The love potion," 1832), *La fille du régiment* ("The daughter of the regiment," presented in Paris in 1840), and *Don Pasquale* (1843) — are repertory standards. But *Lucia* was his most impressive and influential achievement. It brought to a new scale and standard the incorporation of ensemble writing within the *opera seria*, and it provided the prototype for what would become a distinct subgenre of operatic tragedy, the "mad scene." As in the case of Rossini, Donizetti did not invent either of these contributions out of whole cloth; that was not in the nature of the opera biz.

Rather, he crystallized them in practice by providing seemingly unsurpassable models (the sort of thing called a *locus classicus*), thus stimulating legions of emulators.

The reasons for the popularity of Scott's *Bride of Lammermoor* as an operatic source are not far to seek. It was one of his so-called "Waverley novels," mixing Scottish local color with horrific plots, a combination that was irresistible to romantic artists and their audiences. Anything set in Scotland, the mistiest locale within the British Isles, was surefire romantic fare, and the novel was also tinged with a few choice if incidental elements of what was known as Gothic romance: mysterious or uncanny occurrences suggesting the influence of the supernatural, all set against the background of stormy landscapes, graveyards, dark ruins, and dilapidated castles.

FIG. 33-11 Gaetano Donizetti, in a portrait by Giuseppe Rillosi at the Museo Teatrale alla Scala, Milan.

And, of course, it had the central ingredient—thwarted love. Lucy (Lucia) is the daughter of Sir William Ashton, Laird (lord) of Lammermoor, called Enrico in the opera, and cast as her elder brother. She is destined by her mother, Scott's villainess (who never appears in the opera), for a marriage of convenience to the Laird of Bucklaw (Lord Arturo Bucklaw in the opera), a rich man who will save the Lammermoor fortune. But she loves Edgar (Edgardo), the son of the Laird of Ravenswood, her family's mortal enemy. This basic situation, and some of the reasons for it, are set forth in act I of the libretto.

Getting wind of Lucy's attraction to Edgar, Lady Ashton (replaced by Enrico in the opera) coldly dismisses him from contention and sets about breaking her daughter's spirit so that she will assent to the marriage that has been arranged for her. In the novel, Lady Ashton intercepts a letter from Lucy to Edgar; when it is never answered, Lucy is induced to believe that her beloved has abandoned her. In the opera, Enrico contrives a forged letter in which Edgar declares love to another woman. After reading it, Lucia can no longer resist her brother's pressure. She signs the proffered marriage contract. Only then does Edgar manage to break in on the betrothal ceremony and expose the hoax. In the novel, he arrives after the wedding has been performed and immediately reacts by challenging both Sir William Ashton and his son Henry—the prototype of the libretto's Enrico—to mortal combat on the morrow. In the opera, Edgardo directs his rage at Lucia, who (he is led to believe) has abandoned him. In a dramatic confrontation, he tears the ring he had given her off her hand and curses her. This, the height of the plot imbroglio, is the end of act II.

The central scene of the third act is devoted to the wedding and its grisly aftermath, in which Scott's Lucy murders her unwanted husband and appears, raving, among the guests. This episode is portrayed in far greater detail in the libretto than in the original novel. Disoriented, the heroine appears, dripping dagger in hand, believing that she is about to marry Edgardo. She goes through an imaginary ceremony with him, calls on him to meet her in heaven, and convinces one and all that her end is nigh. This famous scene, the mad scene, is sandwiched between a preliminary one (sometimes omitted) in which Enrico and Edgardo belatedly agree to their duel, and the final scene, in which Scott's original ending is given a typically operatic twist. In the novel, Edgar, galloping furiously along the shore to meet his antagonists, is swallowed up in a quicksand. In the opera, Edgardo, waiting for his enemy in the Ravenswood graveyard, learns of Lucia's death. He echoes her promise to meet in heaven, draws his dagger, and stabs himself, thus completing the parallel with the ubiquitous Romeo and Juliet.

Act II, scene 2, sometimes called the act II finale, is the most complexly structured scene in the opera, and the one that best illustrates the way in which elements perfected in *opera buffa* were appropriated by composers of romantic tragedies. In a way, the scene is constructed in just the opposite fashion from the older *opera seria*, often nicknamed "exit opera" for the way in which the da capo arias of old were contrived to precede and motivate exits, which in turn preceded and motivated applause. Romantic opera, especially as it moves in on the dramatic crux, could be nicknamed "entrance opera" for the way in which characters are made to accumulate on stage along with the dramatic tension, until it all boils over in a sonorous ensemble.

The scene, ostensibly an engagement party in a brightly lit, festively decorated hall, begins with two main characters, Enrico and Arturo Bucklaw, on stage, together with a chorus of guests, who begin the act by singing a toast to the lucky groom, to which he graciously responds. This conventional choral opener functions dramatically as the calm before the storm. From this point on to the end of the act, the musical form will be the one with which we are familiar: a cantabile, followed by a transitional passage (or *tempo di mezzo*, "medium tempo") and the cabaletta. Only everything will be cast on a multiple scale. Rather than a cantabile/cabaletta for this character or that, we shall have a cantabile/cabaletta for the entire assembled cast. Thus *buffo* ensemble meets bel canto aria, creating a hybrid that combines features of both so as to project emotion (in a larger house, to a larger audience) more powerfully than ever.

The "recitative" in this scene (so designated in the score) is actually a fine example of extended *parlante*. Arturo asks Enrico where Lucy is; Enrico, knowing her devastated state (brought on by his own deception), warns Arturo that she may be wearing a sad look, but that is because she is in mourning for her mother. All of this takes place over an orchestral melody with a chugging, marchlike accompaniment. It can be construed in a pinch as a contredanse, which some directors actually choreograph for the assembled guests so that the exchange between the principals may be seen as unfolding in "real time." Lucia now enters, looking just as despondent as Enrico has predicted. The music underscoring the *parlante* makes a suitable change in meter, tempo, and key — from a neutral D-major *moderato* to a pathetic C-minor *andante*. She is accompanied and supported by Alisa, her mezzo-soprano sidekick, and Raimondo Bide-the-Bent, her tutor. The number of potential soloists on stage is now five. The unsuspecting Arturo greets her ardently; Enrico, in a hissing undertone, reminds her of her duty. Bide-the-Bent utters a sympathetic aside. Lucia signs the proffered contract.

At this point the sixth main character, Edgardo, bursts upon the scene, disrupting the proceedings and causing Lucia to faint dead away. Needless to say, this forces another change of key and tempo (to Db major, *larghetto*) and of course silences the hubbub of the *parlante*. The action goes into "aria time" for the famous sextet, in which we are made privy to the private ruminations and reactions of all the characters, simultaneously thunderstruck on stage. Another chugging accompaniment starts up, this time a polonaise, one of the most typical cantabile rhythms.

First Edgardo and Enrico, from their diametrically opposing perspectives, give inner voice to their emotions (the former to his enduring love come what may, the latter to remorse) in the kind of gorgeous arching melody a cantabile demands (Ex. 33-11a). As they make their cadence, Lucy (regaining consciousness) and Bide-the-Bent take up the melody, she to lament that she has only fainted, not died, he to continue expressing his pity. Enrico and Edgardo continue as before so that now four singers are in motion, as if in a fugue. When the second stanza is done, the coda begins with Arturo expressing bewilderment, Alisa compassion, and the chorus muttering in amazement. All on stage are now singing at once, and the music moves to the inevitable climax, achieved with a crescendo, an *affrettando* (quickening), and a syncopated "stalling" high note for Lucia, reminiscent of the one for Norma at the ecstatic peak of "Casta diva." Here of course it expresses not ecstasy but utter despair. No meaning in music is ever immanent. Everything depends on context. That is why conventions, in the hands of their best deployers, are not to be confused with stereotypes.

Just as in Rossini's comic finales, where as soon as the tempo seems to reach its very limit it is mind-bogglingly increased, here the climax is immediately repeated, louder than the first time (Ex. 33-11b). It is one of the requisite skills of fine operatic singing to be able to reach what seems like maximum power while keeping something in reserve, so that the maximum can be exceeded without falling into strain. The only difference the second time around is in the orchestration, especially the percussion punctuation at the peak.

But that is just the cantabile. Again, as in *Norma*, it is the cantabile that is generally remembered by name (in this case by Edgardo's incipit, "Chi mi frena") rather than the cabaletta. But the cabaletta (called the *stretta* in ensemble finales) plays a very necessary role in capping off the scene, and the act. With the ending of the sextet, it is as if everyone snaps out of their paralysis into a furious *parlante*, marked *allegro*, to provide the *tempo di mezzo*. Seconded by the chorus, Arturo and Enrico furiously threaten Edgardo, who makes equally furious counterthreats, while Bide-the-Bent tries to referee. Then comes the next plot wrench: the return of the rings, with the revelation that Lucia and Edgardo had secretly plighted their troth. Perhaps the most striking aspect of this commotion is the part assigned to the utterly spent Lucia. It consists of only two notes: a single E, set to a quarter note, on which she makes response ("Sì") to Edgardo's frenzied interrogations; and a single scream, a three-measure high A, with which she responds to his curses. And yet it is (when well performed) the part that the audience remembers.

The curse now sets off the D-major *stretta*, in a jig (or tarantella) rhythm, marked *vivace*. Much simpler than the cantabile, it features a great deal of homorhythmic and even unison singing, and it is cast in a modified da capo form, in which the "A" stanza consists of threats from Enrico, seconded by Arturo and Bide-the-Bent; the "B" consists of defiance from Edgardo, supported by Lucia; a transition allows Alisa to add her horrified voice to the throng, urging Edgardo to leave and save himself; and the return of "A" is set in counterpoint with the opposing parts to provide a frenzied tutti. As in Rossini, the coda is a *stretta* (marked *più allegro*) in which the note values are slyly

EX. 33-11A   Gaetano Donizetti, *Lucia di Lammermoor*, Act II finale, beginning of sextet ("Chi mi frena")

EX. 33-11A (continued)

lengthened so as to allow an increase over what seemed the very limit of speed. Da Ponte himself would no doubt have found this *strepitosissimo* impressive. (It may be confusing to find both the whole fast section of the ensemble and its even faster coda designated by the same term, *stretta*. Probably the section took its name from the headlong coda, one of its most distinctive features.)

As for the mad scene, it is also based on the cantabile/cabaletta format, remodified to produce another sort of dramatic climax. The flexibility with which the basic matrix could respond to new dramatic situations and requirements shows it to be as malleable as its instrumental counterpart, the "sonata form." If the one is a stereotype, then so is the other.

EX. 33-11B   Gaetano Donizetti, *Lucia di Lammermoor*, Act II finale, climax of cantabile

EX. 33-11B *(continued)*

As always, there is an opening *parlante* for Lucia, introduced by horrified *pertichini* from Bide-the-Bent and the chorus. She sings against an extended flute obbligato. (Donizetti had originally wanted to use an "armonica," an instrument invented by Benjamin Franklin in 1761, consisting of water glasses of various sizes concentrically arranged around a spindle; ethereal or "otherworldly" pitched sounds were produced by touching wet fingers to the revolving rims.) What the flute plays is in itself significant, since it is a distorted reprise of Lucia's first aria in act I ("Regnava nel silenzio"), in which she described a ghostly visitation of a long-slain Lammermoor lass who had been haunting the castle (Ex. 33-12ab). The flute thus adds a multileveled commentary to the action, establishing itself as Lucia's demented inner voice and linking her cursed future to a cursed past. Nor is that the only reminiscence motif. When Lucia sees the ghost again, standing between her and Edgardo, the flute (now doubled by the clarinet) recalls the cabaletta of their clandestine love duet in act I ("Verrano a te"), again somewhat deformed (Ex. 33-12cd). The last reminiscence in this heartrending *parlante* is a poignantly elegant embellished reprise of the C-minor music that accompanied Lucia's entrance in the act II finale, now mauled chromatically in a way that at once boosts pathos and intensifies the portrayal of her derangement (Ex. 33-12ef).

EX. 33-12A   Gaetano Donizetti, *Lucia di Lammermoor*, Aria: "Regnava nel silenzio" (Act I)

EX. 33-12B   Gaetano Donizetti, *Lucia di Lammermoor*, Act III, scene 2, introductory flute solo

EX. 33-12C   Gaetano Donizetti, *Lucia di Lammermoor*, Duet: "Verrano a te" (Act I)

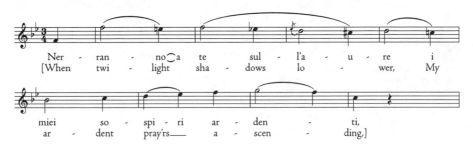

EX. 33-12D   Gaetano Donizetti, *Lucia di Lammermoor*, Act III, scene 2, flute and clarinet

The cantabile aria now begins, as a slow waltz marked *larghetto* and cast in the usual (albeit somewhat deranged) aa′ ba″ format — in the flute (Lucia's alter ego) rather than the voice, which continues its *parlante* for a while, disguising the beginning of the formal lyric. This smudging of boundaries between sections was likely intended as another representation of Lucia's disordered mind, but it was widely adopted thereafter as a "realistic" device. While still relying on the guidance of convention in planning their music, composers could thus give an impression of formal freedom that audiences could interpret as spontaneous emotion. Lucia's lyric entry ("Alfin son tua," "At last I'm yours") comes on the "b" section, accompanied by her horrified onlookers, whose *pertichini* continue the main tune while Lucia, oblivious of them, soars in the mad empyrean. Not until the closing phrase ("Del ciel clemente") does the prima donna sing the main tune at last, accompanied by the flute obbligato (Ex. 33-13a). But by now the tune is virtually buried in coloratura and crowned by a duet cadenza that Donizetti, relying on the taste and training of his performers, never dreamed of insulting them by actually composing. This interpolated cadenza, ironically enough (considering that Donizetti did not write it), is probably the most famous spot in the opera (although not in the score), and another *locus classicus* for earnest emulators and parodists alike.

The *tempo di mezzo* is a lengthy *parlante* for several soloists and chorus, touched off by Enrico's arrival on the scene. He witnesses Lucia's delirium in which, unaware of his

EX. 33-12E   Gaetano Donizetti, *Lucia di Lammermoor*, cello motif from Act II finale

EX. 33-12F   Gaetano Donizetti, *Lucia di Lammermoor*, Act III, scene 2, violin motif

EX. 33-13A   Gaetano Donizetti, *Lucia di Lammermoor*, Act III, scene 2 ("mad scene"), Cantabile: "Del ciel clemente"

55

EX. 33-13A (*continued*)

EX. 33-13B   Gaetano Donizetti, *Lucia di Lammermoor*, Act III, scene 2 ("mad scene"), Cabaletta, "Spargi d'amaro pianto"

EX. 33-13B (continued)

presence, she curses his cruelty in what seems at first like the start of the cabaletta (*allegro mosso* in G♭ major: "Ah! vittima fui d'un crudel fratello," "Ah, I was the victim of a cruel brother"). But the passage reaches a quick ensemble climax and then subsides, paving the way to the true cabaletta (Ex. 33-13b), in a quicker waltz time, marked *moderato*, accompanied as before by the flute ("Spargi d'amaro pianto," "Shed bitter tears"). Each of its two stanzas is followed by a response from all present, the second of them including Lucia herself, who now imagines herself in heaven awaiting Edgardo's arrival, her voice alone occupying a stratospheric space almost an octave above the tessitura of the choral sopranos.

The mad scene from *Lucia* is not only an exemplary operatic number, inexhaustibly instructive to anyone who wants to understand what makes the genre tick, it also crystallizes certain aspects and paradoxes of romanticism with extraordinary clarity. The magnificent irony whereby Lucia's madness, an unmitigated catastrophe to its observers, is a balm and solace to her, is graphically realized in the contrast between the stressed musical style of the *pertichini*, the *parlanti*, and everything else that represents the outer world and its inhabitants, and the perfect harmony and beauty of Lucia's own contributions, especially as regards her duetting with the flute, which (as the audience instantly apprehends) only she can "hear." That is already a mark of opera's special power: its ability to let us in through music on the unexpressed thoughts and emotions of its characters, a terrain inaccessible to spoken drama (unless, like Eugene O'Neill in his dubiously experimental, much-mocked *Strange Interlude* of 1928, the author is willing to abuse the device of the "aside" far beyond the willingness of any audience to suspend its disbelief). There is far more to it, however. The beautiful harmony of voice and flute, conjuring up a better place than the one occupied by the sane characters (or, for that matter, the audience), is a perfect metaphor for romanticism's aspirations. All art — all romantic art, anyway — to the extent that it aspires to "the condition of music" (in Walter Pater's famous phrase) aspires to be a beautiful or comforting lie.

Or is it the (higher) truth? To say so is plainly utopian, but that seems to be the message many audiences have wished to draw from art. How does such a message compare with other utopian messages, including religious and political ones, and with what consequences? These are questions to keep in mind from now until the end of the book. First broached by romanticism, they have been the most pressing esthetic questions of the nineteenth and twentieth centuries. And music, the most inherently (or at least potentially) unworldly and utopian of the arts, has been their most insistent harbinger.

The Music Trance

Romantic Characterstücke; Schubert's Career

THE I AND THE WE

One of the great questions stirred—or restirred—by romanticism was the question of where truth lay. Older concepts of truth had depended on revelation (as in religion) or on authority and the power of enforcement (as in social hierarchies). The Enlightenment as defined by Kant depended for its notion of truth on the assumption of an indwelling endowment (as in his categorical imperative, the "moral law within").[1] The Enlightenment as defined by the Encyclopedists held truth to be external but universal, deducible through the disciplined (or "scientific") exercise of reason—thus available to all and consequently "objective."

Whether revealed, enforced, innate, or rationally deduced, all of these concepts of truth had one thing in common: they could be formulated as "the" truth (or, to recall Michel Foucault's phrase, "the uniform truth"). For this reason, the distinctions between them have proved unstable. If by the ostensible exercise of reason, for example, two equally enlightened persons reach opposite "objective" conclusions, the one with the greater power is likely to prevail, instituting one version of "the" truth by force and collapsing the difference between science and authority. Powerful churchmen, for example during the Inquisition, collapsed the difference between revelation and authority. And the only way of accepting the notion of an innate law is to rely on faith, thus collapsing the difference between the innate and the revealed. Might, ultimately, could still make right.

By the beginning of the nineteenth century, history had provided sobering examples of the way the best-intentioned Enlightenment could degenerate into intolerance and dogmatism, culminating in the naked exercise of power. The most recent and chilling was the speed with which the French Revolution, which had billed itself as the triumph of enlightenment over authority, had produced the Terror. The contradiction had been prefigured in Jean-Jacques Rousseau's strange notion (expressed in his *Social Contract*) of imposing freedom by force;[2] and it would have an even bloodier echo in the twentieth century in the aftermath of the Russian Revolution. Enlightenment and the sense of universal mission with which it endowed (or infected) its adherents would also be perverted, later in the nineteenth century, into a justification for imperialism, the forcible imposition of Western institutions on other cultures and societies in the name of reason and altruism ("the white man's burden"[3]), but also in the name of economic exploitation.

Romanticism provided an alternative to these notions of truth by removing the definite article. Truth (not "the" truth) is found in individual consciousness (or conscience), not decreed by public power. What was rejected was not the notion of truth but the notion of universalism. Instead, romanticism prized the particular and the unique (as we may recall from the preamble to the same Rousseau's *Confessions*). Truth is therefore relative, at least to a degree, to the individual vantage point and therefore to some degree subjective.

The ideal became one not of uniform correct belief but one of sincerity — or, more strongly put, authenticity — of belief and utterance. Perhaps needless to say, relativism can degenerate into the law of the jungle even more easily than universalism can, since it requires little or no rationalization. If there is nothing to support my belief beyond the strength with which I hold or assert it, that strength will all too predictably translate into force if it meets with opposition. Such a view offers little prospect of community or social cooperation.

In its purest or most radical form, then, romantic individualism turned inward from public life, espousing the pessimistic social and civic passivity we have already observed in late Beethoven, and finding refuge in "estheticism" (Keats: "Beauty is truth, truth beauty"[4]). Its political impact, then, was negligible; but its impact on art — and music above all — was decisive. Romantic estheticism is the source of the still potent belief that art and politics are mutually indifferent if not mutually hostile terrains.

Far from politically passive, however, was another strain of romanticism — one that substituted collective consciousness for individual consciousness as the arbiter of truth claims. The human collectivity most commonly invoked for this purpose was the "nation" — a new concept and a notoriously protean (not to say a slippery) one. One thing was certain, however: a nation, unlike a state, was not necessarily a political entity. It was not primarily defined by dynasties or by territorial boundaries. Rather, a nation was defined by a collective consciousness (or "culture"), comprising language, customs, religion, and "historical experience."

Not surprisingly, the romantic concept of nation — and its even more slippery corollaries like "national character," "national spirit," or "national pride" — gained maximum currency where nations were most obviously distinct from states, whether because many small states (like the principalities and dukedoms then occupying the territory of modern Germany and Italy) divided peoples who had language, etc., in common, or because a large state (like the Austrian Holy Roman Empire) comprised regional populations that differed in these same regards.

And not surprisingly, the various ideal or hypothetical components of national character did not necessarily work together in reality: German speakers were divided by religion, Italian coreligionists by language. (What we now call "Italian" was spoken in the early nineteenth century by only a tiny fraction — some five percent — of the population of the Italian peninsula). Nor could anyone really say for sure what constituted a shared history, or precisely what that had to do with nationhood, since the linguistically and religiously diverse subjects of the Austrian emperor or the Russian czar certainly had a history in common. There were also the related but distinguishable concepts of ethnicity (shared "blood" or biological endowment) and of race, which played roles of varying significance and volatility in conceptualizing nationhood in various parts of Europe.

Vagueness of this kind is a great stimulus to theorizing, and there have been countless theories of nationhood. So-called "modernization" theories emphasize the importance of literacy to the spread of "imagined community" over areas larger than individual cities, and identify the middle class, in its struggle for political equality with the hereditary aristocracy, as the primary historical agent of national consciousness, rather than the peasantry or the still small urban working class.[5] Whatever the definition, the politically active phase of national consciousness arose when for political or economic reasons — that is, reasons having to do with various sorts of worldly power — it seemed desirable to redraw the map so as to make nations ("blood") and states ("soil") coincide. That wish and the actions to which it gave rise are commonly denoted by the word *nationalism*. Like every other human idea or program of action, it too could turn ugly. Preoccupation with "I" and "we" all too easily turned into preoccupation with "us and them" — self and other, often with dire consequences for the latter.

The ugliness, though, came later. In its early phases, romantic individualism (idealizing the "I") and romantic nationalism (idealizing the "we") had benign cultural effects that transformed the arts. In this chapter we will explore the musical effects of the big I; in the next, of the big We.

PRIVATE MUSIC

With its belief in the authenticity of the solitary "I," romanticism fostered a great burst of somewhat paradoxically "private" art. The paradox in the case of music, of course, is implicit in the act of publication or performance — a public display of privacy. But of course making one's private soul known to the world was, like all art, an act of representation, not to be confused (except to the extent that the confusion served art's purposes) with "reality." The representation of private lives in published biographies, autobiographies, and diaries (genres that boomed during the nineteenth century) was a reflection of — and an example to — the aspirations of middle-class "self-made men" and their families, who were the primary consumers of this new romantic art.

And consumption took place, increasingly, at home. The industrial revolution affected the arts by facilitating their dissemination and domestic use. Cheap editions of books for home reading, addressed to a much enlarged urban (and newly literate) public, and of music for home singing and playing, created new opportunities for authors and composers, and lent new prestige and popularity to the genres that were best suited to private consumption. In literature, this meant a new emphasis on lyric poetry — little poems that vividly expressed or evoked moods and stimulated reverie, encouraging psychological withdrawal from the world and contemplation of one's "inwardness" (from the German, *Innigkeit* or *Innerlichkeit*).

In music, where domestic consumption was further stimulated by the mass-production of pianos and other household instruments, the "inward" spirit found expression in actual settings of lyric poems or "lyrics" in an intimate style that did not require vocal virtuosity, and with manageable piano accompaniments that were often adaptable to guitar, harp, or other parlor instruments. Even more private and *innig* were the instrumental equivalents of lyric poems—short piano pieces, sometimes actually called "Songs Without Words," that evoked moods and stimulated reverie, according to romantic thinking, with even more unfettered immediacy than words themselves could do, whether read silently or sung aloud.

The closeness of the poetic and musical genres both in content and in effect is evident in their very names: a lyric poem, after all, means a "verbal song"; and as we are about to see, the early pieces for the parlor piano were often given names that evoked poetic genres. The closeness can also be savored by comparing the ways in which poets and musicians were typically described. The critic and essayist William Hazlitt (1778–1830) wrote marvelously of his contemporary the poet William Wordsworth (1770–1850), who introduced romantic poetry to England with a volume called *Lyrical Ballads* (1798), observing that "it is as if there were nothing but himself and the universe. He lives in the busy solitude of his own heart."[6] And here is Franz Liszt's somewhat wordier description of another contemporary (and near countryman) of Hazlitt's and Wordsworth's, the Irish pianist-composer John Field (1782–1837):

> In writing as in playing, Field was intent only on expressing his inner feelings for his own gratification. It would be impossible to imagine a more unabashed indifference to the public than his. He enchanted his public without knowing it or wishing it. His nearly immobile posture, his expressionless face did not attract notice. His glance did not rove . . . . It was not hard to see that he was his own chief audience. His calm was all but sleepy, and could be neither disturbed nor affected by the thoughts of the impression his playing made on his hearers . . . . Art was for him in itself sufficient reward for any sacrifice . . . . Field sang for himself alone.[7]

Notice that in the case of a performing art, a new level of representation comes into play: the artist's representation of himself to his audience. Field's meticulously crafted public impersonation of solitude (described by Liszt, another great pianist, in collusion) leaves no doubt that a state of "artistic solitude" had come to represent artistic truth. It was the way a public performer in the heyday of romanticism "did sincerity." And not only sincerity: disinterestedness had also to be simulated in the name of art "for art's sake." Also very telling is the name of the pianistic genre in which Field specialized, the genre in which Liszt had caught him, as it were, in the act of performing: it was called the nocturne—a French adaptation of the Italian *notturno*, "night piece." The word itself was not new to music: Haydn, Mozart, and their contemporaries wrote many *notturni*. One, by Mozart, is famous as *Eine kleine Nachtmusik*, "a little night music," using the German equivalent of the term. But in the eighteenth century the *notturno*, like the similarly named *serenata* ("evening music"), was a social genre: music for soirées, evening parties. And it was an eminently sociable music: frothy, witty, lighthearted—music to party by.

The word and its attendant music, along with the very idea of the night, had changed enormously in their connotations by the time Field wrote his Nocturnes. In his hands they became the very emblem of solitude and inwardness. To quote Liszt: "from their very first sounds we are immediately transported to those hours when the soul, released from the day's burdens, retreats into itself and soars aloft to secret regions of star and sky." Such a music is not without precedent: recall C. P. E. Bach and his Fantasias for the tiny-voiced clavichord, midnight pieces by necessity that shared features with Field's Nocturnes as Liszt described them, especially as concerned the relationship between form and expression. Field's Nocturnes, like Bach's Fantasias, had a similar purpose: "to infuse the keyboard with feelings and dreams," to quote Liszt,

> and to free music from the constraints imposed until then by regular and "official" form. Before him they all had of necessity to be cast as sonatas or rondos or some such. Field, contrariwise, introduced a genre that belonged to none of these existing categories, in which feeling and melody reigned supreme, and which moved freely, without the fetters and constraints of any preconceived form.

Again this is not entirely true, historically. Artists have always loved to rewrite history to enhance their self-image. Beethoven himself, the past master of "official" form, wrote intimate pieces for the piano. Significantly, though, he called them *bagatelles*, "trifles," pieces of no account. Now they were important. And Liszt's twin emphasis on simulated spontaneity and meticulously crafted naturalness is another reminder that C. P. E. Bach's fantasy style, known in its day as *Empfindsamkeit* ("hyperexpressivity"), was a harbinger of the later romanticism. In view of their geographical origin (Berlin) and their social (or rather, asocial) use, C. P. E. Bach's fantasias could be called bourgeois romanticism's musical debut.

Next in line after Bach as progenitor of the romantic "piano lyric" (often called *Characterstück* in German or *Pièce caractéristique* in French) were a pair of Bohemians, Jan Ladislav Dussek (or Dusìk, 1760–1812) and Václav Jan Tomášek (1774–1850). Dussek, an actual pupil of C. P. E. Bach, was like Field a peripatetic virtuoso, whose career took him from the Netherlands to Germany to Russia to Paris and finally to London, where he became a regular participant in Salomon's concerts, appearing in 1792 alongside Haydn. In addition to his "official" sonatas and rondos and such, Dussek composed many pieces in a "pathetic" (pathos-filled) improvisatory style that particularly thrilled his audiences.

One of them, *The Sufferings of the Queen of France* (1793), dedicated to the memory of the recently beheaded Marie Antoinette (a former patron of Dussek's), was a runaway best-seller, appearing till the end of the decade in many editions. A fairly lengthy composition in ten sections, each with a descriptive heading, it is actually a rather old-fashioned piece in concept. It has forebears going back beyond C. P. E. Bach to his father Johann Sebastian's *Capriccio on the Departure of His Beloved Brother*, and even further back to Johann Kuhnau's so-called Biblical Sonatas (*Musicalische Vorstellung einiger biblischer Historien* or "Musical representations of several stories from the Bible"), which when published in 1700 carried a preface from the author maintaining even then that illustrative music as such was nothing new.

Kuhnau cited one especially relevant forerunner, Johann Jakob Froberger and his famous harpsichord *Tombeau* or "funeral oration" on the death of the lutenist Blancheroche, composed in Paris in 1657. Its concluding page (Ex. 34-1a) contains a graphic illustration of its dedicatee's accidental death by falling down a flight of stairs.

Compare Dussek's guillotine (Ex. 34-1b), which intrudes (in C major) upon the Queen's last prayer (in E major). This harmonic relationship—the "flat submediant"—will be this chapter's idée fixe.

The only thing that could be called "romantic" here is the extravagance of the effect. Descriptive (or "programmatic") music as such does not necessarily meet romantic criteria of inwardness or subjectivity. Indeed, explicit labeling, as Rousseau had pointed out long before, works against the romantic ideal (or as a romantic might say, against the nature of music) by guiding and limiting the listener's reaction. Literalism also runs a great risk of bathos: can you suppress a grin at the sight of the performance direction (*devotamente*, "devoutly") that accompanies the notation of the Queen's prayer? (It is prefigured with even greater unintended comedy when "The Sentence of Death," marked *allegro con furia*, is followed by "Her Resignation to Her Fate," marked *adagio innocente*.) The somewhat younger Tomášek, who spent his entire career as a freelance performer and pedagogue in Prague, was unlike Dussek a self-confessed romantic who opposed the music of the fashionable concert stage (including Dussek's), solemnly declaring that "truth is art's only crown."[8] His character pieces contrast tellingly with Dussek's. Where Dussek's were explicitly illustrative, with titles to explain and justify the sometimes bizarre effects and the "formlessness" of the music, Tomášek used titles derived from classical poetic genres that did not disclose specific content but rather advertised a general "lyric" (and, from a romantic point of view, a more subjective and genuine) expressivity. Dussek represented Marie Antoinette's joys and sufferings, Tomášek his own—and, by implication, ours.

EX. 34-1A   Johann Jakob Froberger, end of *Tombeau de M. Blancheroche*

EX. 34-1B   Jan Ladislav Dussek, *The Sufferings of the Queen of France,* no. 9

Tomášek's main genre, associated with him as the nocturne is associated with Field, was the *eclogue*—a pastoral poem (literally a dialogue of shepherds) and one of the Roman poet Virgil's favorite forms. In Tomášek's hands it was a gentle lyric, usually cast in a simple scherzo-and-trio form, that occasionally used stylized evocations of rustic music (bagpipe drones, "horn fifths," and so on) to evoke an air of "naivety," of emotional innocence. (Despite the claims of the composer's later countrymen, responding to a later political agenda, these folkish effects should not be confused with Czech nationalism.) For more intense and personal expression, Tomášek invoked the ancient genres of rhapsody and dithyramb. The former comes from the Greek *rhapsoidos*, meaning a singer of epic tales, and betokens a dramatic recitation. Dithyramb, originally a song or hymn to the God Dionysus, meant for Tomášek and later composers a particularly impassioned utterance.

The Eclogues were published in seven sets of six between 1807 and 1819. The first set, op. 35, dedicated by Tomášek "à son ami J. Field," preceded the appearance of Field's first nocturnes by five years. Some of Field's nocturnes were written earlier, however. They circulated before publication, often with titles like Serenade, Romance, or (perhaps significantly) Pastorale. In any case, the dreamy atmosphere associated with Field, and through him with the whole repertory of domestic romanticism, certainly pervades the Eclogues of his Bohemian friend.

In the very first one (op. 35, no. 1; Ex. 34-2), that atmosphere is conjured up by a harmonic wash for which the liberal use of the sustaining pedal, while not explicitly indicated in the notation, is absolutely required. Romantic piano music was preeminently "pedal music." It is unimaginable without the sonorous "fill" that the pedal was designed to provide, and which inspired composers and performers with many of their most evocatively "pianistic" effects.

EX. 34-2   Václav Jan Tomášek, *Eclogue*, Op. 35, no. 1, beginning

Equally important to the atmosphere of naive sincerity, inwardness, and "truth" are the frequent dips into "flat submediant" harmonies, like the sudden excursion to D♭ major in measure 15 (♭VI with respect not to the original tonic but to the local one, F). This is the romantic color-chord par excellence. We have seen an important precedent for its expressive use in the Cavatina from Beethoven's B♭-major Quartet, op. 130 (Ex. 31-10), where the flat submediant harmony introduces the unforgettable *beklemmt* ("agonized") passage for the first violin, in which the imitation of a broken voice is combined with the chromatically darkened harmony to endow the passage with the authenticity (that is, the simulacrum) of direct "heart to heart" communication.

Modulation to the flat submediant became a convention signaling that the music that followed it was just such a communication. It marked a kind of boundary between inner and outer experience and its sounding came to signify the crossing of that edge, endowing the music on the other side with an uncanny aura. The new dimension that these harmonies contributed to romantic music can best be compared, perhaps, to the goal that the great romantic diarist Henri Amiel (1821–81) set himself in his *Journal intime*: "Instead of living on the surface, one takes possession of one's inwardness." The sounding of the flat submediant meant taking that plunge beneath the surface.

Tomášek used the flat submediant relation most tellingly in his dithyrambs, the impassioned "Dionysian hymns" in which he gave expression to his most inward moods. In these expansive pieces, the composer no longer sought to project naivety. Their emotional pressure is high, their range of expression more copious and complex. They are stretched, so to speak, on a broad ternary frame, in which a nobly lyrical—indeed operatic—middle section is flanked by turbulence on either side, implying an island of inward repose amid life's turmoil. In two of the three dithyrambs in his op. 65 (1818), Tomášek cast the middle section in the flat submediant key, approached in both instances from the original dominant via a deceptive cadence. Ex. 34-3 shows how C major impinges on E major in no. 2; no. 3 plunges from F into D♭. (The first dithyramb is in C minor, and its middle section is cast in the customary key of the relative major, also a mediant relationship but an expected one, and therefore not "marked" as "characteristically" expressive.)

ALTERED CONSCIOUSNESS

The effect of these modulations on the music's temporality, that is the audience's experience of time, is comparable to the effect of an operatic scene in which static "aria time" supervenes on the action-time of recitative. To evoke such an introspective effect in instrumental music, as we have long since observed, is precisely the act whereby instrumental music becomes romantic. It was the effect against which Goethe—romanticism's most formidable opponent, sometimes misread as a romantic himself because he described what he opposed so compellingly—issued his dire warning in *Faust* (1808).

Faust will lose his soul to the devil Mephistopheles, the latter warns, as soon as he calls out to the passing moment, "Stop, stay awhile, thou art so fair!" ("Weile doch, du bist so schön"). That moment, the moment in which *ethos* (responsible action)

EX. 34-3   Use of flat submediant in Václav Jan Tomášek, *Dithyramb*, Op. 65, no. 2, mm. 36–58

is sacrificed to *pathos* (passive experience, surrender to feeling), will be the moment of damnation. That is the moment romanticism celebrates. Small wonder then that romantics were so often called *poètes maudits* (accursed poets, poets of the damned). Goethe's famous last words were "Mehr Licht!" ([Give me] more light!). Romantics, as Liszt has already told us with reference to Field, were the poets of the night.

In his fourth "night piece" or Nocturne (1817), Field uses mediants and submediants alike to work his dark magic. The music is cast, like that of Tomášek's Eclogues and Dithyrambs (indeed, like most character pieces), in a simple there-and-back ternary form — albeit one somewhat disguised, in keeping with Liszt's comments on Field's sublime "formlessness," by the avoidance of sectional repeats and by the constant forward motion of the left-hand accompaniment. The chief articulator of form here is the harmonic trajectory, an old concept marked with new expressive associations.

The music almost palpably slips into reverie in the middle section (Ex. 34-4a), where the harmony shifts from the A major of the outer sections into C major, and when C major gives way to its parallel minor. And when after that C minor gives way to a circle of fifths that plunges flatward as far as its Neapolitan region (D♭ major in m. 36), we can feel the deepening of the music trance (call it the composer's, the performer's, our own as we wish; distinctions become blurred with the quickening of subjectivity).

We have had occasion once before to speak of a music trance, when examining the aria "Casta diva" from Bellini's *Norma* (Ex. 33-10), the archetypical bel canto aria. And indeed, comparing Field's melodic line and flowingly arpeggiated accompaniment with Bellini's will show the source of the pianist's inspiration: not Bellini himself, who in 1817 had not yet begun to compose, but the operatic style on which Bellini himself drew — as much a performing as a composing style. Where Tomášek had taken the scherzo (or minuet) and trio as his formal template, Field took the da capo aria. The consequent evocation of the human voice served him the way it had served Beethoven, as a means of communicating his musical message that much more sincerely and urgently. The composed mimicry of spontaneous embellishment (which, as Liszt informs us, Field freely varied in true bel canto style when performing his nocturnes) was one of the features of the domestic-romantic idiom that listeners prized most of all, because it added to the music another dimension of seemingly free impulse, at once bountiful and unconstrained. It imparted to the musical experience yet another dimension of subjective truth (the only kind of truth there was).

The connection between trances or reveries and artistic response was much enhanced in early nineteenth-century thinking by the increasing interest just then (and the concomitant increase in understanding) of mesmerism, a practice of thera-peutic trance-induction pioneered by the Austrian physician Franz Anton Mesmer (1734–1815), an acquaintance of the Mozarts. It was rechristened "neurohypnotism" (from "nervous sleep"), later shortened to hypnotism, around 1840 by James Braid (1795–1860), a Scottish surgeon. Mesmer thought that the hypnotic trance was pro-duced by the influence of an invisible magnetic fluid that passed from the soul of the doctor to that of the patient. That is why he called it "animal magnetism," or soul-magnetism. Braid thought it was the product of eye fatigue, transmitted from the

EX. 34-4A John Field, Nocturne no. 4 in A major, mm. 24–37

eye to the cerebral cortex in the brain, to which the eye is connected, where conscious thought processes take place. By paralyzing the functions of the cerebral cortex, Braid thought, the unconscious mind was brought in contact with external reality and could be subjected to conscious control.

What all early researchers into hypnotism believed was that it proved the existence of a level of reality that transcended the world of the senses. That level was where the true self lay. An entranced subject was more truly him- or her*self* than a person in the normal waking state. Any stimulus that could produce a trance phenomenon actually produced a state traditionally associated with poetic or artistic inspiration, in which—to quote Mesmer's contemporary, the Swiss esthetic theorist Johann Georg Sulzer—one "turns all one's attention to that which goes on in one's soul, forgetting the outer circumstances that surround one."[9] The trance state was thus associated with the state of "inwardness" so prized by the romantics, and even with a state of inspiration.

One of the prime stimuli that could produce these effects, it was long recognized, was music. Mesmer himself used the unearthly sound of music played on the armonica (or "glass harmonica"), already mentioned in the previous chapter in connection with Lucia di Lammermoor's mad scene, as an aid to trance induction. In many late eighteenth-century "magic operas" and early romantic operas beginning with Mozart's *Magic Flute* (1791), the armonica was used to accompany scenes of spell-casting or entrancement. The armonica parts in operas still in repertory—perhaps the most recent one being Glinka's *Ruslan and Lyudmila* (1842)—are usually played today on celesta or glockenspiel.

So the idea of music as trance-induction, and of trance-induction as a means of "taking possession of one's inwardness" and therefore a high romantic art ideal, has (or had at first) a more concrete and literal aspect than might seem to be the case. There was a genuine aura of what romantics called "natural supernaturalism"—natural access to transcendent experience—in the romantic idea, eloquently expressed by the philosopher Johann Gottfried von Herder in 1799, that "in the mirror of tones the human heart learns to know itself."[10]

To return to Field's Nocturne, the harmonic "far-out point" (FOP), D♭, is enharmonically reconfigured as C♯ by way of retransition (Ex. 34-4b). The means of accomplishing this involves another mediant relationship: the augmented sixth chord on the last beat of measure 42, which immediately identifies its bass note, D, as the sixth degree of an as yet unstated (and, as it turns out, never stated) tonic (F♯), of which the C♯-major triad that lasts six bars in figuration is the dominant. Its status as sudden flat submediant is what gives the chord its powerful charge. A large chapter in the history of nineteenth-century harmony would recount the ways in which, over the course of the century, composers learned how to deploy and control the chord of the augmented sixth, and exploit that transcendent, hypnotic charge.

SALON CULTURE

Like most of Field's nocturnes, the one in A major was composed, published, and for a long time chiefly performed in Russia, where Field had settled in 1803. He had come with his mentor Muzio Clementi (1752–1832), an Italian pianist who had become a major piano manufacturer, with headquarters in London. Clementi left Field behind as a kind of trade representative, who by his playing and teaching and commercial propaganda would stimulate the sale of Clementi pianos to a new clientele. Neither

EX. 34-4B   John Field, Nocturne no. 4 in A major, mm. 41–45

master nor pupil foresaw that Field would spend the rest of his life in St. Petersburg and (from 1821) in Moscow.

Field's presence in the Russian capitals, where he had numerous pupils and disciples, was among the catalysts in the process whereby, somewhat belatedly, Russia joined the nations of western Europe as a major producer of music in the tradition of which this book is a history. Perhaps the most notable musician in the Russian "Field tradition" was Maria Agata Szymanowska (1789–1831), a Polish noblewoman who, after a stellar international career as a pianist, settled in St. Petersburg in 1821, maintained a brilliant salon, and began publishing nocturnes in 1825. Mikhail Glinka (1804–57), the composer of the first important Russian operas, was also (very briefly) a pupil of Field.

But the reason for dwelling a bit on Field's Russian career has less to do with burgeoning Russian nationalism (to which he, an immigrant Irishman writing in a cosmopolitan style, had little to contribute) than it has to do with the social situation in which Field, and his music, were nurtured there — a social milieu that in a sense encapsulated the special nature of Field's music (and that of many other composers), poised on a kind of cusp between the private and the public spheres.

That domain was the *salon*, a word already broached in connection with Szymanowska (and, in the previous chapter, with Rossini). The word is French (the language of high society everywhere in Europe), and literally means "a big room," the kind found in the large town houses of aristocrats or *nouveaux riches* ("the newly rich," that is, those who had earned their money in trade), where large gatherings of invited guests assembled. In English it was called the drawing room, short for "withdrawing room," the room to which the company withdrew after dinner for conversation and entertainment. By extension, the word *salon* became synonymous with the assembled company itself, especially when that company was a "big" company, consisting of social lions, leaders of public fashion, politicians, or artists, including performing artists. The latter would be there by invitation if they were big enough figures to enjoy social prestige in their own right (or if, like Rossini or Szymanowska, they were the hosts). Just as often they were hired entertainers.

To maintain a salon was to have an open house on a designated day (*jour fixe*) each week or fortnight, and to have a regular roster of important guests. There has been nothing like it as a performance venue since the mid- to late nineteenth century, but it was the chief catalyst of the "domestic-romantic" music we are now surveying. Only in such an environment does the idea of a "public display of privacy" lose its paradoxical, even faintly ridiculous mien. Salons, as exclusive gatherings, partook of both domains, and encouraged a form of music making that had high prestige but addressed relatively small elite audiences — addressing them, moreover, and in true romantic fashion, as individuals (as the historian Peter Gay wittily implied when he defined romanticism as "a vast exercise in shared solitude").

The music a pianist like Field composed for salon performance (whether by himself or by one of his fashionable lady pupils) served the same social purpose, for both composer and audience, as the concerto had served for Mozart. A statistical survey of Field's output bears this out: he started his career as a public musician in London, with a concerto (in E♭, 1799), made his early name in Russia with more concertos, but after 1822 composed only for solo piano or for piano intimately accompanied by a string quartet *ad libitum*. He had shifted his field of operations from the concert hall to the salon, and his music responded to the change with an ever-increasing quotient of *Innigkeit*.

To jump ahead briefly to Frédéric Chopin (1810–49), the last and most famous representative of the "Field tradition," the fact that — after an early group of concertos and other orchestrally accompanied pieces composed in his native Warsaw — his output consisted almost entirely of works for solo piano in small forms was due not only to his personal or "disinterested" esthetic predilections, but also to the ready support his creative and performing activities were receiving from Paris "salon culture."

The salon, in other words, was a new vehicle for the channeling of art patronage, based on a newly negotiated symbiosis between social and artistic elites. Music played at salons, much of it written to be played there, was marked by its milieu as socially elite. Reciprocally, its presence there, especially when played by its creators, marked the occasion and the assembled company as culturally elite. Each elite helped define and support the other. There were material benefits, too, for pianist-composers in social contacts that led to fashionable pupils, mainly the daughters of those in attendance. That was how Field (and later, Chopin) earned a living.

The material side of things was of course banished from the official discourse of romanticism. For the official view, consult the famous painting shown in Fig. 34-1: *Liszt at the Piano*, by the Austrian genre specialist Josef Danhauser (1805–45), a minor artist who nevertheless made a major statement here in producing what has become perhaps the most widely reproduced, and widely commented-on, depiction of early nineteenth-century musical life. It is in reality no such thing, but rather a fantasized scene that did not take place and never could have taken place. It renders a salon not as it actually was but as an artist might have idealized it, populated almost exclusively by artists (four writers and four composers) who have gathered to partake "disinterestedly" in art for the sake of art.

FIG. 34-1   *Liszt at the Piano* (1840) by Josef Danhauser.

Seated furthest left is the French poet Alfred de Musset (1810–57), author of the famous novel *La confession d'un enfant du siècle*, one of the earliest examples of autobiographical fiction, a quintessentially romantic genre. Seated next to Musset is Amandine Aurore Lucie Dupin (1804–76), the Baroness Dudevant, who under the pseudonym George Sand was one of the most prolific novelists of the day, as well as the author of a truly immense autobiography. Her masculine pen name as well as her masculine attire and her trademark cigar (which the artist has made sure to include in the picture) identify her as a fighter for women's rights, including free love. She fought, of course, by the lights of her time, when women sought equality with men by, as it were, becoming "social men," as if playing out the role of the operatic *musico* in real life. Inverting (but thereby nevertheless asserting) the romantic formula of "public privacy," George Sand's private love life was quite public long before she actually wrote about it. Her most highly publicized extramarital liaisons were with Musset, as shown (thus dating the scene depicted to the early 1830s), and with Chopin.

Behind and between Sand and Musset stands Victor Hugo (1802–85), master of all genres of romantic literature, and author — in the prefaces to his historical dramas *Cromwell* (1827) and *Hernani* (1830), performing which had brought about near-riots and fisticuffs in the theater — of perhaps the most militant manifestos ever penned on behalf of romantic art. ("Living form in place of dead form," he called it in the former; "liberalism in literature" in the latter.) To the right of Hugo are two composers. Hector Berlioz (1803–69), to whom we will be formally introduced in a later chapter, was often compared with Victor Hugo as a militant romantic; of all important contemporary musicians he was perhaps the least beholden to salon culture and its intimate media. Embracing him is Rossini, whose "purely sensuous art" Berlioz loathed and, as critic, publicly excoriated. Although he would later run a famous salon himself, in this picture Rossini is for all sorts of reasons (reasons anyone who has read the previous chapter could easily list) completely, even a bit comically, out of place. The Austrian painter, in an early version of the notorious historiographical myth described in the previous chapter, has colonized him on behalf of the big bust on the piano.

Before we get to the big bust, let us identify the remaining living figure, nestled submissively to the right of Liszt. She is the Countess Marie d'Agoult (1805–76), presumably the nominal hostess of the evening, who under the George-Sand-like pseudonym Daniel Stern was a minor French writer, but who was best known both during her lifetime and in history for her sexual liaison with Liszt, to whom she bore three daughters, one of whom (Cosima) will figure again in our narrative. She is probably posed with her back to the viewer because the painter did not know her face and could not make her recognizable.

This painting is famous not only for its cast of characters but for its implicit (and possibly inadvertent) commentary not just on their gathering, but on the whole discourse of romanticism. It is a preeminently a portrait of shared solitude. All present are lost in a music trance, even (or especially) Liszt himself, who is sitting with his back to his hearers, eyes fixed on the big bust—none other than (who else?) Beethoven, the patron saint of creative isolation and all artistic truth. By a skillful trick of perspective, Beethoven has become a floating presence, a true divinity: although presumably supported by the pile of music atop the piano, his image can also be optically construed as resting on the distant horizon, dominating the whole landscape beyond.

And what an imposing, outsized Beethoven it is, this bust, even if confined to quarters—a barrel-chested, broad-shouldered, bullnecked Arnold Schwarzenegger of a Beethoven, a god not only of artistic culture but of physical culture as well. Why such machismo?

As usual, machismo masks nervousness, a nervousness related to the middle-class solidification of gender roles and identities noted in the previous chapter with regard to the newly "naturalized" assignment of voice types in opera. There was something feminine—uncomfortably feminine for "self-made men"—about the passivity of romantic listening. Salons, often if not usually hosted by rich or titled women (like the Countess d'Agoult and the Baroness Dudevant), where the music (unless performed by its composers) was usually performed by women, were increasingly looked upon as a women's world; and as the music historian Jeffrey Kallberg has shown, the connotation spread to the music typically played there, particularly to the nocturne, its emblematic salon genre. By 1841, one German writer unearthed by Kallberg charged the nocturne with "a twofold error" consisting, in the first place, of "dawdling," and in the second, of "falling into the effeminate and languishing, which displeases stronger souls and altogether tires the listener."[11] By 1844, another writer was complaining of the "soft, rapturous, tender, lyrical, almost womanly character of the Fieldian cantilena."[12]

Ironically enough, then, it was precisely from the early to middle nineteenth century, the heyday of musical romanticism, that the stigma of effeminacy—and of license, too, symbolized by the libertine, transvestite figure of George Sand and the adulterous Marie d'Agoult—began to attach itself to music, making musicians uneasy in a society where conformity to standardized sexual roles (and role-playing) was becoming more and more a requirement. By 1909, a critic could warn that exposure to a certain nocturne by Chopin "bewitches and unmans" a listener who is incautious enough to "tarry too long in its treacherous atmosphere."[13] This unease, and the misogyny to which it gave rise, were among the factors that conspired, beginning around the middle of the century, to cast the high-prestige notion of "salon music" into disrepute—a disrepute that has grown apace, so that the phrase is most often used today as a term of abuse, dismissing a composer as shallow or a work as trivially pretty. Rossini's late career as a social lion, and the *Péchés de vieillesse* and *Quelques riens* he composed for performance at his own salon, also did their bit to recharacterize the nature of the salon (or return it to its eighteenth-century status) as a merry place where music functioned as aristocratic entertainment—a double sin for those who believed that art should have no social function beyond "disinterested" esthetic edification (that is, trance-induction). There was also the stigma of sensuality. At the soirée, described in the previous chapter, where Rossini discussed bel canto with his wealthy interlocutors, the discussion of music took place over fine cognac and imported cigars. A social milieu that put music in the category—or even the proximity—of "vicious pleasures" could only sully its reputation with a romanticism that was becoming increasingly imbued with Victorian values.

The last straw was the *petit-embourgeoisement* of the salon, its loss of social cachet. In today's French the word *salon* simply means "the living room" in any house or apartment. The change came about not through democratization, but by the ambition of middle-class households during the Victorian Age to enhance their social prestige by aping what the French called the *grande bourgeoisie*, the urban aristocracies of birth and wealth. A cynical sub-industry arose among music publishers in the later nineteenth century that catered to this pretense by supplying tacky mass-produced imitations of salon genres to grace the imitation salons in "petty bourgeois" homes. By then, moreover, the music that had inhabited the high-prestige salons of old had moved decisively into the concert hall, impelled by the canonization of some of its chief composers.

But beware: the "tackiness" of the later product has been defined from a grand bourgeois point of view unwittingly adopted by historians loyal to Field and (especially) Chopin. The tackiness inhered as much in the mass-production and the cheap dissemination as it did in any ostensive defect of the product itself. When Carl Dahlhaus, for example, speaks of "the deadly mixture of sentimental tunefulness and mechanical figuration"[14] found in what he calls "pseudosalon music," and defines the latter as "pieces that were intended to delude provincial middle-class audiences into a musical daydream of salons they were not allowed to enter,"[15] it is hard to miss the note of social snobbery.

All of these bad qualities, perhaps needless to add, have been found in Field and Chopin, too, by those who have needed to find them. More often than not, what is tacky about tacky music turns out to be the people who listen to it. What really happened to salon culture in the later nineteenth century was that, by inundating the market with music that targeted the petty bourgeoisie, the music publishers of the nineteenth century managed to render the salon, and many of its musical genres, "*déclassés*," no longer capable of creating the sense of an elite occasion. Let this brief account of the salon, its culture, and its fluctuating reputation serve to remind us once again how accurately (and how often) attitudes about art encode social attitudes.

SCHUBERT: A LIFE IN ART

The early romantic composer whose works now loom in history as the most decisive, all-transforming "crossing of the edge" into inwardness was a composer who lived his short life in relative obscurity, and whose enormous influence, both on his creative peers and on the listening habits of audiences, was almost entirely a posthumous one. In a way this is unsurprising, even fitting, since the music of Franz Schubert (1797–1828) reflected, in its exploration of the inner "I," one of the most outwardly uneventful, essentially private lives any composer of major standing was ever destined to live.

Unlike the "Vienna classics" Haydn, Mozart, and Beethoven, Schubert, the son of a schoolmaster, was actually a native Viennese. At the age of eleven he was accepted, like Haydn before him, as a choirboy in the imperial court chapel. There he took instruction with Antonio Salieri, still the imperial Kapellmeister. In addition to his chapel duties, Schubert played violin in (and occasionally conducted) a student orchestra organized by the twenty-year-old Josef von Spaun (1788–1865), then studying law at the University of Vienna. Spaun, who spent his career in the civil service supervising lotteries, would be Schubert's lifelong friend and, because he survived long into the period of Schubert's posthumous fame, became the chief source of biographical information about the composer.

After his voice broke, Schubert briefly became an assistant teacher, then a young master, in his father's school. By the end of the year 1816, however, encouraged by devoted friends whose families promised financial support, Schubert had renounced steady employment for full-time composition. (Nevertheless, over the next two years he would occasionally return to teaching at his father's request, and he twice briefly accepted employment as music tutor to the children of a minor member of the Eszterházy family, famous for its patronage of Haydn.) By the age of nineteen he was the author of six operas (mainly singspiels, short comic works in German with spoken dialogue), five symphonies, sixteen string

FIG. 34-2   Franz Schubert, portrait in oils by Josef Willibrord Mähler.

quartets (composed for family recreation), dozens of dances for piano or small chamber ensemble, and literally hundreds of songs set to verses by contemporary poets. The latter included some early masterpieces, never to be surpassed, including *Gretchen am Spinnrade* ("Little Margaret at the spinning wheel"), to a passage from Goethe's *Faust*, composed at seventeen, and *Erlkönig* ("The Elf King"), to a ballad or narrative poem by Goethe, composed the next year. Small wonder that he inspired reverence among his friends, and appeared to their wealthier parents to be a good investment.

In the autumn of 1817 Rossini conquered Vienna and Schubert, hearing him for the first time, was liberated by the experience. Until then (as seems inevitable for a Viennese) he had considered Beethoven the only possible model for composition in large forms, and a daunting one. This constraint is most obvious in his Fourth Symphony, composed early in 1816; it is cast in the "Beethoven key" (C minor) and subtitled "Tragic." (This subtitle, unlike most, was actually the composer's.) Schubert's reputedly "Mozartean" Fifth Symphony, in B♭ major, composed later the same year, is as clearly modeled on Beethoven's Fourth Symphony (in the same key) as his Fourth Symphony had been modeled on Beethoven's Fifth. To Spaun he confided, "I hope to be able to make something out of myself, but who can do anything after Beethoven?"[16]

FIG. 34-3   Stadtkonvikt in Vienna, the monastery school where Schubert lived while he was a choirboy at St. Stephen's cathedral (drawing by Franz Gerasch).

The works he composed soon after his brush with Rossini — notably two overtures "im italienischen Stile" (in the Italian style) and the Sixth Symphony in C major, all completed between October 1817 and February 1818 — show a new face. The symphony, in particular, incorporated a vein of Italianate melody that was no longer customary in such works (often played, à la Rossini, by solo winds). The long tunes loosened up the structure and began to impart to Schubert's large-scale compositions the discursiveness (or "heavenly length," as Robert Schumann called it[17]) that so enraptured the later romantics who discovered them upon their posthumous publication.

Beginning around 1817, Schubert began to find some public champions, mainly singers (one of them a nobleman) with whom the composer began appearing as song accompanist in fashionable Viennese salons. In March 1818, he had a "concert debut" of sorts when one of his Italian overtures was performed by a restaurant orchestra. In 1820, one of his singspiels ran for five performances at the same Vienna theater where *Fidelio* had its premiere, and Schubert was engaged thereafter to write some incidental music to other shows. A breakthrough occurred in 1821 when, thanks to a subscription undertaken by the composer's friends, a number of songs (including *Erlkönig*, which thus became his "opus 1," and *Gretchen am Spinnrade*) were published.

Their sales earned the twenty-four-year-old composer an income that, however meager at first, was nevertheless connected with his creative work. From then on, as the Viennese music historian Otto Biba has established,[18] Schubert managed to eke out a living from the products of his pen, and was the only composer in Vienna at the time who was officially classified as a *freischaffender Komponist* — a "freelance composer" who neither gave lessons nor worked at a civil service sinecure nor enjoyed aristocratic patronage in support of his musical vocation. He was, albeit in a small way, a commercial success, and a bit of an economic pioneer.

From 1822, the list of Schubert's major works begins to accumulate: the Mass in A♭ major, the unfinished Symphony in B minor that even as a two-movement torso has become a repertory staple, and the "Wanderer" Fantasy for piano which, published in 1823 as op. 15, was the first of Schubert's larger works to be printed during his lifetime. It is named after the song that provided the theme for variations in the second of its four connected movements; there are similar song-variation movements in Schubert's Quintet in A major ("The Trout," 1819) and his Quartet in D minor ("Death and the Maiden," 1824).

Eighteen twenty-two was also the year of his first serious illness, a bout of syphilis that incapacitated him for several months and forced him to return to his paternal home. His financial resources depleted, Schubert was forced to accept lump sums rather than royalty contracts for the publication of some of his most popular songs. By the middle of 1823, he had been moved to the Vienna municipal hospital and was expected (at the age of twenty-six) to die. At this low point he produced one of his greatest works, the song cycle *Die schöne Müllerin* ("The beautiful miller maid"), a kind of novel-in-lyrics that ends with a lovelorn suicide.

From this point to the end of his woefully truncated life, which ended at the age of thirty-one (some say from typhus or typhoid fever, others say alcoholism, still others tertiary syphilis), Schubert's health would be precarious. But apart from the intermittent physical sufferings of the last years, and the unexpectedly grim finale, his life was no romantic scenario but a placid existence devoted almost entirely to creative work. To recount it is basically to offer a chronicle of composition, as one of his friends, the painter Moritz von Schwind (1804–71), already hinted in mock-exasperation in 1824: "If you go to see him during the day, he says, 'Hello, how are you?—Good' and goes on writing."[19] It was seemingly a life lived almost entirely inside the heart and head—and yet what could be more romantic than that? The inner life was the only life, according to romantic doctrine; and Schubert's music was of a sort that seemed to give access to it, making the composer, despite the absence of outward personal drama (or indeed of any intense personal intimacies, at least reliably recorded ones), the subject of intense human interest and vicarious personal identification.

The access, of course, is illusory, but such is the abiding influence of romanticism on today's conventional thinking about the arts that we need constantly to remind ourselves that they deal in representations, not realities. The memoirs of his friends show Schubert to have been far from reclusive (except, as Schwind found out, in the afternoon). Musicological research has revealed him not to have been without worldly ambition, nor was he devoid of social recognition. Medical history assures us that his life span was neither as short nor his illnesses as egregious within the conditions and expectations of his time as they would be in ours. But nothing will prevent those affected by the music from creating its composer in its image. That is an integral part of the romantic experience: the beautiful lie (or higher truth) of a supreme fiction. As the critic Alex Ross has written, "The man is not quite there; the music is another thing altogether. Its presence—its immediacy—is tremendous,"[20] and creates for us a sense of its creator's presence that the mere facts of his life will not efface.

The masterpieces, meanwhile, continued to mount: the "late" piano sonatas and character pieces, the "late" quartets, the dark and troubled song cycle *Die Winterreise* ("The winter journey"). The last year of Schubert's life produced an astonishing series: the C-major Symphony (later nicknamed "the Great" to distinguish it from the "Little" C-major Symphony of 1817), the two piano trios, the Mass in E♭ major, the C-major String Quintet, the last three piano sonatas, the F-minor Fantasie for piano duet, four-

FIG. 34-4   Schubert singing with his friends, as drawn by one of them, Moritz von Schwind.

teen of his greatest songs collected in two

volumes for publication—posthumous publication, as it turned out, under the title *Schwanengesang* ("Swan song").

Whether measured by quantity or by quality, the list (which could be augmented by a slew of minor works) strains belief, as indeed does Schubert's output overall. His earliest known compositions are dated 1810, so that his whole career as a composer lasted no more than eighteen years, during which—by the reckoning of Otto Erich Deutsch (1883–1967), the compiler of a thematic catalogue of Schubert's works modeled on Ludwig von Köchel's *Mozart-Verzeichnis*—he amassed a total of 998 works, "an outburst of composition without parallel in the history of music,"[21] in the provocative yet unchallengeable words of his biographer, Maurice Brown.

PRIVATIZING THE PUBLIC SPHERE

Out of this near-thousand "Deutsch numbers," some of which actually represent groups of songs or short piano pieces (so that the total of actual compositions is well in excess of 1,000), a little over 200 were published during Schubert's lifetime, of which 134 (almost precisely two-thirds) were songs. The proportion is representative: Schubert's songs total around 630, accounting for almost precisely two-thirds of the entries in the Deutsch catalogue. The remainder of the published works breaks down as follows:

> 22 secular choruses, including two for mixed voices, one for female voices, and nineteen for male chorus (*Männerchor*);
>
> 19 groups of dances for piano (totaling 167 individual items, most of them tiny), including waltzes, *Ländler* (a slower version of the waltz), écossaises, *Deutsche tänze* (cf. Mozart's "Teitsch," a souped-up minuet on the way to a waltz), galops (fast dances in duple time, danced in "longways sets" with couples in a line, usually the concluding number at a ball), and cotillons (a more elaborate dance performed in "squares," which also often served as a ballroom finale);
>
> 15 publications for piano duet (four hands at one keyboard), totaling 49 individual items (mainly polonaises and marches, including the still popular *Marches militaires*, op. 51; but also an arrangement of one of Schubert's opera overtures, and one sonata);
>
> 7 works for piano solo, including three sonatas, the "Wanderer" Fantasy, a group of two Impromptus, a group of six *Momens musicals* (soon to be republished with a corrected French title as *Moments musicaux*), and a single waltz variation published in Diabelli's famous collection of 1824;
>
> 5 liturgical settings in Latin, including one complete Mass and a *Deutsches Requiem* or *Trauermesse* (a setting of the funeral rite in German), originally published as the work of the composer's brother Ferdinand to help him with a job application;
>
> 2 full-length chamber compositions: a string quartet in A minor, published in 1824 (with a dedication to Ignaz Schuppanzigh, the famous quartet leader) as op. 29, and a piano trio in E♭ major, published in 1828 as op. 100.

This list is very revealing of the nature of the music business at the time, and of Schubert's willingness to work within market requirements, quite belying the withdrawn image his posthumous reputation has assigned him. With few exceptions, the list is confined to utilitarian, sociable, and domestic genres — "Biedermeier" genres, as contemptuous aristocrats called them (after "Papa Biedermeier," the proverbially obtuse paterfamilias celebrated in humorous verses and cartoons), meaning stuff that was cheap and cozy. At the time of his death, then, Schubert was no famished genius but a composer of solid, albeit largely local reputation. Within his seemingly unpretentious limits he was regarded as a *beliebter Tonsetzer*, a "favorite composer," by an appreciative public, albeit a public largely unaware that behind closed doors he was vying with Beethoven as a composer of quartets and symphonies and (rather less successfully) with Rossini as a composer of operas.

That situation may have been on the point of changing at the time of his death. During his last year Schubert carried on negotiations with some northern German firms who showed a characteristically North German interest in "the highest in art" (as the composer put it),[22] and his largest work to see print in his lifetime, the Trio, was published by the Leipzig firm of Probst. But as long as he was writing for the local Viennese market, he was happy to meet its demands. His dances, for example, were not *Vortragsmusik* ("performance music" or "music for listening") but convivial *Gebrauchsmusik* ("music for active use"), dances to be danced to. The *Männerchöre* ("male choruses") were written for a lucrative market that had been created by the proliferation of Viennese *Männergesangvereine*, men's singing clubs. These works, now among his most obscure, were the Schubert compositions most often performed in public at the time.

Piano duet playing was a convivial activity that lasted into the twentieth century, when the dissemination of sound recordings largely killed it off. Most orchestral works were published in piano four-hands arrangements to create a market for them; making them kept many hacks employed. (Schubert, however, had no access to their services, and it is quite indicative of public taste that of all his orchestral music it was the overture to the opera *Alfonso and Estrella*, an imitation of Rossini, that was chosen for publication in this form.) Even the large-scale works, the three piano sonatas and the two chamber pieces, were of a kind that could be enjoyed at home, whether in solitude or in company.

None of Schubert's compositions in large public media had any circulation to speak of during his lifetime. One singspiel (a farce of mistaken identity called *Die Zwillingsbrüder*, "The twin brothers") made it briefly to the stage, as we have seen, in 1820. None of the other dozen stage works was ever produced until after Schubert's death (sometimes very long after: *Der Spiegelritter*, the earliest one, had its first production in 1949). The only tune from a Schubert opera that musicians or music lovers are likely to know today is that of a duet in the singspiel *Die Freunde von Salamanka* ("The friends from Salamanca"), and only because Schubert used it for a set of variations in his Octet in F major for winds and strings. (The six-movement octet, a sort of suite, was first published complete in 1889, although the variations movement had already appeared in 1853 as part of a four-movement "sonatafied" version; the opera remained unperformed until the Schubert centennial celebrations of 1928.) Nor did Schubert ever hear one of his symphonies performed in public, although (as Biba discovered) the first five, with the perhaps significant exception of the "Tragic" Fourth, were performed by a band numbering about thirty at the salons of Otto Hatwig, a wealthy amateur who led the violin section (with Schubert himself sitting among the violas). The first Schubert symphony to be published was the "Great" C-major, in 1840; the "Unfinished" had to wait until 1867.

Only one full-evening's concert of Schubert's works was ever given during his lifetime. It took place on 26 March 1828 in a small concert room owned by the Vienna Gesellschaft der Musikfreunde (Society of Friends of Music), one of the city's three municipal concert bureaus, which since 1818 had been including Schubert's works in its so-called *Musikalische Abendunterhaltungen* ("Evening musical entertainments"). But even on this occasion the program consisted of works in domestic and sociable genres: a quartet movement, the E♭-major Trio, a *Männerchor*, and seven songs, most of them performed by the baritone Johann Michael Vogl (1768–1840) with the composer at the piano. The little hall was packed with friends. The composer took in a respectable "gate." But the Italian violin virtuoso Niccolò Paganini (1782–1840), a public sensation even greater than Rossini, had picked that very week to make his Vienna debut, and garnered all the press notices.

Perhaps the best measure of Schubert's lack of affinity for the public concert stage is the fact that he never wrote a concerto, despite receiving a commission in 1818 to write one. Later on, when he had become a posthumous "classic" and good box office, Liszt made a concerto arrangement of the "Wanderer" Fantasy, Schubert's showiest piano composition. Similar salvage operations have been attempted on the two string sonatas. The one for violin and piano, in three movements without pause, is also titled Fantasie; and like the "Wanderer" Fantasy it has a slow movement based on one of Schubert's songs, *Sei mir gegrüsst* ("Loving greetings"). The other, now played by cellists, was composed for *arpeggione*, a briefly popular, soon obsolete instrument resembling a bowed guitar.

But there is little in Schubert that sustains a "concerto" mood. His works flourished best within the private circle of his friends, in the "shared solitude" of what they called "Schubertiads," gatherings that fell somewhere between domestic get-togethers and full-fledged salons (Fig. 34-6). Nor did his larger, more public concert works (at least the later ones) compromise the

FIG. 34-5 Schubert making music with Josephine Fröhlich and Johann Michael Vogl (pencil sketch by Ferdinand Georg Waldmüller, 1827).

FIG. 34-6   A "Schubertiad" (Schubert evening) at the home of Joseph von Spaun (drawing by Moritz von Schwind, 1868).

mood of lyric introspection, for rendering which Schubert evolved a matchless and in some ways radically innovative technique.

Quite the contrary: through Schubert the mood of lyric introspection — of privacy — invaded and suffused the public genres. Schubert's mature sonatas and symphonies rarely strike a heroic, "Beethovenian" attitude. Notwithstanding the occasional dramatic outburst, they are discursive, ruminative, luminous works that sooner induce reverie than excitement. Their peak moments more readily suggest diffusion of rapture than dramatic climax. Their tonal/thematic closures, in particular, substitute the serene satisfactions of "crystallization, of finely adjusted machinery clicking gently into place" (as the Schubert scholar Daniel Coren once eloquently put it) for the more strenuous gratifications of victory through struggle.[23]

FIG. 34-7   *Andante de la Symphonie en la* (Andante from the Symphony in A; i.e., the second movement — actually Allegretto — from Beethoven's Seventh Symphony), by Eugène Lami (1840).

Once they achieved widespread dissemination, a process that only began in the 1840s, Schubert's sonatas, symphonies, and major chamber works enabled larger audiences than ever to experience music trances and shared solitude, and "take possession of their inwardness," the way a group of Parisian concertgoers is shown doing in Figure 34-7, a watercolor by Eugène Lami, painted in 1840, titled *Andante de la Symphonie en La* — that is, the second movement (actually marked *allegretto*) from the A-major Symphony (no. 7) by, yes, Beethoven — but an uncharacteristically "Schubertian" movement that fits the description in the previous paragraph to a T. The last two Schubert symphonies, first performed in 1850s and 1860s, had an enormous influence on composers of the generation born between the 1820s and the 1840s (from Anton Bruckner to Antonín Dvořák), helping in this way to revive their genre, which was then (as we shall see) in temporary decline.

CROSSING THE EDGE

To encompass a legacy as enormous and as important as Schubert's within the confines of a narrative like this requires strategy. The nature of Schubert's career, as just narrated, suggests that we begin with music published during his lifetime, which had some circulation among his historical contemporaries, and only afterward branch out into posthumous terrain. Thus we will be proceeding from the intimate domestic genres in which Schubert's unique construction of musical subjectivity was formed, into larger genres that through Schubert (quite unbeknownst to his contemporaries) became infected with the esthetic of intimacy.

We can pick up the stylistic and analytical thread exactly where we left it with Tomášek and Field, by starting with a character piece for piano. Schubert knew the works of Tomášek, and was personally friendly with one of Tomášek's pupils, Jan Vaclav Voříšek (1791–1825), a transplanted Bohemian who was Schubert's near contemporary, and who appeared as pianist at many of the same salons and *Abendunterhaltungen* as Schubert before his own almost equally untimely death. In addition to eclogues and rhapsodies, genres pioneered by his teacher, Voìšek also composed some impetuous character pieces to which he gave the name Impromptu (French for "offhand," or "on the spur of the moment"). They were supposed to give the effect, prized by salon romantics and their audiences, of sudden, untamed inspiration.

Like other types of character piece that we have seen, Voříšek's Impromptus were usually cast in a simple there-and-back ("ternary" or "aba") form. Schubert gave the name to eight similarly structured pieces, all written in 1827, of which two were published that same year. The second of these will remind us of Tomášek and Field in the way it "crosses the edge" from the tonic to the quintessentially romantic region of the flat submediant. But Schubert's handling of the by-now familiar maneuver is an especially bold one that links the flat-sixth technique with another tonally destabilizing technique, that of "modal mixture," the infiltration within a major key of harmonies drawn from its parallel minor (or, more rarely, the other way round).

The sudden "impromptu" modulation in m. 83 that articulates the form of the piece — E♭ major to B minor — looks (and sounds) very remote indeed. But, as always, what strikes the naive ear as impromptu is actually the result of a crafty strategy, consisting in this case of a double mixture. The many digressions into the parallel minor during the first section — one of them (mm. 25–32) going through a complete circle of fifths that touches on D♭, G♭, and C♭ in addition to the signature flats — prepare the listener for the wildly accented G♭ in m. 81 that brings the first section to its precipitous close. There is even a precedent (in the circle of fifths progression) for interpreting the G♭-major chord that follows as a dominant, furnishing a quick transition to the middle section. But when the new dominant makes its resolution to C♭ (the amply foreshadowed flat submediant key), the expected major is replaced wholesale by its parallel minor, spelled enharmonically as B minor to avoid an inundation of double flats (Ex. 34-5a).

This key, the parallel minor of the flat submediant, is sustained as an alternate home tonality much longer than its counterparts in Tomášek and Field. It is decorated with some fairly remote auxiliaries of its own — secondary dominants, Neapolitan sixths — that serve to promote its status as a stable region to the point where we can easily forget the instability of its traditional relationship to the original tonic. It is even given its own flat submediant, albeit in a context (m. 100) that temporarily identifies the harmony as the "Neapolitan to the dominant of the original flat submediant." A mouthful like that is the equivalent of "third cousin on the mother's side twice removed."

EX. 34-5A   Franz Schubert, Impromptu in E-flat, Op. 90, no. 2, mm. 77–106

The relationship can be traced logically, and is therefore intelligible, but its distance, not the logic of its description, is what registers. The logic, while demonstrable, is beside the point. To insist on demonstrating it works against the intended effect.

So stable does the remote secondary tonality come to seem that its return "home," signaled by the descent of the bass B to B♭ (the original dominant) in measure 159, comes not as the normal resolution of ♭VI to V, but as another jolt administered "impromptu" (Ex. 34-5b). The whole process is replayed in compressed and intensified form in the coda, where with really diabolical cleverness Schubert juxtaposes i–V progressions in B minor against V–i progressions in E♭ minor, so that the ear scarcely knows which to choose as its point of orientation. The tonic has been thoroughly destabilized in very novel fashion, and when it is finally reasserted it remains colored by its antagonist, with G♭ (the dominant of B minor) in place of G natural in the tonic triad. Another way of saying this, of course, is to say that the piece ends in the parallel minor.

EX. 34-5B   Franz Schubert, Impromptu in E-flat, Op. 90, no. 2, mm. 155–70

Yet another way of saying it, one that suggests the full innovative potential of Schubert's harmonic and tonal freedom, is to say that the concept of "the key of E♭" now encompasses both major and minor, with all the constituent harmonies of either mode available at all times for arbitrary, "impromptu" (read: affective) substitutions. And what goes for the tonic goes for all the secondary tonalities as well, even the "key of ♭VI," which can be interchangeably expressed as C♭ major or as B minor. The range of harmonic navigation has been augmented exponentially.

This has been a mild example. For a richer, more radical and suggestive taste we can sample one of the *Moments musicaux*. The six pieces that make up the set, while all of them vaguely ternary in format, were not conceived as a unit. They accumulated over several years, and a couple of them were published individually in "almanacs" (albums of miscellaneous pieces assembled by publishers for holiday sale) before the set as a whole was issued. The second of them (in F minor), which retains its independent popularity and is often used as a teaching piece, was originally printed in a Vienna publisher's almanac for 1823 as "Air russe" ("Russian tune"), a banal title Schubert had nothing to do with. The sixth *Moment musical*, in A♭ major (Ex. 34-6), was also given a picturesque name by the publishers when it appeared in an album called *Guirlandes* ("Garlands") in 1825. They called it "Plaintes d'un Troubadour" ("The laments of a troubadour"), evidently pitching it to an unsophisticated public that held fast to the older, pre-Romantic idea of music as imitation of outer reality (objects, "real things") rather than a representation of inwardness or an expression of the inexpressible.

EX. 34-6   Franz Schubert, *Moment musical* no. 6 (D. 780)

EX. 34-6 *(continued)*

The idea of a weeping troubadour was surely prompted by the droopy suspensions in the opening phrases, the kind of thing that had been called a *Seufzer* (sigh) since the days of Heinrich Schütz, if not earlier. That much is a cliché. What makes this piece so rare an experience has nothing to do with that, and everything to do with the idea of a "musical moment," whether the title was Schubert's idea or the publisher's. The *moment* (in German, *Augenblick* — "the twinkling of an eye") had a special meaning for romantics, as we have seen. It was the thing Faust was cautioned not to give himself up to — a stopping of time's forward march, a subjective reverie. A piece of instrumental music called an *Augenblick* was a piece in "aria time," or time-out-of-time. A piece that stops time is a piece that represents (or induces) the music trance.

And indeed, one can actually hear time stop (and resume) in this music, when the harmony slips out of the circle of fifths into uncannily prolonged submediant regions that interrupt and suspend its customary progressions — and then slips back again. These marvelous effects are projected against the old minuet or scherzo-and-trio form (or perhaps more to the point by now, Tomašek's "eclogue" form) in which two "binaries" make up a "ternary." The first sixteen-bar period encapsulates a "normal" binary procedure: eight bars out (I–V) and eight bars back (V–I). The return trip makes its customary stop along the way at a FOP, namely III, expressed as C major in keeping with Schubert's expanded version of tonal functions that admits modal mixture on every level.

What gives the C major chord its uncustomary stability, so that it does not immediately register as the dominant of vi (which never materializes), is the way it has been introduced: by way of its own dominant seventh (in $\frac{4}{3}$ position), its constituent intervals chromatically "altered" so that the chord contains an augmented sixth — two leading tones, B and D♭, both of them seeking resolution, in contrary motion, to C. This "altered" version of the dominant (christened "French sixth" sometime during the nineteenth century) was a favorite chord of Schubert's because of its power to change the course of harmony so unexpectedly and yet decisively. Both chromatic alterations — the use of the augmented sixth as a dominant-intensifier and the use of the modal mixture to transform a single secondary function — are fleeting harbingers of more radical harmonic transformations to come.

The second or complementary period, beginning at the pickup to m. 17, is way out of proportion with respect to the first: sixty-one measures vs. sixteen! It is the "uncannily prolonged" mediant excursions — interruptions in the normal flow of time — that so bloat its length. The period begins right off on the flat submediant (F♭), with a chord informally called the "German sixth," a major triad to which an augmented sixth has been added in order to mandate, through the sixth's implied resolution, another harmonic change of course. When the augmented sixth has achieved its goal (movement by contrary half steps outward to the octave), the chord produced (in m. 18) is the minor form of the tonic — and indeed, the whole eight-bar phrase thus introduced is cast in the parallel minor — the kind of shift we are learning to expect from Schubert.

The next phrase, beginning with the pickup to measure 25, is the uncanny one. At m. 28, the chord previously interpreted as i, the minor tonic triad of A♭, and which had previously proceeded through ii$^6_5$ to V in A♭ minor, now suddenly veers back to ♭VI and is reinterpreted as a pivot chord (iii$_6$) to the *key* of the flat submediant. As in the Impromptu, op. 90, no. 2, the ♭VI harmony has to be enharmonically respelled (as E major) if it is to function as a tonic without a hopelessly complicated notation. But the whole passage enclosed within the new key signature (mm. 29–39) is in fact a prolongation of ♭VI, the purple color-chord of romantic introspection, now promoted to the status of a temporary tonic. It is like passing into another world, another quality of time, another state of consciousness. Nowhere does Schubert more palpably cross the edge of inwardness.

And then, just as E major is confirmed by a cadence in the eleventh measure of its reign, the key signature switches back, the enharmonic spelling is reversed, and a D-natural, insinuated (in m. 41) into what is once again spelled as an F♭ major triad, forces a re-resolution of the chord as a German sixth again, and a return from the shadow world back into the familiar surroundings of A♭. The resumption of the original plaintive tune at the pickup to m. 54 has closure written all over it. By the time m. 61 is reached, after eight uneventful bars of recapitulation, we have confidently foreseen the end.

But instead of the anticipated perfunctory satisfaction, we are in for another sublime vagary, even more remarkably "out of time" than the first. In m. 62, Schubert introduces another modal mixture to complicate the harmony, producing a really fierce dissonance: a major seventh suspended over a minor triad. He resolves it as he did before (compare mm. 62–63 with mm. 1–2), but introduces a chromatic passing tone (C♭) along the way that is fraught with enharmonic potential. That potential is immediately realized when the relationship between the unstable C♭ and the relatively stable B♭ (only relatively stable because the chord it belongs to, a half-diminished seventh, is so dissonant) is reversed. The B♭ moves back whence it came, but the intervening signature change, right in the middle of measure 65, recasts the C♭ as a B♮, and reidentifies the B♭ in retrospect as an A♯.

In effect, both the B♭ in the "soprano" and the D♭ in the bass at the beginning of measure 65 are resolved as if they had been appoggiaturas all along rather than the root and third of a "relatively stable" supertonic in A♭. The chord thus landed on at the end of m. 65 is enharmonically equivalent to the augmented-sixth chord last heard in m. 41, and it will once again act as the pivot for a crossing of the edge — one that will take us even further into the interior realm than the first. The voicing of the chord in question — the "$\frac{4}{2}$" position, the tensest possible — immediately reidentifies the chord not as a German sixth in A♭ but as a dominant seventh in drastic need of resolution to its tonic.

Just for that reason, of course, Schubert employs the stalling tactic we have by now observed both in Beethoven and in Bellini, reiterating the $\frac{4}{2}$ chord three times before allowing the inevitable to take place. The goal of the resolution, as of any dominant seventh in the $\frac{4}{2}$ position, is to a triad in the $\frac{6}{3}$ position. The root is A, a half step above the original tonic — so very close, one might say, and yet (by normal fifth relations) so very far. Only think of it enharmonically, as B♭♭, and Schubert's strategy is revealed: it is the tonicized Neapolitan sixth of A♭, further disguised by its being maneuvered, through a passing $\frac{4}{3}$ at the end of m. 68, to its root position.

But immediately after touching down in measure 69, the A-major chord is revoiced once again, through the same passing $\frac{4}{3}$, to its first inversion, allowing its perfectly normal resolution, in measure 70, as a Neapolitan to the dominant of the original key, awaiting resolution at last. Yet once again, of course, as soon as the end has heaved into view, the composer must stave it off, lingering on the far side of the edge through one more quiet spin to the tonicized Neapolitan, and one more repossession of A♭, this time in a resigned, indeed a spent, *pianissimo*.

Quite the most remarkable thing about the final chord is that it is not a chord at all, but a hollow doubled octave. Its hollowness has an affective significance, to be sure. (It is what prompted the words "resigned" and "spent" in the previous paragraph.) But it has another aspect as well, equally important. In a piece so rife with modal mixtures and so dependent on them for its quality of feeling, an unambiguously major or an unambiguously minor concluding chord might seem too partial a resolution of its tensions.

Or perhaps the word "unambiguously" is poorly chosen. It is not that the A♭ tonality, or its quality as home, has become ambiguous. Quite the contrary. But its content, its store of possible connections and nuances, has been greatly augmented and enriched, and will no longer suffer delimitation. Expressive necessity—the need to represent new qualities of subjectivity, of inwardness—has mothered the invention of a whole range of expanded tonal relations. Any key can now be thought of as encompassing, and controlling, a double mode, and a new ambit of related keys available for "tonicization"—for setting up as alternate harmonic goals—including several that had not formerly figured among normal diatonic relations.

This little *Moment musical* has demonstrated two such—the flat submediant and the Neapolitan. In previous diatonic practice, even Beethoven's at its limits, these harmonies were always regarded and employed as "pre-dominants" or "dominant preparations"—chords "on the way" to a stable harmony rather than potentially stable harmonies in their own right. The transformation of chords that had formerly implied dynamic process and motion into potentially stable, static harmonies is what lends music that exploits the new technique the quintessentially romantic quality of timelessness or "music trance." The implication of motion is suspended; and since (to paraphrase the Greek philosopher Zeno) time is the measure of motion and motion the measure of time, the suspension of implied motion implies the suspension of time. That is what makes "aria time" available to instrumental music, and no one ever profited more from its availability than Schubert.

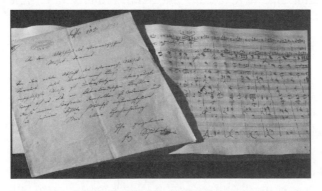

FIG. 34-8   Schubert's "Great" C Major Symphony, together with his letter dedicating it to the Gesellschaft der Musikfreunde, Vienna (which in fact did not perform it).

ONLY CONNECT

For an example of "aria time" impinging on the progress of a more extended musical argument, we can turn to a *locus classicus*, the codetta from the first movement of the "Great" C-major Symphony, Schubert's last. This movement was Schubert's longest and most complex orchestral composition in "sonata form."

But whereas we have learned from Beethoven to expect such a piece to form one single-minded, overarching trajectory through struggle to the inevitable victory, Schubert is likely to entice us — and entrance us — with islands of mysterious repose amid the hurly-burly, interrupting the forward thrust of the circle of fifths and calling out with Faust to the passing moment, "Stop, stay awhile!"

The function of a codetta is to confirm closure in the secondary key (in this case G major), and so this codetta does. But Schubert's way of establishing the key is to take an elaborate walk around it, shadowing it on both sides with mediants, B above (established through its dominant in m. 184) and E♭ below (approached via a deceptive cadence directly from G in m. 190). The submediant tonality is prolonged for a total of thirty-eight measures, to m. 227, where it is forced back to G (in a manner recalling the *Moment musical*) by the addition of an augmented sixth. During its period of sway, it is temporarily resolved as a dominant (mm. 199–210), rocking back and forth with its tonic $^6_4$, characteristically expressed in the parallel minor, producing a tonality (A♭ minor) that could be described either as the minor flat submediant of the original tonic (C) or as the minor Neapolitan of the local tonic (G).

And then the A♭-minor triad is turned into a pivot through its C♭ (spelled B), which is applied as a dominant to an F♭-minor passage (spelled E minor) that could be viewed either as the minor Neapolitan of the E♭ (the local flat submediant), or as submediant in its own right to the momentary A♭ minor. The F♭(E) minor is treated almost exactly the same way that Beethoven treats the same tonal digression in the first movement of the *Eroica* Symphony. It is led back to the E♭ whence it sprang (soon to be resolved through the augmented sixth back to G, the reigning tonic).

EX. 34-7   Harmonic abstract of Franz Schubert, Symphony no. 9 ("Great"), I, mm. 181–240

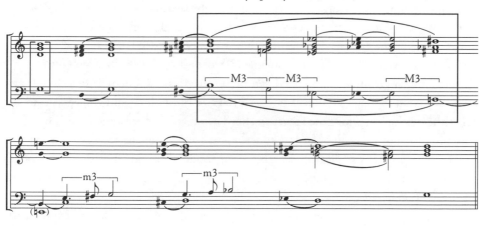

As shown in the analytical chart given as Ex. 34-7, which may be compared with the score, the passage between the B-minor triad in measure 185 and the dominant seventh on B in measure 212 amounts to a sequence of flat submediants, creating a closed circle (enclosed in a box) that could be excised from the analytical chart without disturbing the coherence of the surrounding circle of fifths that gives the codetta its tonally functional import. But of course the really memorable and affecting music is contained precisely within the box. Most memorable of all is the A♭-minor episode, rendered uncanny by the virtually unprecedented use of a solo trombone. It shows up in the analysis simply as a digression within a digression.

Again, it is the remoteness of the progression that appeals to the imagination, and its attendant static quality of time, rather than its logic — even though, as in the case of the Impromptu or the *Moment musical*, the logic of even the most remote connections can easily be demonstrated, and their relationship to the active harmonic ingredients easily understood. Moreover, and somewhat perversely if one insists on measuring Schubert's procedures by a Beethovenian standard of efficiency, the actual running time of the different harmonic areas and individual chords seems as if by design to vary inversely with their functional caliber.

Once again it should be emphasized that, contrary to what is often said about these processes, they do not render tonality — that is, the structure of key functions and relations — in any way ambiguous. Tonal coherence is not weakened or diluted by an increased range of relations and possible connections, but enormously enhanced. Departures and returns can now cover far more ground than ever, and mean more than ever. More territory is "hierarchized," brought under the direct control of the tonic.

But while tonality itself is not rendered ambiguous, the nature and behavior of many of its constituent harmonies certainly are so rendered. Homologous chords — chords identical in intervallic structure (hence in sound) but different in function — can now be used interchangeably with marvelous effect. We have just seen how the German sixth and the dominant seventh, chords that sound the same but resolve differently, can be freely interchanged so that the effective tonic can appear to fluctuate by a semitone. (Compare once again the resolution of the German sixth of A♭ in mm. 41 – 43 of the *Moment musical* and the enharmonically equivalent dominant seventh of A in mm. 65 – 67, or the two resolutions of E♭ in the symphony extract.)

The harmonic vocabulary of romantic introspection is one in which, *as a matter of course*, any augmented sixth chord can be resolved as a dominant seventh and vice versa, any triad in first inversion can be resolved as a Neapolitan and vice versa, and any constituent tone in a diminished seventh chord can resolve as a leading tone. The whole panoply of major and minor degree functions is freely available for use, and any one of them can function at pleasure as a pivot for modulation. In all of these techniques and more, Schubert was the chief pioneer, precisely because his art was nurtured in the intimacy of domestic genres.

Pride of place is still given to mediant relations as a source of inward expressivity, especially the dusky flat submediant where, one could say, it all began. In fact, the flat submediant often functions in "late Schubert" as a constant shadow to the tonic, so that the music seems perpetually to hover on that "edge" of inwardness. Perhaps the most famous example is the opening of the first movement of Schubert's last piano sonata, in B♭ (D960), completed only a couple of months before his death in the fall of 1828 (Ex. 34-8).

The first insinuation of the flat submediant comes after the first phrase of the opening theme, in a ghostly trilled G♭ (the lowest G♭ on the keyboard of Schubert's time) that immediately falls back a semitone to the dominant. After the second phrase, the trill is repeated—only this time it is measured, and applied as a "Phrygian" half step above the tonic. The B♭ and C♭ thus sounded act as a pivot, becoming the third and fourth degrees of the scale of G♭ major. The third phrase of the melody begins on the same pitch as the previous two, but that pitch has now been reidentified as the third scale degree rather than the first, and the melody continues in the key of the flat submediant for fourteen measures in a single unbroken phrase, culminating on the fifteenth downbeat on an unexpected, but enormously strategic E♮.

EX. 34-8   Franz Schubert, Sonata in B-flat, D. 960, I, beginning

EX. 34-8 (continued)

That E♮, of course, creates an augmented sixth against the ostensible tonic, forcing resolution by contrary semitones to F. But the F, when it comes, is treated as the bass of a tonic $^6_4$, capping the opening theme with a radiant return to the original tonic, comparable in its effect to the manner in which the first theme of Beethoven's *Eroica* Symphony had reached its climax a quarter of a century before. Schubert, in this case, was at once vying with Beethoven and updating him by adapting his strategy of reiterated, climax-driven thematic presentation to his newly subjectivized harmonic vocabulary.

Nor are we finished with the flat submediant even yet. Just at the point where the first theme should be making its long-deferred final cadence (m. 45), the tonic triad is preempted by the diminished-seventh chord that shares its third and fifth. This deceptive cadence plays the traditional eliding role, familiar to us from sonata first movements ever since the days of the Bach sons. It signals the move toward the secondary key area where, since the days of the youngest Bach son, we have learned to expect a lyrical "second theme." Schubert, from what we know of him, would seem the least likely composer to frustrate that expectation.

Nor will he, but the treatment of the diminished-seventh chord introduced in measure 45 requires comment. It receives an unusual resolution that Schubert did a great deal to popularize in his published music, for it further expands the range of available harmonic connections. Normally (which is to say, traditionally) the diminished-seventh chord is built on the leading tone, and its resolution coincides with the progression of the leading tone to the tonic. Its first use as a modulating agent came about when its other constituent tones were resolved as ersatz leading tones, as sketched (in B♭ major, the key of Schubert's sonata) in Ex. 34-9a, turning the diminished-seventh chord into a pivot that could lead to four different keys, pitched (like the tones of the diminished-seventh chord itself) a minor third apart.

In the resolution demonstrated in Ex. 34-8, one of the tones of the diminished-seventh chord is treated like an appoggiatura, resolving not up (as would a leading tone) but down, thus turning the chord into a dominant seventh which resolves the usual way, with a root progression along the circle of fifths (Ex. 34-9b). Of course the same effect can be obtained by treating the remaining three notes in the chord as appoggiaturas to a single held tone, enabling four more resolutions (Ex. 34-9c). And this last model suggests a further decorative refinement of the chord, in which, by the use of multiple neighbors, a diminished-seventh chord can embellish a single triad — normally, but not necessarily, the tonic (Ex. 34-9d).

The progression demonstrated in the Sonata (Ex. 34-8) is the one shown in the first two "bars" of Ex. 34-9b, where Schubert's enharmonic spelling shift is also illustrated.

EX. 34-9A   Cyclic resolutions of diminished-seventh chords, leading tone to tonic

EX. 34-9B   Cyclic resolutions of diminished-seventh chords, single appoggiatura to dominant

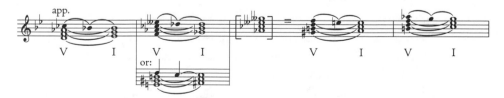

EX. 34-9C   Cyclic resolutions of diminished-seventh chords, triple appoggiatura to dominant

EX. 34-9D   Cyclic resolutions of diminished-seventh chords, neighbors to a triad

The key thus established is once again the key of the flat submediant, incarnated this time in the parallel minor as in the Impromptu, op. 90, no. 2 (Ex. 34-5). On this appearance the key is less stable; it will be dissolved the same way it had been created, through the use of a diminished-seventh appoggiatura, which leads it eventually to the expected dominant, F major. It has the quality of a mirage, or a will-o'-the-wisp.

But note that a single tonality, G♭/F♯, has shadowed both primary functions of the key of B♭, playing submediant to the tonic and Neapolitan to the dominant. This not only tinges both functions with what Romantic poets called *Doppelgänger* (ghostly or hallucinatory doubles), but also mitigates their opposition, showing that on the other side of the mysterious "edge" the tonic and the dominant share a hidden common ground. At the same time it relativizes the 150-year hegemony of the circle of fifths as sole arbiter of tonal coherence, positing two other cyclic models — thirds and semitones — as equally viable tonal administrators, the first accessible through mediant relationships, the other through Neapolitans. And finally, since the flat submediant is the "dominant of the Neapolitan," this opposition among disparate harmonic routes — fifths, thirds, semitones — may be relativized in turn, and freely intermixed.

Never had so many routes of harmonic navigation been open to composers, so many ways of making connections, so many methods of creating and controlling fluctuations of harmonic tension. And to the extent that these fluctuations were understood as metaphors or analogues to nuances of feeling, never had there been such a supple means of recording and, as it were, "graphing" the movements of the sentient subjective self — and all, in instrumental music, without any reference to externally motivating "objects." Never had "absolute music" been so articulately expressive of the verbally inexpressible.

NEW CYCLES

The alternative harmonic routes — cycles of thirds and semitones — could also function by themselves, liberated (as it were) from the dominance of the cycle of fifths, and herein lay the most profoundly subversive potential of Schubertian (and post-Schubertian) harmony. As often happens, what begins as a representational artifice can exert an independent fascination as a technical device; an expressive means can become an end in itself, pursued for the sheer pleasure of the entrancing patterns it makes available. As we have already glimpsed fleetingly in the Impromptu in E♭, op. 90, no. 2, there was a tendency to intensify the emotionally charged flat-submediant relationship by embodying it in sequences, giving the flat submediant a flat submediant of its own. The G-major harmony in m. 100 of the Impromptu (Ex. 34-5a) stands in the same relationship to the key of the middle section as does the key of the middle section to the key of the outer sections. The three keys, in fact, could be placed in an "interval cycle" similar to the circle of fifths, that is, a sequence of moves by identical intervals that continues until the point of departure is regained: E♭ – C♭/B – G – E♭.

This cycle of thirds is present in the Impromptu only by implication. It is stated fully and explicitly as a continuous succession in the passage from the "Great" C-major Symphony shown in Ex. 34-7. And it reaches a kind of epitome in the fourth movement of Schubert's last string quartet, in G major (1826 [D887], never performed or published during his lifetime) a dizzy whirligig of a movement in which many novel interval cycles are demonstrated and experimented with. In the context of a Haydnesque *moto perpetuo* ("perpetual motion machine"), long a source of exhilarating musical humor, the idea of harmonic cycles is not only of absorbing technical interest but poetically appropriate as well (Ex. 34-10). Just as in the symphony extract, the cycle is broken, and normal tonal "functionality" resumed, when one of the harmonies (C♭, suddenly respelled as B) finally resolves along the circle of fifths.

On a more "structural" level, Schubert used the cycle of major thirds to organize the overall key sequence in the four-movement "Wanderer" Fantasy. Its movements, all played *attacca* (without any intervening pause), end respectively in C major, E major, A♭ major, and C major. (The second movement, which ends in E, begins with a quotation of the song *Der Wanderer* in the relative key of C♯ minor.) And on a more explicitly "affective" level, the cycle of major thirds produces a terrifying blast of eerie sublimity when geared to the text of the Sanctus in Schubert's Mass in E♭ major another product of his final wonder year, 1828. The Mass Sanctus, we may recall, is a representation of the song of the angelic hosts surrounding God's throne. Schubert's use of the cycle of thirds here was surely an attempt to render the scene in as sublime or "unearthly" a manner as possible (Ex. 34-11). Once again, as we have come to expect from Schubert, major and minor triads are freely mixed—more for the sake of unpredictability here than for that of subjective expressivity (hard to attribute with any confidence to an angel). Even the E♭ triad, when it recurs, is replaced by its minor variant to enhance its freshness — or its strangeness. ("It is the addition of strangeness to beauty," Walter Pater said, "that constitutes the romantic character in art.")[24]

And now for the strangest, most unearthly touch of all: notice the orchestral bass line, in which passing tones have been inserted between the roots of all the third-related triads. These passing tones bisect each major third into major seconds, thus producing one of the earliest seriously intended whole-tone scales in the history of European music. (Mozart, we may recall, had used one previously in his "Musical Joke" serenade, but only to represent out-of-tune violin playing.)

As a theoretical concept, the whole-tone scale had been known since the sixteenth century. That is, since the sixteenth century it had been known that six whole steps add up to an octave in equal temperament. Music theorists and composers had made occasional (usually jocular) references to this phenomenon. The German organist Jakob Paix, for example, in a volume of canons published in 1590, printed a canon by Josquin des Prez under the rubric *in hexatono* ("at six whole steps"), leaving it to the reader to figure out with a chuckle that the piece was just an ordinary canon at the octave.

For another example, the Roman composer Giovanni Maria Nanino (1543–1607), a pupil of Palestrina, wrote an ingenious canon in 1605 as a memorial for Pope Leo XI, who had died the same year he was installed. Subtitled "Ascendit in celum" ("He ascends into Heaven"), it consists of a phrase that is to be sung each time a whole

EX. 34-10   Franz Schubert, Quartet in G major, IV, modulatory sequence step higher than the last (Ex. 34-12). But since there is an imitation at the fifth before the repetition at the second, the actual mechanism by which the canon perpetually ascends is the circle of fifths rather than the whole-tone scale. Before the nineteenth century nobody could find any serious musical use for a scale that did not contain any perfect intervals.

Now there was such a use, and Schubert was perhaps its earliest exponent. The earliest instance known to the present author comes from Schubert's Octet in F major for winds and strings, composed in 1824 and first performed in public at a concert put on by the violinist Ignaz Schuppanzigh on 16 April 1827 (just three weeks after Beethoven's death), at which Beethoven's great advocate put Schubert forth as the great man's successor. The octet is indeed one of Schubert's most Beethovenian compositions in inspiration, although the work of Beethoven's that provided the model for it, the Septet, op. 20, is early and relatively relaxed (Schubertian?) Beethoven. But Beethoven never wrote a passage like the one in Ex. 34-13.

Although the cello plays a deceptively ascending figuration, its first notes in each measure collectively describe a descending progression of major thirds, a closed

EX. 34-11   Franz Schubert, Mass in E-flat, Sanctus, beginning

EX. 34-12   Giovanni Maria Nanino, "Ascendit in celum" canon (1605)

EX. 34-13   Franz Schubert, Octet, VI, mm. 172–77

"sequence of flat submediants"—C, A♭, E, C, (A♭)—like the one shown in Ex. 34-11 from the Mass. Over this root progression, no fewer than three whole-tone scales descend as the violins and viola connect, with passing tones, the roots (in syncopation, to avoid parallels), fifths, and thirds of the resultant minor triads in contrary motion to the bass. All the earliest whole-tone scales functioned the way these do, as a means of connecting the roots (and, as we see, not only the roots) in a symmetrically apportioned, descending cycle of major thirds—a characteristic pattern or template that grew out of the romantic penchant for flat-submediant harmony, and now offered an alternative means of tonal navigation to the traditional circle of fifths.

Schubert eventually experimented with analogous cycles of minor thirds as well, in which the linked tonalities all lie along an implied diminished-seventh chord (as laid out explicitly, if only "theoretically," in Ex. 34-9). Here, too, a novel scale emerges from the part writing if passing tones are inserted between the successive chord roots, as Schubert demonstrated in another passage from the vertiginous finale of the G-major Quartet (Ex. 34-14a), where the wild harmonic gyrations undergo a *stretta*—an acceleration in sheer pace and an expansion of modulatory compass.

The peculiar restlessness of the harmony is insured by the use of the $\frac{6}{4}$ position for all the nodal points in the cycle of minor thirds, implying a cadence ceaselessly deferred and lending the passage the bearing of a frenzied, unappeasable pursuit. The emergent scale can be traced in the second violin part, which connects the chord roots with passing tones. Where the scale that emerged in this way from the cycle of major thirds consisted of a descent by whole steps, the cycle of minor thirds yields a scale that descends by alternating whole steps and half steps (Ex. 34-14b).

Like the whole-tone scale, it proved extremely suggestive to the composers who became acquainted with Schubert's posthumously published instrumental works at midcentury—particularly Liszt, who passed it along in turn to many other composers. One of them, the Russian composer Nikolai Rimsky-Korsakov (1844–1908), confessed in 1906 that Schubert, in his view, was the fountainhead of what he considered to be modern music, "the first composer in whom one can meet such bold and unexpected modulations."[25] (And, in saying this, he gave valuable testimony to the nineteenth

EX. 34-14A   Franz Schubert, Quartet in G major, IV, another modulatory sequence

EX. 34-14A   (*continued*)

EX. 34-14B   Franz Schubert, Quartet in G major, IV, demonstration of the scale that emerges from the interpolated passing tones

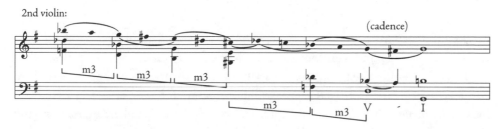

century's primary criterion of musical modernity.) Owing to the delayed publication of his works, the implications of Schubert's tonal and harmonic experiments were still being worked out (albeit in entirely different technical and expressive contexts) almost a century after his death.

B-MINOR MOODS

As promised earlier, an extended look at one of Schubert's larger, more public works will confirm the influence of the private genres in which he so excelled. That influence—an influence Schubert absorbed from his environment and then transmitted to his posthumous posterity (curiously skipping a generation, as we have seen, owing to delayed publication) — is what produced the ultimate "romanticization" of the larger instrumental forms, as practiced by German composers (and others in the Germanic orbit) in the later nineteenth century. The obvious starting place is Schubert's fortuitously emblematic "Unfinished" Symphony of 1822. The following discussion should be read with score in hand.

This famous work has few precedents in the symphonic literature — not for being unfinished (for which there are precedents within every composer's legacy, including five other unfinished symphonies in Schubert's own) but for being cast in the key of B minor. Associated with the darkest, grimmest, most "pathetic" moods, the key had been pretty well avoided by earlier composers of symphonies, which fully accords with the history of a genre that had originated in theatrical and convivial milieus. The only previous B-minor symphony by a major composer was one of the set of six (for strings only) that C. P. E. Bach had written for (and dedicated to) Baron van Swieten in 1773. Haydn had written a symphony in B major in 1772, and cast its second movement, a plaintive siciliana, in the parallel minor. Both of these symphonies had partaken of the "stormy stressful" style of their decade, associated (explicitly in Bach's case) with the idea of *Empfindsamkeit*, "hyperexpressivity." Schubert's symphony breathes a similarly special atmosphere, equally far from the traditional symphonic air of public celebration. It is usually referred to as number 8 because it was first published in 1866, a quarter of a century after the "Great" C-major symphony, which was actually written three years later. When another unfinished symphony (just a sketch in E major) was completed by an editor and published in piano score in 1884, it was given the number 7, and the "Great" Symphony was promoted to the magic Beethovenian number 9. The "Unfinished" retained its position as number 8, even though it was the seventh performable symphony in order of composition.

No one knows why the piece remained unfinished. The manuscript full score breaks off after two pages of the Scherzo. A more complete piano sketch showing the whole Scherzo and a melodic outline of the Trio has enabled several scholars to "finish the Unfinished," opportunistically tacking on the B-minor entr'acte from Schubert's incidental score to *Rosamunde* (a play that ran for two performances in 1823) by way of finale.[26] There is no real evidence that this was Schubert's intention, and the idea of a torso that consisted of two pathos-filled movements and ended with a slow movement (and in the "wrong key") appealed powerfully to romantic sensibilities, enhancing the symphony's popularity and making it, with Beethoven's Fifth and Ninth, one of the symphonies that most haunted the memories and imaginations of later composers. Its reach extended at least until 1893, when the canonized torso may have suggested to the Russian composer Pyotr Ilyich Chaikovsky (who had already recalled the "Unfinished" Symphony in his ballet *Swan Lake*) the striking idea of ending his Sixth Symphony — also cast in rare B minor, and subtitled "Pathétique" — with a slow movement.

Both the impulse to emulate Beethoven and the distance that separates Schubert from his older contemporary are evident from the symphony's very outset. As early as his op. 1, we have observed in Beethoven the habit of preceding the first theme in a sonata movement with an assertive "preface theme" to take over the function of a slow introduction and command the audience's attention. Often, especially when in a minor key as in the Trio, op. 1, no. 3 (Ex. 32-2), or the Fifth Symphony (Ex. 32-5), the preface theme achieves this objective by being played in a peremptory unison. Schubert begins the first movement of his B-minor Symphony with a patently Beethovenian preface theme *all'unisono*—indeed at first it almost seems a paraphrase of the one that opens the Trio—but its character is the very opposite of assertive (Ex. 34-15). For such a mysteriously ill-defined beginning in Beethoven there is only one precedent: the Ninth Symphony—no precedent at all because Schubert's symphony was composed before the Ninth was performed.

EX. 34-15   Franz Schubert, Symphony no. 8 ("Unfinished"), mm. 1–8

On closer examination, this quintessentially romantic opening gesture turns out to be an embellished plunge from tonic to dominant—the descending-tetrachord motif that ever since the seventeenth century has functioned (in the words of Ellen Rosand) as "an emblem of lament." We should not be surprised to find Schubert refurbishing an ancient convention; conventions, after all, are what make communications intelligible. But neither should we be surprised to find him investing it with a personal, "subjective" stamp in the form of a deliberately skewed phrase rhythm, its eight bars divided as asymmetrically as possible (2+3+3), with the last segment consisting of a single sustained tone (the equivalent of a "composed fermata"—another inverse reference to Beethoven's Fifth?). The effect is less to stun the audience than to draw it in, to allow its members to "take possession of their inwardness."

The tremulous accompaniment figure that starts up in m. 9 to introduce the "first theme" is reminiscent—perhaps deliberately reminiscent—of the opening of Mozart's G-minor symphony, K550. The texture of the theme itself, however, in which the string section accompanies the wind section, is one we have not seen in a Mozart symphony, nor any symphony. That texture was Rossini's specialty (as we observed in the overture to *The Barber of Seville* Ex. 33-4), and it was Schubert's peculiar historical mission as a writer of symphonies (though one studiously ignored, unless hotly contested, by German historians) to reconcile a new brand of Italian theater music with the Austro-German concert symphony, as if refreshing the genre with a new infusion from its original source.

(For another example of pure Rossini in Schubert, see the rhapsodically dilated second theme in the first movement of the String Quintet in C major [mm. 58–138], scored first for the two cellos and then the two violins: it is a Rossinian operatic ensemble in every respect, even down to the chugging accompaniment, except insofar as it embodies a characteristically Schubertian mesmerizing pass into the local flat submediant, and its serenely radiant reversal. At the very end, moreover, just as in a

Rossinian ensemble, the characters regroup, first cello and first violin — leading man and leading lady? — doubling at the octave [mm. 127–138] for perhaps the most soaringly Italianate melodic passage Schubert ever wrote.)

Even less like a concert symphony and more like a Rossini overture is the way the first theme in the "Unfinished" proceeds to the second. Never in the symphonies of Haydn, Mozart, or Beethoven — not even in the piano sonatas of the Bach sons! — had a first theme made a full cadence in the tonic, as Schubert's does so demonstratively in measure 38. The whole point of a "sonata allegro," as practiced by its pre-Schubertian masters, was to elide that cadence (dramatically in symphonies, subtly in chamber music) into a modulatory bridge, and not allow a full cadence in the tonic until the very end of the movement. Schubert not only allows the first theme to finish, but follows it with an obviously "patched-in" four-bar linkup (mm. 38–41) to an equally stable second theme, as if almost defiantly to advertise a lack of interest in "transitions." For such a seemingly perfunctory linkage of themes we again have to look to the overture to *The Barber of Seville*; and even there it had taken place in the truncated "recapitulation" rather than the more exacting "exposition."

But here the resemblance to Rossini ends, for Schubert's procedure is anything but perfunctory. Notice the peculiar structure of the four-bar link, played by the horns and bassoons. It has the same rhythmic skew as the "preface theme," dividing not 2+2 but 3+1. And the "3" consists of the same sort of long-held unison pitch as the last three measures of the preface. It is another "composed fermata," or time-out-of-time, and its purpose, like that of all fermatas, is to interrupt the rhythmic momentum. Whereas a Beethoven fermata either comes on a rest or is followed by a rest, thus compounding the forward thrust with suspense, Schubert's is on a quiet continuous sound that has the opposite effect. It neutralizes the thrust, replacing suspense (which quickens consciousness) with relaxation, deepening the music trance.

Neither in Mozart nor in Beethoven nor in Rossini, moreover, have we ever encountered a second theme that is more than twice the length of the first theme. It, too, comes to a full cadence (m. 104) before being replaced by another long-held unison to initiate a quickie transition. And that unison is a B, the cadence note of the first theme. The whole second theme, for all that it is the longest sustained span in the movement so far, could be snipped right out with no loss of tonal coherence. It is an island of repose, a fair and fleeting *Augenblick* magnified into what philosophers call a "specious present" — a considerable duration that nevertheless represents instantaneousness. It is, in short, a *moment musical*.

And as befits that status, it is cast not in the expected key of a second theme in the minor — that is, the mediant (III) — but in the romantically charged submediant. (Again, the only Beethovenian "precedent" comes in the as-yet-unheard Ninth Symphony.) The theme (Ex. 34-16a), as was so often the case in Schubert's impromptus and *moments musicaux*, is redolent of domestic music: it has even been associated with a specific Viennese popular song (Ex. 34-16b), the rhythm of which also permeates the theme of the posthumously published Impromptu in A♭ major, op. 142, no. 2 (Ex. 34-16c).

EX. 34-16A   Franz Schubert, Symphony no. 8 ("Unfinished"), I, second theme

EX. 34-16B   A possible source for the second theme of Schubert's Symphony no. 8 ("Unfinished"), I

EX. 34-16C   Franz Schubert, Impromptu, Op. 142, no. 2, beginning

The theme is even constructed a bit like an impromptu or a *moment musical*, in something like a miniature aba form of its own. Its middle section is approached in a radically romantic, psychologically "realistic" way: the theme trails off right before its implied cadence (m. 61) in simulation of a mental vagary, and after a measure's unsettled pause resumes in what seems a neurotically distorted form, the melody transferred to the massed winds supported by a unanticipated switch to the minor subdominant harmony in the abruptly *tremolando* strings and the suddenly roused trombones. The interval is wrong—a descending fifth (mistakenly recalling the first theme?) instead of a fourth; the right interval, sounded on the next try, is seemingly not recognized. A third stab brings the chord without which a romantic vagary is not complete: the flat submediant (E♭)—with respect to the original tonic the submediant's flat submediant, completing an implied cycle of major thirds, Schubert's as yet unpatented specialty.

The chord picks up its augmented sixth in m. 68, but its resolution is delayed by a whole series of feints, most strikingly (m. 71) to a diminished seventh chord that resolves two bars later according to the pattern illustrated in Ex. 34-9b, and in so doing initiates a little development section in which a motive derived from the third measure of the theme is put through a series of attempted, then frustrated, circles of fifths. The storm and stress having been dissipated by the cadence in m. 93, the theme is resumed in a stable but asymmetrically phrased (five-bar) variant, providing the closure of double return, and also providing reconciliation between the formerly opposed winds and strings.

The actual development section, famously, is based throughout on the preface theme — the one theme that had been originally presented in a harmonically open-ended form requiring closure on the tonic. (Beethoven had used the preface theme similarly, albeit less single-mindedly, in op. 1, no. 3.) Never had an augmented sixth been more evocatively employed than in the uncanny beginning of the section (mm. 114–127), and never had it been more unconventionally handled: prepared as the submediant of E minor, it proceeds as the Neapolitan (!) of the original key, leading to the original dominant, expressed in its most dissonant form replete with minor ninth and prolonged earsplittingly, it could even seem sadistically, over a span of twelve measures (mm. 134–145).

Of course the resolution of this grating dissonance is going to have to be deceptive — otherwise the development section will have achieved its harmonic purpose so prematurely as to make its continuation redundant. And so another series of feints is in the offing, far more dramatic because the scale is so much greater and the stakes are so much higher. The first of these feints (mm. 145–146) will involve an even more unconventional placement and conduct of an augmented sixth, producing one of the most violent deceptive cadences Schubert ever attempted.

What makes the dominant ninth so tense is the extraordinary pressure of the ninth itself (the G in the present context) to descend to the root. And so, by moving the bass up to an A-natural (already a violent move because it creates a false relation with the A♯ in the dominant chord), and then resolving the dominant seventh thus created against the G as if it were a German sixth (in the hypothetical key of C♯), Schubert manages to force the G to resolve in measure 146 as if it were an ✕ upward to G♯ rather than downward to the long-awaited dominant root. The resolution that had been insisted upon, or pled for, over the preceding twelve bars is not only thwarted but preempted, leaving the properly mesmerized listener, who had been programmed to identify with the G and its desires, exhausted and disoriented.

The diversionary ploy has its price: an unwanted cadence on C♯ now looms. It too must be frustrated. So Schubert preempts the arrival of its tonic with a diminished seventh chord, screamed out by the whole orchestra (m. 154), that reharmonizes the G♯ and directs it still further up, to A, presaging resolution to D. This time resolution is forestalled by precisely reversing the feint employed in measure 73, now transforming the dominant of D into a diminished seventh chord that is given an unconventional "outward" resolution of the kind more usually associated with augmented sixths. The resolution redirects the harmony back to E minor, the development's point of departure and the subdominant of the original key.

This time it takes Schubert forty-four measures to regain the dominant ninth (the only unusual harmonic effect along the way being the strangely voiced augmented Neapolitan in mm. 194–197, in the "wrong" inversion and again tinged with an augmented sixth), and its resolution finally brings closure to the preface theme, initiating a fairly placid recapitulation. Here the most noteworthy touch is the rerouting of the first theme (by means of some poignant stabs of harmony in mm. 229–231 and 238–240) so that it cadences in the dominant (where it "should" have cadenced in the exposition). But however unconventional this may appear, it is done for the sake of conformity to convention, for it enables the recapitulation of the second theme in the customary mediant key (D major). The coda (mm. 328 ff) rounds the movement off with a very demonstrative closure of the preface theme (with a few nostalgic nods at the subdominant, where the theme had spent so much time in the development).

The first movement of the "Unfinished" Symphony, then, is a virtual textbook of submediant relations — many of them unprecedented in symphonic writing and astonishing in their assured virtuosity — and how they can be used to create both mood and form. In this way the symphony becomes a study of how the intimate and domestic forms ("lower" forms in the conventional, covertly social hierarchy of genres, to which Schubert outwardly subscribed) in which Schubert chiefly made his reputation, and in which he acquired his submediant skills, could affect the "higher" forms and infect them with *Innerlichkeit*, assimilating them to the mood music of the urban bourgeoisie.

CONSTRUCTIONS OF IDENTITY

The key of the second movement, Andante con moto, bears an unusual but thoroughly Schubertian relation to that of the first: it is cast in the subdominant of the parallel major, projecting the concept of modal mixture from the level of local harmonization to that of "macrostructure," the relationships that give coherence to the whole multimovement sequence. Where the first movement had been a study in submediant relations, the second admits a much wider spectrum of third-relations to its purview. In part this is because its form is more loosely sectional, less "teleological," than that of the first. Rather than a goal-directed sonata design, organized around a single overriding progress to closure, the movement is put together very much like the slow movement of Mozart's E♭-major Symphony, K. 543 (Ex. 30-1), which could very well have been its model: a slow rondo (or, alternatively, a slow minuet or *Ländler* with two trios) in which both episodes are based on the same melodic material but contrast radically in key, both with the framing sections and with each other.

Even if we ignore for the moment the many strongly colored "local" harmonies that attract our ear (beginning with the unconventionally "inverted" German sixth in measure 14 whose many recurrences will be a major point of reference) and take note only of chords that are "tonicized" by cadences and so contribute to the articulation of the movement's form, we encounter an amazingly diverse and wide-ranging assortment, beginning with the brief excursion from the tonic E to the "parallel mediant" G (the mediant of the parallel minor, tonicized in m. 22) and back, which defines the shape of the opening section.

The first episode (beginning with the four-bar unharmonized preface at m. 60) starts out in that Schubertian rarity, the ordinary diatonic submediant or relative minor. Remaining true to our plan and ignoring the beautifully executed (but cadentially unconfirmed) excursion to the parallel mediant (F major) at m. 74, we arrive at a mode switch at m. 83, immediately followed by the enharmonic recasting of C♯ major as D♭. (Note that we have had cadences by now on three members of a cycle of minor thirds encircling the tonic: E major, G major "above", D♭ major "below.") Parenthetically we might note that the clarinet and flute exchange that takes place during this excursion into D♭ major (mm. 90–95) removes any doubt that we are dealing here with a *Ländler*, an adapted (and locally Viennese) ballroom dance — that is, a Mozartean device updated by a composer who, unlike Mozart, "speaks Viennese like any other Viennese" (in the words of the poet August Heinrich Hoffmann von Fallersleben).[27]

A return to C♯ minor provides a pivot to the submediant, A, at m. 109, suitably equipped with what sounds like an augmented sixth, just as, knowing Schubert, one might expect. But the chord is spelled as a dominant seventh, with G-natural instead of F✕, and so it resolves, into a remarkable "flat side" circle of fifths that touches down on D, the Neapolitan (m. 111); G, the parallel mediant of the original key (m. 121); and finally C, the parallel or "flat" submediant (m. 129), preparing the retransition to E major for the medial return of the "rondo" theme.

The section that now begins (m. 142) is identical to the first section as far as m. 186, where it is suddenly rerouted to the subdominant to prepare for the second episode, which begins (m. 201) in the parallel subdominant, A minor, soon to be replaced by A major at m. 223. This key may be unremarkable with respect to the original tonic; but compared with its counterpart in the first episode, it is in the magical flat submediant key. At m. 244 the parallel tonic is briefly sounded as a pivot to the same "flat side" excursion along the circle of fifths as we heard in the first episode, only this time it moves much more quickly than before, because it is zeroing in on the original tonic from C, the original flat submediant (m. 250), to F, the Neapolitan (m. 252), which makes its conventional resolution to the dominant, and thence home.

The final section is not a full recapitulation or rondo frame; rather it is a coda based on the original thematic material, with some enharmonic interplay between diatonic and chromaticized mediants that is at once witty and touching. First G♯ minor (III) is emphasized by an ordinary dominant embellishment (mm. 270–271, repeated in 277–278), then the four-bar violin preface is extended by an extra pair of measures that takes it (where else?) to C, the flat submediant, which then pivots ear-tinglingly to *its* flat submediant, A♭ (m. 286), completing a cycle of major thirds, perhaps the earliest one in all of Schubert to have been explicitly enunciated in direct succession. And finally, in another characteristically Schubertian move, the violin preface, now adapted to the key of A♭ major, is converted at the end to the parallel minor, by replacing the expected C with a C♭. This is an especially disorienting move, since it involves an unaccompanied arpeggio (mm. 292–295) that describes an augmented octave. But of course it is also an especially strategic move, since that disorienting C♭, reinterpreted enharmonically, turns out to be the original dominant. Its resolution secures the final closure (Ex. 34-17).

This quick return from seemingly remote parts once again resonates with Mozart; recall the slow movement of his G-major Piano Concerto, K. 453 (Ex. 30-5c). Recall, too, that Mozart's clever progression has been given contradictory interpretations. Some have interpreted the distance as real, in which case the pleasing artifice by which it is so quickly traversed seems an ingratiating mask worn by violence; others have interpreted the distance as illusory, in which case the harmonic sleight-of-hand comes off as irony (see chapter 30). The former interpretation casts the music as tragic, the latter as comic.

The interpretation of Schubert's harmony is beset with similar differences of opinion; but the stakes have seemed greater with him, and the disagreements have been more heated. Perhaps that is because his music, constructing a more emphatically private and personal space than Mozart's, claims a greater personal investment from listeners. That would certainly be in keeping with romantic ideals, and to that extent, perhaps, the controversy has been a measure of Schubert's artistic success. But the grounds of Schubertian contention have been no more confined (or confinable) to artistic matters than in the case of Mozart. With Mozart, aesthetic debate was connected with social

EX. 34-17   Franz Schubert, Symphony no. 8 ("Unfinished"), II, mm. 280–300

EX. 34-17 (*continued*)

issues. With Schubert, again very much in the spirit of romanticism, it is connected with issues of personal identity.

The latest controversy began with what scholars call "external" evidence — the interpretation of facts about Schubert's life, not the interpretation of his scores. In 1989 Maynard Solomon, a highly respected biographer of Beethoven and Mozart, published an article in which he interpreted certain passages in diaries and letters, both Schubert's and those of his friends, as coded references to the composer's participation in what Solomon called the "male homosexual subculture" of the Austrian capital.[28]

Solomon's most compelling piece of evidence was a diary entry in which one of Schubert's friends wrote that Schubert, being "out of sorts," is in need of "young peacocks, like Benvenuto Cellini." (Cellini, the great sixteenth-century sculptor and goldsmith, used references to game birds in his autobiography as a euphemism for the young boys he pursued for erotic purposes.) Later, a younger scholar, Kristina Muxfeldt, noted that among the song texts Schubert had set were poems by Count August von Platen, in the style of Persian love lyrics known as ghazals, that were full of transparent references to homosexual love. Schubert's settings of these poems, she observed, were unusually intense in harmony, even for him.[29]

These readings and findings, while original and unwontedly specific, were not really news. Schubert's venereal disease, which may have hastened his death, had long since led to speculations concerning what one writer, as early as 1857, called *passions mauvaises*, "evil passions."[30] The judgment implied by the word *mauvais* reflected the moral standards of 1857, well into the Victorian age, when sexual roles, as observed in the previous chapter, were hardening. The judgment also obviously partook of the mythology of the *poète maudit*, equally anachronistic for Schubert. In Schubert's time imputation of homosexual tastes or activities carried less stigma than they did at midcentury (here, many would contend, our own time is in agreement with Schubert's), and were less bound up with issues of identity (but here our time differs profoundly from his). In any case, it is doubtful whether these matters would have excited as much controversy as they have, had some critics not begun to find corroborating "internal" evidence — that is, evidence in "the music itself."

Those who believed they had found such evidence claimed to locate it precisely in the novel harmonic and tonal relationships that we have been investigating, the very aspects of Schubert's style that historians have prized as his signal contribution to the art of music, and on which many music lovers have founded their special sense of intimacy with the composer. In an essay entitled "Constructions of Subjectivity in Schubert's Music," Susan McClary, a versatile and imaginative scholar whose readings of Bach and Mozart have already figured in this book, made a direct connection between Schubert's special genius for musically representing the romantic "I" and his alleged homoerotic leanings. Where Solomon's prize exhibit had been a journal entry and Muxfeldt's had been a song text, McClary's was the second movement of the "Unfinished" Symphony, the composition we have just surveyed.

McClary interprets the freewheeling mediant relationships and sleight-of-hand modulations that we have been tracing as analogous (or more exactly, homologous) to promiscuous personal relationships. Mediants are to fifths, she argues, as gay is to straight — in both cases (to simplify a bit) what is represented is pleasurable deviance from a socially mandated norm. "On some level," she writes, "centered key identity almost ceases to matter, as Schubert frames chromatic mutation and wandering as sensually gratifying." In Schubert's "enharmonic and oblique modulations," as McClary interprets them, "identities are easily shed, exchanged, fused, and reestablished, as in the magical pivot between E and A♭ major near the end."[31] Finally, pursuing homologies between her description of Schubert's musical behavior and recent descriptions of gay male behavior, she quotes a literary critic who, while employing a nearly impenetrable professional jargon, seems to be making a similar point about the pleasures of promiscuity: "Subjectivity within male coupling is episodic, cognized and recognized as stroboscopic fluctuations of intense (yet dislocated, asymmetrical, decentered) awareness of self-as-other and self-for-other."[32]

Whether this argument holds up depends primarily on how much evidentiary weight an analogy can be made to bear. (Analogies and homologies are partial similarities that have been singled out for the purpose of comparison. If the motivating premise is embraced a priori, as it is here, an analogical argument becomes dangerously liable to the trap of circularity.) But the controversy in which this argument participates is little concerned with the fine points of rhetoric. Rather, it has served as a diagnostic of contemporary attitudes toward sexual deviance. Those made uneasy by the thought of it have been quick to label the argument as an "assault" on Schubert, as one scholar has put it,[33] or an attempt to appropriate his name and reputation on behalf of a political agenda.[34]

What all sides to the debate agree upon, however, is that profound and possibly "subterranean" matters of personal identity are at stake, and that Schubert's music has the power of representing them. The very thought was a product of Schubert's time. Except in a few late works, not even Beethoven is so interpreted by anyone, but Schubert is so interpreted by everyone. That is the continuing triumph of romanticism.

Volkstümlichkeit

The Romantic Lied; Mendelssohn's Career; the Two Nationalisms

THE LIED IS BORN

Although German-speaking composers have been prominent in the last several chapters (and will remain so for several chapters to come), and despite the frequent claim that their prominence raised the German "art music" tradition in the nineteenth century to the status of general standard and model (at least within the instrumental domain), the fact is that only two important musical genres were actually German in origin, and one of them was vocal.

The romantic *Charakterstück* for piano (to call it by its German name) was one of these, and the other was the romantic *Lied* (plural *Lieder*), the setting of a lyric poem for solo voice accompanied by the piano or (at first) some other "parlor" instrument, a genre so German that it has retained its German name in English writing. Both the character piece and the lied have cognate genres in other national traditions. The romantic character piece is in some obvious ways comparable to the fancifully titled harpsichord *pièces* by seventeenth- and eighteenth-century French *clavecinistes* like François Couperin (see Ex. 25-12). But there were two important differences. The French genre was "imitative" while the German one was "expressive," in keeping with the great change in esthetic sensibility that the word "romantic" declares. And the French genre descended from the dance suite while the German one descended from the fantasia. The two genres, it thus transpires, were not genetically linked. The one did not lead to the other, and so the romantic *Charakterstück* is entitled to be considered an independent genre, as indigenously German as the romanticism to which it gave form and expression.

Similarly, the lied can be superficially compared with many previous forms of accompanied solo song, going all the way back to the monodies of the early seventeenth-century Florentines, or the English "lute ayres" of the same period. (The latter may look even more closely akin to the lied, since it had a fully composed accompaniment rather than a figured bass.) Indeed, the at times intense and personal expressivity of those earlier genres does seem to prefigure the primary esthetic aim of romantic lyricism. But again, the lineages were dissimilar. The monody and ayre descended respectively from the madrigal and the recitation of epic poetry. They were court genres, not domestic ones, and they were both quickly subsumed into the nascent opera. There is no genetic link between them and the lied.

Like the *Charakterstück*, the romantic lied originated in Berlin, the Prussian capital, and once again that curious protoromantic C. P. E. Bach (who wrote some two hundred lieder) played a crucial role in its birth. From the very beginning, moreover, the lied was associated not only with the idea of *Empfindsamkeit* or personal expressivity, but also with the idea of *Volkstümlichkeit* or "folklikeness." The two ideals may seem at first incongruous, since the simplicities of folk song may not seem on the face of it the likeliest channel for the expression of a unique personal psychology. But in fact, as already hinted in the previous chapter, German romanticism saw personal and collective expression as mystically linked, each depending on the other for authenticity. It was in the lied that the romantic "I" bonded musically with the romantic "We." Accordingly, the earliest lieder were in effect imitation folk songs with simple melodies that, while reflecting the mood of the poem, could be easily sung by nonprofessionals at home. The accompaniments were also kept simple and were (in theory, anyway) regarded as optional. The person chiefly responsible for the theory was a Berlin lawyer named Christian Gottfried Krause (1719–70), who first described the lied in a book published in 1752 under the title *Von der musikalischen Poesie* ("On poetry for music"), and then got several of his friends, including C. P. E. Bach, to furnish examples of it. Thus, rather unusually, the description of the genre actually preceded its earliest specimens. It was decidedly a cultivation, a "hothouse growth."

The first book of actual lieder was published in 1753 under the title *Oden mit Melodien* ("Odes with melodies"). An ode, which means a poem of praise sung to the lyre (whence lyric), was a time-honored classical genre that could be either public (choral) and grandiose, addressed to an assembled audience (as in the Greek drama or the odes of Pindar), or personal and intimate, addressed to a loved one (as in the odes of Sappho, or, in Roman times, of Horace and Catullus). It was the latter type, of course, that furnished the German romantics with their model. The model of models was Anacreon, a Greek lyric poet of the sixth century BCE, whose widely imitated "Anacreontic" verses celebrated the joys of wine and love.

Americans may know about Anacreon because the drinking song that (in Francis Scott Key's *contrafactum*) became "The Star-Spangled Banner" was originally called "To Anacreon in Heaven." It was the more personal, amorous side of Anacreon that inspired the verses by Karl Wilhelm Ramler (1725–98) that (chosen by Krause and set at his instigation to suitably "*Volkstümlich*" melodies) laid the foundation for the romantic lied. *Amint* (Aminta), one of C. P. E. Bach's contributions to Krause's *Oden mit Melodien*, will give an idea of that foundation (Ex. 35-1). Its simple melody returns with every verse in the manner of a folk song. The simple three-part texture, completely written out even though it could easily be "realized" by a skilled continuo player, is additional evidence that the song is meant for home consumption by the relatively unskilled. The performance direction, *Mit Affekt* ("emotionally"), connoting an urban, sophisticated, self-aware manner seemingly at odds with the rustic simplicity of the tune, is a perfect paradigm of what we might call the "lied sensibility" with its unique crossbreeding of the I and the We.

THE DISCOVERY OF THE FOLK

This crossbreeding, which implied the impossibility of a particular "I" without a particular "We," was in large part the brainchild of a Prussian preacher named Johann

EX. 35-1   C. P. E. Bach, *Amint* (Wotquenne 199, no. 11)

Gottfried von Herder (1744–1803), who provided the main intellectual bridge between the *Sturm und Drang* movement of the 1770s and the later German romanticism. His basic idea may seem all too obvious to us, heirs as we are to two centuries of romantic thinking; but in its day it was a revolutionary notion. Very simply, Herder contended that there was no universal human nature and no universal human truth, no "sensus communis" as posited by his one-time mentor Kant. Rather, he argued, each human society, each epoch of human history, each and every human collectivity was a unique entity — and uniquely valuable. Human difference was as worthy of study and respect, and could be as morally instructive, as human alikeness.

This idea has been given various names, among them historicism, particularism, and relativism. Herder did not invent it out of whole cloth; parts of it were actually derived from the writings of Jean-Jacques Rousseau and the *philosophes*, who were among the most ardent upholders of Enlightenment and its gospel of universality. But the specific emphases Herder gave his eclectic intellectual compound, and the consequences he drew from it, mark his thinking as particularly romantic, and particularly German. Through him, paradoxically enough, aspects of German particularist thinking became universal. They provided the necessary philosophical foundation for all nineteenth- and twentieth-century nationalist thought.

It seems only natural and right that human particularity and diversity should have appeared natural and right to a German thinker. The German-speaking lands were then, and to some extent remain even now, a political and religious crazy quilt. And the idea of valuing particularity and diversity arose in reaction to the universalist, Enlightened assumption that progress lay in political consolidation and uniformity. To a French thinker, the politically fragmented German scene looked not only backward but weak; and shortly after Herder's death Napoleon would prove the point by force of arms. Herder's particularism and the German nationalism that grew out of it were in part an expression of resentment against French condescension, to say nothing of the French military threat.

Looking for the bedrock of irreducible human difference, Herder fastened on language. In his influential tract *Über den Ursprung der Sprache* ("On the origin of language," 1772), he argued that without language a human being would not be human. But language could only be learned socially, that is, in a community. Thus human singularity had its limits. A human was human only in the society of other humans, and the natural definer of societies was language. Since there could be no thought without language, it followed that human thought, too, was a social or community product — neither wholly individual nor wholly universal. Thus to view humanity only as a totality was to miss the very specifics that made people human. These were to be sought in language communities, each of which (since it had its own language) had its own characteristic mode of thought, its own essential personality.

An Enlightened thinker might conclude that each language was merely a particular way of expressing universal truths. Herder insisted, rather, that each language manifested or (to put it biblically) revealed unique values and ideas that constituted each language community's specific contribution to the treasury of world culture. Moreover (and this was the most subversive part of all), since there is no general or a priori scale against which particular languages can be measured, no language, hence no language community, can be held to be superior or inferior to any other.

When the concept of language is extended to cover other aspects of learned behavior or expressive culture — customs, dress, art — those aspects will be seen as essential constituents of a precious collective spirit or personality. That spirit embodies a truth separate from but equal to the truths embodied by all other spirits. In such thinking the concept of "authenticity" — faithfulness to one's essential spirit — was born. It became an explicit goal of the arts, not just their inherent nature, to express the specific truth of the community they served.

These ideas put an entirely new complexion on the whole concept of folklore. Until the late eighteenth century, folklore, or local vernacular culture, was associated chiefly with the peasantry, and was therefore assigned a low cultural or intellectual prestige. Now folklore was seen as embodying the essential authentic wisdom of a language community or *nation*. Its cultural stock soared. It was zealously collected and studied, both for the sake of defining national characteristics and for the sake of comparing them. The brothers Jacob and Wilhelm Grimm, philologists (students of language) by training, compiled their epoch-making collections of folktales (*Kinder- und Hausmärchen*, "Children's and household tales," 2 vols, 1812 – 15) under the direct influence of Herder's teachings. They followed up on these with an even more ambitious two-volume collection of German folk myths and legends, *Deutsche Sagen* ("German sagas," 1816 – 18). By the middle of the nineteenth century their efforts had been duplicated in almost every European country.

The great explosion of published folklore and its artistic imitations did a great deal to enhance the national consciousness of all peoples, but especially those in two categories: localized minority populations (like the Latvians or Letts, the original object of Herder's collecting interest) whose languages were not spoken across political boundaries, and (at the opposite extreme) large, politically divided groups like the Germans, whose languages were widely dispersed across many borders. The boundary between the collected and the created, or between the discovered and the invented, was at first a soft one, easily traversed. It was not always possible to distinguish between what was collected from the folk and what was contributed by the editors, most of whom were poets as well as scholars, and did not distinguish rigorously between artistic and scholarly practice.

The most illustrative case was that of the *Kalevala* ("Land of heroes"), the national epic of the Finns, who in the early nineteenth century lived under Swedish and, later, Russian rule. First published in 1835, it was based on lore collected from the mouths of peasants but then heavily edited and organized into a single coherent narrative by its compiler, the poet Elias Lönnrot (1802–84). It never existed in antiquity in the imposing form in which it was published, and which served to imbue the modern Finns — that is, the urban, educated, cosmopolitan classes of Finnish society — with a sense of kinship and national cohesion. Nor do the ironies stop there. The distinctively incantatory trochaic meter of the poem (the result of the particular accentual patterns of the Finnish language), when translated into English, provided the model for Henry Wadsworth Longfellow's *Song of Hiawatha* (1855), which purported to provide the United States of America, a country of mixed ethnicity and less than a century old, with a sort of borrowed national epic that would lend it a borrowed sense of cultural independence from Europe.

In the area that concerns us most directly, Herder himself made one of the earliest fundamental contributions, with his enormous comparative anthology of folk songs from all countries, *Stimmen der Völker in Liedern* ("Voices of the peoples in Songs," 2 vols., 1778–79). In it, he actually coined the term *Volkslied* (folk song), now universally used to denote what had formerly been called a "simple" or "rustic" or "peasant" song. His collection was followed, and so far as Germany was concerned superseded, by the greatest of all German folk song anthologies, *Des Knaben Wunderhorn* ("The youth's magic horn"), brought out by the poets Achim von Arnim and Clemens Brentano in three volumes between 1805 and 1808. Verses from this book, which contained no original melodies, continued to be set as lieder by German composers throughout the century and far beyond.

In some ways this "discovery of the folk" was a mere recycling of an ancient idea, that of "primitivism," the belief that the qualities of technologically backward or chronologically early cultures are superior to those of contemporary civilization, or more generally, that it is those things that are least socialized, least civilized — children, peasants, "savages," raw emotion, plain speech — that are closest to truth. The most recent and dogmatic upholder of primitivistic ideas had been Jean-Jacques Rousseau, whose *Social Contract* begins with the unforgettable declaration that "man was born free and is everywhere in chains." No one had ever more effectively asserted the superiority of unspoiled "nature" over decadent "culture."

KULTUR

But the Herder/Grimm phase did contain a new wrinkle, namely the idea that the superior truth of unspoiled natural man was a plural truth. The next step in the romantic nationalist program was to determine and define the specific truth embodied in each cultural community. Here is where the motivating resentment or inferiority complex finally began to break the surface of German nationalism. Not surprisingly, the values celebrated in the German tales — the "Prince Charming" values of honesty, seriousness, simplicity, fidelity, sincerity, and so on — were projected onto the German language community, which in its political fragmentation, economic backwardness, and military weakness (its primitiveness, in short) represented a sort of peasantry among peoples, with all that that had come to imply as to authenticity. It alone valued *das rein Geistige*, "the purely spiritual," or *das Innige*, "the inward," as opposed to the superficiality, the amorality, the craftiness and artifice of contemporary civilization, as chiefly represented by the hated oppressor empire, France.

The word "culture" itself—or rather *Kultur*, to incorporate the special resonance the word had for the Germans—began to symbolize the values through which the German romantics set themselves apart from other peoples. As the German social historian Norbert Elias has put it,

> The concept of *Kultur* mirrors the self-consciousness of a nation which had constantly to seek out and constitute its boundaries anew, in a political as well as a spiritual sense, and again and again had to ask itself: "What really is our identity?" The orientation of the German concept of culture, with its tendency toward demarcation and the emphasis on and detailing of differences between groups, corresponds to this historical process.[1]

The answer to the question "What is German?" (*Was ist deutsch?*) arose most clearly in the romantic lied, a genre that was inspired, one is tempted to say, by that burning question of national identity. In the light of contemporary philosophy and politics (and the links between them), the mission of the lied to unite the "I" and the "We" takes on a newly clarified sense of purpose.

The rediscovery of the folk and the consequent fever of collecting had an enormous impact on German poetry as well as the music to which it was set. Many poets, led by Goethe (a close friend, as it happens, of Herder's), began writing in a calculatedly *volkstümlich* style so as to capture some of the forgotten wisdom that *das Volk* had conserved through the ages of cosmopolitanism, hyperliteracy, and Enlightenment. It was a neat switch on the concept of "the Dark Ages." The dark, especially in its natural forest habitat, was in its mystery and intuitive "second sight" now deemed light's superior as teacher of *lore*—that is, nation-specific traditional knowledge.

LYRICS AND NARRATIVES

The imitation folk poetry of German romanticism came in two main formal types: lyrics and narratives. The lyrics were often cast as "dance songs" of a type that will ring a bell with anyone who remembers the early chapters of this book, for they resemble the stanza-and-refrain forms used in medieval poetry, and not by accident: next to contemporary "folk" or oral culture, the expressive culture of medieval times, precisely because they were the Dark Ages, was newly valued by romantics as a storehouse of unsullied lore.

Goethe's most famous song-with-refrain, owing to the large number of musical settings it attracted, was *Heidenröslein* ("Heath rose"), one of his earliest lyrics, first published in 1773. It was reissued in 1794 in a book of *Lyrischen Gedichte* (poems for music) set by his musical collaborator Johann Friedrich Reichardt (1752–1814), the first great figure in the history of the lied, with more than fifteen hundred to his credit (Ex. 35-2). The text, a sustained metaphor for the "deflowering" of a maiden, consists in fact of a narrative; but the actual narrative genre (a matter of form as well as content) was something else:

Sah ein Knab' ein Röslein stehn,	A boy saw a rose growing,
Röslein auf der Heiden,	a rose upon the heath.
war so jung und morgenschön,	It was so young and morning-fresh,
lief er schnell, es nah zu sehn,	he quickly ran to look at it up close.
sah's mit vielen Freuden.	He looked at it with much joy.
Röslein, Röslein, Röslein rot,	Rose, rose, red rose,
Röslein auf der Heiden.	Rose upon the heath.
Knabe sprach: Ich breche dich,	The boy said, I'll pluck you,
Röslein auf der Heiden!	Rose upon the heath!
Röslein sprach: Ich steche dich,	The rose said, I'll prick you
dass du ewig denkst an mich,	so that you'll always think of me,
und ich will's nicht leiden.	for I won't suffer it.
Röslein, etc.	Rose, etc.
Und der wilde Kanbe brach	And the savage boy picked
's Röslein auf der heiden;	the rose upon the heath;
Röslein wehrte sich und stach,	the rose, defending itself, pricked away,
half ihr doch kein Weh und Ach,	but its aches and pains availed it not;
musst' es eben leiden.	it had to suffer all the same.
Röslein, etc.	Rose, etc.

The change from setting neoclassical or "Anacreontic" verses, as in Ex. 35-1, to setting *volkstümlich* poetry like this produced the mature German romantic lied. The change is often described as one between two generations of composers, or between a

EX. 35-2   J. F. Reichardt, *Heidenröslein*

EX. 35-2 (continued)

first and a second "Berlin song school." The real change, however, was in the nature of the words they set.

The main narrative genre of *volkstümlich* romantic poetry was called the *ballad*, another term with medieval (or pseudo-medieval) roots: compare the Italian *ballata* or its prototype, the *balada* of the troubadours (called *chanson balladé* in northern France). The German term obviously reflects a faulty etymology, since a *chanson balladé* is, quite literally, a "danced song" rather than a narrative. The Germans were not responsible for the mix-up, however; the term *ballad* was first used in England, as early as the fourteenth century, to designate a sung narrative poem, often one that included dramatic dialogue between humans and supernatural beings, and that typically ended in disaster.

As a folk genre the ballad flourished mainly in the British Isles and Scandinavia, lands of mist and frost that fascinated the German romantics. The earliest German romantic ballads were in fact translations from English and Scandinavian originals — or rather, imitations of Herder's translations in his *Volkslieder* — and had no "true" German folk prototype at all. In this they resembled the *Kalevala*: they were contemporary creations manufactured to supply a desired ancient heritage. Far and away the most famous German ballad of this kind was Goethe's *Erlkönig* ("The elf king"), written hard on the heels of Herder in 1782 and first published as part of a singspiel libretto called *Die Fischerin* ("The fisherman's wife"). It achieved fame when republished, again in a setting by Reichardt, in the *Lyrischen Gedichte* of 1794 (Ex. 35-3 shows the grisly end):

Wer reitet so spät durch Nacht und Wind?	Who rides so late through night and wind?
Es ist der Vater mit seinem Kind:	It is the father with his child.
er hat den Knaben wohl in dem Arm,	He holds the boy in his arms,
er fasst ihn sicher, er hält ihn warm.	he clasps him firmly, he keeps him warm.

—Mein Sohn, was birgst du so bang dein Gesicht?
—Siehst, Vater, du den Erlkönig nicht?
Den Erlenkönig mit Kron' und Schweif?
—Mein Sohn, es ist ein Nebelstreif.

"Du liebes Kind, komm, geh mit mir!
Gar schöne Spiele spiel ich mit dir;
manch' bunte Blumen sind an dem Strand;
meine Mutter hat manch' gülden Gewand."

—Mein Vater, mein Vater, und hörest du nicht,
was Erlenkönig mir leise verspricht?
—Sei ruhig, bleibe ruhig, mein Kind:
in dürren Blättern säuselt der Wind.

"Willst, feiner Knabe, du mit mir gehn?
Meine Töchter sollen dich warten schön;
Meine Töchter führen den nächtlichen Reihn
und wiegen und tanzen und singen dich ein."

—Mein Vater, mein Vater, und siehst du nicht dort
Erlkönigs Töchter am düstern Ort?
—Mein Sohn, mein Sohn, ich seh es genau:
es scheinen die alten Weiden so grau.

"Ich liebe dich, mich reizt deine schöne Gestalt;
und bist du nicht willig, so brauch ich Gewalt."
—Mein Vater, mein Vater, jetzt fasst er mich an!
Erlkönig hat mir ein Leids getan!

Dem Vater grauset's, er reitet geschwind,
er hält in den Armen das ächzende Kind,
erreicht den Hof mit Müh' und Not:
in seinen Armen das Kind war tot.

"My son, why do you hide your face so fearfully?"
"Father, don't you see the Elf King?
The Elf King with his crown and train?"
"My son, it is a patch of mist."

"Come dear child, go with me!
I will play beautiful games with you;
many are the bright flowers on the shore,
my mother has many robes of gold."

"My father, my father, and do you not hear
what the Elf King softly promises me?"
"Be calm, keep calm, my child:
in dry leaves the wind is rustling."

"Will you go with me, brave boy?
My daughters shall tend you nicely.
My daughters will lead the dancing each night
and will lull and dance and sing for you."

"My father, my father, don't you see over there
the Elf King's daughters in that deserted spot?"
"My son, my son, I see it perfectly,
the old willows look so gray."

"I love you, I am charmed by your good looks,
and if you are not willing, I shall have to use force."
"My father, my father, he's clutching me now!
The Elf King has hurt me!"

The father shudders, he rides apace;
in his arms he holds the groaning child.
Sweating and straining he reaches the courtyard;
in his arms the child lay dead.

Though very elaborately and effectively disguised with specifically Germanic and romantic surface features, Goethe's pseudo-folkish ballad belongs to an ancient mythological tradition with origins going back at least as far as the Greeks: the "siren song" or song of fatal seduction, usually addressed by supernatural women to natural men, and most often given a maritime setting, as in the *Odyssey* (or in the form of another German romantic nature being, the *Lorelei* or Rhine mermaid). Goethe's immediate model was Herder's translation of a Danish folk ballad in which Herr Oluf, a knight, riding at night to summon guests to his wedding, meets up not with the Elf King himself but with one of the Elf King's daughters, who tries to lure him in a lethal dance but, failing, mortally curses him along with his bride and mother.

Goethe's variation ostensibly removes the element of sexual allure (but perhaps only succeeds in displacing it interestingly), while surrounding the horse and rider with a whole syllabus of Germanic nature mythology, according to which the forest harbors a nocturnal spirit world, invisible to the fully mature and civilized father, but terrifyingly apparent to his unspoiled son. The father thinks he "sees perfectly"

EX. 35-3   J. F. Reichardt, *Erlkönig*, ending

FIG. 35-1   Moritz von Schwind, *Erlkönig*.

and is in control of things. He is powerless, however, against the spirits, who flaunt their ascendancy by taking the child. Thus the romantically nostalgic or neoprimitivist themes of hidden reality, invisible truth, the superiority of nature over culture (in none of which, incidentally, did Goethe really believe) are clothed in the imagery and diction of folklore to lend them supreme authority.

THE LIED GROWS UP: HAYDN, MOZART, BEETHOVEN

Until the end of the eighteenth century, and even a bit beyond, the lied was considered a lowly genre, the province of "specialist" composers (i.e., hacks) like Reichardt and his "Second Berlin School" contemporaries Johann Abraham Peter Schulz (1747–1800) and Carl Friedrich Zelter (1758–1832), Goethe's favorite, who as director of the Berlin Singakademie played a leading part in the Bach revival, another manifestation of burgeoning German nationalism.

What Goethe liked about Zelter's settings was their modesty and true *Volkstümlichkeit*. (He broke with Reichardt a year after the *Lyrische Gedichte* were published because, as he put it, Reichardt had a "forward and impertinent nature" and thought himself Goethe's artistic equal.)[2] What he disliked in the settings of others (emphatically including Schubert) was the oversensitive, overcomplicated response to each successive line in a poem that "smothered" the words in musical artistry. Far from showing him musically insensitive, though, the fear shows how easily distracted (or to put it positively, how strongly attracted) Goethe was by music. He wrote to Zelter in 1809 that however wary he may have felt, as a poet, toward music carelessly applied, no lyric poem was complete without it. Only when set and sung, he wrote, is a poem's inspiration released into "the free and beautiful element of sensory experience." In a wonderful formulation, he concluded that, when listening to beautiful words beautifully set and sung, "we think and feel at once, and are enraptured."[3]

But the lied nevertheless remained a low-prestige affair, which is why Schubert's Viennese forebears, whose careers were oriented toward the aristocracy for support, cultivated it so little. Aristocracy, as ever, stood for cosmopolitan "civilization," not particular *Kultur*. Between 1781 and 1803, Haydn composed no more than three dozen lieder with keyboard accompaniment in the style, more or less, of the "first" Berlin song school. (Compare that with fifteen "canzonettas" to English texts composed in London in 1794–95, and a walloping four hundred British folk song arrangements with obbligato strings, commissioned by publishers in London and Edinburgh.)

One of Haydn's most *volkstümlich* songs, though, has become exceedingly famous: *Gott, erhalte Franz den Kaiser!* ("God save the Emperor Franz!"), better known as the *Kaiserhymne* ("Emperor's hymn"), which with various words and at various times has seen duty as national anthem for three countries (Ex. 35-4). The first was Austria, from the year of its composition, 1797, until 1918, when the last Habsburg emperor (Karl I) was deposed. Next came Germany, from 1922 to 1950, sung to a poem by Hoffmann von Fallersleben that dates from 1841 and begins "Deutschland, Deutschland über alles" ("Germany above all else"). Since 1950 the melody has served the Federal Republic of Germany ("West Germany" until 1990), sung to the words "Einigkeit und Recht und Freiheit" ("Unity, Justice, and Freedom").

Haydn's hymn was composed under the inspiration of "God Save the King," the earliest of all national anthems in the modern sense (first used in 1745 but, like the British "unwritten constitution," never formally adopted). Equally to the point, it was composed in direct "rebuttal" to *La Marseillaise*, the French revolutionary hymn that was officially adopted as the anthem of the Directory government in 1795 and has been in continuous use ever since. True, Haydn's hymn celebrated an imperial dynasty rather than a nation in the modern sense. But the concept of nationhood had developed by the late 1790s to the point where the "folklike" style was the only way one could embody a national sentiment that aspired to cross-cut all social classes. Later, in a gesture that found a number of echoes, as we have seen, in Schubert, Haydn cast the slow movement of his Quartet in C major, op. 76, no. 3, as a set of variations on "Gott, erhalte Franz den Kaiser!" so that the quartet is now known as the "Emperor" Quartet.

Mozart, who composed some sixty freestanding (or "insert") arias with orchestra (all but five in Italian, the operatic lingua franca), left only half that many songs with keyboard accompaniment (all but four in German, his native tongue). One, at least, is a masterpiece — or so Goethe thought. The text of *Das Veilchen* ("The little violet"), Mozart's only Goethe setting (composed around 1785), was extracted, like *Erlkönig*, from a singspiel libretto (*Erwin und Elmire*, 1775). Curiously reversing the sexual roles in *Heidenröslein*, the flower is cast this time as the spurned male lover, trampled underfoot.

Mozart's setting sports an appropriately *volkstümlich* opening theme, first given by the piano in the form of a ritornello, then repeated by the voice; and it makes some nicely

EX. 35-4   Joseph Haydn, *Kaiserhymne* (*Gott erhalte Franz den Kaiser!*)

restrained illustrative use of the piano (to paint, for example, the maiden's "carefree step"). But it is really a miniaturized aria, with an opening section that modulates to the dominant, a middle section in the parallel minor with a poignant far-out point on ♭VI, and a return to the original key "doubled" by a final thematic and textual reference (Mozart's idea!) to the opening stanza for the sake of a proper da capo closure.

Beethoven's involvement with the lied was about as deep as Mozart's: in a composing career that lasted twice as long, he composed about twice as many lieder (not counting 168 purely mercenary folk song arrangements, mostly at the instigation of the same British publishers who tempted Haydn). His song output does contain one major work, however: *An die ferne Geliebte* ("To the distant beloved"), op. 98, completed in 1816 and published with a dedication to his patron, Prince Lobkowitz. Rather than a single song, it is a set of six, all linked by composed transitions and ending with a thematic recollection of the first, thanks to which it bears the subtitle *Liederkreis*, literally a "circle of songs." In English the term is *song cycle*.

Beethoven's, though not quite the first, is the earliest song cycle to survive in active repertory. The cyclic idea seems originally to have been an English one, as befits the land where the modern novel had its birth. For at its most elaborate a song cycle could be compared with a novel in songs, just as the earliest English novels, like Samuel Richardson's *Pamela* (1740), were cast in the form of letters—discrete utterances between which the reader or listener was left to infer the connections that produced the plot.

The poems Beethoven set, by Alois Jeitteles, an obscure Jewish medical student in Vienna (later a famous physician), interweave nature imagery with personal pathos. There is a lot of rustic imagery in the music—echoes off the mountainside, birdsong, and the like. Though written out for the sake of the changing, often illustrative accompaniments, the individual songs conform (allowing for a bit of ornamental variation) to the stanzaic (or "strophic") structure of folk songs, with a single melody repeated for every verse unit.

Beethoven's songs, in other words, are still *Lieder im Volkston* or *volkstümliche Lieder* (folklike songs) but with a much stronger admixture of personal sentiment than we have seen in previous lieder. Song no. 2, the most rustic in the set, also has the most "pathetic" harmonies where the text refers to "inner pain." The very fluid tempo also serves to instill a sense of subjective sentiment into the music. Even when not specified by the composer, a fluctuating tempo, called *tempo rubato* or "stolen time," suggesting spontaneity of feeling, would become an essential component of "romantic" performing style.

Joseph Kerman has pointed out that "the lied grew up in reaction to the 'art music' of Italian opera, cantata, and canzonet," just as the *Kultur* of German romanticism was a reaction to the artifices of "civilization." Therefore, he adds, the English term "art song," which is sometimes used as a translation for "lied," is "miserably confusing."[4] But Beethoven succeeded, while maintaining the unaffected "natural" tone without which lieder are not lieder, in reweighting the scales on the side of art. With him, art and nature, craft and spontaneity, are brought into a more traditional equilibrium. Not surprisingly, Goethe hated his songs; Beethoven was the "smotherer" supreme.

Ex. 35-5 samples the first, second, and last songs from *An die ferne Geliebte*, including the transition into no. 6 as a reminder that the individual songs are connected by the piano. The general style is not all that far removed from that of Reichardt: indeed, the middle stanza of the second song (Ex. 35-5b), in which the voice chants a monotone while the piano takes over the tune, was probably modeled on Reichardt's effective (hence widely imitated) "transcription" of the Elf King's insinuating whisper in Ex. 35-3. Like Mozart, Beethoven tampered with the ending of the text, planting a "pre-echo" of the final lines at the end of the first song so that the cycle can "come full circle" with wistful hopes of vicarious union through shared song.

The ending of the cycle resonates powerfully, of course, with Beethoven's well-publicized loneliness, well known to every listener. Here the composer's "I" decisively preempts the traditional "We," but forges a new We (and, in its subjective sentimentality, an equally German one) by enlisting the listener's sympathy. And yet it is still important, whenever biographical resonances impinge on the way we interpret romantic art, to distinguish the "persona" embodied in the art from the person who lived the life. From what we know of his life, the actual Beethoven (as often observed) sang most readily "to the *safely* distant beloved." The da capo effect that unifies the cycle operates on several levels. There is the literal musical quotation at the end (where, ironically, it is actually the poet who is "quoting" the extra stanza that the composer had planted earlier, not that a listener would know), which involves a change of meter and tempo (Ex. 35-5d). And there is a coda suffused with motivic reminiscences, culminating in a striking reminiscence of the first phrase in the final cadence, forcing one last poignant retrospect. But upon examination, the main tune of the sixth song turns out to be a variation of the opening melody in anticipation of its literal return. It retains the contour up to E♭, down to F, and up again to C (see Ex. 35-5e).

EX. 35-5A   Ludwig van Beethoven, *An die ferne Geliebte*, no. 1, mm. 1–9

EX. 35-5B   Ludwig van Beethoven, *An die ferne Geliebte*, no. 2, middle stanza

EX. 35-5C   Ludwig van Beethoven, *An die ferne Geliebte*, no. 6, mm. 1–16

EX. 35-5C   (continued)

EX. 35-5D   Ludwig van Beethoven, *An die ferne Geliebte*, cyclic return

EX. 35-5E   Ludwig van Beethoven, *An die ferne Geliebte*, the motivic relationship between the first and last songs

SCHUBERT AND ROMANTIC IRONY

Yet for all the structural excellence and expressivity of *An die ferne Geliebte*, the lied remained for Beethoven a minor genre. The first major composer for whom it was a major genre—hence the composer through whom the lied became a major (and an indispensable) genre in any history of European "art" music—was Schubert, as already implied in the previous chapter. A full understanding of Schubert's romanticism is impossible without understanding how his lieder newly negotiated the relationship of "I" and "We."

In investigating them, we shall reencounter many of the same devices (particularly harmonic devices) that we have already associated with the subjective and spiritual side of romanticism, only this time they will be approached by way of *Volkstümlichkeit*. To attempt to assign priority here—to decide whether Schubert's songs "influenced" his instrumental music or the other way around—would be fruitless, and it would miss the point. Take, for a first example, *Lachen und Weinen* (Ex. 35-6), composed in 1823 to a poem by Friedrich Rückert (1788–1866). In overall form and character it is simple, sincere, and as *volkstümlich* as you please, but the antithesis at the heart of the poem—"Laughing and Crying," apparently unmotivated but of course motivated by love—is expressed by artful modal mixtures of a kind that eventually became absolutely basic to Schubert's harmonic idiom. Compare, for example, the beginnings of the exposition (Ex. 35-7a) and recapitulation (Ex. 35-7b) in the first movement of the G-major String Quartet, which we already know to be one of Schubert's harmonically most adventurous compositions.

EX. 35-6   Franz Schubert, *Lachen und Weinen*, D. 777

EX. 35-6 (continued)

The quartet shows the same reversal as the song: the initial switch from major to minor comes back as minor-to-major. Nor is the switch in either case just a static exchange. The initial mode switch in the song sends the melody off into an asymmetrical pair of phrases that include an "affective" dominant-ninth chord and an "entranced" flat submediant. The corresponding reversed switch in the second half of the song sends the melody off into an equally asymmetrical phrase that cadences on the subdominant,

EX. 35-7A   Franz Schubert, Quartet in G, D. 887, I, mm. 1–10

EX. 35-7B   Franz Schubert, Quartet in G, D. 887, I, analogous spot in recap

approached by a "V of IV" that thoroughly destabilizes the tonic. At these points subjectivity (the "I") comes graphically to the fore, but in a way that can only be appreciated in dialectical, even ironic opposition to the folkish "We" with which each stanza begins (and ends). When absorbed into the "absolute" medium of the string quartet, these effects retain their expressive potency, but are no longer limited in their connotation to the simple emotional opposites defined by the poem.

Or take the opening of "Am Meer" ("By the sea"), a song composed for the *Schwanengesang* collection in 1828 to words by Heinrich Heine (1797–1856), the most outlandishly subjective and ironic of all romantic poets (Ex. 35-8a); or else take the opening of *Die Allmacht* ("The Almighty"), a majestic hymn composed in 1825 to words by the composer's friend Johann Ladislaus Pyrker (Ex. 35-8b). These songs give off an aura of the sublime—in Wordsworth's unimprovable lines, "The sense of God, or whatsoe'er is dim/Or vast in its own being"[5]—obtained by juxtaposing the tonic in brusque unruly fashion with chromatic chords of a kind that normally precede the dominant.

Approached this way, such chords, in the words of the famous music theorist Heinrich Schenker, "plunge into the very midst of spiritual experience."[6] Indeed, in "Am Meer," a song of truly bizarre imagery (the lover's tears, a metaphor for sexual intercourse, when imbibed become a deadly soul poison), the uncanny chord comes first, so that the song begins with a shiver of uncanny subjectivity. It evokes or exposes *Innigkeit* in a spectacularly violent way, suggesting (in Kerman's words now) "everything in the world that is inward, sentient, and arcane."[7] More literally, perhaps, but also more chillingly, the unprepared augmented sixth chord in *Am Meer* might seem to symbolize the poisoned kiss itself.

Without the eccentric context provided by the poem, one thinks, such a progression could have no meaning at all. But then one hears the very opening of the Quintet in C major (Ex. 35-8c), composed the same year as "Am Meer," and one has to think again. The same kind of uncanny juxtaposition materializes—even uncannier, because the diminished seventh proceeds not to the dominant, as in *Die Allmacht*, but circles right back to the tonic, the oscillations of E and E♭ hair-raisingly evoking modal mixture of the most destabilizing kind, with all its emotional implications intact. Yet it materializes in an imaginatively open-ended context, all the more arcane for its being wordless.

In which context did such arcane eloquence originate? Impossible — tantalizingly, blessedly impossible — to say. The combination of an extreme subjective expressive immediacy and an unspecified or "objectless" context is what gave rise to the sublime romantic notion of "absolute music" — one of the most potent, but also one of the most widely misunderstood, of all romantic concepts. Schubert's opening gesture in the quintet, more vividly than almost any other single idea that could be quoted in an example, gives an inkling of what one later composer (Richard Wagner) would mean when he spoke of music as "saying the unsayable,"[8] or what another later composer (Felix Mendelssohn) would mean when he said that the meaning of music is not too indefinite for translation into words, but far too definite.[9]

EX. 35-8A   Franz Schubert, *Schwanengesang*, opening of "Am Meer"

What these admittedly extreme examples also show is that by the end of his career, Schubert no longer distinguished between the possibilities of the lied and those of the more "artistic" genres against which the lied, as Kerman reminds us, had originally rebelled. This is not to say that Schubert did not share the general views of his time where the relative importance of genres was concerned. One of his most frequently quoted letters is the one to his friend Franz von Schober (30 November 1823) in which, with reference to the song cycle *Die schöne Müllerin* ("The beautiful miller maid"), now regarded as one of his masterpieces, he complained that "since my opera I have composed nothing but a few songs to Müller."[10] (The poet of the cycle, Wilhelm Müller, was probably moved to write it by the implied pun on his own name, which means "miller.") The opera (*Fierabras*) has been forgotten, but at the time it seemed to Schubert the more important work by far.

Still, there was nothing in the realm of harmonic invention, formal experiment, psychological nuance or even keyboard virtuosity, that was "too good" for a Schubert

E X. 35-8B   Franz Schubert, opening of *Die Allmacht*

EX. 35-8C   Franz Schubert, opening of Quintet in C

lied—with one conspicuous exception. Vocal (or "operatic") floridity remained forbidden to the genre. Occasional cadential ornaments aside, there is never a hint
of coloratura. On the rare occasions where Schubert allots more than two notes
to a syllable of text, it is almost always for the sake of invoking some "preverbal"
form of vocal expression—like the moan of pain that accompanies the word "Weh"
(woe) in "Wasserfluth" ("The water current"), the fifth song in that gloomiest of
song cycles, *Die Winterreise* (Ex. 35-9). The basic vocal idiom is always that of the
Volksweise (folk tune), the "natural" music representing the "We," inflected by eccentric
details of melody, harmony, or accompaniment that at extreme moments allow the "I"
to intrude.

The only exceptions to this rule are for the sake of irony, a sake that can justify the
suspension of any rule. Irony—saying one thing and meaning another—is sometimes
regarded (especially by poets who specialize in it) as being somehow inaccessible to

EX. 35-9   Franz Schubert, "Wasserfluth" (from *Die Winterreise*, no. 5), mm. 1–14

EX. 35-9   (continued)

From   its fount my burn - ing   woe,_____ From   its fount my burn - ing
To___ the brook thou soon shalt flow,_____ To___ the brook thou soon shalt
dur - stig ein   das hei - sse   Weh,_____ dur - stig ein___ das hei - sse
nimmt dich bald das Bäch - lein   auf,_____ nimmt dich bald das Bäch - lein

woe.
flow.
Weh.
auf.

music. W. H. Auden, one of the great poets of the twentieth century, writing in collaboration with Chester Kallman, once permitted himself to assert that

> since music, generally speaking, can express only one thing at a time, it is ill adapted to verses which express mixed or ambiguous feelings, and prefers poems which either express one emotional state or successively contrast two states.[11]

Beginning with Schubert, though, there is scarcely a composer of song (or opera) who did not contradict this blunt dictum on practically every page, for irony (with its stronger relative, sarcasm) is one of the romantic artist's most indispensable tools. Even if Auden and Kallman's basic premise were true, that music "can express only one thing at a time," music in conjunction with a text can easily express "mixed or ambiguous feelings," or downright contradictory ones, with breathtaking and often heartrending effect. But of course we have already seen that Auden and Kallman's basic premise is untrue. Just recall all the harmonic "puns" encountered in the previous chapter — for example between the dominant-seventh chord, which resolves straightforwardly by fifth progression, and the "German sixth," which resolves obliquely by half step — and the ways in which Schubert is able to exploit such ambivalences in order to express an enormous range of ambiguous feelings even in the absence of words.

In "Der Müller und der Bach" ("The miller and the brook"), the next-to-last song in *Die schöne Müllerin*, irony works on a number of levels that together make this ostensibly pretty song an agonizing heartbreaker. This cycle is an especially "novelistic" one. It follows one of the stereotypical novel plots: boy meets girl; boy gets girl; boy loses girl to a rival. The dénouement is tragic: thwarted in love, the hero kills himself; and "The Miller and the Brook" records the very moment when the fatal decision is made.

Like Goethe's *Erlkönig*, the poem features the folkloric device of nature-made-animate: the journeyman miller and the brook engage in a dialogue. Only this time the device is not "naive." The poet does not affect belief in the reality of the brook's voice; it is clearly delusional, turning the song into a typically novelistic interior dialogue. That is the first, purely textual, irony. The second irony consists in the unusually florid (="pretty") style of the setting, with its decorative melodic curlicues at cadences that do not always carry particularly charged words. Clearly, the youth is putting on tragic airs, at least at first (Ex. 35-10a).

The youth sings of his broken heart; the brook offers consolation (Ex. 35-10b), not only in its cheery babbling (the pianist's right hand!), but by a typical mode switch into the major. At the youth's reentry the mode switches back, but the brook's babbling continues: a synthesis. When the youth takes up the brook's major mode at the very last line, however, it marks no return to a solaced mood, but marks instead the moment at which his will to live is vanquished by his grief, which must find relief at any cost (Ex. 35-10c). And this, of course, is the third, most poignant irony. Comparison with *Lachen und Weinen* (Ex. 35-6) will drive the point home. In that song, as in "The Miller and the Brook" up to the last stanza, the mode symbolism is straightforward: major is happy, minor is sad. At the end of "The Miller and the Brook," however, minor is sad and major is sadder. As before (for example, in Donizetti's *Lucia di Lammermoor*, discussed in chapter 33), as always, the irony comes about through a mastery of conventional codes that is so sure as to permit their idiosyncratic manipulation.

EX. 35-10A   Franz Schubert, *Die schöne Müllerin*, "Der Müller und der Bach," mm. 1–10

144

EX. 35-10B Franz Schubert, *Die schöne Müllerin*, "Der Müller und der Bach," mm. 29–40

Der Bach

Und wenn sich die Lie-be dem Schmerz ent-ringt, ein Stern-lein, ein neu-es, am

Him-mel er-blinkt, ein Stern-lein, ein neu-es, am Him-mel er-blinkt.

EX. 35-10C Franz Schubert, *Die schöne Müllerin*, "Der Müller und der Bach," mm. 71–82

Ach, un-ten, da un-ten, die küh-le Ruh'! Ach, Bäch-lein, lie-bes Bäch-lein, so

sin-ge nur zu, ach, Bäch-lein, lie-bes Bächlein, so sin-ge nur zu.

That mastery of irony, coupled with an unparalleled capacity to find the psychological or "interior" dimension in the poems he put to music, set Schubert apart from his songwriting contemporaries from the very beginning of his songwriting career. At first, like most composers of lieder, he worked within the limits of the *volkstümlich* lyric as established by Goethe. Two of his early hits, both written during his teens, were settings of the very poems given above as Goethean models together with their settings by Reichardt.

Schubert's *Heidenröslein* and his *Erlkönig* were both composed in 1815, when he was all of eighteen years old. They are a perennial classroom pair. The former illustrates the "strophic" type of setting favored by Goethe and his chosen musicians, in which only a single model musical stanza is composed and reused, just as in a folk song, as many times as the poem has stanzas, fulfilling the romantic ideal of naturalness. The latter exemplifies the more artistic kind of setting that Goethe claimed to despise, in which the musical setting follows the poem's meaning rather than its form, proceeding straight through without regular internal repetitions, each verse inspiring its own musical counterpart. There is no good single term to cover this kind of setting, since as a type it is defined basically by what it does *not* do, namely set the text "strophically." What it does do has to be separately described each time or else presented without comment, since part of the point of avoiding the strophic style was to make the setting sui generis — that is, constituting a class of its own. This, too, was a romantic ideal: Herder himself was obsessed with the notion of being sui generis to the point of inventing a German equivalent, *urwüchsig* (roughly, "growing from scratch"), from which he derived the rather monstrous abstract noun *Urwüchsigkeit* to define the quality of uniqueness that he valued above all. He applied these terms first of all to languages and language communities, of course, rather than to individuals. For *urwüchsig* lied settings "nonstrophic" would be as good (or bad) a term as any. What has in fact become standard is the equally clumsy and uninformative "through-composed," a direct translation of the German *durchkomponiert*.

While it is customary to say that the strophic form is "natural" and the through-composed is "artistic" (and while we are following custom here), there is no reason why strophic settings could not be artistic in the highest degree. Schubert's *Heidenröslein* (Ex. 35-11) seems as natural (or "artless") an imitation folk song as could be desired, distinguished above all by the memorable perkiness of its thrice-repeated strain. But Goethe's poem (see above) has a booby-trap in the form of an asymmetrical five-line stanza (rhyme-scheme ab/aab). Schubert found a wonderful solution to the problem of making the melody reflect the parallelism of the two unequal half verses and at the same time making the three-line group (terzet) as coherent a unit as the two-line group (couplet).

The couplet does what comes "naturally." Its two lines each occupy two measures, and each of the four measures contains a single harmony, the whole describing a perfect cadence: $I - ii(^4_2) - V(^6_5 - ^4_2) - I(^6_3 - ^5_3)$. The "artistic" challenge comes with the terzet, where it becomes necessary to invent a three-stage harmonic design. First, by inflecting the C (the third of the ii chord) to C♯ on its second appearance (m. 6), Schubert turns it into a V^4_2 of V, a more restless harmony; next, by ending the second line of the terzet with a deceptive cadence (iii instead of V, the expected resolution), Schubert makes a third phrase (=line) necessary. Moreover, the five-line verse now ends with a half cadence on V, and it is left to the two-line refrain (mm. 11–14) to route the harmony back to the tonic. Thus the three cadences (couplet-terzet-refrain) together comprise an unshakably stable I-V-I progression, imparting a like shapeliness and stability to the stanza despite its asymmetry.

But now take an even closer look, at the placement of the harmonies not only with respect to one another, but also with respect to the words. In the second and the third stanzas (the ones supposedly left "to chance" or "to take care of themselves" in strophic settings), the tensest (most chromatic and dissonant) harmony—the "V_2^4 of V"—coincides with the promise and then the delivery of the rose's painful retaliation ("Ich steche dich," " . . . und stach"). Formal strategy and poetic meaning have thoroughly interpenetrated, as in only the most "artful" poems and songs. The eighteen-year-old Schubert was already a past master of art-concealing art.

EX. 35-11   Franz Schubert, *Heidenröslein*, model stanza

EX. 35-11 (continued)

REPRESENTATIONS OF CONSCIOUSNESS

Heidenröslein was written in August 1815, *Erlkönig* in December. In between came sixty
other songs, three choruses, a piano sonata, a set of twelve dances, a cantata, and an
opera. By then Schubert was a seasoned composer of dramatic ballads; *Erlkönig* was his
seventeenth essay in that genre. His earlier settings had relied a great deal on operatic

devices, particularly the use of recitative for the narrator's lines. In *Erlkönig*, recitative has shrunk down to just a single line: the horrifying final one in which the child's death is revealed. Elsewhere the momentum is maintained at considerable cost to the poor pianist's right arm, to which the horse's incessant hoofbeats are assigned. (That triplet pulse, although never before so boldly rendered, was already traditional in setting this poem: compare Reichardt in Ex. 35-3.)

Besides the horse, there are four "roles" in this narration, each characterized in relief against the unremitting gallop — the increasingly distraught child, the desperately consoling father, the grimly deadpan narrator who sets the scene and tells the outcome, and, of course, the sinisterly beguiling title character. It is when the Elf King sings that the pianist gets a bit of relief, owing to Schubert's uncanny knack for ironic characterization. The sweet crooning of the sprite — sweet, that is, until he loses patience at the end of his third speech — so occupies the attention of the terrified but fascinated child that the hoofbeats fade into the background, only to return with redoubled force at each panicked outcry from child to father. That insidious ironic sweetness — experienced, as it were, from the threatened child's perspective — is much scarier than any conventional spookiness (like Reichardt's monotone chant) could be.

What keeps the dramatic pressure so high is not just the relentless (and potentially monotonous) rhythm, but also the tonal scheme. The Elf King, of course, always sings in major keys, in contrast with the horror music surrounding his interventions. They are, first, the relative major (B♭), then the subdominant major (C), and finally the inevitable submediant (E♭), poised strategically for a return to the tonic. In the long horrific middle of the song, however, from the Elf King's first appeal to the child until his last, successive cadences are pitched hair-raisingly on ascending half steps. Using capital letters to represent major keys and lower case for minor, the unprecedented progression of tonics is B♭ – b – C – c♯ – d – E♭.

Also perhaps unprecedented is the level of dissonance at the boy's outcries, "Mein Vater! Mein Vater!" At these points the harmony could be described as a dominant ninth chord with the root assigned to the pianist's horsy right hand. The voice has the ninth, pitched above, and the left hand has the seventh, pitched below. The result is a virtual "tone cluster" (D against E♭ and C the first time; E against F and D the second time; finally F against G♭ and E♭). Ex. 35-12 shows the end of the Elf King's first appeal (in B♭), the child's dissonant recoil to the sound of hoofbeats, and the modulations to B minor (father) and C major (the Elf King's second try). As in the case of the cycles of thirds investigated in the previous chapter, the harmonic logic of these progressions, within the rules of composition Schubert was taught, can certainly be demonstrated. That logic, however, is not what appeals so strongly to the listener's imagination; rather it is the calculated impression (or illusion) of wild abandon. The mark of a successful innovation, on the terms of the game as Schubert and his contemporaries played it, was to be at the same time novel and intelligible. That is a difficult assignment, here carried off by the eighteen-year-old Schubert seemingly at the prompting of a spontaneous (hence effortless) inspiration.

EX. 35-12   Franz Schubert, *Erlkönig*, mm. 66–85

Even Goethe, finally, was impressed with this song. Schubert sent him a copy in 1816 with a request for permission to dedicate the song to the poet, but received no reply. The poet was no doubt offended by the young composer's impudent failure to respect the poem's stanza structure — just the thing we post-romantics tend to value most highly in the song today. Fourteen years later, and two years after Schubert's death, a young singer, Wilhelmine Schröder-Devrient (1804–60; soon to become the most famous dramatic soprano in Europe), sang it in the aged Goethe's presence and bowled him over. "I had already heard this song, and it meant nothing to me," Goethe's literary assistant and biographer Johann Peter Eckermann recorded him saying, "but sung like this, it conjures up a great picture before my eyes."[12]

Another song that ineluctably conjures up a picture is *Gretchen am Spinnrade* ("Little Margaret at the spinning wheel"), a famous set piece extracted from Goethe's dramatic poem *Faust*. Schubert's first masterpiece, it was written over a year earlier than *Erlkönig*, in 1814, when the composer was only seventeen. It is not a "still" but a "moving picture" that is conjured, a dramatic scene. On one level of motion, the "micro" level, we have the spinning wheel, rendered in wonderful detail: the oscillating right hand figure, marked *sempre ligato*, shows the wheel turning; the left hand thumb, marked *sempre staccato*, suggests its clicking; and the occasional pickups in the bass represent Gretchen's foot on the pedal (Ex. 35-13a). But this static representation turns dynamic, and we come to the "macro" level of depiction, when Gretchen, remembering Faust's kiss, momentarily forgets to spin, and the piano falls silent, only to start up again with the foot-on-pedal figure (Ex. 35-13b).

As in *Erlkönig*, what really keeps this scene in motion, far beyond the mechanism of mere scenic description, is the fluidly mobile tonal scheme, more an aspect of narration — and then? and then? — than depiction. The music begins and ends stably in D minor — or so it seems. On closer inspection, we notice a significant lack. The initial D-minor chord, whose figurations establish the picture of the spinning wheel, is never confirmed as tonic by a cadence. (The apparent V–I progressions in the bass, representing the working of the foot pedal, are not accompanied by changing cadential harmonies; they take place entirely within the continuously sounding tonic.)

In fact, the first chord that follows the tonic is a chord that destabilizes it: C major (m. 7), relative to which the first chord is not i but ii. The ostensible key of C is confirmed (albeit very weakly) by a cadence in m. 11, but slips back to the original tonic by m. 13. Still, though, there has been no strong cadence to D minor; the dominant harmony on the weak beat of m. 12 that pulls the music back toward D is lacking its crucial third, that is, the leading tone. The key of D minor is more solidly established than before, but still very weakly.

The original tonic is reestablished in m. 30 to accommodate the textual refrain ("Meine ruh ist hin . . . "), and only now is the chord of D minor preceded (in m. 29) by its fully expressed dominant. From here to the end of the song the key of D minor will return only with the refrain. Each time, moreover, Schubert will exploit the refrain's tonally open-ended character to launch a new modulation as Gretchen's memory ranges back over the events she is reliving. Most of the next section, in which she recalls Faust's physical presence and his kiss, moves as before through A minor to F major, but at m. 55 begins an intensifying progression similar to the one noted in the middle of *Erlkönig*, in which tonicizing cadences occur on successive steps of a scale — here G, A♭, and B♭, the last finally enhanced with an electric G♯ and resolved as an augmented sixth to the original dominant (enhanced with a shocking ninth) for the culminating recollection of the kiss.

All during this passage, the representation of the spinning wheel has been losing definition. The first thing to go (beginning in m. 51) is the click-click-click of the left thumb; later (m. 66), as we know, the turning figure itself is stilled. As Charles Rosen observes, the actual object of Schubert's representation "is not the spinning but Gretchen's consciousness of it," just as the actual object of representation in *Erlkönig* was not the Elf King "as he really is" (there is, after all, no such thing — or so we think) but the child's consciousness of him.[13]

In both cases, consciousness of the "objective" surroundings (spinning wheel, hoofbeats) recedes as the "subjective" vision grows more vivid. The representation of "inwardness" as it interacts with and triumphs over the perception of external reality is the true romantic dimension here, the source of the music's uncanny power. "Objective" representation, whether of spinning wheels or horses' hooves, was old hat, esthetically uninteresting in itself; its "subjective" manipulation is the startling new effect, prompted in Schubert's imagination by those "inward" aspects of the poem to which he was uniquely attentive.

To return to Gretchen: after the next refrain (mm. 73 ff), the music goes off on another "intensifying progression," with successive cadences on E♭ (m. 86), F (m. 88), G (m. 90), and finally — after a long digression over a dominant pedal — on A (m. 97), treated immediately as the dominant of the original key, which allows the song to end with a final tonic refrain. What we have gone through (along with Gretchen, so to speak), is an extended "stream of consciousness" represented by the widely ranging harmony, its cadential processes and goals kept weakly defined on the surface (but, of course, at all times firmly directed and controlled from behind the scenes). A deliberately attenuated tonal coherence serves the purposes of psychological realism. The generic language of tonal harmony, one often hears it said, has been subverted in the interests of specific portraiture.

But of course that's only how things look. In fact, nothing has been subverted. Rather, a new task, that of representing a unique human exercise of memory in musical terms, has given rise to a new technique, a new way of using an existing vocabulary. Indeed, it was a musical need (tonal closure), one that no poet has reason to heed, that prompted Schubert to end his setting with a final refrain, absent in the original poem. Schubert's use of a refrain shows the way in which "strophic" and "through-composed" procedures, often presented as mutually exclusive stances or alternatives, actually work in harness, allowing individual lieder to assume a great variety of shapes, and turning the tension between the "shapely" (*ontic*) and the "dynamically progressing" (*gignetic*) aspects of form to expressive account.

From this earliest Schubert lied masterpiece let us jump to one of the latest — *Der Doppelgänger* ("The double," from the *Schwanengesang* cycle) — for a last look at Schubert's transformation of the genre (Ex. 35-14). It is one of the few songs in which Schubert tackled the burgeoning "urban" romantic theme of mental disintegration, presented by poets of a post-Goethe generation without the sugar-coating of nature painting or folklore, and by composers who set their work without a reassuring veneer of *Volkstümlichkeit*. Without that veneer, which leaves open an interpretive escape hatch (was it really the Elf King? was it the child's delusion? was it marsh gas after all?), psychological realism — the reality of psychological disturbance brought about by the stress of urban living — is confronted head-on.

EX. 35-13A   Franz Schubert, *Gretchen am Spinnrade*, mm. 1–17

EX. 35-13B   Franz Schubert, *Gretchen am Spinnrade*, mm. 63–75

The poet most closely associated with the depiction of extreme or neurotic mental states triggered by thwarted desire was Heinrich Heine, Schubert's exact though much longer-lived contemporary. More precisely, as the Schubert scholar Richard Kramer points out, Heine ruminates ironically on the "bitter aftertaste"[14] of love, rather than on the more familiar romantic theme of ecstatic anticipation, as for example in Beethoven's *An die ferne Geliebte*. *Der Doppelgänger*, from Heine's *Buch der Lieder* ("Songbook," 1827), the only book of his that Schubert lived to see, opened up a theme that would haunt romantic artists to the end of the century, and indeed beyond, as a metaphor for existential loneliness: the theme of dissociation, "out of body" experience. The poet, returning to the scene of an unhappy love, encounters a stranger who turns out to be himself, endlessly replaying the futile exertions of the past.

The mood of the poem is obsessional, to say the least, and so it may not completely surprise us that, just this once, Schubert chose the old-fashioned ground-bass form for his setting (Ex. 35-14). Here it functions not only as formal unifier but as metaphor. The four notes outlined by the outer voices in the chords played before the voice enters contain a very unstable interval, the diminished fourth A♯-D, that perpetually forces an obligatory resolution of the D (only "hearable" in B minor as an appoggiatura) to C♯. The motive, turned into an ostinato that continually forces the same resolution, figures the compulsively repetitive behavior the poem describes. Running through the song like an idée fixe, an incessant thought, it provides a frame for the voice's breathless phrases in quasi-recitative. (Schubert reused the motive, which he seems to have derived, diminished fourth and all, from the subject of the C♯-minor fugue in Book I of Bach's *Well-Tempered Clavier*, to evoke a sense of uncanny awe in the Agnus Dei from his Mass in E♭ major, also the product of his last year, in which the motive modulates terrifyingly from the relative minor to the frightful, flat-filled parallel minor.)

There are two fixed and two variable notes in the ostinato. The B and the D are unalterable, whereas the A♯ and C♯, once their functions have become accustomed and predictable, are often lowered from their normal positions in the scale of B minor — the A♯ to a "modal" A♮ and the C♯ to a "Phrygian" C♮ — to enhance the effect of weirdness and abnormality. It is on one of the eerie Phrygian alterations, of course, that the singer recognizes his own horrifying image in the stranger — a German sixth (m. 41) that if normally resolved would lead out of the tonic key to its subdominant (as *almost* happens at the very end: one could, if one tried, hear the last two measures as a half cadence on the dominant in E minor). The chord does not proceed normally, however, but rather (in m. 42) resolves as an appoggiatura to a French sixth chord that serves as an altered dominant of B.

But now, in a fashion that anticipates one of the bedrock tenets of Freudian psychoanalysis, confrontation with — and acknowledgment of — the specter from the past brings relief (albeit temporary) from the obsessional pattern: the basso ostinato is replaced in mm. 42–54, corresponding to the lines addressed directly to the uncanny double, by another pattern that first rises by semitones and then briefly escapes to the major mediant. (The psychoanalytic resonance, which we have had occasion to mark as early as Mozart — see Ex. 30-1 and its attendant discussion — should neither disconcert nor be discounted as anachronistic; Freud repeatedly confessed his debt to the psychological insights of the romantic poets.)

ROMANTIC NATIONALISM

With this thoroughly urbanized and neurotic song we have strayed pretty far from the state of nature, as did the lied itself in the generations after Schubert. The solo song became increasingly a site for subjective lyric expression, the more intense or even grotesque the better, leaving collective subjectivity to the larger, more literally collective choral and dramatic genres. The traditional *volkstümliches Lied* became once again the domain of specialist composers, like Carl Loewe (1796–1869), who, though actually a couple of months older than Schubert, is usually thought of as belonging to a later generation since he lived so much longer. He remained faithful to the ballad and other genres of story-song into the 1860s, and also, in the spirit of Herder, set Slavic and Jewish folk texts in addition to German ones.

Loewe's setting of *Erlkönig* (Ex. 35-15) was one of his earliest ballads. It was composed in 1818, a year later than Schubert's, but before Schubert's was published. By the time Loewe published his setting in 1824, however, Schubert's had been in print for three years and was already famous. So Loewe's version has to be seen as a competing setting, justified by its difference from its predecessor. The differences, as it happens,

EX. 35-14   Franz Schubert, *Der Doppelgänger*

EX. 35-14 (continued)

all point in the direction of a greater nature mysticism, a more naive romanticism. Like Schubert (or, for that matter, like Reichardt), Loewe uses a compound meter that reflects the strong hoofbeat iambs and anapests of Goethe's poem. But his rhythm is less relentless than Schubert's; he seems more interested in the evocation of a static, atemporal sphere — the Elf King's supernatural domain — into which the horse and its riders have intruded.

The evocation of timelessness though tremolos — an essentially orchestral device (based on a bowing effect) and something of a rarity in piano music — pervades the song from beginning to end, and palpably surrounds the child whenever the Elf King speaks (Ex. 35-15a). At these moments the horse and its headlong charge pass into oblivion, and the music is even more insidiously sweet and inviting than Schubert (who never gives up the human perspective entirely) had made it. Perhaps most significantly, the Elf King's appeals to the boy are set to melodic phrases reminiscent of horn signals. Not only does that lend them a harmonic immobility that deepens the boy's music trance, so to speak, but the timbre of the hunting horn — in German, *Waldhorn* or "forest horn" — had long since become the primary tone color of supernatural timelessness for German romantics, evoking the "forest primeval," as Longfellow would later put it in his romantic poem *Evangeline*.

Another "anti-Schubertian," anti-ironic touch comes at the very end (Ex. 35-15b), where Loewe eschews the distancing operatic manner to which Schubert still made recourse. He allows the rhythmic motion to come to a stop in the middle of the last line, to create a proper storyteller's suspense, but then accompanies the final word, "*tot*" (dead), with a horror-harmony rather than Schubert's recitative-punctuating formal cadence (the musical equivalent of a deadpan "throwaway"). Loewe clearly "believes" more in the supernatural content of the poem than Schubert did. That folkish naivety (or "faux-naivety") characterized Loewe's ballads to the very end.

THE LITURGY OF NATIONHOOD

Otherwise, the *volkstümliches Lied* was fast transforming itself into the frankly and literally patriotic *Vaterlandslied*, sometimes called the *Rheinlied* after the symbolically charged river Rhine, the quintessential emblem of Germany. Such songs were composed in quantity as the idea of German cultural unity, primed by anti-Napoleonic resentment and sparked by Herderian folk-romanticism, was transformed into a political agenda. A "textbook" example of the genre is *Was ist des Deutschen Vaterland* ("What is a German's fatherland?"), a famous poem by Ernst Moritz Arndt (1769–1860), a professor of history and a fierce publicist in the cause of German nationalism, set to music in 1825 by Gustav Reichardt (no relation to Johann), a Berlin conductor and singing teacher.

The poem, drafted in 1813 at the very height of Napoleonic resistance, is basically a long list of German-speaking territories, each offered as an answer to the title question and resoundingly rejected with the same refrain: "Oh no, no, no! His fatherland must be greater than that." The last two stanzas, musically set off from the rest, contain the true (that is, politically correct) answer.

EX. 35-15A   Carl Loewe, *Erlkönig*, mm. 27–34

EX. 35-15B   Carl Loewe, *Erlkönig*, ending

142. Des Deutschen Vaterland.

Ernst Moritz Arndt. (1813.)

FIG. 35-2 *Des Deutschen Vaterland* as published in Ludwig Christian Erk's *Deutscher Liederschatz* (Treasury of German Songs, 1859–1872).

FIG. 35-2   (continued)

Was ist des Deutschen Vaterland?	What is a German's fatherland?
so nenne endlich mir das Land!	Tell me its name at last!
So weit die deutsche Zunge klingt	As far and wide as the German tongue resounds
und Gott im Himmel Lieder singt:	and God in Heaven sings lieder:
Das soll es sein,	That it must be!
das, wack'rer Deutscher, nenne dein!	That, gallant German, call thine own!
Das ganze Deutschland soll es sein!	All of Germany must it be!
o Gott vom Himmel, sieh' darein,	O God, look down from Heaven
und gib uns rechten deutschen Muth,	and give us true German spirit,
dass wir es lieben treu und gut.	so that we love it truly and well.

Reichardt's setting is only one of many settings the famous poem received. For the most part a rather ordinary if spirited *volkstümlich* march, it nevertheless contains a stroke of true German genius when, at the mention of God singing lieder (!), and again at the plea for "rechten deutschen Muth," the music takes a turn toward the Schubertian visionary terrain of mediants and submediants to inspire a music trance of nationalist fervor. As a result, according to Ludwig Erk (1807–83), the latter-day Herderian from whose posthumous collection *Deutscher Liederschatz* ("Treasury of German songs") Fig. 35-2 is taken, "this song was in the decades 1830–70 one of the German songs in most widespread use, and had great political significance." No less significantly, he adds that "since the ideal of a united German empire has become a reality, our song has begun to be forgotten." Mission accomplished.

But it was also the original mission of a great deal of music that did not pass so quickly into oblivion. Under the impetus of romantic nationalism, choral music came into its own. It enjoyed a rebirth that can only be compared with its original "birth" for European music history as the continent-uniting music of the medieval Christian church, the first music deemed important enough to be recorded in notation. That implied trajectory, from chant to lied and from church to folk, testifies to the transformation romanticism wrought not only in the way one thought about nation, but also the way one thought about art. Both concepts were sacralized, made holy, in the process of their romantic redefinition.

Romantic choral music was associated not only with *Gemütlichkeit*, the conviviality of social singing, celebrated in the *Männerchor* texts for which Schubert had supplied such a mountain of music, but also with mass choral festivals—social singing on a cosmic scale that provided European nationalism with its very hotbed.

These affairs had originated in the aftermath of the French Revolution as an explicit attempt to put the nation-state in the place formerly occupied by God and king in the popular imagination. Beginning in 1794 (Revolutionary Year III), the Cult of the Supreme Being—code for the revolutionary State—was established. Significantly enough, this cult replaced an earlier cult of the Goddess of Reason, which proved musically barren. The new cult inspired a rich liturgy, some of it actually modeled on that of the Catholic church. Its exercises culminated in the singing of revolutionary hymns by *choeurs universels*, choirs embracing all present. The men's choral societies that flourished in the German-speaking countries, and the choral festivals that brought them together in monster assemblies, were echoes, so to speak, of the French "universal choirs"—albeit adapted, after the post-Napoleonic restoration, to a political sentiment that was literally counter-revolutionary.

The Swiss educator Hans Georg Nägeli, one of the leaders of the "Liederkranz" or singing-society movement, frankly confessed the aspirations that motivated its growth and spread. For a Swiss like Nägeli, such aspirations were best described as civic, concerned with social order. For Germans, they were better described as nationalistic in the most literal sense of the word: concerned with nation-building. No matter how the political cause may be described, what served and sustained it musically was ever the same. "Take hordes of people," Nägeli wrote in 1826,

> take them by hundreds, by thousands, bring them into human interaction, and interaction where each is at liberty to express his personality in feelings and words, where he receives at the same time like-minded impressions from all the others, where he becomes aware in the most intuitive and multifarious way possible of his human self-sufficiency and camaraderie, where he radiates and breathes love, instantly, with every breath—and can this be anything other than choral singing?[15]

One could hardly hope to find a better illustration of romantic nationalism—the "I" finding fulfillment in the "We." But now let us recall some memorable words by St. Basil, the founder of Christian monasticism, quoted in the very first chapter of this book. For him, too, choral music was first of all a means of promoting fellowship: "A psalm forms friendships, unites those separated, conciliates those at enmity . . . . So that psalmody, bringing about choral singing, a bond, as it were, toward unity, joins the people into a harmonious union of one choir."

But where Basil saw choral singing as bringing harmony to a monastic community of perhaps hundreds, Nägeli and his contemporaries saw it as uniting whole nations numbering perhaps millions, the sort of "imagined community" that had no way at all of being imagined in St. Basil's time, or for many centuries thereafter.

THE ORATORIO REBORN

Not that modern concepts of nationhood could not be projected on the ancient past. Indeed, such projections—to be blunt, such figments of imaginary history—were the inevitable product and propagator of modern nationalism wherever it appeared. We have already seen the Biblical Hebrews cast as protonationalists by Handel and his English oratorio librettists for the benefit of an audience now regarded as the first true European nationalists in the modern sense of the word. And it was the spread of modern nationalism in the aftermath of Napoleon's defeat that mainly accounted for the nineteenth-century rebirth of the "Handelian" oratorio in Germany, where it had never thrived before, alongside the nationalistic "Bach revival," which also began with an oratorio, albeit of a different sort: the St. Matthew Passion, performed in Berlin under the twenty-year-old Felix Mendelssohn, a pupil of Carl Friedrich Zelter (Goethe's intimate), in 1829.

That event was a tremendous watershed in the growth of German choral music. In its wake, literally hundreds of German oratorios were composed for performances at summer choral festivals that, first organized in 1814, had reached grandiose proportions by the 1830s, with throngs of performers holding forth before even bigger throngs of spectators, all hungry for nationalistic edification.

In keeping with the nature of the venue, festival oratorios nominally followed the Handelian rather than the Bachian model: secular works on (usually) sacred themes, rather than actual service music. But just as in Handelian times, the sacred was interpreted metaphorically, as a stand-in for the national. Indeed, one German critic was even moved to reclaim Handel (suitably re-umlauted as Händel) for a German sensibility that Handel never knew, declaring that the score of *Judas Maccabeus*, just revived in translation for a music festival on the Rhine, "breathes the deep seriousness of the German spirit and expresses the most joyful *volkstümlich* enthusiasm."[16]

In keeping with the old genre's new purposes, a new theme was added to the traditional biblical and Apocryphal subject matter on which Handel's oratorios had drawn: legendary plots from the history of the Christian church, many of them based on episodes from Torquato Tasso's *Gerusalemme liberata* ("Jerusalem delivered"), a sixteenth-century epic poem set at the time of the First Crusade. One such oratorio, *Die Zerstörung Jerusalems* ("The devastation of Jerusalem"), first performed at a festival in Leipzig (Bach's city) in 1832, was the work of Carl Loewe, already familiar to us for his *volkstümlich* ballads.

Loewe's lifetime fame came not only as balladeer but also as the most prolific composer of nation-building festival oratorios. His work thus provides a link between the *volkstümlich* and the *feierlich*—between the folkish and the sacred—and makes all the more obvious the nationalistic subtext behind the "Jerusalem" theme. Just as Handel's audiences recognized themselves in his choruses of Israelites, so German nationalists read a parallel between Jerusalem's fate (sacked but then delivered) and the one they wishfully predicted for their own country, first disunited and devastated but then united and triumphant.

Later Loewe oratorios featured legendary figures from German history. *Gutenberg*, first performed in Mainz, the great printer's city, in 1836, celebrated the four-hundredth anniversary of his first experiments with moveable type. *Johann Hus*, first performed in Berlin in 1842, commemorated the fifteenth-century religious martyr. Loewe even composed an oratorio called *Palestrina* (1841) that recounted the legend of the Pope Marcellus Mass (see chapter 16) through which the great religious composer was reputed to have saved the art of music. Because his work was "inspired" rather than "correct," Palestrina counted as an honorary romantic—and, it followed, an honorary German.

Quite the most remarkable aspect of Loewe's oratorios, from the historical if not the artistic point of view, is the way they managed to hybridize one exclusively Bachian element into the otherwise Handelian mold. Like the Bach Passions and cantatas, almost all of them (even *Palestrina*!) incorporated the traditional German-language *geistliche Lieder* (spiritual songs) popularly known as "chorales" into the musico-dramatic proceedings, both in simple four-part harmonizations (*Cantionalsätze*, as we learned to call them in chapter 18) and in more elaborate fugal or cantus-firmus settings.

What may seem at first surprising about this is the chorale's association with actual worship services. There were those, in fact, who thought the use of chorales inappropriate for festival rather than actual service use. They were in the minority, however. Chorales were retained for the same reason that Martin Luther had originally sponsored them: their use, whether sung by a congregation or merely heard by an audience, furthered *Gemeinschaft*, the sense of community that could as easily foster nationalism as Protestantism.

What is truly remarkable, though, and remains so even on reflection, is the fact that Loewe was a devout Catholic, who advertised his religion as his main artistic inspiration. Equally remarkable is the fact that the most important of the German choral festivals, for Loewe as much as anyone else, was the Lower Rhine Festival (*Niederrheinisches Musikfest*), inaugurated in 1817 with gala performances of Haydn's oratorios, and by the 1830s the site of music pilgrimages from near and far. Its main site was Düsseldorf, with subsidiary performances in the neighboring cities of Cologne, Wuppertal, and Aachen (Aix-la-Chapelle), the French border city. Although these cities had passed from the Holy Roman Empire to Prussia in the post-Napoleonic settlement of 1815, their historical ties were to the Rhineland, and their dominant religion remained Catholic.

The assignment to Lutheran Prussia of historically Catholic territories was an enormous spur to German unification, which eventually happened in 1870 under Prussian hegemony. (And the assignment to a post-Napoleonic, militant Prussia of territories bordering on France, it has been frequently observed with benefit of hindsight, made two world wars inevitable.) As a result of these political changes, and as a further cultural spur to unification, Catholic composers now felt free and even called upon to incorporate Lutheran chorales into works that were then performed by largely Catholic assemblies of musicians for largely Catholic audiences. In other words, the Lutheran repertory of chorales was now, in apparent defiance of a sometimes bloody history, considered the common property of all Germans irrespective of creed. A religious repertory was in effect co-opted in the name of a nation.

There could be no greater testimony to the ascendancy of the national — and eventually the nationalist — ideal and its transformatory power in post-Napoleonic Europe. Now nation trumped even religion as a definer of human community, and the chorale became for all intents and purposes a brand of spiritual folklore — *Volkstümlichkeit* made holy. This revolution in the meaning of the chorale was explicitly recognized — indeed proclaimed — in 1819 by the same Ernst Moritz Arndt whose celebrated patriotic poem *Des Deutschen Vaterland* gave rise to all those enthusiastic musical settings. In a Herder-inspired pamphlet entitled *Vom dem Worte und dem Kirchenliede* ("On language and church song"), Arndt called for the revival of the chorale and its enshrinement in a common songbook for the use of all Christian Germans.

"Such a project," one historian has dryly observed, "was of course a liturgical impossibility."[17] But by the 1820s it was no longer a cultural impossibility, as culture became increasingly identified with nation rather than faith. Near the end of his life, Ernst Ludwig Gerber (1746–1819), a great musical lexicographer and the first scholarly historian of German music, pled for the recognition of chorales as the closest thing modern Germany had to genuine folk songs. Later Herder-inspired research, as we know, revealed that Germany actually had a rich surviving folk heritage; but Gerber's idea, however mistaken, was nevertheless symptomatic of the way chorales were now being understood.

Like folk songs, chorales were ancient (or at least "historical") artifacts of nationhood, bearers of the national spirit. Along with the folk song revival, the chorale revival might help reverse the universal spiritual decline of modern Europe that wore the sheep's clothing of Enlightenment. As Glenn Stanley, a historian of the German oratorio, has put it, the chorale came to be seen as "an image of a former, better time," in which the nation's spirituality was as yet "a culture unperverted by secular influences."[18] More colorfully, the German romantic poet Novalis, writing as early as 1802, saw the salvation of all music in the chorale revival, if it succeeded in counteracting "the hatred of religion that came with the Enlightenment and reduced the infinite creative music of the universe to the monotonous rattling of an infernal mill."[19]

MENDELSSOHN AND CIVIC NATIONALISM

To see the chorale in action in its new and highly fraught cultural context, we can survey the way it is employed in *Paulus* ("St. Paul"), an oratorio by Felix Mendelssohn (1809–47), composed between 1832 and 1836 and performed to great acclaim in Düsseldorf under the twenty-seven-year-old composer's already experienced baton at the 1836 Lower Rhine Music Festival. Choosing this piece will offer a further perspective on the relationship between religious and national culture in Germany as mediated by the oratorio, since the composer was by birth neither a Protestant nor a Catholic, but a Jew.

The plot of Mendelssohn's oratorio, assembled from scripture by the composer with the assistance of his friend, the Lutheran theologian Julius Schubring, concerned the career of the Apostle Paul of Tarsus, born a Jew, who, after an early career as a persecutor of Jewish heretics (i.e., Christians), received a divine revelation on the road to Damascus and devoted the rest of his life to preaching the Gospel of Christ to the Gentiles. (For a previous musical representation of Paul's conversion, by Heinrich Schütz, see Ex. 21-14.) As the story of a convert, a Jew turned Christian, it was the story of Mendelssohn as well. By choosing to write an oratorio, moreover, the composer was acting exactly in the Apostle's footsteps, turning away from his own former community and preaching the Gospel to the gentiles. The autobiographical component ran deep, and surely helped motivate the choice of subject.

Jakob Ludwig Felix Mendelssohn was the grandson of Moses Mendelssohn (1729–86), the famous Jewish philosopher who has already made a brief appearance in this book as an apostle of eighteenth-century Enlightenment. Yet despite descent from what might be called the German-Jewish aristocracy, the future composer's father Abraham Mendelssohn, a banker, had his children baptized in 1816 to facilitate their assimilation, as "emancipated Jews" — Jews who enjoyed full civil rights — into German society. (Abraham himself and his wife converted to Protestantism in 1822 and signaled the fact by adding the Christian surname Bartholdy to the family name; the composer is sometimes called Felix Mendelssohn Bartholdy.) Mendelssohn's oratorio thus became in its way an allegory not only of the composer's own career, but of the family history as well.

Yet like the genre to which it belonged, it was also an allegory of the German nation, thanks to the chorales. Nor was this the first time chorales had played a symbolic role in a work by Mendelssohn. In 1829, right after his epochal *St. Matthew Passion* performance, he had accepted a commission for a symphony, now known as the "Reformation" Symphony, to be performed the next year in commemoration of

FIG. 35-3   Felix Mendelssohn, pencil portrait by Johann Joseph Schmeller (1830).

the three-hundredth anniversary of the "Augsburg Confession," which marked the official beginning of German Protestantism as a genuine "ism" and a national church. Traditional Lutheran music figures in various parts of the symphony.

The slow introduction to the first movement, for example, made the Lutheran response formula known as the "Dresden Amen" familiar to concert audiences. (It was first used in a *Passio germanica* — German Passion oratorio — by a sixteenth-century Dresden cantor named Joseph Schlegel, who possibly composed it; but it quickly became "traditional.") The finale was an impressive chorale fantasia on Luther's hymn "Ein' feste Burg" ("A mighty fortress"), in which the "episodes" outlined a concurrent symphonic-binary ("sonata form") structure. In its combination of novelty and antiquarianism, virtuosity and spirituality, all in the name of a national religious commemoration that presaged a national regeneration, the symphony was an apt symbol of a moment in the life of the German nation, and put its twenty-one-year-old composer at the forefront of the nation's musical establishment.

Or would have, had the celebration for which the work was commissioned not been called off. Mendelssohn did eventually reach the pinnacle of German civic music life, albeit a bit more slowly than at first predicted, but it was *Paulus*, rather than the "Reformation" Symphony, that proved the breakthrough composition.

The oratorio was conceived in the wake of the eventual first performances of the symphony, which took place in Berlin and London, under the composer's baton, in 1832. Where *Ein' feste Burg* had been the inevitable choice to symbolize the Reformation itself, the chief chorale in *Paulus* is "Wachet auf, ruft uns die Stimme" (usually translated "Sleepers, wake! a voice is calling"), on which J. S. Bach had based one of his most famous cantatas (BWV140). It was an equally inevitable choice for an oratorio that is all about receiving God's call and spreading God's truth.

The Overture is in effect a prelude and fugue for a traditionally brass-heavy "festival" orchestra (updated with trombones and "serpent" or S-shaped proto-tuba) in which the chorale melody is heard first, straightforwardly harmonized, in the prelude and then, stripped down to its first line, as a motto-style cantus firmus sounding in proclamatory counterpoint, mainly in the winds, against the working out of the fugue, mainly in the strings. The climax comes with the regaining of the prelude's major mode and the full statement of the chorale in massed winds against continuing rushing figuration in the strings.

This is Mendelssohn at his most retrospective or "historical." But it is important to keep in mind the primary purpose or function of this stylistic retrospectivism, and the reason why it was so highly valued by audiences: it furthered the agenda of cultural nationalism by creating the conditions through which — to quote Ernst Moritz Arndt yet one more time — "history enters life and life itself becomes part of history."[20] Such music advanced the high ethical cause of public edification. Its style as such was a function of its purpose.

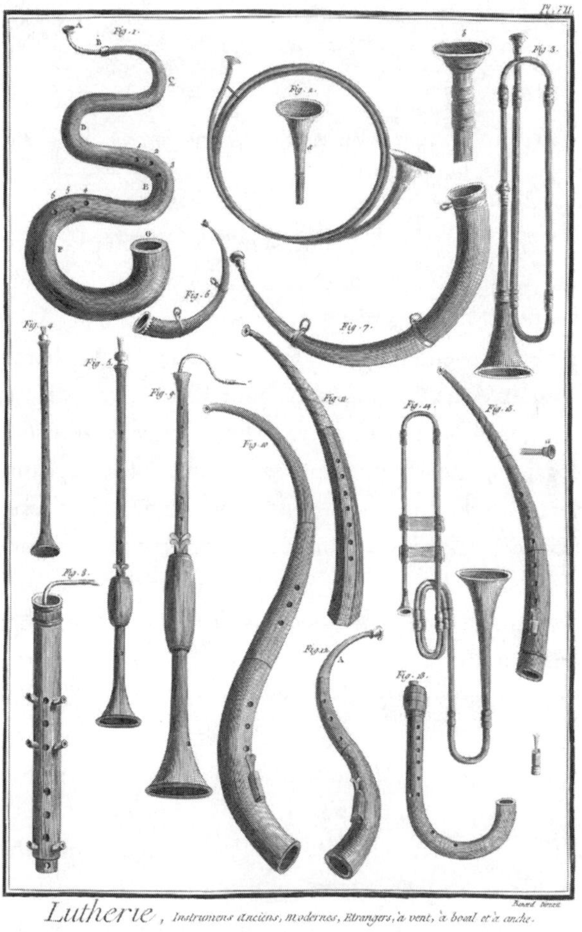

The Overture is answered, as it were, by the chorale setting that follows the scene of Paul's conversion (Ex. 35-16). This is a setting very much in the style of certain Bach chorales, in which a simple harmonization is accompanied by orchestral "illustrations." Here the illustration consists of massed brass fanfares to provide a properly gleaming recollection of the divine manifestation, in which the voice of God is described in scripture as being accompanied by a blinding light. Heinrich Schütz (Ex. 21-14) had used a full chorus in echo style to represent

FIG. 35-4 Wind and brass instruments, as illustrated in Diderot's *Encyclopédie*. The serpent is at the upper left.

that voice; Mendelssohn used the choral sopranos and altos, divided into four parts, accompanied by an aureole of winds and brass.

Because of the brass interventions, it is unlikely that the audience (representing the "congregation") could have joined in the singing of the chorale. But there was nothing to prevent their joining in the singing of the first chorale in *Paulus* (Ex. 35-17) and literally becoming a *Gemeinschaft*, a "community" of coreligionists or compatriots. Mendelssohn did not specifically call for such audience participation, and probably did not expect it. Other latter-day oratorio composers, however, did call for it; and even where the audience remained silent, it was clear to all that a simple chorale setting like Ex. 35-17 represented the singing of a *Gemeinschaft* that symbolically included all those present.

EX. 35-16 Felix Mendelssohn, *Paulus*, Chorale (no. 16), beginning

EX. 35-17   Felix Mendelssohn, *Paulus*, Chorale (no. 2), beginning

The remaining chorale settings in *Paulus* are two. "O Jesu Christe, wahres Licht" ("O Jesus Christ, light of truth"), another chorale that makes reference to Paul's conversion, is set in a somewhat more elaborate style than Ex. 35-16, with a full-fledged ritornello, replete with imitative counterpoint, that intervenes between the lines of every verse. The last chorale setting, by far the most significant both symbolically and musically, is the one sampled in Ex. 35-18. Here Paul, having found his true calling, is addressing the Heathen, who have just mistaken him and his miracle-performing companion Barnabas for the gods Jupiter and Mercury. He rebukes them for their idolatry, preaching that "God does not reside in temples made by human hands." Instead, he exhorts them, "You yourselves are God's temple, and the Spirit of God dwells in you."

These words are then given illustration by Mendelssohn in a remarkable exchange between St. Paul and the chorus. Paul sings, "Aber unser Gott ist im Himmel, er schaffet Alles was er will" ("But our God is in heaven; he creates all according to his will"). The melody to which the Apostle sings these words is not a chorale; rather it is a *volkstümlich* tune of a type that can be plausibly transferred to a crowd of Heathen "folks." When they take up the refrain, however, their counterpoint, doubled discreetly by the strings, becomes the background or accompaniment to a chorale melody sung by the second sopranos (till now held in reserve), illustrating the notion that their singing bodies, providing a "home" for the chorale melody, are indeed the dwelling-place of God's spirit.

And what chorale melody do the second sopranos sing in Ex. 35-18? None other than "Wir glauben all' an einen Gott" ("We all believe in one God"), the tune to which, from the time of the very earliest Lutheran hymnbooks, Luther's translation of the Nicene creed was sung. The whole first verse of the Lutheran creed passes in review, enshrined in an oratorio given its first performance before an audience largely made up of Catholics, to consecrate an ideal of national religious union. There could be no greater testimony to the link that German romanticism had forged between language, folk, and "spirit" in the name of Nation. Through his ostensibly sacred work, Mendelssohn actually emerges as perhaps the nineteenth century's most important — and successful — civic musician.

EX. 35-18   Felix Mendelssohn, *Paulus*, last part of no. 36, *con molto di moto*, mm. 122–49

EX. 35-18 (continued)

He was duly recognized and rewarded as such, and given the opportunity to lead his soon-to-be-united nation to musical greatness. In 1833, after his first appearances as conductor at the Lower Rhine Music Festival (which did for Handel in Germany what Mendelssohn's 1829 Passion had already done for Bach), he was appointed music director of the Catholic city of Düsseldorf, a tenure that culminated in the first performance of *Paulus*. Next he was appointed chief conductor of the Leipzig Gewandhaus (Drapers' Hall) orchestra concerts, which became, as a result of his appointment, the most prestigious music directorship in all of Protestant Germany. He held this post with great distinction for a dozen years, 1835–47, in the course of which he did more than any other single musician to reinvent not only German, but all of modern concert life in the form that we now know it.

Under Mendelssohn's directorship, subscription seasons were extended to increase the orchestra members' pay and insure their exclusive loyalty, so that standards of performance could rise. "Serious" programming was introduced, with symphonies performed *seriatim* (that is, complete and without interpolations between the movements) and "classic" repertory, including Bach (an old Leipziger), maintained alongside performances of new works. An international roster of "name" soloists regularly appeared with the orchestra. Mendelssohn himself conducted not only choral works, the traditional job of the music director or Kapellmeister, but symphonies as well (formerly directed from his chair by the leader of the first violins, still known for this reason as the "concertmaster"). Mendelssohn also appeared regularly as concerto soloist, as chamber-music

FIG. 35-5 The Leipzig Gewandhaus (Market Hall) as sketched by Mendelssohn.

performer, and as organist in sacred concerts. As significant an event as his Berlin Bach and his Düsseldorf Handel premieres was Mendelssohn's Leipzig premiere of Schubert's "Great" C-major Symphony in 1839.

From 1843, Mendelssohn added the role of director of the newly founded Leipzig Conservatory (soon regarded as Europe's finest training school for composers) to his civic duties. In the same year he was also made director of the Berlin Cathedral Choir and conductor of the symphonic subscription concerts of the Berlin Opera Orchestra. From around 1840 he was the uncrowned composer (and conductor) laureate of England, too, where his protégé Prince Franz Karl August Albert Emanuel of Saxe-Coburg-Gotha (1819–61), a talented organist and composer, had, by marrying Queen Victoria, become the Prince Consort of the realm (known to his subjects as Prince Albert).

Mendelssohn's preeminence in England was cemented by his second oratorio, *Elijah* (*Elias* in German), completed ten years after *Paulus* and first performed (in English) at the 1846 Birmingham Festival, the grandest and most triumphal of British musical ceremonials, bloated up to gargantuan proportions in competition with the German festivals. The chorus numbered more than 300, the orchestra 130. (By then, though, the total personnel at the Lower Rhine Festival numbered 631; henceforth, when it came to nationalism, Germany would never be outdone.) As obviously Handelian as *Paulus* was Bachian, the chorale-less *Elijah* remained, alongside Handel's *Messiah*, an invariable British festival item, performed as an annual national sacrament to the end of the Victorian era.

Another sidelight on Mendelssohn's status as pan-German and pan-Protestant culture hero, and the status of his musical idiom as the lingua franca of German liberal nationalism, is the way his musical style was appropriated by so-called Reformed Judaism. This was a modernizing movement that arose around 1825 within the German Jewish community in response to civil emancipation. It surprised and to a degree displeased the gentile establishment that had predicted wholesale conversion and assimilation — in effect, the disappearance of urban Jewry — to follow upon the granting of civil rights. Instead, many German Jewish congregations began aping the outward forms of Protestant worship — the structuring of the service around a German-language sermon; the use of music in a contemporary style, performed by choirs and organs; sometimes even the adoption of Sunday rather than Saturday as the Sabbath — but without renouncing the actual Jewish liturgy.

The earliest musical luminary of Reformed Judaism was the Vienna cantor Solomon Sulzer (1804–90), who commissioned from his friend Schubert, in the last summer of the latter's life, a choral setting in Hebrew of Psalm 92 (*Tov l'hodos*, "It is good to give thanks"). The greatest choirmaster-composer for the reformed synagogue was Louis Lewandowski (1821–94), who came to Berlin from the Polish-speaking part of East Prussia at the age of twelve, became the protégé of the banker Arnold Mendelssohn (the composer's cousin), and was sent, the first Jewish pupil ever, to study composition at the Berlin Academy of Arts, from which he graduated with honors, having composed and conducted a symphony, the traditional *Habilitationsstück* or graduation piece.

Lewandowski's collected liturgical works, issued in three volumes issued between 1871 and 1882, enshrine Mendelssohn's elegantly polished yet *volkstümlich* choral style as a sort of homage to the liberal spirit of emancipation and reform at a time when, as we will shortly see, the tenor of music, of politics, and of musical politics were all turning against Mendelssohn and liberalism alike (Ex. 35-19).

But perhaps the best measure of Mendelssohn's public stature during the last decade of his life was the unanimous homage rendered him in the Leipzig press, at once the most influential and the most factionalized music press in Germany, if not all of Europe. Writing in the old and respectable *Allgemeine musikalische Zeitung* ("Universal musical times"), the editor, Carl Ferdinand Becker, declared in 1842 that Mendelssohn's works and deeds could be "only contemplated, never criticized." Mendelssohn's fellow composer Robert Schumann, writing in the "opposition" paper *Neue Zeitschrift für Musik* ("New journal for music") of which he was the founding editor, as early as 1840 dubbed Mendelssohn "the Mozart of the nineteenth century." Mendelssohn's only serious career disappointment, after the cancellation of the Augsburg Reformation Festival, was his failure in 1832 to be elected director of the Berlin Singakademie to replace his teacher Zelter. (A decade later the post, like any post in Germany, would surely have been his for the asking.) But he paid the price of his success: he died of apparent

EX. 35-19   Louis Lewandowski, *Ma towu oholecho Jaakow* ("How goodly are thy tents, O Jacob"), opening psalm for sabbath morning service (*Todah w'simrah*, I, no. 1)

EX. 35-19   (continued)

How goodly are Thy tents, O Jacob, Thy dwelling-places, O Israel.
And I, through Thy abundant kindness, will enter.

overwork, following a series of strokes, in the fall of 1847, aged thirty-eight. A large statuary monument to him was erected outside the Leipzig Gewandhaus. Until its dismantling by the Nazi government in 1937, it was one of two major musical memorials in the city, the other being the monument to Bach in front of the St. Thomas Church.

NATIONALISM TAKES A TURN

Yet less than three years after Mendelssohn's death, in September 1850, an article appeared in the *Neue Zeitschrift für Musik* (by then no longer edited by Schumann) that set in motion a backlash against him from which his reputation has never fully recovered,

FIG. 35-6   Monument to Mendelssohn by the sculptor Werner Stein, which stood in front of the Leipzig Gewandhaus from 1892 to 1937.

and put a whole new complexion on the idea of German nationalism, indeed of nationalism as such. The article, signed K. Freigedank ("K. Free-thought"), was called *Das Judenthum in der Musik* ("Jewry in music"), and it made the claim that Jews, being not merely culturally or religiously but biologically—that is, racially—distinct from gentile Christians, could not contribute to gentile musical traditions, only dilute them. There could be no such thing as assimilation, only mutually corrupting mixture. A Jew might become a Christian by converting (as Mendelssohn had done), but never a true gentile (hence never a true German).

As long as nationalism was conceived in linguistic, cultural, and civic terms, it could be a force for liberal reform and tolerance. To that extent it maintained continuity, despite its romantic origins, with Enlightenment thinking. A concept of a united Germany could encompass not only the union of Catholic and Protestant under a single flag, but could also envision civic commonalty with Jews, even unconverted ones, so long as all citizens shared a common language, a common cultural patrimony and a common political allegiance. During the 1830s and 40s, the period now known to German historians as the *Vormärz* (because it preceded the abortive revolution of March 1848), German musical culture had proved the liberality and inclusiveness of its nationalism by allowing an assimilated Jew to become, in effect, its president.

Mendelssohn, for his part, was an enthusiastic cultural nationalist, even a bit of a German chauvinist, as his letters, with their many smug if affectionate comments about the musical cultures of England, France, and Italy, attest. The libretto of *Paulus*, which begins with the story of the stoning by the Jews of St. Stephen, the first Christian martyr, even betrays an anti-Judaic sentiment.

But there is a profound difference between the anti-Judaism of the *Paulus* libretto and the sentiment displayed in *Das Judenthum in der Musik*, to which we now apply the label anti-Semitism (a term coined—by its adherents!—in France in the 1890s). That difference, moreover, is directly congruent with the difference between the liberal or inclusive nationalism of the early nineteenth century and the racialist, exclusive nationalism that took its place in the decades following 1848 and that is with us still. A religion may be changed or shed, as a culture may be embraced or renounced. An ethnicity, however, is essential, immutable, and (to use the favored nineteenth-century word) "organic." A nationalism based on ethnicity is no longer synonymous with patriotism. It has become obsessed not with culture but with nature, symbolized by *Blut und Boden* (blood and soil).

Thus, for the author of *Das Judenthum in der Musik*, even Mendelssohn's undoubted genius could not save him from the pitfalls of his race. He could not "call forth in us that deep, that heart-searching effect which we await from Music," because his art has no "genuine fount of life amid the folk," and can therefore only be "reflective," never "instinctive." His choice of Bach rather than Beethoven as his model was the result of a stunted, "inorganic" personality: "the speech of Beethoven can be spoken only by a whole, entire, warm-breathed human being," while "Bach's language can be mimicked, at a pinch, by any musician who thoroughly understands his business," because in Bach "the formal still has the upper hand" over "the purely human expression." In sly reference to E. T. A. Hoffmann's bedrock romantic tenets, the author denied Mendelssohn, or any Jew, the ability to rise above mere glib, social articulateness and achieve "expression of an unsayable content." Yet in seeming paradox, the most conclusive proof of Mendelssohn's impotence (and his unworthiness of comparison with Mozart) was his failure to write a great opera. Oratorio—"sexless opera-embryos"—was the highest level to which his Jewish spirit could aspire. The only authentic emotional expression Mendelssohn could achieve was the "soft and mournful resignation" found in his piano pieces, where the author of the article affected to discern a genuine and moving response to the composer's own consciousness of his racial inadequacy.

Finally, the author warned, Germany's acceptance of this musician as its musical president was only the most obvious sign of the "be-Jewing" (*Verjüdung*) of the nation in the name of Enlightened liberality. The Jewish influence must be thrown off if the nation is to achieve organic greatness, its heroic destiny.[21]

With contents that by the late twentieth century could only be regarded with alarm, such an article would hardly be worth quoting in a book like this but for three factors that conspired to make it in its day, and (alas) have allowed it to remain into ours, a force to be reckoned with. In the first place, it is the most vivid symptom to be found in musical writings of a change in the nature of nationalism that all modern historians now recognize as a major crux in the history of modern Europe (and, after the blood-soaked twentieth century, in the history of the entire modern world).

Second, it paints a picture of Mendelssohn that has remained influential even after its motives have been forgotten, owing to the radical opposition it constructs between retrospectivism or conservatism (stemming, in this case, from Bach) and "revolutionary" progressivism (stemming from Beethoven) as historical forces. This dubious opposition, originating in ugly politics, has nevertheless remained a basic tenet of music historiography since the middle of the nineteenth century. It has been influential, moreover, not only on historians but on composers as well, which has made it a major influence on the actual history of composition, not merely its historiography.

Third and most immediately consequential: as many readers guessed, and as he himself revealed in 1869, "K. Freigedank" turned out to be Richard Wagner (1813–83), an envious fellow composer and a native Leipziger (and, though it is usually forgotten owing to the very different shapes of their careers, a member of the same generation as Mendelssohn) who would shortly become in his own right one of the towering figures in music history. Wagner's words achieved an almost scriptural authority for his innumerable followers, and he was probably the most potent single "influence" on many succeeding generations of composers everywhere. As hardly need be added in view of his pronouncements on Mendelssohn's limitations, his main domain was opera.

His authority was such that by the end of the 1860s, Wagner was (in Carl Dahlhaus's words) the "uncrowned king of German music."[22] Comparison of that epithet and the one we have applied to Mendelssohn — "president of German musical culture" — not only goes a long way toward explaining Wagner's obsessive antagonism toward the figure he displaced, but is also quite suggestive of the trajectory along which the parallel histories of music and of Germany would proceed over the course of the nineteenth century.

EPILOGUE: TWO PRODIGIES

As already hinted in Schumann's comparison with Mozart, Felix Mendelssohn was arguably the greatest composing prodigy in the history of European music. He was not exploited by his parents the way Leopold Mozart exploited Wolfgang. He was not taken on concert tours as a child and did not develop an early freakish fame. Nor, though coming close (with fourteen symphonies for strings and one for full "classical" orchestra completed by his sixteenth birthday), did he quite have the child Mozart's amazing facility. But it was not until the age of nineteen, with the violin concertos of 1775 (see chapter 30), that Mozart began writing music in a style, and of a quality, that was entirely his own, while Mendelssohn produced works as early as the age of sixteen that have to be considered mature masterpieces, the equal of anything anyone was writing at the time.

His Octet (or double quartet) in E♭ major for strings, op. 20 (1825), and especially his Overture to Shakespeare's *Midsummer Night's Dream*, op. 21 (1826), originally written as a piano duet, treat extended forms with complete mastery, and are stylistically original to boot. The Overture, particularly its opening section with its depiction of Shakespeare's fairies, sounded a new note of "fantastic romanticism" — a light, scurrying, "elfin" style to which Mendelssohn returned repeatedly in later life (almost always, curiously enough, in the key of E), and that, though widely imitated, remained his virtually patented property (Ex. 35-20).

His infatuation with Bach and Handel, nurtured by his rigorous, counterpoint-saturated training with Zelter, is also reflected in his earliest compositions, not only in purely academic exercises (for example, a long series of fugues for string quartet) but also in his first masterpiece. The climactic moments in the Octet's fugal finale (Ex. 35-21) are crowned by exuberant quotations from Handel's *Messiah* ("And He shall reign forever and ever" from the Hallelujah Chorus), which are later subjected to a very rigorous and complicated contrapuntal development.

These examples, impressive as they are, have a down side from the most exigently romantic point of view. They give evidence that Mendelssohn never outgrew his precocious youthful style. Like many musicians from highly cultured, affluent families, used to having his material and emotional needs easily met, he remained stylistically conservative and expressively reserved, disinclined to use his music as an outlet for the

EX. 35-20A   Felix Mendelssohn's "elfin" style, opening of *Midsummer Night's Dream* Overture, Op. 21 (1826), mm. 8–15

EX. 35-20B   Felix Mendelssohn's "elfin" style, opening of Rondo capriccioso, Op. 14 (1827), mm. 1–4

EX. 35-20C   Felix Mendelssohn's "elfin" style, Violin Concerto, Op. 64 (1844), beginning of last movement, mm. 3–10

display of "inwardness" or strong personal emotion, and feeling no need to attract attention with a display of "revolutionary" novelty. Throughout his short career he remained comfortably faithful to the musical status quo — that is, the "classical" forms, as they were already thought of by his time. His version of romanticism, already evident in his earliest works, consisted in musical "pictorialism" of a fairly conventional, objective

EX. 35-21   Felix Mendelssohn, Octet, Op. 20, IV, mm. 22–33

EX. 35-21 (*continued*)

nature (though exquisitely wrought), and in a predilection for a "national character" that was as often exotic as German.

Thus two of his five mature symphonies, in the spirit of Herder, incorporate *volkstümlich* souvenirs from countries to which he had traveled: no. 4 in A major (1833) ends with a finale in tarantella style and is called the "Italian," while no. 3 in A minor (1842) incorporates highland tunes and is called the "Scottish." (As the dates indicate, Mendelssohn's symphonies were published in an order that had little to do with their actual chronology.)

The one genre in which Mendelssohn could be regarded as a pioneer arose to suit a need created by his practical activity as conductor and concert programmer: the so-called concert overture, a freestanding, poetically titled orchestral piece (usually in something akin to "first movement" or "sonata" form) that served as a curtain raiser to a concert rather than an opera. The one most frequently played today is another Scots-inspired piece, *Die Hebriden* (The Hebrides; also known as "Fingal's Cave"), composed in 1830, when Mendelssohn was twenty-one. In 1842, Mendelssohn added several additional pieces, including the famous Wedding March, to his *Midsummer Night's Dream* Overture to make up an incidental score that could either be used to decorate the play or be performed in its own right as a suite.

Mendelssohn, in short, although he played a highly visible part in the general discourse of romanticism (especially its nationalistic strain), was anything but a "*poète maudit.*" His was the music of a well-adjusted, self-confident social animal, embodying civic virtue in his public works and the bliss of domesticity in his private ones, particularly his numerous albums of *Lieder ohne Worte* ("Songs without Words"), gently lyrical (and not too difficult) character pieces for piano that spread his fame into countless homes. Until its sadly premature expiration, his was a dream career like Haydn's, pursued under altogether different social conditions, but just as successfully.

It was different with the Mendelssohn family's other musical prodigy. By the time Felix Mendelssohn was born, his older sister Fanny (1805–47) had already shown signs of unusual gifts. She began piano studies in 1812, after the family had moved to Berlin, first with her mother and later (together with her brother) with Ludwig Berger, the Prussian capital's most distinguished teacher. She also underwent the same training in theory and composition as her brother, with Zelter, and enrolled in Zelter's Singakademie to study voice in 1820. Her first composition, a song in honor of her father's birthday, was written in 1819, when she was fourteen. Felix's earliest compositions, stimulated by her example, date from the next year.

It was Fanny Mendelssohn who originated the genre "Songs without Words," originally called *Lieder für das Pianoforte* or "Songs for Piano" and modeled at first on some cantabile (singing-style) études by Berger. She produced in all more than 500 compositions, including 250 songs, more than 125 piano works, a string quartet, a piano trio, and an orchestral overture. Her most extended works, like her brother's, were choral, written at a time when she was conducting an amateur choir that gave regular concerts in Berlin. They included two cantatas for soloists, chorus, and orchestra: *Hiob* ("Job") and *Lobgesang* ("Hymn of praise"), the latter bearing the same title as Felix's Symphony no. 2, which like Beethoven's Ninth has a choral finale. Her magnum opus is the *Oratorium nach den Bildern der Bibel* ("Oratorio on biblical scenes"), completed along with the cantatas in 1831, the most active year of her composing career, when she was twenty-five (and a year before Felix began composing *Paulus*, his first oratorio, on which he frequently consulted with Fanny).

Virtually none of Fanny Mendelssohn's music became known during her lifetime beyond the circle of her family and the friends who frequented her Sunday salons; and after her marriage

FIG. 35-7 Fanny Mendelssohn Hensel, drawn in 1829 by her husband, Wilhelm Hensel.

(to the Prussian court painter Wilhelm Hensel) and the birth of her son (Sebastian, named after Bach), she experienced a severe falling-off of inspiration (or "the mood to compose," as she put it in a letter to Felix). Both her isolation and (probably) her creative blocks were the result of the discouragement she received, from her father and later from her brother, when it came to pursuing a career. Her father forbade her to publish her music or perform in public lest she become ambitious and compromise the feminine virtues of *"love, obedience, tolerance and resignation"* (read: submission) on which the stability of family life depended, as he put it to her in a letter (the grim italics were his).[23]

Instead, eight of her lieder were published in 1827 and 1830 in books of songs by her brother, and under his name. Once only, after her father's death, did she appear as a concert pianist, performing a concerto by Felix at a charity affair in 1838. Only in 1846, a year before her death, when she was forty years old, did her thirty-seven-year-old brother give her permission to accept the invitation of two Berlin publishing houses to issue small albums of her lieder and her Songs without Words. A few more publications, including the Trio, appeared at Felix's instigation after her death (like her brother's, from a sudden stroke), so that her catalogue includes eleven "opuses."

Her music, like her brother's, is the product of their social background and training: stylistically conservative, technically polished, and emotionally reserved. In the genres that she cultivated extensively (basically the "women's" or "salon" genres of keyboard miniature and lied) her output bears entirely favorable comparison with his, as the two songs given in Ex. 35-22 will show. They were printed side by side in Felix's *Zwölf Lieder* ("12 songs"), op. 9 (1830). One of them is by Fanny (but which?).

Many, in fact, regarded Fanny as Felix's potential peer. One was Goethe, who ended a letter to the sixteen- year-old Felix Mendelssohn with "regards to your equally talented sister."[24] Another was the French composer Charles Gounod, who met her

EX. 35-22A   *Ferne* (text by J. G. Droysen), Op. 9, no. 9, mm. 1–12

EX. 35-22B *Verlust* (text by H. Heine), Op. 9, no. 10, mm. 1–19

much later in life, on vacation in Rome in 1840, and was amazed to discover her "rare ability as a composer."[25] The life of Fanny Mendelssohn Hensel is compelling proof that women's failure to "compete" with men on the compositional playing field has been the result of social prejudice and patriarchal mores (which in the nineteenth century granted only men the right to make the decisions in bourgeois households), not the "natural" deficiency that defenders of the status quo dependably allege. The matter is especially poignant in the case of the Mendelssohns, who epitomized enlightened, emancipated, and assimilated Jewry, since Fanny's fate exposed the limits to emancipation, and the internal resistance to it, just as the posthumous backlash against Felix exposed the limits, and the external resistance, to assimilation.

Nations, States, and Peoples

Romantic Opera in Germany (Mozart, Weber), France (Auber, Meyerbeer), and Russia (Glinka)

I. PEASANTS (GERMANY)

MR. NATURAL

Up to now we have seen peasants on the operatic stage only as accessories. They represented their class, not their country. The elevation of *Volkstümlichkeit* to the status of a romantic ideal changed all that. It happened first, of course, in Germany, the land where *das Volk* was first "discovered." And the first operas in which the new concept of *das Volk* showed up were the nineteenth century descendants of the vernacular comic operas known as singspiels, "plays with singing."

Up to now, comic opera, for us, has mainly meant *opera buffa*: the sung-through Italian genre that, starting out as modest intermezzi, conquered the music theaters of the world by the 1750s and (as we saw in chapter 33) had been exerting a strong influence on serious opera as well. In countries like France, Germany, and England, which had thriving spoken theaters, there was another route to comic opera. In these countries (but never in Italy) simple musical numbers—often based on "timbres" (the tunes of well-known folk or popular songs) and meant for the untrained voices of actors—were inserted into spoken comedies for added entertainment or sentimental value. The French name for the genre that resulted is the most revealing: *comédies mêlées d'ariettes*, "comedies mixed with little songs."

It went without saying that only a character "simple" enough to sing a simple song could credibly sing one in the context of such a play, and so mixing little songs into comedies led to an enormous increase in rural settings. The most popular plots were ones in which (following a tradition going all the way back to the medieval "pastourelle") honest peasant lovers won out over the machinations of wicked squires, or in which aristocrats (even kings) learned about virtue from the simple manners of country folk.

A vivid example is *Le roi et le fermier* ("The king and the farmer," 1762), a comedy by the popular playwright Michel-Jean Sedaine (1719–97), with "morceaux de musique" (pieces of music) by Pierre-Alexandre Monsigny (1729–1817), a talented noble amateur. A king, traveling incognito, intervenes to rescue a farmer girl who has been abducted by a villainous aristocrat. The king is charmed by the country singing, evidence of the singers' purity of heart. But convention decreed that, once having identified himself, the king leave the stage before the final number, a lowly *vaudeville*, a strophic affair in which every character takes a turn, hardly befitting a king's dignity. (The term *vaudeville* had a very complicated history, extending from fifteenth-century comic songs that flourished in the "valley of Vire" — *Vau de Vire* — in northern France, all the way to the variety shows of the early twentieth century. In the eighteenth century it seems to have been a corruption of *voix de ville*, "city tunes," even though it was applied to songs sung on stage by rustic characters.)

Le roi et le fermier was an adaptation from an English model, and the English theater bequeathed to the continent another kind of spectacle "mixed with music": the "magic play," in which, following a tradition that went back to the seventeenth-century Restoration stage, music was used to differentiate supernatural characters (fairies, sorcerers, and the like) from natural ones. Both varieties of musicalized theater, the peasant comedy or *comédie mêlée d'ariettes* (=*Singspiel*) and the magic play (=*Zauberspiel*), fed into the German stage, eventually producing a hybrid, called *Zauberoper* ("magic opera," perhaps better translated as "fable" or "fairy-tale" opera), that flourished briefly as a craze in Vienna's suburban theaters.

The craze lasted from the 1780s into the early nineteenth century, and we have it to thank for Mozart's last operatic masterpiece, *Die Zauberflöte* ("The magic flute"), commissioned by its librettist Emanuel Schikaneder (1751–1812), a singing actor who ran one of those suburban theaters, the Theater auf der Wieden, where Mozart's singspiel was first performed on 30 September 1791, a couple of months before the composer's death.

It was in *Die Zauberflöte*, rather than in his small and insignificant output of lieder, that Mozart came into really fruitful contact with the *volkstümlich* style. It is only one of the many categories represented in the opera, a magnificent farrago or variety show encompassing just about every conceivable style from the most serious to the most farcical, from the most exotic to the most indigenous, and from the most archaic to the most up-to-date. The all-encompassing mixture (under the aegis of "Egyptian" — that is, Masonic — rites) was code for the universalist message of the Enlightenment, and we have already taken note of *Die Zauberflöte* (in chapter 30) in connection with its lofty philosophical outlook.

Reapproaching it now from the single standpoint of the *volkstümlich* is hardly going to do it justice. But singling out this one strand from its rich tapestry will serve our present purpose. Not that the *volkstümlich* is in any way an inconspicuous component. On the contrary, it is associated with one of the opera's most memorable characters: Papageno, the Queen of the Night's birdcatcher, played in the original production (and partly improvised in the slapstick "Hans Wurst" or Punch-and-Judy tradition) by Schikaneder himself (see Fig. 28-10).

Papageno fulfills a traditional role for a peasant character in *Die Zauberflöte* — the Sancho Panza role, so to speak, serving the opera's hero Tamino, a Javanese prince on a noble quest, as wisecracking "vulgar" (i.e., folksy) sidekick, the way Sancho Panza served the knight errant Don Quixote in Cervantes's famous novel. But in his magic, half-man/half-bird aspect he also symbolizes, or begins to symbolize, the specifically romantic mystique of *das Volk* in a way that no previous operatic character whom we have met has done.

The birdcatcher enters in act I, dressed in his suit of feathers and playing his little pipe, singing as straightforward an imitation folk song as any eighteenth-century composer had ever put on paper (Ex. 36-1a). Although headed "Arie," like all the solo numbers in the opera, it is just a strophic lied (compare Schubert's *Heidenröslein* in chapter 35) with an introduction and the most minimal ritornello imaginable—just

EX. 36-1A   W. A. Mozart, *Die Zauberflöte* no. 2, Papageno's aria ("Der Vogelfänger bin ich ja")

the five notes of Papageno's panpipe plus a cadence. It is a sort of "Ur-musik," as the Germans would say — a primeval music close to the state of nature. And of course his natural drives are what Papageno celebrates in song, particularly the drive to catch a "bird" and reproduce himself through her.

Just as Papageno's music seems close to the imagined origins of music, so Papageno's utterances often seem close to the origins of speech and language, as if embodying Herder's concept of the origin of human culture(s). Early in the action, Papageno is punished for boasting by having his mouth padlocked, so that he can only gesticulate and hum, "Mmmm-mmm-mmm." Still, he manages to communicate in this way with Tamino. When the lock is removed, he announces that now he'll "chatter forth afresh," but truly. Papageno gets to break through from primeval utterance (*Ursprache*) to language even more graphically at the other end of the opera, during the act II finale, when he is finally granted his heart's desire: a wife (Papagena), through whom he will raise his brood (i.e., a basic human "community"). The two confront one another and, as if reborn in happiness, say each other's names as if uttering their first words (Ex. 36-1b).

In this gentle slapstick of foreplay and procreation, we are privileged to witness in metaphor the decisive moment, described by Herder, when humans became truly

EX. 36-1B   W. A. Mozart, *Die Zauberflöte* Act II finale, Papageno/Papagena duet

human, forming communities through language: "The human race in its childhood formed language for itself precisely as it is stammered by the immature," 'Herder wrote; "it is the babbling vocabulary of the nursery.'" Or as Mozart and Schikaneder put it, "Pa-pa-pa-pa-pa-pa-pa." Thus in *Die Zauberflöte*, the peasant characters begin to represent something beyond a single, simple social class. They begin their long career in art as symbol for the human race itself, differentiated by language into nations.

DER FREISCHÜTZ

The decisive step that turned opera not into an attempted Enlightened mirror of all humanity at once, as in *Die Zauberflöte*, but rather a romantic mirror of a specified nation, was taken when whole casts were assembled from the peasant class—not just sidekicks and "comic relievers," but heroes and heroines, villains, and all the rest. Once peasants—people of the soil—were not merely an element of contrast, they could begin to represent the soil itself, from which the nation drew its sustenance and what Herder called its *Urwüchsigkeit*, or "autochthony." Their music, too, could provide something more than incidental or decorative trappings. It could become a stylistic bedrock for scenes of all types, including the most dramatic, even tragic ones.

The first opera to achieve the status of national emblem or mirror in the nineteenth century was *Der Freischütz* (1821), by Carl Maria von Weber (1786–1826). The title, literally translated, means "The free marksman," which conveys little to anyone unfamiliar with the German folk legend (*Volkssage*) on which it is based. For this reason, the opera is sometimes called *The Magic Bullet* in English. Its legendary source was first published in 1810 in a best-selling collection of ghost stories (*Gespensterbuch*) by Johann August Apel and Friedrich Laun.

Weber, a cousin of Mozart's wife, Constanze, was born into a distinguished family of musicians. His parents ran a traveling singspiel theater, so he grew up intimately familiar with the existing repertory of popular music-plays in German. Only when the family's tours were interrupted, whether by his mother's illnesses or by the Napoleonic Wars, did they stay in one place long enough for their son to get any regular schooling. One of his early teachers was Michael Haydn, Joseph's brother, under whose supervision the precocious composer produced his third singspiel (but first successful one), *Peter Schmoll und seine Nachtbarn* (Peter Schmoll and his Neighbors), first performed in March 1803, when the composer was all of sixteen. The story, a

FIG. 36-1 Carl Maria von Weber, engraving by C. A. Schwerdgeburth (1823) after a portrait by Carl Christian Vogel von Vogelstein.

sentimental yarn about a family of refugees from the French Revolution and their fate in Germany, was a timely one.

In September 1803, Weber journeyed to Vienna to study with the aging Joseph Haydn, but the latter, increasingly enfeebled with what would probably be diagnosed today as Alzheimer's disease, declined to take on a new pupil. Instead, Weber spent a year as apprentice to Georg Joseph Vogler (1749–1814), known as Abbé (or Abt) Vogler because of his youthful position as court chaplain at Mannheim. Vogler was a rather eccentric composer (Mozart once called him "a faker pure and simple"),[2] but a remarkable teacher whose theories of distant modulation and whose interest in all kinds of exotic musics stimulated Weber's composerly imagination.

Vogler's influence may be seen in his pupil's incidental music to *Turandot, Prinzessin von China* ("Turandot, the Princess of China," 1809), a "theatrical fable" by the Venetian dramatist Carlo Gozzi (1720–1806) in Schiller's translation. All seven numbers are based on a purportedly authentic *air chinois* (Chinese song) Weber found in Rousseau's *Dictionnaire de musique* of 1768. (Rousseau's source was *A Description of the Empire of China*, published by the traveler Jean-Baptiste Du Halde in 1738; see Fig. 36-2.) Later, Gozzi's play became the basis for a famous opera by Giacomo Puccini; later still, the *air chinois* turned up in an orchestral work by Paul Hindemith called *Symphonic Metamorphoses on Themes by Carl Maria von Weber* (!). The beginning of Weber's overture, one of the earliest European compositions to incorporate an Asian theme other than an Islamic ("Turkish") one, is given in Ex. 36-2.

Exoticism or orientalism may seem a far cry from nationalism. In light of what nationalism has become, it *is* a far cry. But in their early phases, nationalism and

E X. 36-2   Carl Maria von Weber, beginning of Overture to *Turandot*

mm. 32 - 44

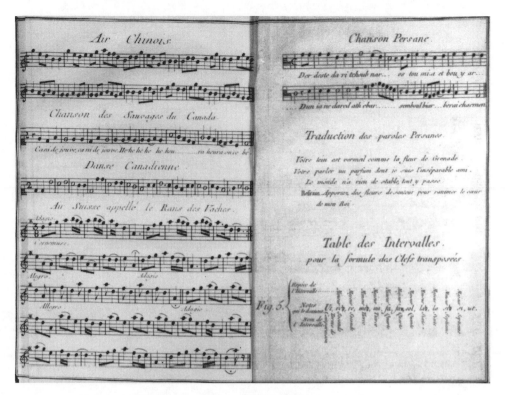

FIG. 36-2 Chinese, Native American, Swiss, and Persian tunes as they appear in Jean-Jacques Rousseau's *Dictionnaire de musique* (1768). The *Air chinois* at top left went into Weber's incidental music for Gozzi's *Turandot* (1809), thence into Paul Hindemith's *Symphonic Metamorphosis after Themes by Carl Maria von Weber* (1943).

exoticism were opposite sides of the same coin. They both reflected an interest, at least potentially benign, in human difference (ours from them, theirs from us). Weber's own predilections led him in many directions where settings and "local colors" were concerned. After the *Turandot* music he composed a one-act singspiel called *Abu Hassan* (on a subject drawn from the *Arabian Nights*), with a conventionally "eastern" coloration similar to the one in Mozart's *Abduction from the Seraglio*. After *Der Freischütz* he began *Die drei Pintos*, an opera (never finished) with a Spanish setting; then came *Euryanthe* (1823), set in France in the age of chivalry; then *Oberon* (1826), set partly in "fairyland," partly in Africa, and partly (again) in medieval France.

All of these settings can be called "typically romantic," since romanticism, as we learned in chapter 33, was as much drawn to the long ago, the far away, and the never-never as it was to the celebration of self. And the self that romanticism celebrated (whether personal or collective) was in any case a "romanticized" (that is, idealized and often mythologized) sense of self. The idealization of the peasantry in romantic opera was actually the idealization of a nation's mythic origins, not the peasants as they actually were, or the conditions in which they actually lived (rarely matters to celebrate).

Most important of all: if *Der Freischütz* looms now as Weber's most important work because of its role in "inserting" opera, so to speak, into the history of nationalism, that is due entirely to its reception by the composer's contemporaries, and later by posterity.

It is not necessarily an indication, let alone the result, of the composer's intentions. Critics never tire of pointing out that in its musical style and forms the opera owes as much or more to the international theatrical mainstream of its day (that is, to Italian and—say it softly!—even French models) than it does to the *Volkslied* movement.

It is also probably true that Weber was originally attracted to the story of *Der Freischütz* more for its ghostliness than for its local color. Horror stories and other manifestations of "black romanticism" were very much in vogue at the time. It was the age, after all, of Mary Shelley's immortal *Frankenstein* (1818). A few years after *Der Freischütz*, Heinrich August Marschner (1795–1861), a younger contemporary of Weber's who was widely regarded as his heir, scored a big hit with a *"grosse romantische Oper"* called *Der Vampyr* (1828), a title that needs no translation, with a plot (loosely based on Byron) that needs no description.

One may even concede that the circumstances of the opera's first production—the inaugural musical offering at the newly rebuilt national theater in Berlin, the Prussian capital—were, at least at the outset, more powerful than the composer's intentions or even the work's specific contents in creating its aura as an event in the life of the nation. National significance, like historical significance and even artistic significance, is a two-way street. It is the product of an interaction between an object (the work) and its consumers (reception), and arises in the course of a performance history.

That said, however, it is entirely appropriate to quote an encomium addressed to *Der Freischütz* in 1909, as it approached its centenary, by the American music critic Henry Krehbiel (1854–1923), who was himself of German extraction and presumably knew whereof he wrote. "There never was an opera," Krehbiel enthused, "and there is no likelihood that there ever will be one, so intimately bound up with the loves, feelings, sentiments, emotions, superstitions, social customs, and racial characteristics of a people."[3] The reference to race is dated, but Krehbiel speaks truly on behalf of the composer's countrymen. At a time when Germans were yearning for symbols around which they could construct a sentiment of *Einheit*, of their unity and singularity as a people, Weber provided one, and it was accepted with joy.

The "two-way street" worked in an especially graphic way where *Der Freischütz* was concerned. By 1824, an English writer touring Germany, struck by the way its "beautiful national melodies" were "sung in Germany, by all classes, down to the peasant, the hunter and the laborer," concluded from this that Weber, lacking the ability to invent his own tunes, had filled his opera with folk songs. In fact Weber borrowed nothing, not even the bridal chorus expressly subtitled "Volkslied" (Ex. 36-3). Yet by 1824, according to the English writer's testimony, the song (and many others from the opera) had *become* a *Volkslied*. It had entered the popular oral tradition. Sung by actual hunters and peasants who did not know the opera, it had gained acceptance not just as a *volkstümliches Lied*, a "song in folk style," but as an actual folk song.

None of this can be said for *Der Vampyr*, or for Weber's other operas. It was the nation, not Weber, who made his ghost-story opera a national opera. Its significance for German nationalists of a later time rested on that prior acceptance by the nation at large. It was then that the opera picked up its freight of ideology. Wagner, living in

Paris in 1841, took the opportunity presented by the French premiere of *Der Freischütz* at the Grand Opéra to send this chauvinistic dispatch to the newspapers back home, in which Weber's name is never even mentioned, as if the opera were the collective issue of the German *Volk*:

> O my magnificent German fatherland, how must I love thee, how must I gush over thee, if for no other reason than that *Der Freischütz* rose from thy soil! How must I love the German folk that loves *Der Freischütz*, that even now believes in the wonders of artless legend, that even now, in manhood, feels the same sweet mysterious thrills that made its heart beat fast in youth! Ah, thou adorable German daydream! Thou nature-rapture, bliss in forests, gloaming, stars, moon,

EX. 36-3   Carl Maria von Weber, *Der Freischütz* no. 14, "Volkslied"

EX. 36-3 (continued)

village clock-chimes striking seven! How happy he who understands thee, who can believe, feel, dream, delight with thee! How happy I am to be a German![4]

"Das deutsche Volk," extolled by Wagner, is Papageno writ large, a whole nation of Mr. Naturals — or of Maxes, to name the wholesome, handsome, gullible hero of Weber's opera. Like many legends from many countries, the plot is a basic yarn of good and evil involving a Faust-like pact with the devil:

> Max, the tenor title character, a hunter and forest ranger, is gulled by Caspar, another forester and a sinister bass, into going with him to the "Black Huntsman" Samiel's abode in the Wolf's Glen, the very depths of the forest, there to secure his diabolical aid. The next day Max, who has been suffering a slump, must face a test of marksmanship on which his whole future depends. If he wins the match he will succeed Cuno, the chief ranger to the local prince, and marry Cuno's daughter Agathe, whom he loves (and who loves him).
>
> In the Wolf's Glen Caspar, coached by Samiel, forges the seven magic infallible bullets that he and Max will use on the morrow. What Caspar does not tell Max is that the seventh bullet goes not where the marksman directs it, but wherever Samiel may wish. When the Prince lets fly a white dove and Max aims the seventh bullet at it, Agathe (who has had a prophetic dream) cries out that she is the dove. Too late: the gun is fired, and she falls — but only in a faint. It is Caspar, the evil tempter, whom Samiel has killed with the seventh bullet. Max confesses his misdeed, is forgiven, granted the position he sought, and wins Agathe's hand.

Perhaps needless to say, the original folk legend had ended in a bloodbath. The happy ending, in which the benevolent prince intervenes the way a *deus ex machina* (a god lowered in a machine) might have done in an ancient *opera seria*, was a concession to the requirements of the comic opera genre, as contemporary audiences knew perfectly well. But despite its many conventional aspects, the opera did contain some real novelties, and it was these that enabled audiences to point to *Der Freischütz* as something new under the sun — something new and *theirs*.

One is the Overture, which has quite deservedly become a concert staple. Even so, its frequent detachment from the opera is somewhat ironic, because one of its chief claims to historical fame is its close integration with the drama that follows it. With a single conspicuous exception, all its themes are taken from vocal numbers inside the opera. This is something we have seen previously only in the overture to *Don Giovanni*, and there only in the slow introduction, where the opera's dénouement is foreshadowed.

Probably prompted by Beethoven's *Coriolan* and *Egmont* overtures, neither of which actually precedes an opera, Weber made the *Freischütz* Overture an instrumental précis of the whole drama to follow. Foreshadowed in advance of Weber only by a few French composers, by the second half of the nineteenth century such a procedure would be standard, even de rigueur. And as it became so, it became routinized in the form of the casual medley or "potpourri" overture — literally a mixed bag (even more literally, a "rotten pot") of themes. Weber still observed the formalities of "sonata-allegro" form, and like Beethoven drew dramatic meaning from them. Leaving the slow introduction aside for the moment and beginning with the *molto vivace*, we can trace both the first theme in C minor and the transitional clarinet melody, marked *con molto passione*, to

Max's first aria, in which he feels an inexplicable foreboding as Samiel steals across the stage behind him (Ex. 36-4a). The full-blown "second theme" at m. 123 comes from Agathe's aria in act II, in which, by contrast, she expresses her joyful hopes for the future (Ex. 36-4b). The stormy bridge material (mm. 53–86) is drawn from the horror music in the forging scene at the Wolf's Glen.

It will surely not pass unnoticed by anyone hearing it that the overture's "recapitulation" recapitulates not only the themes but also the C-minor/C-major trajectory associated with Beethoven's *Kampf und Sieg* (battle-and-victory) scenarios. Indeed Weber dramatizes things even more emphatically than Beethoven ever did by detaching the C-major recap of the second theme from the rest and preceding it with a snatch of dark "forest music" from the slow introduction followed by a fanfare—in short, turning it into a "Victory Symphony," as Beethoven put it in the *Egmont* Overture. Agathe's optimism, voiced cautiously (in E♭) in the exposition, is now proclaimed from the rooftops, telegraphing the joyous resolution of the drama. (And while we are on the subject, it is time to reveal that calling Beethoven's minor-major progressions the *Kampf und Sieg* scenario was already a slightly ironic allusion-in-advance to Weber, who actually wrote an oratorio with that title in the fateful year 1815, to commemorate Wellington's victory over Napoleon at Waterloo.) This pointed reference in the *Freischütz* Overture

EX. 36-4A   Carl Maria von Weber, *Der Freischütz* no. 3, Allegro con fuoco

EX. 36-4B   Carl Maria von Weber, *Der Freischütz* no. 8, Vivace con fuoco, mm. 2–11

to Beethoven's rhetoric of contrasts has many counterparts in the opera, where time and again dark and light are strikingly juxtaposed. The most famous instance is the beginning of act III, which opens on Agathe's sunlit room after the midnight horrors at the Wolf's Glen at the end of act II. She sings a paean to the sun's warmth in harmonious duet with a solo cello. This scene was repeatedly cited by later composers and critics (and not only German ones) as a model of how all the elements in opera — poetry, music, scene-painting, lighting — can interact to intensify a single impression.[5] It was a major stimulus on the theory and practice of composers (most notably Wagner) who saw in opera a "union of all the arts."

We have been holding the slow introduction to the *Freischütz* Overture in reserve because it contains the one important musical passage without a direct counterpart in the body of the opera: the "aria" for four concertante French horns (*Waldhörner* — "forest horns"! — in German), or to be more precise, for two pairs of horns, one in C, the other in F, that alternately call to one another and croon together over a bed of murmuring strings (Ex. 36-5). It seems a normal enough way to set the scene for an opera about hunters (and one that had plenty of eighteenth-century precedents), but as sheer sound it was an unprecedented and electrifying effect that forever changed the nature of orchestral horn writing.

Until then horn parts had hardly differed from trumpet parts except in range. Now the horn became for German composers the *Naturlaut*—"nature sound"—par excellence, instantly evoking the whole panoply of romantic nature mysticism. After Weber, a quartet became the normal orchestral horn complement everywhere, not just

EX. 36-5   Carl Maria von Weber, *Der Freischütz* Overture, mm. 9–36

EX. 36-5 (continued)

in Germany. But what made Weber's horns sound particularly "German," hence (to recall Krehbiel) "intimately bound up with the loves, feelings, etc., of a people," was the close harmony, equivalent in range and "voicing" to the style of the *Männerchor*, the men's-chorus idiom that instantly evoked nationalistic singing societies with their patriotic hymns and "Rheinlieder." Weber's horn quartet, in other words, effectively mediated between the human (vocal) and ghostly (forest) domains, giving the first real taste of what Paul Bekker (1882–1937), a historian of orchestration, called "the orchestra of romantic illusion."[6]

As soon as the horns have finished (m. 25), the strings begin an eerie unmeasured tremolo, a device that has been traced back as far as Niccolò Piccinni in 1781, but not yet a commonplace in 1821. It makes all the more explicit the supernatural connotations of the forest-horn music; and in the very next measure harmonic color joins orchestral color to transport us to the world of the baleful nature spirits on whom Max and Caspar will be calling: the tremolo veers into a rootless diminished-seventh chord that is held out for four measures before returning to the harmony whence it sprang. It is a magnificent amplification, so to speak, of the sublime opening of Schubert's C-major Quintet (Ex. 35-8c).

Eeriness is compounded by the use of the clarinets in their lowest register, and the thudding notes of the timpani, marked "solo" (albeit supported by the double basses, pizzicato, for greater pitch definition). We definitely get the feeling that not only the cello melody beginning at m. 27, but also the harmony and the orchestral timbres will be returning later with dramatic significance — or, in other words, that these atomic musical particles (a single chord, a timpani stroke) have become "motivic."

The significant return comes, of course, in the act II finale, the midnight forging scene known as "The Wolf's Glen" (Fig. 36-3). The whole scene is a series of ghastly apparitions or *Geistererscheinungen* that (as the music historian Anthony Newcomb was first to demonstrate in detail) reproduces the effects of a phantasmagoria, an exhibition of optical illusions produced by a "magic lantern" or light projector.[7] Phantasmagorias were a popular form of mass entertainment in the early nineteenth century, invented by a French engineer named Étienne-Gaspard Robert (or Robertson) and first shown to the public in Paris in 1798.

Some phantasmagorias, like Robertson's own, were frankly presented as light shows, or demonstrations of an ingenious scientific

FIG. 36-3 Scene from *Der Freischütz*, lithograph by Adam and Holstein after Johann Heinrich Ramberg (1763–1840).

apparatus. Others were billed by charlatans as supernatural events in which "actual" specters were raised: the prophet Samuel (cf. Samiel!), originally raised by the Witch of Endor at the behest of King Saul; a witches' sabbath; a *"nonne sanglante"* (nun with bleeding stigmata); a *"danse macabre"* (dance of death), and the like. Weber was only the first of many composers who took a cue from the phantasmagoria shows: in later chapters we will observe a Witches' Sabbath orchestrally evoked by Hector Berlioz (1830), and an orchestral *Danse macabre* conjured up by Camille Saint-Saëns (1874).

To achieve the musical equivalent of a light show implies a musical analogy with visual imagery. The operative correspondence or common denominator—the *tertium quid* (third element), to put it in terms of logic—is *color*, which in music means effects of "chromatic" harmony (from *chroma*, color in Greek) and effects of timbre ("tone color"). The Wolf's Glen scene in *Der Freischütz*, more than any previous musical conception, abounds in such effects; and what is more, it links them in a way already noted in the Overture, where a chromatic harmony (the diminished seventh chord) is expressed through a rare timbre (unmeasured string tremolo).

That very effect is the chief connecting tissue in the Wolf's Glen, which otherwise consists of an explosive succession of brief, blindingly colored and contrasted episodes. The scene opens in the key of F♯ minor, as distant from the key of the Overture as a key can be. As soon as the "chorus of invisible spirits" intones its "Uhui! Uhui," however, the tonic chord is replaced with the very same diminished-seventh (C – E♭ – F♯ – A) tremolo that we have seen strategically prolonged in the overture. It, too, functions as a *tertium quid*, bearing the same intervallic relationship to C minor as to F♯ minor: as spelled in parentheses above, the first two notes are the root and third of the former and the remaining ones are the root and third of the latter, identifying it as C minor's "tritone complement." The whole scene will be an oscillation between these two tritonally related keys: Weber was no doubt recalling the tritone's medieval nickname of *diabolus in musica*, part of musicological folklore to this day. But it is the mediator of the progression, the diminished seventh chord, redolent as it is of the Dungeon Scene from Beethoven's *Fidelio* (Ex. 33-1a), that is the scene's really characteristic harmony. It sounds whenever the devil Samiel is invoked (becoming, in effect, his identifying motive), and is sustained for as many as eight measures at a stretch.

The scene takes shape through an ever-accelerating progression of images. It begins with another miracle of media coordination to set beside the scene in Agathe's room, but at the opposite extreme, with every component conspiring to project gloom. The orchestration—once again combining low-or "chalumeau"-register clarinets and tremolando strings, to which a soft trombone choir and faint glowering bassoons are added—reinforces the murk onstage. When the unseen spirits wail and the harmony turns dissonant, the stage direction, in which an intermittently visible full moon "throws a lurid light over all," is matched by a pair of piccolos in octaves, adding their sinister glint to the unison woodwind choir. This music, "coloristic" to an unprecedented degree, continued to reverberate in the work of opera composers, and eventually "symphony composers" as well, for the rest of the century.

The vocal writing effectively mediates between song and "melodrama," or accompanied speech. The voice of Samiel is never set to music; it remains an unintegrated alien presence throughout the scene. Max's first terrified outcry is preceded by an uncanny horn blast first heard in the Overture (m. 93). The first phantasmic vision is that of Max's mother in her grave; next comes Agathe, appearing to Max alone as a hallucination. When she seems about to plunge to her death in a waterfall, the orchestra sounds another reprise from the Overture (rushing strings at m. 249).

Then the actual bullet-casting begins. Each of the seven bullets, counted off by Caspar and eerily echoed by an offstage voice, is accompanied, exactly as in a light show, by a fleeting hallucination, the orchestra assuming the role of magic lantern, projecting bizarre orchestral colors in dazzlingly quick succession to parallel the flashing stage lights.

- At the shout of "One!" night birds with glowing eyes come flying out of the trees and flap their wings. Measured trills in the strings accompany glinting diminished seventh chords (the Samiel-harmony!) in the winds.
- At "Two!" a black boar comes crashing through the bushes and darts across the stage. A rumbling of the bass instruments over a diminished fourth is accompanied by the tremolando strings: the rumble's low notes are harmonized by the Samiel chord.
- At "Three!" a hurricane bends the tops of the forest trees. The music is clearly adapted from the Storm (fourth movement) in Beethoven's "Pastoral" Symphony.
- At "Four!" an invisible coach, of which only the supporting fiery wheels can be seen, rattles across the stage to precipitate triplets reminiscent of Schubert's *Erlkönig*.
- At "Five!" the "Wild Hunt," a ghostly mirage replete with horses and dogs, appears in midair. The phantasmic hunters egg their hounds on to the sounding brass of the orchestral horns.
- At "Six!" volcanic eruptions break out, accompanied by a reprise of the whole madly squalling thematic transition from the Overture (m. 61 ff), but this time veering off into tonal regions (F♯ minor, A♭ minor) never even broached in the Overture's development section.
- At its height, at the count of "Seven!" Samiel himself appears; Caspar and Max fall in a dead faint; the full orchestra, rolling timpani predominating, negotiates an unprecedented juxtaposition of the keys of C minor and F♯ minor, with a single reiterated diminished seventh chord the sole intermediary.

Though Weber's "Wolf's Glen" looms in retrospect as a watershed of musical romanticism, and though the idea seems paradoxical given the subject matter, many German artists at the time suspected it of excessive "realism." That is because it gave its imaginative or (in the language of the time) "fantastic" contents a visually explicit representation. In so doing it contradicted Beethoven's precept, in describing the "Pastoral" Symphony, that music should aim at *mehr Ausdruck der Empfindung als Mahlerey*, "more the expression of feeling than painting." What Weber had accomplished, with unprecedented success, was frankly painting, and some of his contemporaries were offended by it.

By implication, they included E. T. A. Hoffmann himself, the foremost German theorist of musical romanticism. In an essay on theatrical direction published in 1818, he had warned that:

> Nothing is more ridiculous than to bring the spectator to the point where he, without needing to contribute anything from his own imagination, actually believes in the painted palaces, tress, and rocks . . . . First and foremost one must take care to avoid anything unseemly; then one must rely on a deep understanding of the genuinely fantastic, which will work upon and free up the fantasy of the spectator. The stage set should not itself, as an independent striking image, attract the eye of the spectator. Rather the spectator should come to feel, as the action progresses and without being aware of it, the effect of the stage set in which the action takes place.[8]

This is exactly the kind of argument that people advanced, in the early days of mass-produced and widely available television, on behalf of radio: it enlisted the listener's imagination ("the mind's eye") rather than dulled imagination with explicit imagery. Then, as before (and as always), there was a covert social component to the criticism. It came out *almost* explicitly in a letter from Zelter to Goethe after the *Freischütz* premiere. After praising the music, he mocked the staging of the Wolf's Glen scene, replete with "clouds of dust and smoke," and added that "children and women are crazy about it."[9]

Newcomb argues convincingly that the scene's obvious debt to the phantasmagoria shows — a street and fairground entertainment, not a "high art" — was the aspect that evoked the criticism, and that it concealed social snobbery: aristocratic scorn for the "peasant" tastes of street and fairground spectators. It was only after the opera's canonization as mirror or mystical embodiment of German nationhood that such criticism was silenced. But that was the point, exactly. It took precisely such a "lowering" of taste to give the work such an elevated status. Thanks to it, "peasantry," as figurative proxy for the nation, was not only represented in the work but actually incorporated into it. Whether described as a debasement of aristocracy or as an elevation of peasantry, a truly national art, like the idea of nation itself, gave differing social classes a common ground, and a common bond.

II. HISTORY (FRANCE)

OPERA AND REVOLUTION

There was another route to nation through opera. The musical stage became the favored site, in the age of burgeoning nationalism, for the idealized or allegorical reenactment of every nation's history. If largeness of conception automatically meant significance of achievement, historical opera would rank first in the history of opera, since history-in-music became the overriding preoccupation of the venerable Paris Opera (the Académie Royale de Musique). In the period of the so-called July Monarchy

(1830–1848), the Académie Royale became the site of the hugest opera spectacles ever attempted anywhere. Never was art more directly involved with or inspired by politics, and never was politics more directly concerned with national destiny.

The Parisian predilection for the "monster spectacle" was a direct reflection of France's self-image as the great political monolith of Western Europe. It had been so under the Bourbon monarchy, when the French court opera had flourished, and so it remained after the revolution. At a time when the maps of Germany and Italy were crazy quilts of little principalities and city-states, and the multinational Hapsburg ("Holy Roman") Empire was slowly crumbling under its own dead weight, France was the same large centralized entity it had been since the fifteenth century, the only continental European country that looked on an early nineteenth-century political map pretty much the way it looks now.

Its political fortunes may have been volatile, what with three revolutions in little more than fifty years and a perpetual pendulum swing during the nineteenth century between republican and imperial rule. But its territorial integrity was stable, and its military was mighty. It took the whole "concert of Europe," the massed armies of every other major European country, even Russia, to beat its armies back during the Napoleonic Wars. Even when subdued, France remained a giant and "the one to beat," and its arts establishment continued to reflect that traditional self-image.

The Paris Opera's post-Napoleonic recovery was signaled by the building of a new home for it in 1821, the Salle Le Peletier (named after the street on which it stood), with a seating capacity of around two thousand. That was indeed large for the time, even if the Metropolitan Opera House in New York (both the old house in use from 1883 to 1966 and the one at Lincoln Center that replaced it) accommodated almost twice that number. The difference is that for all its size, the Paris Opera was in 1821 still a government-subsidized enterprise that, while encouraged to recoup its expenditures, did not have to do so.

Even after the July Revolution, government involvement with the theater remained strong and decisive, reflecting the even more fundamental fact that in nineteenth-century France (and, to a considerable extent, in many European countries even today) opera was considered a national asset and an instrument of national policy, while in twentieth-century America it is considered a luxury product and is expected, therefore, to earn a profit — not that it can really do so without philanthropic and (to a small and incessantly contested degree) public support.

The new house was not only large, it was also superbly equipped. In 1822 it became the first opera house to use gas lighting instead of candles, around 1830 the first to use limelight, and in 1849 the first to use electricity. Its stage machinery was comparably advanced. Composers and librettists were encouraged to exploit it in consultation with a specially appointed stage manager (*metteur en scène*), the first such official in the history of opera, who from 1827 supervised a staging committee consisting of specialists in machine construction, lighting, set-design, and costumery.

This renewed emphasis on the visual reflected, just as it did in Weber's Germany, a deliberate modernization and popularization of an ancient and aristocratic art. All the design and mechanical innovations on which the Académie now prided itself had long since been standard equipment for the melodramas, peepshows, dioramas, and vaudeville comedies displayed at the so-called boulevard theaters visited by the bourgeoisie. The Académie Royale now wanted to attract that audience, not only because its patronage was lucrative, but also because the bourgeoisie increasingly defined the concept of "nation" in France, even after the post-Napoleonic Restoration, and the Académie now thought of itself, in a way it could never have done under the old regime, as a *national* theater.

The first opera to benefit from this state-supported grandiosity in production was a five-act monster titled *La muette de Portici* ("The mute girl of Portici," 1828, sometimes called *Masaniello* or *Fenella* after its leading characters), by Daniel-François-Esprit Auber (1782–1871), to a libretto by Eugène Scribe (1791–1861). Some said (and say) that Scribe was the greatest librettist of the nineteenth century, some that he was the worst. What all must agree is that he was the century's most prolific and influential dramatist. As the arbiter of the so-called *pièce bien faite* (well-made play), and creator of literally dozens of libretti set by every composer of the period (some more than once), Scribe was the nineteenth-century Metastasio.

Even his admirers admit that Scribe's librettos are full of hackneyed language and theatrical clichés. What he was uniquely gifted for doing, however, was what librettists were paid to do—that is, exploit resources and create opportunities. In the words of Louis Véron (1798–1867), Scribe's nominal boss as director of the Opéra in its glory days:

> For a long time people have thought that nothing was easier to compose than a poem for opera. What a huge literary error! An opera in five acts can only come alive by means of a very dramatic scenario bringing into play the grandest passions of the human heart and strong historical interest. This dramatic action, however, ought to be able to be comprehended by the eye like the action of a ballet. It is necessary that the chorus play an impassioned role in it and be so to speak one of the interesting characters of the play. Each act ought to offer contrasts in settings, costumes, and above all in ably prepared situations. The librettos of M. Scribe offer this abundance of ideas, these dramatic situations, and fulfill all the conditions for variety of setting (*mise-en-scène*) that the construction of an opera in five acts demands. When one has at one's disposal the most enormous theater, an orchestra of more than eighty musicians, nearly eighty chorus members male and female, eighty supernumeraries ["spear-carriers" or "extras," walk-on actors who do not speak or sing but augment the spectacle], not counting children, a company of sixty *machinistes* [highly skilled stagehands] for moving sets, the public listens and expects great things from you. You fail in your mission if so many resources only serve you to put on comic operas or vaudevilles![10]

And that is why there were five acts: it was the standard format for tragedies, "great" plays. In collaboration with Véron, with Charles Duponchel (1794–1868) and Pierre Cicéri (1782–1868), *metteurs en scène*, and with a *pléiade* of gifted composers, beginning with Auber and also including Jacques Fromental Halévy (1799–1862) and especially Giacomo Meyerbeer (1791–1864), Scribe masterminded a new and epoch-making genre called "grand opera," or (since it was associated specifically with the Paris Opera house) *grand opéra*. The enduring repertoire of late nineteenth-century opera—above all the operas of Verdi and Wagner (falsely supposed to be antipodes)—is fundamentally beholden, both musically and dramatically, to *grand opéra*, and historically incomprehensible without knowledge of it.

La muette de Portici, slightly predating both the July Revolution and the advent of Véron, set the tone for these mighty collaborative efforts, and became their model. Just as Véron described, a passionate love intrigue is played out in it against a vast historical panorama, with intense dramatic confrontations alternating with immense crowd scenes and extravagant scenic effects. It was to motivate the crowd scenes that the historical background initially became so important, and it was his skill at aiming acts unerringly toward grandiose dénouements that made Scribe such a successful librettist for the genre.

To get crowds moving on stage, popular uprisings were handy, and so *La muette de Portici* is projected against the background of an insurrection led by the Neapolitan fisherman-revolutionist Tommaso Aniello (called Masaniello) against Spanish rule in 1647. It was a popular subject at the time. A stirring literary account of it, Raimond de Moirmoiron's *Mémoires sur la revolution de Naples de 1647*, published in 1825, had already been turned to theatrical account in an *opéra comique* with music by the transplanted Neapolitan Michele Carafa, a friend of Rossini, which in turn restimulated literary endeavors: several "book versions" (commercial spin-offs from the opera) like the pseudonymously authored *Masaniello, histoire du soulèvement de Naples en 1647* ("Masaniello: The Story of the Naples Rebellion of 1647") were being hawked in the Paris bookstalls.

In addition, a spectacular "diorama" (pictorial projection with lighting effects) called the "Eruption of Mount Vesuvius" was being displayed on the boulevard, at the theater of Louis Daguerre, the future photographic pioneer. To compete with all of these at once, a tragic twist was envisioned, and that made necessary the five-act *tragédie lyrique* format that would henceforth become standard once again, as it had been in the days of Louis XIV.

A three-act *opéra comique* libretto on the subject of Masaniello, by a staff hack named Germain Delavigne, was already the theater's property. It was to "play-doctor" that version into a "well-made" lyric tragedy that Scribe was engaged. The tragic treatment meant replacing spoken dialogue with fully accompanied recitative; that already meant lengthening the piece, since singing takes so much longer than speaking. It also meant interpolating ballet into at least two of the acts as had been de rigueur at the Académie Royale since Lully's time. These requirements were even applied to existing operas when staged by the Académie Royale. The production of Weber's *Der Freischütz* that Wagner described (and, for home consumption, derided) in 1841 had been fitted out with orchestrally accompanied recitatives, composed on commission by Berlioz, who also orchestrated a well-known piano piece of Weber's—"Invitation to the Dance" (*Aufforderung zum Tanze*), a *rondeau brilliant* in waltz time (1819)—to serve as the interpolated ballet.

Above all, tragedy implied an ill-fated love intrigue. In meeting this last requirement Scribe was faced with a quandary. Owing to the unexpected departure of one of the

Académie's leading ladies, only one dramatic soprano was available for the new opera, not enough to populate a traditional love triangle. Scribe's inspired solution was to raid the ballet (another genre that was having a popular rebirth at the Académie Royale), where miming to music had long since been brought to a high degree of expressive precision. The use of a mime character as operatic protagonist was not completely unprecedented (there is one, for example, in *Silvana*, an early opera by Weber). But the idea was novel enough, and the Académie's stable of attractive ballerinas popular enough, to stimulate advance interest in the new work among the social classes the theater now wanted to woo. And so the "mute girl" was not only included in the cast but even made the title character.

Thus arrived at, the love triangle in the opera's foreground became that of Alphonse, the Spanish viceroy's rakish son, who is betrothed to the Spanish princess Elvira, but who has seduced and abandoned the mute fishermaid Fenella, whose spunky pantomimes provide not only piquant entertainment—especially as played at the premiere by the ballerina Lise Noblet (1801–52), a famous beauty reputedly "kept" by Count Claparède, a wizened military hero who was the crony of the Vicomte de Martignac, the Minister of the Interior (whose office oversaw all theaters), and consequently a focal point for gossip (Fig. 36-4)—but also the primary incitement for the background matter, her brother Masaniello's rebellion.

Scribe's technique for relating libidinous foreground to historical background is shown off to perfection by his scenario for the opera's culmination, the fifth act. It is essentially a refinement (if that is the word) on the "entrance opera" technique described in chapter 33 in connection with Donizetti, in which characters accumulate on stage as the plot thickens. Set at the gateway to the Viceroy's palace, now occupied by Masaniello's victorious troops, and with an ominously smoking Mount Vesuvius visible at stage rear, the act proceeds in two great waves.

Wave the first: the act begins, just as act II had begun, with a barcarolle, a decorative, seemingly innocent "genre" number for Pietro, one of Masaniello's henchmen, and his companions, wine cups in hand. Between the barcarolle's stanzas, however, Pietro reveals that Masaniello has betrayed the revolution he has set in motion, that he (Pietro) has punished Masaniello with a slow poison, and that Masaniello will soon be dead. Borella, another revolutionist, rushes in with a crowd of fishermen and issues a call to arms against Alphonse's

FIG. 36-4   Lise Noblet as Fenella in Auber's *La muette de Portici* (1828). Lithograph by Lemercier after a drawing by Achille Deveria.

forces, who are poised to attack. The crowd responds with panic, not only at the threatened bloodshed but also at the volcano's impending eruption. They call for Masaniello. He arrives, clearly deranged from the effects of the poison, singing an incoherent reprise of the act II barcarolle (i.e., a "mad scene"), while Vesuvius and the Viceroy's advancing army both rumble in the orchestral background. Fenella rouses him from his reverie and, becoming aware of the situation, Masaniello leads everyone off but Fenella, who is left alone onstage, miming prayer.

Wave the second: the first to enter this time is Elvira, who warns Fenella to flee. Next Alphonse arrives with news that Masaniello has perished at the hands of his own followers, incited by Pietro. As the massed choruses (fishermen, fisherwomen, revolutionists, Spanish soldiers) reenter the stage, Vesuvius erupts. On learning of her brother's death Fenella is overcome with grief. To general horror, she throws herself into the burning lava that has begun to inundate the stage.

Musically speaking, what is most remarkable about this act is its breakneck dramatic tempo: a matter not of clock time or of musical tempo as normally defined, but of structure. As listed in the score, there are only two "numbers": the opening barcarolle and a colossal unbroken finale that takes in all the rest of the action. As we may remember from the days of Mozart and Da Ponte, a finale is a section in which musical numbers never close with full cadences (i.e., signals to applaud), but are subsumed into an unbroken continuity, further emphasized by frequent, sometimes remote, harmonic modulations reflecting the vicissitudes on stage.

We have previously seen the ensemble finale, long the exclusive preserve of the comic opera where it originated, adapted to tragic ends in the Italian operas of the 1830s (Bellini) and 1840s (Donizetti). Rossini, in his late *opere serie* for Naples, had also adapted it in this way. Having come to Paris and produced some of these operas in French translation, Rossini was part of the background to the Scribian finale as well. But before Scribe there was no precedent for a whole act that was in effect a continuous finale, which is to say a fluid dramatic or "organic" continuity uninterrupted by individual "numbers." As Wagner wrote in wonder, spectators perceived *La muette de Portici* as "something completely novel," because "one was always kept in suspense and transported by a complete act in its entirety."[11] This will be a very important point to remember when considering the various operatic "reforms" of the later nineteenth century, most of which (but particularly Wagner's own) were attempts to achieve precisely this "numberless" continuity. Remembering this is all the more pertinent in view of an implicit, often forgotten, irony. Idealistic reformers of opera were wont to look back derisively on the French *grand opéra*, giving it in retrospect a reputation for opportunistic, exploitative commercial cynicism that is certainly supported by many of the details in this account of its origins and of the genesis of *La muette de Portici*. Surely no operatic genre was ever devised with a more constant and fretful eye toward its public reception. And yet two of the principal tenets of late-century "reformist" opera—the emphasis on uniting all media (poetry, music, setting, spectacle) in mutually reinforcing collaboration, and the achievement of "numberless" continuity—were powerfully anticipated by the *grand opéra* not in opposition to public taste but in the very act of courting it.

And yet public taste—a protean, discrepant thing—has rarely if ever been successfully controlled or anticipated from "above"; nor does public reception ever completely match creative intention. The adventures of *La muette de Portici* provide one of the most pointed illustrations of these truths. That story, the story of its reception, is its truest claim on our attention.

The opera was planned during the period of the so-called Bourbon Restoration, toward the end of the stormy and reactionary reign of Charles X, the brother of Louis XVI, the last monarch of the old regime (beheaded during the Reign of Terror). Charles had succeeded his other brother, Louis XVIII, who had been placed on the throne by the "concert of Europe" following Napoleon's defeat. By 1827 the political atmosphere was tense and theatrical censorship was severe. In such circumstances an opera about a revolution, even one as removed in time and place as Masaniello's, might seem the very last thing the Académie Royale, France's most official musical stage, would consider offering for public view. In fact, however, the opera was planned by the theatrical directorate in direct collaboration with the king's chief minister, the Vicomte de Martignac, in an effort to sway liberal opinion away from renewed revolutionary action.

The revolution depicted in the opera is not only abortive but disastrous for all concerned. By the fourth act it has gone out of Masaniello's control and descended into mob rule. Masaniello turns against his former companions (even offering his protection to Alphonse and Elvira) in an effort to stop the senseless bloodshed. He becomes, improbably enough, the embodiment of order, and is condemned by the senseless mob for his moderation. It is only Fenella's final act of suicidal desperation that brings everyone to their senses. The opera's last lines, spoken "in one voice" by all the surviving characters and choruses, suggest that the natural disaster (the eruption of Vesuvius) was a divine punishment for the civil disaster they had wrought:

Grâce pour notre crime!	Mercy for our crime!
Grand Dieu! protège-nous!	Great God! Protect us!
Et que cette victime	And let this one victim
Suffise à ton courroux!	Appease your anger!

As Karin Pendle, a historian of the *grand opéra*, observes, the intended moral of the opera was that in Masaniello's revolution, and by implication in all revolutions, "the losers are not primarily the leaders but rather the masses of people who have been taken advantage of by both sides." It was "the mood of the times," she adds, that "dictated the content of *La muette de Portici*," and "its warning was there for all who had ears to hear."[12] And yet as Jane Fulcher, a rival historian of the *grand opéra*, points out, many among the public had ears for another message altogether, and managed to find it in the opera by "reading" the work opportunistically and selectively, the way large, heterogeneous modern audiences always interpret works of art.

The outcome of the drama finally mattered less to the public than the manner in which the crowd, with which the public identified, was portrayed. "In the end," writes Fulcher,

> the depiction of the people was the work's most gripping aspect: the people depicted as grand and heroic, through most of the work, on the first royal stage . . . . The blocking of the crowd scenes presented them as an active and self-assured group, now themselves in a position to inspire fear and awe in the authorities. Moreover, their choral scenes, by far the most musically powerful parts of the work, similarly projected a sense of dignity and pride that clashed openly with what occurred at the opera's end.[13]

So completely did bourgeois audiences identify, against official expectation, with the powerfully portrayed peasant revolutionaries, as to turn the opera into a virtual "accessory before the fact" to the revolution of 1830, the so-called July Revolution, in which political power was decisively wrested by the bourgeoisie from the aristocracy for good and all.

This reading of the opera against the official grain was much abetted by the means of its public dissemination. Operas were published and popularized not only as complete works, but in separate "numbers" as well. Individual numbers were encoded in barrel organ cylinders and became street music. They were issued in sheet music and enjoyed independent sales as home music. One item from *La muette de Portici* that became an instant, runaway best-seller was the act II duet for Masaniello and Pietro, "Amour sacré de la patrie" ("Sacred love of fatherland," Ex. 36-6).

Detached from its original context, this exhilarating marchlike number could serve as many contradictory purposes as could patriotism itself, teaching government and governed alike that works of art could be freely appropriated, in an age of mass dissemination, for use as political weapons. It became customary for audiences to applaud the revolutionary duet with special show-stopping fervor, turning the occasion into a virtual antigovernment demonstration. What the nineteenth century learned from the *grand opéra* was that works of art could be dangerous. They were dangerous not necessarily by design but by virtue of their ambiguity — and, consequently, the different ways in which they could be used. In an age of emergent mass politics, music had become a potential rabble-rouser. Opera could now not only mirror but actually make the history of nations. In extreme cases it could even help make the nation.

Just how literally this was the case was driven home when *La muette de Portici* was exported, first to Germany, next, and fatefully, to Belgium. The political situation in the Low Countries, particularly among the French-speaking Belgians or Walloons, was much closer to that portrayed in the opera than the situation in France, where the opera had already proved politically explosive. Like Masaniello's Neapolitans, the Belgians had been living under Hapsburg domination since 1815, when the Congress of Vienna had peremptorily assigned the Belgian provinces to the United Kingdom of the Netherlands, a de facto Austrian protectorate. The July Revolution in France had emboldened Belgian patriots to seek independence. They demanded a performance of

La muette de Portici, banned by the nervous Austrians, as the price of their participation in birthday celebrations for the Dutch king, William of Orange, scheduled for 24 August.

La muette, heavily cut, opened the very next day, Wednesday, 25 August 1830, at the Théâtre de la Monnaie in Brussels. As usual, the authorities cut the wrong numbers. The scenes of mob violence were gone, but "Amour sacré de la patrie" remained. Having circulated for two years in sheet and street music, it was widely known by heart. By the end of the number, the whole audience seemed to be on its feet, singing along. The chief of police sent a scout outside to assess the mood of the mob that had collected on the theater square. The scout returned and reported that the chief was to be assassinated in his box at the end of the performance.

By the end of the fourth act, most of the audience had left the theater and had joined the crowd, which swept into and occupied the offices of the main Brussels newspaper, the city courthouse, and the Hôtel de Ville, the seat of government. The decisive moment came with the storming of the municipal armory and the distribution of weapons to the rioters. Over the next few days the revolt spread to other cities. Unable to contain the crowds, the Dutch forces withdrew. By the next year, with the connivance of the anti-French coalition of "powers," Prince Leopold of Saxe-Coburg-Gotha (uncle of the soon-to-be-crowned Queen Victoria of England) had been elected King of the Belgians. His descendants reign to this day.

EX. 36-6   Daniel-François-Esprit Auber, *La muette de Portici* no. 8, duo, "Amour sacrée de la patrie," mm. 48–56

Historians debate the spontaneity of the Belgian uprising, and its precise relationship to the operatic performance that seemed to spark it. Was the demonstration an unpremeditated reaction to the patriotic duet or was the duet the prearranged signal to begin the demonstration? The latter, admittedly, seems more likely to be the case, since according to all reports the police anticipated the demonstration (if not its strength) and had put the theater square under guard.

Yet how much of a difference, finally, do these admissions and qualifications make? Unaffected is the status of the musical performance — and, secondarily, of the work performed — as a political act. It is clear, moreover, that the effect of the performance on Belgian history had nothing at all to do with the conception of the work or the intentions of its creators. But again, what difference did that make to the Brussels demonstrators, and what difference should it make to us?

BOURGEOIS KINGS

The Belgian insurrection of August 1830 differed very significantly from its French counterpart of the previous month (the so-called July Revolution), to which it is often likened. The one was a revolt of patriots against an imposed foreign regime. The other was a revolt by an aristocracy of wealth (the *haute bourgeoisie* or upper middle class) against an aristocracy of birth. It put an end to the Bourbon dynasty once and for all, but, remembering the post-revolutionary Reign of Terror and fearful of the "proletariat" (the industrialized and newly populous urban working class), the victors, headed by the venerable Marquis de Lafayette of American revolutionary fame, held back from redeclaring republican rule. Instead, a liberal constitutional monarchy, respectful of individual rights (and particularly the rights of private property), was declared by the newly empowered legislature or Chamber of Deputies, a stronghold of bourgeois interests.

At its head stood Louis Philippe (1773–1850), the gray-suited, umbrella-toting "citizen king," whose father, the Duke of Orléans, had been an active revolutionary (under the name Philippe Égalité) but had been martyred by the Terror. The new king stood for the protection of bourgeois interests against aristocrat and proletarian alike. Especially after a number of variously motivated attempts were made on his life, the France his reign represented became a bastion of "conservative liberalism," a strong secular state committed to economic growth and the securing of all attendant rights and privileges. The "July Monarchy" was thus at once a beacon of religious and civil tolerance and bulwark of political stability, bitterly opposed in the name of these values to all clericalism and aristocratic resurgence, but to all revolutionary or socialist tendencies as well. It was a brief European foretaste of "Americanism," the sort of capitalistic economic liberalism that only became a world force much later with the emergence of the United States as a world power.

And its art exhibited traces of precocious Americanism as well; it is hard nowadays to overlook the many parallels between the luxuriance and the implied values of the July Monarchy's most exalted art product — the *grand opéra*, which reached its zenith under Louis Philippe — and those of the Hollywood movie industry: the same basis in popular spectacle, the same emphasis on high-tech "production values" and "special effects," the same preoccupation with richly appointed semi-fantastic historical settings, and the same enthusiastic, anachronistic reinforcement of contemporary middle-class values by means of epic dramaturgy.

And by no means least: the same social tolerance in the name of economic expansion, exemplified in the hospitality shown both by Hollywood and by the Académie Royale under Louis Philippe to enterprising Jewish talent. Both Halévy and Meyerbeer, the grand opera's leading lights, were Jews (and Meyerbeer was a foreigner to boot). But both were welcomed as creators of artistic showpieces of a specifically national type, in which the French nation in its most militantly bourgeois phase took an intense patriotic pride.

Indeed, Halévy's most successful opera, *La Juive* ("The Jewess", 1835), to a book by Scribe, is an impassioned indictment of religious bigotry. That is not what packed them in, though. It was, rather, the staging by Duponchel and Cicéri that bowled audiences over with its conspicuous consumption and its "cast of thousands," causing one reviewer to exult that "the Opéra may become a power capable of throwing its armies into the balance of power in Europe."[14] The gold standard for opulence, however, was set the next year by *Les Huguenots*, Meyerbeer's masterpiece, which also clothed a liberal bourgeois plea for religious tolerance in raiment of unbelievable, Versailles-rivaling splendor.

The composer of *Les Huguenots* was born Jakob Liebmann Meyer Beer to a wealthy Berlin family, comparable to the Mendelssohns but if anything even richer and more acculturated. It was a mark of his sense of security that the composer's father, Juda Herz Beer, a sugar merchant and an elder in the municipal synagogue, never converted or had his children baptized. His mother, Amalia, the daughter

of perhaps the most prosperous banker in Berlin, actually made her son swear never to renounce his hereditary faith; and while the composer was a totally assimilated and cosmopolitan citizen of Europe, and never religiously observant, he honored his pledge and was eventually brought back to Berlin for burial, amid huge publicity, in the city's Jewish cemetery.

His career is if anything an even more impressive illustration than Mendelssohn's of the opportunities that opened up to "emancipated Jews" in the early optimistic decades of the nineteenth century. Trained first as a piano virtuoso, he was able to perform Mozart's D-minor Piano Concerto at the age of ten. Two years later he enrolled in the Berlin Singakademie where, a couple of decades ahead of Mendelssohn, he studied

FIG. 36-5   Meyerbeer, photographed in 1855 by Félix Nadar.

theory and beginning composition (counterpoint) with Carl Friedrich Zelter. In 1810, having embarked on a professional career and contracted his last two names into "Meyerbeer," he began two years of lessons (alongside Weber, from then on a friend) with Abbé Vogler.

Meyerbeer landed a court Kapellmeister's post in 1813, the same year that his second German singspiel was produced to indifferent success. Wishing to devote himself to theatrical composition, and therefore unhappy with the prospect of a life spent in small-time court service, he took the advice of Antonio Salieri (still the Vienna court composer), quit his job, and went to Italy to learn the tricks of the opera trade. Actually, it was not much of a gamble. Thanks to his family's fortune, Meyerbeer was financially independent throughout his life. Indeed, he was one of the richest men in Europe, and in later years knew how to use his money to manipulate the press. (His biographer, Heinz Becker, credits him with the invention of "the modern press conference with refreshments.")[15]

He spent eight miraculously successful years (1816–24) in Italy (Venice, Padua, Milan) much as Handel had done a century before him, Italianizing not only his style but even his first name (to Giacomo). By the time of his last Italian opera, *Il crociato in Egitto* (The Crusader in Egypt, 1824), a *melodramma eroico* on the Rossini model (and the last important opera, incidentally, to feature a major role for a castrato), Meyerbeer was recognized as Rossini's most viable rival. (His viability was most effectively, if backhandedly, acknowledged by Rossini himself, who never tired of denigrating Meyerbeer's work, especially after he had quit the scene and Meyerbeer continued to thrive.) *Il crociato* was a deliberate bid to attract the attention of the Paris opera houses, by then regarded (thanks precisely to their status as an official national establishment) as the Mecca of the operatic world. After a trial Paris production of another of his Italian operas in 1826, he was at last favored (a year later than Rossini) with an actual Paris commission. The commission came not from the Académie Royale but from the director of the Opéra Comique, with whom the composer had struck up a friendship. For that house one was expected to write three-act operas with spoken dialogue and happy endings: by then it was a firmly established principle that a tragic opera ended with at least one death and a comic opera with at least one marriage. Before he could embark on the project, however, he was sidetracked by a request from the widow of Weber, who had just died unexpectedly in London, to complete his friend's singspiel, *Die drei Pintos.*

There are probably the makings of a psychological novel in Meyerbeer's lifelong failure to keep this promise. (He finally returned the still-unfinished score to the Weber family a quarter of a century later, appeasing them with a large indemnity; the opera was eventually completed — in 1887! — by a young opera conductor named Gustav Mahler, who went on to become a major composer of symphonies but never wrote an opera of his own.) The temporary delay had a fateful and, for Meyerbeer, a very happy consequence, however. While he was ostensibly occupied with the abortive *Drei Pintos* project, the success of Auber's *Muette de Portici* created a demand for more operas on a like heroic scale, and Meyerbeer thus got in on the ground floor, so to speak, of the nascent *grand opéra.*

The original Opéra Comique commission—*Robert le diable* ("Robert the devil"), vaguely based on an old Norman legend—would have been something of a chip off *Der Freischütz*, already popular at the Opéra Comique in a free adaptation called *Robin des bois* ("Robin Hood"). Robert, one of several knights set to compete for the hand of Princess Isabelle, is tempted by his sinister friend Bertram, just as Max is tempted in *Der Freischütz* by his friend Caspar, to enhance his chances of success with supernatural aid. Bertram turns out to be not a man but a demon, and not Robert's friend but his father. He comes within a hair's breadth of claiming Robert's soul, but is defeated in the end by Alice, Robert's foster sister.

In the five-act *grand opéra* version eventually presented at the Académie Royale, Bertram is swallowed up in an earthquake at the very end, and Robert is led off to the altar, where Isabelle is waiting. (Thus the marriage survived from the *opéra comique* conception, but what is actually shown on stage is Bertram's hellish Don Giovanni-ish demise.) The obligatory third-act ballet is a counterpart to Weber's "Wolf's Glen," with a fiery "Valse infernale" representing a demoniac orgy in a deserted cave, and most spectacularly (as well as most obviously indebted to the phantasmagoria shows) a swirling dance for a whole convent-cemetery's worth of risen nuns' corpses. This was as much an opera to see as to hear, and it has been argued that the real hero behind *Robert le diable* was Cicéri, the designer. But it made Meyerbeer the toast of Paris (and the object of furious resentment back home). The Jewish parvenu became the bourgeois king of the opera, to match the one at the helm of government. He maintained his preeminence with three more grand opera scores, each with an elephantine gestation period and a behemoth of a production, spaced out over a period of thirty years.

While maintaining *Robert le diable*'s colossal scale and reliance on awe-inspiring spectacle, the operas that followed differed significantly from the prototype as dramatic conceptions. It was not an artistic difference alone, but one that matched the changes in the political climate. Owing to the snail's pace at which the cumbersome Paris production machine had to operate—whereas Italian productions typically went from contract-signing to opening night in a matter of weeks, the process normally

FIG. 36-6 Edgar Degas (1834–1917), *The Ballet from "Robert le Diable"* (1871).

lasted from three to twelve years in Paris — a grand opera production could sometimes be curiously out of joint with the times by the time it reached the stage.

Robert le diable was a case in point. Although first presented in 1831, in the first year of the July Monarchy, the score was commissioned and supplied in the waning years of the restoration. However thrilling, it was at heart a frivolous *diablerie* ("deviltry," to use the term current at the cheap boulevard theaters) with a facile, unproblematic moral and a rather smugly happy end, in which good and bad characters alike receive their just deserts. The works actually created in the period of the ascendant bourgeoisie, in contrast, employed the same dazzling theatrical rhetoric to produce uniformly horrifying dénouements, investing them, however artificially, with a gripping moral urgency.

M. Elizabeth C. Bartlet, a historian of the Paris musical stage, has caught their common denominator with succinct precision. In the grand operas of the July Monarchy, she writes, "sympathetic characters are crushed by forces beyond their control."[16] The portrayal of these forces as human rather than supernatural was the reason why every grand opera commissioned after 1830 had to have an explicit historical setting, usually a well-defined "time of troubles" brought about by irreconcilable factional strife. And the forces being human, they are subject to moral judgment and can serve as cautionary examples. The moral is always the same: "Don't let things get out of control! Resolve your differences!" Naked conflict, intransigence, prejudice, as every grand opera shows us time and again, lead inevitably to destruction.

Rarely if ever does the opera appear to take sides within the conflict portrayed. It sides, ostensibly, against conflict itself. As George Sand was quick to discern (and to approve), however, there was an implicit political bias in *grand opéra*. It proceeded, she noted, from a "new liberal theory of history according to which, far from being the exclusive property of revolutionists, terrorism was attributed primarily to the aristocratic nobles, kings, princes and gentlemen."[17]

In *Les Huguenots* (1836) these political morals are drawn with particular clarity thanks to the trusty Romeo-and-Juliet formula. A pair of star-crossed lovers, Raoul (Protestant) and Valentine (Catholic), are caught in the Reformation's web. They meet their doom in the course of the infamous St. Bartholomew's Day massacre of 1572, in which many hundreds of Huguenots (French Calvinists) were shot dead in the streets of Paris at the behest of Catherine de' Medici, the Italian-born queen mother. The entire fifth act of the opera was given over to a reenactment of the horrible event, at the end of which the auditorium famously reeked of gunpowder and buckshot, adding yet another sensory element to the media-saturation for which the *grand opéra* was famed. Like *La Juive*, which preceded it by a year, *Les Huguenots* is an indictment of religious fanaticism and an implicit declaration of bourgeois liberalism.

In *Le prophète* (1849), the setting is sixteenth-century Holland and Germany, where another fanatical religious movement, that of the Anabaptists ("Rebaptizers" rejecting infant baptism), held sway. The Anabaptists, whose main tactic was fomenting peasant revolts, could be looked upon as the extreme left wing of the early Reformation movement. The title character is John of Leiden (Jean in the opera), who declared himself the resurrected King David and declared a theocratic "kingdom of Zion" in the town of Münster in 1534. After presiding over this self-created polygamous religious commune for about a year, John was defeated by the Catholic prince bishop whom he had deposed and was publicly tortured to death along with his followers.

In the opera, Jean is portrayed as a good-natured innkeeper gulled by crafty thieves posing as Anabaptists into becoming their religious figurehead. He is disillusioned in the end, with tragic results for himself, Berthe his betrothed (who stabs herself when she learns the tyrannical "prophet's" identity), and his mother Fidès, who dies with Jean in the catastrophic explosion of his palace, which he himself has engineered as an act of expiation. In this opera the political subtext is especially obvious. As the poet and critic Théophile Gautier (1811–72) wittily observed, "the Anabaptists and the peasants have dialogue that one could believe to have been drawn from the prose of communistic journals" such as were proliferating in the period leading up to the abortive proletarian revolutions of 1848.[18] Again there was an irony engendered by delayed production. By the time it was staged, the revolution of which it sought to forewarn had already taken place and France was again a republic.

L'Africaine ("The African girl"), the last Scribe-Meyerbeer collaboration, was not produced until 1865, a year after the composer's death. Once again the historical setting is the sixteenth century, the "age of exploration," but the exotic geographical setting ("an island in the Indian Ocean") is semi-fantastical. And once again religious fanaticism (this time the Iberian inquisition) is cast as a destructive force, though this time it has a rival in the collision and mutual corruption of European and African mores.

The two main characters are the Portuguese explorer Vasco da Gama and Sélika, an "African" (actually Hindu) queen he has brought back to Portugal as a slave and concubine. Taking her back with him on a subsequent expedition, Vasco is defeated and captured by Sélika's tribe. In the end, though, she demonstrates her superior magnanimity by first marrying him rather than having him killed, and then letting him go back to Portugal with Inès, his European betrothed. In a final scene reminiscent of the Dido-and-Aeneas theme so beloved of the *opera seria* composers of yore, Sélika, like Dido (also an African queen), poisons herself on a promontory overlooking the sea as Vasco and his fleet depart.

GRANDEST OF THE GRAND

As Wagner's appreciation of *La muette de Portici* has already suggested, a *grand opéra* cannot be fairly sampled as a musical achievement at any level short of an entire act. The fourth act of *Les Huguenots* is the inevitable choice, not only because it has long been acclaimed as the greatest, if not the "grandest" single act in all of *grand opéra*, but also (if paradoxically) because it is an interestingly atypical work that reveals the genre's conceptual Achilles' heel even as it suggests the ways in which its virtues would later be absorbed into the international operatic mainstream.

It is often said that *grand opéra* killed the bel canto, just as bourgeois pretension and "conspicuous consumption" killed aristocratic grace. As evidence, its amazing paucity of solo numbers is often cited. Arias, the dramatic as well as the musical focal points in Italian operas, became merely occasional and decorative, often sung *ad libitum*. Single characters rarely got to occupy the stage long enough to sing one. And while every grand opera score contained its share of "detachable" numbers (numbers intended for a life outside the opera on the recital stage and in homes), they are often throwaways, used for the purpose of narrative exposition rather than emotional effusion, and are written in a simple ballad (strophic) style more often than in the gripping sequence of accelerating tempos that one gets in Italian opera.

In *Les Huguenots* only two characters are given real arias to sing. Both of them are decidedly minor characters, and their big moments come early in the evening, before the plot has had a chance to thicken much. One is Marguerite, the Queen of Navarre, who gets a traditionally regal coloratura aria at the beginning of act II to establish it, in keeping with the "act-oriented" principle of Scribian librettos, as the "feminine" act (replete with a then-licentious bathing scene) to contrast with the all-male cast of act I. The other is Urbain, Marguerite's gawkily flirtatious page, a "trousers" role often compared with that of Cherubino, the Countess Almaviva's androgynous lover-boy in Mozart's *Marriage of Figaro*. (There is also a blustery musket song in act I called "Pif paf pouf!" for the *basso profondo* role of Marcel, an old Huguenot; it was often detached, and became famous, but it is hardly an aria.) It is a superb commentary on the values of *grand opéra* that it should have been Urbain, the most incidental of the major roles in *Les Huguenots*, who was given the opera's most famous aria to sing. But even as an element of décor, the Cavatine du Page ("Nobles seigneurs, salut!" ["Greetings, Noble Lords"]) is a sumptuous and revealing tidbit. It deserves a peek for the way it brought a note of frank sexual suggestiveness into operatic music, making winkingly overt what had always been an implicit component of opera's appeal.

Marguerite has sent Urbain into the stag party that is act I with a summons for Raoul, the male lead. The demonstratively male atmosphere of the act makes the *travesti* character's sexual ambiguity all the more piquant. The character is a boy, but the singer is a woman among men, and the composer plays the gag for all it is worth. Urbain is marked as "exotic" (i.e., sexy) by his vocal range, to be sure; but also by his coloratura flourishes at the beginning and the end, which provide a musical equivalent to the ironically obsequious courtly bows that surely accompanied them in the stage business. His lascivious allure is also underscored by Scribe: the Count of Nevers (the host on whose party he has intruded) pointedly addresses Urbain as "beau page"—literally "handsome page," but to be understood as "pretty boy."

But all of these (and the gorgeously sensuous orchestration besides) are secondary to the main attraction, the lilting waltz rhythms in which Urbain's creamy cantabile phrases are cast, as close to a belly dance as a meter could get within a strictly European setting. It is a compound waltz, in fact, implying in its $\frac{9}{8}$ meter two levels of curvaceous ternary movement, whirls within whirls (and still more whirls when the writing includes sixteenth-note triplets). Urbain's melody behaves like a veritable ballerina—pirouettes (twirls) cynically placed on the word "*honneur*," jetés (leaps) on "Chevaliers," spectacular *fouettés en tournant* (whip-arounds) to characterize the coquettish series of "*nons*" in the middle section.

Most coaxing of all are the *battements* (flutters) alternating with *tendus* (stretches) — the staccato repeated notes alternating with languorous "sighing" pairs (marked *dolce e legato* in the composer's manuscript) — in the middle section, where the page promises "glory and bliss" to the lucky recipient of her mistress's summons. There is technical interest here in the composer's apparently superfluous use of the words *staccato* and *legato* to denote what might already seem sufficiently explicit in the dots and slurs (Fig. 36-7). Spotlighted in this way they tell the conductor to reinforce the distinction by adjusting the tempo — something that was becoming more and more the rule in

FIG. 36-7   Autograph score of the Page's cavatina from act I of Meyerbeer's *Les Huguenots* (1836).

romantic orchestral practice, now that baton conducting was coming in. A new kind of virtuoso — the podium virtuoso — was emerging.

And he was emerging amid controversy. That Meyerbeer asks for the conductor's intervention here is evidence that he saw the innovation as useful. Others affected disapproval, especially where the sacralized repertory of "absolute music" was concerned. There is a passage in a treatise on conducting by Felix Weingartner (1863–1942), who saw himself as a reformer of the art, in which he protested what he described as the distortions wrought by the podium virtuosi of his student days. The chief culprit was Hans von Bülow (1830–94), probably the late nineteenth century's most celebrated maestro. The passage Weingartner chose for illustrating von Bülow's sins was one from Beethoven's *Egmont* Overture that exhibits exactly the same contrast in articulation that Meyerbeer called for in Urbain's cavatina (Ex. 36-7).

EX. 36-7   Ludwig van Beethoven's *Egmont* Overture, second theme

Weingartner carped that Bülow "leaped at once from *allegro* into an *andante grave*" at this point, "thereby destroying the uniform tempo" marked by the composer. The historical evidence (including Meyerbeer's notation) suggests that Weingartner's protests were actually bent not toward the restoration of a lost propriety but at a new ideal of regularity that we will later associate with twentieth-century modernism. Ironically enough, the tradition of tempo fluidity Weingartner was trying to stamp out (and which was effectively eliminated from most twentieth-century performances) was a tradition largely instituted by the very figure whose unsullied texts Weingartner was trying to restore. For Beethoven was one of the first baton conductors, and all who have given ear-witness testimony on his performances agree, to quote one of them, that he was "much concerned to achieve a proper *tempo rubato*."[19] It is altogether possible, even likely, that Meyerbeer, German by birth, was trying through his notation to acquaint French musicians with the freewheeling "Beethovenian" approach to tempo he had imbibed in his youth.

But it was a new expressive purpose to which Meyerbeer sought to put the style. His page's cavatina is worlds away from the *Innerlichkeit* of German romanticism, and Meyerbeer's use of coloratura is equally far from that of his Italian contemporaries, Bellini and Donizetti. The page's delivery is not self-revealing. It is a facade. The only affect projected (if one can call it an affect) is that of coquetry. For high romantic emotion one must turn, in a *grand opéra*, to the "production numbers": the *morceaux d'ensemble*, as they were called.

Vocal virtuosity will certainly not be lacking. Not for nothing were performances of *Les Huguenots* billed as *les nuits de sept étoiles* — "nights of seven stars" — and ticket prices raised. With seven roles demanding singers of the absolute first rank it was the highest-priced of all operas for all concerned, including the management. But it was a new kind of virtuoso singing that Meyerbeer required in dramatic (as opposed to decorative) roles: a forceful rather than graceful virtuosity that demanded an extension of the full (or "chest") voice almost to the top of the range, with a concomitantly lessened dependence on refined falsetto ("head-voice") singing. This is the kind of heroic singing style we know today as "operatic." For better or worse, we owe it, in the first instance, to Meyerbeer.

The fourth act of *Les Huguenots* contains just three big numbers. First there is a "scene," a hectic recitative number in which Valentine, now married and unavailable, hides her illicit Protestant lover Raoul from her father St. Bris, the mastermind of the St. Bartholomew's Day plot. After the first performances, Meyerbeer added a brief romance for Valentine alone so as to give the opera's female lead a lyrical moment to balance Raoul's little air at the beginning of act V. Its two to three minutes' duration, believe it or not, is the only span of time in the entire four-hour show when the stage is occupied by a single soliloquizing character expressing strong emotion. This was indeed a new kind of opera!

What follows next is one of Scribe's most powerful "dramatic tableaus," to which Meyerbeer composed his most famous *morceau d'ensemble*: the Conspiracy and Blessing of the Daggers (*Conjuration et bénédiction des poignards*). Here is where the St. Bartholomew's Day massacre is plotted. The first section, the *conjuration*, is baritone St. Bris's big moment. He leads the taking of the oath with a big rabble-rousing tune ("Pour cette cause sainte"/"For this holy cause") whose resemblance to *La Marseillaise*, whether calculated or not, is patent — and potent (Ex. 36-8).

Treated at first as if it were the beginning of an aria, its second half is immediately taken up by St. Bris and Nevers (now Valentine's husband), as a duet accompanied by shouts of assent from the chorus of Catholic lords, and a pair of countermelodies (in contrary motion, of course) for Tavannes, an ardent coconspirator, and the horrified Valentine (sung "aside" to the audience, cadenza and all). Having thus been given a monumental exposition, the tune will come back as a kind of rondo theme (or "double return") to bind up the whole tableau. In between its appearances Nevers, realizing that it is not a battle but a craven massacre of innocents that is being planned, angrily withdraws. With fine irony, Meyerbeer gives him the hushed yet nevertheless crowning

EX. 36-8   Giacomo Meyerbeer, *Les Huguenots*, "Pour cette cause sainte," compared with La Marseillaise

reprise of the tune so bumptiously put forth by St. Bris, as Nevers claims the honorable position that St. Bris in his cowardice has abdicated.

After Nevers has stalked off the stage, and Valentine has been shooed away by her father, the actual plot is hatched, following which three monks enter, bearing baskets full of white scarves that will serve on the morrow as identification badges for Catholics during the bloodbath. (During their entrance, Valentine, having escaped from her room, returns unnoticed to the stage and sings an arioso reminding the audience about the concealed presence of Raoul.)

The preparation for the blessing of the daggers is a moment of brutally degraded pomp, characterized musically by the dotted rhythms of the old French overture. The actual blessing (Ex. 36-9) is intoned to a weird chord progression that shows Meyerbeer to have been paying attention to the latest developments in German music: the tonic, Ab, is shadowed by major thirds below (E major) and above (C major), completing an uncanny "thirds cycle" before the C-major chord resolves as a dominant to F.

After an anathema has been pronounced on the Huguenots, and an oath taken to spare no one, be it graybeard, woman, or child, the stage erupts in a bloodthirsty

EX. 36-9 Giacomo Meyerbeer, *Les Huguenots*, Act IV (blessing scene)

allegro furioso that functions as a sort of choral cabaletta. Meyerbeer's virtuosity in the scoring of this sonorous explosion (still using "natural" brass instruments) was widely admired and emulated, perennially cited in orchestration treatises beginning with Berlioz's in 1843. What seems almost a greater achievement, though, is the way in which the composer managed to scale the sonority down by degrees to pianissimo as the conspirators disperse.

Here, the most fully populated moment of the tableau, was where Scribe thought the act was over. And so it was when the opera went into rehearsal in June 1835. It was Adolphe Nourrit (1802–39), the leading tenor of the Opéra, playing Raoul, who demanded that he and his leading lady — Cornélie Falcon (1812–97), his protégé and mistress, in the role of Valentine — be given a proper love scene. It was not an easy thing to rationalize, and Scribe refused to supply it. Meyerbeer turned to a friend, Émile Deschamps, for the requisite text.

In the end, the strangely motivated Grand Duo went like this: Raoul emerges from hiding and immediately makes for the door, so that he can warn his fellow Huguenots of the impending catastrophe. The desperate Valentine, losing her head and trying to detain him, blurts out that she loves him. Thunderstruck ("Tu l'as dit!"/"You said it!"), Raoul asks to hear her say it again, over and over. This provides the slow "cavatine" portion of the duet, set in the exotically "remote" key of G♭ major and marked *andante amoroso* (Ex. 36-10). But finally, hearing the local church bells give out the fatal signal (on F, followed by a blast of brass on a jarring C♮ that may remind us of Weber's Wolf Glen tritones), he tears himself away and runs to his coreligionists' aid, thus providing the pretexts for a concluding "stretta" or fast finish.

What seemed to Scribe a contrived situation, improbable to the point of absurdity, became irresistible theater when realized. The freezing of the action into "aria time" at this terribly fraught juncture — just long enough for the two doomed characters to catch a moment's "inward" bliss before being predictably crushed by the inexorable march of external events — brought audiences to a frenzy of empathy. It was instantly the most successful number in the opera, chiefly responsible for the work's becoming the first grand opera to reach a thousand documented performances (in Paris in 1900); and it has retained its reputation as a masterpiece even as Meyerbeer's music has fallen out of the active repertory and his name has sunk, in many quarters, into low repute.

What brought the opera up to this self-surpassing level was the introduction of a new member into the planning board, so to speak, to join the composer, the librettist, the theater manager, the stage director, and the designer. Or rather, it was the readmittance to lost privilege of an old member, the oldest one of all, namely the singer. Never before in a grand opera, and never since, did a solo singer's voice dominate the work's most memorable moment. That made *Les Huguenots* at once the greatest *grand opéra* and an atypical one. It fused the novel, timely values of *grand opéra* with the foundational, "eternal" verities of all public music drama, as set in stone in Venice almost exactly two hundred years before. Opera has always thrived — and, it seems, can only thrive — on voice-inspired empathy.

EX. 36-10   Giacomo Meyerbeer, *Les Huguenots*, Act IV ("Cavatine," *andante amoroso*)

Until then not particularly known for its intimacy, Meyerbeer's music, especially in the cavatine that capitalized on Nourrit's extraordinary range and timbre, set a standard of tenderness that long remained a touchstone. In the witty words of Hugh Macdonald, a historian of French opera, "'Tu l'as dit' is a classic love duet: at least it is of a type that immediately became a classic," owing to its many imitators. "Echoes of this duet are heard throughout the nineteenth century, not just for its orchestral and vocal style but for its key. I doubt if any composer familiar with *Les Huguenots* (and what composer was not?) was free to use G♭ in any other way."[20]

VAGARIES OF RECEPTION

Macdonald's long list of Meyerbeer's debtors and emulators has its ironies. For one thing it shows that, whatever the enabling conditions that brought forth Meyerbeer's work, its artistic and historical significance is not at all tantamount to, or exhausted by, its now-forgotten political significance. Even in its own time, the opera circulated in a variety of guises thanks to the many touchy government censorships that held sway in post-Napoleonic Europe. It was banned outright in French Protestant cities; in Vienna, and later in St. Petersburg, it became *The Guelphs and the Ghibellines* with the action transferred to thirteenth-century Italy; in Munich the setting was changed to seventeenth-century England and the warring factions became Anglicans and Puritans.

But whatever the ostensible subject, a composer's colleagues, rivals, and progeny constitute an audience in their own right, one that (like all audiences) receives its impressions selectively and reads opportunistically, according to its predilections and its needs. So the other irony — that the list of Meyerbeer's debtors contains some who were far from his professed admirers — is in the end not so surprising. Most noteworthy is the prominence among them of Richard Wagner, whose hostility to Meyerbeer was of a piece with his denigration of Mendelssohn.

In *Das Judenthum in der Musik*, Wagner steered clear of naming Meyerbeer's name as well as his own (probably because Meyerbeer was then technically an employee of the Prussian court and enjoyed its protection), but nobody had any trouble guessing the identity of "a far-famed Jew composer of our day" who "has addressed himself and his products to a section of our public whose total confusion of musical taste was less caused by him than exploited by him to his profit." This charlatan "writes operas for Paris, and sends them touring round the world." His is an art designed to titillate "that section of our citizen society whose only reason for attending the opera is utter boredom." His success, Wagner argued, is "proof of the ineptitude of the present musical epoch," since "the Jews could never have taken possession of our art until our art began to show signs of what they have now demonstrably brought to light — namely, its inner incapacity for life."

To clinch the point, Wagner triumphantly asserted that "so long as the art of Music had a real organic life-need in it, down to the epochs of Mozart and Beethoven, there was nowhere to be found a Jew composer," just as "at the time when Goethe and Schiller sang among us, we certainly knew nothing of a poetizing Jew."[21] In other words, Wagner claimed, it was not a change in the legal and social status of affluent Jews (their so-called emancipation) that made possible their participation in the arts, but rather the degeneration of the arts themselves, which had degraded them to a level susceptible to Jewish infiltration.

This diatribe did not go unanswered. One answer, appearing in the same journal as the original screed, went beyond the defense or vindication of individuals. Instead, it managed to engage Wagner's (or "Herr Freigedank's") arguments at a profound and culturally significant level. The author, Eduard Bernsdorf, was a member of a distinguished German family of diplomats. (His nephew, who called himself Johann-Heinrich von Bernstorff, served as German ambassador to Washington in the years immediately preceding the First World War.) Bernsdorf's main point was that Wagner's diagnosis of the state of contemporary art and society was accurate, but that it was merely witless scapegoating to attribute it all to Jewish influence. "What he says about Meyerbeer is in many respects true," Bernsdorf allowed, "but not because Meyerbeer is a Jew but because Meyerbeer is a man of the nineteenth century."[22]

A man of the nineteenth century—a "modern man," that is, in the eyes of contemporaries—meant a beneficiary of progress in commerce and technology. The works of Meyerbeer—or rather their success—epitomized this benefit. Nineteenth-century improvements in transport and communications (e.g., the railroad, the telegraph) shrank distances dramatically, and enabled a truer cosmopolitanism than ever before. Of this, too, Meyerbeer had been a conspicuous beneficiary. A great deal of romantic ideology—especially where it involved the purity of nations and ethnicities (and particularly where it took on an exclusionary or xenophobic tinge, as it did with Wagner)—was a direct reaction to this new cosmopolitanism born of urbanization and improved communications. In many ways, then, romanticism had become antimodern and reactionary. This was the kind of romanticism Wagner's tract espoused.

And to such romantics, the Jew—who had achieved civil rights and emerged as a force in gentile society concurrently with (and partly as a result of) urbanization as well as the technological and commercial modernization of Europe—became the symbol of everything they found threatening in modern life. Defenders of German *Kultur* began to see Jews not only as tainted by commerce ("merchants") and as spreaders of "modernity," but as the henchmen of the hated French with their cosmopolitan mores and their unregenerate Enlightened "civilization." What better focal point for such a phobia, then, than "a far-famed Jew composer" who "writes operas for Paris, and sends them touring round the world"?

These ancient debates would hardly merit airing in a book like this if they were merely ancient debates. Sadly, however, aspects of Wagner's anti-Semitic diatribe (motivated partly by personal spite, Meyerbeer having been his indispensable benefactor but having ceased his financial support in 1846) continue to surface, sometimes unwittingly, in present-day discussions of Meyerbeer, and continue, often unwittingly, to influence contemporary thinking about art. The most influential music history text of the mid-twentieth century (and still in print), Paul Henry Lang's *Music in Western Civilization*, paraphrases Wagner almost word for word, imputing the same "boredom" to Meyerbeer's audience (in a quote cribbed from Voltaire): "One goes to see a tragedy to be moved, to the Opéra one goes either for want of any other interest or to facilitate digestion."[23]

Then comes a fusillade of dated antibourgeois rhetoric, presented (one hopes) in naive ignorance of its former status as anti-Semitic code: Meyerbeer's operas were "written and composed for the use of merchants"; his work represented "the invasion of the bourgeois spirit, the pursuit of money and pleasure," which "abolished the sincere atmosphere of the first fervors of the romantic movement"; they represented the sinister intrusion of "a foreigner" into the domain of French art, when "a certain Jacob Liebmann Beer came to France" and "deliberately set out to utilize the weaknesses of the French character"; they are not a legitimate genre because they lack "a foundation in nature."[24] The only thing missing is Wagner's magnificent string of epithets summing up what he (and many since) perceived as the cynicism of *Les Huguenots*, the opera to which he was most indebted, and that consequently caused him the most distress: "a monstrous piebald, historico-romantic, diabolico-religious, fanatico-libidinous, sacro-frivolous, mysterio-criminal, autolytico-sentimental dramatic hotchpotch."[25]

But the worst of it, for the Germans, was the fact that so much of the music in *Les Huguenots* seemed to be deliberately ugly. "The horrible is Meyerbeer's element," wrote Robert Schumann, another composer-turned-journalist, when the work was given in Leipzig in 1837.[26] That made Meyerbeer, in German eyes, not a romantic but another base realist, willing to sacrifice art's transcendent domain to the depiction of grim, filthy, or (worst of all) ordinary reality. The other side of realism was the importation into art of the musical artifacts of "external reality," made all the more intolerable in the case of *Les Huguenots* by the fact that one of these artifacts was a Protestant chorale—indeed the most famous of all chorales, Luther's own *Ein' feste Burg*, invoked not for its spiritual content but as a trademark to identify the Protestant faction.

Literally from the beginning of the opera (the Overture) to the end (the act V massacre), *Ein' feste Burg* haunts the opera (see Ex. 36-11), sometimes merely quoted (for example, by the doughty old Marcel in act 1), sometimes "developed" (as in the massacre). All parties to the device—composer, audience, critics—were aware that it was not historically "true" to use a Lutheran melody to represent the Calvinist Huguenots. The melody was selected not for its literal truth but for its "verisimilitude"—a distinction that is crucial to an understanding of artistic realism.

What is "verisimilar" is what *seems* true (*vraisemblable* in French), not necessarily what *is* true. When it came to musical "semiosis"—the creation of musical "signs"—what counted above all was legibility: not "is it the literal truth?" but "can it be read?" Only *Ein' feste Burg*, Meyerbeer realized, would instantly and automatically register with uninitiated audiences as "Protestant." Within the context of the artwork it alone, consequently, would elicit a "true" response. That is why another name for verisimilitude is "artistic truth." What is most important to realize is that artistic truth was as "real" a truth as any other kind. For one thing, it immediately set at nought all political censorship. Hearing *Ein' feste Burg* ring out in an opera retitled *The Guelphs and Ghibellines* immediately erased the censor's cover and revealed the work's "true" and original intent.

So it was not the actual, factual falsity of the symbol that made it anathema to German romantics, but rather the profane use to which Meyerbeer had put it, as well as the potentially corrupting effect such a usage might have on the audience. "I am no moralist," Schumann wrote, moralizing, "but it enrages a good Protestant to hear his dearest chorale shrieked out on the boards, to see the bloodiest drama in the whole history of his religion degraded to the level of an annual fair farce, in order to raise money and noise with it." And even more pointedly, "one is often inclined to grasp one's brow, to feel whether all up there is in the right condition, when one reflects on Meyerbeer's success in healthy, musical Germany."

This time, however, there was no question of anti-Semitic code, because the work with which Schumann invidiously contrasted Meyerbeer's degrading spectacle was Mendelssohn's *Paulus*, "a work of pure art," in which "the resumption of the chorale," as Schumann put it, served the purposes of true religious feeling and, beyond that, the expression of *das innerliche Herz*, "the inward heart," romantic art's only true domain.[27]

III. PEASANTS AND HISTORY (RUSSIA)

A NEWCOMER TO THE TRADITION

Perhaps the most piquant case history involving the relationship between music (particularly opera) and ideas of nationhood was that of Russia, which emerged as a European musical "power" at about the same point in its history as its emergence as a political and diplomatic power. Consequential musical contacts between Russia and Western Europe were a result of the "Westernizing" campaign of Tsar Peter I ("the Great," reigned 1682–1725), and mainly occurred, to begin with, in Peter's new capital,

EX. 36-11A   *Ein' feste Burg* in *Les Huguenots*, Overture, mm. 1–13

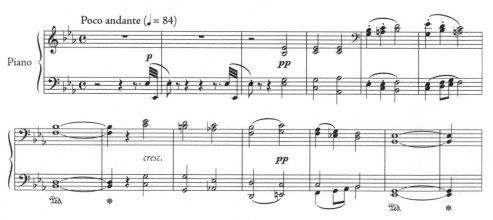

St. Petersburg, named for the Tsar's patron saint. Over the course of a rough century beginning in the 1730s, Russia participated in the musical commerce of Europe first as a consumer only, then as a producer for home consumption, and finally as an exporter.

Since the period in which Russia emerged as a musical power was precisely the period when Herderian ideas about the essential reality of national character — and

EX. 36-11B   *Ein' feste Burg* in *Les Huguenots*, Act I, "Choral"

the merits of cultural difference—were gaining credence, it is not surprising that the second phase of Russian participation, that of domestic production, should have placed a premium on national "markings," often secured by the incorporation of "natural artifacts" from the surrounding peasant culture, newly valued under Herder's influence.

EX. 36-11C   *Ein' feste Burg* in *Les Huguenots*, Act V, height of the massacre

The first published collection of transcribed Russian folk songs (*narodnïye pesni*, a term directly translated from Herder's *Volkslieder*), arranged for voice and parlor piano, was issued in 1790. It was compiled by an aristocratic admirer of Herder named Nikolai Lvov, with musical arrangements contributed by a hired hand, an immigrant Bohemian pianist named Johann Gottfried (or Jan Bogumir) Pratsch. The Lvov-Pratsch collection immediately became an avidly mined quarry of raw thematic material for composers in the European tradition (including such Europeans as Beethoven, who mined it for his "Razumovsky" Quartets, op. 59).

Later, when Russia became a musical exporter in its own right, the cultural-commercial value of its product was much enhanced by its exoticism, providing another incentive for national coloration. Utilizing Russian peasant lore within literate or "fine-art" musical products is often seen as an example of Russian "nationalism" in music, and the term can be justified in various contexts so long as it is not forgotten that the nations of Western Europe were just as nationalistic as Russia in the post-Napoleonic period. Indeed, Russia received its notions about national character, and its nationalistic aspirations, from the West; Russian "nationalistic" music has therefore to be regarded as an aspect of the country's musical Westernization.

For the only Russian music to which the word "nationalistic" is ever applied is the music composed by urban Russians with elite Western training, in Western forms, and for Western media. The truly indigenous music of Russia, that is its folk music, is never called nationalistic, because it has no sense of an "other" against which its character is to be measured, and without a sense of the other there cannot any true self-consciousness. "And what should they know of England who only England know?"[28] asked the British poet Rudyard Kipling in the heyday of imperialist expansion. The same question is worth asking of any country that seeks national self-assertion, whether in art, in politics, or in art politics.

In any event, no other country was ever more conscious of the power and value of musical "semiosis" — musical "sign" language, often involving the appropriation of musical symbols "from life" — than Russia. As long as there has been a significant school of Russian composers in the European art music tradition, there has been a musically defined mythology of the Russian nation and its history, and it has often sought expression through the incorporation — or more precisely, the "professional assimilation" — of folklore.

The presence of that "significant school" in Russia is often dated precisely to the year 1836, the same year that witnessed the Paris premiere of *Les Huguenots*. And the crucial event that gave that year its significance in Russian musical history was also an operatic premiere: that of *A Life for the Tsar*, a "patriotic heroic-tragic opera" by Mikhail Ivanovich Glinka (1804–57).

This was not by a long way the first Russian opera, let alone the first opera premiered in Russia. The history of music as a continuously practiced secular fine art in the European literate tradition begins for Russia in the year 1735, ten years after the death of Peter the Great, when his niece, the Empress Anne (or Anna Ioannovna, reigned 1730–40), decided to import a resident troupe of Italian opera singers to adorn her court with elegant imported entertainments. Anne's operatic project could be called a continuation of Peter's legacy into a new cultural sphere.

The main reasons why Russia had stood culturally apart from Western Europe until the advent of Peter the Great were two: first, Russia accepted Christianity (in 988) from Byzantium, the seat of the Greek (Eastern) Orthodox Church; and second, from around 1240 until 1480 Russia was ruled as a conquered territory by the Mongol empire, from a seat in Central Asia. Under the suzerainty of an Islamic empire, the Russians and their local rulers, while still Christian, were for two centuries politically and economically cut off from all other Christian states. By the time the Muscovite princes were able to shake off their Muslim overlords, Byzantium and all the former Greek territories had fallen to the Ottoman Turks, another Islamic empire. Thus Russia had become an isolated Orthodox power, and took pride in viewing itself as the "Third Rome," the true seat of Christendom.

Up to the time of Peter, virtually the only literate musical tradition in Russia was that of Church chant and its derivative polyphonic genres, preserved in a neumatic notation of a kind that had not been used in Western Europe since the days of the Carolingians. So alien was the secular art music of the West from any indigenous Russian music that the Russian vocabulary distinguished radically between the two. Russian chant was called *peniye* ("singing"). All Western art music, whether vocal or instrumental, was called *musika*, later changed to *muzïka*. (The sign *ï* represents a Russian vowel similar to the English short *i*, but pronounced much further back in the mouth; in Russian transliterations, the letter *i* stands for the same sound as the Italian *i*, namely the English long *e*.)

The first Russian *musika* treatises and practical scores, which began appearing in the late seventeenth century, disseminated what was known as *partesnoye peniye* ("part-singing") or *khorovïye kontsertï* ("choral concertos"): that is, *a cappella* adaptations of Venetian-style "concerted" motets for the use of Orthodox choirs in what is now the Ukraine, an area bordering on Catholic Poland. (They had to be *a cappella* because the Orthodox Church, strictly interpreting the last line of Psalm 150—"Let everything that has breath praise the Lord!"—forbade the use of inanimate instruments for divine praises.) One of these treatises, the *Grammatika musikiyskaya* (1675) by the Ukrainian singer and composer Nikolai Diletsky, has the curious distinction (as we have known since chapter 24) of containing the earliest graphic representation of the complete chromatic circle of fifths.

The earliest indigenous secular genre of *muzïka* practiced in Russia was called the *kant*. *Kanty* were simply songs in *partesnoye peniye* or choral concerto style furnished with secular texts of any kind. These genres were short-lived and fairly primitive attempts at hybridizing native Russian genres with high-prestige Western styles.

The Italian opera, though at first a wholly imported court luxury that had no contact at all with native genres (or even native musicians), eventually took root and thrived. The first opera to have its premiere on Russian soil was *Il finto Nino, overo La Semiramide riconosciuta* ("The feigned child;" or, "Semiramis recognized"), an *opera seria* by Franceso Araja or Araia (1709–70), the Naples-born maestro of Anne's troupe.

(Should this be called the first Russian opera?) Araja stayed in St. Petersburg until 1762, through the reigns of Anne and her three immediate successors. In 1755, he composed an *opera seria*, *Tsefal i Prokris* ("Cephalus and Procris"), to a libretto in Russian by the court poet Alexander Sumarokov (1718–77), to be enacted before the court of the Empress Elizabeth by a cast of serfs. (Or was this "the first Russian opera"?)

Araja was succeeded, during the long reign of the Empress Catherine II ("the Great," reigned 1762–96) by a very distinguished line of St. Petersburg *maestri di cappella*: Vincenzo Manfredini (served 1762–65), Baldassare Galuppi (1765–68), Tommaso Traetta (1768–75), Giovanni Paisiello (1776–83), Giuseppe Sarti (1784–1801, with interruptions), Domenico Cimarosa (1787–91), and Vincente Martín y Soler (1790–1804, with interruptions). These were among the biggest names in all of Europe. Catherine lured them to her cold, remote capital by offering them huge "hardship wages," and they definitely put St. Petersburg (which in terms of international diplomacy stood for all of Russia) on the international musical map. One of the most famous operas of the late eighteenth century, Paisiello's *Barber of Seville* (1782), had its premiere in the Russian capital. Sarti, Catherine's special favorite, was Mozart's closest rival in fame and prestige (as Mozart acknowledged by quoting his music in *Don Giovanni*).

Two changes that took place under Catherine had far-reaching, if not necessarily intended, significance for the eventual growth of a national school of composition. First, comic operas (often French ones, with spoken dialogue) were performed at Catherine's court alongside the more serious Italian fare. And second, native-born composers began to receive training from the maestri, mostly in order to furnish modest comic operas in the Frenchy popular style that the maestri felt it beneath their dignity to compose.

Thus the first European-style comic opera by a native composer to receive performance in Russia was *Anyuta* ("Little Annie"), a *comédie mêlée d'ariettes* presented at the empress's summer residence in 1772, in which the vocal numbers were sung to the tunes of well-known folk or popular tunes. It was modeled, by one of Catherine's court poets, directly on a French favorite called *Annette et Lubin*. The musical arrangements, by a composer whose name has been forgotten, have not survived, but the work, artistically insignificant as it must have been, is historically famous because according to some people's definition, *this* was "the first Russian opera."

Meanwhile, two talented Ukrainian-born lads, Maxim Berezovsky (1745–77) and Dmitri Bortnyansky (1751–1825), were sent by Catherine in the late 1760s (probably after apprenticeship with Galuppi) to complete their studies in Italy with the famous Bolognese pedagogue "Padre" Giovanni Battista Martini. Both of them had opera seria performed in Italy before returning to Russia and being put to work modernizing (that is, Italianizing) the repertoire of the Imperial Chapel Choir, replacing traditional *peniye* with arty Italianate *muzïka*. Berezovsky's opera, *Demofoonte* (1773), to a libretto by Metastasio himself, received performance first. As the earliest opera by a native Russian composer with an entirely original score (albeit sung in Italian, and never performed in Russia), maybe this was "the first Russian opera."

Or maybe that distinction belongs to *Misfortune on Account of a Coach* (*Neschast'ye ot karetï*, 1779), an *opéra comique* (or singspiel, or whatever) by Vasily Pashkevich

(1742–97), one of Catherine's court musicians, which was the first opera by a native Russian composer (unless, as his surname seems to suggest, he turns out to have been a Polish immigrant) to a Russian libretto, performed in Russia. By the end of the century there were dozens of Russian musical comedies by Russian composers in existence, some of them quite elaborate and expertly composed.

By the time *A Life for the Tsar* was produced, they numbered in the hundreds and included a few that could bear comparison with the finest German singspiels. At least one — *Askold's Grave* (*Askol'dova mogila*, 1835) by Alexey Nikolayevich Verstovsky (1799–1862) — counts as a full-fledged "Russian romantic opera," fully comparable (indeed heavily indebted) to Weber's *Der Freischütz*. So why was Glinka's opera immediately greeted (in the words of the novelist Nikolai Gogol) as "a wonderful beginning"?[29] And why does Glinka, rather than Verstovsky, now have such an unshakeable historical position as the founding father of the "Russian national school"?

Glinka's was not even the first Russian opera to employ a markedly "Russian" (that is, folkishly Russian) style. Such a style was virtually built into the Russian singspiel genre, which as far back as *Anyuta* had employed popular songs to match their stock of peasant or otherwise lowborn characters, just as popular, folk, or folk-style (*volkstümlich*) tunes were doing in comic operas everywhere in Europe. They normally featured at least one "Papageno type" as a matter of course, and a Papageno had to sing folk songs, whether real or invented.

A vivid example of the Russian brand of this standard-issue eighteenth-century *Volkstümlichkeit* comes from *Yamshchiki na podstave* ("The post-coachmen at the relay station," 1787), with words by Count Lvov (soon to compile his folk-song anthology), and music by an emancipated serf, Yevstigney Fomin, whose backwoods given name betrays his peasant origins. This number shows a trio of rustics named Timofey, Yan'ka, and Fadeyevna (Timothy, Johnny, and "Thaddeus's little girl") going into a dance to entertain their owner, the local *barin* (landowning lord). Verisimilitude is achieved by the use of a famous tune ("The Birch Tree") that became more and more famous over the course of the nineteenth century as composer after composer borrowed it for local color, and by the use of pizzicato strings to imitate the balalaika, a sort of triangular-bellied Russian banjo (Ex. 36-12).

Glinka's music never got any more "Russian" than this. Likewise, *Askold's Grave*, whose composer Verstovsky outlived Glinka and could never understand his rival's immediately recognized historical status, much less come to terms with it, contains a wealth of beguiling choral "fakesongs" (well-counterfeited folk songs) to characterize the opera's peasants. One of them (Ex. 36-13), called "The Moon Shone at Midnight," is sung in authentic responsorial style, with a solo "intoner" (*zapevala*) and a choir that answers in rough-hewn "harmonizations" (*podgoloski*, literally "undervoices"). Others show the slippery modal "mutability" (*peremennost'* in Russian) exhibited by many Russian folk songs, with cadences that alternate between the tonic and the "natural minor" seventh degree. These choruses are every bit as authentically "national" as anything Glinka ever wrote. They display many idiosyncrasies of performance style, like the "voice-throwings" or octave leaps at the ends of phrases, that are neatly drawn from life. So why, finally, did Glinka and not Verstovsky get the credit for ushering true *narodnost'* (nationhood) into Russian musical art and thereby establishing the Russian national school? Did it have to do with something more (or at least other) than folklore?

For answers to these questions we must turn to contemporary witnesses. In a review that appeared in a Moscow newspaper shortly after the premiere of *A Life for the Tsar*, a would-be composer named Yanuariy Neverov, who had studied briefly in Berlin and had his head stuffed full of Herderian romanticism, declared that "delightful Russian tunes" by themselves would never create a truly national style. For that you needed more than tunes; in fact you needed more than a musical style. You had to achieve the "organic unity" that comes from a "dominating idea."[30] Glinka, in other words, was

EX. 36-12 Yevstigney Fomin, *Yamshchiki na podstave*, no. 8

truly *narodnïy* (nation-embodying) because he was ideologically, not merely decoratively, *narodnïy*. He used his folk or folklike melodies, in a manner that precisely corresponded to the difference between Mozart's *Volkstümlichkeit* and Weber's, or between the peasant folksiness of the Enlightenment and the national folksiness of romanticism, not merely to evoke a pleasant peasant flavor or provide a tasty condiment to the main dramatic course, but to evoke an all-encompassing idea of Russia that lay at the heart of the dramatic conception. That, and only that, was true *narodnost'*.

Neverov, and many others since, have noted that, paradoxically enough, there is actually less direct quotation of folk sources, less purely stylistic *Volkstümlichkeit*, in Glinka than in Verstovsky, or in many a forgotten eighteenth-century singspiel. His greater *narodnost'*, according to Neverov, came not from literal imitation of reality but, in true romantic fashion, from his own *innerliche Herz*, which, like that of any artistic genius, had been formed in the spirit of his nation. "Mr. Glinka has set about things differently" from Verstovsky, the critic wrote. "He has looked deeply into the character of our folk music, has observed all its characteristics, has studied and assimilated it — and then has given full freedom to his own fantasy," thus producing "images that are purely Russian, native, clear, comprehensible, familiar to us simply because they breathe a pure *narodnost'*, because we hear in them native sounds." But also because "all these Russian images are created by the composer in such a way that *in the aggregate*, in their cohesion, they have been marshalled and deployed in defense of Russia."[31]

There is a lot here to unpack, even before we get to the musical text itself. In the first place, Neverov is calling attention to Glinka's greater seriousness and his mastery of a self-consciously advanced international technique. This last was absolutely unprecedented in a Russian musician. To Neverov, *A Life for the Tsar*, and nothing

E X. 36-13   Alexey Nikolayevich Verstovsky, *Askold's Grave*, no. 10

earlier, was "the first Russian opera," simply because it was the first Russian opera that was truly an opera, not a singspiel. It is sung throughout, thus becoming the first Russian opera to employ accompanied recitative as well as the full range of arias and ensembles. It competed ambitiously with the operas of Europe on every front, overcoming all taint of provincialism and successfully combining the virtues of many national schools.

Not only because of its musical continuity, but also because of its large-scale virtuoso vocal numbers in accelerating tempos, its multipartite ensembles and monumental finales, *A Life for the Tsar* demonstrated its composer's complete mastery of what in chapter 33 was called the "Code Rossini," the full panoply of sophisticated Italian conventions. But the opera was also "French" in its liberal use of "recalling themes," its ample choruses, and its popular tone, all characteristics of the old "rescue" genre, and of the nascent *grand opéra* as well, showing Glinka to have been entirely up-to-date, abreast of all the latest European developments. There is even a second-act ballet, just as there would have had to be in Paris. And finally, the opera was "German" in its harmonic complexity and the prominence accorded its rich, colorful orchestra. It had bigness and greatness stamped all over it. It was, in short, a bid for recognition as a major player on the world stage, such as Russia herself was making in post-Napoleonic European diplomacy.

Glinka's *narodnost'* was thus paradoxically proved by his cosmopolitan eclecticism. But this seems more paradoxical to us than it did to the composer's contemporaries. Combining or "organically" uniting the best of the West — or, more generally, the best of the rest — was one highly preferred way of asserting Russianness (*narodnost'*) for members of Glinka's and Neverov's generation. It affirmed the universality of Russian culture, hence its superiority to all other cultures. Thus Neverov could praise Glinka's recitatives (the one area in which he had no competition from any other Russian composer) as the world's finest, because "they unite the expressivity and dramatic flexibility of the German with the melodiousness of the Italian."

It was a deliberate synthesis of opposites at which Glinka was aiming. To recall the anti-Rossinian strictures of Prince Odoyevsky, the "Russian Hoffmann" and a friend of Glinka's (quoted in chapter 33), Russians drew an even sharper distinction than the Germans themselves between the "spirituality" of German romanticism and the "sensuality" of Italian opera. In German this was the opposition of *Geist* and *Sinnlichkeit*; the Russian equivalents were *dukh* and *chuvstvennost'*. German music in Russian eyes was all *dukh*, brains without beauty; Italian music was all *chuvstvennost'*, beauty without brains. Glinka resolved that his music, Russian music, would uniquely have both brains and beauty.

Because he grew up in a country that until the 1860s lacked the institutional means for training professional composers (i.e., conservatories), Glinka is often looked upon as a "naive" or self-taught composer, with all the limitations on technique that would seem to imply. That is a serious misapprehension. Despite a late start, and despite his being, as an aristocrat, an avocational musician (the only kind that in early nineteenth-century Russia had the leisure to indulge in composition), Glinka had an exceptionally well-rounded professional education in music — but one acquired the old-fashioned way, by apprenticeship and practical experience.

FIG. 36-8   Glinka conducting a chamber ensemble, in a drawing by V. Tauber.

After childhood and adolescent music instruction in piano and violin, both on his ancestral estate and at an exclusive boarding school in St. Petersburg, and after teaching himself the rudiments of form and orchestration by rehearsing and conducting his uncle's serf orchestra in the classical repertory, Glinka apprenticed himself at the age of twenty-four to Leopoldo Zamboni, the principal coach for the visiting Italian opera troupe, briefly mentioned in chapter 33, that was headed by Leopoldo's father Luigi, a famous *buffo* bass who had "created" the role of Figaro in Rossini's *Barber of Seville*. Zamboni schooled his local apprentice in the forms and conventions of Italian opera, as well as elementary counterpoint. Over the next two years Glinka attended the rehearsals and the extremely idiomatic Zamboni-led St. Petersburg performances of over a dozen Rossini operas.

In 1830 Glinka went abroad for an extended stay. In Milan he became personally acquainted with Bellini and Donizetti and under their supervision wrote creditable imitations of their work. Thus he acquired beauty. Then he went after brains, making straight for the Teutonic source. He spent the winter of 1833–34 in Berlin, under the tutelage of Siegfried Dehn (1799–1858), the most sought-after German pedagogue of the day, who through a combination of strict counterpoint and idealistic aesthetics "not only put my knowledge in order, but also my ideas on art,"[32] as Glinka would put it in his memoirs. He returned to Russia shortly before his thirtieth birthday, the possessor of a fully professional, perhaps uniquely cosmopolitan, European technique.

And on top of all that he was "ideologically Russian." The final element in the mix that made Glinka's opera the foundation of a national school had only marginally to do with musical style, but everything to do with the specific Russian concept of *narodnost'* (nationhood) that then reigned. While it clothed itself, like all such romantic notions, in the rhetoric of antiquity, the *narodnost'* embodied in Glinka's opera was a brand-new doctrine, promulgated as part of the general, Europe-wide post-Napoleonic reaction by Tsar Nikolai I (reigned 1825–55), the most reactionary crowned head on the continent. It was no progressive thing.

On the second of April 1833, Count Sergey Uvarov, the Tsar's newly appointed minister of education, circulated a letter to the heads of all educational districts in the Russian empire, stating that "our common obligation consists in this, that the education of the people be conducted, according to the Supreme intention of our August Monarch, in the joint spirit of Orthodoxy, autocracy, and nationhood."[33] This troika of interdependent values to which Russians would henceforth be expected to subscribe — *pravoslaviye, samoderzhaviye, narodnost'* in Russian — was formulated thus in direct rebuttal to the familiar French revolutionary slogan, *Liberté, Égalité, Fraternité* ("liberty, equality, fraternity"). In this company *narodnost'* would function as "a worthy tool of the government,"[34] as Uvarov put it, or (as quite accurately, if maliciously, paraphrased in Soviet times) as "an ideological weapon in support of serfdom and autocracy."[35] The "Russian nation" was conceived entirely in dynastic and religious terms, autocracy (absolute monarchy) being related to Orthodoxy as "the ultimate link between the power of man and the power of God."

These last words were written by Vasily Zhukovsky (1783–1852), Glinka's friend and mentor, who was himself an outstanding romantic poet as well as a government censor, and who authored the text to the fifth act or epilogue of *A Life for the Tsar*, a magnificent pageant of religious veneration that celebrates the birth of the nation in the person of the tsar. This was the brand of "nationalism" — Official Nationalism, as it came to be called — that was embodied in Uvarov's slogan, in Zhukovsky's poetry, in Glinka's opera, and in Neverov's critique.

Immediately after his return to Russia in 1834, Glinka joined Zhukovsky's literary salon. "When I declared my ambition to undertake an opera in Russian," Glinka recalled in his memoirs, "Zhukovsky sincerely approved of my intention and suggested the subject of Ivan Susanin."[36] It was a predictable choice, even an inevitable one. For one of the cornerstones of Official Nationalism was the creation of a romantic national mythology, "a sense of the present based on a remodeled past," in the apt words of Hubert Babinski, a historian of Russian literature. "Legend and history," Babinski continues,

> were a pleasing combination, and one sees among some Poles and Russians of this time that odd cultural phenomenon in which a legendary past is created to antedate and form a basis for recorded history. Not having an *Iliad* or an *Aeneid* [that is, an authentic national epic], they wrote their own mythical past from folklore, inspired by Herder's idea of creating a national consciousness out of national myths.[37]

Glinka's maiden opera, the first Russian opera that was really an opera and the earliest to achieve permanent repertory status, hence the cornerstone of the national repertory, was created out of just such a didactic mythography.

The legend of Ivan Susanin had a tenuous documentary basis: a concession conferred in 1619 by Tsar Mikhail Fyodorovich on a peasant named Bodgan Sobinin, and renewed to Sobinin's heirs by every subsequent ruler all the way down to Nikolai I, granting dispensation from certain taxes and obligations in recognition of the merits of Sobinin's father-in-law, Ivan Susanin, who,

> suffering at the hands of said Polish and Lithuanian persons immeasurable torments on Our account, did not tell said Polish and Lithuanian persons where

We were at the time, and said Polish and Lithuanian persons did torture him to death.[38]

That is to say, the peasant Ivan Susanin had at the cost of his life concealed from a Polish search party the whereabouts of Mikhail Fyodorovich, the sixteen-year-old scion of an old noble family named Romanov, who had been elected tsar by a popular assembly in February 1613, thus ending a "time of troubles" regarding the Russian succession and founding the Romanov dynasty that would rule Russia until 1917. The name of Ivan Susanin entered historical literature in 1792 and his heroic martyrdom was embroidered and immortalized by Sergey Nikolayevich Glinka, the composer's cousin, in his *Russian History for Purposes of Upbringing*, published in 1817, since which time it went into all children's textbooks and became part of every Russian's patriotic consciousness.

Timely parallels with Susanin's deed were suggested by the activities of peasant partisans in the Patriotic War of 1812 against Napoleon. In the aftermath of that war "Ivan Susanin" became a fixture of Russian romantic literature. There was even a singspiel on the subject by a transplanted Italian composer named Catterino Cavos, performed in 1815, the year of the post-Napoleonic restoration. Since a singspiel had to have a happy ending, Cavos's Susanin gets rescued at the last minute by a detachment of troops led by Sobinin. Glinka's tragic hero dies his historical death, hence the title of the opera. It was Tsar Nikolai's idea, actually; at first the opera was simply to be called *Ivan Susanin*. The direct participation of the tsar in its very naming suggests the context into which the opera should be placed. It reflects above all Glinka's enthusiastic commitment to the doctrine of Official Nationalism and his determination to embody it in symbolic sounds.

As the composer put it in his memoirs, his root conception of the drama's shape lay in the opposition of musical styles, Russian vs. Polish. This basic structural antithesis has many surface manifestations. The Poles (the hated "other") are at all times and places represented by stereotyped dance genres in triple meter (polonaise, mazurka) or highly syncopated duple (krakowiak). They express themselves only collectively, in impersonal choral declamation. Choral recitative was something Meyerbeer, too, was experimenting with; but Glinka's purpose was different. By never letting a Polish character sing as an individual person, he effectively "dehumanized" the enemy the way good war propaganda always does.

The "Russian" music (that is, the music the Russian characters get to sing) is at all times highly personal and lyrical. To a very small extent — two instances, both involving the title character — it draws upon existing folk melodies. Susanin's very first *réplique* (sung line) in act 1 — "How can you think of getting married at a time like this?" (addressed to his daughter Antonida and Sobinin) — is based on a tune Glinka once heard a coachman sing, and which he noted down in his memoirs (Ex. 36-14a; Fig. 36-9). At the other end of the opera, the triumphant moment when Susanin reveals to the Poles that he has led them all to their death in the woods instead of to the tsar, motives from the same tune are accompanied by a basso ostinato (Ex. 36-14b) derived from one of the most famous Russian folk songs, "Downstream on Mother Volga" ("Vniz po matushke po Volge," Ex. 36-14c).

EX. 36-14A   Folklore in Mikhail Ivanovich Glinka's *A Life for the Tsar*, Susanin's "Chto gadat' o svad'be"

How can there be a wedding when such a storm is brewing?

EX. 36-14B   Folklore in Mikhail Ivanovich Glinka's *A Life for the Tsar*, Susanin's "Tuda zavyol ya vas"

I have taken you where not even the grey wolf ever runs.

The only other demonstrably folkloric element in the opera (just as in Verstovsky's operas) were the choruses. One of them, a girls' wedding song in act III, while set to an original melody, translates the traditional five-syllable (*pentonic*) line of actual peasant wedding songs into a five-beat meter notated with a time signature of $\frac{5}{4}$, one of the earliest such usages in European art music (Ex. 36-14d). Otherwise, the Russian

EX. 36-14C   Folklore in Mikhail Ivanovich Glinka's *A Life for the Tsar*, "Vniz po matushke po Volge"

Down the mother Volga, along its wide expanse...

EX. 36-14D   Folklore in Mikhail Ivanovich Glinka's *A Life for the Tsar*, Girls' chorus: "Razgulyalasya, razlivalasya"

music is modeled on the idiom of the contemporary sentimental "romance," an urban professional genre in which the Russian folk melos had been put through an Italianate refinery. Again, the objective was not to be "authentic," but "legible" to an audience of urban operagoers. Legibility, in short, *meant* authenticity.

FIG. 36-9   Coachman's song (quoted in the first line Susanin sings in *A Life for the Tsar*) as jotted by Glinka in the manuscript of his memoirs.

Very much in the manner of the *grand opéra*, the rhythm of the contrast between Russian and Polish musics unfolds at first at the rate of entire acts. After a first act consisting of Russian peasant choruses and romancelike arias and ensembles for the principles, the second act is entirely given over to Polish dances. Thereafter the rhythm of contrast is accelerated to reflect the mounting dramatic tension. The Poles' approach in act III is telegraphed by a few strategic orchestral allusions to the act II polonaise. Their colloquies with Susanin in acts III and IV are always couched (on both sides) in stereotyped generic terms. At the tensest moment in act III, where the Poles forcibly seize Susanin and he cries out "God, save the Tsar!" Polish (triple) and Russian (duple) rhythms are briefly superimposed (Ex. 36-15).

Far more important than the sheer amount of folk or folklike material in the score is the use to which the material is put. This was Glinka's great breakthrough, and the reason why he is fairly regarded by Russian music historiography as a founding father. As Rossini-hating Prince Odoyevsky was first to discern and celebrate, what

EX. 36-15   Mikhail Ivanovich Glinka, *A Life for the Tsar*, Act III, montage of "Russian" and "Polish" styles

EX. 36-15   *(continued)*

— I fear nothing, not even death! I will lay down my life for the Tsar, for Russia!
— Damned mule, shall we kill him?
— What good would it do?
— We run others through for not knowing, so it'll serve him right

Glinka "proved" in *A Life for the Tsar* was that "Russian melody may be elevated to a tragic style." In so doing, Odoyevsky declared, Glinka had introduced "a new element in art," one that had repercussions not only for Russian music, but for all music in the European tradition.[39]

What Odoyevsky meant by "a new element" was that Glinka had *without loss of scale* integrated the national material into the stuff of his "heroic" drama instead of relegating it, as was customary, to the decorative periphery. Of the dramatic crux, including Susanin's act IV solo *scena*, which strongly resembles Florestan's dungeon scene in *Fidelio* (on which it may very well have been modeled), but where the national style is nevertheless particularly marked, Odoyevsky wrote, "One must hear it to be convinced of the feasibility of such a union, which until now has been considered an unrealizable dream."

One reason why it had been so considered, as we have seen, was that before Glinka Russian composers had never aspired to the tragic style at all. What made it "feasible" was that the main characters in Glinka's opera were all peasants, hence eligible, within the conventions of the day, to espouse a folkish idiom (even an Italianized, urbanized one). But the tragic style nevertheless ennobles Susanin. He is not "just" a peasant; he has become an embodiment of the nation, a veritable icon, and so had the Russian folk idiom.

But while this made the opera musically progressive, it remained politically and socially reactionary; for the most advanced of all of Glinka's musicodramatic techniques was one that enabled him to harp from beginning to end on the opera's overriding theme of zealous submission to divinely ordained dynastic authority. The epilogue, which portrays Mikhail Romanov's triumphant entrance into Moscow following Susanin's sacrifice and the rout of the Poles, is built around a choral anthem (Ex. 36-16; Glinka called it a "hymn-march") proclaimed by massed Meyerbeerian forces, including not one but two wind bands on stage, to a text by Zhukovsky that culminates in the following quatrain:

Slav'sya, slav'sya nash russkiy Tsar',	Glory, glory to thee our Russian Caesar,
Gospodom danniy nam Tsar'-gosudar'!	Our sovereign given us by God!
Da budet bessmerten tvoy tsarskiy rod!	May thy royal line be immortal!
Da im blagodenstvuyet russkiy narod!	May the Russian people prosper through it!

Glinka's setting of these words is in a recognizable "period" style — the style of the seventeenth- and eighteenth-century *kanty*, the three- and four-part polyphonic songs mentioned above as the earliest Westernized secular genre in Russian music.

EX. 36-16   Mikhail Ivanovich Glinka, *A Life for the Tsar*, Epilogue, mm. 1–16

EX. 36-16   (continued)

(Ironically, and possibly unknown to Glinka, their ancestry was part Polish.) In Peter the Great's time such songs, chorally sung, were often used for civic panegyrics, in which form they were known as "Vivats." The *Slav'sya* or "Glorification" theme in Ex. 36-16 is motivically — that is, "organically" — related to that of Susanin's retort to the Poles in Ex. 36-15 (on the defiant words *"ne strashus',"* "I'm not afraid"), which was derived in turn from the opening peasant chorus in act 1 (and through that relationship related to the opening phrase of the overture; see Ex. 36-17).

But that only begins to describe its unifying role. As the composer and critic Alexander Serov (1820–71) first pointed out in an essay published in 1859, the *Slav'sya* theme, which in nineteenth-century Russia became virtually a second national anthem, is foreshadowed throughout the opera wherever the topic of dynastic legitimacy (that is,

EX. 36-17A   Prefigurings of the *Slav'sya* theme in *A Life for the Tsar*, Epilogue, "Hymn-March," mm. 1–4

EX. 36-17B   Prefigurings of the *Slav'sya* theme in *A Life for the Tsar* Act I, opening chorus

(In blizzard, in storm)

the divine right of the tsar) is broached (Ex. 36-18). The approach is gradual, beginning in act I with a minor-mode reference to the first two bars of the theme when Susanin (seconded by the chorus) dreams of "A Tsar! A lawful Tsar!" In act III, when news arrives of Mikhail's election, Susanin and his household bless their good fortune by falling to their knees in prayer: "Lord! Love our Tsar! Make him glorious!"—and between their lines the strings insinuate the same fragment of the *Slav'sya* theme, only this time in the major. When later in the same act the Poles demand to be taken to the tsar, Susanin defies them with an extended if somewhat simplified snatch of the *Slav'sya* theme, disguised mainly in tempo, and sung in the "remote," hence highly emotional key of D♭ major:

Vïsok i svyat nash tsarskiy dom	Our Tsar's home is a high and holy place,
I krepost' bozhiya krugom!	Surrounded with God's staunch strength!
Pod neyu sila Rusi tseloy,	Beneath it is the power of all of Russia,
A na stene v odezhde beloy	And on the walls, dressed all in white,
Stoyat krïlatïye vozhdi!	Winged angels stand guard!

Thus *A Life for the Tsar* is thematically unified in both verbal and musical dimensions by the tenets of Official Nationalism. The irony, of course, is that Glinka adapted the techniques by which he achieved this broadly developed musicodramatic plan from the French rescue operas of the revolutionary period and applied them to an opera where rescue is thwarted, and in which the political sentiment was literally counterrevolutionary. No wonder, then, that the opera became the mandatory season opener for the Russian Imperial Theaters; and no wonder that the libretto had to be superseded under Soviet power (which had a censorship as strict as Nikolai's,

EX. 36-17C   Prefigurings of the *Slav'sya* theme in *A Life for the Tsar* beginning of Overture

EX. 36-18A   More prefigurings of the *Slav'sya* theme in *A Life for the Tsar* Act I, no. 4 (voices only)

EX. 36-18B   More prefigurings of the *Slav'sya* theme in *A Life for the Tsar* Act III, no. 11 (quartet)

but of a rather different political complexion) by a new one that replaced devotion to the Romanov dynasty with abstract commitment to national liberation, and to an anachronistically secular concept of the Russian nation.

That malleability, as we have had ample opportunity to observe, was highly characteristic of nineteenth-century "national" opera, which was the product of an intense, continuing, and never entirely settled negotiation between musical style and "extramusical" associations. But since such associations are never entirely lacking, and cannot be, it is finally inappropriate to call them extramusical. They are as much a part of the work as the notes. The meaning of the work arises out of a process of interpretation in which the relationship between the notes and the associations to which they give rise is in a perpetual state of definition and redefinition. And that is why interpretation requires both an object and an interpreting subject, and why, therefore, it can never be either entirely "objective" or entirely "subjective" to the exclusion of the other.

Virtuosos

PAGANINI AND LISZT

STIMULUS

The enlargement and social broadening of the musical public in response to new economic, demographic, and technological conditions was the great nineteenth-century musical change. Its most immediate effect, and one with an eventually profound if sometimes indirect influence on all performing and composing activity, is often called "the democratization of taste." Attitudes toward it vary with attitudes toward democracy itself. From the aristocratic standpoint the democratization of taste meant the debasement of taste. From the standpoint of the bourgeoisie it meant the enlivening, the enrichment, but above all the enhanced accessibility and social relevance of art.

From the point of view of artists, the democratization of taste meant a new competitiveness, as institutional or household patronage gave way to the collective patronage of a ticket-buying public. The surest road to success no longer lay in reaching high, toward a secure career-niche at the most exclusive social plane, but in reaching wide, "packing them in." The ability to astonish as well as move became paramount. The age, in short, of the itinerant virtuoso was born. We are still living in it.

There were always itinerant musicians — "wand'ring minstrels," vagabond players, street serenaders. The difference was that such musicians, especially the instrumentalists, had formerly subsisted at the margins of society, only remotely involved with the literate traditions we have been tracing, which were the product and preserve of the higher social echelons. The new nineteenth-century itinerants, by contrast, were the stars of the musical world, and took their place among the literate tradition's primary bearers and beneficiaries.

For our purposes, the line begins with the Italian violinist Niccolò Paganini (1782–1840). He was not the first of the new breed, to be sure, and came from the land that had the longest, most illustrious tradition of string virtuosity. But he made a career of unprecedented brilliance and notoriety, arousing in its wake an unprecedented degree of envy and zealous emulation that went far beyond the confines of his — or any particular — instrument. In the pithy summary of the violinist-historian Boris Schwarz, "by his development of technique, his exceptional skills and his extreme personal magnetism," Paganini "not only contributed to the history of the violin as its most famous virtuoso, but drew the attention of Romantic composers to the significance of virtuosity as an element of art."[1]

FIG. 37-1   Paganini, statuette by Jean-Pierre Dantan, 1832.

He was born in the northern coastal city of Genoa, then as now Italy's chief seaport and commercial center. As a transport hub Genoa received many foreign visitors, especially from Central Europe, for which it was the main trade outlet. And so it was that a flashy Polish violinist, August Duranowski, happened to give a concert at the Genoese church of San Filippo Neri and aroused the jealous admiration of the twelve-year-old Paganini, whose precocious talents were then just emerging, with his "multitude of technical tricks," as Paganini later confessed to a biographer.

The other main formative influence came directly from the "classical" tradition of Italian string virtuosity, when Paganini rediscovered *L'arte del violino*, a set of twelve concertos by Pietro Locatelli (1695–1764), published in Amsterdam in 1733, each sporting a pair of enormous unaccompanied cadenzas called *capricci ad libitum*. Paganini modeled his first published composition, *24 Caprices* for unaccompanied violin, directly on Locatelli's *capricci*, and even incorporated a theme from one of them into the first in his own set, as if flaunting his outdone predecessor as a trophy. The technical standard Paganini set with this publication was as much on the cutting edge of virtuosity as Locatelli's had been seventy years before, incorporating not only Duranowski's bag of tricks but a whole array of which Paganini was the inventor, and which, until the *Caprices* were published, nobody else could duplicate. They remain a benchmark of consummate virtuosity to this day.

All twenty-four are thought to have been completed by 1805, when Paganini was serving as court soloist to the Princess Elisa Baciocchi, Napoleon Bonaparte's sister, recently installed by her brother as viceroy in the Italian city-state of Lucca. By 1809, armed with the caprices, Paganini felt ready to renounce the security of a court appointment and ply his trade as a free musical entrepreneur in a style "calculated for the great masses" (as he put it to another violinist composer, Louis Spohr, for whom he declined to play in private).[2]

A patient, purposeful sort, Paganini confined his activities to Italy for almost twenty years before attempting the conquest of the European capitals. During this time he composed a number of concertos, which he would need for orchestral appearances in the big European centers, and, in 1820, published the caprices, with a half-deferential, half-challenging dedication *Agli artisti*, "to the artists," that is, his rivals. The book was met, probably just as Paganini hoped, with scorn and disbelief, and widely pronounced unplayable. In 1828, delayed longer than he intended by several serious illnesses that left him with a cadaverous look he would later turn famously to his advantage, Paganini finally headed across the Alps.

The first city on the invader's map was Vienna. A measure of his effect there can be found in the recollection of Schubert's friend Eduard Bauernfeld that in the aftermath of his one-and-only benefit concert (described in chapter 34), Schubert insisted on treating

Bauernfeld to one of Paganini's recitals, saying, "I have stacks of money now — so come on. We'll never hear his like again!"[3] (Afterward, Schubert wrote to another friend, "I have heard an angel sing.")[4] After appearances in Prague, then another Austrian city, Paganini hit the German states to the north, playing eleven concerts in Berlin alone. He appeared before Goethe in Weimar (the poet's response: "I have heard something meteoric"); before Heine (who left a fictional memoir of the occasion) in Hamburg; before Robert Schumann (then a budding composer, later a powerful critic) in Frankfurt; and (taking a detour) before Tsar Nikolai I in Warsaw. By now, having had all his teeth extracted on account of jaw disease, Paganini eschewed the use of dentures during concerts, to give his face an even more frightfully sunken aspect.

The only dissenting voice on record is that of old Spohr, who finally caught Paganini's act in Kassel: "In his composition and his style there is a strange mixture of consummate genius, childishness and lack of taste that alternately charms and repels."[5] But it is not clear that Paganini's admirers would have described him any differently; in the new spirit of the time the virtuoso actively cultivated repulsion as an aspect of his charm. It is an aspect of romanticism — (mis)labeled "realism" — that we have already observed in the work of Weber and Meyerbeer, among others.

Finally, in 1831, Paganini reached Paris, where his series of ten concerts at the new opera house inspired press scandals and slander campaigns as if to prove the completeness of his triumph. The same reception greeted him the next year in London, another city with a powerful press. But Paganini knew how to exploit publicity, responding to charges of venality by playing free concerts, reaping praise for his generosity and paeans for his playing, and then, having thus created a fury of demand, charging enormously inflated prices for his remaining appearances.

In Paris, Paganini made a conquest of another composer-critic in Hector Berlioz, who thought enough of Paganini to favor him not with the viola concerto that Paganini requested of him, but rather a big programmatic symphony (*Harold in Italy*) based on Lord Byron's poem *Childe Harold*, with a viola obbligato that symbolized the romantic loner, the archetype of the age, testifying to the new role the virtuoso protagonist was assuming at the pinnacle of modern art. The most fateful — indeed prophetic — encounter in Paris, however (though Paganini was not aware of it), was with the nineteen-year-old Franz Liszt, who, sitting unnoticed and incredulous in the hall, heard the great virtuoso perform the fabled caprices in addition to his Second Concerto.

And then, in 1834, after only six years, the whirlwind was over. Continued ill-health forced Paganini, now a wealthy man, back into semiretirement in Italy, where he briefly accepted a position — for a man of his means a sinecure, really — as *maestro di cappella* at the ducal court of Parma. Later, like Rossini before him but less luckily, he ventured into business, sponsoring an ill-fated gambling casino in Paris over which he lost a good part of his fortune. On his deathbed he refused the ministrations of a priest, for which reason the church denied him a religious burial. For five years his body was stored in a cellar in Nice, occupying a discarded olive oil vat, until the Grand Duchess of Parma intervened to have him interred. His dark exploits thus continued even after his death.

Needless to say, and for all sorts of reasons, Paganini was a legend in his lifetime. His effective international career lasted a mere six years, but its long-term historical impact must far exceed that of any other single-handed burst of musical activity of comparable duration. It went far beyond the matter of his instrumental technique, peerless and influential though that was. With his gaunt and gangling appearance and his demoniac temperament, Paganini almost single-handedly forged the romantic mystique of virtuosity as a superhuman, even diabolical endowment. He was Faust come to life—a role model for countless geniuses, charlatans, entertainers, and adolescents ever since his first appearances abroad.

His ability to dominate and mesmerize an audience created a whole new relationship—a far more romantic relationship—between artist and collective patronage than had ever existed before. Fig. 37-2, a famous caricature (*Paganini, Master-Magician*) by the painter and poet L. P. A. Burmeister (alias Lyser, 1804–70), replete with cabalistic symbols, a dance of death, and a hypnotized maiden, effectively sums up his extraordinary image, and helps account for the hostility toward Paganini on the part of the church that ultimately refused him burial. That hostility, his quick burnout, and his perpetual association with wasting disease only enhanced his fiendish aura, turning him, despite the commercial nature of his career and his abundant worldly success, into one of the century's authentic *poètes maudits*.

For an idea—probably only a dim idea—of what the shouting was all about, we can turn to Paganini's written legacy. There we will see technical innovation galore, but what is more important, we will see it allied to a new poetic idea of virtuosity and

F I G. 37-2   Niccolò Paganini, in a caricature, *Paganini, Master-Magician* (1819), by Lyser.

its role in musical expression. That poetic idea comes across best not in Paganini's concertos but in his shorter pieces. The five concertos, underneath the fireworks rather ordinary works from the formal or craftsmanly point of view, are proof of the composer's traditional schooling and competence. (In his teens Paganini had studied composition quite seriously, eventually with Ferdinando Paer, the composer of the first *Leonora* opera.) The only glimmer they contain of Paganini's uniqueness is the finale of the Second (1826), a rondo based—typically for the day—on a folk tune, a popular Neapolitan tarantella called *La campanella* ("The church bell").

That finale, while full of bravura ("show-offery"), remains well within the bounds of the *style brillant* or "sparkling style," the ingratiatingly decorative or ornamental virtuosity well known to the eighteenth century and valued by aristocratic audiences as evidence of their investment, so to speak, in quality goods. The First Concerto (1817), still a popular concert piece, shows how far a composer could go in an effort to "sparkle" in this way. The orchestral parts are written in E♭ but the solo part is written in D major for a violin tuned a half step sharp. In this way, not only will the timbre take on extra brilliance, but all the open-string resonance and multiple stoppings available in D major will remain available at the higher pitch.

Nowadays, possibly because concerto-quality violins have become so inordinately valuable on the art market, because modernized instruments are already under so much greater tension than in Paganini's day, and because concert pitch has actually risen in the twentieth century, no violinist is willing to risk damaging a Strad by tuning it high, and the concerto is performed "honestly," with all instruments written and sounding in D major. Paganini did not need to worry so; at the time of his death (in relatively straitened circumstances) he owned seven Stradivarius violins, two by Amati, and four (including his favorite) by Guarneri del Gesù. He could afford to be casual about his charlatanry.

The caprices and the variation sets were the pieces in which Paganini turned virtuosity into something new and frightening, in the tradition of romantic realism ("black romanticism"). He made it the vehicle for "thinking new thoughts"—that is, projecting aggressively novel, sometimes grotesquely novel musical ideas—and in so doing inspired generations of artists to do the same. His signature piece, *Le streghe* ("The witches," 1813), a set of variations on a theme from a comic opera by Franz Xaver Süssmayr (the Mozart pupil who completed his teacher's requiem), played heavily into the demoniac image Paganini was cultivating. The violinistic technical novelties were now motivated by a shocking poetic idea.

A good example of such grotesquerie is the motive on which the Caprice no. 13 is based (Ex. 37-1a). Basically a study in parallel thirds featuring Paganini's trademark device of playing whole melodies on single strings (or, as here, a pair of strings) with spectacular swooping shifts, the caprice quickly acquired the nickname "Le rire du diable" ("The devil's laugh") owing to the chilling chromatic descent with portato bowings. Caprice no. 17 (Ex. 37-1b) is another combination of weirdly striking ideas—diatonic and later chromatic runs often involving complicated "downshifting" on a single string (one of the most difficult violinistic tricks to bring off cleanly) juxtaposed with ascending double stops in a contrasting register—that startle and astonish as much as they "please." The middle section (Ex. 37-1c) is played entirely in octaves: another Paganini specialty of which he was, if not the originator, the chief popularizer, making its emulation a must for all competitors (and in so doing, "advancing" the normal technique of the instrument).

Caprice no. 24, the most famous of the *Caprices*, combines the genres of technical study and bravura variations. For fairly obvious reasons, variations make an ideal showcase for virtuosity. Here, successive variations on the brief and businesslike binary *tema* (Ex. 37-1d) feature in turn the "thrown" (*jeté*) bow stroke, legato string-crossings, octaves, downshifting, broken octaves, parallel thirds and sixths, and so on. Variation 9 (Ex. 37-1e) was the shocker. It introduced a technique of which Paganini was indeed the inventor, the so-called left-hand pizzicato, in which (at the spots marked "+") the fingers of the left hand are drawn sharply off the strings they stop, thus plucking the pitch prepared by the next lower finger. (This effect, obviously, can be executed only on descending scales or arpeggios or on open strings) The best measure of Paganini's spell on later generations of composers, by the way, is the number of major figures who wrote their own sets of bravura variations on the theme of Caprice no. 24. Besides Liszt, whose transcription we will be viewing shortly, they include Robert Schumann (1810–56), Johannes Brahms (1833–97), Sergey Rachmaninoff (1873–1943), Boris Blacher (1903–75), and Witold Lutostawski (1913–94).

The only aspect of Paganiniana that the Caprices do not illustrate is the violinist's pioneering use of harmonics, both natural and (to an extent previously unattempted) "artificial," in which a lower left-hand finger stops a note that will serve as fundamental to a harmonic produced by a higher finger. It is altogether possible that Paganini performed the Caprices with harmonics that he deliberately held back (as a "trade secret") from publishing. All of the concert pieces (concertos and variation sets) that

EX. 37-1A   Niccolò Paganini, Caprice, Op. 1, no. 13 ("Rire du diable")

EX. 37-1B   Niccolò Paganini, Caprice, Op. 1, no. 17 (Andante)

EX. 37-1C   Niccolò Paganini, Caprice, Op. 1, no. 17, middle section

EX. 37-1D   Niccolò Paganini, Caprice, Op. 1, no. 24, Tema

EX. 37-1E   Niccolò Paganini, Caprice, Op. 1, no. 24, Variation 9

were finally published from manuscript after Paganini's death are liberally strewn with them, and all reviewers mention "flageolet tones" as Paganini's pièce de résistance.

Most striking of all is an autograph document that has happened to survive, headed *"Segreto comunicato e raccomandato da Paganini al suo caro amico L. G. Germi: Armonici a doppie corde di terza"* (Secret passed along and recommended by Paganini to his dear friend L. G. Germi: Harmonics in double stops at the interval of a third), in which the complicated fingerings he had worked out for playing whole scales of parallel thirds in artificial harmonics are divulged to a comrade violinist, who is implored in a note at the foot of the page "to tear up the present paper as soon as you have read it, and not to let yourself be seen performing it, because they will steal the secret from you" (Fig. 37-3).

For Paganini at full strength, then, only a variation set will do. There are many spectacular items from which to choose, from the set on the French revolutionary hymn *La carmagnole* (1795), composed during his year of study with Paer, to the sets on *God Save the King* and *St. Patrick's Day*, composed (perhaps needless to say) for his

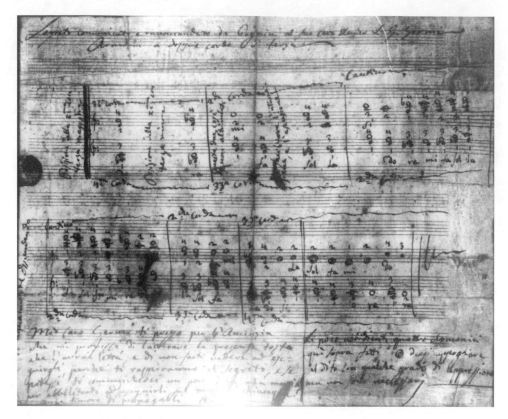

FIG. 37-3 *"Segreto comunicato da Paganini."*

British tour, to the most famous one of all, the Introduction and Variations on "Dal tuo stellato soglio" ("From thy starry throne") from Rossini's biblical opera *Mosè*, played entirely on the low G string (1819). For us, however, the most resonant choice will be the set simply titled *I palpiti* ("Heart throbs," 1819), based on the celebrated aria from Rossini's *Tancredi* at which we took a long look in chapter 33. Like the first concerto, it is composed for a *scordatura* ("mistuned") violin, notated in A major but sounding a half step higher, in B♭.

An operatic scena in its own right, it begins with a slow introduction marked *larghetto e cantabile* to stand in for the obligatory cantabile with which any Rossini cavatina started up. Then comes a section marked *Recit.: con grande espress.* (Ex. 37-2a) to function as transition, in pure operatic style, to the famous cabaletta, "Di tanti palpiti," on which the variations will finally be played. By so elaborately evoking the operatic context, Paganini is in effect declaring equal rights for instrumental virtuosity, challenging on their home turf the laurels of the declining castrati and the ascendant *musici* (sopranos and altos in trousers), for centuries the undefeated international champions of musical Europe. Paganini's ultimate triumph, in fact, was to earn concert fees that equaled and finally exceeded those of opera stars.

Since a cabaletta is always cast in strophic form, one could say that Paganini's variations represent a four-stanza aria. The first stanza (Ex. 37-2b) is more or less what Rossini wrote. The second and fourth will remind us of the devices already encountered in the caprices. The third, however, is unique—the longest spate of (practically) uninterrupted *armonici a doppie corde di terza* Paganini ever committed to paper (Ex. 37-2c). Even here, though, and characteristically, Paganini did not commit the "secret" itself to paper. All he notated was the result, not the means of achieving it. For that, an edited part for the soloist (Ex. 37-2d) has to be supplied, by a violinist familiar with the technique that Paganini guarded so closely during his lifetime,

EX. 37-2A   Niccolò Paganini, *I palpiti*, Recitativo

EX. 37-2B   Niccolò Paganini, *I palpiti*, Theme

EX. 37-2C   Niccolò Paganini, *I palpiti*, Variation II, mm. 1–12

confiding it only once, to Germi. (In 1831, however, a German violinist named Karl Guhr, who had figured it out after hearing Paganini in Frankfurt, spilled the beans: he published a book, *Über Paganinis Kunst die Violine zu spielen* [On Paganini's Art of Violin Playing] containing tables similar to the one shown in Fig. 37-3.)

RESPONSE

By the time the nineteen-year-old Liszt heard Paganini in Paris he had himself been a concert artist for almost ten years, and a working composer for more than five. He was born in the village of Raiding (now Dobojan) in the vicinity of the old Hungarian town of Sopron (then called Ödenburg) near the Austrian border. As the alternate naming of the localities suggests, the region had a mixed Hungarian and German culture. The composer's family name is German, but spelled in the Hungarian fashion. (If it were spelled List, it would be pronounced "Lisht" in Hungarian.) His father was an overseer at the court of Prince Nikolaus Esterházy, the nephew and namesake of Haydn's patron. His mother hailed from Krems, a town in lower Austria. Liszt grew up speaking German, not Hungarian, although he showed an early interest in the music of Gypsy bands, and later in life drew on his experience with it to construct an exotically Hungarian "persona" for himself with which to fascinate audiences.

In the spring of 1821, before he turned ten, the boy and his family moved to Vienna so that he could develop his precocious gifts. He studied piano with Carl Czerny

EX. 37-2D   Niccolò Paganini, *I palpiti*, Variation II as edited

FIG. 37-4 Franz Liszt in 1860 with his daughter Cosima (1837–1930), then married to the pianist and conductor Hans von Bülow, later to Richard Wagner.

(1791–1857), a pupil and disciple of the still-living Beethoven, and composition with old Antonio Salieri, *still* (aged seventy) the nominal Imperial Kapellmeister. Czerny lost no time presenting Liszt as a prodigy. His first Vienna concert took place in December 1822, the second in April 1823. At the latter, Beethoven is reputed to have planted an anointing kiss on the eleven-year-old soloist's forehead; in later life, Liszt recalled having been taken to Beethoven's quarters by Czerny and receiving the kiss there. In any case, having received Beethoven's blessing, Liszt was asked to contribute a variation to Diabelli's famous "patriotic anthology" (Ex. 37-3).

Liszt's international concert career began that fall. On the way to Paris, he gave concerts in a whole string of south German towns. In the French capital he studied composition with Paer and with Anton Reicha (1770–1836), the leading theory professor at the Paris Conservatory (where Liszt was refused admission because of his foreign nationality). After a sensational Paris debut in May 1824, Liszt conquered London with a program that featured the twelve-year-old prodigy, amid the sundry vocal and orchestral numbers that the "variety show" format of contemporary concerts required, showing off his talents in a concerto by Johann Nepomuk Hummel (1778–1837), a set of orchestrally accompanied variations by his teacher Czerny, and an "Extempore Fantasia on a written Thema, which Master Liszt respectfully requests may be given to him by any Person in the Company."

All of this music, no doubt including the "extempore fantasia," was virtuoso fare in the light and blithesome *style brillant* purveyed by the popular performers of the day, and so were Liszt's early compositions, as their very titles proclaim: *Variations brillantes sur un thème de G. Rossini*, or *Impromptu brillant* [i.e., a medley] *sur des thèmes de Rossini et Spontini*. His first noteworthy original composition, called *Étude en douze exercices*, consisted of twelve Czernyesque "concert studies," display pieces without orchestra for use on the road, in which (in the words of Alan Walker, Liszt's biographer), "the boy makes the keyboard sparkle from one end to the other."[6] In probable collaboration with his other teacher, Paer, the young prodigy also fulfilled a commission from the Académie Royale de Musique for a one-act opera, *Don Sanche, ou Le château d'amour* ("Don Sanchez, or the castle of love"), premiered at the Salle Le Peletier on 17 October 1825, five days before the composer's fourteenth birthday. Though he lived another sixty years, it would be his only work for the operatic stage. His destiny lay on a stage of a different kind.

EX. 37-3   Franz Liszt's "Diabelli Variation" (Variation 24 from Diabelli's "Patriotic Anthology")

And then came Paganini. "Quel homme, quel violon, quel artiste!" Liszt gushed in a letter to a friend. "What a man, what a violin, what an artist! O God, what pain and suffering, what torment in those four strings!"[7] The restless and ambitious prodigy had grasped something more than the rest of Paganini's audience: he knew that in order to equal the Italian's achievement and join him at the pinnacle of instrumental mastery he would have to submit to a tremendous test of endurance. He became obsessed with the famous response of the Italian painter Correggio, reported in Giorgio Vasari's *Lives of the Artists*, to a masterpiece by Raphael: "Anch'io sono pittore!" ("I, too, am a painter!"). Although, like many others, Liszt misattributed the remark to Michelangelo, he understood it well; he knew that it was not a boast but an acknowledgment of responsibility, a promise of self-sacrifice.

The prodigy went into seclusion, a seclusion he described enthusiastically in a famous letter to his pupil Pierre Wolff, dated 2 May 1832. He was reinventing his technique from the bottom up, spending four to five hours a day on "trills, sixths, octaves, tremolos, double notes and cadenzas," but also reinventing the expressive purposes the technique would serve, for which reason he spent an equal amount of time devouring Beethoven, Bach, Mozart, and Weber, along with the literary classics he never read in school (because he didn't go to any): Homer, the Bible, Plato, Locke, as well as the latest romantic fare—Lord Byron, Victor Hugo, and especially *Harmonies poétiques et religieuses* of the French poet Alphonse de Lamartine, which he tried at various times to "translate" into music. "If I don't go mad," he promised, at the end of the ordeal "you will find in me an artist! Yes, an artist such as is required today."[8]

The first creative fruit of Liszt's seclusion was a series of Paganini transcriptions in which the pianist sought equivalents on his instrument to the violinist's sublime *diableries*. Before the year 1832 was out Liszt had composed a *Grande fantaisie de bravoure sur La Clochette de Paganini* (Big Bravura Fantasy on Paganini's "Campanella"), based on one of the pieces he had actually heard Paganini perform, the finale of the Second Concerto. One little section is actually called "Variation à la Paganini," and it is, inevitably, a study in leaping around the topmost register of the instrument, the way Paganini could do with his patented harmonics (Ex. 37-4). Elsewhere, Liszt makes no attempt actually to imitate the violin, preferring instead to create in pianistic terms the frightening atmosphere of "black romanticism" that Paganini uniquely evoked, at the very opposite extreme from the "brilliant" or "sparkling" style of traditional instrumental virtuosity.

There was, briefly, another side to this goal, as Liszt dabbled for a while in revolutionary politics. In the circles he frequented—notably the utopian religious socialists who called themselves "Saint-Simonians" (after Claude-Henri de Rouvroy, Comte de Saint-Simon, a philosopher who wished to marry traditional religion with modern science)—"an artist such as is required today" meant an artist willing to "seek out the PEOPLE and GOD, go from one to the other; improve, moralize, console man, bless and glorify God," so that "*all classes of society*, finally, will merge in a common religious sentiment, grand and sublime."[9] These quotes, capitals, italics, and all, are from an essay by Liszt that appeared in a Paris newspaper during the years of his

Paganinian self-transformation. Art, as he wished to practice it, would be an instrument of social transformation. The virtuoso would become a sublime, rabble-rousing public orator on behalf of social progress, much as the poet had become in the person of Victor Hugo.

While it cannot be said that Liszt actually played such a role in life, his imagining it is already powerful testimony to the new status and concept of musical virtuosity. The

EX. 37-4 "Variation à la Paganini" from Franz Liszt, *Grande fantaisie de bravoure sur La Clochette de Paganini*

*) All the notes with the stems turned downward must be played with the left hand.

magnetic, socially engaged performer-virtuoso (which in those days implied a composer, too) was the public face of romanticism, as the Beethovenian or Schubertian ideal of withdrawn and concentrated subjectivity was the private face. While the national side of this dichotomy can easily be (and certainly has been) overdrawn, it nevertheless accords with a long tradition that Liszt's self-transformation, and its literary expression, were stimulated and realized in the French capital in the heady atmosphere of the July Monarchy.

Liszt's final tribute to Paganini was a new set of concert studies, *Études d'exécution transcendante d'après Paganini* ("Etudes for transcendental technique after Paganini"), first published in 1838 (by which time several of them existed in various manuscript versions) and reissued with revisions in 1851, reflecting refinements the composer had introduced over the years in the course of performing them. Besides a streamlined version of *La campanella*, the set included five of Paganini's Caprices freely transcribed, including two of these given above in Ex. 37-1a. Liszt's versions are shown in Ex. 37-5.

Liszt's transcriptions hew pretty close to the originals, while greatly magnifying their effect in the true spirit of emulation, succeeding brilliantly in having them sound as though they were originally conceived for the piano. They are especially full of surprises — in range, in texture, in harmony — for listeners who know the originals (and that makes it especially fun to follow Liszt's transcriptions from Paganini's score). In the E♭ Etude, Liszt pulls off an especially apt surprise by accompanying Paganini's octaves (split between the two hands phrase by phrase) with some pseudo-Bachian imitative counterpoint by inversion, showing off "erudition" as an especially prizable aspect of the new virtuosity (Ex. 37-5b).

EX. 37-5A   Franz Liszt, *Paganini Etudes* (1851 ed.), no. 2, mm. 6–11

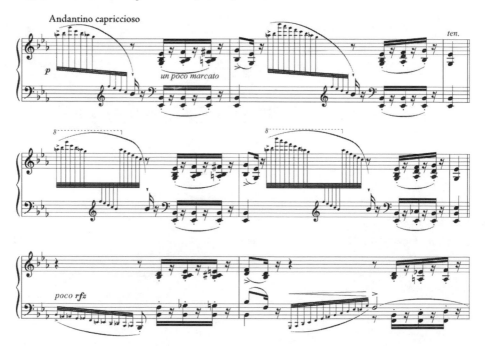

In the A-minor variations, which Liszt made the finale of his set just as Paganini had done, the pianist occasionally manages to set the theme off in one hand against Paganini's variation in the other, and in the last variation (Ex. 37-5d) reaches a level of sheer sonority that was in itself a pianistic breakthrough; one can easily imagine it being greeted with scenes of mass hysteria like the one shown in the famous Berlin caricature of 1842 (Fig. 37-5), manifestations such as had formerly been confined to the opera house. On the way, a number of witty allusions to past piano masterpieces pass in review; perhaps the most resonant for us is the reference to the rapt final movement

EX. 37-5B   Franz Liszt, *Paganini Etudes* (1851 ed.), no. 2, mm. 24–28

EX. 37-5C   Franz Liszt, *Paganini Etudes* (1851 ed.), no. 6, mm. 1–16

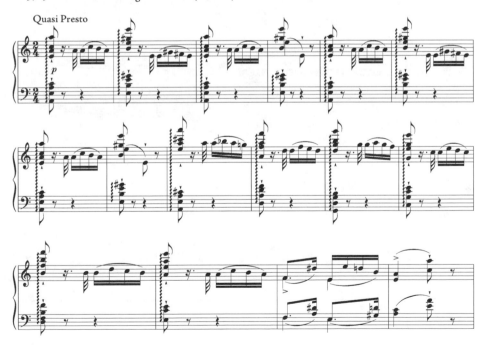

of Beethoven's last sonata (op. III) in Variation 10 (Ex. 37-5e). It was surely a matter to ponder and debate, whether by placing Beethoven in proximity with Paganini, Liszt had debased the former or ennobled the latter. Either way, the underlying point remained the same—the new virtuosity was a truly all-encompassing medium.

Caricatures like the one in Fig. 37-5, set beside the one in Fig. 37-2, are all the evidence we need that Liszt made fair claim to Paganini's mantle as demonic possessor of all who heard him. Concerts like his were cathartically purging in a way that only rock concerts have remained in our time, and the cult of worshiped personality that he inspired is something to which only rock musicians openly aspire now. His consciousness and cultivation of "dark forces" came most clearly to the fore, just as it had with Paganini, when after his self-transformation he made a *reprise de contact* with opera.

His *Réminiscences de Don Juan* (1841), known informally as the "Don Juan Fantasy," while ostensibly a potpourri on "airs" from Mozart's *Don Giovanni*, is quite obviously more than that. Charles Rosen calls it Liszt's self-portrait (for, like many champion performers, though not the relatively old and unbeautiful Paganini, he nurtured a reputation as a "Don Juan" himself; Paganini's turn came long after his death, in an

EX. 37-5D   Franz Liszt, *Paganini Etudes* (1851 ed.), no. 6, var. 11, mm. 1–4

EX. 37-5E   Franz Liszt, *Paganini Etudes* (1851 ed.), no. 6, var. 10, mm. 1–8

Più moderato

FIG. 37-5   "Franz Liszt Exerts His Spell on the Ladies in the Audience," caricature from the periodical *Berlin, wie es ist . . . und trinkt* (mid-1840s). The name of the journal, "Berlin, as it is . . . and drinks," is a rather clumsy pun (*ist* means "is"; *isst* means "eats").

endearingly ridiculous Viennese operetta by Franz Lehar).[10] But Liszt's Fantasy also makes an astonishing comment on the opera, and on the way romantic audiences interpreted it.

By juxtaposing the Don's seduction of Zerlina, evoked through a set of variations on their duet, "Là ci darem la mano" ("There, give me your hand"), and the Statue's seizure of the Don—which, as Liszt brilliantly reminds us by suddenly citing it (Ex. 37-6a), happens on an almost identical line ("Dammi la mano in pegno!" ["Give me your hand in pledge"])—Liszt casts Mozart's hero as predator and prey alike, at once stalker and stalked. The medley starts right off with the Statue's ghastly speech in the graveyard: "You'll laugh your last laugh ere daybreak," made more gruesome than Mozart had made it by eliding out the recitative that connects and harmonically joins its two tonally remote lines.

Next comes the wild diminished-seventh chord that brings the Statue on stage for the final confrontation, and a repetition of the graveyard speech, now accompanied by the violin figuration that attends the Statue's later appearance. Thus the two grimmest, most "diabolical" scenes in the opera are conflated in a devil's brew that will eventually include the scary syncopations and scales familiar from the Overture's introduction, the Statue's horrifying line "It is not human food I eat," and ending with a shuddering join (Ex. 37-6b), over a sustained harmony, between the Statue's graveyard intonations and Don Giovanni's lecherous "come hither" to Zerlina ("Vieni, vieni").

That kind of intensifying conflation, the very opposite of the loose stringing of tunes implied by designations such as "medley" or "potpourri," runs through the whole of Liszt's Fantasy. Later, the statue's creepy chromatic scales will rumble sarcastically beneath the coda of the seduction duet, where the Don sings to Zerlina, "Andiam, andiam, mio bene" ("Let's go, my sweet"), turning the line before our ears—provided we can recall the words when hearing the music—into the Statue's leering summons to perdition. Even more pointed is the irony when the grandiose bravura paraphrase of Don Giovanni's "Champagne" aria that finishes the medley, rather than providing the ultimate in "sparkling" virtuosity, is darkly framed by the Statue's chromatically

EX. 37-6A   Franz Liszt, *Réminiscences de Don Juan*, transition to "Duetto" ("Là ci darem la mano")

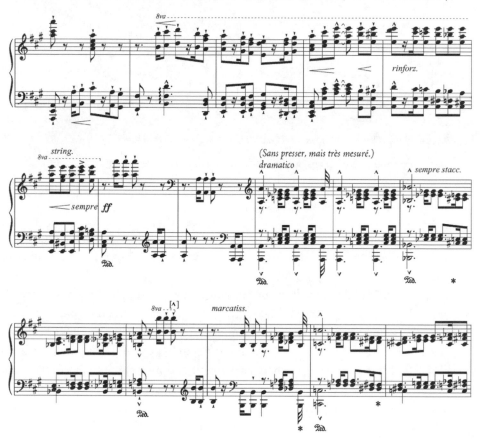

EX. 37-6B   Franz Liszt, *Réminiscences de Don Juan*, juxtaposition of Seduction and Perdition

tortured line, "Ah, tempo più non v'è" ("You're out of time"). As the aria races to its frenzied climax (marked *più animato* and *fortissississimo*), one hears the Statue's clanking tread in the bass, represented by the violin figuration from the finale, inexorably keeping pace (Ex. 37-6c). The last word is the Statue's — a taunting reminder of his opening graveyard threat, transposed up a half step in triumph.

George Bernard Shaw, who earned his living as a concert reviewer before his playwriting career took off, recognized the special quality of the "Don Juan Fantasy."

> When you hear the terrible progression of the statue's invitation suddenly echoing through the harmonies accompanying Juan's seductive *Andiam, andiam, mio bene,* you cannot help accepting it as a stroke of genius — that is, if you know your Don Giovanni *au fond* [through and through],

he wrote, paying tribute as well to the "riotous ecstasy" of the "Champagne" aria, and the way it is "translated from song into symphony, from the individual to the abstract," by virtue of Liszt's transcendent virtuosity, recognized as an integral part of the poetic idea. That is music criticism of a high order.[11]

But so is the fantasy itself. While surely "readable" in conventional moralizing terms, as a divine judgment on the Don's lascivious conduct, Liszt's juxtapositions impose a new layer of romantic interpretation on Mozart's opera. Without the use of words, Liszt interprets the opera very much the way it was interpreted in the Danish philosopher Søren Kierkegaard's almost exactly contemporaneous tract *Either/Or* (1843), a bible of

EX. 37-6C   Franz Liszt, *Réminiscences de Don Juan,* "Champagne" aria accompanied by "Statue's tread"

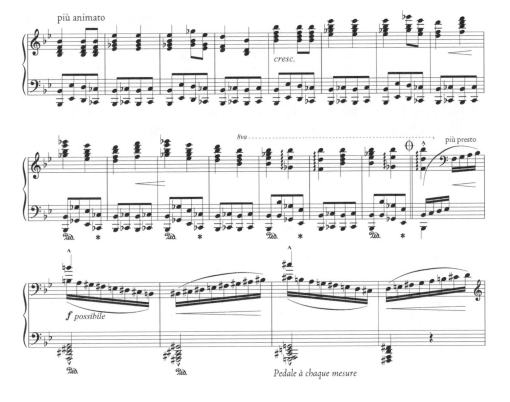

"existentialism," where *Don Giovanni* is said to reveal the links between the erotic and the demonic, and between love and death as the only truly transcendent experiences.

Kierkegaard claimed that the opera disclosed the secret of all music, and its hold on us. Listening to Liszt's fantasy, one is hard pressed to disagree; but, if that is so, then it took the new virtuosity to finally unleash music's essential power. Nor should one allow this remark to pass without noting that in pursuit of the thematic or conceptual unity that would haunt romantic artists from then on, Liszt has allowed himself to forget all about tonal unity, up to now the chief criterion of coherence, at least for instrumental music. He quotes everything in its original key, which allows the piece to begin in fantasialike tonal limbo, proceed to A major, and end quite nonchalantly in B♭ major.

After emerging from his chrysalis of self-imposed labor, Liszt spent about a decade (1838–48) crisscrossing Europe in a cyclone of touring and concert-giving that revolutionized the musical life of the continent, and its music business as well. It was not just the level of his playing that was unprecedented. Liszt was the first virtuoso to dare appear solo for an entire evening, thus inventing the instrumental "recital" as we know it today. And Liszt was the first traveling virtuoso to retain the services of a personal impresario, or what we would now call a manager, an advance man who handled his professional correspondence, booked his halls, advertised his appearances, negotiated and collected his fees, and took care of his personal needs (even preparing his food) on the road. The powerful modern concert booking agencies and "artist managements" that run (and sometimes ruin) the lives of musical performers today are the descendents of Gaetano Belloni ("Liszt's poodle," as an envious Heinrich Heine dubbed him),[12] who served Liszt in this capacity from 1840 to 1847.

Belloni was also suspected of hiring claques (or paying "ovation expenses," as Heine dryly put it), but there is no evidence that Liszt ever needed one—quite the contrary, if contemporary observers and reviewers are to be believed. The novelty of his solo recitals, and the nature of his touring repertoire, are both fascinatingly revealed in a memoir by Vladimir Stasov (1824–1906), a prolific Russian writer on the arts, who attended Liszt's St. Petersburg debut in April 1842.

"Everything about this concert was unusual," Stasov recalled:

> First of all, Liszt appeared alone on the stage throughout the entire concert: there were no other performers—no orchestra, singers or any other instrumental soloists whatsoever. This was something unheard of, utterly novel, even somewhat brazen. What conceit! What vanity! As if to say, "All you need is me. Listen only to me—you don't need anyone else." Then, this idea of having a small stage erected in the very center of the hall like an islet in the middle of an ocean, a throne high above the heads of the crowd, from which to pour forth his mighty torrents of sound. And then, what music he chose for his programmes: not just piano pieces, his own, his true metier—no, this could not satisfy his boundless conceit—he had to be both an orchestra and human voices. He took Beethoven's [concert aria] "Adelaide," Schubert's songs—and dared to replace male and female voices, to play them on the piano alone! He took large orchestral works, overtures, symphonies—and played them too, all alone, in place of a whole orchestra, without any assistance, without the sound of a single violin, French horn, kettledrum! And in such an immense hall! What a strange fellow![13]

There were two pianos set up on the stage, and Liszt alternated between them, "facing first one, then the other half of the hall," as Stasov recollected. In addition to the vocal numbers to which Stasov referred, the program included Rossini's *William Tell* Overture, Liszt's "Don Juan Fantasy," and the sextet from Donizetti's *Lucia di Lammermoor*, act II (Ex. 33-11). The only item that was not an arrangement from another medium was the grand finale, Liszt's own showstopping *Galop chromatique*, a tour de force of velocity, but something of a throwback to the old *style brillant*. At his second St. Petersburg concert, the program included the "scherzo and finale" (including the storm) from Beethoven's *Pastoral* Symphony. Only at the third concert, when he played Beethoven's "Moonlight" Sonata, did Liszt play the sort of repertoire that is now considered standard "recital" fare.

The inclusion of so much orchestral repertory in keyboard arrangement was partly Liszt's own predilection, partly a reflection of the "provincial" venue (an outlying capital with, as yet, no full-time resident orchestra), and partly a concession to the expectations of an audience used to variety entertainment at public concerts. (The kind of repertoire we now associate with solo recitals — sonatas and other "purely" instrumental compositions — were still reserved, in the main, for salons; Liszt played many, by invitation, at aristocratic St. Petersburg residences.) The program, in short, could be called a traditional one; all that was not traditional was the uniform medium — and, of course the unheard-of style of the playing, which caused Stasov and his companion at the recital to vow "that thenceforth and forever, that day, April 8, 1842, would be sacred to us, and we would never forget a single second of it till our dying day."[14]

THE CONCERTO TRANSFORMED

It was inevitable that a new concept of instrumental virtuosity should have brought about a reconceptualization of the musical genre in which such virtuosity was traditionally exhibited. Accordingly, the nineteenth-century concerto — under the impact of the new virtuosity, but also under the impact of more general notions of romantic heroism and individualism to which the new virtuosity was itself a response — underwent a thorough transformation in form and conceptual content alike, and took on a new expressive significance.

Like so many other romantic reconceptualizations, this one can be traced back — if desired — to Beethoven. And of course such a tracing *was* desired by the protagonists of the change, for whom the titanic figure of Beethoven provided the ideal precedent and validation. Beethoven himself inherited the concerto — both as a form and as an "idea" — from Mozart. The directness of the succession can be seen most dramatically, perhaps, in Beethoven's Concerto no. 3 in C minor, op. 37 (1800), the first movement of which is so obviously modeled on that of Mozart's C-minor concerto, K. 491 (1786), by all odds Mozart's most "Beethovenian" work (Ex. 37-7a; for the Mozart, see Ex. 32-1b).

The Beethoven and Mozart themes are of course orchestral themes. The Mozartean concerto that Beethoven inherited was the "symphonized" variant of the old ritornello form, examined in some detail in chapter 30, in which a full-blown (but harmonically static) orchestral "exposition" stands in for the first ritornello, to be repeated (now in harmonically dynamic form) with the participation of the solo instrument upon its entry. Even though, as we know from accounts of actual performances, the soloist participated in a supporting role in all the tuttis, and even though the featured solo entrance could be mighty dramatic (as can be certainly be seen in Example 37-7b), the delayed solo entrance, and the elaborateness of the orchestral preface to it, tended

EX. 37-7A   Ludwig van Beethoven, Piano Concerto no. 3, I, opening theme (mm. 1–8)

EX. 37-7B   Ludwig van Beethoven, Piano Concerto no. 3, I, first solo entrance

to equalize the roles of soloist and orchestra. The concept of concerto that Mozart's continued to uphold was one of cooperation or conspiracy — that is, "concerted action" (as per the Italian *concertare*: to plan together, to hatch a plot, etc.) — rather than one of contest or opposition (for which the relevant Italian verb is *contrastare*).

The new virtuosity decisively altered the balance of forces in favor of the soloist, the lonely romantic "hero." And so the beginning of Beethoven's next concerto, the Fourth, op. 58 (1805), is widely regarded as a romantic watershed (see Ex. 37-8), as its proximity to the *Eroica* Symphony (op. 55) seems to advertise. To open with the soloist rather than the orchestra was indeed a novelty (though not wholly unprecedented), even if the quietness of the exchange gives little inkling of heroism. The entry of the orchestra on a "remote" harmony ("V of vi" only in retrospect!) does tend to put the two forces somewhat at odds, and can be justly read as "romantic." (The opposition of forces is far more obvious in the second movement, known to have been intended by Beethoven as a portrayal of "Orpheus in Hades," with the piano cast as the protagonist and the orchestral strings as the Furies; some scholars, notably Owen Jander, have suggested that the entire concerto be "decoded" in the light of that reading.)[15] Immediately after this exchange, however, the music settles into the familiar pattern; the soloist must wait almost seventy measures before regaining the spotlight.

The opening of Beethoven's Concerto no. 5 in E♭ major, op. 73 (1809), cast in the "Eroica" key and subtitled "The Emperor" on account of its commanding size, is indisputably, indeed supremely, heroic. The work actually begins with a cadenza — or rather with three cadenzas, each embellishing the next harmony in a cadential succession. Even after this magnificent self-assertion, though, the solo instrument must recede to its traditional subordinate role, calmly awaiting its turn for formal reentry, which only takes place in m. 104.

Real integration of solo and tutti in a single thematic exposition had to await the advent of the generation born in the first decade of the new century. There was a forerunner of sorts in Weber's *Konzertstück* in F minor for piano and orchestra (1821), a single-movement "concert piece" more or less in the form of a traditional symphonic first movement with slow introduction, but with the piano and the orchestra freely sharing the thematic material from the outset. The unusual relationship of the performing forces had an "external" motivation in the form of a "program" or plot line, akin to the one that motivated the slow movement of Beethoven's fourth concerto. The piano is cast as a protagonist, the wife of a knight-crusader anxiously awaiting, then joyfully greeting, his return.

The three mature concertos by Mendelssohn, by contrast, treat the new relationship of soloist and orchestra as standard operating procedure, requiring no special justification. The new relationship involves not only the sharing of thematic material between the forces, but also the nature and the role of the cadenza. In his two piano concertos — in G minor, op. 25 (1831), and D minor, op. 40 (1837) — the cadenza, rather than preceding the final tutti, forms a transition that joins the first and second movements in an unbroken continuity. In the Violin Concerto in E minor, op. 64 (1844), Mendelssohn's last orchestral work, the cadenza, fully written out (although marked *ad*

EX. 37-8   Ludwig van Beethoven, Piano Concerto no. 4, I, mm. 1–14

libitum, meaning that the tempo should be free), is cast in the role of "retransitioner," elegantly bridging the development and recapitulation. The reentry of the first theme against the soloist's continuing arpeggios is a justly celebrated moment.

Also very elegant is the way in which the solo violin and the orchestra share the thematic material in the exposition and recapitulation. At the outset, it is the violin, singing in its most brilliant register, that gets to announce the soaring opening theme. The second theme, by contrast, is played by a wind choir over a violin pedal (the new tonic key having been neatly calculated to coincide with the soloist's lowest open string). In the recapitulation, the orchestra gets both themes: the first scintillatingly accompanied by the violin's continuing figuration as noted, the second presented as it was in the exposition, but with enriched instrumental colors.

Hand in hand with the integration of solo and tutti, in Mendelssohn's influential conception, went the compacting and streamlining of the overall form by means of transitions, minimizing formal breaks and creating an impression of "organic" structural unity. Behind it stood an even more influential idea, enunciated by Goethe, Mendelssohn's (and Germany's) benevolent mentor, that artistic form should imitate the forms (*Gestalten*) of nature, first among which was the *Urpflanze*, the "primal plant," nature's microcosm, all of whose parts were symbiotic.[16] While scientific in "form," this idea was quite mystically romantic in "content" (compare William Blake's *Auguries of Innocence*: "To see a world in a grain of sand/And a heaven in a wild flower"). Its influence led to new concepts of form founded primarily on thematic rather than tonal relations; we will be much preoccupied with them in chapters to come. But while romantic in its striving after organic unity, and while that organicism allows the soloist greater "thematic" prominence than previously the norm, Mendelssohn's concerto concept is nevertheless anything but heroic. The virtuosity it calls for is of the "brilliant," ingratiating sort, and the soloist and orchestra are forever deferring to one another, graciously concerned that each get its share. That carefully maintained equality could even be called the perfection of the Mozartean concerto ideal. In any case it was a short-lived moment of amicable equilibrium, soon to be upended by the new virtuosity.

Liszt's long-gestating Concerto no. 1, cast not by any accident or oversight in the *Eroica*-cum-*Emperor* key of E♭ major, was sketched five years before Mendelssohn's Violin Concerto, and completed five years after it; but it seems to come from another "period" altogether (not to say another planet). It is dedicated to Henry Litolff (1818–91), a French pianist-composer of English birth, who was experimenting with a new and enlarged concerto concept that he called *concerto symphonique*.

In a way this new genre was a modernization of an old one: the *symphonie concertante* (or *sinfonia concertante*), a symphony with important obbligato parts for a group of virtuoso soloists—itself a modernization of an even older form, the concerto grosso. Haydn and Mozart had written examples (Haydn for a concertino of mixed winds and strings; Mozart, respectively, for woodwind quartet and for violin and viola in tandem). The *symphonie concertante* flourished especially in Paris, as a regularly featured attraction at the Concert Spirituel. It even had a specialist composer, the Italian-born violinist Giuseppe Maria Cambini (1746–1825), who wrote more than eighty.

Litolff's *concertos symphoniques* differed from *symphonies concertantes* mainly in medium: a single piano soloist and a large orchestra that carried most of the thematic weight. Liszt's debt to Litolff is evident not only in the dedication of the concerto, and in its weighty "bigness" rather than brilliance of conception, but also (and most specifically) in its colorful orchestration that included piccolo and triangle, instruments first used by Litolff in the context of a keyboard concerto. Yet where Litolff's concertos were expansive four-movement affairs, Liszt opted, in keeping with the new "Goethean" fashion, for an even greater "organic" compression than Mendelssohn's.

His model here, perhaps surprisingly, was Schubert, still a composer of fairly local Viennese reputation at the time. The point of contact was Schubert's *Wanderer Fantasy*, his most virtuosic piano work, which Liszt began including in his concerts in the 1840s, and even arranged later as a concerto with orchestra. As noted in chapter 34, its four movements are all linked by transitions, so that the work is played without interruption. The "organic" continuity thus created, moreover, proceeds through a complete (and typically Schubertian) circle of major thirds, the four movements cadencing respectively in C major, E major, A♭ major, and C. As we shall see, Liszt became fascinated with this harmonic procedure and made it "typically Lisztian," in the process disseminating it widely, thanks to his enormous fame and prestige, and to the high-powered assertiveness with which his virtuoso manner could project substantive stylistic novelties.

It is that manner, and that assertiveness, with which we are mainly concerned at present, and they hit the listener like a cannon blast in the opening phrases of the First Concerto (Ex. 37-9a), modeled in their rhetoric so closely on the opening blast

EX. 37-9A   Franz Liszt, Piano Concerto no. 1, mm. 1–4

from Beethoven's Fifth that their novelty, in seeming paradox, is all the more vividly displayed. Two peremptory unison phrases in sequence, set off by fermatas: but where Beethoven's phrases were degrees of the diatonic scale, Liszt's are chromatic segments that give no hint of a tonal orientation in themselves. They speak, in short, the language not of the sonata but of the fantasia.

Between the two of them they encompass four half steps descending two at a time, or (to put it the other way round) two whole steps that together descend a major third.

EX. 37-9B   Franz Liszt, Piano Concerto no. 1, mm. 14–23

At first Liszt chooses to interpret the final note of the descent as an enharmonically notated flat submediant (albeit disguised by the fermataed wind chord that harmonizes it as the fifth of an enharmonically notated "Neapolitan"), resolving straightaway to the dominant, on which the piano makes its *Emperor* Concerto–like entry, leading to a frankly marked cadenza (even more frankly labeled *grandioso*) that puts the opening chromatic idea through a little development section which circles back to the dominant to prepare for an orchestral reentry that (we have every reason to assume) will serve as expository ritornello.

EX. 37-9B (*continued*)

And so it appears to do (Ex. 37-9b), until the piano cuts it off in measure 17 with another cadenza, which modulates to the Neapolitan key forecast in the opening bars. The orchestra tries again in the new key, only to be cut off for the third time by the piano (m. 23). By now there can be no doubt who is running the show. The soloist repeatedly, sometimes quite violently, seizes the spotlight, each time in order to display another facet of his personality—and the masculine pronoun seems justified not only

EX. 37-9C   Franz Liszt, Piano Concerto no. 1, mm. 25–37

by the aggressive nature of the pianist's interventions, but by his seductive advances on individual members of the supporting band. This third cadenza, for example, trails off into a long meditative episode (the second theme?) in which the piano is joined, beginning in measure 25, by several other solo instruments (clarinet, violins, cello) for confiding, seemingly amorous exchanges (Ex. 37-9c).

The overall form of the piece is likewise a display of various facets of a single entity: four linked episodes standing in (as per the *Wanderer* Fantasy) for movements, in which the last closes the tonal circle initiated by the first, and in which the middle episodes assume the characters of the traditional cantabile slow movement (*quasi adagio* at m. 99) and, abetted by the frolicsome triangle, the traditional scherzo (*allegretto vivace* at m. 175).

All of these facet-episodes, however, are motivically linked. The initial sequenced phrase, like the one that begins Beethoven's Fifth, shows up in the most various guises. Perhaps the most important is the one that first appears in the piano at m. 61 (Ex. 37-9d),

EX. 37-9D   Franz Liszt, Piano Concerto no. 1, mm. 61–70

EX. 37-9D (*continued*)

a passage in bravura double octaves marked *con impeto* (with abandon), in which the chromatic descent is extended to encompass an entire octave — and then three octaves (!), so that the passage traverses the entire keyboard. It returns in m. 292 to form a bridge between the scherzo and the finale; and, played presto at m. 494, it returns again (this time in the tonic) to bring the whole concerto to a close.

At once "organic" and quite unconventional is the concerto's tonal organization or "key scheme." The tonal space traversed by the original sequence, both in its four-half-step entirety (E♭–B) and in its two constituent phrases (E♭–D♭; D♭–B), governs many of the concerto's defining tonal relationships. The most "local" of these is the harmonization given the octave passage just described in Ex. 37-9d. The full chromatic scale occupies three beats, each containing four notes. Thus each beat contains the four-descending-half-step motive, and each repetition of the motive is harmonized with a root position triad, thus filling out a complete Schubertian cycle of major thirds to match the melodic completion of the chromatic scale: F♯–D–B♭–F♯. (On its last appearance the harmonization is "in the tonic" [i.e., E♭–B–G–E♭] exactly reproducing the root progression in the Sanctus from Schubert's Mass in E♭ major, cited in Ex. 34-11.)

The same relations, at the "global" level, define the tonal shape of the concerto as a whole. The work opens and closes in its nominal tonic, E♭. The Quasi adagio is cast in B major, and the bridge to the last movement (*allegro animato* at m. 292) is cast in C♯ (=D♭) major. This last, being a repetition of the octaves passage, is also harmonized by a circle of major thirds, C♯–A–F–C♯, one that exactly fills in the gaps, so to speak, between notes in the "tonic" circle described in the previous paragraph. The two circles of thirds are related exactly the way the opening pair of thematic statements relates to the chromatic scale: major thirds (four-half-step segments) subdivided into major seconds (two-half-step segments). Thus a thematic idea is interpreted harmonically to provide a tonal coherence based not on the generic circle of fifths but (as in some late works of Schubert) on an ad hoc circle of thirds. This is striking evidence indeed of the gradual shift from key to theme and motive as prime form-definer as the concept of "organic" unity took hold.

Particularly telling, from the standpoint of "organic" construction (or unity-within-diversity), are the thematic reprises in contrasting tempos and "characters." The Concerto's finale contains four such reprises, turning it into a sort of "recapitulation" of the whole. Most radically altered are two: the solo flute theme that is first heard *piano* (and marked *dolce, espressivo*) at m. 155, the slow movement's quiet coda, returns *forte* (marked *appassionato*) at m. 321 to round off the mercurial transition (*poco a poco più animato*) into the finale.

Most striking of all is the reuse of the ruminative main theme of the Quasi adagio — utterly transformed in key, tempo, and articulation, differently harmonized, and differently continued — as the propulsive main theme of the finale (*allegro marziale animato*). Actually, the Adagio theme is divided into two new themes, each with an independent continuation: compare mm. 108–110 of the big piano solo in the Adagio with mm. 352 ff in the finale, and mm. 110–112 with mm. 368 ff (see Ex. 37-10).

Liszt eventually gave a name to this fusing of variation technique with that of symphonic development and recapitulation. He called it "thematic transformation" (*thematische Verwandlung*). He proudly described it in a letter to his uncle Eduard (also a pianist) as "the *binding together* and rounding off of a whole piece at its close," and added that the idea "is somewhat my own."[17] Clearly, though, it drew on a great deal of existing

EX. 37-10A   Franz Liszt, Piano Concerto no. 1, Adagio, mm. 108–112

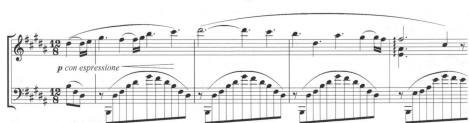

EX. 37-10B   Franz Liszt, Piano Concerto no. 1, Finale, mm. 352–56

EX. 37-10C   Franz Liszt, Piano Concerto no. 1, Finale, mm. 368–72

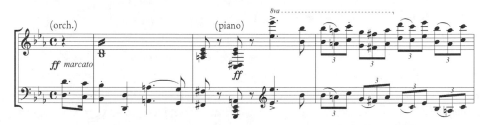

lore, both compositional and "philosophical" or aesthetic, and synthesized it in a manner that, depending on the point of view, could be variously described as unprecedentedly free or unprecedentedly rigorous. Either way, it could all be traced back to Beethoven, whose achievement could be similarly (variously and contradictorily) described.

Such technical and formal observations could be multiplied practically *ad libitum*: consider, for example, the fairly long stretch (mm. 320–37), where in a footnote Liszt directs the conductor's attention to "the rhythm of the first theme in the kettledrum," another idea ("abstracted rhythm") plainly — and proudly — appropriated from Beethoven's Fifth. They evince — or advertise — not only a wish to achieve a tight "organic" construction, but its realization as well. They testify, too, and somewhat ostentatiously, to the composer's impressive organizational skills: virtuoso composing to match virtuoso playing. And yet the result, for all its tightness and control, is a unique and unpredictable form; and the impression the concerto makes (and is designed to make) in its unfolding is that of a spontaneously inspired fantasia, an untrammeled train of associative thought, in which the soloist, the dominant personality, enjoys a hitherto unprecedented freedom to lead the orchestra — and the audience — whither he will.

A DIVIDED CULTURE

For these reasons, among others, Liszt's concerto, and the compositional approach it embodied, despite their claim of descent from Beethoven, were widely regarded by cultured musicians at the time as monstrosities. It is precisely at this point, in fact, that a chronic rift begins to open up between a compositional avant-garde, to which Liszt and many other "creative virtuosos" belonged, and a conservative establishment. This rift has been a constant factor in the history of European (and Euro-American) music ever since, and reached a crisis in the twentieth century. To a considerable extent, its story will be the main story of this book from now on.

Among the factors contributing to the rift was the wide and rapid spread of conservatories, to the point where they became the standard institutions of higher musical education everywhere, so that composers, no less than pianists and violinists, received a standard training administered with the aid of didactic texts. Conservatories are preservative institutions, both by etymology and by ideology. As originally noted in chapter 23, conservatories are called that because they were originally orphanages (*conservatorio* in Italian), preserving the lives of children, to whom musical training was given to make them employable. By the end of the eighteenth century, the word had lost that literal meaning, and designated instead a public institution whose primary purpose was the preservation of musical standards through standardized instruction.

As soon as those standards began to apply to composition, the idea of "classical music" (with a canonized "classical period" or golden age to validate its practices) was born, and with that came the notion of a classical tradition that had to be preserved through education in "classical forms." We have seen that the "classical period" received its official christening (from the Leipzig critic Johann Wendt) in 1836, the year of *Les Huguenots* and *A Life for the Tsar*. Most significantly, the theory of "sonata form" (as a tripartite or "aba" construction unfolding through a bithematic exposition, a development, and a recapitulation) dates from this period, not that of Haydn or Beethoven.

The books that first describe the form in these terms and give instruction in composing along these lines were the textbooks written by the transplanted Bohemian

FIG. 37-6   "We're delighted! Held in thrall! Jenny has turned the heads of all," caricature of a concert by Jenny Lind (the "Swedish nightingale," as P. T. Barnum dubbed her), Hamburg, 1845. Now it's the gentlemen's turn to run amok.

Anton Reicha for use at the Paris Conservatory (*Traité de haute composition musicale*, 3 vols, 1824–26) and Adolf Bernhard Marx for Berlin and Leipzig (*Die Lehre von der musikalischen Composition*, 4 vols, 1837–47). Thus by 1847, one could say that the conservatory canonization of the classical period, and of classical forms, was complete. Its dominant historical idea was that of a sacralized heritage — a golden age, a "classical period" — from which no advance was possible, only propagation or decline. Tradition meant maintenance.

As against that pessimistic view was another idea of history — the one vouchsafed by nineteenth-century science (Darwin, Comte) — that saw history as perpetual progressive evolution. According to this happy, self-confident outlook, tradition meant advance, and the heritage of the past was raw material to be transformed. That was the idea Liszt espoused in word and musical deed. It, too, claimed validating descent from Haydn, Mozart, and (especially) Beethoven, as Liszt's deliberate allusions to Beethoven emphatically attest, but it regarded their legacy not as a perfected heritage but as part of a dynamic process that continued into the present.

The conservatory view, it could seem, was an Enlightened backlash: a sui generis form such as Liszt achieved in his concerto was something atrocious rather than admirable, no matter how demonstrable its thematic coherence, because it represented merely subjective rather than universal truth. Its arbitrary freedoms were merely "liberties" that diminished the value of the product. And the attempt to create the impression of "improvisatory" spontaneity of gesture is unmasked as contradictory, even ludicrous, the moment someone other than the composer plays the piece. In an even tougher, more literalistic variant of such a stricture, the very participation of the orchestra makes pretentious nonsense of the composition's — that is, the composer's — willful uniqueness.

But while such criticism surely underestimates an audience's powers of empathy (or of what writers and critics of fiction call "the willing suspension of disbelief"),[18] it contains a nub of truth that points to a genuine paradox. What Mendelssohn's jeweled Violin Concerto and Liszt's impetuously "temperamental" Concerto in E♭ have in common — and where they differ from every previous "classical" concerto we have examined (including Mendelssohn's own piano concertos, intended as vehicles for his own performances) — is that they contain no provision at all for actual improvisation. Their every note is preplanned and put in place, hence controlled, by the composer — even (or should we say especially?) their cadenzas, which now take on a previously unaspired-to "structural" role. Mozart, who lived at a time, and played before audiences, that valued truly spontaneous behavior at musical performances (both from the player and from the listener), would have been quite dumbfounded, not to say aghast.

Mendelssohn and Liszt were brought up at the tail end of that "Mozartean" time. They were both steeped in the art of genuine improvisation, and displayed it with alacrity. In a fascinating letter to his sister Fanny, dated 30 January 1836, Mendelssohn described his cadenzas to a concerto by Mozart (the D-minor, K. 466), performed ex tempore the day before to great success. After jotting down a few passages to show how he had cleverly juxtaposed and developed two of Mozart's themes, he added that one of the second violin players,

> an old musician, said to me afterwards, when he met me in the corridor, that he had heard it played in the same hall by Mozart himself, but since that day he had heard no one introduce such good cadenzas as I did yesterday — which gave me very great pleasure.[19]

As for Liszt, we not only have the evidence of his London program, already quoted, that he was in the habit early on of ending his appearances with "Extempore Fantasias" on submitted themes, but also a curious complaint from Glinka, quoted by Stasov, that

> sometimes Liszt played magnificently, like no one else in the world, but other times intolerably, in a highly affected manner, dragging tempi and adding to the works of others, even to those of Chopin, Beethoven, Weber, and Bach a lot of embellishments of his own that were often tasteless, worthless and meaningless.[20]

This remark of Glinka's is wonderful testimony to the change of taste (perceived as a change in ethics) that was taking place under the impact of changing customs and institutions, and in response to the new musical "work-concept" that arose in the wake of Beethoven and his romantic reception. Glinka, as we learned in the previous chapter, had spent a year in Berlin, where he had "had his ideas on music put in order" by Siegfried Dehn, an apostle of the new "classicism" that was passing itself off as antiquarianism, a return to old (or eternal) values.

His strictures against Liszt were not received all that well by Glinka's Russian interlocutors, one of whom commented (in the language of Russian high society), "Allons donc, allons donc, tout cela ce n'est que rivalité de métier!" ("Come now, come now, all that is just professional jealousy"). But eventually the idea that musical scores are inviolable texts, and that improvisation is a debased form of musical art, affected even Liszt, as his meticulously notated, "organic" piano concerto confirms. By 1849, not even spontaneity could be "merely" spontaneous. And pianists trained in conservatories spent all their time (like Liszt in 1832) on "trills, sixths, octaves, tremolos, double notes and cadenzas"—but not on their own cadenzas. Improvisation was no longer part of the curriculum, and by the end of the century, for artists in the European literate tradition, it had become a lost art—which is to say, the literate tradition had become more truly and literally and exclusively literate. There are now probably hundreds if not thousands of conservatory-trained pianists in the world whose techniques at trills, octaves, and double notes are the equal of Liszt's, but hardly a one who can end a concert with an extempore fantasia. Should we call this progress?

Critics

SCHUMANN AND BERLIOZ

THE PUBLIC SPHERE

The same explosion of musical activity into public life that gave rise to the new virtuosity (or found an outlet in it) also gave rise to a new musical profession altogether: that of critic, someone who evaluates music and musicians professionally, for the benefit of nonprofessionals and nonpractitioners.

This last proviso is necessary in order to distinguish the music critics who flourished in the nineteenth century in response to a new public need from other writers about music, such as theorists and pedagogues. Theoretical and didactic writings have existed as long as there has been a literate tradition of music, but they address an audience of professionals, would-be professionals, and amateur practitioners on matters of professional or practical concern. It was a new musical market—new patterns of musical consumption by a broad nonprofessional public—that required the mediation of public advisers and public spokesmen.

The very idea of a "public sphere"—an arena of free speech and debate, a "marketplace of ideas" in which everyone had, at least in principle, a stake and therefore a right to participate—was a novelty in continental Europe. In England it had a longer history, which we have traced as far back as the time of Handel; but on the Continent it was an idea associated above all with the Enlightenment and the faith it placed in the dissemination of knowledge, and the exercise of reason, as guarantors of political freedom. In the public sphere privileged status was accorded, at least in theory, not to wealth, not to birth, but to persuasiveness; and persuasion, ideally, flowed from expertise. Power flowed to the expert from the ability to influence or even mold public opinion. As the concept of the public-at-large grew by leaps and bounds during the nineteenth century owing to urbanization and educational reform, and as the idea grew popular that ultimate political power resided in it, many vied for the power to shape its views.

The supreme instrument for the exercise of this power in an age of exploding literacy was the press, and the role of musical expert molding public opinion on music and musicians was exercised both in the columns of daily newspapers and in specialized musical journals addressed not only to musicians but to the concertgoing and music-purchasing public at large. To become a public expert and a power in the public sphere of music, one either gained employment at a newspaper or founded a journal. Perhaps the earliest musical journalism that looks like what we now think of as criticism in the modern sense was the columns of Joseph Addison about the

London (Italian) opera stage, which appeared in *The Spectator* beginning in 1711. The first specialized music journal was *Critica musica*, published and edited in Hamburg (Germany's main commercial center) by the composer and theorist Johann Mattheson between 1722 and 1725.

Addison, a lawyer and politician and definitely not a musician (although he did write a libretto or two), was the prototype for the "critic as public spokesman." Mattheson, who was a very distinguished musician indeed, was the prototype for the "critic as public adviser." The two types have coexisted ever since. Their interests (in both senses of the word) do not necessarily coincide. In the 1940s in New York, for example, the two most influential music reviewers classically embodied the dichotomy. Olin Downes (1886–1955), who wrote for the *New York Times*, was a musical amateur whose previous paid involvement with the art had amounted to playing the piano to accompany exercise classes and singing lessons. Virgil Thomson (1896–1989), who wrote for the *Herald Tribune*, was an important composer who remained active as such throughout his tenure with the newspaper. The one was as militant a public representative or mouthpiece as the other was a public preceptor. It was a rare day when their reviews agreed about anything.

It is Thomson, whom we will meet again in a later chapter, whose writings have remained in print and are considered in retrospect to be a significant ingredient in the history of their times. This may not be altogether fair; Downes, who wrote for the more powerful paper, probably had a more decisive impact at the time on musicians' careers and composers' reputations. But it is understandable that history has favored Thomson. It is the very conflict of interest in composer critics that claims the attention of history. Their words are inevitably read as advocacy—even propaganda—rather than objective judgment.

This may lessen their effectiveness in the short run, but it serves in retrospect as a lens through which to consider not only their own work as composers, or that of their subjects, but also, more broadly, the nature of the relationship between the creator of musical works and the audience that received them—the relationship, to put it in "market" terms, between producer and consumer. As already intimated in the previous chapter, that relationship was subject to strains during the nineteenth century owing to the contradictions that emerged, not only between the ideals of romanticism and the realities of the market, or between romanticism and Enlightenment, but even within romanticism itself. As a result, composer critics tend to be profoundly ambivalent figures, and fascinating ones.

There were many interesting composer critics over the course of the nineteenth century, including Alexander Serov (1820–71) and César Cui (1835–1918), both opera composers, in Russia, and Hugo Wolf (1860–1903) in Germany. Liszt himself published a good deal of critical prose (often ghostwritten by his aristocratic mistresses, the Comtesse d'Agoult and the Princess Sayn-Wittgenstein). There were also, to be sure, some very influential and culturally significant noncomposing critics, including Eduard Hanslick (1825–1904) in Vienna and George Bernard Shaw (1856–1950) in London.

The birth of modern musical criticism is usually traced to the founding at Leipzig, in 1798, of the *Allgemeine musikalische Zeitung* ("Universal music news"), a "musical newspaper for the general public," to give its name the proper nuance. Friedrich Rochlitz (1769–1842), its first editor, was an amateur musician, trained as a theologian, who had worked as a professional journalist and translator before specializing in music criticism. Rochlitz kept his post at the helm for two decades, and became the most influential musical tastemaker in Germany. The journal itself lasted until 1848. The momentous early articles on Beethoven by E. T. A. Hoffmann, which played such a crucial role in defining the romantic outlook on music (see chapter 31), were all published in the *Allgemeine musikalische Zeitung* during Rochlitz's tenure.

Two early composer critics stand out as historical figures by reason of their eminence in both their domains. As it happens, one of them went the newspaper route and the other founded a journal. Hector Berlioz (1803–69) worked regularly as reviewer and essayist for the *Journal des débats*, the leading Paris daily, from 1834 to 1863, and wrote for a number of other publications besides. He did it for a livelihood, and (so he said) reluctantly, since his composing earned him little or nothing until the last decade of his life.

Robert Schumann (1810–56) became involved in criticism at just about the same time. He planned and wrote a prospectus for his Leipzig magazine, the *Neue Zeitschrift für Musik* ("New music journal"), in 1833. As the place of publication already suggests, Schumann's journal was intended at the outset as a direct challenge or alternative to the *Allgemeine musikalische Zeitung*, which had grown conservative and "philistine," and hostile to the elite faction Schumann wished to champion. The first issue appeared on 3 April 1834. Schumann edited it single-handedly (and filled its columns almost single-handedly) throughout its first decade. Since 1844 it has had many other editors, and still exists, at least in name.

WHAT IS A PHILISTINE?

The Philistines, in history, were a non-Semitic (probably Greek) people who settled on the Mediterranean coast, in a region now named Palestine after them, around 1200 BCE. In the Bible, of course, they figure as the historical enemies of the Israelites, God's "chosen people." It is easy to see how the term could be applied to the opponents of any chosen, or self-chosen, group. In the early nineteenth century the name was applied by artists imbued with the ideals of romanticism to those perceived as their

FIG. 38-1 Robert Schumann, drawing from a daguerreotype by Johann Anton Völlner, Hamburg, March 1850.

enemies, namely the materialistic, hedonistic "crowd," indifferent to culture and content with commonplace entertainment.

Already a tension within romanticism is exposed, because that crowd, with its "democratized" taste, was now the primary source of support for artists, and many romantic artists, notably Liszt, took sustenance from it and actively wooed it. For an idea of romantic ambivalence toward the public, we might recall that it was none other than Liszt who defined for us (in his memoir of John Field, quoted in chapter 34) the romantic ideal of subjective privacy and public indifference. It could hardly be said that Liszt practiced what he seemed there to be preaching.

Schumann, who as a critic did holy battle with the philistines more persistently, and more explicitly, than any other, was also not without ambivalences or inner conflicts on this score. He began his career as a would-be virtuoso of the new school, inspired by Paganini, whose *Caprices* he also arranged for piano around the same time as did Liszt, and whose musical portrait he painted over and over again. His pianistic ambitions came to grief in 1832, when he injured his right hand by overpractice with the aid of a mechanical contrivance intended to free the ring finger from its physiological dependence on the middle finger.

An alternative hypothesis is that Schumann's weakened fingers were the result of mercury poisoning induced during treatment for syphilitic symptoms, which ultimately affected his brain and led to the mental illness that finally incapacitated him. His frustration, and the "sour grapes" to which it gave rise, may have played its part in engendering the hyperbolic idealism that informed Schumann's criticism. But that was no impediment; rather, by attracting attention to him and making his work influential, Schumann's animus became the source of his power.

In one of his early reviews in the *Neue Zeitschrift für Musik*, for example, Schumann warned creative artists of the "poisoned flowers" (the temptations) in their path, namely "the applause of the vulgar crowd and the fixed gaze of sentimental women."[1] By the time he came to write his famous comparison of Meyerbeer's *Les Huguenots* and Mendelssohn's *Paulus* (sampled in chapter 36), Schumann had no hesitation in condemning Meyerbeer's base motives, when the only evidence for that baseness was his success with "the masses."

Yet one need only compare the drawings of Liszt and Paganini, both of them artists without whom musical romanticism is inconceivable, in Figures 37-1 and 37-4, to savor the contrast between romantic theory and romantic practice. The situation becomes even more complicated when Schumann's stormy courtship (replete with elopements and lawsuits) and marriage to Clara Wieck (1819–96), his piano teacher's daughter and a famous virtuoso in her own right, is taken into account. Clara, who like Fanny Mendelssohn was a major composing talent quashed by antifeminine prejudices, seconded her husband's strictures against virtuosity and publicity with alacrity, and there is no reason to doubt her sincerity, or his. But neither she nor he ever lived up to them in life, or meant to. It was not hypocrisy but what psychologists call dissociation (or, more vulgarly, "compartmentalization") that allowed romantic idealists the ability to achieve sufficient compromise with reality conditions to survive, often very happily indeed.

It was in his fantasy life, to which he gave almost novelistic expression in his criticism, that Schumann lived up to his ideals, and inspired legions of romantic artists with similar fantasies. His reviews often took the form of narratives, little stories in the lives of the Davidsbündler, the members of the imaginary "Davidsbund," the "League of David" who fought the Goliaths of the Philistine press, on the one hand, and, on the other (no less menacing), the authoritarian mind-set of the conservatory.

The cast of characters included, in the first place, Florestan and Eusebius, Schumann's alter egos. The former, named after Beethoven's imprisoned freedom-fighter, represented his embattled *"innerliches 'Ich,'"* his "inmost I," a concept we have associated with German romanticism from its Beethovenian beginning. Eusebius, named after an early

FIG. 38-2 Robert and Clara Schumann (née Wieck), daguerreotype by Johann Anton Völlner, Hamburg, March 1850.

church historian, later adjudged a heretic (as Schumann must have known), represented Schumann's gentler, more moderate nature in contrast and occasional opposition to the more choleric Florestan.

Thus Schumann acknowledged within himself the ambivalences endemic to the composer critic's role, torn between the artist's intransigence and the detachment of the public arbiter. A third regular character, Meister Raro, originally represented Schumann's teacher, Friedrich Wieck. Thus we have a virtual Freudian trinity: the rash and reckless Florestan (id), the milder, more sociable Eusebius (ego), and the reproving Raro (superego). As Freud constantly maintained, his psychoanalytic theory was strongly prefigured in romantic literature, and here is a choice bit of evidence.

A Schumannian review typically consisted not of a direct critique but of a reported conversation among the Davidsbündler — a public airing of private response, a comparison of subjective experiences in an imagined private space. By the use of what Sanna Pederson, a historian of music criticism, calls "framing strategies," Schumann encouraged his readers, first, to have (and to trust) strong empathic responses to the music they heard or played, and, second, to try to explain them in terms of the composer's achievement.[2]

Such a review, writes Pederson, is not so much informative or didactic as *performative*, promoting a model of behavior rather than advancing a specific opinion. The act of selecting a work for such a discussion implicitly raises it to the level of high (or "autonomous") art, and the serious, confiding nature of the discussion serves as a counterweight to the mindless applause that validates music in the public marketplace. By aspiring to the model of behavior exemplified by the Davidsbund, Schumann's reading public could transcend philistinism and join his imagined elite community of disinterested artistic natures.

Above all, Schumann encouraged his readers to look for more than sensory stimulation in music, but rather seek in it the same mental and spiritual delight they sought in literature. In this he swam distinctly not only against the tide of philistinism but also against that of the Enlightenment, which had relegated music (in the words of Kant) to the category of "enjoyment more than culture."[3] By contrast, John Daverio, a Schumann biographer and a historian of romanticism, went so far as to identify Schumann's ideal as being one of "music as literature," meaning not (or not always) a music that has a literary plot line or "program," but rather music that has a complexity of meaning, an "intellectual substance," comparable to that of the most artistic literature.[4]

LITERARY MUSIC

Schumann most clearly and convincingly aimed at this complexity in his character pieces for piano and his songs, the private genres in which Schubert had set the standard. He was very conscious of Schubert as a forebear — exceptionally so for the time, when most German composers sought preceptors chiefly in Beethoven and (lately) in Bach, and were striving mightily to build a national repertory in the "public" forms of symphony and oratorio. Schumann venerated the great Bs, too, and emulated them in his large orchestral and choral works, which he wrote with increasing frequency as his career progressed, and especially after he succeeded Mendelssohn and Hiller as music director at Düsseldorf in 1849.

At the outset of his career, though, in his Davidsbündler period, Schumann was among the few who found special inspiration in Schubert, in whom he saw a sort of musical novelist. In a letter to Friedrich Wieck, Schumann compared Schubert directly to the popular romantic novelist Johann Paul Friedrich Richter (1763–1825), who wrote under the pseudonym Jean Paul. The comparison is especially revealing because Schumann is known to have secretly modeled some of his early piano pieces on favorite passages in works by Jean Paul, especially *Die Flegeljahre* ("years of indiscretion"), a long bildungsroman (novel of coming-of-age) in four volumes with which many young romantics ardently identified. Schumann's own identification with this novel was such that he consciously modeled the personalities of his literary alter egos, Eusebius and Florestan, on the twin brothers Walt and Vult, the novel's joint heroes.

More generally, if literary music was Schumann's ideal, he could have found no better model for it than Jean Paul's musicalized literature, in which musical experiences and occasions often trigger major *Erlebnisse* (emotional epiphanies, transcendental moments) in the novels. Jean Paul was a skilled amateur pianist who habitually put himself in the mood to write by improvising *Sturm und Drang* fantasias at the keyboard. Thus, music of a particular free-flowing style congenial to the romantic temperament may even have helped the writer find his unique and fascinating literary voice, with its apparently meandering, erratically digressive manner.

So this is what Schumann meant when he wrote to Wieck that "when I play Schubert, it is as though I were reading a composed novel of Jean Paul."[5] What was most remarkable in Schubert, he went on, was his "psychological" quality: "What a diary is to others, in which they set down their momentary feelings, etc., music paper really was to Schubert, to which he entrusted his every mood, and his whole soul, musical through-and-through, wrote notes where others use words." Schumann's choice of words ("momentary feelings") was surely an allusion, conscious or not, to Schubert's *Moments musicaux*, and we will find in Schumann a similar preoccupation with harmonic nuance and ambiguity. Indeed, prompted by Schubert's example, Schumann went further and became the master of the unconsummated harmonic gesture, one of the most potent of all romantic "musico-literary" effects.

Since we have approached Schumann by way of Schubert, it would make sense to look first at one of his song cycles ("novels in song"), in which he successfully emulated Schubert's most characteristic achievement — so successfully that it is fair to call Schumann's the only cycles that truly rival Schubert's in stature and in frequency of performance. Fully five of them were written in a single year, 1840, during which Schumann produced an astonishing sum of 140 lieder. The great "song year" was also the year of his marriage to Clara Wieck, who was about to reach majority, after years of legal travail.

As Schumann's Florestan once said, "I do not like those whose life is not in unison with their works."[6] Schumann's commitment to art song, that is to composing endless variations on the theme of love, can hardly be read any other way than in light of Florestan's dictum. But whether it was a case of art spontaneously imitating life, as romantic doctrine would have it, or one of life imitating art in conformity with romantic doctrine, is more difficult to say. Hardest of all to decide is how much significance such biographical resonance should be accorded in our appreciation of the works. That is an unsettled, and unsettleable, debate of long standing. We will engage the issue, but don't expect solutions.

Variations on the theme of love must include some sad ones, of course, and this already casts some doubt, in the present instance, on the simple proposition that an artist's works, no matter how romantic, are the direct outgrowth and expression of lived experience. Indeed, the outstanding product of 1840, Schumann's year of long-deferred conjugal bliss, was *Dichterliebe* ("Poet's love"), op. 48, a set of love songs to lyrics by Heinrich Heine that trace the most dismal emotional trajectory imaginable, a painful saga of unrequited love.

Dismal, yes, but not tragic, the way Schubert's *Die schöne Müllerin* is tragic, for the cycle ends not with suicide but (as Heine tells us) with renunciation and (as Schumann tells us) with eventual healing.

FIG. 38-3   Heinrich Heine as drawn by Wilhelm Hensel, 1829.

Heine was the great master of emotional ambivalence, and that made him the perfect partner for Schumann. From chapter 34, we may recall Heine as the author of the weird ironic poems that drew from Schubert, in the last year of his life, some of his most extravagant harmonic vagaries. Schumann was the first composer to set Heine's verse in quantity.

The sixteen songs in *Dichterliebe* (out of twenty originally composed in a single feverish week at the end of May) are all settings of poems from Heine's early collection, *Lyrisches Intermezzo*, which contains sixty-six poems. Schumann's selection begins with Heine's no. 1 and ends with Heine's no. 66, so that the cycle can be viewed as a sort of condensation of the book. Ex. 38-1 amounts to a condensation of that condensation, sampling the first pair of songs, the last song, and two *Erlebnisse* from within the cycle.

The first song, "Im wunderschönen Monat Mai" ("In the ravishing month of May"), is an especially good candidate for reading as a direct translation of lived experience, since it concerns longing that is felt during the very month in which Schumann, then longing for union with Clara, is known to have composed the song. A question, though: exactly what difference does it make to the listener to know these facts? And another: are the feelings of fictional characters, as embodied in art, less real than those of their creators? Whatever our response to these questions—hence whatever the "source" of the emotion expressed in the song (whether Schumann's life, Heine's life, or that of the fictional "poet" of the title)—the task of the "literary" musician remains the same. It is to find a musical embodiment of the emotion that will complement, and hopefully intensify, the verbal one, thus to arouse a sympathetic vibration in the beholder (for it is ultimately the beholder's life that is of greatest concern—at least to the beholder).

EX. 38-1A Robert Schumann, *Dichterliebe*, Op. 47, no. 1 ("Im wunderschönen Monat Mai")

EX. 38-1A (continued)

In the lovely month of May,
when all the buds were bursting,
then within my heart
love broke forth.

In the lovely month of May,
when all the birds were singing
then I confessed to her
my longing and desire.

The nature of that embodiment is apparent from the very first downbeat, in which the entering left hand creates a strident dissonance, a major seventh, against the tied upbeat in the right. That dissonance we immediately recognize as a suspension. (We may even wish to call it an "unprepared" suspension since it is not preceded by a consonance between the parts, but only by a single note in one.) We know how a suspension must resolve. Therefore, we feel a "longing" to hear a B — a longing that by a common convention we may wish to ascribe to the C♯ itself, thence to the singer of the song (even though he has not sung anything as yet). Nor is our longing immediately satisfied: the dissonant note is held over an arpeggiation of five tones, three of them also dissonant against C♯, during which the suspension, the first harmonic gesture in the song, remains unconsummated.

To dispose of a common objection to "musico-literary" interpretation: our longing to hear the B is admittedly created not by the sounds alone and unassisted, but in response to cultural conditioning (that is, what we have learned from our previous experience with suspensions). That only makes the device more apt, since the association of amorous longing with springtime (on an analogy, stated in the poem itself, with the burgeoning of plant life, or in conditioned response to hearing the songs of the returning birds) is also a cultural construction, not an instinct. (Humans, after all, unlike most animals, do not experience natural "heat," or seasonal periods of sexual appetite.) These are not meaningful objections; it is no news to anybody that human beings live and act in a state of culture, not unmediated nature.

The local resolution of C♯ to B occurs during a larger progression that could be viewed as complementary in function: a B minor triad in first inversion moves to a dominant seventh on C♯. The repetition of this progression in mm. 3–4 produces another sort of frustrated longing, through another "unconsummated harmonic gesture," as the dominant seventh fails to resolve to its implied tonic, F♯. The song's key signature, that of F♯ minor, corroborates that aural impression. Even without looking at the music (but all the more keenly if we happen to be looking) we are conditioned to interpret the progression as $iv_6 - V_7$ in F♯ minor.

In m. 5, where the voice enters, another frustrating oscillation between dominant and subdominant seems to get underway. But the vocal phrase reroutes the progression toward a cadence in A major, also a possible reading of the key signature. Now we are conditioned retrospectively to interpret the B minor triad as a pivot, changing its function from minor subdominant to major supertonic. This new implied cadence — $ii_6 - V_7 - I$ — is confirmed in measure 6. It seems to identify the "real" key of the piece as A major, and the piano's four-bar prelude as a feint.

But lest we be lulled prematurely into a false sense of tonal security, let us recall that if the opening bars were a harmonic feint, then the dominant seventh of F♯ minor is still unresolved. It is still an unconsummated harmonic gesture, and still hangs over our perception of the apparent "perfect" cadence in m. 6, coloring it with a pesky sense of ambiguity (of possible "III-ness") that renders it fragile. And in fact it turns out to be impermanent. The voice repeats the cadence on A in m. 8, but then moves on (m. 10) to a cadence on B minor, achieved through an appoggiatura (another "longing" tone — and look what an assortment of appoggiaturas show up to second it in the piano part!), and finally (m. 12) to a cadence on D major to finish up the stanza, approached through another appoggiatura, G-natural, that actually contradicts the key signature. If D major is in fact the tonic of this song, then *everything* up to now has been a feint.

The returning piano figuration in m. 12 (in which the G♯–F♯ effectively cancels the voice's G-natural, which had proceeded to F♯ in the same register) shows the excursion to D major to have been the harmonic feint. D major in root position links up smoothly with the inverted B-minor chord from before, and the interrupted cadence — or rather, the unconsummated oscillation — of iv$_6$ and V$_7$ in F♯ minor is resumed to link the two strophes, the second being a harmonic replay of the first, repeating at the end (over the very word *Verlangen*, "desire") the unconfirmed — and unconfirmable — excursion to D major.

So what, then, is the function of the D-major triad, on which the voice makes its illusory cadence? Like the inverted B-minor triad — the other chord with D in the bass — it is a pivot that links the signature-sharing keys of F♯ minor and A major, and preempts their cadential fulfillment. The voice part begins and ends on harmonic pivots, hovering perpetually on a cusp between two keys, both sanctioned by the signature but neither cadentially confirmed. Since a pivot is by definition a harmony with a dual (or multiple) function within a piece or progression, the tonality of the song thus hovers undecidedly — and undecidably — in an unprecedented "in between" region, fraught with ambiguity in the most genuine and literal sense of the word. Which key is it in? Both and neither.

In its refusal to settle the matter of keys, the entire song thus prolongs a single unconsummated harmonic gesture — expressed most dramatically by the piano's forever-oscillating, never-cadencing ritornello — that finds its "objective correlative" (its fixed semantic counterpart) on the literary plane. That final line, "my longing and desire," has the last word in a profoundly musical sense, made palpable by the very last note in the song — a B that in context functions as an unresolved, unconsummated seventh. After it dies away the air veritably tingles with the longing and desire it has created/symbolized/embodied.

Of course this is only the first song in a cycle of sixteen. We can hope, like the singer (as we are left imagining him), that resolution and consummation will come in the next song (Ex. 38-1b). That is not only an emotional but an esthetic plus: the unresolved seventh demands that the cycle continue, heightening the sense of "organic" unity that binds it into an artistic whole transcending the sum of its parts.

But does resolution come? The first harmony in the second song consists of two notes: A and C♯. They are both part of the F♯-minor chord the first song leaves us longing for, but the defining root is missing. The same two notes are equally members of the A-major triad, the first song's undecidable alternative tonic. Thus Schumann has found another way to defer an unequivocal statement — which accords perfectly with the sense of the second song, which is one big "if." As the bass moves down the scale, the full F♯-minor triad is sounded briefly on the second beat. But this is no unequivocal statement: the chord occurs in a weak rhythmic position, and the bass moves right on down to D — the first song's dread pivot note. The "if" remains resolved.

It is never resolved at all in the poem, and yet we notice that eventually the song does cadence firmly — and repeatedly — on A, the "wrong" goal, disconfirming the first song's closing gesture and perhaps telegraphing the ultimate frustration of the poet's amorous longing. But do these cadences on A really give an answer, even if "wrong"? Does the music of the second song dispel the disquieting ambiguities of the first?

A closer look at the relationship between the voice and the accompaniment shows that ambiguities remain, and that Schumann has merely found another way to leave harmonic gestures unconsummated.

Each of the singer's phrases contains two lines of the poem. Each verse couplet, though punctuated with commas rather than periods to maintain a sense of rhetorical urgency, contains a complete sentence, and each of them is punctuated in the setting, as we have seen, by a cadence. But the voice part ends every time on the supertonic, over a dominant chord, extended with a fermata. Every one of the singer's gestures, even the last, is thus demonstratively left unconsummated, preserving the open-endedness of the "if." Harmonic closure comes only in the accompaniment, *pianissimo*, like an echo — or perhaps a reflected thought, suggesting imaginary fulfillment of the singer's iffy wish.

Like Schubert before him, Schumann had a special genius for expressing in music a condition contrary to fact — the most subjective (hence romantic) thing that

EX. 38-1B   Robert Schumann, *Dichterliebe*, Op. 47, no. 2 (*Aus meinen Thränen*)

From my tears spring up
many blooming flowers,
and my sighs become
a chorus of nightingales.

And if you love me, child,
I give you all the flowers,
and before your window shall sound
the song of the nightingale.

music can do. And so we are prepared to grasp the irony with which the most seemingly definite and unequivocally consummated musical gestures in the cycle are undermined, turning consummation itself into a species of unconsummation. This paradoxical effect is the one for which Heine was especially famous; and the most famous example of all examples of it is the huge complaint called "Ich grolle nicht" ("I'm not complaining"), which Schumann set as the seventh song in *Dichterliebe*. Ex. 38-1c shows its second half.

EX. 38-1C   Robert Schumann, *Dichterliebe*, Op. 47, no. 7 ("Ich grolle nicht"), mm. 16–end

EX. 38-1C *(continued)*

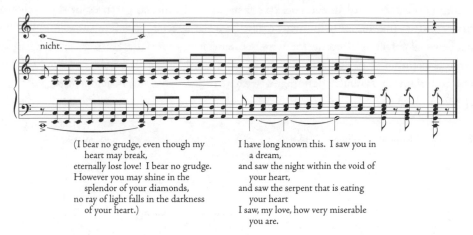

nicht.

(I bear no grudge, even though my
    heart may break,
eternally lost love! I bear no grudge.
However you may shine in the
    splendor of your diamonds,
no ray of light falls in the darkness
    of your heart.)

I have long known this. I saw you in
    a dream,
and saw the night within the void of
    your heart,
and saw the serpent that is eating
    your heart
I saw, my love, how very miserable
    you are.

In this emotional turning point, the disillusioned poet lashes out at the love object who has rejected him. The poem is a rant, ably seconded by the pounding repeated chords in the pianist's right hand with their regular accents, and by the operatic ascent to the high note (famously an afterthought entered in proofs, but what of that?) to match the most extravagant poetic metaphor of the poet's rage. The setting is full of uncommonly straightforward word painting, sometimes verging on the corny (like the six-beat dilation on the word *längst*, "long"). All of this belaboring of the obvious can only be a signal that none of it is true.

And so the harmony confirms. The description of the poet's dream, in which the surface mood is what the Germans call *Schadenfreude* (gloating at another's misfortune), is undermined by the tortured harmony (every chord containing a dissonance!) that shows it is the singer, not the one figuratively sung to, who is truly *elend* (miserable). The most complete unmasking of the surface pretense, of course, comes right at the end, where the final refrain (Schumann's idea) is accompanied by the baldest IV – V – I imaginable, followed by a ranting postlude that does nothing except insist on the finality of the cadence, and capped by a quite gratuitously banged out I_4^6 – V – I. The most definite tonal assertion in the whole cycle accompanies its most

FIG. 38-4 Program of a subscription concert given in Düsseldorf (20 February 1851) at which Robert Schumann conducted Beethoven's Fifth Symphony and Clara Schumann played Weber's *Concertstück* (Concert Piece) in F Minor under her husband's baton. As was usual at the time, there are songs and piano solos between the orchestral offerings, but nothing by Schumann.

flagrant lie—"I'm not complaining," indeed! If the truth is ambiguous, the implication seems to be, only ambiguity can be true.

In song no. 12, of which the first half is given in Ex. 38-1d, nature becomes animate in good *volkstümlich* fashion. But Heine and Schumann remain incorrigibly urbane artists. Their folklikeness is never innocent. It continually veers over into the Schubertian twilight world of morbid self-absorption, an adamantly bourgeois domain. The harmony described by the piano's first arpeggio is an old Schubertian ploy, most familiar to us from the *Moments musicaux* (Ex. 34-6), a German sixth that is homophonous with a dominant seventh and hence contains the promise of double meaning. Its first alternative resolution (that is, the first instance of "doubleness") comes in measure 9, at the moment when the flowers first speak to the poet from "their world" (meaning, of course, from his own "inner space"). Their actual words are set off later by a slower tempo and a modulation to the key of the diatonic submediant, itself an instance of doubleness since the German sixth occurs on the chromaticized ("flat") submediant, through which safe return to the tonic is made two measures later.

EX. 38-1D   Robert Schumann, *Dichterliebe*, Op. 47, no. 12 (*Am leuchtenden Sommermorgen*), mm. 1–9

In the bright summer morning
I walk about the garden,
The flowers are whispering
    and talking,

As so often happens in *Dichterliebe*, the voice part in this song ends on an unconsummated dominant, to be resolved "inwardly," in the accompaniment. That resolution takes place through one of the longest of the many extended piano postludes in the cycle. The postlude begins with a recapitulation of the piano's opening phrase, which had already recurred as a ritornello between the verses, thus suggesting that the poet's pensive stroll continues. But now he wanders wordlessly. It is as if Schumann were invoking Heine's own famous dictum, "When words fail, music speaks." By seeming to supplement musically the poet's uncompleted thought, the composer invites the listener to complete them imaginatively, as a poet might do by ending a line with an ellipsis (" . . . ").

The listener's imagination is called upon again, even more urgently and explicitly, at the very end of the cycle. The last song—in which the love born at the beginning of the cycle, having died, is buried—is bitter and angry, another rant. The singer mocks his own grief with a parody of a merry song, and puffs it up with hyperbolic comparisons between love's coffin and the most enormous things he can think of (beer casks, bridges, cathedrals). Only at the end does the mood begin to soften. But the voice drops out (as usual, on an unconsummated harmony) before the change of mood is consummated. It is transferred first to the "thought music" in the piano, where we are at first surprised to hear a reprise of the postlude from no. 12, putting us back, as it were, in the summer garden for more tranquil recollection (Ex. 38-1e).

EX. 38-1E   Robert Schumann, *Dichterliebe*, Op. 47, no. 16 ("Die alten, bösen Lieder"), mm. 53–67

EX. 38-1E (*continued*)

But then (m. 59) we are more than surprised; we may even be confused to hear what sounds like another song start up, but without the singer. This extra song is short but (unlike many of the actual songs in the cycle) melodically and harmonically complete. It does not allude to any previous song in the cycle. The texture, homophonic rather than arpeggiated, ineluctably suggests words, which we must supply (or at least whose import we must divine) in our imagination, influenced in part, to be sure, by the sensuous qualities of the music, but also, perhaps more strongly, by our own "take" on the situations conveyed by the whole cycle to this point.

So it is not just the beholder's imagination that is engaged, but the beholder's subjectivity, meaning the beholder's own unique combination of experience and inclination. As early as 1794, when the idea of the "esthetic" was new and romanticism was green, Friedrich Schiller commented on the need for this act of completion on the part of the beholder, and the way that it enriches the experience of art, when he wrote that "the real and express content that the poet puts in his work remains always finite; the possible content that he allows us to contribute is an infinite quality."[7]

By "poet," of course, Schiller meant to include all artists, and he surely meant to imply that all art inevitably shared the property to which he called attention. Nevertheless, once the idea was abroad there were many artists who were not content to leave the property latent or implicit. Romantic artists who wished most fully to realize Schiller's idea were the ones most inclined to leave important things deliberately unsaid. Among composers it was Schumann, with his boundlessly varied unconsummated gestures, who realized it in the highest and most principled degree. That is what the notion of "literary music," in the profoundest sense, connoted.

HOW MUSIC POSES QUESTIONS

To savor the experience of literary music without the concurrent medium of words we may consider two piano compositions from Schumann's freshest, most idealistic period, one of them tiny, the other grand. A proviso first: although words do not figure *concurrently* in piano music, they are often present in the form of titles, epigraphs, textual allusions, and so on. These definitely and purposefully mediate the effect of the notes and should be thought of as part of the work rather than as an "extramusical" expendable or a mere concession to "unmusical" beholders. The latter view gained a lot of currency in the twentieth century, owing to the confusion of the romantic idea of "absolute music" with a vein of antiromantic formalism that later invaded musical thought. It will be discussed at the proper time.

Schumann never intended any such strict conceptual segregation of media. He did not distinguish between the contribution of the music and that of words to the effect of his compositions. In fact he abhorred such distinctions, enthusiastically committed to the view (as he once put it in an aphorism) that "the aesthetics of one art is that of the others too; only the materials differ."[8] This little maxim of Schumann's could be looked upon as heralding the late-nineteenth-century ideal of media-synthesis or "union of all the arts" (sometimes designated *Gesamtkunstwerk* — "collective work of art" — based on a misunderstanding of one of Wagner's pet terms; see chapter 42). Schumann himself never aimed at anything so grandiose.

The nature of Schumann's interplay of words and textless music is very piquantly illustrated in the third number in the series of *Phantasiestücke* ("Fantasy pieces"), op. 12, a group of seven character pieces composed in 1837 (Ex. 38-2). Marked to be played "slowly and delicately," it is one of Schumann's most diminutive keyboard creations, only forty-two bars long (albeit with the last twenty-six repeated), consisting mainly of repetitions of a single motive, a dotted "neighbor progression" that is stated in the first measure and thereafter given various continuations.

The texture, like that of the piano's "extra song" at the conclusion of *Dichterliebe*, is clearly homophonic, especially at the beginning, and therefore lyrical. More than one voice seems to be singing, however. If we mark occurrences of the motive phrase, we can identify soprano and alto entries in the first section (up to the double bar), joined in the second section by a rather insistent bass whose entries are dramatized by the player's rather extreme crossing of hands at the keyboard.

All of this may be easily noticed, and even interpreted in light of the music's familiar harmonic trajectory (FOP in the midsection and a double return to conclude), without knowledge of the title, deliberately withheld from the music as printed in Ex. 38-2. That title is *Warum?*, German for "Why?" What does knowing it add to the experience of the music?

It certainly couldn't be said that the title clarifies or explains anything. A title that is itself a question only contributes another enigma. It prompts speculation, though, which is to say the active intervention of the beholder's imagination. One might speculate that the first phrase, which adds an unusual ascending major sixth to the neighbor motive, mimics an interrogative inflection. In that case, the "why" is the unsung text of the "song." One might speculate that the interplay of voices represents a lovers' colloquy. (But there are three voices — a ménage à trois?) One might speculate that the interrogative title is just a reference to the insistence with which the generating motive

EX. 38-2   Robert Schumann, *Phantasiestücke*, Op. 12, no. 3

EX. 38-2 *(continued)*

is propounded. Or one might even speculate that the title is ironically self-referential ("why this title?") in a way that Heine might have approved. Or one might speculate something else. (Here's one: is it by chance that the "motive phrase" in Schumann's *Warum?* coincides with an urgent phrase in a then very popular opera by Francesco Morlacchi, an Italian working in Germany, in which the male lead, Tebaldo, sings a kind of duet with his absent beloved, Isolina, as shown in Ex. 38-3?) Chances are, though, that one will do more speculating with knowledge of the title than one would do otherwise. A mind engaged in speculation is a mind receptive and alert.

EX. 38-3 Francesco Morlacchi, *Tebaldo ed Isolina* (1822), Act II, Scena e romanza: "Caro suono lusinghier"

So it should not embarrass or perplex us unduly to find in the presence (or absence) of titles an added complexity rather than an explanation. That seems to be the idea. Schumann himself was inconsistent and sometimes vacillating about applying them. They were much more frequently afterthoughts than motivating concepts. In several cases the composer added, changed, or deleted them in successive editions of his works. Another set of piano pieces from 1837 carries an autobiographical collective title—*Davidsbündlertänze* ("Dances of the members of the League of David")—about which Schumann was profoundly ambivalent. In the first edition the individual pieces were "signed" by Florestan and Eusebius, and carried descriptive commentaries describing their antics. All of that disappeared in the second edition, and subsequent ones as well. This, too, prompts questions and speculations—as in this memorable passage from a celebrated article on Schumann's esthetics by Edward Lippman:

> Did Schumann come to feel that guides to the meaning of his works were really not necessary? that the content was sufficiently obvious without them? or that the public had become educated and no longer needed the help it did originally? Did he feel that the headings restricted the imagination, or that they were a danger because they might be misconstrued? or did he always regret having permitted any small glimpse into his personal affairs and feelings? Perhaps the headings did not give the significance of the music at all, or even provide an index to its significance; they might have arisen as an additional poetic expression inspired by the music, which the composer could easily feel to be expendable. Or again, in removing them, Schumann might actually have changed rather than concealed the meaning of the music; did the pieces in fact remain the same without their titles?[9]

One's head spins. And one is grateful to Lippman, who, by allowing his spinning head this unusual public exposure, gave one of the best insights ever into the nature of literary music.

The pinnacle was reached in Schumann's *Phantasie*, op. 17, a monumental three-movement work composed in 1836 and dedicated to Liszt, that is in everything but name a sonata on the most heroic Beethovenian scale. Between 1832 and 1838, Schumann wrote three actual piano sonatas, of which one is comparably grand. (He originally published it under the title *Concert sans orchestre*, "Concerto without orchestra.") The original working title of the *Phantasie* itself was *Grosse Sonate für das Pianoforte* ("Great big sonata for piano"). So why the change?

The change was dictated by the concept of literary music, or rather by Schumann's sensitivity to its implications. Unlike the other sonatas, this one was freighted from the beginning with a heavy cargo of literary ideas. The first movement was drafted in the early summer of 1836 as an independent composition called *Ruines: Fantasie pour le Pianoforte*. The work was temporarily renamed Sonata by late fall, when it picked up its additional movements. In this form it was envisioned as a memorial to Beethoven, inspired by the news (which Schumann had published in the *Neue Zeitschrift für Musik*) that a committee had been formed in Bonn, led by the great literary scholar August Wilhelm von Schlegel (1767–1845), to raise funds for the erection of a monument to the Master at his birthplace, where Schlegel served as professor of art and literary history. Schumann's rather optimistic idea was to contribute the proceeds from the sale of a hundred copies of his *Grosse Sonate* to the monument fund, but the project foundered until Liszt rescued it with a promise to contribute his concert earnings. Thanks almost single-handedly to Liszt, the monument was finally erected in 1845 and unveiled on the seventy-fifth anniversary of Beethoven's birth.

In December 1836, Schumann proposed the piece to a prospective publisher under the name *Grosse Sonate f. d. Pianoforte für Beethovens Denkmal* ("Sonata for Beethoven's

FIG. 38-5 Friedrich von Schlegel, charcoal drawing by Philipp Veit, ca. 1805.

monument"), and listed the three movements as "Ruinen/Trophäen/Palmen" (Ruins, Trophies, Palms). The titles of the new movements were intended in their original, ancient Greek meanings, which resonated both with the antique aura of veneration suggested by the first movement, and with the idea of the Beethoven monument. Trophies were memorials (war spoils displayed on pillars) erected in commemoration of victory, the most "Beethovenian" of all concepts; "palms" were the ceremonial palm branches awarded at victory celebrations.

To all of this Schumann now added an epigraph from a poem, *Die Gebüsche* ("The bushes"), by A. W. von Schlegel's even more distinguished brother Friedrich (1772–1829). It has been suggested that Schumann knew these lines not from Schlegel's poem directly,[10] but only from Schubert's setting of it, to which the music of the *Phantasie*'s final movement briefly alludes. But even if that is so, Friedrich von Schlegel was a culture hero with whom Schumann had to identify, if only by reputation. Famous both as a romantic philosopher and as a classical scholar, he was the author of *Die Griechen und Römer* ("The Greeks and Romans"), a long-standard survey of classical civilization, and he wrote lyric poetry as well. The range of his interests and writings, in other words, runs the gamut of moods in the *Phantasie* from the most public and monumental to the most inward, even secret. The epigraph tantalizingly invokes the latter, in a fashion reminiscent of the other occult or unfulfilled gestures we have encountered in Schumann's literary music:

Durch alle Töne tönet	Through all the sounds
Im bunten Erdentraum	In the motley dream of earthly life
Ein leiser Ton gezogen	There sounds a soft, long drawn-out sound
Für den der heimlich lauschet.	For the one who overhears in secret.

Many have guessed at the identity of this secret sound; one can never know for sure. But what made the "Ruins" fantasy an apt basis for the Beethoven tribute to begin with was the fact that, as we will shortly learn, it already contained a secret quotation from Beethoven, to which Schumann added others, even more veiled and less definite, when he came to write the Trophies and Palms. As usual, he toyed a good deal with the titles and headings. Shortly before the work was printed in 1838 he made a wholesale substitution, in which only the heading of the first movement survived: *Dichtungen: Ruinen, Siegesbogen, Sternbild* ("Poems: Ruins, Triumphal Arch, Constellation"). At the very last minute, when the music was already in proofs, Schumann suffered cold feet, changed *Dichtungen* back to *Phantasie*, and dropped the rest, even "Ruinen," the original motivating image.

This is quite a stew of representation and allusion, enigma and erasure, and the more we know of the work's history the thicker (and, it could seem, the more contradictory) the stew becomes. There are many who would claim that Schumann's right to withdraw the titles should be respected and that they should not be divulged lest they unduly influence, hence constrain, a listener's understanding. Indeed, the chance that listeners might think of the titles as constraints was probably what dissuaded Schumann from publishing them (although he kept the epigraph). But as long as we regard the titles as stimuli rather than as confines to the imagination they can function for us as "images that yet fresh images beget," the way Schumann, in his confident moods, intended. (The quoted line is from W. B. Yeats's nostalgic "Byzantium," a poem whose resonances for musical interpretation were first plumbed by Anthony Newcomb.)[11]

But in fact Schumann did not mean to withdraw the titles entirely. His actual direction to the publisher was to replace each title with an asterism — three stars in triangular formation (thus: ⁂), a device often used in nineteenth-century typography to signal an omission, often the name of an anonymous author, or a dedicatee. The Russian composer-critic César Cui, for example, used an asterism as his journalistic nom de plume throughout his career. Obviously, there is a huge difference between simply omitting a title (which may as well never have existed as far as the reader is concerned) and signaling its omission. To do the latter is to challenge the reader to guess it, or invent one. A new question is posed. Nothing is removed from the stew. Indeed, the stew only thickens with the revelation that something (presumably something private) is being concealed. The listener is again involved, again asked to speculate, again rendered receptive and alert.

The posthumous publication of Schumann's private correspondence in 1885 added a great deal to the pot willy-nilly. In 1838, he had written to Clara Wieck, his then distant beloved, that the original "Ruinen" fantasy was conceived as "a deep lament for you,"[12] implying that it was his own life that lay in ruins. A year later, after the whole *Phantasie* had been published, he wrote to her that in order to understand it, "you will have to transport yourself into the unhappy summer of 1836, when I renounced you."[13] A couple of months after that, he wrote, "Aren't *you* the 'tone' in the motto? I almost think so."[14]

We need not pounce at this or shout Eureka. In the first place, as Charles Rosen wisely reminds us, Schumann (perhaps teasingly, perhaps candidly) left the matter in doubt. "As a listener to his own music, not as a composer, he has understood how his love for Clara can be poured into the mold of his work,"[15] and left a model by which other listeners may pour their own loves into the music they hear, if that is their pleasure, for music, especially Schumann's "literary music," is "made to be filled with *our experience*" (italics added). And as Rosen rightly warns, "too firm an identification of an element in a work with an aspect of the artist's life does not further understanding but blocks it," as does any reading so definitive as to foreclose the begetting of fresh images.

Still and all, there is one spot in the first movement of the *Phantasie* on which every interpretive trajectory in the foregoing discussion can converge, and that is the spot marked Adagio, fifteen measures before the end (Ex. 38-4a). Comparison with Ex. 35-5e will reveal its identity as a variant of the opening/closing song in Beethoven's *An die ferne Geliebte* ("To the distant beloved"). That, of course, *was* Clara in 1836. But it was also a Beethoven "ruin," a disfigured shard from the Beethoven composition that, perhaps more than any other, contained a poignant message for the composer of the *Phantasie*.

EX. 38-4A   Robert Schumann, *Phantasie*, Op. 17, I, mm. 295–end

It has a poignant resonance for the music's secret overhearer, too, whether or not the listener is aware of any biographical resonances. For the music is contrived in such a way that the whole movement up to the point of recall seems to function as a gigantic upbeat to it. And here is the most decisive reason why the piece had to be renamed *Phantasie*, even after *Grosse Sonate* and *Dichtungen* had been tried out. "We are accustomed to judge a thing from the name it bears,"[16] Schumann had written in 1835 in the pages of the *Neue Zeitschrift für Musik*. "We make certain demands upon a fantasy, others upon a sonata." Thinking back now to some other fantasies we have met, notably those by C. P. E. Bach in chapter 27 and Mozart in chapter 30, we may recall "tonal vagrancy" as perhaps their most salient shared characteristic. What a sonata normally announces at the outset — a firmly settled, cadential establishment of the tonic — a fantasy only arrives at later, and sometimes not until the end. That is what we expect in a fantasy, or as Schumann would say, what we demand from it.

Now look at Ex. 38-4b, the beginning of "Ruinen," marked "to be played in an extravagant and passionate manner throughout." There can be no doubt that turbulent swirl, consisting of a root, fifth, seventh, and ninth, is expressing a dominant function, "longing" extravagantly and passionately for the tonic. (With two "unprepared" dissonances, moreover, and one more — C, a fourth — that enters with the melody, the harmony seems to begin not at the beginning but in process, as one might expect in a fragment or shard — or ruin — torn off from some larger unheard entity.) It would make an instructively frustrating exercise to pursue the harmonic implications of the opening gesture through the movement to find the moment where the gesture is consummated. But as the reader has probably guessed, that moment does not happen unequivocally until the allusion to *An die ferne Geliebte* makes its tranquil, consoling C-major close in m. 299.

In between, every threatened consummation is provocatively attenuated or evaded: in m. 13 by an ordinary deceptive cadence made a little garish by the application of a

EX. 38-4B   Robert Schumann, *Phantasie*, Op. 17, I, mm. 1–19

diminished seventh; later by the use of modulating pivots that introduce long roving episodes; elsewhere by turning I at the last minute into V of IV (a notorious anti-sonata digression into the subdominant); and so on. About one-third of the way through, the opening material, both melodic and harmonic, returns. Some, noting the double return, have called this a recapitulation; but to give such a name to the resumption of a still-unconsummated dominant is not to uphold but fatally to undermine everything "sonata form" has ever stood for.

Something else "fantasia" has stood for, at least since we investigated Mozart's C-minor Fantasia, K. 475 (Ex. 30-8), has been the seemingly random or illogical extemporaneous introduction of new material (often harmonically stable) to disrupt and destabilize the thematic and harmonic continuity of the whole. A classic instance takes place about half-way through Schumann's first movement, where the still-unresolved dominant harmony dissolves into an out-of-time arabesque or curlicue (incongruously played low and slow), and is succeeded by what can only be described as a lengthy interpolated character piece in C minor, which Schumann originally marked "Romanza" (romance, normally a vocal form), then changed to "Erzählend im Legendenton" (told in the manner of a legend), which was finally printed simply as "Im Legendenton."

The functional relationship of its key to the sought-after tonic resolution is attenuated by a connecting phrase in G minor, so that C minor, when it comes, no longer sounds like the resolution of the harmony, but instead like another — yet another — feint. The theme that articulates it has some connection with the main body of the movement (specifically, with some episodic material first presented in the "alto" in mm. 33–37). But its quality of interpolation, of downright intrusion, is patent, and amply confirmed at its conclusion, almost a hundred bars later, where the "main body" resumes just where it had broken off — or rather, *been* broken off by the intruder. If the whole "Im Legendenton" episode were spliced out, an unbroken continuity would be restored. The interpolation makes no contribution at all to the clarification of the structure. It answers no questions, only poses new ones, further thickens the stew.

And so it is that when the opening material recurs a second time at m. 286, it *still* has the character of an unconsummated gesture, and the quotation from *An die ferne Geliebte* can function as the single consummation toward which the entire movement has been striving. It is a thematic consummation as well as a harmonic one, for as Charles Rosen and John Daverio have both convincingly pointed out (and as the reader can easily confirm by listening), most of the main themes in the first movement of the *Phantasie* are related motivically (if sometimes somewhat indirectly) to the melody of the final song in *An die ferne Geliebte* (albeit not always to the part quoted), and can be construed as derivations from it.

Seeing the whole movement in this light accords even better with the motto from Schlegel, which speaks of a tone sounding *throughout*, not just at the end. (And just to multiply possibilities, consider in the light of the Schlegel motto the enigmatic single tones that sound softly forth as weak local harmonic resolutions at two spots, of which the first is shown in Ex. 38-4c.) What is provided at the end, then, is not a new idea but a synthesis: the simplest, most concentrated possible statement of ideas that have been formerly propounded in a diffuse and complicated manner, with varied or even contradictory implications. The quotation from Beethoven is no longer merely a quotation—that is, something brought in from outside—but the realization of impulses from within, and their reconciliation.

EX. 38-4C   Robert Schumann, *Phantasie*, Op. 17, I, mm. 77–81

More "organic" than that form can hardly get. It is a compositional tour de force. And yet while the movement could not be more clearly articulated or "directional" from the dramatic or gestural standpoint (that is, as an unfolding of thematic and harmonic impulses in time, and their ultimate convergence in repose), it is enigmatic in the extreme when approached from the standpoint of traditional conservatory "Formenlehre" (textbook study of form), which emphasizes the standardized arrangement of sections within a whole.

The first movement of the *Phantasie* thus has a doubly enigmatic status: originally a self-contained composition, when contemplated in isolation from its companion movements it becomes a "fragment" or a ruin in a new sense. Friedrich von Schlegel himself called attention to the romantic mystique of fragments. "Many of the works of the ancients have become fragments,"[17] he noted. But then he added, "Many of the works of the moderns are fragments as soon as they are written." This may sound like a complaint. Some, indeed, might have wished to say it in complaint, as Schlegel was mockingly suggesting. But Schlegel heartily approved. His love of fragments is closely related to Schumann's obsession with unconsummated gestures, withheld information, and the rest. The notion of a fragment demands that the beholder relate it to something larger, yet absent, to be supplied by an engaged imagination.

The beholder, in other words, must *add* something, once again confirming Schiller's marvelous insight that art's hold on our imaginations comes not (or not only) from what the composer puts in, but from what we ourselves are forced to contribute before we can take anything out. It follows from this that our perception of an artwork is never entirely objective. That much is a truism. But what also follows is the less common admission that it is never entirely subjective, either. Artistic engagement, and whatever knowledge (or self-knowledge) may emerge from it, is therefore the product of an interaction between the object submitted to the public gaze and the subjects who do the gazing. Neither can ever be excluded. Or so Schiller and Schumann (and every other romantic artist) insist.

Far from a truism, this has always been a hotly debated issue, for its implications are vast and potentially very disquieting. If we can never know or understand an artwork with complete objectivity (or with any other kind of completeness), where does that leave us with respect to other kinds of knowledge? Perhaps the intentionally incomplete statements with which romantic artists insist on tantalizing us do not really differ in kind from other statements, including those that purport to be entirely complete and unproblematical. Perhaps completeness of utterance is only a disguise worn by partiality. Perhaps romantic techniques of propounding intentional and unanswerable questions within the experience of art products, while seemingly novel and even radical, are only an extreme manifestation of a universal condition of knowledge. That would make romantic artists the greatest realists of all.

ANXIETY AND RECOIL

We have already noted that as Schumann's career progressed, his activities became more public. In his case publicity seems to have acted as a restraint. His later music showed increasing mastery of technique, but also a tendency to conform to public expectations. As a hotheaded Davidsbündler and maverick journalist, he summed up his attitude toward such expectations in a quintessentially romantic aphorism: "People say, 'It pleased,' or 'It did not please'; as if there were nothing higher than to please people!"[18] (Imagine Mozart's reaction to this!) As a civic music director and the head of a large family, Schumann inclined toward "classicism," as the term was then beginning to be understood.

A subtle and revealing illustration of the change in Schumann's attitudes and their "socio-esthetic" implications was the fate of another fantasy that became a fragment. What began life as a one-movement *Fantaisie* in A minor for piano and orchestra, composed in 1841, later found a home as the first movement of a conventional three-movement concerto (op. 54), completed in 1845. The complete concerto is a justly popular repertory item. It has perhaps the most perfectly realized balance of forces of any standard piano concerto, with the soloist and the orchestra cooperating in all the thematic presentations, as well as in the transitional, episodic, and developmental passages. The only concerto that may be said to surpass it in these respects is Mendelssohn's Violin Concerto, completed two years later and possibly under its influence.

When it functions as the first movement of a "normal" concerto, what we are most apt to notice about the former *Fantaisie* is what is most normal about it. Unlike the opening movement of the *Phantasie* for piano solo, its unfolding can easily be reconciled with the conventions of "sonata form," which is what made it potentially an appropriate beginning for a "classical" concerto in the first place. Tearing it loose from that context, at once turning it into a fragment and returning it to its former estate as a freestanding composition, will expose its more experimental side.

The first thing we are apt to notice now is that its various sections, all of which may be related, if desired, to the conventional sonata design, have different, sometimes highly contrasting, tempos: *allegro affettuoso* to begin; *animato* at m. 67; *andante espressivo* at m. 151; *più animato* at m. 200; *tempo primo* at m. 249; and, after the written-out cadenza, *allegro molto* at m. 448. But then, in seeming contradiction, we notice that at each of these highly contrasted spots, the thematic material is the same: or rather, that (with the exception of the "tempo primo" that functions as a literal restatement or "recapitulation") each section is based on a variation—or, to speak Lisztianly, a "transformation"—of the same thematic idea, in which a common opening phrase is given a new continuation each time (Ex. 38-5).

EX. 38-5   Thematic transformations in Robert Schumann's *Fantaisie* for Piano and Orchestra

Viewed this way, the *Fantaisie* looks less like a sonata movement than like a set of linked character pieces that might have been variously signed "F" (for Florestan) or "E" (Eusebius). Yet considering the placement of the slowest and the fastest tempos, the *Fantaisie* seems at the same time to sum up within itself the outward shape of a complete and conventional three-movement concerto, making its later incorporation into such a work seem a redundancy. In its sui generis yet elaborately overdetermined form, the concerto can support many interpretations, which is to say that there are many plausible answers to the implicit questions it poses.

Ultimately, that is the point. The one-movement composition, which seems in effect to anticipate Liszt's innovations (though far less flamboyantly) in its compression and its thematic transformations, asks far more of its hearers than the popular three-movement concerto in which it was eventually embedded, and which Clara Schumann premiered (with Mendelssohn conducting) at the Leipzig Gewandhaus on New Year's Day 1846. By then, the enigmatic "literary" quality he had prized as a youth had come to

FIG. 38-6   The old pontoon bridge over the Rhine at Düsseldorf, from which Schumann plunged in a suicide attempt on 27 February 1854.

trouble and torment the composer, who was increasingly given to fits of nervous tension and melancholy that (as he noted in his diary) gave his life "an *idée fixe*: the fear of going mad."[19] This "fixed idea" or obsession made Schumann morbidly sensitive to symptoms of "irrationality" in his early output, and even caused him to revise some of his most remarkable compositions to render them more conventional, hence less threatening to his own peace of mind. It was almost as if the romantic conviction that his life and his work were esoterically commingled gave Schumann the idea that altering the work might alter his fate — a neurotic symptom in itself. His fears were eventually borne out, or perhaps fulfilled themselves: Schumann spent his last two years in an asylum following a suicide attempt. "Classicism," for him, was a retreat from a threatened abyss. In this he was the first of many.

INSTRUMENTAL DRAMA

More forthright, less inhibited, in fact downright exhibitionistic (many thought) was the self-dramatizing romanticism of Berlioz, Schumann's closest French counterpart. His was the dynamic, scathing, somewhat scandalous romanticism of Victor Hugo, whose works were known to cause riots in the theater. Civic engagement was what French romantics sought in the afterglow of their heroic revolution, which surrounded the word *citoyen* (citizen) with an aureole. Berlioz the citizen-composer followed in the footsteps of his teacher, Jean-François Le Sueur (1760–1837), who had been the Inspecteur du Conservatoire from the very founding of that great institution in

1795. That job obligated Le Sueur to furnish the grand hymns for mass singing at the yearly revolutionary commemorations (*Fêtes de la Révolution*).

The French tradition of civic ceremonial music reached its very height in Berlioz's *Grande messe des morts*, op. 5 (1837), a colossal requiem Mass for tenor solo, six-part chorus, and orchestra augmented by eight pairs of timpani and four separate brass bands placed at the four corners of the performing space for the Dies Irae sequence, an epic evocation of the last judgment replete with trumpets to wake the dead. It was performed in the mammoth Dôme des Invalides, burial place of France's national heroes, on 5 December 1837 at a commemorational ceremony organized by the July Monarchy's ministry of the interior.

FIG. 38-7   Hector Berlioz in an engraving by E. Metzmacher after a photograph by Félix Nadar (1857).

Two years later, Berlioz received another official commission, to accompany the solemn tenth-anniversary commemoration of the July Revolution itself on 28 July 1840. This time Berlioz dispensed with the chorus, aiming in by-then time-honored romantic fashion at the more elemental and "universal" message that the "metalanguage" of instrumental music alone could convey. The result was the *Grande symphonie funèbre et triomphale* ("Grand funereal and triumphal symphony"), scored for an enormous yet ambulatory military band, and performed in procession through the streets of Paris (thanks to which, as Berlioz recalled in his memoirs, the piece turned into an unintentional canon between the front instruments and the rear). The first and last movements are marches, the first lugubrious and the second — headed "Apothéose" ("Apotheosis"), from the Greek for exaltation to godly rank — ebullient. In between came the masterstroke: an "Oraison funèbre," or eulogy to the revolutionary dead, declaimed by a solo trombone from the steps of the Invalides, to music originally composed for a scene from an abandoned historical opera, *Les francs-juges* ("The judges of the secret court").

FIG. 38-8   Berlioz conducting massed choruses; caricature by Gustave Doré (1832–1883) in *Journal pour rire*, 27 June 1850.

Berlioz's seminal work, however, was one in which he summoned all the techniques of public address for the purpose of private disclosure. It is officially titled *Épisode de la vie d'un artiste, Symphonie fantastique en cinq parties* ("Episode in the life of an artist: a fantastic symphony in five movements"). The title may be translated as the "Symphony of Fantasies," but the word *fantastique* also had for Berlioz and his contemporaries a wealth of "Hoffmannesque" resonances, denoting something strange, grotesque, uncanny, unearthly — in short, romantic. The whole symphony was composed in a "mental boil"[20] (as Berlioz later recollected in tranquility) from January to April 1830. Inspired by biographical circumstances comparable to those that surrounded Schumann's *Phantasie*, and perhaps having comparable artistic ends, Berlioz's symphony nevertheless differs so completely from Schumann's work in its artistic means and "ethos" (moral tone) that between them the two works represent a sort of gamut. Comparing them will be an exercise in what the intellectual historian Arthur Lovejoy called "the discrimination of romanticisms."[21]

Like Schumann a few years later, in 1827 Berlioz conceived an all-consuming passion for what then seemed an unattainable object. In September of that year he attended a performance of *Hamlet* by a touring English company performing in the original language; and, though he knew no English at the time, he was smitten both by Shakespeare, who would thereafter be (with Virgil) his model of all artistic models (thus making Berlioz, like Schumann, a "literary" musician to the core), and by Harriet Smithson, the Irish actress who played Ophelia.

FIG. 38-9   Harriet Smithson as Juliet to Charles Kemble's Romeo, Paris, Odéon Theater, September 1827.

Shakespeare was available for immediate possession: over the course of his career Berlioz composed three major works on Shakespearean subjects — a concert overture, *Le roi Lear* (King Lear, 1831); a "dramatic symphony," *Roméo et Juliette*, actually a sort of secular oratorio for soloists, chorus, and orchestra, in which all the love music, significantly, is wordless (1839); and finally a comic opera, *Béatrice et Bénédict* (1862), after *Much Ado About Nothing*. Miss Smithson was not available. Berlioz spent the next two years in vain and hopeless pursuit, which culminated (just as it had with Schumann) in a temporary embittered renunciation that bore immediate musical fruit, in Berlioz's case the *Symphonie fantastique*.

(Eventually he succeeded, against all expectation, in wooing Miss Smithson. They were married in 1833. But, as his biographer Hugh Macdonald puts it, for Berlioz there was no clear distinction between the real Harriet Smithson and the idealized embodiment of Shakespeare's heroines.... [A] relationship that had begun on an ideal level could only spoil in the glare of everyday reality, and the wholly Romantic conjunction of the artist with the ideal woman came to a bitter end.[22]

They never divorced, but separated around 1842; she died in obscurity in 1854.)

Where Schumann sought to sublimate the biographical stimulus that motivated the *Phantasie* to the point where it is arguably no longer essential or even relevant to the work's interpretation, and was careful to enfold its subjective content in a sphinxlike sheath that engaged the listener's own subjectivity, Berlioz let everything hang out, leaving nothing, or so it seemed, to the imagination. What was billed as the symphony's motivating scenario was actually distributed to audiences in their program books (hence the word "programmatic" to describe the relationship between the work's verbal and musical dimensions). Although the composer had his qualms and vacillations about the program leaflet (or, simply, the symphony's "program," as we usually say now), rewrote it three times, and occasionally decided not to have it handed out, he eventually had it published in the first edition of the score in 1845, and since then it has been unquestionably (and by the composer's express avowal) as essential a part of the symphony as the libretto is in any opera. An explicit and occasionally detailed narrative, it goes far beyond anything Schumann ever attempted with his titles or headings:

NOTE

The composer's intention has been to develop, insofar as they contain musical possibilities, various situations in the life of an artist. The outline of the instrumental drama, which lacks the help of words, needs to be explained in advance. The following program should thus be considered as the spoken text of an opera, serving to introduce the musical movements, whose character and expression it motivates. The distribution of this program to the audience, at concerts where this symphony is to be performed, is indispensable for a complete understanding of the dramatic outline of the work.

PROGRAM

1. *Reveries — Passions.* The author imagines that a young musician, afflicted with that moral disease that a well-known writer [Chateaubriand] calls the *vague des passions* ["surge of indefinite passion," roughly, readiness for a big emotional experience], sees for the first time a woman who embodies all the charms of the ideal being he has imagined in his dreams, and he falls desperately in love with her. Through an odd whim, whenever the beloved image appears before the mind's eye of the artist it is linked with a musical thought whose character, passionate but at the same time noble and shy, he finds similar to the one he attributes to his beloved.

This melodic image and the model it reflects pursue him incessantly like a double *idée fixe.* That is the reason for the constant appearance, in every movement of the symphony, of the melody that begins the first Allegro. The passage from this state of melancholy reverie, interrupted by a few fits of groundless joy, to one of frenzied passion, with its stirrings of fury, of jealousy, its return of tenderness, its tears, its religious consolations — this is the subject of the first movement.

2. *A ball.* The artist finds himself in the most varied situations — in the midst of the tumult of a party, in the peaceful contemplation of the beauties of nature;

but everywhere, in town, in the country, the beloved image appears before him and disturbs his peace of mind.

3. *Scene in the country.* Finding himself one evening in the country, he hears in the distance two shepherds piping a *ranz des vaches* [Swiss cow call] in dialogue. This pastoral duet, the scenery, the quiet rustling of the trees gently brushed by the wind, the hopes he has recently found some reason to entertain — all concur in affording his heart an unaccustomed calm, and in giving a more cheerful tint to his ideas. He reflects upon his isolation; he hopes that his loneliness will soon be over. — But what if she were deceiving him! — This mingling of hope and fear, these ideas of happiness disturbed by black presentiments, form the subject of the Adagio. At the end one of the shepherds again takes up the *ranz des vaches*; the other no longer replies. — Distant sound of thunder — loneliness — silence.

4. *March to the scaffold.* Convinced that his love is unappreciated [or as the first draft had it, "Convinced not only that his adored one does not return his love, but that she is incapable of understanding it and moreover has become unworthy of it"], the artist poisons himself with opium. The dose of the narcotic, too weak to kill him, plunges him into a sleep accompanied by the most horrible visions. He dreams that he has killed his beloved, that he is condemned and led to the scaffold, and that he is witnessing his own execution. The procession moves forward to the sounds of a march that is now sombre and fierce, now brilliant and solemn, in which the muffled noise of heavy steps gives way without transition to the noisiest clamor. At the end of the march the first four measures of the *idée fixe* reappear, like a last thought of love interrupted by the fatal blow.

5. *Dream of a Witches' Sabbath.* He sees himself at the Sabbath, in the midst of a frightful troop of ghosts, sorcerers, monsters of every kind, come together for his funeral. Strange noises, groans, bursts of laughter, distant cries which other cries seem to answer. The beloved melody appears again, but it has lost its character of nobility and diffidence; it is no more than a dance tune, mean, trivial, and grotesque: it is she, coming to join the Sabbath [or, according to the first draft, "it is the loved one coming to the Sabbath to attend the funeral procession of her victim; she is now only a prostitute, fit to take part in a debauch"]. — A roar of joy at her arrival. — She takes part in the devilish orgy. — Funeral knell, burlesque parody of the *Dies irae* (the hymn sung in the funeral rites of the Catholic Church). Sabbath round dance. The Sabbath round and the *Dies irae* combined.[23]

The degree to which this program was truly autobiographical is of course unknowable, and (many would say) irrelevant. Berlioz, to begin with, is not known to have been a "substance abuser," but he is known to have been fascinated with Thomas De Quincey's pseudo-autobiographical *Confessions of an English Opium-Eater* (1822), a novel replete with dream visions every bit as bizarre and spectacular as the composer's. (Berlioz read it in Alfred de Musset's translation in 1828.) Besides, the program follows too many literary and dramatic conventions to have been wholly spontaneous or life-prompted. (In any case, the most spontaneous moments in the first draft — namely the misogynistic outbursts against the beloved, here most clearly identifiable with the actual Harriet Smithson who had wounded the actual Hector Berlioz — were removed on reflection.) The five-movement format is often traced back to Beethoven's "Pastoral" Symphony, also a descriptive work (though on nothing approaching such a level of detail). It may indeed have served as a model — or a "validator," as Beethoven so often served his varied progeny. The Beethoven symphony is neither narrative nor enactment, however, but a series of mood pictures in the eighteenth-century tradition of the *sinfonia caratteristica* ("characteristic" or descriptive symphony). There really was no musical precedent for a scenario-symphony such as Berlioz was offering, and so it may be more appropriate to seek its precedent in the contemporary theater, where the five-act "Shakespearean" tragedies and histories of Hugo, Berlioz's almost exact contemporary, were setting the pace. The incipient *grand opéra* was also a five-act affair, and it seems right to regard the *Symphonie fantastique* as a sort of opera — or "instrumental drama," as Berlioz calls it himself — for orchestra.

But what an orchestra! Whether in terms of sheer size or diversity of timbres, this was at the time the biggest band ever assembled outside an opera house (though Berlioz himself would exceed it in his choral works). To balance the unprecedented twenty-three wind and brass players (including parts for two ophicleides, now played on tubas), Berlioz specified a minimum of sixty strings. In addition the score calls for two harps and five percussion players, four of whom must simultaneously produce timpani rolls at the end of the third movement, with its famous depiction of distant thunder. (They also perform on two other kinds of drum, cymbals, and tubular chimes; all five players have their hands full at the end of the fourth movement.)

Thus a total of not less than 91 musicians is called for, including the virtuoso conductor. At the first performance, Berlioz had hoped for about 220 but settled for 130. The mastery — not only of mass but of detail — with which he handled this gargantuan band, even at this early stage of his career, has unquestionably been his greatest legacy. "Berlioz's sound," as Edward T. Cone, a later composer-critic, put it, "has been in the ears of composers ever since, even when they have reacted most strongly against it," or when they felt (as many people once felt about movies, and some still do about TV) that its colorfulness and realism preempted, and thereby stunted, the listener's imaginative faculties.[24]

The first performance was conducted by François-Antoine Habeneck (1781–1849), an old-fashioned violinist-conductor, who beat time with his bow. Dissatisfied, Berlioz resolved to learn to conduct himself, and became one of the earliest virtuoso baton conductors. The orchestra, in fact, was the only instrument he played well. Almost alone among major composers in having virtually no keyboard skills, he was most competent on flageolet (or whistle-flute) and guitar, both instruments associated mainly with nonliterate repertories, and both as a result instruments for which he never had occasion to write. Thus Berlioz, far more than pianistically skilled composers, had to think directly in terms of orchestral colors, for which he developed an unparalleled ear.

As a result, however, his manner of writing often transgressed the usual rules of voice leading, traditionally learned at the keyboard. Because of his huge ambition in the face of seeming technical liabilities, Berlioz could never entirely shake the reputation of a crank, or of flaunting his "originality in itialics," as the fastidious Mendelssohn put it.[25] As if to compensate for his lack of more traditional skills, Berlioz's expertise in the newest techniques of orchestration and conducting was phenomenal, and pathbreaking. In 1843 he published a textbook on orchestration, only the third book of its kind and the first to give a full description of all contemporary instruments and their possibilities, many of them pioneered in his own work. As updated by Richard Strauss in 1904 the book is still in print. Berlioz, in short, was the prototype of the avant-garde or antitraditional composer. (Not that he, a worshipper of Beethoven and Gluck, would have so characterized himself.) If the size and timbral variety of the orchestra in the *Symphonie fantastique* is another reason for associating it conceptually with dramatic rather than traditionally "symphonic" music, the really decisive reason for doing so is the way in which Berlioz adapted the specifically operatic device of the "reminiscence motif" to organize the symphony in both narrative and formal dimensions. As the program states, the image of the beloved haunts the symphony from start to finish in the form of an obsessively recurring melody, which Berlioz, using a phrase we have already encountered in Schumann (though not as a musical term), called the idée fixe. It is, in short, a musical symbol that could perhaps be compared, not only in its deployment but in its object of depiction, with Schumann's symbolic quotation from Beethoven's *An die ferne Geliebte* in his *Phantasie*.

Again, though, it should be kept in mind that what in Schumann was a nebula (or "stew") of potential meanings becomes with Berlioz an explicit, sharply focused image whose unequivocal referent is given within the work itself — signaled first in the program, then corroborated in the music — and which may be apprehended "objectively" by the beholder. Indeed, thanks to Berlioz's orchestral skills, our first experience of the idée fixe is almost physically palpable. The best entrée into the symphony, both as an object and as an idea, would be to trace its peregrinations through the work, much as one might trace a character's appearances in a drama or even a novel.

The first presentation of the idée fixe, given in Ex. 38-6 in Franz Liszt's concert transcription, is the most graphic piece of "body portraiture" we have encountered since Mozart (in *The Abduction from the Seraglio*, Ex. 28-6), and the body portrayed is not "hers" but "his," that is, the smitten "artist's." It is the physiological reaction — the irregular heartbeats or "palpitations" in the accompanying parts — rather than the melody itself that is the real tour de force of "imitation" here, reminding us that before taking courage and staking everything on his musical vocation Berlioz had spent two years, at his father's behest, as "a reluctant and unsatisfactory medical student" (in the words of his biographer D. Kern Holoman).[26]

Or rather, we have here a fairly complicated interplay between an abstract and arbitrary symbol (the idée fixe melody) and the realistic imitation of nature (the palpitating accompaniment). Berlioz's music will play on the blurry cusp between these two types of representation throughout the symphony. That is what lends it such fascination. The "beloved" melody, which needs to be instantly recognized on every recurrence, is given a very distinctive, arching profile, rising up in quick fitful leaps, then making slow, smooth, syncopated descents that seem to hover out of time. In its skittish avoidance of surface symmetries, in its rhythmic contrasts, and in its slow, laborious progress to its climactic high C, this forty-bar arialike melody is plainly intended as a sort of stylistic archetype, in keeping with its role as romantic "ideal." The whole first movement in which this instrumental aria occurs is a C-major sonata allegro thoroughly recast in operatic terms. The extended slow symphonic introduction in the parallel minor, evidently intended as a representation of the *vague des passions*, is

EX. 38-6 Hector Berlioz, *Symphonie fantastique*, the idée fixe in Liszt's transcription

EX. 38-6 *(continued)*

in fact a little da capo aria with coda whose melody was originally that of a song Berlioz had composed at the age of twelve in response to his own first passionate stirrings; its "objective" suitability to the expressive purpose was thus putatively assured. The coda, in a technique well-learned from Beethoven, is built over a submediant pedal that will resolve to the Allegro as a "flat" submediant.

The exposition begins (as the program states) with the idée fixe. Its melody, too, was adapted from an older, discarded vocal composition: *Herminie*, a cantata Berlioz had composed to a prescribed "neoclassical" text in 1828 in an unsuccessful bid for the Prix de Rome, a stipend given by the government to support promising young musicians during a two-year creative sojourn in Italy. (Berlioz won it in 1830 with another neoclassical cantata, *Sardanapale*.) In its original context, the melody that symbolized an idealized Harriet Smithson had expressed the hopeless love of Erminia, a Saracen woman, for the Christian knight Tancred, as related in *Gerusalemme liberata* ("Jerusalem delivered"), Torquato Tasso's sixteenth-century epic of the Crusades.

The second theme is a long while a-borning, but makes its decisive cadence on the dominant exactly where Berlioz marks the first ending. The two themes of the exposition, the "instrumental drama's" protagonists, stalk one another through the rather meandering development section. The process of the meandering seems, incidentally, to have been modeled directly on the beginning of the development section in the first movement of Beethoven's *Eroica* Symphony, first performed in Paris under Habeneck only two years earlier: compare Berlioz's modulations by ascending half steps at measures 168 ff, each stage prepared by a flat submediant, with Beethoven's right after the first movement's double bar (Ex. 38-7). The technique of modulation by half step, only a starting point for Beethoven, is maintained by Berlioz through the development section with unprecedented consistency. Rarely if ever had a stretch of music of comparable length so relied on half-step rather than fifth relations for its harmonic coherence.

EX. 38-7A   Ludwig van Beethoven, Symphony no. 3, I, mm. 182–90

EX. 38-7B   Hector Berlioz, *Symphonie fantastique*, I, mm. 168–81

This is a purely thematic development on the new textbook model, which Berlioz must have learned from Anton Reicha, his conservatory professor, who had literally "written the book" on the subject. Its technique of constant half-step motion precludes the reaching of any well-defined FOP (harmonic "far out point"), nor is the retransition defined by much of a dominant pedal (just four bars, mm. 408–411). There is a completely unexpected (and, in terms of "normal" sonata procedure, unexpectable) reprise of the idée fixe in the dominant right in the midst of things, and a double return that comes not as the resolution of a long-building tension but as the culmination of another series of ascending half steps, intensified by the use of a motivic sequence and a long crescendo, both long-established devices for producing operatic climaxes.

Lastly, when it comes time to wind things down for the "religious consolation" at the end, the half steps turn around and begin descending through another motivic sequence ingeniously derived from the idée fixe by flattening out its rhythmic design into undifferentiated quarter notes. The crescendo becomes a diminuendo, and the tempo gradually slackens into long-sustained chords played "by the whole orchestra as softly as possible." The theme-based development, while it no longer betrays its genetic link to the binary dance form of old and no longer charts a compelling tonal course, acquires in compensation a new narrative flexibility. At the very least it effectively indoctrinates the audience to respond like the artist himself to every strategic recurrence of the idée fixe. From here on to the end of the symphony, the general tactic will be to have the idée fixe impinge upon a new dramatic "terrain," in each case evoked by the use of "characteristic" music — that is, generic music associated "in life" with a specific place or function. The function of the idée fixe in every case except the last will be to make a familiar environment seem suddenly strange, transformed by the injection of strong emotion. In the last case, the process will work in the opposite way, the environment (not familiar this time but "fantastic") serving to transform the idée fixe.

Thus, in the second movement or "act," the ball scene is evoked in the most direct way possible, by the use of actual ballroom music, in this case a waltz (by then a commonplace in operatic ballets). The harp music, too, is an element of characteristic "setting." A ubiquitous instrument at domestic soirées and parties (especially in France), and lately a standard presence in the theater, the harp was making its symphonic debut in this movement. (As a concerto soloist it had a minor eighteenth-century history, again mainly French.) As late as 1896, César Franck's use of the harp in a nonprogrammatic symphony gave rise to controversy.

The idée fixe occurs twice in the movement, with strikingly different dramatic effects. A sudden modulation to — where else? — the flat submediant prepares its first appearance, and the cellos and basses react, as before, with palpitations. These, however, are quickly subsumed into the waltz figuration and the oompah-pah accompaniment; the beloved is spotted dancing from afar. Toward the end, however, the artist and his beloved come suddenly face to face, and the surrounding music suddenly disappears (save a slight ripple of half-heard harp music, inserted for verisimilitude). It

FIG. 38-10   Double-action harp by Erard, ca. 1860.

is a classic "moment out of time" of a type we have encountered before in instrumental music only in Schubertian trances, represented here by the usual dip into the flat submediant, and also by some "uncountably" sustained tones in the flute and horn. In opera, of course, juxtapositions of "real time" and "stop time" had been of the essence from the very first.

In the third movement, the ambient sounds are provided by the "pipers" (oboe and English horn), and the thunder (timpani and tremolando strings). There is a long rounded aria that represents the artist's presence, even though it is not always in "his" vocal range. (Compare the movement titled "Roméo seul"—Romeo alone—in the *Roméo et Juliette* symphony.) It is first sung by the first violins and flute in unison; its reprise in the dominant (mm. 69 ff) takes place an eleventh lower, strategically placed in the "male" register so that when interrupted by the idée fixe it can continue to play "the artist" in reaction to it. Their collision comes somewhat in advance of the beloved's actual musical appearance, signalled by the artist's agitation at the thought of her. Berlioz marks a *tremolo très serré*—"very close" or "unmeasured" tremolo—and in so doing once again becomes one of the first to transfer an orchestral effect from the opera house (where its history goes back to the days of Gluck and Piccinni) to the "pure" instrumental domain (Ex. 38-8).

EX. 38-8   Hector Berlioz, *Symphonie fantastique*, III, mm. 87–92

EX. 38-8 (*continued*)

The thunder, we are thus given to understand, has gone "within." The impassioned duet between the idée fixe and the rhythmically erratic interjections of the panting, stammering protagonist is violently cut off on a note of irresolute despair — literally a chromatic note (cf. m. 24 in Ex. 38-6) that allows the harmony to veer off in a dangerously flatward direction before equilibrium is laboriously regained. At the recapitulation, Berlioz succeeds in investing timbre alone with representational significance. The pizzicato strings play an embellished reprise of the opening aria, while the flute and clarinet, the instruments that had just played the idée fixe in unison, contribute countermelodies.

To speak the language of the program, hope gains the upper hand over fear at the beginning of the coda, where motives from the protagonist's aria in the strings are allowed to coexist in harmonically peaceful counterpoint with motives from the idée fixe, still in the flute and clarinet. But the equation of inner and outer turmoil through the use of tremolo reintroduces a note of forlorn disquiet when the English horn resumes the *ranz des vaches* and is answered not by the oboe, its erstwhile partner (identified since then with the idée fixe, another absent partner), but by the distant thunder of the four timpani.

The fourth movement, the "March to the Scaffold," enjoyed a separate popularity during the nineteenth century as an orchestral showpiece in its own right, which seems fair enough given the frequency with which colorful orchestral excerpts from operas are performed at concerts. (But many nonprogrammatic symphonic movements were similarly extracted in those days: a special favorite, as already implied in an earlier chapter by Lami's painting [Fig. 34-7], was the Allegretto from Beethoven's Seventh Symphony, which Berlioz himself first encountered as the slow movement of the Fifth, thanks to Habeneck's substitution.) In fact, the movement began life as an operatic excerpt. Like the middle movement of the *Symphonie funèbre et triomphale*, it was lifted from the abandoned score for *Les francs-juges*.

All Berlioz had to do in order to adapt it to its new purpose was change the ending, which now contains the movement's single fleeting reference to the idée fixe (Ex. 38-9). What follows is perhaps the most explicitly illustrative music in the score: the short sharp shock of the guillotine blade in m. 169; the head rolling into the basket (pizzicati in the same measure); and the hats-in-the-air fanfare to conclude, reminding us that public executions were once a form of popular entertainment. Like the similarly literalistic representation of the plagues in Handel's *Israel in Egypt*, this is inevitably a moment of high comedy despite the grisliness of the subject and the ostensible seriousness of the program.

THE LIMITS OF MUSIC

The comic literalism of the ending to the March to the Scaffold gives us our opportunity, before turning to the symphony's wholly fantastic concluding movement, briefly to

FIG. 38-11   Execution of Louis XVI by guillotine, 1793 (anonymous engraving, late eighteenth century).

EX. 38-9   Hector Berlioz, *Symphonie fantastique*, IV, mm. 174–end

compare romantic theory and practice. When wearing his critic's rather than his composer's hat, Berlioz was known to rail at literal depiction as a lapse of style or taste, and a transgression against the true spirit of romanticism. In a fascinating essay of 1837, "De l'Imitation musicale" ("On imitation in music," or as aptly paraphrased by its translator, Jacques Barzun, "The limits of music"), he tried to formulate a romantic theory of musical depiction, supporting it with examples, both positive and negative, from the literature. It is easy to see that the article was motivated not only by the failure of previous writers (such as Giuseppe Carpani, whose biography of Haydn furnished the immediate pretext) to come up with an adequate theory, but also by the criticism that the *Symphonie fantastique* had been receiving from conservative musicians, in particular from François-Joseph Fétis (1784–1871), the influential editor of the *Revue musicale*, the leading Paris music magazine.

Berlioz begins by admitting that misconceived or inappropriate imitations of nature can produce unintentional comedy, and not only in music. Writing of the great tragedian François-Joseph Talma (1763–1826), whose portrayal of Orestes in Racine's *Andromaque* was considered by many the most glorious achievement of the French dramatic stage, Berlioz had the effrontery to remark of the recently deceased tragedian that when he

> used to hiss the *s*'s as he exclaimed, "*Pour qui sont ces serpents qui sifflent sur vos têtes?* [For whom are those snakes that hiss around your heads?]," far from being terrifying he always made me want to laugh. For it seemed to me clear, then as now, that this solicitude of Orestes to imitate the hissing of serpents when his soul is filled with terror, his heart with despair, and his head with ghostly visions, was directly opposed to any idea we may form of what is dramatically natural and likely. Obviously Orestes is not *describing* the Furies; he imagines that he is actually seeing them. He hails them, pleads with them, defies them; and one must be a very docile spectator not to find comic a piece of imitation ascribed to such a sufferer at such a juncture.[27]

Berlioz hazards four rules to govern the use of descriptive or illustrative devices in music: If we are to accept imitation among musical devices without detracting from music's independent power or nobleness, the first condition is that imitation shall virtually never be an *end* but only a *means*; that it shall never be considered (except very rarely) the main musical idea, but only the complement of that idea, joined to the main idea in a logical and natural manner.

> The second condition to making imitation acceptable is that it shall concern something worthy of holding the listener's attention, and that it shall not (at least in serious works) be used to render sounds, motions, or objects that belong outside the sphere which art cannot desert without self-degradation.
>
> The third condition is that the imitation, without aping reality as by an exact substitution of nature for art, shall nonetheless be close enough for the composer's intent to avoid misconception in the minds of an attentive audience.
>
> The fourth and last condition is that this physical imitation shall never occur in the very spot where *emotional* imitation (expressiveness) is called for, and thus encroach with descriptive futilities when the drama is proceeding apace and passion alone deserves a voice.[28]

When it comes to the examples, we are not surprised to find Beethoven cited at first as a model of correct procedure.

But then Berlioz turns around and audaciously cites him as a transgressor—a move calculated, at the very least, to attract attention. The citation of Handel's *Israel in Egypt* is (again) no surprise to us (recall chapter 26). But note that Berlioz cites it from hearsay, and inaccurately. Handel's oratorios, continually in active repertory in England and lately revived in Germany, were still terra incognita in France.

It might seem as if the "Storm" in the Pastoral Symphony were a magnificent exception to our first rule which allows imitation only as a means and not as an end. For this symphonic movement is wholly given over to the reproduction of the divers noises heard during a violent storm which breaks suddenly over some village festivities. First a few drops of rain, then the rising wind, the thunder grumbling dully in the distance, the birds seeking shelter; finally the approaching gale, the boughs that split, men and animals scattering with cries of dismay, the shattering bolts of lightning, the floodgates of heaven opening, the elements let loose — chaos.

And yet this sublime depiction, which outstrips anything that had ever been attempted in the genre, actually falls within the category of *contrasts* and *dramatic effects*, which are required by the scope of the work. For it is preceded and followed by gentle and smiling scenes to which it acts as a foil. That this is so may be tested by imagining this storm transplanted into another composition in which its presence would not be motivated: it would unquestionably lose a great deal of its effectiveness. Hence this piece of imitation is strictly speaking a means of achieving contrast, devised and managed with the incalculable power of genius.

In *Fidelio*, on the other hand, a work by the same composer, we find another piece of musical imitation of very different purport from the one just reviewed. It occurs in the famous duet at the grave: the jailer and Fidelio dig the place where Florestan is to be buried. Halfway through their toil the pair unearth a large rock and roll it with difficulty to one side. At that point the double basses of the orchestra play a strange and very brief figure — not to be confused with the

EX. 38-10   Ludwig van Beethoven, *Fidelio*, Act II, no. 12 ("Es ist nicht leicht!" "Nur etwas noch!"), mm. 1–4

ostinato phrase of the basses which runs through the whole piece—by which it is said Beethoven wished to imitate *the dull sound of the rolling stone* [Ex. 38-10].

Now this imitation, being in no way necessary either to the drama or to the effectiveness of the music, is really an end in itself for the composer: he imitates in order to imitate—and at once he falls into error, for there is in such imitation no poetry, no drama, no truth. It is a sad piece of childishness, which one is equally grieved and surprised to have to complain of in a great master. The same could be said of Handel, if it be true—as is commonly said—that in his oratorio *Israel in Egypt* he tried to reproduce the flight of locusts, and this to the point of shaping accordingly the rhythmic figure of the vocal parts. Surely that is a regrettable imitation of a subject even more regrettable—unworthy of music in general and of the noble and elevated style of the oratorio.[29]

There is no need for us to render a judgment of the end of the fourth movement of the *Symphonie fantastique* according to these criteria. (Our judgments should, and inevitably will, reflect our criteria, not Berlioz's.) What is most pertinent is Berlioz's insistence that what is at stake are the proper limits of musical representation—ultimately the proper limits of artistic representation in general, and even more broadly, the limits of properly artistic subject matter. That is indeed a perpetually contested boundary, and will remain one as long as anyone feels a personal stake in art.

VARIETIES OF REPRESENTATION

Returning now to the *Symphonie fantastique*, the fifth and last movement, in which the artist imagines his own bizarre funeral, was at first notorious for all the deliberately ugly music it contains. One can hardly hear the opening bars, with their interminably sustained diminished-seventh chords, without thinking of Weber's "Wolf's Glen," a work Berlioz revered and, both as critic and as composer, did his best to propagate. (His interpolated recitatives, composed on commission, allowed *Der Freischütz* to be performed at the Académie Royale, the bona fide "Paris Opera," rather than at the Opéra Comique.) But Berlioz's music, unlike Weber's, had to do the work of the whole "production." It is surely with *Der Freischütz* in mind that D. Kern Holoman praises "the ghostly beginning of the last movement, with the eight-part *divisi* strings articulating a dramatic sonority, the whole concept as splendid as the curtain rising on an eerie stage lit in green and purple."[30] With such a task to perform, it is no wonder either that the first part of the "Dream of the Witches' Sabbath" is the part of the *Symphonie fantastique* with the most detailed program, or that every event it details is unmistakably represented in the music. The program, and the "unmistakability" of the representation, were alone what justified the outrageous musical effects.

The whole slow introduction (Larghetto) can be related, as Holoman suggests, to the "unearthly sounds, groans, shrieks of laughter" listed in the program, but the "unearthly cries, to which others seem to respond" have a more specific referent in the woodwind semaphores in Ex. 38-11, answered by the muted valve horn (a very recent invention, introduced in concert only two years before, and specified here for the first time). The "unearthliness" was due not only to the literally unheard-of timbre, but to the octave glissandos, which (as Berlioz knew full well) have to be "faked."

EX. 38-11   Hector Berlioz, *Symphonie fantastique*, V, mm. 7–11

The character-transformation of the idée fixe into "an ignoble dance tune, trivial and grotesque," previewed at m. 21 and played in full at m. 41 (Ex. 38-12), was another device borrowed straight from the opera, but one destined for a long career in orchestral music (as we have already begun to see), largely thanks to Liszt, who attended the premiere performance of the *Symphonie fantastique* and immediately introduced himself to Berlioz, with whom he maintained a cordial friendship until the latter's death. (Berlioz conducted the premiere performance, in Weimar, of Liszt's E♭-major Concerto, where the device of thematic transformation received a workout; Schumann, too, not only knew but had even reviewed the *Symphonie fantastique* by the time he wrote the *Fantaisie in A minor* for piano and orchestra that eventually became the first movement of his Concerto.) Once again timbre plays a hitherto unprecedented role in characterization: to depict his beloved in a fright wig Berlioz used yet another instrument new to the

EX. 38-12   Hector Berlioz, *Symphonie fantastique*, V, mm. 40–54

EX. 38-12   (*continued*)

symphony orchestra, the small, shrill-sounding E♭ clarinet, employed previously only in military bands.

Between the preview and the full statement comes the most radically disruptive and "incoherent" musical event in the score: the sudden tutti on E♭ that interrupts the C-major statement of the tune after its seventh bar. This moment is again carefully given its precise "objective" referent in the program — "a howl of joy greets her arrival" — without which the music would have been simply incomprehensible.

But now comes a profound change in the relationship between the music and the scenario, which from this moment is nothing more than a list of musical events such as might be found in any concert program. For this most fantastic episode of the Fantastic Symphony verbal justification was no longer necessary because a different (and older) kind of musical symbolism had kicked in, one that drew its referents not from within the work but from a wider range of reference on which the composer could rely because he shared it with his audience.

That shared asset was the musical treasury of the Church, the most traditional symbolic repository of all. Berlioz's appropriation of the stern medieval Dies Irae melody (Ex. 3-7b) and his burlesque treatment of it were a little risqué at a time when representations of religious services on the opera stage were subject to censorship, but it was essential to his "objective" or naturalistic purposes to employ an artifact from "reality," even if it served to illustrate a figment of fantasy.

Yet even here the device seems to have had its source not in real life but in literature. The Dies Irae, sung offstage in the original Latin, was employed as a stage effect in the cathedral scene from Goethe's *Faust*, a play Berlioz placed almost on a level with Shakespeare. Associations with *Faust*, a play all about diabolical havoc, would seem to have furnished the pretext for Berlioz's strange use of the chant to symbolize not divine redemption (as in the liturgy) but devilish fun and games. Such was the force of Berlioz's example that it irrevocably changed the chant's significance for composers to come, who inevitably associated it neither with Goethe nor with God, but with the unholy jigs in the *Symphonie fantastique*.

Not only the Dies Irae device but the midnight chimes that accompanied it (Ex. 38-13) were theatrical borrowings, making use of an instrument that had to be carted to the concert hall directly from the opera house. The most striking musical effect in the Dies Irae travesty is the irregularity with which the eight-measure peal of the chimes (spaced now three, now five bars apart) impinges on the rhythmically regular Dies Irae variations. That seemingly uncoordinated (but of course meticulously calculated) relationship was another "naturalistic" touch: the singers and the bell ringers, working independently, seemingly come together only from the chance perspective of the onlooker (that is, the audience).

EX. 38-13   Hector Berlioz, *Symphonie fantastique*, V, mm. 121–146

The chant variations proceed in a curiously academic, even pedantic manner, by strict diminution. But that is only the first of Berlioz's ironic borrowings from conservatory routine. The *Ronde dus abbat* ("Witches' round dance") itself is introduced through an ungainly but altogether "correct" fugal exposition, and the climactic section, in which the round dance and the Dies Irae are combined, is a cantus firmus exercise such as every counterpoint pupil is still forced to write. (It remained a favorite device with Berlioz: compare the climax of the overture to his opera *Benvenuto Cellini*, in which all the themes are his own, including the cantus firmus.)

All of these devices work together to make the latter part of the symphony's finale a piece of mock church music in the academic manner — just the sort of thing a well-trained musician might imagine under the influence of opium. The effect of the incongruity between the "learned," somewhat archaic compositional devices and the garish program (to say nothing of the orchestration, which reaches a peak of wildness with the *col legno* at fig. 83, where the violinists and violists are asked, for the first time in an orchestral score, to "strike the string with the wood of the bow"), is a source of humor to those in the know, and by the end one is *almost* convinced that the sophisticated composer's tongue is in his cheek.

Whether or not it was intended, Berlioz's fellow composers appreciated the joke, and appropriated it. Burlesque Dies Iraes — in which the Church's most terrifying musical artifact, describing the Last Judgment in appalling detail, was defaced, distorted, covered with composerly graffiti of every kind — became something of a rage or a blasphemous sport in the wake of the *Symphonie fantastique*. Most directly inspired by it was Liszt's *Totentanz* ("Dance of death"), a one-movement piano concerto subtitled "Paraphrase über 'Dies Irae' in der Form einer Variation" (1838, revised and published 1859). Funniest of all was the *Danse macabre*, an orchestral showpiece by Camille Saint-Saëns (1874), that thoroughly defanged the chant, doing to it what Berlioz had done to his idée fixe (Ex. 38-14).

The last major contribution to this odd little tradition was the *Rhapsody on a Theme by Paganini* (1934) by the Russian pianist-composer Sergey Rachmaninoff, a

EX. 38-14   Camille Saint-Saëns, Dies Irae in *Danse macabre* one-movement concerto consisting for the most part of variations on the theme of Paganini's twenty-fourth Caprice, with the Dies Irae thrown in as a reminder of Paganini's "diabolical" persona. By now the tradition (or traditions, for Paganini's Caprice had spawned another) has become entirely jocular, but its improbable longevity perhaps testifies to the ambivalence with which audiences reacted to Berlioz's original appropriation of the tune, and a wish to settle the uneasy questions it raised.

DISCRIMINATING ROMANTICISMS

Now what would Schumann have made of all this? We don't have to guess, because Schumann devoted the lengthiest critical article of his career to the *Symphonie fantastique*, issued in the *Neue Zeitschrift für Musik* in six installments between 3 July and 14 August 1835. Its length was due in part to its being not just a review but a defense against the captious reviews of others, notably François-Joseph Fétis, whose review Schumann printed in translation over two issues of the journal preceding his own. It was so detailed and diligent that Schumann later submitted it, successfully, for a doctor's degree.

The first installment was a shout of poetic enthusiasm, signed Florestan. The rest was a sober, highly technical descriptive commentary, signed "R. Schumann." The use of his real name was treatment accorded only a few works that Schumann took especially seriously. It already tells us as much as the actual words of the review about Schumann's attitude toward his French contemporary and counterpart, and the fact that it was based on Liszt's piano transcription rather than on the full score (unpublished until 1845) or on an actual hearing (which Schumann could not experience until 1843 when Berlioz visited Leipzig) makes it all the more a triumph of empathy. But Schumann's was nevertheless one of the most peculiar reviews that the *Symphonie fantastique* ever received, and that is why it is so revealing to us of the contrasting attitudes we may otherwise be inclined to lump together under the general rubric of romanticism. There was in fact no such "general rubric" at the time, as the review itself makes clear.

Only after spending five installments lauding the symphony and minutely describing it for his readers both as sound and as expression, providing in the process no fewer than twelve notated examples to refute Fétis's charge that Berlioz was technically incompetent, does Schumann even mention the program. He gives it, grudgingly and with many omissions, as an afterthought, and brings the whole six-part series of ardent notices to a close with this amazing sermon:

> Thus the program. All Germany is happy to let him keep it: such signposts always have something unworthy and charlatan-like about them! In any event the five titles would have been enough; word of mouth would have served to hand down the more circumstantial account, which would certainly arouse interest because of the personality of the composer who lived through the events of the symphony himself. In a word, the German, with his delicacy of feeling and his aversion to personal revelation, dislikes having his thoughts so rudely directed; he was already offended that Beethoven should not trust him to divine the sense of the *Pastoral* Symphony without assistance. Men experience a certain timidity before the genius's workshop: they prefer to know nothing about the origins, tools, and

secrets of creation, just as Nature herself reveals a certain sensitivity when she covers over her roots with earth. So let the artist lock himself up with his woes; we should experience too many horrors if we could witness the birth of every work of art!

But Berlioz was writing primarily for his French compatriots, who are not greatly impressed by refinements of modesty. I can imagine them, leaflet in hand, reading and applauding their countryman who has depicted it all so well; the music by itself does not interest them.

Whether a listener unfamiliar with the composer's intent would find that the music suggested pictures similar to those he wished to draw, I cannot tell, since I read the program before hearing the music. Once the eye has been led to a given point, the ear no longer judges independently. But if you ask whether music can really do what Berlioz demands of it in his symphony [as Fétis had tried emphatically to deny], then try to associate with it different or contrasting images.

At first the program spoiled my own enjoyment, my freedom of imagination. But as it receded more and more into the background and my own fancy began to work, I found not only that it was all indeed there, but what is more, that it was almost always embodied in warm, living sound.[31]

The persiflage about national stereotypes, while certainly revealing of contemporary attitudes (attitudes still with us, alas, and still dire), seems a bit beside the point. At issue, ultimately, is freedom of imagination, as Schumann finally gets around to saying in the last paragraph. Music, he insists, that leaves too little to the listener's "own fancy," that excludes the listener from the co-creative process, finally leaves the listener (out in the) cold. The alternative, for Schumann, is certainly not music without expressive (or even descriptive) content, but rather a music that by leaving such content undefined to a degree — by asking "Warum?" — allows and even forces the listener to participate in its creation. It is the music that requires this involvement on the part of the listener that affords the experience of what would later be called "absolute" music — a music absolutely, rather than merely particularly, expressive.

Did Berlioz disagree? Maybe not: after Fétis derided his efforts, he tried to clarify them, saying now that the program did not provide a scenario for the music but rather functioned the way spoken dialogue functioned in a comic opera with respect to the arias. It set them up, prepared the listener to receive their expressive content in its fullness, but did not compete with them or duplicate their meaning. (On another occasion he compared the program to the Greek chorus in ancient tragedies.) This was taken at the time as a retreat rather than a clarification.

It may have been so. It may have been the reason why he never wrote another program to accompany his later instrumental compositions, even though all of them had literary associations. It may even have been one of the reasons why Berlioz declared himself in later life, exasperated at the obstacles he still encountered in getting his works produced in his own country, to be "three-quarters German" as a musician.[32] Minus the animus that motivated it, this was an avowal of faith in instrumental music and its capacity to communicate its expressive content without the help of words. That is the crux on which the discrimination of musical romanticisms depends.

Self and Other

CHOPIN AND GOTTSCHALK AS EXOTICS; ORIENTALISM

All these poets write as if they were ill, and as though the whole world were a hospital.
—GOETHE TO HIS AMANUENSIS ECKERMANN, 20 SEPTEMBER (1827)

GENIUS AND STRANGER

"Hats off, gentlemen, a genius!" exclaimed Eusebius on Wednesday morning, 7 December 1831, in the dignified pages of the *Allgemeine musikalische Zeitung*.[1] With these words the twenty-one-year-old Schumann, making his critical debut three years before founding his own journal, welcomed the twenty-one-year-old piano virtuoso Frédéric Chopin into the ranks of published composers and introduced him to German music lovers, for whom previously he had hardly been a name. Also appearing for the first time in print were Schumann's *Davidsbündler*: the article would have been historic even were it not for the clairvoyance with which one genius had recognized another. But the opening has become a catchphrase; the composer it heralded soon proved to be the very embodiment of everything that the word genius implied in the early nineteenth century, and only Schumann spotted him—or even *could* have spotted him, one easily believes—so early.

Even more than a genius, Chopin was music's supreme *poète maudit*. An intruder from an alien terrain, he captivated and mystified with a strange fascination. (Even in 1831 Schumann described himself as being transfixed in Chopin's presence by "strange basilisk eyes," naming a mythical creature that killed with a glance.) And then he wasted mysteriously away, dying of "consumption" (tuberculosis), the most romantic of diseases, before his fortieth birthday.

One of the most romantic things about Chopin was his place of origin. Despite his French surname, he was a Pole, baptized with the name Fryderyk Franciszek Chopin in Zelazowa

FIG. 39-1   *Chopin Evoking Memories of Poland*, by Jan Styka.

FIG. 39-2   Chopin at the Radziwill salon (Hendrik Siemirdzki, 1887).

Wola, a settlement near Warsaw, where he was born in 1810 to the family of a French expatriate, Nicolas Chopin, who had come there in 1787 for reasons unknown and stayed on there to avoid conscription in the French revolutionary army. The future composer's father married a cultured Polish woman and raised his children as Polish patriots.

But although Polish patriotism burned brightly at the time, and would greatly increase, there was no such thing as Poland. In 1795 the country had been swallowed up by Russia, Prussia, and Austria, its powerful perfidious neighbors, in what was called the Third Partition. Its king was forced to abdicate, and it disappeared from the map of Europe until 1918, when it was restored after all three of its devourers had been defeated in the First World War. Like the Jews, those who identified as Poles now constituted a diaspora, a "scattering" among other nations.

The part of Poland in which Chopin was born had been incorporated into Russia, and he was legally a subject of the Russian tsar. But a Russian was the very last thing Chopin would have called himself. In the context of post-Revolutionary romantic politics, as we have seen, nation was no longer synonymous with state. Indeed Schumann, in a later review, noted wryly that "if the mighty autocrat of the North"—that is, Tsar Nikolai I, who had put down a major Polish rebellion in 1831—"knew what a dangerous enemy threatened him in Chopin's works," simple and pretty as many of them were, "he would forbid this music. Chopin's works are guns buried in flowers."[2] Chopin thus became the first major European composer to be actively touted abroad as a nationalist. "And because this nationalism is in deep mourning," Schumann wrote, alluding to Poland's tragic fate, "it attracts us all the more firmly to this thoughtful artist."

Indeed, it was only because the exiled Chopin's nationalism was an oppressed and offended nationalism that Schumann noticed it as nationalism at all. Although the romanticism to which he so ardently subscribed was, as we have seen, very much the product of German nationalism, Schumann did not think of himself as a nationalist. He was already used to thinking of the values of his nation, at least those to which he personally subscribed, as the general values of humanity, thus professing an unwitting double standard—we now call it ethnocentrism—that perpetuated the oppression with which he consciously sympathized on Chopin's behalf.

There was of course a residual social component to Schumann's double standard as well. In the early nineteenth century most Slavic languages were regarded as peasant vernaculars (and their speakers, implicitly, as peasants), especially within large multinational imperial states like Austria and even Russia, itself a Slavic state but with a French-speaking court, and an arrogant overlord to many smaller Slavic linguistic groups. Austria encompassed many Slavic-speaking territories: Bohemia and Slovakia, Western Poland (Galicia), and Croatia, to name only the largest. A speaker of Czech, Polish, or Serbo-Croatian, however, could achieve no social advancement within the empire unless he or she spoke German, the language of civil administration, and preferably French as well, the diplomatic and high-society lingua franca.

The linguistic hierarchy translated directly into a cultural and social hierarchy based on political power, inspiring rebellion. Herder's utopian brotherhood of nations, one of the bedrocks of romanticism, had been predicated on the God-given uniqueness and equality of all languages—something utterly contradicted by social and political realities. Herder had come to his idealistic vision by studying the local Lettish (or Latvian) folklore in the environs of Riga, a German-speaking enclave within the Russian empire. Herder-inspired attempts to turn Slavic vernaculars into literary languages, as precondition for national liberation, were just beginning in Chopin's time. His countryman Adam Mickiewicz (1798–1855) composed epics, dramas, sonnets, and ballads in the Polish language. Modern Czech literature began with the national historian František Palacký (1798–1876). The first Ukrainian writer to win an international reputation for writing in his mother tongue was the poet Taras Shevchenko (1814–61).

Significantly enough, in view of Schumann's comment about Chopin's "guns amid flowers," all three of these writers faced political persecution from imperial authorities who recognized in their work a threat to Germanic or Russian hegemony. Mickiewicz and Palacký took active part in national insurrections (in 1830 and 1848 respectively) and spent a good part of their lives, like Chopin, abroad. But whereas Chopin lived abroad by choice, in pursuit of his fortune, the writers were true political exiles whose romantic luster, perhaps somewhat undeservedly, rubbed off on the composer, too. In the real world languages and their speakers were far from equal, but in the world of art oppression carried (and still carries) a cachet.

NATIONAL OR UNIVERSAL?

Schumann had bought enthusiastically into Herder's brotherly vision of human diversity, and expressed it in one of his own household maxims: "Listen closely to folk songs; they are an inexhaustible mine of the most beautiful melodies and will give you a glimpse into the character of different nations."[3] But in another maxim, and with no apparent sense of contradiction, Schumann also wrote that "Music speaks the most universal of languages, one by which the soul is freely, yet *indefinably* moved; only then is it at home." To move the soul freely and indefinably, and so to realize its highest aim, music had to be "unmarked" by any defining (thus delimiting) national character. To Schumann, though probably not (at first) to Chopin, German music was unmarked. That is how one naturally tends to hear the music that surrounds one, until one is made aware of the existence of other musics. Thereafter one's own music can be heard as unmarked not by default but only by ideology.

This patronizing ambivalence toward nationalism—as something only "others" possessed or professed, and as something attractive but limiting—on the part of a member of a dominant culture shows very clearly through Schumann's critique of Chopin's composerly "nature" (a word that almost always needs quotation marks when applied to artists and art works):

> In his origin, in the fate of his country, we find the explanation of his great qualities and of his defects. When speaking of grace, enthusiasm, presence of mind, nobility, and warmth of feeling, who does not say Chopin? But also, when it is a question of oddity, morbid eccentricity, even wildness and hate. All of Chopin's earlier creations bear this impress of intense nationalism.
>
> But Art requires more. The minor interests of the soil on which he was born had to sacrifice themselves to the universal ones. Chopin's later works begin to lose something of their all too Sarmatian physiognomy, and their expression tends little by little to approach the general ideal first created by the divine Greeks; so that by a different road we finally rejoin Mozart.
>
> I say "little by little"; for he never can, nor should he completely disown his origin. But the further he departs from it, the greater will his significance in the world of art become.[4]

Chopin shared Schumann's ambivalence. He felt his Polish patriotism deeply and sincerely, and also traded on his exotic origins (his "Sarmatian physiognomy" as Schumann put it, affecting Latin) when it came to promoting himself and his works in European society. But he also very consciously modeled his art, and particularly his craft, on the most "universal" examples. Schumann called him "the pupil of the first masters—Beethoven, Schubert, Field,"[5] and went on enthusiastically to proclaim that "the first molded his mind in boldness, the second his heart in tenderness, and the third his hand in flexibility." It was probably Schumann's own repressed nationalism that caused him to overrate Beethoven's formative influence on Chopin (though it was not an insignificant factor) and prevented him from noticing how much Chopin's florid melodic style had borrowed from Italian bel canto opera, of which Chopin had become an enthusiastic connoisseur even in Warsaw.

More recently, Charles Rosen[6] has rightly emphasized Chopin's devotion to Bach, whom he regarded (the way Schumann regarded Beethoven) as the great founder. While (unlike Mendelssohn) he rarely imitated Bach directly, and as a Catholic probably dismissed Bach's vocal music from consideration (if he even knew of it), Chopin's early study of the *Well-Tempered Clavier* deeply influenced the contrapuntal precision of his style, turning him into perhaps the most fastidious and polished craftsman of his day.

In at least two of his publications — a cycle of twenty-four preludes for piano in all the major and minor keys (1839) and a set of studies (Études) published in 1833 — he paid Bach's didactic works conspicuous tribute; and when the painter Eugène Delacroix asked him to define musical logic, Chopin responded by playing a Bach fugue, noting that "to know the fugue deeply is to be acquainted with the element of all reason and all consistency in music."[7]

Not that Chopin ever wrote a fugue (or even a fugato) for public performance or print. Bach's actual style, let alone the genres in which he worked, was regarded (except by professional Germans like Mendelssohn) as irrevocably obsolete. But Chopin's compositions in "abstract" genres strove for logic and stylistic consistency, and proclaimed the composer's universal aspirations, just as his pieces based on Polish national dances declared his national origins and proclaimed aspirations of a different sort. The two strains, however, were not in stylistic conflict, and the progression Schumann claimed to note in Chopin from the national to the universal was a figment of the critic's imagination. Chopin's most Bach-like composition (Étude in C major, op. 10, no. 2, imitative of the opening prelude in the *Well-Tempered Clavier*) was written in 1830, and his very last composition, written only weeks before his death in 1849, was a Polish dance (Mazurka in F minor, op. 68, no. 4).

OR EXOTIC?

Chopin's prodigious gifts manifested themselves very early, and inevitably took him away from his homeland, which then offered a musician little scope for a career. He published his first polonaise in 1817 at the near-Mozartian age of seven and made his public debut with orchestra the next year, playing a concerto by Adalbert Gyrowetz (or Jírovec), a very old-fashioned Bohemian composer whose Haydnesque works upheld the unmarked "universal" style. Ironically enough, his first recognition from on high came from Tsar Alexander I, elder brother of the "northern autocrat" Chopin would later so come to hate, who heard him in Warsaw in 1825 and rewarded him with a diamond ring.

Only after finishing high school in 1826 did Chopin enter the local conservatory for full-time music instruction. As a pianist he was already fully formed. His main interest now lay in composition. The first composition that gained him wide notice, a brilliant set of variations for piano and orchestra on "Là ci darem la mano," the duet from *Don Giovanni* on which Liszt would later base his mighty "Don Juan Fantasy" (Ex. 37-5), was composed in 1827, while at the conservatory. (This was the composition that Schumann so prophetically reviewed in 1831, in Chopin's arrangement for piano without orchestra, published as op. 2.) Chopin's foreign debut with orchestra took place in Vienna in 1829. And here he made a fateful discovery, when he noticed that the audience reacted with greatest interest not to his variations on the work by Vienna's favorite son, with which he sought to flatter them, but to his *Krakowiak*, a concert rondo based on a catchy syncopated Polish dance. As in the case of many another Eastern European composer, Chopin's style became more national as his career became more international. Exoticism sells, especially when presented as nationalism (nationalism with "tourist appeal," as the musicologist James Parakilas adroitly termed it in a recent study of Chopin). It provides opportunities, but (as we know from Schumann's ambivalent appreciation) it also fetters. This is a dilemma that all "peripheral" artists have had to face since the establishment of Germanic hegemony in "classical music."

His success in Vienna gave Chopin hopes of a stellar career like Paganini's. He returned to Warsaw where (like Paganini before him) he composed a pair of concertos (in E minor and F minor respectively), plus a *Fantasia on Polish Airs* with orchestra, for use on the road. The concertos combined sparkling pianism with tourist appeal: both their finales are in the style of folk dances (a duple-time *ozwodny* in no. 1, which was actually completed later; a triple-time mazurka in no. 2), and in the first concerto the opening theme has the characteristically stilted gait of a polonaise. Second themes in both concertos employ the texture and florid ornamentation of Field's dreamy nocturnes, which Chopin would later develop into a major genre of his own. A little later, back in Vienna at the start of his first big tour, Chopin wrote a *Grande polonaise* for piano and orchestra in the *Eroica* key of E-flat major. It marked his most determined effort to win popular success on a Paganinian (or, later, Lisztian) scale.

He never won it. Disappointed by his reception in Vienna on second exposure, he cancelled a scheduled Italian tour and made for London, Field's territory, "by way of Paris," as he put it in a letter home. After a few concerts en route in southern Germany (where he was much distressed to receive the news of the sack of Warsaw by Tsar Nikolai's army and resolved not to return to Poland until it was free) he arrived in the French capital in September 1831. And there he stayed.

Paris, then in the first flush of Louis Philippe's July Monarchy, appealed to Chopin not (as sometimes assumed) for any reason pertaining to his father's origins, but rather by virtue of its lively intellectual life as the cosmopolitan capital of the nineteenth century, and its high bourgeois salon culture. After his brilliant debut (26 February 1832), at which he played his F minor concerto and his Mozart variations, Chopin found himself a social lion. Patronage came his way from the Rothschilds, the most prominent family of European bankers; the most prestigious hostesses showered him with invitations to grace their salons; and his appearances there made him the most sought-after piano teacher in the city, servicing a high-paying clientele of society belles, some of them very talented and gratifying to teach. Henceforth Chopin was able to renounce the concert hall. From

FIG. 39-3 Chopin, drawing by E. Radziwill at the Chopin Society, Warsaw.

FIG. 39-4   George Sand's property at Nohant, *La Mare au Diable: Bois de Chanteloup*, drawing by her son, Maurice Dudevant.

1838 until 1848, when forced back onstage by material need, he gave no public performances at all.

With the larger public he now communicated solely through publication. He became friendly with Liszt, Berlioz, Meyerbeer, and Bellini, with literary figures such as Balzac and Heine, and with painters like Delacroix, who produced a famous portrait of him in 1838 that now hangs in the Louvre (Fig. 39-5). Their deference surrounded his name with an aura. So did his ten-year liaison with the writer George Sand (Aurore Dudevant), who made veiled references to him in her novels beginning in 1836, and with whom he wintered rather scandalously at Majorca, the Spanish island resort, in 1839. Beginning that year, Chopin spent his summers, and did most of his composing, at George Sand's baronial estate at Nohant, about 150 miles southwest of Paris. In the city, he lived in luxurious seclusion.

THE PINNACLE OF SALON MUSIC

Moving as he did in rarefied social echelons to which no other musician had entrée

FIG. 39-5   Portrait of Chopin by Eugène Delacroix.

(making him look, not altogether wrongly, like a snob and a social climber to Mickiewicz and other members of the exiled Polish intelligentsia), Chopin cultivated an extremely refined manner that was reflected directly in the style of his performances and compositions. The line between the two was fairly blurry; for as many witnesses report, most of Chopin's compositions began at the keyboard, where they were worked up on the basis of improvisations that he later struggled hard to write down. Although his notation is meticulous, his music continued to evolve in performance as long as he continued to play it (or to teach it), and his manuscripts abound in variants that make them an adventurous player's paradise but an editor's and bibliographer's nightmare.

Having withdrawn from public performance, Chopin had no further need of the orchestra or indeed of any playing partners. After 1831 nearly all his works would be piano solos; the only exceptions were a handful of songs to Polish texts and a cello sonata, one of his last compositions, composed out of friendship with the cellist Auguste Franchomme (1808–84). He took great satisfaction in the fact that the public, who rarely saw him, regarded him primarily as a creative artist rather than a virtuoso. Most impressive of all was the awed respect shown him by other pianists, many of whom made a point of featuring his works alongside (or even in preference to) their own. The ability to play Chopin idiomatically is still probably the paramount qualifying yardstick for a concert pianist today.

Although he wrote three sonatas (highly unconventional except the first, a student work), Chopin's piano works consist overwhelmingly of character pieces: twenty-one nocturnes, twenty-seven études (literally technical studies, but actually virtuoso concert works), twenty-six preludes, four ballades, four rondos, four scherzos, four impromptus (including a "Fantaisie-impromptu"), and several one-of-a-kind items composed late in his career: a *Fantaisie* (1841), a *Berceuse* or lullaby (1844), and a *Barcarolle* (1846). The lion's share of his output, however, and in some ways the most significant, were the sublimated ballroom dances: sixteen polonaises, twenty waltzes, above all the sixty-one mazurkas, aphoristic miniatures of which most (forty-two) were written after settling in Paris. The études and preludes are often programmed in sets (two sets of ten études, opp. 10 and 25; twenty-four preludes, op. 28), and seem to have been put in an effective performance order by the composer. The rest are freestanding salon pieces, to be chosen and presented at the performer's discretion.

We too have to exercise discretion in choosing and presenting for examination a tiny sample from such a rich assortment. No such sample can hope to be representative. The only solution seems to be to concentrate on the extremes, hoping that that will serve to suggest the amazing scope of Chopin's seemingly one-sided and restricted output, and show how and why this mysterious stranger became such an emblematic (and emblematically contradictory) figure: of "genius," of romantic suffering, of artistic perfection, of sickliness and effeminacy, of nationalism, of exoticism, of universality.

THE CHOPINESQUE MINIATURE

On the miniature extreme, no composer ever exceeded Chopin's mastery of the romantic fragment, the most suggestively romantic statement of all. No one ever thematized the idea as vividly as did Chopin when he invented a new genre, the freestanding prelude, to embody it. A prelude, after all, is by definition incomplete. The *New Harvard Dictionary of Music* defines it as "a composition establishing the pitch or key of a following piece."[8] So far we have encountered the prelude only as the first item in a keyboard suite, or as paired with a fugue. Before Chopin, several pianist composers had provided books of preludes for practical concert use, mere modulatory transitions between recital items for pianists who were incapable of improvising their own. Collections of this kind had been published by the Italian-born London-based Muzio Clementi, not only a virtuoso but a piano manufacturer (1787); by the Slovakian-born Johann Nepomuk Hummel (*24 Präludien*, op. 67, 1814); and by Ignaz Moscheles (1794–1870), a Bohemian-born pianist based in London, whose celebrated book of didactic models for improvisations, *50 Präludien*, op. 73 (1827), Chopin probably knew and took (along with the *Well-Tempered Clavier*) for a model.

But Chopin's preludes were not didactic. They were vividly if enigmatically expressive performance pieces, albeit in an "improvisatory" style; and their novelty, instantly perceived, proved influential. The evocative genre Chopin thus created, a prelude to everything and nothing (or, if one insists on being tiresomely literalistic, to the next prelude), was widely imitated by later romantics and post-romantics such as the Russians Alexander Scriabin, Sergey Rachmaninoff, and Dmitriy Shostakovich; the Frenchmen Claude Debussy and Olivier Messiaen; the American George Gershwin, and the Argentine Alberto Ginastera, the date of whose "American Preludes" of 1944 illustrates the impressive chronological reach of Chopin's hold on the imaginations of later pianist composers.

Like the preludes and fugues of the *Well-Tempered Clavier* or the didactic sets by Clementi et al., Chopin's covered all the major and minor keys, which is why the set contained precisely twenty-four. His ordering was different from his predecessors, who put the keys through a rising sequence of semitones, with each major key followed by its parallel minor. Chopin's ordering already suggests that his set was not a mere compendium but a performance entity, for the sequence of keys is much closer to the

EX. 39-1   Frédéric Chopin, Prelude, Op. 28, no. 1

EX. 39-1 (*continued*)

sequences of actual harmonic practice: a circle of fifths, with each major key followed by its relative minor (C major, A minor, G major, E minor, etc.).

The first, in C major (Ex. 39-1), perfectly exemplifies the paradoxical, imagination-captivating nature of the genre, being at once fragmentary and whole, complete and yet not complete, sufficient yet insufficient. (Compare Oscar Wilde on the "perfect pleasure" of a cigarette: "it is exquisite, yet it leaves one unsatisfied.")[9] The opening, with its suggestion of a parallel period (compare mm. 1–8 with 9–12) is a feint. The second phrase, which promises to balance the first, instead soars aloft into a chromatic ascent that thrillingly overshoots its goal in m. 21 by means of an appoggiatura and only subsides harmonically in m. 25, having grown to exactly twice its expected length. Melodic satisfaction does not come until m. 29, with the sounding of the soprano C so calculatedly withheld at m. 25, where instead the harmonically equivalent m. 1 had been reprised.

But when melodic satisfaction is granted, harmonic stability is withdrawn by suspending the subdominant in the right hand over the root-fifth pedal in the left (a quintessentially Chopinesque touch!). Full subsidence is not achieved until the final arpeggio in m. 33, so that the forthright initial eight-bar phrase has been answered by an elusively asymmetrical twenty-five-bar continuation. The skillful prolongation of the melodic-harmonic resolution makes for a very satisfying conclusion on one level; and yet the piece has not been rounded off. It is a paradoxically single ("aphoristic") statement of the sort of idea that usually demands contrast and repetition: complete yet incomplete, fully formed yet inchoate. It is at once a highly unconventional, sui generis shape and a fastidiously, consummately planned one. The music sounds at once spontaneous and very finely wrought (especially in texture).

EX. 39-2   Frédéric Chopin, Prelude, Op. 28, no. 2

The cryptic second prelude (Ex. 39-2) is one of the most written-about pieces in the whole much-written-about romantic repertoire. It is an out-and-out grotesque (from *grottesca*, originally referring to wall decorations in ancient excavated cave dwellings or grottos): a deliberately, fancifully ugly or absurd utterance. Fancifully ugly is the dissonant left-hand accompaniment, with its chromatic middle-voice neighbors that so frequently interfere with and distort the effect of the harmony-tones, as for example in mm. 5 and 10, with their crabby diminished octaves formed by the friction of chromatic neighbors against diatonic suspensions.

Fancifully absurd is the harmonic vagary. The piece begins, straightforwardly enough, as if in E minor, but the first melodic phrase effects a detour to G, the ostensible relative major. The movement to B minor at m. 9 sets up the false expectation that the whole maneuver will be symmetrically repeated in the dominant; but when the moment of truth comes, in m. 11, the anticipated D is distorted to D♯, obfuscating the tonal orientation and making for some more willful clashes in the part writing. The next phrase is famous for the functional undecideability of the harmony. Where it's leading is anyone's guess. When cadence is finally made on A minor, it seems arbitrarily tacked on — almost mockingly so, given the incongruous little chorale (marked *sostenuto*) that introduces it. If we take the three cadential points G, D (anticipated if never actually realized), and A as marking the prelude's trajectory, we have an instance of willful harmonic movement swimming directly against the current of the circle of fifths.

Thus (to quote the musical deconstructionist Rose Rosengard Subotnik) the A-minor cadence, "rather than constituting the only conceivable and thus logically necessary end to the piece" as longstanding harmonic practice would require, merely intrudes upon it as "a forcible and contingent end, more rhetorical than harmonically logical in its persuasiveness."[10] Subotnik links this radical arbitrariness to the general rejection of "Enlightened" premises in post-Napoleonic Europe, and the potentially sinister romantic exaltation of "personal" over universal truth.

In any case, this is no end-accented progression like the one in the opening movement of Schumann's *Phantasie* (Ex. 38-4). There is no thwarted inevitability about the harmonic trajectory, although (and this should be taken as a caution) analysis can always be employed in hindsight to suggest the opposite. As Subotnik points out, "every pitch in this piece has harmonic aspects that can, in retrospect, be related in some fashion to the tonal identity of the final cadence," and is thus "susceptible to an ex post facto, empirical explanation of what actually (or historically) happened."[11] But such an analysis will not provide what tonal analysis, when truly pertinent, ought to provide — namely, an account of "the necessary realization of a logical premise." (Justification of willful behavior ex post facto, which analysis is designed to accomplish in the name of genius, is just what thinkers like Edmund Burke viewed as the potentially sinister or corrupting side effect of romanticism on reason.)

Yet while Chopin's prelude is "on purpose" a put-on thing from beginning to end, the part writing, however arbitrary the effect, is contrapuntally pristine, rendering the piece at once academically impeccable and poetically fractious. Those primarily committed to academic respectability must respect it, even as they wonder at the grotesquerie (and possibly try to explain it away). Those primarily committed to poetic fractiousness will wonder at the cool "aristocratic" control of the *facture* (the "making," the technical handling or management of materials) which with Chopin was such an indispensable point of honor. There is, in short, something in this piece to bewilder everyone, and something for everyone to admire. It was when both of these elements were present and impossible to disengage from one another that romantics were most apt to speak, as Schumann did, of genius.

Such genius was often linked with the demonic, as we have seen, or with madness or physical illness (and there were many in the nineteenth century who deduced from this the false converse that madness or physical infirmity were signs of genius). Thus Chopin's lifelong sickliness and his death from consumption became in the minds of many the virtual content and message of his art, turning his compositions into what the contemporary French poet Charles Baudelaire called *Fleurs du mal* ("flowers of illness," or "poisoned flowers") and greatly increasing the fascination they wielded over suggestible imaginations.

George Sand made specific allusion to the A-minor prelude in two different memoirs of her life with Chopin. In one, she depicted him composing it while actually coughing blood, becoming an object of "horror and fright to the population"[12] and leading to the couple's eviction from their Majorcan retreat. In the other, she attempts through biography to account for the prelude's strange effect on listeners. It came to him, she writes,

> through an evening of dismal rain — it casts the soul into a terrible dejection. [My son] Maurice and I had left him in good health one morning to go shopping in Palma for things we needed at our "encampment." The rain came in overflowing torrents. We made three leagues in six hours, only to return in the middle of a flood. We got back in absolute dark, shoeless, having been abandoned by our driver to cross unheard of perils. We hurried, knowing how our sick one would worry. Indeed he had, but now was as though congealed in a kind of quiet desperation, and, weeping, he was playing his wonderful Prelude. Seeing us come in, he got up with a cry, then said with a bewildered air and a strange tone, "Ah, I was sure that you were dead."[13]

On the basis of these biographical embroideries, it became fashionable to maintain that Chopin's music, in the words of the mid-century French critic Hippolyte Barbedette (and the Preludes particularly by virtue of their great "artistic value"), exerted a dangerous influence on ordinary mortals. "Chopin," he opined,

> was a sick man who enjoyed suffering, and did not want to be cured. He poured out his pain in adorable accents — his sweet melancholy language which he invented to express his sadness. One feels it irresistibly and is suddenly willess before its charm; since music is above all a vague and inexplicit language, he who plays Chopin's music, for the little he is under the spell of such melancholy thought, will inevitably end by imagining that it is his own thought he expresses. He will really believe in suffering, along with him who knew so well how to weep. Conclusion: Chopin's music is essentially unhealthy. That is its allure and also its danger.[14]

This one-sided but culturally significant view of Chopin is of course contradicted by many of his best-known pieces, including the very next prelude, a light, outdoorsy, altogether unproblematic vivace in G major. The pianistically undemanding E-minor largo that follows it (Ex. 39-3) has become hackneyed over the years by naively emotive, amateurish performances (like the one given — in a satirized attempt at seduction — by the Jack Nicholson character in the movie *Five Easy Pieces*). What can make such performances seem naive is the fact that for all its *espressivo* melancholy and harmonic subtlety this is actually one of the more mannerly preludes. It is a formally straightforward binary design in which two parallel periods of equal duration proceed without feint or detour first (mm. 1–12) to a dominant half-close, and then (mm. 13–25), more emphatically, to a full stop on the tonic.

It is the highly chromatic (or "chromatized") harmony that has made this prelude popular. But its chromaticism, far from enigmatic or confusing like that of the second prelude, consists rather of a lucid, regular, and very intelligible application of chromatic

EX. 39-3 Frédéric Chopin, Prelude, Op. 28, no. 4

passing tones to all three voices in a contrapuntally pristine though rhythmically way-ward series of 7–6 suspensions. (In the first period, for example, the sevenths are sounded at m. 2, m. 4, the middle of m. 6, m. 9, and m. 10; their respective resolutions come at the middle of m. 3, the third quarter of m. 4, the middle of m. 8, and the second quarter of m. 9.) Harmony based on a suspension chain rather than a root progression by fifths was the very opposite of a novel device. Its origins lay in the ground-basses of the sixteenth and seventeenth centuries, and it was already a deliberate archaism when Mozart briefly revived it (also in chromaticized form) in his C-minor Fantasy, K. 475 (Ex. 30-8). We have not seen it since. Its very old-fashionedness made it esoteric and exotic, and therefore striking, when Chopin used it. It testifies nevertheless to his unusually thorough and conservative grounding in counterpoint, partly the result of his having been trained in a remote and "backward" corner of Eastern Europe rather than in one of the musical capitals of the continent. In its paradoxical way it was a token of his Polishness.

NATIONALISM AS A MEDIUM

The more obvious tokens of Chopin's Polishness are to be found, naturally enough, in his Polish dances, the polonaises and especially the mazurkas, which were of all his works the ones most prized by his contemporaries as characteristically or authentically "Chopinesque." The man, in other words, was equated with (reduced to?) the group from which he hailed, as is usually the case with "others." Yet here, as everywhere, Chopin was eclectic, or rather syncretic, forging a personal and very distinctive style out of heterogeneous, in some ways even incongruous, ingredients. The authentically national — meaning, in France, the authentically exotic — was only one of those ingredients.

The "mazurka," as it was known abroad (largely thanks to Chopin) was the national dance of the Mazurs, the settlers of the Mazowsze plains surrounding Warsaw. Danced by couples either in circles or in country dance sets, it came in various types — the moderate *kujawiak*, the faster *mazurek*, the very rapid *oberek*, all represented among Chopin's mazurkas. What all types had in common was a strongly accented triple meter, with the strongest accents (usually on the second or third beat) marked by a tap of the heel. Thus even the fastest mazurkas are distinctly felt "in three," unlike the waltz which, except for the slowest specimens, is normally counted "in one," with never an accent except on the downbeat.

So characteristically Polish did Polish patriots consider this dance that a traditional mazurka melody, "Dombrowski's mazurka" (*Mazurek Dąbrowskiego*) — so called because it was played in 1806 as an anthem to greet the briefly victorious Polish legion under General Jan Dombrowski (also spelled Dąbrowski) that fought the hated Prussians, Austrians, and Russians on the side of Napoleon — became the national anthem of the resurrected Polish republic after World War I (Ex. 39-4). The melody illustrates the most characteristic mazurka pattern: a dotted rhythm on the first beat, followed by an accent.

EX. 39-4 *Mazurek Dąbrowskiego*

Jesz - cze Pol - ska   nie zgi - nę - ła,____ kie - dy my   ży - je - my

(Poland still is ours for ever, long as Poles remain)

The first set of mazurkas Chopin composed as an exile from Poland, and therefore as nostalgia or exotica rather than in a spirit of insular nationalism, was the set of four published in 1834 as op. 17. All of them feature the characteristic heel-tapping rhythm exemplified in Ex. 39-4. All four are cast, like the vast majority of Chopin's mazurkas, in the ternary da capo form of the *kujawiak* rather than the more common successive strains (AABB, AABBCC, etc.) of the *mazurek*. Although it can be justified in "national" terms, this was already an accommodation to the common practice of the "art" tradition, with its minuets (or scherzos) and trios. Another touch that is especially characteristic of the mazurkas is the use of tonic (and occasionally tonic-fifth) pedals. All four mazurkas in op. 17 show it. The midsections of nos. 1 and 4 maintain it throughout; it is more intermittent, yet quite unmistakable, in the remaining pieces. It is, of course, a trace of folklore, the mazurka being primevally accompanied in its natural habitat by the *duda* or Polish bagpipe, which could produce either a tonic or tonic-fifth drone. Leaping melodic grace notes, though often thought of as especially Chopinesque, may be another bagpipe effect, since briefly stopping another pitch on the "chanter" or melody pipe is the only way one can articulate repeated notes given the bagpipe's unremitting air stream, which the player cannot "tongue" or interrupt in any way.

But all such life traces are filtered, in Chopin's French-period mazurkas, through a gauze of nostalgic memory conjured up by stinging or slithery chromatic harmony. In op. 17, no. 1, the effect is achieved by the use of modal mixtures and auxiliary dissonances to add a pungency that registers as poignancy to melodic reprises. The last phrase of op. 17, no. 2 (Ex. 39-5), with its play of passing chromatics (including the Lydian raised fourth degree) and appoggiaturas, epitomizes the slithery style, as does the second half of the midsection, all played over a tonic pedal.

EX. 39-5   Frédéric Chopin, Mazurka, Op. 17, no. 2

By contrast, the surprising delayed harmonization of the opening note in op. 17, no. 3 (Ex. 39-6), turning what is by rights a consonant diatonic note into a dissonant chromatic suspension, is especially stinging. The major-minor instability of the third degree will persist throughout the piece, as will the instability of the fourth degree, ever tottering between the folklike Lydian tritone and the perfect common-practice interval over various local tonics.

EX. 39-6   Frédéric Chopin, Mazurka, Op. 17, No. 3, mm. 1–4

HARMONIC DISSOLUTION

All such effects pale, however, before the extraordinary maneuvers of op. 17, no. 4, one of Chopin's most haunting fragments, in which denatured and strangely tinctured reminiscences of the mazurka seem to hover in a kind of harmonic ether. The characteristic accompaniment pattern of the "authentic" mazurka, the steady oompah-pah against which the shifting melodic accents rebound, prominent in the first two mazurkas and only slightly attenuated in the third, is now almost altogether gone, replaced by a mid-register pulsation marked *sotto voce* ("in an undertone" — see Ex. 39-7a).

EX. 39-7A   Frédéric Chopin, Mazurka, Op. 17, no. 4, mm. 1–20

EX. 39-7B   Frédéric Chopin, Mazurka, Op. 17, no. 4, end

The repeated harmonic progression in Ex. 39-7a is a variant of the Chopinesque suspension chain we encountered in Ex. 39-3, even closer this time to the ancient *passus duriusculus* ground bass, cadencing alternately on V and on I. The grafting of this basso ostinato to a melody voice full of mazurka rhythms is already a fantastic amalgam, made stranger still by the admixture of Italianate *fioritura* (most closely associated, at the keyboard, with the nocturne) on melodic repetitions (as in m. 15).

But for the romantic sense of evocative incompletion at fullest strength, nothing can compare with the ending of this mazurka (Ex. 39-7b). The idea is simplicity itself: a closing repetition of the mazurka's first four bars, which in their harmonic open-endedness had made an effective preface (or "prelude") to the dance. In a postlude, the same open-endedness is uncanny. Ending on an F major $^{6}_{3}$ (or, perhaps more to the point, a tonic triad with an appoggiatura to its fifth left unresolved) gives a sense that the piece has not ended but merely passed out of earshot (as the notation *perdendosi*, "getting lost," corroborates). Nothing can follow such an ending without spoiling its special mood of enchantment. To do it justice, silence must palpably hang in the air — a silence that seems to throb with unheard music. Not for nothing, then, did Chopin choose to end the set with this mazurka, even if the four pieces were not necessarily meant to form a concert sequence.

There is a huge difference between the fragmentary quality of Schumann's *Phantasie*, which begins in medias res but comes to a definite close, and the far more disquieting sense of incompletion Chopin achieves in the A-minor mazurka. The closest Schumann came to it was in "Child Falling Asleep" (*Kind im Einschlummern*), the next-to-last of his *Kinderscenen* ("Scenes of childhood"), op. 15, a programmatic piece in which the implied narrative — the child nodding off before the end is reached — explains and justifies the effect. Even so, Schumann continued a circle of fifths from the end of "Child Falling Asleep" into the beginning of the last piece in the set, "The Poet Speaks" (*Der Dichter spricht*), so that the harmony at the end of the first piece does find resolution of sorts in the other, albeit in a different key (Ex. 39-8).

EX. 39-8   Robert Schumann, *Kinderscenen*, end of no. 12 and beginning of no. 13

E X. 39-8 (continued)

Der Dichter spricht

No. 13

More direct echo or emulation of Chopin's uncompleted fragment can be found in composers of the next generation. Stephen Heller (1813 – 88), a Hungarian-born pianist composer who made his home, like Chopin, in Paris, was only three years Chopin's junior, but he had barely achieved notice by the time of the Polish composer's death, and then only as a composer of technical studies. His more important works mainly belong to later decades. First among them was a set of character pieces with the emblematically romantic title *Spaziergänge eines Einsamen* ("Solitary rambles"), published in 1851. The last item, a harried vivace, ends the cycle with an unresolved diminished-seventh chord, the equivalent of ending a letter or a story or—most typically—a lyric poem with an ellipsis ("..."). Except for the startling effect at the end (startling, that is, in retrospect, when one realizes that it *was* the end), the piece is fairly innocuous, and so were the many popular stories and poems that abused the device of ellipsis, turning it eventually into a cliché (Ex. 39-9).

E X. 39-9   Stephen Heller, *Spaziergänge eines Einsamen*, Op. 78, end of no. 6

Liszt was among the abusers. He wrote a whole series of *Valses oubliées* (Forgotten waltzes) that popularized the effect of "dissolved" tonality as a representation of hazy memory ("balls of youth recalled in old age . . ."), and even an experimental "Bagatelle in No Key" (*Bagatelle ohne Tonart*), composed in 1885, the last full year of Liszt's life, but unpublished until 1956 (Ex. 39-10). The touted suspension of tonality is the result of a series of unusual deceptive cadences whereby dominant-seventh chords are converted into diminished sevenths, one of which is allowed, as in Heller's piece, to finish the piece, if not conclude it.

EX. 39-10   Franz Liszt, *Bagatelle ohne Tonart*, mm. 169–end

The interesting question such pieces raise — one that (for reasons to be examined in due course) was on many minds in 1956 when Liszt's bagatelle was published amid considerable publicity — is whether such devices, which may be said to have originated with Chopin, necessarily weaken the structural role of tonality. The answer, pretty clearly, is that they do not, any more than the rhetorical use of ellipsis, or of incorrect or nonstandard grammar in literature, weakens the everyday efficacy of grammar. To end a piece with an unresolved appoggiatura, or more radically with a diminished-seventh chord, honors the requirement of tonal closure in the breach rather the observance, but honor is in any case paid. If anything, frustration heightens the sense of expectation.

There is not the slightest doubt as to the expected conclusion in Chopin's mazurka or Heller's "Ramble." Not even in Liszt's bagatelle can there be any real debate as to the identity of the harmonic goal that has been rhetorically left unreached; the last functional chord being a clear dominant of A minor, that is clearly the key avoided. There is no ambiguity, and surely no tonal incoherence. The startling effect of arbitrary rupture is entirely a matter of rhetoric rather than structure. The object of the rhetoric is the affirmation precisely of the right to be arbitrary, to please oneself: in a word, the time-honored romantic right to subjectivity.

PLAYING "ROMANTICALLY"

The other area in which the rights of the romantic subject are paramount in Chopin is in the realm of performance practice, particularly the crucial matter of *tempo rubato*. Chopin's playing was so unusually marked by it that there were those among his contemporaries who actually thought that he had invented the technique of arbitrarily "stealing" time from some notes so as to lengthen others for expressive effect, an arbitrary act being referable to no standard save the actor's subjective desire for it. Chopin was indeed one of the first to use the actual word *rubato* as an explicit if fuzzy performance direction, rather than relying only on traditional directions for tempo modification like *accelerando* (or *stretto*), *ritenuto*, etc., or else (like several eighteenth-century composers, including C. P. E. Bach and Mozart) indicating its effect with melodic ties and syncopations.

The first such usage came in the first mazurka Chopin published after leaving Poland: the one in F♯ minor, published in 1832 as op. 6, no. 1 (Fig. 39-6). The word is used alongside *ritenuto* and *rallentando*, and probably means a subtler broadening than the more traditional terms imply, here intended to point up the repetition of the opening period and distinguish it (as more expressive or emphatic) from the first playing. If Chopin's own description of tempo rubato is applied, it would appear to mean a slight delay of the melody with respect to the bass, probably not to be righted until the next downbeat.

Chopin always maintained, like Mozart in a famous letter with which Chopin must have

FIG. 39-6 Original edition of Chopin's Mazurka in F-Sharp Minor, op. 6, no. 1 (Leipzig: Kistner, 1832).

been familiar, that for him, *rubato* did not mean a general alteration of tempo but only a dilation of melody over a steadily pulsing accompaniment. Wilhelm von Lenz, a Russian government official who took lessons from both Liszt and Chopin in Paris, reported Chopin as saying that "the left hand is the conductor; it must not waver, or lose ground; do with the right hand what you will and can."[15] Whether Chopin always practiced what Lenz here had him preaching may be questionable. Earwitness reports of his playing are very inconsistent. Mendelssohn accused him in 1834 of playing in the "Parisian spasmodic and impassioned style, too often losing sight of time and sobriety,"[16] and the French music publisher Aristide Farrenc, who had known him throughout his Paris years, chided Chopin in 1861 for the "tempo rubato, of which one makes today a usage so ridiculous and tiring."[17] Hackneyed or exaggerated post-Chopinesque rubato eventually produced a backlash in the early twentieth century, when an "objective" style of playing, characterized by uniform metronomic tempos, became fashionable. Stravinsky, whom we have already identified as a ringleader of the anti-Beethovenian reaction, was at the forefront of this movement, too, receiving "special thanks" from his friend, the Italian composer Vittorio Rieti (1898–1994), "for not asking us to swallow crescendo porridge, pedal sauce, and rubato marmalade."[18]

Needless to say, this "objective" attitude was just as significant a cultural indicator in the early twentieth century as Chopin's style of performance had been in the mid-nineteenth. And what should also go without saying is that Chopin performances in the early twentieth century had to conform to the new attitude if they were to be considered "authentic." Even "Chopin specialists" like the Polish pianist Arthur Rubinstein (1887–1982), who made a special point of presenting themselves as the composer's heirs, performed his works in a much "straighter" fashion than the Chopinists of the preceding generation, the first to leave recorded evidence behind.

The assumption, or claim, was that those earlier pianists, such as Vladimir de Pachmann (1848–1933), had exaggerated and vulgarized the "true" Chopinesque rubato, which Rubinstein's generation had restored to its original dignity. It seems just as likely, however, that Chopin's own playing would have been considered vulgar (full of "porridge, sauce, and marmalade") in Rubinstein's time, and that Rubinstein and his contemporaries had not restored Chopin at all but rather altered him (perhaps unwittingly) to conform to a new set of expectations.

The mazurkas, where Chopin was most apt to include the word *rubato* in his notation, were a special case, and a wonderfully instructive one. A reviewer of Chopin's last public concerts, which took place in London in 1848, wrote that the mazurkas "lose half their characteristic wildness if played without a certain freak and license, impossible to imitate,"[19] and to which the composer alone possessed the key. Most suggestive of all is a memoir by the German (later English) pianist and conductor Charles Hallé (1819–95), who lived in Paris during most of Chopin's residence there and came to know him well. "A remarkable feature of his playing," Hallé recalled,

> was the entire freedom with which he treated the rhythm, but which appeared so natural that for years it had never struck me. It must have been in 1845 or 1846 that I once ventured to observe to him that most of his mazurkas (those dainty jewels),

when played by himself, appeared to be written, not in 3/4, but in 4/4 time, the result of his dwelling so much longer on the first note in the bar. He denied it strenuously, until I made him play one of them and counted audibly four in the bar, which fitted perfectly. Then he laughed and explained that it was the national character of the dance which created the oddity. The more remarkable fact was that you received the impression of a 3/4 rhythm whilst listening to common time. Of course this was not the case with every mazurka, but with many.[20]

Of course one wants to know which ones, exactly, but Hallé did not say. The most plausible suggestion is that the distension applies mainly to the basic mazurka rhythm noted in Ex. 39-4, beginning with a dotted figure that might easily be extended beyond a beat's duration in the interests of enhancing its noble effect. But note that this time Chopin explained the practice not by referring to the expressive dimension of the music, let alone his feelings, but instead referred to its "national character," an impersonal criterion.

The question thus legitimately arises as to whether the application of tempo rubato, even the kind that affects not just the melody but the general tempo, is really as arbitrary and romantic as it may seem, or whether it may be governed by rules of rhetoric that have their origin not in an individual's subjective expressive impulse, but in the intersubjective expressive conventions of the musical community. And from this arises the further thought, disturbing to some, that what we subjectively perceive as our own personal expressive impulses may in fact be grounded to a greater extent than we realize in the historically contingent values of the communities to which we belong.

But none of this should really be surprising, let alone disturbing. Artists like Chopin, who in their composing and performing created a highly prized impression of extreme subjective spontaneity and unique original inspiration, but whose work was nevertheless intelligible to the nonprofessional audience that it addressed, were obviously working within the boundaries of the normal (which is to say, the conventional), even as their more adventurous conceptions, like the A-minor Mazurka, served to extend those boundaries (or "push the envelope," as the saying lately goes). When the boundaries have been thus extended, what was once considered radical behavior will seem normal, and may eventually (as in the work of Stephen Heller, or the reputed abusers of rubato) become hackneyed.

THE CHOPINESQUE SUBLIME

Strangely enough, the pieces in which Chopin strayed furthest beyond the boundaries of what his contemporaries thought normal and intelligible were his two mature sonatas (in B♭ minor, op. 35, published in 1840, and in B minor, op. 58, published in 1845), works belonging to the most traditional and classical genre to which Chopin applied himself. It was precisely his failure or unwillingness to reckon with the obligations of genre, the expectations to which title words give rise, that made his sonatas hard to understand. To recall Schumann's point, quoted in the previous chapter, "we are accustomed to judge a thing from the name it bears," and, more pointedly, "we make certain demands upon a fantasy, others upon a sonata." Later, confronted with Chopin's B♭ minor sonata, the same Schumann expressed his bemusement in one of his funniest paragraphs:

The idea of calling it a sonata is a caprice, if not a jest, for he has simply bound together four of his wildest children, to smuggle them under this name into a place to which they could not else have penetrated. Let us imagine some good country cantor visiting a musical city for the purpose of making artistic purchases. All the newest compositions are laid before him, but he does not care to know them; finally, some rogue hands him a sonata: "Ah, yes, that is something for me, a composition of the good old days," says he delighted, and buys it at once. At home he takes up the piece, and I am much mistaken if he does not vow, by every musical divinity, that this is no sonata style but rank blasphemy, even before he has painfully ground out the first page at the keyboard. But Chopin has achieved his goal: he has penetrated into the cantor's residence; and who knows whether, in years to come, in the same dwelling there may not be born some romantic grandson who some day will dust off the sonata, play it, and think to himself, "This man was no fool!"[21]

Schumann was exaggerating. The sonata is not as weird as all that. It has a first movement that is recognizably in sonata form, even if the recapitulation of the first theme (and with it, the dramatic double return) has been elided out. It has a scherzo replete with trio. The famous (to Schumann, repellent) slow movement is cast, just like the one in Beethoven's *Eroica*, as a *Marche funèbre*, a funeral march.

EX. 39-11   Frédéric Chopin, Sonata in B-flat minor, IV

The finale, a presto to be played sotto voce throughout, still gives pause, however (Ex. 39-11). It is indeed a wild child, unique and well-nigh indescribable: a moto perpetuo, but for the last chord all in octaves (that is, without harmony), all spun out of a six-note motive but without literal repetitions except for an ironically formal recapitulation as if to take the place of the one missing from the first movement. Bach might have called it a prelude (no wonder it comes at the end!). It elicited from Schumann a virtual accusation of sadism:

That which in the last movement is given to us under the name "finale" resembles mockery more than any kind of music. Yet we must confess that even from this joyless, unmelodious movement an original and terrifying spirit breathes on us which holds down with mailed fist everything that seeks to resist, so that we listen fascinated and uncomplaining to the end—though not to praise; for this is not music.[22]

On the contrary, Chopin must have taken this as the very highest praise (and so, of course, Schumann must have intended, master of irony that he was). But what should seem by now both striking and characteristic is the way in which the music paradoxically achieves its extreme modernity by way of archaism. Except for the chromatic and dissonant implied harmony, the piece that so astounded and even offended nineteenth-century musicians would have struck their early eighteenth-century counterparts (who encountered unaccompanied preludes every day) as downright conventional, at least in appearance.

SONATA LATER ON

And now for Chopin's heroic side, exemplified chiefly by the regal or military polonaises, the chillingly macabre or ironic scherzos, a few of the nocturnes (composed as if expressly to counter the genre's association with the feminine)—but above all by the ballades, like the preludes a genre that Chopin invented (or reinvented at the keyboard), and that later spread far and wide. The ballade was the repository for Chopin's most serious expressions of Polish nationalism. It was universally understood in that vein by his contemporaries; and in its widespread influence it helped establish what James Parakilas has aptly called "a uniform, international nationalism"[23] as a primary constituent of European (and, incipiently, Euro-American) art music in the nineteenth century.

Up to now the romantic ballad has been in our experience a vocal genre, based on poems (like Goethe's *Erlkönig*) that emulated narrative folk songs. Taking Goethe's poem, known to us (from chapter 35) in settings by Reichardt, Schubert, and Loewe, as our archetype of the genre, we could further stipulate that a ballad typically concerns a horrific situation of some kind, and that it proceeds through a combination of straight narration and dramatic dialogue to a climactic denouement (". . . in his arms, the child lay dead!"). It was, so to speak, an end-accented genre.

The British Isles and Scandinavia were the home of the authentic folk prototypes, circulated by Herder and other collectors of the late eighteenth century, on which professional poets in other countries fashioned their literary ballads, often with the pretense that they were drawing on local oral tradition. That was the case with Goethe, and that was certainly the case with Mickiewicz, the Polish national poet and cultural hero of the Polish diaspora, who brought the ballad to Poland in his first book, *Ballady i romanse* (1822). In the introduction, Mickiewicz called the ballad "a tale based on the events of common life or on the annals of chivalry."[24] It was in order to give Poland its own chivalric poetry, testifying imaginatively to a Polish knightly past, that Mickiewicz invented Polish balladry. All over Eastern Europe poetry was being used in this way to remodel the past as a basis for present aspirations and in hopes of a better future.

Like Chopin, Mickiewicz lived in Paris after the failed rebellion of 1831. He was at the center of an émigré community to which the composer was far more peripherally attached. But Chopin was very much aware of his work and even told Schumann, on a visit to Leipzig in 1841, that his ballads (of which he had by then written two, the second dedicated to Schumann) were modeled on "certain poems of Mickiewicz."[25] This avowal, plus the fact that the early German editions called the pieces *Balladen ohne Worte* ("Ballads without words"), has led many Chopinists off on wild goose chases to find the actual poems by Mickiewicz whose contents were embodied in Chopin's music (or even secretly set to it). But Chopin probably never meant to imply such a thing. Like Mendelssohn in his *Lieder ohne Worte*, he probably intended what we would nowadays call a structural analogy (more precisely, a homology) between the sung and instrumental media, in which the very absence of words served to liberate the poetic utterance and make it at once more intense and more universal in its appeal.

That, at any rate, seems to be what George Sand sought to convey in a passage from her memoirs that purported to summarize Chopin's views on the meaning of music, thoughts she managed to extract from him despite his inclination to "talk little and pour out his heart only at his piano." Here, according to the woman who knew him best, is Chopin's esthetic credo:

> Where the instruments alone take charge of translating it, the musical drama flies on its own wings and does not claim to be translated by the listener. It expresses itself by a state of mind it induces in you by force or gently. When Beethoven unchains the storm [in the *Pastoral* Symphony], he does not strive to paint the pallid glimmer of lightning and to make us hear the crash of thunder. He renders the shiver, the feeling of wonder, the terror of nature of which man is aware and which he shares in experiencing it . . . . The beauty of musical language consists in taking hold of the heart or imagination, without being condemned to pedestrian reasoning. It maintains itself in an ideal sphere where the listener who is not musically educated still delights in the vagueness, while the musician savors this great logic that presides over the masters' magnificent issue of thought.[26]

These points, whether expressed in Chopin's words or Sand's, apply with particular force to the Ballades, which are by definition story pieces, but without any specified subject matter. Chopin in effect has announced an intention to do something similar to what Berlioz did in his *Symphonie fantastique*, but has foresworn as futile and even trivializing the use of a programmatic guide to interpretation. Rather, by the use of instrumental music, he now sought to duplicate (and even to surpass) not the content but rather the *effect* of Mickiewicz's nationalistic narrative poetry. Anticipating by half a century the favorite maxim of the French symbolist poet Stéphane Mallarmé, Chopin sought to *peindre, non la chose, l'effet qu'elle produit*: "paint not the thing but the effect it produces."[27]

The means were all ready to hand, but had never been coordinated in precisely the way that Chopin now proposed to deploy them. The means in question were those of the traditional sonata, as dramatized by Beethoven and lyricalized by Schubert. The unprecedented deployment reflected the characteristic structure and rhetoric of the poetic ballad. It was one of the most sophisticated and successful mutual adaptations of music and literature ever achieved in a century that was practically dedicated to that achievement. No wonder it was influential.

To represent narrative content by means of techniques borrowed from sonata form was an inevitable solution. By its very nature the process of thematic development—in which musical events seem to be not merely juxtaposed but causally connected, so that the past conditions the present and the present (both thematically and tonally) forecasts the future—has a compelling narrative aspect. And by its very nature the newly radicalized contrast in thematic content—in which a lyrically expansive "second subject" (in an increasingly "remote" alternate key) had lately begun to assert equal rights and claim equal time—implied an equally compelling dramatic potential. There was even the latent possibility of a traditional narrative "frame" if one deployed the traditional slow introduction and coda in tandem.

Let us turn now to Chopin's Ballade in G minor, op. 23, now known as the First, completed in 1835 (having possibly been sketched as early as 1831, in the immediate aftermath of the Polish revolt) and published in 1836. The relationship of its spectacularly end-accented overall shape to the narrative shape of, say, *Erlkönig* is obvious. From a briefly loud and "weighty" (*pesante*) opening largo the piece has quieted down to piano by m. 4 and settled into a ruminative moderato by m. 9 (Ex. 39-12a). There is no challenge to either the soft dynamic or the deliberate tempo until the fortieth measure (Ex. 39-12b), where a sudden forte, accompanied by the marking *agitato* (soon succeeded by *sempre più mosso*), begins foretelling the general trajectory the piece will follow (albeit not without incidental detours) until *il più forte possibile* ("the greatest possible loudness") is reached in m. 206, preparing the way for a final explosion of fireworks, *presto con fuoco*, two bars later, to be played at the greatest possible speed (Ex. 39-12c). The whole Ballade is in effect a single magnificently sustained, ten-minute, 264-bar dramatic crescendo that continually gathers momentum from portentous introduction to cabaletta-like coda. Nothing could be further removed from the small aphoristic or sectional forms with which we have up to now associated Chopin's name. The piece shows him to have been capable of formal planning on a colossal scale few had attempted since Beethoven, however novel or sui generis the relationship of the constituent parts.

EX. 39-12A   Frédéric Chopin, Ballade no. 1 in G minor, mm. 1–17

EX. 39-12A (*continued*)

EX. 39-12B Frédéric Chopin, Ballade no. 1 in G minor, mm. 40–44

EX. 39-12C Frédéric Chopin, Ballade no. 1 in G minor, mm. 206–212

To compare the coda to a cabaletta is to add an operatic ingredient to the Ballade's eclectic recipe alongside the elements drawn from the practice of sonata form and the rhetoric of narrative poetry. That impression is corroborated at the other end of the piece, to return to Ex. 39-12a, in the bare-octaves introduction (Largo), which, though exceeding the range of any actual singer, is unmistakably vocal in style, comprising three phrases of evident recitative, each one shorter, hence more urgent, than the last. The first phrase arpeggiates a harmony that is retrospectively identified by the following cadence as a Neapolitan sixth. The last phrase is left hanging (m. 7) on a remarkably evocative chord containing three dissonances — two appoggiaturas and one suspension — over a dominant root. This chord was so striking to nineteenth-century musicians that Frederick Niecks, author of an early biography of Chopin, called it "the emotional key-note of the whole poem."[28]

The way in which the first theme of the Moderato begins (m. 8) — with an arpeggio that resolves the keynote chord's charged dissonances one by one (E♭ to D, G to F♯ by octave displacement, B♭ to A by direct melodic succession) — is evidence of the composer's narrative skill: the bard's exordium ends on a note of suspense, leading the listener with urgent expectations into the unfolding drama. What is of greatest relevance right now, however, is the fact that the two main harmonic events of the narrator's Introduction, the Neapolitan sixth and the keynote chord, both return in the coda (cabaletta), after having gone unheard throughout the main body of the Ballade. The Neapolitan sixth is taken up at the height of the *presto con fuoco* (m. 216) and the cadence it initiates is then repeated obsessively three more times (Ex. 39-12d). The keynote chord, meanwhile (or rather its constituent notes in the form of an arpeggio), returns at m. 257 (Ex. 39-12e) in the form of a recitative phrase in octaves that keenly recalls the rhetoric of the "bard's exordium." It serves to introduce the horrifically dissonant final outburst before the end, just as a brief phrase of recitative ("in his arms . . . " — on the Neapolitan!) had preceded the catastrophic denouement in Schubert's setting of *Erlkönig*.

EX. 39-12D   Frédéric Chopin, Ballade no. 1 in G minor, mm. 216–22

EX. 39-12E   Frédéric Chopin, Ballade no. 1 in G minor, mm. 257–end

EX. 39-12E   *(continued)*

Both Schubert and Chopin used the recitative and the Neapolitan harmony in response to the narrative framing device in the poems their music served to transmit. In Schubert's case it was an actual poem, Goethe's ballad about the Elf King. In Chopin's case it was the imaginary or conceptual ballad of which his music was the embodiment. In both cases, however, the narrator speaks in his own voice exactly twice: in the first stanza (Introduction) and in the last (cabaletta). In between comes the main action, carried not by the narrator but by the "principals"—in Chopin's case the two main themes, plus a couple of nonrecurring episodes.

Very much unlike the narrator's choppy phrases of recitative, which we interpret as a conventional representation of speaking, both of the Ballade's main themes are cast in full lyrical periods, suggesting singers' voices. The first, in a manner quite unlike standard sonata procedure, comes to a full close before the first episode begins. There is no cadential elision at this point, as we normally expect to find in a sonata. But the situation remains sufficiently sonatalike so that we recognize what follows as an episode, not a theme; we not only expect a modulation, but we specifically expect one to the major. And so we are prepared to know the second theme when we hear it (Ex. 39-12f), even though it comes not in the "classical" relative major but in the Schubertian submediant.

EX. 39-12F   Frédéric Chopin, Ballade no. 1 in G minor, mm. 68–82

EX. 39-12F   (*continued*)

This second theme, unlike the first, ends with a dissolve on every appearance—another departure from what we might take to be the sonata-ish straight-and-narrow. Its first dissolution is accompanied by a restive return of the first theme over the dominant pedal, acting as a bridge to set up the climactic statement of the second theme in A major, at a tritone's remove from its first statement, thus most dramatically—even melodramatically—providing the tonal far-out point (FOP). This climax is set up by means of a typically operatic stall (Ex. 39-12g), the kind of thing that prepares the soprano's high note in Bellini and Donizetti, composers from whom Chopin learned an enormous amount, not only about bel canto lyricism, but about dramatic pacing as well.

EX. 39-12G   Frédéric Chopin, Ballade no. 1 in G minor, mm. 98–109

The episode that follows next is sometimes called the "waltz episode" owing to the character of the accompaniment. Unlike typical sonata episodes it does not modulate, but rather prepares the return of E♭ for the final statement of the second theme. This is followed by the final statement of the first theme, again in the agitated dominant-pedal mode replete with stalling tactics, but in *its* original key, thus completing a tonal palindrome:

g – E♭ – A – E♭ – g (upper case denoting major, lower case minor). The superimposition of this closed tonal progression, with its suggestion of "ternary form," over the steadily gathering momentum of the Ballade's narrative unfolding is further proof of the eclectic complexity of design that undergirds its thrillingly immediate and emotional impress.

Now this description of the Ballade's sequence of events has gone out of its way to call attention to those aspects of its unfolding that do not conform to the normal sonata-form template. Chiefly these departures have to do with the order in which things happen. The second theme is recapitulated before the first. The FOP occurs not at the climax of development but at the moment of greatest lyrical expanse. Development as such is deployed in brief setups to offset lyrical high points rather than as a modulatory agent. The coda has an entirely unconventional relationship to the introduction, as we have already observed.

Because of these apparent deviations from standard operating procedure, some have been reluctant to compare Chopin's Ballade with the sonatas of earlier composers or to locate the source of its rhetoric in sonata procedures, even if we are less likely now to assume, as did the otherwise admiring Niecks, that such deviations merely demonstrate Chopin's incapacity for handling large classical forms. And yet the shapes and gestures that give form to the Ballade — the bithematic exposition, the motivic reconfigurations of the first theme, the recapitulation (never mind in what order), the elaborate coda (never mind its contents) — all had their origins and sole precedents in symphonies and sonatas, and derived their meaning (as narrative, as drama) from the listener's recognition of that fact.

Chopin had so internalized the morphology of the sonata, one might say, that he could deploy its elements in idiosyncratic ways that actually resemble the oral techniques of a folk balladeer, who (as Goethe remarked) has his pregnant subject — his figures, their actions and emotions — so deep in his mind that he does not know how he will bring it to light. He can begin lyrically, epically, dramatically and proceed, changing the form at will, either to hurry to the end or to delay it considerably.

So Chopin changed the form of the sonata to suit his narrative purposes. Perhaps, then, it would be best to say, not that Chopin's Ballades are in a modified sonata form (which fails to consider, or even obscures, the reasons for modification), but that they represent the sonata later on, the way French or Spanish is Latin later on. Recognizable elements of an older vocabulary and syntax have been newly configured and positioned to serve new rhetorical and expressive aims; and it would make no greater sense to interpret the new configurations as decline or deterioration in the handling of form than it would to regard French (as many once surely did) as a deteriorated Latin.

The extra recurrences of the main themes, seemingly at odds with sonata procedures, are crucial to our perception of the Ballade as a ballad, which, besides being a narrative, is also a strophic song, unfolding in recurrent stanzas. By synthesizing strophic and sonata principles, Chopin brilliantly solved the problem of capturing the relationship in a ballad between the recurrent tune and the ever-evolving narrative content. Every time the first theme recurs, to pick the most obvious example, its continuation is different: the first time it gives way to the first episode, the second time to the lyrical climax, and the third time to the coda-cabaletta. Thus it is invested each time with a new narrative function, just as each repeated melodic stanza is invested in a poetic ballad with new words.

But if the Ballade is a narrative, what kind of a story is it telling? George Sand's explanation, that the instrumental medium substitutes feeling content for object content, is not quite sufficient, whether or not it carries the composer's authority. Feelings can as easily be evoked by pictures (like Beethoven's storm picture in the *Pastoral* Symphony, to cite Sand's or Chopin's own example) as by stories. Why a story — and a folk story at that?

NATIONALISM AS A MESSAGE

The Polish-American musicologist Karol Berger has argued that Chopin invented the instrumental Ballade as a vehicle to tell the story of Poland as he and his fellow émigrés conceived it — not the story of Poland's lamentable past (although that past is surely referred to) but the story of its future. "Personal and collective identities always have narrative structure," Berger writes. "We identify ourselves by means of the stories we tell about ourselves, stories about where we have come from, and where we are going."[29] The story Chopin told in the Ballade was a modified and (by means of his music) universalized version of the story Mickiewicz and other exiled Polish intellectuals were telling about Poland — that is, about themselves. It was a story of impending revolution.

In the words of the Polish-born Oxford historian Sir Lewis Namier, from his famous essay "1848: The Revolution of the Intellectuals," exiled Polish patriots felt in the aftermath of their crushed revolt of 1830–1831 that

> Poland's resurrection could only come through a war between the Partitioning Powers, or the defeat of all three (as happened in 1918); that this presupposed a general upheaval, a world war or a world revolution; that the July Monarchy [newly installed in France, where they lived] offered no base against the Powers of the Holy Alliance [namely Prussia, Russia, and Austria, Poland's occupiers]; and that a new revolution was needed to mobilize popular forces in France and give the signal to Europe. They waited for 1848.[30]

The 1848 revolutions also failed, but we have Chopin's response to them in the form of a letter to a compatriot then living in New York. War and revolution were a heavy price to pay, he wrote. They "will not happen without horrors, but at the end of it all there is Poland, magnificent, great; in a word, Poland."[31] The G-minor Ballade, composed some twelve to fifteen years earlier, was a prophecy. Berger relates its narrative to that of the biblical exodus, with its "structure of past enslavement, present exile and future rebirth preserved but modulated to stress the dimension of the future."[32] That emphasis is what conditioned the Ballade's thrilling trajectory from a subdued beginning to a blaze of fiery, even tragic glory.

This interpretation carries conviction on the basis of evidence both internal and external. Beyond the general gathering of momentum over the course of the whole movement, Berger specifically emphasizes the contrast between the drooping contour of the main theme (particularly if its beginning is heard as a continuation of the "emotional key-note" in mm. 6–7) and the stunning upward surges, practically covering the length of the keyboard, that set off the narrator's valedictory recitatives in the Ballade's final measures, one of which actually replays, fortissimo, the keynote phrase. In the context of a folk or national genre like the ballad/Ballade (even one with spurious literary origins), these surges and keynotes carry the force of a political harangue.

And that is where the external evidence fits in. It is remarkable that Chopin's Ballade was almost universally interpreted as the composer's most seriously nationalistic endeavor despite the fact that, unlike the polonaises and mazurkas, its musical style is not at all marked as specifically Polish. Indeed, the only national reference made in the course of the foregoing stylistic and formal analysis was to the Italian opera, then regarded, along with German symphonism, as an international or universal genre. And there are Germanic resonances in the piece as well, beginning with its very opening, where the octave-unison writing and the Neapolitan harmony have recalled to many listeners the opening bars of Beethoven's Piano Sonata no. 23 in F minor, op. 57 (the "Appassionata").

Chopin, in other words, pulled off the extraordinary feat of telling a national story using only universal ingredients. That, in its way, is the Ballade's most compelling association with the political and cultural discourses that surrounded and conditioned the revolution of 1848, which (as Namier insisted) "was universally expected" by the intellectual classes all over Europe, and at the same time "was super-national as none before or after."[33] Glossing this characterization, Berger defines that universal expectation as the hope that "the future revolution should complete the unfinished business of 1789 and universally replace the principle of dynastic property with that of national sovereignty."[34] Poland, a murdered country whose national sovereignty had been forcibly eradicated to add to the property of three European dynasties, was the great emblem of 1848, and Chopin, in his Ballade, displayed that emblem to all of Europe in a language all could understand, and respond to, as theirs.

So the national question, while originally posed in terms of folklore (or *Volkstümlichkeit*, "folklikeness"), nevertheless quickly transcended folklore. The reception of Chopin's Ballade, like that of many other national monuments in tones, proved that nationalism in music is not defined by style alone, or even necessarily, but by a much more complex interaction between creative intentions and critical perceptions.

Given the import of his work, and the aspirations it embodied, the final chapter of Chopin's life was a tragicomical anticlimax. His affair with George Sand ended in 1847 as a result of envious intrigues by her children, leaving him depressed and disinclined to work. The immediate effect of the outbreak of the long-awaited 1848 revolution, when it hit Paris, was the interruption of Chopin's income from teaching, forcing him to take up residence in England where he again became the darling of fashionable society. He stayed there for eight months, returning to Paris in November, having earned (or been given) enough money to maintain a residence. His longstanding tuberculosis claimed him less than a year later. He died surrounded by fellow Poles including his sister, who had come to his bedside from Warsaw; but he was buried in Paris like a grand seigneur after a funeral attended by three thousand mourners, at which Mozart's Requiem was performed.

AMERICA JOINS IN

A composer whose career began very much like Chopin's, but later diverged owing to his failure to attain a comparable level of social prestige, was Louis Moreau Gottschalk (1829–69), a native of New Orleans who was the first American-born composer to make his mark within the European tradition of fine-art music. His father, London-born and Leipzig-educated, was a prosperous merchant from a highly assimilated (possibly converted) German-Jewish family like Mendelssohn's; his mother, a skilled amateur pianist and operatic singer, was the daughter of a celebrated French Creole baker who had fled to Louisiana as a refugee from the Haitian slave revolts of the 1790s. His socially ambitious parents identified wholeheartedly with European high culture and brought up their children in an atmosphere effectively shielded from the local popular culture by a well-developed salon and opera-house network. As soon as their gifted son had received his basic training from the local cathedral organist, he was packed off to Paris, aged thirteen, for finishing.

Gottschalk was an extraordinarily precocious talent. Before he turned sixteen he gave a recital at which he played Chopin's E-minor Concerto before an audience that included Chopin himself, who paid enthusiastic respects backstage and (according to Gottschalk) declared him the future "king of pianists."[35] Yet like the young Chopin before him, Gottschalk found he could not break through to real recognition from the European public except as an exotic — which is what turned him, very much against the current of his upbringing, into an American (or, more precisely, a Louisiana Creole) nationalist.

In quick succession he published three sets of bravura variations — *Bamboula, danse des nègres*, op. 2; *La savane, ballade créole*, op. 3; *Le bananier* ("The banana tree"), *chanson nègre*, op. 4 — that have been aptly dubbed a "Louisiana trilogy" by Gilbert Chase,[36] a leading musical Americanist. They established for him a reputation, at age nineteen, of being (in the words of an enraptured Paris reviewer) a rude prodigy who composed "wild, languishing, indescribable" things that bore "no resemblance to any other European music."[37]

Although French was his first language, Gottschalk was not really a Creole, since he descended only on his mother's side from French settlers. Nor, despite his own testimony (accepted by his early biographers), is there any reason to assume that his "Louisiana trilogy" was

FIG. 39-7 Louis Moreau Gottschalk, wood engraving after a drawing by Henry Louis Stephens, published in *Vanity Fair*, 11 October 1862.

based on exotic memories from his childhood. *La savane* ("The savannah"), for example, which bears the Chopinesque designation *ballade*, was supposedly inspired by a legend that the live oaks in the swamps surrounding New Orleans had grown up out of the skeletons of runaway slaves. According to his program note, the boy Gottschalk heard this legend from his governess, a mulatto slave girl named Sally, who punctuated her narrative with snatches of the mournful slave song on which the bravura variations are based. French audiences were not likely to notice that this so-called slave song was a minor-mode variant of "Skip to My Lou, My Darling," an old English dance tune that is still an American nursery staple.

But even if Gottschalk's "Creole" music was no more authentic than this, the piano style in which he couched it did give his music a convincingly personal imprint (hence authentic in another, perhaps more important sense), and one that proved unexpectedly fertile in America. The startlingly original *Bamboula*, apparently composed in 1844–45 when Gottschalk, aged just fifteen, was recovering from an attack of typhoid fever, was issued by the Paris publisher Escudier in 1849. The title is supposedly the name, in New Orleans black patois, of an African-style drum made of bamboo, and the piece is purportedly an evocation of Saturday night social dancing at the Place Congo (Congo Square), a hall frequented by *les gens de couleur*, New Orleans' free mulatto or mixed-blood population, who were largely of Caribbean descent.

None of this can be confirmed. The tunes are not recognizably West Indian, nor was the very sheltered Gottschalk likely to have been taken as a lad to witness such goings-on at first hand. But in evoking the bamboula drum, whether real or imaginary, Gottschalk devised an angular, dryly percussive style of piano playing (Ex. 39-13), full of hocketing exchanges between the hands and reinforced in the notation by many polyglot reminders to the player to keep it up ("*très rhythmé*," "*sostenuto il canto, staccato l'accompagnement*," "*pesante il basso*," etc.). The touch, and consequently the texture, is exceptionally differentiated, the two hands (and sometimes two lines within a single hand) being radically contrasted. There is even a spot where the right hand is required to play legato and rubato while the left hand carries the warning "*la basse toujours rhythmée*," and (even more unusually) there are whole sections in which the damper pedal is held in abeyance.

This special piano touch, "wild and indescribable" to listeners used to Chopin and Liszt, later became the foundation of ragtime, especially when Gottschalk added syncopated Latin American rhythms to the mix (as in his "Souvenir de Porto Rico, Marche des Gibaros") during a strange Caribbean interlude that lasted from 1857 to 1862 (Ex. 39-14). The hocketing hands-exchange technique reached its peak in *The Banjo* (1854), composed while Gottschalk was living in Spain and briefly enjoying court patronage. At the end (Ex. 39-15a) there is a lengthy bravura coda or cadenza based on the melody of his compatriot Stephen Foster's then brand-new *Camptown Races* (1850), in which the accompaniment was already fashioned to resemble banjo-picking (Ex. 39-15b).

While Foster (1826–64) wrote music for consumption in homely domestic venues or minstrel shows, Gottschalk's bravura exercises in Americana, it is important to

EX. 39-13   Louis Moreau Gottschalk, *Bamboula*, mm. 1–24

remember, were composed for European audiences. He returned to America early in 1853 for what he expected to be a whirlwind tour, but his father's death later that year turned him willy-nilly into the family breadwinner. From then on he made his career entirely on the terms of the burgeoning American music trade, not on those of the European salon culture to which he had expected to return. He would not be Chopin's successor as society lap dog after all. His destiny lay in the uniquely American business of popularizing high culture.

He stepped up the frequency of his concert tours to unprecedented levels, causing him chronic exhaustion and periods of burnout, and considerably shortening his life in consequence. Thanks to the boom in American railway construction that coincided exactly with his peak concertizing period, Gottschalk covered more miles in less time than any other virtuoso of the day, playing not only big cities but small mill and mining towns from coast to coast and bringing European fine-art music to audiences of a kind that would never have heard it in Europe. Toward the end of his concert career he calculated that between 1853 and 1865 he had given 1,100 recitals and logged more than 95,000 miles by rail.

And he did all this not in twelve years, actually, but in only seven, since (as already mentioned) he spent the years 1857 to 1862, following a nervous breakdown, leading a vagabond existence in the Caribbean, playing little but composing much. His works from

FIG. 39-8   Stephen Foster, portrait by Thomas Hicks.

this period included a one-act opera (*Escenas campestres* [Rural Scenes]), a symphony (*La nuit des tropiques* [The Tropical Night]), and a new crop of "Latin" piano works like the one in Ex. 39-14, which he could later purvey to American audiences as the kind of exotic fare with which he had formerly regaled Paris.

But he also composed quantities of precisely the kind of sentimental commercial music his European experience had taught him to despise — sentimental parlor-piano compositions with titles like *The Last Hope* (1854), *The Maiden's Blush* (1863), *The Dying Poet* (1864), and *Morte!* (1868). It practically goes without saying that these compositions, intended for home consumption, were not in the least nationalistic. Quite the contrary: just as to aristocratic European audiences Gottschalk had represented untamed America, so to the "vulgar" American public, both those who came to hear him play and those who purchased the sheet music afterward to play at home, he represented European "class."

EX. 39-14   Louis Moreau Gottschalk, *Souvenir de Porto Rico, Marche des Gibaros*

EX. 39-14 *(continued)*

A vivid case in point is the single piece of Americana he composed in America: a rousing pastiche of patriotic songs called *Union*, with which he would end his concerts during the Civil War. After a stormy martial introduction and an ornate arrangement of "The Star-Spangled Banner," during which audiences presumably stood at attention, there came a contrapuntal juxtaposition of "Yankee Doodle" and "Hail Columbia," a far more learned, even academic sort of exercise than he would have dreamed of playing before European audiences who heard conservatory-trained musicians every day.

EX. 39-15A   Louis Moreau Gottschalk, the Foster-quoting section of *The Banjo*

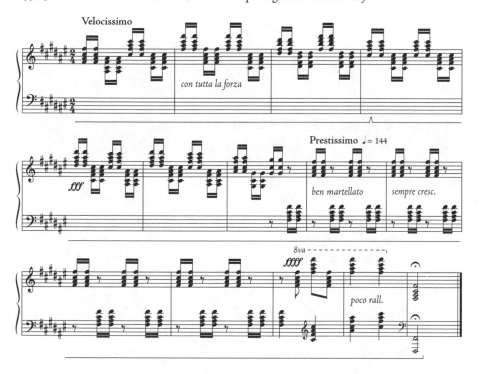

EX. 39-15B   The corresponding snatch of Foster's "Camptown Races"

The first statement of "Hail Columbia" is European in another way as well: as an exercise in the most recondite, most sophisticated sort of slithery "continental" harmonization, indebted above all to Chopin (Ex. 39-16a). If *Bamboula* and *Souvenir de Porto Rico* gave a foretaste of ragtime, this passage is a prophecy of the vogue for sentimental barbershop quartet singing that flourished as a sort of American *Männerchor* movement for forty years or so beginning in the 1890s (see Ex. 39-16b).

Gottschalk was forced to leave the United States in 1865 to avoid prosecution on a charge (later declared unfounded) of statutory rape. He spent the last four years of his life, as his biographer and performing champion Jeanne Behrend put it, "skirting much of the outer rim of South America — six months in Peru, one year in Chile, two years in Argentina and Uruguay, seven and a half months in Brazil."[38] During this final period Gottschalk became a sort of P. T. Barnum of music, or perhaps an American Berlioz, taking popularization to new heights in monster concerts that he organized wherever he went at the expense of the Chickering piano manufacturing firm of Boston, the inventor of the cast-iron frame (hence the perfecter of the modern grand piano), which had made Gottschalk an official trade representative. In South America this musical son of New Orleans now represented Yankee enterprise.

The pinnacle was reached in Rio de Janeiro on 24 November 1869 with the cooperation of the Brazilian Emperor Pedro II, who placed the massed bands of the National Guard, the Imperial Army and Navy, and three municipal orchestras at Gottschalk's disposal. "Just think of 800 performers and 80 drums to lead,"[39] he exulted, exaggerating only slightly, in a letter to a friend. The concert went "crescendo," starting with Gottschalk alone on stage playing a Lisztian potpourri on themes from Charles Gounod's popular operatic version of Goethe's *Faust*, followed by a new *Tarantella* for piano and orchestra. Then the curtain went up on the great mass of performers, 650 in all. After the Brazilian national anthem played (according to the *Anglo Brazilian Times*) by "forty young ladies on twenty-five pianos" (Chickerings, of course), came the Grand March from Meyerbeer's *Le prophète*, a movement from Gottschalk's own "Tropical Night" Symphony, and as grand finale a new work of Gottschalk's, composed for the occasion and dedicated to the Emperor: *Marcha solemne brasileira*, replete with backstage cannon fire. A repetition of the entire program was scheduled for the day after next, with a solo performance by Gottschalk on the evening in between.

EX. 39-16A   Louis Moreau Gottschalk, *Union*, mm. 11–24

No novelist would dare invent what happened next for fear of losing credibility. Gottschalk collapsed during that intervening performance right in the midst of *Morte!* (She's Dead), one of his popular potboilers, and had to be carried from the stage back to his hotel room. The second *concerto monstro* had to be postponed, then canceled. Gottschalk never played again. He died on 18 December from the consequences of a ruptured abdominal abscess.

ART AND DEMOCRACY

As an emissary from America to Europe, then from Europe to America, and finally between Americas; as a mediator between low culture and high society, and then

EX. 39-16B   Chorus from "Home on the Range," arranged for barbershop quartet by Ozzie Westley, mm. 17–end

between high culture and "low" society; as a shuttler between culture and commerce; and as a perpetual peripatetic whose selfhood was always defined by some sort of otherness, Gottschalk led an emblematically liminal existence — an existence on the borders — that defined a particularly "American" moment in the history of European music. It was a moment of confrontation that presaged the hardening of categories and the closing of borders.

The United States, the exemplary creation of Enlightened universalist politics, posed a perpetual threat to the European status quo. What it threatened was the security of traditional hierarchy. The American experience, which began with a revolution, was viewed in Europe as an experiment in social leveling, hardly less ominous than the revolutionary movements that were gathering force seemingly everywhere on the European continent between 1830 and 1848. Backlash against Americanism — defined in terms of commercialism, mechanical technology, and indifference if not sheer hostility to quality or excellence in matters of culture and conduct — was already well advanced by the time the young Gottschalk sailed for Europe in 1842. Pierre Zimmermann, the head of the piano department at the Paris Consevatoire, would not even allow an American boy to audition (even one who spoke perfect French and had been trained at home by Frenchmen), because "America produces steam engines, not musicians."[40] Instead Gottschalk studied in Paris with the German-born Charles Hallé, Chopin's friend.

The democratic, nonhierarchical spirit of nineteenth-century America, however partial or limited (in view of the simultaneous existence, until 1865, of Negro slavery, to pick only the most obvious contradiction), has been looked upon by some American cultural historians as having fostered a kind of populist golden age of art. Gottschalk's successful if overly strenuous career as an American public entertainer between 1853 and 1865, and his later activity as a grandiose musical impresario in Latin America, might seem to support the historian Lawrence Levine's contention that "in the nineteenth century, especially in the first half, Americans, in addition to whatever specific cultures they were part of, shared a public culture less hierarchically organized, less fragmented into relatively rigid adjectival boxes [i.e., "high" vs. "low"] than their descendants [i.e., we] were to experience a century later,"[41] and that the loss of this sense of a shared heterogeneous popular culture, including the portion later defined and fenced off as "high," was a grievous one for the subsequent development of art in America, and even throughout the world.

There is truth in this view, and we will explore it. It is most immediately demonstrated in the opposition Gottschalk faced from fastidious critics in America such as John Sullivan Dwight (1813–93), inevitably a Bostonian, who was an early advocate of what Levine calls "fragmentation,"[42] and who deplored Gottschalk's popularizing and Americanizing efforts. But it is a one-sided view. Gottschalk, and other American artists, had their social troubles in America, too, owing not to their being Americans, but to their being artists. The place of charismatic individuals in a society that puts a social and political premium on ordinariness or conformity can be precarious, as Gottschalk's eventual fate bore out.

The morals charge and the attendant scandal that led to his exile from America reflected the social stigma and suspicion that attached to artists in American society. Indeed, the stigma and suspicion have lasted into our own time, as witness the perpetual difficulties encountered in establishing and administering government art patronage in America. Recall, for example, the persistent efforts in the 1980s and 1990s to dismantle the federal government's National Endowment for the Arts, and the moral vilification some American artists have personally suffered in consequence of those efforts at the hands of politicians who saw an electoral advantage in persecuting them.

Here European attitudes can be shown to differ considerably, in the direction of tolerance. Both Liszt and Chopin, as we already know, lived openly with women to whom they were not married (and who were married, or had been married, to others), and suffered little or no social stigma in consequence. In the case of Liszt, his reputation as a womanizer was in fact a distinct career advantage. Chopin and George Sand were once notoriously refused accommodations in Majorca, it is true. The reason, however, was not their depraved liaison, but rather Chopin's manifestly poor health.

STEREOTYPING THE OTHER: "ORIENTALISM"

So far in this chapter we have observed the tensions between the universal and the particular, and between the nationalistic and the exotic, from the perspective of expatriated composers highly conscious of themselves as outsiders, presenting a sense of self that is to a large extent constructed out of a sense of difference. It is unlikely that Chopin would have written so many mazurkas, or Gottschalk his "Louisiana trilogy," had they stayed at home all their lives. There are, of course, other perspectives. There is the domestic or patriotic national consciousness that we have observed by now in many romantic artists, in which the assertion of national identity serves a different social purpose, emphasizing community rather than peculiarity, sameness rather than difference, social cohesion rather than social division.

And there is yet another perspective, in which members of one community represent an alien or exotic community for their own purposes and their own consumption. This kind of exoticism could be looked upon as a sort of inverse nationalism, since very often the purpose of representing (and, almost invariably, of stereotyping) the other is the bolstering of one's own sense of community by contrast. It is an act not of ecumenism or world fellowship in the spirit of Herder, but one of invidious distinction, of "marking off," ultimately of exclusion.

The most widespread and time-honored guise that this kind of exoticism has worn in the European musical tradition is that of "orientalism," the musical representation of non-European (generally Asian) peoples. We have encountered it as far back as Mozart, in his singspiel *Die Entführung aus dem Serail* ("Abduction from the Seraglio") of 1782, and encountered it again in Beethoven (*Die Ruinen von Athen*), in Rossini (*L'Italiana in Algeri*), and in Weber (*Turandot*; also *Abu Hassan*, an 1811 singspiel based on the *Arabian Nights*). Even by Mozart's time it had a long history. "Turkish" operas — operas making fun of Turks or other Muslims — were a Vienna specialty (in still-conscious reaction to the Ottoman siege of 1683). Lully's incidental music to Molière's play *Le bourgeois gentilhomme* had lampooned the Turks (Europe's most formidable antagonists since the time of the Crusades) even earlier, in 1670; and there are isolated examples going back to the sixteenth century.

European musical representation of the Orient enjoyed an enormous renewed vogue during the nineteenth century, thanks in particular to a historical and economic turnabout whereby the Europeans, rather than the Asians, became the expansionist aggressors. One can almost exactly coordinate manifestations of musical (as well as artistic, literary, and scholarly) orientalism with the movements of colonial and imperialist armies, beginning with Napoleon's Egyptian campaigns of 1798–99 — a scholarly bonanza above all owing to the discovery of the Rosetta stone, and the subsequent publication of the twenty-four-volume *Description of Egypt* by Edme François Jomard, a geographer and antiquarian who had traveled with Napoleon's army between 1809 and 1813.

Together with the sumptuously illustrated album *Voyage in Lower and Upper Egypt* by Baron Dominique Denon, another member of Napoleon's entourage who later became the chief curator of the Louvre, Jomard's work touched off a French craze for all things "Near Eastern." The Vicomte de Chateaubriand published a best-selling travel book, the semi-imaginary *Itinerary from Paris to Jerusalem*, in 1811; Victor Hugo's wholly imaginary *Les Orientales*, a book of exotic poems, followed in 1829. Accordingly, the first place to look for signs of a new romantic wave in musical orientalia is France.

The wave reached an early crest in the work of Félicien David (1810–76), a specialist in the Eastern mode, who made a pilgrimage to Egypt in 1833–35 by way of the Turkish cities of Constantinople (Istanbul) and Smyrna (Izmir). He noted down Arab and Turkish tunes wherever he went, and after first publishing a large series of piano pieces based on them (*Mélodies orientales*, twenty-two pieces in seven books, 1836), summed up his impressions of the East in a monumental "Ode-Symphony" (a symphony with voices in the manner of Beethoven's Ninth) called *Le Désert*, which had its deliriously successful premiere in December 1844 and remained a concert staple for a couple of decades thereafter, although like its author it is virtually forgotten today.

The direct influence of Beethoven's Ninth is apparent from the very outset, which evokes the infinite desert expanse (as Beethoven had evoked the cosmos) with a seemingly endless pedal tone on C against which a welter of motives for future development (some seemingly in C, others in F, still others in A♭) alternate with "melodramas" for a speaking narrator, a device borrowed from *Lélio, or Returning to Life* (*Lélio, ou le retour à la vie*), the now-forgotten sequel to the *Symphonie fantastique* by Berlioz, who was quick to proclaim his imitator's work a masterpiece.

Thereafter the work proceeds in three long movements, each comprising several unrelated episodes or scenes (although there is a sort of recapitulation of the opening at the very end), the whole representing a caravan slowly crossing the desert, encountering a sandstorm, passing mosques, offering a prayer to Allah, and so forth. The voices are all male, but the second movement contains

FIG. 39-9   Title page of first edition of Felicien David's *Le Désert* (Paris, 1845).

a "Danse des almées" (Dance of the "Almahs," Egyptian belly dancers, regarded by Europeans as prostitutes) that supplies what would prove to be the most durable, indeed indispensable, ingredient in European musical orientalism (Ex. 39-17a). The most famous episode in *Le Désert* was the call of the muezzin, the crier who, standing in the balcony of a minaret or mosque turret, at stated hours five times daily, intones the call summoning the faithful to prayer (Ex. 39-17b).

Both the dance and the muezzin's cry were based on authentic source material, personally observed by the composer on location; indeed, in the final melisma of the muezzin's call, he seems to have tried to give an impression of microtones. In any case, David received the compliment of recognition from an Arab delegation in native dress, attending the premiere as the guests of the French government, much to the audience's delight.

The vogue for *Le Désert* came quickly to an end, however; by 1857, Berlioz, who as press critic had acclaimed it, was calling it in private correspondence "a curious specimen of silly music."[43] The reason for its fall from favor may have had to do, at least in part, with its excessive "verisimilitude," with its being, paradoxically enough, too faithful (and uncritical) a portrait of the East, and too little a story. The main

EX. 39-17A   Félicien David, *Le Désert, Danse des almées*

EX. 39-17B   Félicien David, *Le Désert*, Muezzin's call

thrust of French musical orientalism quickly turned toward opera rather than song or symphony, where a certain repertoire of archetypal tales emerged to lend moral, social, and political significance to the exercise.

The list of orientalist operas that ensued would include works by almost every French composer of any reputation at all from the middle to the end of the century. By David himself there was *Lalla-Roukh* (1862), after a story about the love life of an Indian princess by the Irish poet Thomas Moore. By Meyerbeer there was *L'Africaine*

(1865), which (its title notwithstanding) also concerns the love of an Indian princess, in this case for Vasco da Gama, the Portuguese explorer. By Léo Delibes (1836–91) there was *Lakmé* (1883), yet another tale about the love of an Indian princess (and priest's daughter), this time for an English officer. By Jules Massenet (1842–1912) there was *Le roi de Lahore* ("The King of Lahore," 1877), in which the title character dies, spends an act in Hindu heaven, and returns to life in the guise of a beggar to claim a virgin priestess for his bride.

By Georges Bizet (1838–75) there were *Les pêcheurs de perles* ("The pearl fishers," 1863), a love triangle—yes, she is a virgin priestess—set in Ceylon (Sri Lanka), and *Djamileh* (1872), about a slave girl who wins the heart of an Egyptian caliph. By Ambroise Thomas (1811–96) there was *Le Caïd* ("The Khayyid," 1849), about the amorous misadventures of a North African chieftain. Finally, by Camille Saint-Saëns (1835–1921) there was *Samson et Dalila* (1877), on the famous biblical story, which of all these operas retains the securest place in repertory today.

Whether comic or tragic, all of these operas are love stories given an unusually frank and sensual treatment that, set in the "occident," would have been considered offensive within the mores of the time. The idea of the Orient as sexual playground gave license for the enjoyment of libidinous fantasies, their immorality diminished by the non-Christian (hence morally irredeemable) setting. The exotic sexpot or sex toy was only one of the stereotypes for which the orientalist manner made allowance: others included acts of despotic violence, depraved luxury, picturesque or orgiastic rites and sacrifices, and so on. Under cover of moral censure an otherwise inadmissible voyeurism could be indulged.

What is more, a repertory of recognizably "oriental" musical devices could be deployed semiotically, as signs or tropes to conjure up the qualities associated with orientalist plots and characters: thus a certain kind of oriental music could signify or conjure up sex(iness), another violence, a third barbarous ritual, even without an explicitly oriental setting. For this technique to work, verisimilitude had to be sacrificed to stereotype, the latter often lacking any authentic counterpart in "oriental" reality.

But that is precisely the point. "Orientalism," as the Arab-American literary critic Edward Said (a leading theorist of the process) has pointed out, "overrode the Orient."[44] Indeed, the very expression "the Orient" is already an example of such overriding, since the East is "the East" only to "the West." The very act of naming it is already constitutive: the name is what brings the thing into being. And that thing is a thing of metaphor, of imaginary geography and historical fiction: a reduced and "totalized" (omnisciently known) other against which we construct our no less reduced and totalized sense of ourselves.

There is no way of fully disengaging this constructed East from "the real one," least of all in artistic representations (which are always conventional). Thus an attempt, like David's *Le Désert*, merely to transcribe the reality of the thing, will quickly pall—will seem artless or naive—next to the really sophisticated fruits of orientalism.

The famous *Bacchanale*, the ballet sequence from act III of *Samson et Dalila*, can serve as an example (Ex. 39-18). The Philistines, an ancient people who have left no musical traces to posterity, are seen carousing before the idol of their god, Dagon, right before Samson brings the temple down to end the opera. Without any authentic source to guide him, thus untempted by the possibility of "real verisimilitude," Saint-Saëns opts for a fancifully exotic mode containing not one (as do some Arabian modes) but two "oriental" augmented seconds (B – A♭, F♯ – E♭), intervals that in various contexts can evoke Arabs or Jews or Gypsies *ad libitum*, or symbolize their attributes (here, orgiastic excess). At the same time the drumbeat accompaniment below is dividing the eighth-notes in every pair of $\frac{2}{4}$ measures into groups following the asymmetrical pattern 3 + 3 + 2, a rhythmic cycle found in many kinds of non-European music including Arabian, but also black Caribbean ("Afro-Cuban") or Latin American.

EX. 39-18   Camille Saint-Saëns, *Samson et Dalila*, Act III, *Bacchanale*

The net result is an imaginary or all-purpose orientalist music that nevertheless communicates a very specific image to properly attuned European listeners. (What it would communicate to Palestinian Arabs, the modern-day descendants of the Philistines, is anybody's guess.) In an orientalist sense it is realer than anything real could be; and if that seems a paradox, an observation by the Russian critic Hermann Laroche may help clarify it. Pondering the "biblical orientalism" in several Russian operas based on Old Testament or Apocryphal subjects, he asked and answered a rhetorical question:

> In what does Alexander Serov's masterly characterization of the extinct Assyrians in his opera *Judith* [1863] consist, or Anton Rubinstein's of the ancient Semites

in his "sacred opera" *The Tower of Babel* [1870]? Obviously in one thing only: the composers have successfully reproduced *our* subjective idea of the Assyrians and the Semites.[45]

Which is to say, they successfully catered, by the use of stereotypes, to contemporary prejudice, as memorably encapsulated in Chateaubriand's *Itinerary* when he wrote of the Turks that they spend their time "ravaging the world or else sleeping on carpets, amidst women and perfumes."[46] Orientalist tropes (figures, turns of phrase) would henceforth pervade the representation of masculine barbarity and feminine voluptuousness alike, and thereby broaden their significance through a process known as metonymy, the representation of a thing by one of its attributes, or vice versa. An orientalist trope could now connote or specify barbarity or voluptuousness in any context.

SEX À LA RUSSE

This process can be traced very vividly in the music of Russian composers, who were if anything even more obsessed with the development of orientalist tropes than were the French. The reason for their obsession was twofold. In the first place, Russia was engaged throughout the nineteenth century in imperialistic expansion into Islamic territories, first in the Caucasus (where the indigenous populations were in fact Christian as well as Muslim), later in what the Russians called "Central Asia," the vast plain or steppe south of Siberia and north of Iran, Afghanistan, and China.

The Caucasian campaigns reached their peak in the immediate post-Napoleonic period and lasted into the 1830s. The Central Asian campaigns were waged from the 1860s to the early 1880s, by which time the entire territory of what would later become the Union of Soviet Socialist Republics (USSR), the world's last surviving multinational empire, was controlled by Russia. In this later phase of its expansion into Islamic Asia, Russia was competing with Great Britain in what Rudyard Kipling, the great poet of British imperialism, called the Great Game[47] a protracted war of conquest against a Muslim Holy League led by the khan of Bokhara (now Uzbekistan).

Unlike the British Empire, or any of the other modern Western European empires (French, Spanish, Portuguese), which were formed in the process of colonization (first of the New World, later of Africa and India), the Russian empire, like the Ottoman (Turkish) and the nearly defunct Hapsburg (Austrian) empires, or like the empires of the ancient world, was a contiguous empire, formed by a continual process of aggrandizement into bordering territories. It occupied a single enormous landmass, and its various peoples intermingled (and intermarried) to a much greater degree than in the Western European empires.

This contiguity and (so to speak) intimacy gave impetus to the other reason why Russian composers were such avid orientalists. The orientalist tropes with which they filled their music distinguished them from the composers of Western Europe, and gave them a means of competing with the older, more established traditions of European art music. To accentuate the "oriental" aspect was for Russian composers a way of asserting their individual identity and their claim to respect and attention as independent musical creators at a time when Russia was just joining the European fine art tradition.

Thus when the arts publicist Vladimir Stasov (1824–1906), a wonderfully energetic and effective propagandist for what he called the "New Russian School" of nationalist composers, looked back in 1882 at "Twenty-Five Years of Russian Art" (the title of one of his most famous essays), he listed "the oriental element"[48] as one of the four major characteristics that justified its assertion of equal rights. (The others were its skepticism of European tradition, which made it independent; its striving for a unique national character, which made it authentic; and its "extreme inclination toward program music," which made it progressive.)

But of course this gave orientalist tropes a far more ambiguous place within the Russian stylistic spectrum than within the French. For French composers, orientalism was exclusively a means of marking the other. For Russian composers, depending which way they were facing, orientalism could also be a means of marking the self. Orientalism was thus attended by the same tensions and ironies as nationalism. Where nationalism could mean authenticity at home and exoticism abroad, orientalism could mean exoticism at home and authenticity abroad. For Russian composers, an orientalist trope could be a sort of self-portrait. That greatly multiplied the range of its possible meanings, of course, and its possible ambiguities. It also made the formation and deployment of orientalist tropes a much more significant and artfully sophisticated phenomenon among Russian composers than among any other European national group.

To witness that formation and deployment we can compare three different settings, made over a period of more than sixty years, of a single poem, an untitled lyric by Alexander Pushkin (1799–1837) dating from 1828. In literal translation, it goes like this:

> Sing not in my presence, O beauty,
> Thy songs of sad Georgia;
> They remind me
> Of another life, a distant shore.
>
> Alas! they remind me,
> Thy cruel melodies,
> Of steppes, of night — and 'neath the moon
> The features of a poor far-off maid.
>
> This lovely, fateful vision
> I can forget on seeing thee;
> But you sing — and before me
> I envision it anew.
>
> Sing not, etc.

The first setting (Ex. 39-19a) is by Glinka, the composer of *A Life for the Tsar* (see chapter 36), but composed five years before that epoch-making opera made him a nationalist. Subtitled "Georgian Song," it incorporates only the first two stanzas of the poem. According to the composer's memoirs, the song's strophic melody, which

EX. 39-19A *Ne poy, krasavitsa* (Pushkin), Glinka's setting, mm. 1–12

EX. 39-19B *Ne poy, krasavitsa* (Pushkin), Miliy Alexeyevich Balakirev's setting, mm. 1–8

EX. 39-19B (*continued*)

he learned from the poet and playwright Alexander Griboyedov (1795–1829), was an authentic Georgian tune, the very one to which Pushkin reputedly composed the poem. From the music alone there is no way of guessing that. Nothing about the song sounds the least bit exotic. The diatonic melody seems perfectly normal to Western ears, Glinka's harmonization unremarkable, the text setting straightforwardly syllabic. Already we have a warning that musical orientalism is a matter not of authenticity but of conventions — conventions that had not yet been established by 1831.

The next setting (Ex. 39-19b) is by Miliy Alexeyevich Balakirev (1837–1910), the founder of what Stasov called the "New Russian School" of avowedly nationalistic composers. (Some reference sources give Balakirev's birth year as 1836, because on the

EX. 39-19C *Ne poy, krasavitsa* (Pushkin), Sergei Rachmaninoff's setting, mm. 1–12

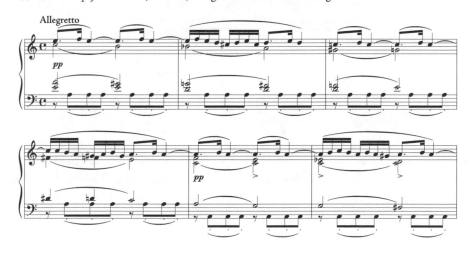

EX. 39-19C (*continued*)

EX. 39-19D *Ne poy, krasavitsa* (Pushkin), Sergei Rachmaninoff's setting, mm. 5–8

day he was born, Russian calendars read 21 December 1836. Russia was then using the Julian or old style calendar, and would until 1918; in Western Europe and America, where the Gregorian or new style calendar was already in use, the date read 2 January 1837. In this book, with its international purview, all dates are given according to the new style.) The New Russian School consisted of a group of self-taught composers who had gathered around the charismatic Balakirev like a sort of real-life Davidsbund, opposing academic authority on the one hand and philistinism on the other. With the aid of Stasov's propaganda, and abetted by the journalistic activity of César Cui (a member of the group), they gradually achieved recognition under a whimsical nickname Stasov had invented for them: *moguchaya kuchka*, which means a "mighty little bunch." The five outstanding members of the circle — Balakirev himself, Cui (1835–1918), Alexander Borodin (1833–87), Modest Musorgsky (1839–81), and Nikolai Rimsky-Korsakov (1844–1908) — are often called the "Mighty Five" in English.

All of them made conspicuous contributions to the orientalist flood tide: Balakirev in an orchestral work called *Tamara* (1882), based on a poem by Mikhail Lermontov; Cui in an opera, *A Prisoner in the Caucasus* (1857; revised 1882), based on a poem by Pushkin; Borodin in an opera, *Prince Igor* (posthumously produced in 1890), and a "musical picture" for orchestra called *In Central Asia* (1880); Musorgsky in an unfinished opera based on the novel *Salammbô* by Gustave Flaubert; and Rimsky-Korsakov in many works including two symphonic suites: *Antar* (1868) and the very popular *Sheherazade* (1888), based on the *Arabian Nights*.

Balakirev's setting of Pushkin's verses in Ex. 39-19b, titled "Georgian Song," was made in 1865, a generation later than Glinka's, and is typical of the orientalism practiced by the Mighty Five. It is as exotic as could be. The melody is full of close little ornaments and melismas like the ones in Félicien David's muezzin's call (see Ex. 39-17b), but also full of telltale augmented seconds like the ones in Saint-Saëns's *Bacchanale* (Ex. 39-8) — even though the singer (that is, the speaker of Pushkin's lines) is not supposed to be an oriental himself but presumably a Russian. Most conspicuously "oriental" of all is the imitation in the accompaniment of Islamic drumming patterns with two pitched drums — the tar (a big frame drum) and the tabla (a higher cylindrical drum played with the individual fingers and capable of producing rapid tattoos).

All of these stylistic effects have plenty of authentic prototypes — but only in Arabian, Turkish, and Persian music, or in the music of those Caucasian regions (Armenia and Azerbaijan) that absorbed influences from traditional Islamic practices. Georgian folk music uses none of them, and sounds nothing at all like Balakirev's "Georgian Song". Balakirev, who lived for long periods in the Caucasus, knew that perfectly well, but he wanted his listeners to get the point, and that meant sacrificing real verisimilitude to something more legible. Russians call it *khudozhestvennaya pravda*: "artistic truth." It is what Laroche had in mind in his comment on operatic representations of ancient oriental peoples. Orientalism again overrides the Orient.

So far, then, we have had an example (Glinka's) that was authentic but not exotic, and one (Balakirev's) that was exotic but not authentic. It is the latter that counts for orientalists (if not for ethnomusicologists) as verisimilar, hence truly oriental. But now consider a third setting of Pushkin's poem: the most famous one, by Sergey Rachmaninoff (1873–1943), written a generation later than Balakirev's, in 1892, when Rachmaninoff, a piano-playing and composing prodigy of nineteen, had just graduated from the Moscow Conservatory (Ex. 39-19c). It is far less verisimilar than Balakirev's and makes no pretense to authenticity. Yet with hardly an augmented second it speaks the sign language of Russian orientalism in a highly developed form, adding a great deal to our experience of the poem.

Rachmaninoff's setting also has conspicuous melismas: not little decorative authentic-sounding ones like Balakirev's, which sound a little strange in the mouth of the poet-speaker, but great sweeping ones that have a motivic consistency deriving from the opening neighbor note. The neighbor-note motif is usually sounded in pairs or in threes, with ties that connect resolution tones to the next preparation tone. The result is a syncopated undulation that is sounded in conjunction with two other distinctive musical gestures to complete a semiotic cluster (a set of signifiers that work together, deriving their meaning from their association): a drone (or drum) bass such as even Glinka had suggested, and—most important of all—a chromatic accompanying line that in this case steadily descends along with the sequences of undulating melismas.

To anyone familiar with the tradition on which it depends, the song's opening ritornello quite specifically conjures up the beautiful oriental maiden the song is about—not the one singing, but the one remembered. And the ritornello also tells us that she was the poet-singer's erotic partner; for the cluster of signs—undulating melisma, chromatic accompanying line, drone—evokes not just "the East" in general, but specifically its voluptuous allure. The syncopated undulation is iconically erotic; its contour paints a picture of languid limbs, writhing torsos, arching necks. The drum bass and the melismas are an echo of the stereotyped Islamic musical idiom that Balakirev had already evoked, sexuality's necessary ticket of admission (for "Western," Christian necks do not arch and writhe).

It is the descending chromatic line, possibly a vestige of the old *passus duriusculus* as mediated through Chopin, that is particularly interesting as an orientalist trope, because it is neither iconically nor stylistically "verisimilar." That is, it is neither realistic sexual portraiture nor specifically Asiatic in style. But though a purely arbitrary convention, it was a widely accepted one: a badge worn by exotic sexpots all over Europe, including France—or rather Spain (once an Islamic region, after all) seen through French eyes—as its most celebrated manifestation in all of opera reveals (Ex. 39-20).

EX. 39-20   Georges Bizet, *Carmen*, Act I, "Habañera," mm. 1–12

EX. 39-20   (continued)

est un oi - seau re - bel - le Que nul ne peut___ ap - pri - voi -

ser,   Et c'est bien en vain qu'on l'ap - pel - le,   S'il lui con -

vient___ de - re - fu - ser.

Love is a wild bird whom nothing can restrain.
One calls upon it in vain, if it is inclined to refuse.

The climax of Rachmaninoff's song (Ex. 39-19d) — undeniably a climax despite the soft dynamic — occurs at the setting of the last two lines, when the chromatic line is suddenly transferred from the middle of the texture to the voice part, at the top. Clearly it is the predominating sign of oriental sensuality, or what the Russians call *nega*, the bliss of gratified desire (or, more excitingly, the promise of it). Its origin as a musical trope lay in Glinka — not in his "Georgian Song," but in *Ruslan and Lyudmila* (1842), his second opera, based on a mock-epic by Pushkin that is set partly in fictitious oriental lands. The composer who brought it to its peak of development was Alexander Borodin, one of the most gifted members of Balakirev's doughty "Davidsbund." Borodin was quite famous during his lifetime, but not as a musician. Like many of Balakirev's associates, he was a Sunday composer. As a chemist with an international reputation, he was one of Russia's leading scientists, and the founder and chief administrator of his country's first women's medical course. He had little spare time for the hobby that

won him immortality, which is one reason why his largest work, the opera *Prince Igor*, was far from finished at the time of his death, although he had been working on it for eighteen years. Based on *The Song of Igor's Campaign*, a genuine epic of the twelfth century and Russia's first literary masterpiece, the opera was a veritable monument to Russian orientalism composed at a time when its plot—a tale of ill-fated hostilities between a Russian prince and Turkic nomads called Polovtsy whose encampments surrounded his domain—was being virtually played out in real life in the Russian empire's wars of aggression in Central Asia.

On the way to it, Borodin also composed a number of shorter works with Eastern themes that could be looked upon as sketches toward his fully elaborated orientalist idiom. One of these spin-offs from

FIG. 39-10   Costume for Borodin's opera *Prince Igor*.

the opera was a short song for contralto called *Arabskaya melodiya* ("Arabian melody"), composed in 1881. The tune is an authentic Arab melody, taken from a book. Again, however, the mode of the tune coincides with the familiar diatonic scale and does not give away its exotic origin to the Western ear. What marks Borodin's song as oriental is the snaking chromatic accompanying line, so obviously related to the one in Rachmaninoff's "Georgian Song" (Ex. 39-21), for which it served as model.

Where Rachmaninoff's chromatic line (like Bizet's in *Carmen*) made a straightforward descent, however, Borodin's (like Glinka's in *Ruslan*) is serpentine, adding a new dimension of erotically iconic undulation. The point at which the change of direction takes place is very significant. The line descends to the fifth degree, then passes chromatically up to the sixth, then down again through the same interpolated half step,

EX. 39-21   Alexander Borodin, *Arabskaya melodiya*, second strophe, mm. 1–8

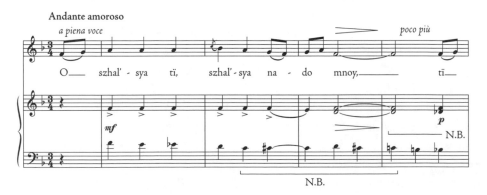

EX. 39-21   (*continued*)

joined now by a middle voice that proceeds to repeat the same double pass twice, not counting a couple of extra undulations between the fifth degree and its chromatic upper neighbor. When the climax is reached — a climax as much sexual as musical — on the words "But even death is sweet to me, the death born of passion for thee" (compare the sixteenth-century madrigal texts in chapter 17), the rhythm of the undulation is excited into diminution and begins to spread out to neighboring scale degrees, ultimately to complete the chromatic gamut, as in Rachmaninoff.

The reversible chromatic pass between the fifth and sixth degrees is the essential *nega* undulation — the essential symbol or "marker" of sex à la russe — as a little snatch from the Chorus of Polovtsian Maidens at the beginning of *Prince Igor*'s second act will prove (Ex. 39-22a). Brief as it is, this little passage deploys the whole orientalist cluster with terrific economy: the text is about creature comfort and gratified desire (in this case the image of nocturnal dew following a sultry day is acting as *nega* metaphor); the sopranos contribute the melodic undulation, here a sort of pedal; the altos contribute the harmonic undulation, from the fifth degree to the sixth and back through a chromatic passing tone each way; and the orchestral bass instruments supply the drum/drone.

And now we are equipped to get the full message from the most famous music in *Prince Igor* (Ex. 39-22b). The famous "Polovtsian Dance" (immortalized for Americans as *Stranger in Paradise*, a pop standard from the Broadway musical *Kismet*) again displays the whole cluster — melodic undulations tied over the beat, a chromatic pass from the sixth scale degree to the fifth, a throbbing drumbeat in the bass, plus, in its orchestral garb, the sound of the English horn, the closest orchestral counterpart to the "snake-charmer's" pipe and another absolutely indispensable orientalist marker.

All of these features are displayed again in the "oriental" theme that confronts a Russian one directly in the "musical picture" *In Central Asia*, which celebrates the contemporary Russian military victories in the east quite directly (Ex. 39-22c). Its first statement, naturally enough, is an English horn solo. The one shown in Ex. 39-22c is the climactic one, in which the chromatic inner voice grows to encompass a whole scale, as in Rachmaninoff's later modeling of it, and (also as in Rachmaninoff's song) moves out from an inner voice to a textural extremity, here the bass. It was a telling touch — and again, a typical one — to extend the length of each phrase in the melody to five bars through one extra languorous undulation ("please, just once more . . . ").

What it tells us is why those hedonistic Central Asians were simply no match for the purposefully advancing Russians.

Nega saturation is maximized in *Prince Igor* by the use of a subplot, not present in the twelfth-century original, involving the romance of the title character's son Vladimir and

EX. 39-22A   Alexander Borodin, *Prince Igor*, Chorus of Polovtsian Maidens

EX. 39-22B   Alexander Borodin, *Prince Igor*, Polovtsian Dance

Konchakovna, the daughter of their captor, the Polovtsian chieftain Khan Konchak. The pretext for her invention (by Stasov, as it happens, who provided Borodin with the opera's scenario) was a single line in the original in which two Polovtsian khans, Gzak and Konchak, consider "entoiling the falconet by means of a fair maiden,"[49] that is, sexually enslaving the young prince.

EX. 39-22C   Alexander Borodin, *In Central Asia*, mm. 175–92

The result was something unique in the annals of opera: an ingénue ("innocent maiden in love") role played not by the usual lyric soprano but by the throatiest contralto imaginable. In the act II love duet, Konchakovna's voice coils all around and beneath Vladimir's tenor to startling effect. The falconet is indeed "entoiled by a fair maiden"—fascinated and emasculated. Never had there been such an emphasis on raised fifths, flattened sixths, and chromatic passes in general. They were the means of his enslavement. Passion mounts in two great waves in which the lovers occupy opposite positions; the *meno mosso* in the middle (Ex. 39-23), cast over the palpably chafing harmony of the dominant minor ninth, is where Konchakovna slides beneath. Her part obsessively applies the flattened sixth scale degree (D♭) to the fifth (C) while Vladimir, having gone through a variety of other chromatic passes, finally adopts hers at the fermata. She then turns around (*allegro appassionato*) and makes another pass at him, from raised fifth to sixth, while he yelps in response, his phrases narrowed down to the sign of chromatic passing in minimal, most concentrated form. The orchestral bass meanwhile gives out one of those complete chromatic descents that signal *nega* at full sensual strength.

They reach their first climax on a question ("Will you/I soon call me/you your/my wife?"), supported in the orchestra by a prolonged harmony rooted on the flat sixth — a harmony we have associated with altered, often ecstatic, emotional states since the days of Schubert, but never so patently sexual as here. The flat submediant finally

EX. 39-23   Alexander Borodin, from *Prince Igor*, Act II, Love Duet

EX. 39-23 (continued)

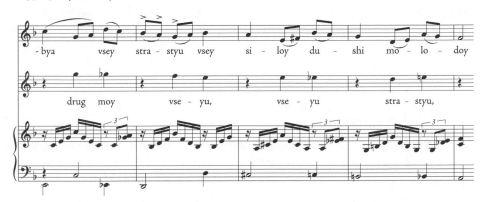

Konchakovna: My sweet, my joy, my delight!
Yes, I love thee with all the passion,
all the strength of my young soul.

Vladimir: O repeat thy words of love,
let me hear them again, my darling!
Love me, my darling, my own,
with all thy passion.

makes its affirmative progress through the dominant to the F major tonic. The change from anxious question to rapt reply itself takes the form, for Vladimir, of a chromatic inflection (the sustained A♭ over ♭VI now trumped at the tonic by a sustained high A-natural). And while they both hold their final notes the orchestra harps repeatedly on the hypnotic undulation of fifth degree and flattened sixth. Vladimir is now thoroughly lost, his manhood *negated*, rendered impotent with respect to his (and his father's) bellicose mission. Prince Igor leaves him behind to perish, the victim of a sinister oriental charm.

THE OTHER IN THE SELF

The view of oriental "difference" as something sinister, and its transference to "ethnic" characters of all kinds, but especially sexy women, was one of the most significant artistic symptoms of the issues at stake in later nineteenth-century cultural politics. The most familiar bearer of orientalist tropes in the standard operatic repertoire, the title character of Bizet's *Carmen* (1875), is not even an "oriental" by the usual definition. As a Spanish Gypsy, however, she is a member of an ethnic minority (one, be it noted, with origins that can be traced to South Asia). For Prosper Mérimée, the author on whose story the opera was based, Carmen's exotic heritage made her an outsider to "mainstream" society and a threat to its denizens and their values. Bizet made this even clearer by casting every one of Carmen's solo numbers in an explicitly designated Spanish or Latin American dance form (habanera, seguidilla, etc.) — exotic, that is, not so much within the opera's stage world as in the world of its French audience.

The judgment of ethnic difference as alluring peril is embodied not only in the music but also in the plot, in which a good soldier, Don José, is (like Borodin's Vladimir) brought to moral ruin and vocational impotence by contact with the ethnic other and her irresistible charms. The story became a veritable archetype in later nineteenth- and early twentieth-century opera, wryly summarized by the music historian Ralph

P. Locke, who notes the omnipresence of a "young, tolerant, brave, possibly naive, white-European tenor-hero" (Borodin's Vladimir, Bizet's Don José, Meyerbeer's Vasco da Gama, and many later counterparts) who "intrudes," in pursuit of love or sex, "into mysterious dark-skinned, colonised territory" and is punished for it, usually along with the sex-object that lured him.[50]

Otherness, in this view, and especially female otherness, is likened to an addiction or a disease, against which Europeans need protection or inoculation. In a way we have come round again to Chopin, whose foreignness and whose diseased condition worked in tandem to mark him in the eyes of Parisians and Londoners both as a fascinating genius and as a toxic presence, the two aspects of his allure inextricably linked (and often read as effeminacy).

The progress of the view can be measured by *Carmen*'s dénouement, in which Don José ruins himself with a "crime of passion," killing his exotic temptress in the throes of jealousy. Although he is the criminal and she the victim, it is he, not she, who is marked by the music as the object of the audience's sympathy. Indeed, Susan McClary has gone so far as to suggest that "the urgency of Bizet's music invites us to desire Carmen's death."[51] The urgency to which McClary refers is the ordinary urgency of "tonal" music for thematic and harmonic closure. If her remark rings true, then, it must follow that along with the uplift and rapture that it affords, music can also serve (even simultaneously) as a dehumanizing influence, dehumanizing both the exotic victim and the momentarily depraved witnesses in the theater — yes, us.

But McClary also reminds us that Carmen's stage death does not end her disquieting hold on our imaginations. "We leave the theater humming her infectious tunes [like Ex. 39-20], and the closure that had seemed so indisputable opens up again."[52] The "other" is irrevocably a part of everyone's consciousness in the ethnically commingled world we now inhabit, and operas like *Carmen* were a part of the process through which Europeans (and lately Euro-Americans, too) came to terms with that new reality — the presence of the other within the self.

As suggested earlier, Russians were conscious of this presence sooner than most. A case in point is Pyotr Ilyich Chaikovsky (1840–93), one of the earliest conservatory-trained Russian composers, who held aloof from Balakirev and his Davidsbund, preferring to work within established institutions and media, becoming (as we shall see) one of the great late nineteenth-century symphonists. He was far less inclined than were the "Mighty Five" to emphasize his "otherness" from Western European culture, less inclined to present himself as an exotic. Apart from a single character in a single opera (*Iolanta*, his last) and a single "Arabian Dance" in a single ballet (*The Nutcracker*, his last and most popular), Chaikovsky never showed the slightest interest in musical portrayals of "the East."

But that does not mean that Chaikovsky did not employ orientalist tropes in his music — far from it. He made extremely telling and effective use of them quite early in his career in a work that seems, on the face of it, quite unrelated in its thematic content to anything oriental: a concert overture (or "Overture-Fantasia," as Chaikovsky called it) on the subject of Shakespeare's tragedy *Romeo and Juliet* (1869; revised 1870, 1880), a work that has long been in the standard orchestral repertory.

Like most concert overtures, it roughly follows sonata form in its sequence of events: slow introduction, bithematic exposition, development, recapitulation, coda. And each of these parts seems to be correlated with a character or plot component in the drama: the slow introduction, in ecclesiastical style, with Friar Laurence; the turbulent first thematic group with the feuding families; the lyrical second thematic group with the balcony scene, and so on.

The frank sensual iconicity of the balcony music is often remarked. One conspicuous reason for that impression is a throbbing, panting countermelody in the horn (see the end of Ex. 39-24b) that unmistakably evokes the physical manifestations of passion. But the love themes evoke *nega* just as surely by means of the orientalist trope we have already observed in *Prince Igor*, namely the strongly marked chromatic pass between the fifth and sixth degrees; and the first love theme (generally associated, though on no particular authority, with Romeo) features, on its first appearance, the equally marked English horn timbre (Ex. 39-24a).

Juliet responds to Romeo's advance with a theme of her own, mirroring his descending chromatic pass with an ascending one that is then maintained as an oscillation (or perhaps an osculation — a prolonged kiss), while Romeo's ecstatic reentry is prepared by reversing the pass once more by way of a transporting augmented-sixth progression (Ex. 39-24b). At the climax, delayed until the recapitulation, Chaikovsky enhances carnality by adding one more chromatic pass at the very zenith of intensity to introduce the last full statement from which the love music will then gradually subside (Ex. 39-24c). This music is easily as steamy as the love duet from *Prince Igor*, and the source of the steam in both, despite their differing subjects and settings, is the same.

EX. 39-24A Pyotr Ilyich Chaikovsky, *Romeo and Juliet* ("Overture-Fantasia"), main love theme (Romeo?)

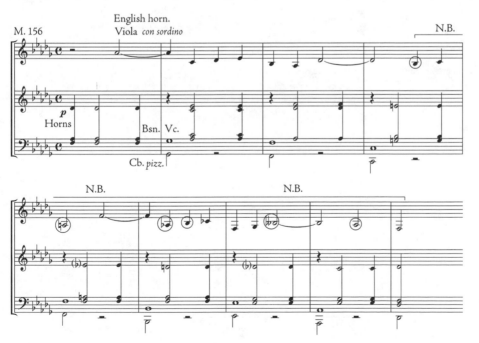

EX. 39-24B Pyotr Ilyich Chaikovsky, *Romeo and Juliet* ("Overture-Fantasia"), subsidiary love theme (Juliet?)

EX. 39-24C Pyotr Ilyich Chaikovsky, *Romeo and Juliet* ("Overture-Fantasia"), climax

For this we have corroboration from the best of witnesses. In a marvelously cruel letter to Chaikovsky, Balakirev, the peerless connoisseur of musical orientalism, reacted to the main themes of the work, which Chaikovsky had sent him for comment while composition was still in progress. To understand what he had to say about the big love theme one must know what Balakirev knew: that Chaikovsky was just then getting over an infatuation with the soprano Désirée Artôt, the one woman known to have aroused the otherwise homosexually inclined Chaikovsky's romantic interest, who had disappointed him by marrying the Spanish baritone Mariano Padilla y Ramos. Balakirev wrote to Chaikovsky that the theme given in Ex. 39-24a was

> simply enchanting. I often play it and have a great wish to kiss you for it. It has everything: *nega*, and love's sweetness, and all the rest. It appears to me that you are lying all naked in the bath and that Artôt-Padilla herself is rubbing your tummy with hot scented suds. I have just one thing to say against this theme: there is little in it of inner spiritual love, only the physical, passionate torment (colored just a wee bit Italian). Really now, Romeo and Juliet are not Persian lovers, but European. I'll try to clarify this by example. I'll cite the first theme that comes to mind in which, in my opinion, love is expressed more inwardly: the second, A♭-major, theme in Schumann's overture *The Bride of Messina*.[53]

Indeed, Schumann's long wet noodle of a love theme (Ex. 39-25), which reaches no climax, does seem as if by design to moderate the orientalism of Chaikovsky's, diluting the chromatic passes and replacing the lascivious English horn with a chaste (or, to use the German buzzword as Balakirev did, an "inward") clarinet.

EX. 39-25   Robert Schumann, *The Bride of Messina* Overture, second theme

EX. 39-25 (*continued*)

Balakirev's letter confirms the impression that Chaikovsky used the orientalist trope metonymically, to conjure up not the East as such but rather its exotic sex appeal. The little tease about Artôt is provocative indeed, precisely because it is so plausible. If, as Balakirev seems to suggest, Chaikovsky had cast himself as Romeo to Artôt's Juliet, then the theme becomes a self-portrait. And if so, then it is a remarkable instance of that phenomenon, noticeable first in Russian music, whereby the eastward gaze is simultaneously a look in the mirror.

Midcentury

THE NEW GERMAN SCHOOL; LISZT'S SYMPHONIC POEMS; HARMONIC EXPLORATIONS

HISTORICISM

Historians generally, and musicologists in particular, are seldom associated with the avant-garde. Their contemplative lifestyle and their antiquarian scholarly interests lend them an air, in uninitiated eyes, of conservatism. But historians of a certain type — or rather, adherents to a certain theory of history — have conspicuously allied themselves with avant-garde movements, seeing themselves not only as passive recorders of events but as active participants in their making. This type of activist historian, the product of a somewhat improbable union of Enlightened and romantic thought, reached a peak of prestige and authority in mid-nineteenth-century Germany, just as German music was reaching its own peak of prestige and authority, and when it was widely believed (not only by musicians) that "music is the sovereign art of the present."[1] The history of that country and that century, and particularly of that music, cannot be fully understood without some knowledge of the history of history.

As a historical method "historicism" has largely died out, victimized by the extremes of distortion and abuse to which its tenets were subjected in the twentieth century. Therefore, the name of its main musical protagonist will probably be new to most readers of this book: Karl Franz Brendel (1811–68), from whom the impressive quotation in the previous paragraph was taken. He may be forgotten today, but his memory is worth reviving. There was no more important figure in the world of German music at midcentury than this man, a doctor of philosophy with only a casual musical education (mainly piano lessons with Friedrich Wieck, Clara Schumann's father), who neither composed nor performed. His impact derived from the nature of his voluminous writings, and the social and political activism through which he put his precepts into practice.

Brendel's great achievement was to write his century's most widely disseminated "universal" and "scientific" history of music: *Geschichte der Musik in Italien, Deutschland und Frankreich von den ersten christlichen Zeiten bis auf die Gegenwart* ("History of Music in Italy, Germany and France from the Earliest Christian Times to the Present"). First published in 1852, by 1906 it had gone through nine editions. The words put in quotes in this paragraph's first sentence constitute the book's inheritance from the Enlightenment. It aspired to say everything that was important, and to say it in a way that put all facts into an overriding system that gave them meaning. The reasons for

FIG. 40-1 Franz Brendel, music historian, editor of the *Neue Zeitschrift für Musik*, and organizer of the *Allgemeiner deutscher Musikverein*.

putting the words in quotes constitute the book's inheritance from romanticism. The limitation, despite the claim of universality, to the richest and most powerful countries of Western Europe is already evidence of the author's commitment to a view of history cast in terms of the progressive realization of an essential European spirit of which those countries were collectively the protagonist. And the science that gave his work system was the one worked out by the romantic (or "idealist") philosopher Georg Wilhelm Friedrich Hegel (1770–1831). It was known as the "dialectic."

In its broadest terms, the Hegelian dialectic has long been a cliché: human history develops according to a process in which one concept (thesis) inevitably gives rise to its opposite (antithesis), which then interacts with the thesis to produce a resolution (synthesis) that in turn becomes the thesis for a new "triad." Thus nothing is static or immutable. The hypothetical or axiomatic first triad that sets history in motion—Being reacting with Negation to produce Becoming—stipulates that all of history must be conceived as a constant state of flux.

So far the theory is irrefutable: the first thing one notices in this or any study of history is that things change under the impact of other things. Everything that can be observed can be described either as a cause or as an effect, hence everything is both cause and effect in an endless chain. This much is not a theory of history but simply a description—or rather, a tautological definition—of how things happen. What sets the Hegelian dialectic apart from other interpretations of the great chain, such as Darwin's theory of biological evolution (first set forth in 1859 and immediately reinterpreted or

FIG. 40-2 Georg Wilhelm Friedrich Hegel, lithograph after a lost painting by Julius Ludwig Sebbers.

misinterpreted in light of the dialectic), is that it purports to show not merely *that* things change or *how* things change, but *why* things change. The stipulation that change has purpose turns random process into law.

The law of history, as Hegel first postulated it in lectures at the University of Berlin that his pupils reconstructed from their notes and published as *Lectures on the Philosophy of History* in 1837, was this: "The history of the world is none other than the progress of the consciousness of Freedom." That is the first sentence of the book, and the notion from which the entire subsequent argument and demonstration is drawn. According to it, all meaningfully or significantly "historical" change (all change, in other words, that is worthy of representation in the dialectic) has contributed to this progress in the realization of human freedom, which Hegel called the progress of the "world soul." If it has not contributed to this progress, then, change has not been historically significant (or, in Hegelian terms, not "historical").

The doctrine remains a tautology, of course. While more specific than the baldly axiomatic statement of the dialectic, it still harbors a confusion of explanation with definition. And it obviously left a lot of things undefined—beginning with "Freedom," which many who called themselves Hegelians interpreted in ways Hegel never would have countenanced. But it was enormously attractive in its optimism, appearing as it did "between the revolutions." And it enabled its followers to believe, in the words of Karl Popper (one of historicism's most implacable foes), "that by contemplating history we may discover the secret, the essence of human destiny."[2] It offered, in sum, the authority of science and consolations of religion; and it was believed in, and defended, not only as history but as prophecy.

The Hegelian dialectic was infinitely adaptable to other philosophies of process. Its great virtue was its power to lend any such process the aspect of systematic logic in support of a purpose (or anything deemed good, true, or beautiful). It was especially fruitful in conjunction with romantic ideas of "organic" growth toward diversification within a higher unity, and here is where it made its greatest impact on the histories of art and politics, and provided a means for yoking the two together.

As the first self-consciously Hegelian historian of music, Brendel cast his narrative in terms of successive emancipations, both of musicians and of the art itself. Before the sixteenth century all was primitive, mere "prehistory," because in Brendel's ears (and here he did not differ from his contemporaries) such music did not intelligibly express the ideas or feelings of individual creators. All musicians were slaves to the mechanical rules of counterpoint, as people generally were enslaved by the dogmas of the medieval Church.

The first great composer, in Brendel's reckoning, was Palestrina, who, reflecting the romantic interpretation of the Renaissance, broke through to true spiritual expressivity. What he expressed, however, was not yet a personal sensibility but rather the collectively held beliefs of his religious community. His art was "sublime" rather than "beautiful," because it continued to address a higher-than-human plane. But while it still fulfilled prescribed ecclesiastical functions, its euphony and expressive power already showed the way toward artistic autonomy.

The phase of "beauty" was reached when the spiritual, freed from its ecclesiastical bonds, could be expressed in fully human (that is, secular) terms. The rise of opera bore witness to it. And the next stage — the fully-fledged "esthetic" — came with the emancipation of music from words in the instrumental masterpieces of the German classical masters. Their music, now able to realize its own essential spirit, able at last to evolve spontaneously and autonomously (that is, according to its own laws), was effectively a metaphor for the advancement of humanity toward ultimate self-realization. The very autonomy of the new instrumental music (implying freedom from all "extramusical" association or constraint) made it a political symbol — hence re-enmeshing it in extramusical ideas. That is a small example of the dialectic in action.

The value of music could be measured best, in the Hegelian view, in terms of the degree to which it embodied its own epoch's evolutionary synthesis and pointed the way to the next. Composers were valuable (or not) to the degree that their actions advanced the tendencies inherent in the musical materials toward further autonomous evolution. Unsurprisingly, the most advanced, hence most valuable, composers were Germans: Bach and Handel (the latter viewed bizarrely as a church musician), who were the last and most consummate representatives of the sublime epoch, and Gluck, Haydn, and Mozart, who brought to its first full fruition the epoch of the esthetic. Needless to say, Beethoven's popular image as music's emancipator supreme received a resounding confirmation.

But the most provocative chapter of Brendel's *History* was the last, because of the way the author maintained his account of progressive emancipation even beyond Beethoven, into what was then the present. This was at the time a very unconventional and risky move, since it potentially threatened the status of Mozart, Haydn, and Beethoven as "classics" — that is, as having set a timeless (and therefore unimprovable) standard. For a German historian, nothing short of the nation's honor was at stake in this historical "fact." Denying it was unthinkable. Brendel got around the problem in two ways. First, he posited that every age (or stage) had its perfect representatives. Hence Bach was not invalidated by Mozart, nor Mozart by Beethoven, and so Beethoven would never be invalidated either; his status was secure. Second, he obediently gave the chapter concerning the present the title *Verfall* (decline), in keeping with what was by then an inescapable art historian's obligation.

And yet the chapter's contents roundly belied its title. The music of the man Brendel singled out as the greatest composer then living carried on the torch, advancing both the progressive consciousness of freedom and the progressive attainment of esthetic (or organic) unity. The ostentatiously Hegelian terms in which the author couched his description of that composer's achievement left no doubt that Brendel saw the latter's work as a new synthesis, a new transcendence begetting a new thesis — a new dawn — for music:

> It is the unity of the poetic and the musical, and the progress to a new consciousness of this unity, that deserves to be called the essential novelty in the artistic creations under discussion. In earlier phases, but especially with Beethoven, the conscious thought — the sovereignty of the poetic Idea — emerges only along with a soaring

of ideals and a gravity of contents, as the end result; but here these factors constitute the point of departure, the foundation of the whole creation. Hence, this conscious side now has a commanding significance. Here we see that earlier process concluded: the summit of thinking, toward which everything strives, has been achieved with precision, and thereby the sovereignty of Idea has been elevated to the status of a governing principle.[3]

Let identification and exemplification wait for a moment while we savor the rhetoric. The high premium placed on embodied consciousness and precision of thought might seem to contradict the usual romantic emphasis on feeling. But as Carl Dahlhaus pointed out in his history of musical esthetics, what is really accomplished is the final proof of an even more fundamental romantic intuition: namely the superiority of instrumental music to vocal.[4] Here Brendel purported to correct not only Beethoven, who in the Ninth Symphony seemed to imply that the incorporation of voices was a breakthrough to a higher unity, but also Hegel himself, who in his own treatise on esthetics had endorsed the eighteenth century's preference for vocal music. Brendel could presume to use the dialectic against its own originator because the system was greater than any person.

That is what gave Brendel's work such enduring prestige and such a lasting influence even among musicians who have never heard of him. As the editor of the book's sixth edition (1875) put it in his Preface, "all contemporary criticism, consciously or unconsciously, is under its sway," because "for the first time a synthesis [!] appeared of material that formerly had only the exterior unity of an arbitrary narrative, showing the history of music to be a great, self-evolving whole under the control of law."[5] Ever since the appearance of Brendel's *History*, historicism has been a force not only in the historiography of music but in its actual history as well.

That is, ever since the middle of the nineteenth century, there has been abroad the idea that the history of music (like the history of everything else) has a purpose, and that the primary obligation of musicians is not to their audience but to that purpose—namely, the furthering of the "evolutionary" progress of the art, for the sake of which any sacrifice is justified. Ever since the middle of the nineteenth century, in other words, the idea that one is morally bound to serve the impersonal aims of history has been one of the most powerful motivating forces, and one of the most exigent criteria of value, in the history of music. As recently as 1993, in a widely noticed review, a critic sought to discredit a new symphony that had enjoyed unusual audience acclaim by declaring that it did not "add anything to the universe of musical possibility."[6] Such criticism has become common, so common as to seem commonplace, even commonsensical. In fact, it depends entirely on the historicist assumptions that Franz Brendel was the first to introduce into musical criticism.

Brendel's own way of putting it was to say that "the essence of today's art" can no longer be realized in "the old naturalistic way"—that is, instinctively or intuitively by musicians out to please their patrons or their listeners—but only with "the intervention of theory and criticism," and by "art's presupposing theory and criticism within itself."[7] The age of creative innocence was over; self-conscious theory, based on a high consciousness of purpose and of history, was the only true path to the future. Furthermore, that consciousness of purpose, being the road to self-realization, made the future graspable in the present. The path of destiny was marked out to those in the know. Others did not matter. The self-conscious few, history's self-appointed "advance guard" or *avant garde*, now saw themselves (following the English poet Percy Bysshe Shelley's famous definition of his own calling) as "the unacknowledged legislators of the world."[8]

Perhaps needless to say, these contentions have been among the most controversial ideas of their time, a time that extends right up to the present and shows little sign of abatement. Their advent marks the beginnings of the modern — or modernist — age of music, which has also been the age of revolutionary politics. Both in art and in politics, it has been the age in which (to quote Richard Kostelanetz, a contemporary American theorist of the avant-garde) "an innovative minority makes the leaps that will be adopted by the many" — or that, according to the theory, ought by rights to be adopted. The invidious comparison implicit in this idea — or rather the elitism, to give it its contemporary *nom de guerre* — has understandably given rise to angry backlashes and counterrevolutions. Since the middle of the nineteenth century, the world of classical music has been a world riven with political factions and contentious publicity.

Of these, too, there is no end in sight, for we still live in the age of historical and theoretical self-consciousness whose birth we are now witnessing, and of which this very book is a product. That self-consciousness — together with the obligations it has been seen to impose on its proponents and the fierce conflicts to which it has given rise — will be something to reckon with on virtually every remaining page of this book. From here on we are truly investigating the history of the present.

THE NEW GERMAN SCHOOL

The first self-conscious proponent of the musical avant-garde was Brendel himself, in his role as activist — a role his historical vision (by his own typically Hegelian avowal) had thrust upon him unbidden. During his youthful piano studies with Friedrich Wieck in Leipzig, Brendel naturally came to know a fellow pupil named Robert Schumann. After receiving his doctorate he returned to Leipzig in 1844 and lectured on music history as preparation for his magnum opus. That plan was temporarily put on hold when Schumann asked him to take over the *Neue Zeitschrift für Musik*. Brendel formally became its editor with the issue of 1 January 1845 and remained in that position for almost a quarter of a century, until his death. Already the established voice of the German musical left, the journal was an effective forum and power base.

To Schumann's eventual consternation, Brendel turned the journal in a frankly political direction when he began agitating in its pages, under the guise of music criticism, for German unification. It should have been no surprise; on the contrary, it was the inevitable nationalistic outcome of commitment to Hegel's teachings, with their emphasis on the realization of the spirit through unity. The political faction that pressed hardest for unification was the group that called themselves the Young Hegelians. For them, the goal of unification was eventual German hegemony over Europe. This new (or neo-) Hegelianism became the philosophical underpinning, in the second half of the century, for a new, aggressive brand of German nationalism, to which Marxism, another radical offshoot of Hegelian thinking, became the antithesis.

The Young Hegelian character of Brendel's activity as spokesman for the German musical left became especially evident in 1859 when in celebration of the twenty-fifth anniversary of the founding of the *Neue Zeitschrift für Musik* the indefatigable editor organized at Weimar, Goethe's town, and in Leipzig, the journal's birthplace, a great convocation of musicians from all parts of Germany, out of which emerged an organization called the Allgemeiner Deutscher Musikverein, the All-German Musical Society, for the purpose of agitation and propaganda on behalf of the musical tendency to which Brendel had devoted the culminating chapter of his *History* seven years before. In his widely publicized keynote address, Brendel christened that faction the New (or neo-) German School. The guest of honor at the convocation, the honorary president of the society, and the figurehead of the New German School was the same man whose music Brendel had held aloft (in the passage from his *History* quoted earlier) as a beacon of "progress to a new consciousness" of music's historical obligation. That man was Franz Liszt.

Liszt? That virtuoso? That eclectic? He wasn't even German! But since we left him in chapter 37 his life had undergone a remarkable change. In 1848, possibly under the influence of Princess Carolyne Sayn-Wittgenstein, a brilliantly intellectual, immensely wealthy Polish noblewoman (née Iwanowska) whom he had met the year before at his recital in Kiev (and who would be to the end of his life not only his mistress but his muse and ghost-writer), Liszt unexpectedly retired from the concert stage and took up full-time residence in Weimar, the capital of a small, secluded, and (by mid nineteenth-century standards) sleepy East German duchy where Bach had once played the organ, and where Liszt had rather perfunctorily been given an honorary court appointment several years earlier. Nobody expected him, an international star, really to fill such a post. As the English novelist George Eliot put it, visiting Weimar on her honeymoon, "One's first feeling is: how could Goethe live here, in this dull, lifeless village?"[9] How much less could the likes of Liszt?

FIG. 40-3   Princess Carolyne Sayn-Wittgenstein with her daughter Marie, lithograph by C. Fischer after a painting by Casanova (1844).

But with the fantastic energy he had formerly devoted to his pianistic career, Liszt now became the court kapellmeister to end all kapellmeisters. The musical establishment of which he assumed the reins was measly: an orchestra of thirty-seven, a chorus of twenty-three and a corps de ballet of four. Liszt had never conducted. But by dint of his personality, his high ambitions, his prestige, and the enthusiastic generosity of his patron, the Grand Duchess Maria Pawlowna of Saxe-Weimar (sister of the Russian tsar Nikolai I), he soon turned the backward town into what his biographer Humphrey Searle called "the Mecca of the avant-garde movement in Germany."[10]

In the first place, Liszt greatly expanded and modernized his equipment, so that the Weimar court orchestra came to represent the midcentury state of the art. Those who composed for it (meaning, in the first instance, Liszt himself and his hired orchestrators) were encouraged to exploit its resources to the hilt. In furtherance of his aim to create the ideal music machine, Liszt summoned from Leipzig the already famous nineteen-year-old prodigy Joseph Joachim (1831–1907), a former protégé of Mendelssohn and Schumann, to preside over the orchestra as Konzertmeister (leader of the first violins) beginning in 1850. After several years of service, however, Joachim's loyalty to his former masters and their attitudes toward the Viennese classics won out over his contractual commitments to the avant-garde and he resigned the post, later becoming (along with his best friend and contemporary Johannes Brahms, another Schumann protégé) one of the New German School's most tireless public detractors.

But Liszt's presence brought many sincere disciples to Weimar, the most important being the composers Joachim Raff (1822–82) and Peter Cornelius (1824–74), and the pianist Hans von Bülow (1830–94), who married Liszt's daughter Cosima and under his tutelage became the great conductor of the age. These younger men, together with Liszt, formed the early nucleus of the New German School. Taking advantage of his protected position as a court musician, Liszt placed himself as conductor at the service of the most advanced, formidable, and politically risky composers of the time, particularly Richard Wagner (then a political exile from Germany). Liszt gave the widely publicized and acclaimed first performance of Wagner's romantic opera *Lohengrin* (on a German knightly legend) in 1850, as well as notable productions of operas by Schumann (*Genoveva*) and Berlioz (*Benvenuto Cellini*).

FIG. 40-4A   Joachim Raff. He and Peter Cornelius, shown in Fig. 40-4b, were two mainstays of the "new German school."

Finally, and most important, Liszt used his abundant remaining time at Weimar to produce a remarkable series of avant-garde compositions of his own, many of which he had roughly conceived at the keyboard during his whirlwind touring years, but had never had the time to work out on paper. Temporarily abandoning the piano, he turned to the orchestra he now led as his medium of choice. At first, since he had no training and little experience as an orchestrator, he farmed out the task to assistants: at first a minor composer of comic operas named August Conradi (1821–73), but later Raff, whom Liszt summoned to Weimar and personally supported for this purpose. Later, having performed the music and had the experience of hearing and revising the scoring of his works in long and painstaking

FIG. 40-4B   Peter Cornelius.

rehearsals (a process Joachim found particularly unendurable), Liszt became a master of ostentatious orchestration in his own right.

The works he produced in this fashion were the ones Brendel extolled in the final chapter of his *History* as "the summit of thinking," the culmination of the whole historical process toward which everything up to that time had striven. Liszt eventually called them *symphonische Dichtungen*, symphonic poems, echoing the Hegelian ideal of "unity of the poetic and the musical." They are single-movement orchestra works, sometimes as long the average symphony, sometimes only as long as a good-size first movement, that are outfitted with titles and (sometimes) brief prefaces to specify the "poetic" content the music will expound.

In their various aspects Liszt's symphonic poems had plenty of precedents. Specific "poetic" content can be found not only in programmatic symphonies like Berlioz's *Symphonie fantastique* or David's *Désert*, but also in the type of theater or opera overture (like Beethoven's *Coriolanus* or *Egmont*, or Weber's *Der Freischütz*) that seek to summarize or otherwise evoke the drama to which they are appended. The closest precedents, perhaps, were Mendelssohn's concert overtures, self-sufficient works to which no drama was appended (although the first of them, *Midsummer Night's Dream*, still took its cue from one). Liszt actually referred to his early symphonic poems as overtures, or sometimes (more vaguely, but also more tellingly) as "free-form compositions," before arriving at the definitive name in 1854, before any of them had been published.

As for compressed single-movement form, Liszt's own piano concertos and Schumann's *Fantaisie* for piano and orchestra provided models that, while lacking any specified poetic or programmatic content, were certainly not lacking in drama. These works (not to mention Berlioz's symphony with its idée fixe) also employed the technique of thematic transformation, or perpetual variation, on which Liszt would rely to give shape (if not conventional form) to his symphonic poems. Why then, in view of so many apparent forerunners, did the symphonic poems seem to so many contemporaries to be not merely a new genre, but a breakthrough to a new artistic plane?

The reason had to do, first of all, with the nature of the poetic content, which in most cases was neither narrative nor pictorial, but philosophical, staking out a loftier expressive sphere than any composer save Beethoven had previously addressed, and doing so, moreover, with an explicitness that seemed to exceed — or at least claimed plausibly to exceed — Beethoven's powers. Liszt himself implied such a claim, which, he maintained, was a contemporary musician's privilege and duty, and the only way of paying Beethoven proper tribute. "Although Dresden and a hundred other cities may 'stop at Beethoven' (to whom, while he lived, they much preferred Haydn and Mozart), that is no reason for Weimar to do so," Liszt wrote to a dubious court official in 1855. "There is no doubt nothing better than to respect, admire and study the illustrious dead," he continued,

> but why not also live with the living? The significance of the musical movement of which Weimar is the real centre lies precisely in this initiative, about which the public understands little, but which is nevertheless important for the continued development of contemporary art.[11]

To many others, of course, in Dresden and a hundred other cities (including Berlin, where during the 1850s Liszt's orchestral music was regularly hissed and jeered), avant-garde posing of this sort, with its haughty implication that the interests of art and its audience had irreconcilably diverged, seemed the most intolerable hubris. And there was more. Liszt and his spokesmen made the patently Hegelian claim that with the symphonic poem he had at last ushered in the age of music's full equality among the arts as a bearer of meaning, a necessary precondition to its "sovereignty."

As usual, the spokesmen made the claim more sweepingly and arrogantly than the master. Liszt's own version (probably drafted by the Princess Sayn-Wittgenstein) took the form of a rather modestly worded *avant-propos* (foreword) meant for distribution at performances of any of his symphonic poems, to silence doubts or disagreements as to his intent. Addressing first the problem of music's suitability to extramusical tasks, he conceded that "the poorest of apprentice landscape painters could give with a few chalk strokes a much more faithful nature picture than a musician operating with all the resources of the best orchestras." But of course there was a *but*. "If these same things are laid open to subjective contemplation, to dreaming, to emotional uplift, have they not a kinship with music, and should not music be able to translate them into its mysterious language?"[12]

This is not so far from what George Sand, speaking for Chopin, said about the content of the latter's music in the previous chapter: one paints not the thing but the emotion to which it gives rise. But Liszt wanted more. He wanted to specify "the thing" rather than leaving it to the listener's imagination. And that justified the use — inherited from Berlioz but very much against the traditional German romantic biases that Schumann had passionately defended in his review (in the "old" *Neue*

Zeitschrift) of the *Symphonie fantastique* — of verbal notes and explanations, in short, of programs. As Liszt put it in the *avant-propos*:

> Since the musician's language is more arbitrary and more uncertain than any other, and lends itself to the most varied interpretations, it is not without value (and most of all not ridiculous, as it is often thought) for the composer to give in a few lines the spiritual sketch of his work and, without falling into petty and detailed explanations, convey the idea which served as the basis for his composition. This will prevent faulty elucidations, hazardous interpretations, idle quarrels with intentions the composer never had, and endless commentaries which rest on nothing.

Brendel went much further, in a handbook *Franz Liszt als Symphoniker* ("Franz Liszt as a symphonist") published in 1859, the year of the great Leipzig Lisztfest. There he made the brazen claim that beginning with Liszt, and only with him, "content creates its own form."[13] If the implied dichotomy between form and content is accepted as real (and this itself was, and remains, a major battle) then Liszt's achievement, as described by Brendel, counts as a double emancipation. On the one hand, content itself is liberated from an earlier state of contingency, and music is thus freed to express it more directly than before. And on the other, composers are freed from their dependency on the traditional *Formenlehre*, the standard repertory of forms in which all previous music, even Beethoven's, had perforce been cast.

In a review of *Harold in Italy*, Berlioz's symphony with viola obbligato, which appeared in the "new" *Neue Zeitschrift* in 1855, Liszt himself (or his ghostwriter) had come out aggressively in favor of programmatic music as "one of the various steps forward which the art has still to take" toward "the poetic solution of instrumental music." He took the offensive against what he called "the purely musical composer," who "only values and emphasizes the formal working-out of his material," and who therefore forfeits "the capacity to derive new formulations from it or to breathe new life into it."[14] Given the Hegelian premises on which Liszt based the argument, "purely musical composers" had good reason to think that they were being declared useless and obsolete.

The last straw was the slogan *la musique de l'avenir*: "the music of the future," or *Zukunftsmusik* (as it became widely known in Germany), along with its derivatives like *Zukunftsmusiker* (musician of the future) for composers of the New German School and *Zukunftskonzerte* (concerts of the future) for performances of their works. The term was apparently coined by the Princess Sayn-Wittgenstein after the premiere of *Lohengrin*, when Brendel suggested that the work was beyond the capacities of present-day audiences. "Very well," came the smug rejoinder, "we are creating the music of the future."[15]

The phrase immediately began resounding in the pages of the *Neue Zeitschrift* and in Liszt's correspondence. Needless to say, it quickly turned counterproductive, a great source of fun for the group's antagonists. Finally, in his 1859 keynote address, Brendel called for its abandonment in favor of "New German School." But by then it was too late. It was pointed out that New German School was a misnomer in any case, since two of its elder statesmen, Liszt and Berlioz, were not German. To this Brendel retorted that it was "common knowledge" that these two had taken "Beethoven as their point of departure and so are German as to their origins."

Warming to the subject, he continued:

The birthplace cannot be considered decisive in matters of the spirit. The two artists would never have become what they are today had they not from the first drawn nourishment from the German spirit and grown strong with it. Therefore, too, Germany must of necessity be the true homeland of their works, and it is in this sense that I suggested the denomination New German School for the entire post-Beethoven development.[16]

While the occasion that elicited it might be written off as a tempest in a teapot, this was a remarkable pronouncement. It testified to a new conception of nationhood and nationalism that had arisen in the wake of Hegel, or rather in the wake of the political activism that Hegel had inspired among the Young Hegelians. Germanness was henceforth no longer to be sought in folklore. One showed oneself a German not ethnically but spiritually, by putting oneself in humanity's vanguard.

The new nationalism appeared to sacrifice the distinctive national coloring that Herder had prized. In a sequel to his *History* called "The Music of the Present and the Holistic Art of the Future" (*Die Musik der Gegenwart, und die Gesammtkunst der Zukunft*, 1854), Brendel had dismissed such coloring as mere surface decoration (*Schmuck*). But the new concept made a far greater claim for the nation than the old. Germany was now viewed as the world-historical (*welthistorisch*) nation in Hegel's sense of the word, the nation that held the key to history and served as the executor of history's grand design, the nation whose actions led the world to its inevitable destiny. And so it came about (according to Arnold Schoenberg, a twentieth-century advocate of the concept) "that German music came to decide the way things developed, as it has for 200 years."[17]

FIG. 40-5 Alphonse de Lamartine, by Henri Decaisne.

THE SYMPHONY LATER ON

Except for the chauvinistic bombast, to be taken on faith or not at all, we can put all this heady rhetoric and theorizing to the test at last by examining one of Liszt's symphonic poems. *Les préludes*, eventually published in 1856 as Symphonic Poem No. 3 with a dedication to Princess Sayn-Wittgenstein, was not the first of the set to be performed. It was the first to have been conceived and sketched, however, possibly as early as 1841; and it is the only one of the thirteen to have survived in standard repertory. It is also one of the shortest and (partly in consequence) one of the most radical, and is for all of these reasons perhaps the most revealing of Liszt's innovative project.

The title is that of a famous poem, from *Nouvelles méditations poétiques* (New Poetic Meditations, 1823) by Alphonse de Lamartine

(1790–1869), one of the loftiest, most philosophical romantic poets. On its first publication, the work was actually titled *Les préludes (d'après Lamartine)* ("The preludes, after Lamartine"), and carried a prefatory note that looked, and was evidently designed to look, like a précis of the poem:

> What else is our life but a series of preludes to that unknown Hymn, the first and solemn note of which is intoned by Death?
>
> Love is the glowing dawn of all existence; but in whose fate are the first delights of happiness not interrupted by some storm, the mortal blast of which dissipates its fine illusions; the fatal lightning of which consumes its altar; and where is the cruelly wounded soul which, on issuing from one of these tempests, does not endeavor to rest his recollection in the calm serenity of life in the countryside? Nevertheless man hardly gives himself up for long to the enjoyment of the beneficent stillness which at first he has shared in Nature's bosom, and when "the trumpet sounds the alarm," he hastens to the dangerous post, whatever the war may be, which calls him to its ranks, in order at last to recover in combat the full consciousness of himself and the entire possession of his energy.

The program has been tailored for music, of course; following the sonorous invocation of the Question (mm. 1–46) it comprises four episodes—Love (mm. 47–108), Storm (mm. 109–181), Bucolic Calm (mm. 182–344), Battle-and-Victory (mm. 345–end, with a recapitulation of the Question at m. 405)—corresponding to the movements of a conventional symphony if not in the most conventional order (yet ending *very* conventionally with *Kampf und Sieg!*). It has been thoroughly Germanized as well, the main trophy of battle being full consciousness of Self, just what Dr. Hegel would have prescribed.

EX. 40-1   Table of themes derived from the main motive in Liszt's *Les préludes* (Symphonic Poem no. 3)

EX. 40-1 *(continued)*

The music, while heavily indebted in concept to Berlioz, self-consciously advertises its descent from Beethoven even as it flaunts its freedom from the formal constraints to which Beethoven had submitted. This, of course, is no mere contradiction; rather it is an "antithesis" that leads to the achievement of the next—higher—liberating synthesis. After a mysterious pair of pizzicato Cs that seemingly invoke the lyre of the muse whom Lamartine summons to his side at the outset of his poem, the Question is broached in the form of a three-note *échappée* figure, plus a continuation (see Ex. 40-1).

The most obvious reason for separating the first three notes from the continuation is that Liszt himself so separates and repeats them in mm. 6–9, thus marking them as an independent motive. A more esoteric reason, yet probably known to a large part of the audience to whom the work was originally addressed, is that Beethoven had already propounded a very similar *échappée* motive (albeit jestingly) as a great philosophical enigma in a note preceding the last movement of his last quartet (F major, op. 135). Under the heading "The Difficult Resolution," the motive and its inversion are set out over the words "Muss es sein?" (Must it be?) and "Es muss sein!" (It must be!) (Ex. 40-2).

EX. 40-2   Ludwig van Beethoven, *Der schwer gefasste Entschluss,* Op. 135

Liszt was not jesting. It was a measure, he (or at least Brendel) would have said, of the long way music had come since Beethoven's day that composers could now give serious treatment to philosophical questions that formerly could only be broached vaguely, or else ruefully mocked. And the treatment Liszt gave the question embodied in the three-note motif is the third and most important reason to consider the motif as an independent entity, since every major theme in the ensuing composition — every answer to the Question (or "prelude to that unknown Hymn") — is fashioned out of the question's intervallic substance, set out in Ex. 40-1.

This was by all odds the most thoroughgoing demonstration Liszt ever gave of his technique of thematic transformation. In light of the preface invoking Lamartine, the conceptual source of the technique can be easily traced to Berlioz's operatically derived idée fixe, the device that had unified the *Symphonie fantastique*, the prototype of all later compositions with specific literary programs. And yet there is a genuinely Beethovenian element as well, in the whittling down of the decisive unit of recognition from a full-fledged theme to a tiny motive. This refinement — the weaving of the whole symphonic fabric out of a motivic thread that comes, in turn, directly out of the poem — seemed as if deliberately meant to justify Brendel's claim that Liszt's symphonic poems ushered in a new age of music in which "content creates its own form."

BUT WHAT DOES IT *REALLY* MEAN?

So it may come as a disquieting (or perhaps an amusing) surprise to learn that the music was mostly conceived in an altogether different poetic context, and thus preexisted the content that supposedly created it. The American Liszt scholar Andrew Bonner has found documentation to confirm the suspicion of earlier writers that what we now know as the symphonic poem *Les préludes* was originally conceived as the overture to *Les quatre élémens* ("The four elements"), a group of four choruses that Liszt wrote in 1844 to words by a minor French poet named Joseph Autran (1813–77), and was largely based on themes drawn from the choruses. It is possible that some retouching — adding a harp part, strengthening a bit of the thematic transformation and making it more obvious — followed the decision to ascribe the content to Lamartine, but the music only follows that content in the most general way, and the program's all-important motivating Question nowhere occurs in Lamartine's poem.

Given the exalted claims that were being made on his behalf, and the contentious critical climate surrounding his work, Liszt was understandably embarrassed, as Bonner notes, "that the program had not in this case determined the music,"[18] and took steps (including the destruction of the overture's original title page) to suppress the composition's early history. These circumstances have magnified the glee with which the record has been set straight, and inspired the claim (by Emil Haraszti, the first to suspect the truth) that the corrected record invalidated the claims of the Zukunftists.

But does it really? The claim was never made, after all, that the music explicitly paraphrased the poetic content, only that it paralleled the content and conveyed its emotional impact to the listener. The means of embodiment and conveyance was and remains symbolic, hence conventional, no matter what the content. The content, therefore, can be viewed as a particular interpretation of the music, just as any symbolic representation has to be interpreted (even one consisting of words, such as an allegory or a parable). The association of the music with the choruses of *Les quatre élémens* was one such interpretation; the ex post facto association with Lamartine was another, just as plausible or appropriate, but no more demonstrably "true." In either case — that is, in both cases equally — the representational tasks that the music had to accomplish conditioned not only its thematic content but its form as well. Take away the symbolic dimension, in either case, and the form loses a significant part of its motivation. This or that program may be attached or discarded; but a program is self-evidently required to account for the sui generis form of the music, its highly characterized and contrasted thematic content (drawing on such recognizable generic types or *topoi* as the stormy, the pastoral, and the military), and its multitude of carefully worked-out motivic relations that subsumes contrast within an overarching narrative unity. The music of *Les préludes* all by itself would likely impress a naive listener (that is, a listener without any preconceptions) the way an obviously allegorical painting might strike a naive viewer. Both might be greatly pleased and moved by the sheer sonorous or visual display; yet both might also be aware that there is a dimension of meaning to which they at the moment lack access.

It comes down, then, to a choice of allegories. Liszt proposed the later one, via Lamartine, as part of a broad agenda to which he and Brendel and the rest of the New German School attached enormous esthetic, historical, and political importance; hence his urgent insistence on only the second associative reading of the music and his deliberate suppression of the first. Yet neither his insistence on the one program, nor Haraszti's insistence on the other as the true meaning of the music, can be supported simply by reading the music. A third program, if advanced authoritatively in the absence of other alternatives, might be just as convincing, hence just as "true." This relativism need trouble us only if we resist the notion that associative meanings of all kinds, however compelling and however necessary, are virtually by definition conventional, hence artificial. And we will be troubled in this way only if we have never given thought to the way in which even the sounds of spoken language acquire their meaning.

These interpretive matters become urgent in proportion to the urgency of the attendant political stakes. In the 1850s and 1860s, the interpretation and evaluation of Liszt's symphonic allegories were tied to the issue of music's continuing need to evolve in the direction that a self-selected vanguard of German composers had pointed out for it, and became furiously contentious. At the same time, as we shall see a couple of chapters hence, Italian operas were being subjected to similar interpretive contests between those who read them as revolutionary allegories and those who preferred to take their plots at face value. In the twentieth century, similar controversies have swirled around the artworks created in the great European totalitarian states, some reading them as allegories of political dissidence, others as allegories of political submission, still others as abstract or transcendent artistic utterances without political association, and their creators maintaining a studied silence.

In all cases these clashing interpretations were (and are often still) advanced in a categorical fashion that can be only supported ideologically (that is, on the basis of belief), never tested empirically (that is, on the basis of observation). But in no case can the necessity for interpretation be seriously questioned. The basic esthetic "fact" that the music embodied and represented a "poetic" content, and did so both in its thematic matter and in its form, is accepted by all of the contending parties, although in all cases some felt that the music was thereby enhanced, others that it was thereby diminished.

These are among the issues first raised by the New German School that have never gone away, and never will. Another cursed question is the matter of who gets to decide which reading is correct, a question that abides whether or not the composer is among the interpreters. It would be an excellent exercise to imagine historical conditions other than the one affecting the interpretation of *Les préludes* (namely the discovery of suppressed documents) under which a composer's own interpretation, if offered at all, might be doubted or impugned or even rejected; and another excellent exercise would be to imagine under just what circumstances the allegorical interpretation of a work of instrumental music becomes desirable and even necessary, so that even without the authority of a program the listener will impose one.

Yet even at their freest and most poetically determined, the symphonic poems of Liszt and his many imitators were still governed by a general approach to coherent form inherited directly from the earlier symphonic (or sonata) literature that the New German School sought, or claimed, to have supplanted. At the global level, the level of overall shape rather than the moment-by-moment unfolding, traces of the standard inherited form — that of the lyricalized or Schubertian sonata — can be most clearly observed.

In *Les préludes*, for example, the standard "there and back" construction that had controlled musical discourse at least since the time of the old dance suite continues to impress its general shape on the sequence of programmatically derived events. The expanded reprise of the introductory climax (*andante maestoso* at m. 35) to form the coda (mm. 405–419) imposes a traditional thematic and tonal symmetry on the whole structure. Furthermore, the relationship between the introductory section (the "invocation of the Question," mm. 1–66) and the first episode (Love, mm. 67–108) is cast very much in the manner of a Schubertian sonata exposition, with a dynamic first theme and a languidly lyrical and dilatory second theme in the key of the mediant.

Then again, it cannot be a mere coincidence that the main Love theme reappears unexpectedly (and, for that matter, without specific programmatic motivation) in the pastoral episode, or that the transition to the martial episode should feature the same theme in C major, the original tonic. That is the effective recapitulation, and it begins, just as Chopin's recapitulations so often did, with the lyrical theme, saving the more commanding main theme for coda-duty. In between, the stormy episode, with its extremes of tonal indeterminacy, bears unmistakable earmarks of the traditional development.

So Liszt's Symphonic Poems, like Chopin's Ballades, represented not a break with previous practice but rather the adaptation of earlier practices to new technical means and new expressive aims. If Chopin's Ballades were sonatas later on, then Liszt's Symphonic Poems were symphonies later on. As the music theorist Richard Kaplan put it in accounting for this phenomenon, so long as "three fundamental aspects of sonata organization" are observed, historical continuity is maintained. These fundamental aspects, in his pithy description, are "a tonal dichotomy which eventually is resolved, a concurrent thematic duality, and a return or recapitulation."[19] We shall see very little large-scale instrumental music from the nineteenth century, no matter how progressive the composer, that does not meet these basic, inherited criteria of coherence.

THE NEW MADRIGALISM

There was another way in which the new emphasis on poetic or literary content affected New German musical style, and it proved ultimately the more subversive one. In curious fashion it paralleled a much earlier striving for the "unity of the poetic and the musical," when in the late sixteenth century the composers of those sophisticated Italian part-songs known as madrigals became carried away with the project of representing strong emotion in their music and infused it with a degree of chromaticism without precedent, and without equal until precisely the moment we are now investigating, when a similar impulse (though now more strongly motivated by philosophical than by emotional content) turned Liszt into the nineteenth century's most zealous harmonic experimenter.

His experiments revolved in oddly systematic fashion around two harmonies with longstanding but limited diatonic application: the diminished-seventh chord and the augmented triad. In ordinary diatonic usage both of these chords often function as altered and intensified dominants. The diminished-seventh chord, built on the leading tone, adds an extra tendency-tone demanding resolution to the fifth degree of the tonic. The augmented triad on the fifth degree adds an extra tendency-tone demanding resolution to the third degree of the tonic. In any case, the altered pitch in an augmented triad is traditionally prepared and resolved as a chromatic passing tone. By treating other tones in these chords as tendency-tones, whether leading tones or passing tones, avenues of quick enharmonic modulation can be opened up. This sort of harmonic punning can be found as early as C. P. E. Bach, and had been a common device since Beethoven (Ex. 40-3).

EX. 40-3A   Normal resolutions of diminished-seventh and augmented triads

Following on these precedents, but particularly on Schubert's usages, Liszt emancipated the diminished seventh and augmented harmonies from their diatonic contexts in two ways. First, he exploited the equidistance of the tones in these rootless harmonies to create circles of major and minor thirds, the former based on the tones of the augmented triad, the latter on those of the diminished-seventh chord. For these, as we have already seen, there were especially salient precedents in Schubert. For the circle of major thirds the precedents were explicit, based on sequences of flat submediants (revisit Ex. 34-11 from Schubert's Mass in E- flat). For the circle of minor thirds the

EX. 40-3B   Ludwig van Beethoven, "Pathétique" Sonata, I, "Tempo I"

EX. 40-3C   Franz Schubert, Quintet in C, I, mm. 11–24

Schubertian precedents were subtler, implicit in the part-writing rather than categorically expressed as harmonic progressions, as in the passage from the G-major Quartet cited in Ex. 34-14.

In his so-called "Mountain Symphony"—actually the Symphonic Poem No. 1 (first sketched in 1847), titled *Ce qu'on entend sur la montagne* ("What one hears atop the mountain") after a poem by Victor Hugo—Liszt contrived an explicit descending circle of minor thirds to match Schubert's major thirds in Ex. 34-11. The keys are even the same, which suggests that the Schubert passage may have been not just a precedent but an actual model. And just as Schubert had connected the bass notes of his circle with passing tones to produce a descending whole-tone scale, so Liszt connected his bass notes to produce a descending tone-semitone or octatonic scale, perhaps the first one ever to be explicitly set out in a single voice (Ex. 40-4).

EX. 40-4   Franz Liszt, Symphonic Poem no. 1, *Ce qu'on entend sur la montagne*

The octatonic scale may thus be counted Liszt's innovation, and it was taken up enthusiastically by many later composers, especially in Russia. The whole-tone scale, by contrast, was already a known quantity by the time Liszt came upon the scene, having been previously adapted from Schubert's original usage by a number

FIG. 40-6   The sorcerer Chernomor in Glinka's *Ruslan and Lyudmila*, costume sketch by A. Roller for the first production (St. Petersburg, 1842).

of composers, again with Russians (who used it to conjure up fantastic or magical effects) in the lead. The original Russian precedent had been set by Glinka, to represent the evil sorcerer Chernomor in his "magic opera" *Ruslan and Lyudmila* (1842). It is quoted in Ex. 40-5 from the popular overture to the opera, where its connection to the circle of major thirds is evident.

Elsewhere in the opera Glinka uses it as an unharmonized scale. When sounded without harmonic support, its construction out of intervals of equal size inhibits any sense of degree-identification, which in turn prevents any sense of functional hierarchy among the pitches. This is just a fancy way of saying that a whole-tone scale is not centered unequivocally on a tonic, but putting it in terms of an abolition of

EX. 40-5 Glinka, Overture to *Ruslan and Lyudmila*

hierarchy casts it in a Hegelian emancipatory light that heightened its appeal to the New Germans as well as the New Russians.

Liszt knew the scale not only from Schubert and Glinka, but also from the overture to an opera called *Mazeppa* by an altogether obscure Russian composer, a noble dilettante named Boris Scheel (1829–1901), who composed under the pen name of Baron Vietinghoff. A friend had sent the overture to Liszt as a sort of joke, since Liszt himself had based a symphonic poem on the legend of Mazeppa, a Ukrainian chieftain whose wild nocturnal ride, tied to the back of a runaway stallion by the enraged husband of his paramour, had been immortalized in another poem by Victor Hugo.

Liszt responded in kind with a humorous letter in which he parodied the tendency of which he himself was the titular figurehead. Although couched in ironic exaggeration, the letter accurately expresses the sense of historical necessity that drove Liszt and his party in their preoccupation with innovation.

When you have the opportunity, will you give my best compliments to the author, and give him also the little scale of chords that I add? It is nothing but a very simple development of the scale, terrifying to all whose long ears protrude
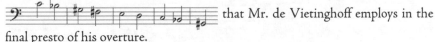 that Mr. de Vietinghoff employs in the final presto of his overture.

[Carl] Tausig [1841–71, a Polish disciple of Liszt] makes pretty fair use of it in his [impromptu for piano] *Das Geisterschiff* ("The Ship of Ghosts"); and in the classes of the Conservatory, where the high art of the mad dog virtuoso is duly taught, the existing elementary exercises of the piano methods
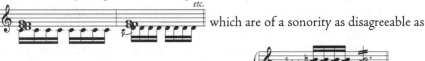 which are of a sonority as disagreeable as

it is incomplete, ought to be replaced by this one which will thus form the unique basis of the method of harmony—all the other chords, in use or not, being merely arbitrary curtailments of it.

In fact it will soon be necessary to complete the system by the admission of quarter and half-quarter tones until something better turns up!

Behold the abyss of progress into which the abominable Musicians of the Future are hurling us! Take care that you do not let yourself be contaminated by this pest of Art![20]

As we shall see in later chapters, every one of the harmonic absurdities Liszt strains to imagine—twelve-note universal harmonies (sometimes expressed, as here, as the superimposition of two whole-tone scales), quarter- and eighth-tones, and all the rest—would eventually be quite seriously advanced in the same spirit as Liszt was advancing his own harmonic novelties: to wit, in the name of progressive emancipation.

Liszt's own use of the whole-tone scale reached a blazing climax, after he had returned to composing for the piano, in *Sursum corda* ("Lift up your hearts," 1867), the last number in the long cycle *Années de pèlerinage* ("Years of pilgrimage"). Although clearly the result of the interpolation of passing tones into a French-sixth chord on F♯ ("V of V" in the key of E major), the effect is one of a harmonic blur preceding the massive return of the main theme in the main key (Ex. 40-6).

EX. 40-6   Franz Liszt, climax of *Sursum corda* (last number in *Années de pèlerinage*)

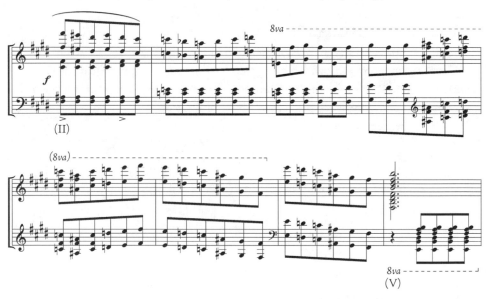

As for the diminished seventh, perhaps the most dramatic use to which Liszt ever put it is found in his single-movement Sonata in B minor for piano (1853), a work dedicated to Schumann as if in return for the dedication of the latter's *Phantasie*, and cast along the same lines as Liszt's own concertos but, at half an hour's duration, grander by far. If provided with a program it would have been a virtual symphonic poem for the keyboard; that Liszt preferred to give it a neutral designation shows him still willing to make generic distinctions that some of his followers would abandon.

Ex. 40-7a shows the first page of the Sonata, containing three themes (or better, motives) that will be subjected to extensive "transformation" over its course. The first is the descending introductory scale marked *lento assai*. Its two occurrences already show the nature of the transformations that lie ahead: the former, beginning as if in the natural minor, is given a Phrygian inflection at the end; the latter, with its two augmented seconds, is cast in what Liszt called the "Gypsy" scale, associated in his mind with his native Hungary. (Naturally it is most commonly found in his famous "Hungarian Rhapsodies" for piano.) The two motives at *allegro energico* together make up what might ordinarily be called the Sonata's first theme, except that from the very beginning they are varied, developed, and transformed quite independently. The former is the one fashioned so strikingly (and from a tonal point of view, so indeterminately) out of appoggiatura-heavy diminished seventh arpeggios. Ex. 40-7b, showing a few of its transformations, gives a heady foretaste of the Sonata's expressive behavior. The resolution of chromatic arpeggios into diatonic ones sets up the basic harmonic polarity that in this Sonata largely preempts the usual tonal dichotomy.

EX. 40-7A   Franz Liszt, Sonata in B minor, mm. 1–17

EX. 40-7B   Franz Liszt, Sonata in B minor, transformations of diminished-seventh motive (mm. 18 – 22, 55 – 60, 125 – 34, 385 – 88)

EX. 40-7B   (continued)

Most radical of all are the passages in which Liszt allows diminished sevenths and augmented triads to succeed one another in parallel motion (that is, as consonances), usually by semitones along a chromatic scale, thus invoking another uniform-interval cycle devoid of any built-in degree hierarchy, so that traditional harmonic functions are held in abeyance. The Storm section of *Les préludes* contains a famous instance using the diminished-seventh chord. Even more celebrated is the theme heard at the very outset of Liszt's monumental trilogy of symphonic poems known as the *Faust-Symphonie* (1857), in which each movement purports to describe one of Goethe's characters (Faust, Gretchen, and Mephistopheles in that order).

The theme seems to mirror the title character's fateful quest of occult knowledge (Ex. 40-8a). Following the initial A♭, it consists of four augmented triads arpeggiated in a descending semitonal sequence that exhausts all the pitches of the chromatic scale. Again, the use of chords of uniform intervallic structure, deployed along a scale that is similarly uniform, prevents any tone (even the first one) from emerging as a

EX. 40-8A   Franz Liszt, *Faust-Symphonie*, opening

functional center and creates an appropriate sense of aimless meandering. Perhaps even more remarkable is the similarly indeterminate harmonic progression that follows, in which the minor triad on the second beat of measure 5, owing to its harmonic environment, the voice-leading, and the rhythmic placement, clearly seems to resolve as a pseudo-suspension to yet another augmented triad, which the ear has by now been conditioned to accept as a normative — hence, a stable — harmony.

The first definite cadence — to a manifestly Beethovenian C minor — comes with the change in tempo from the introductory *lento assai* to the main body of the movement, *allegro agitato ed appassionato*. Passionate agitation is evoked by piling on a heap of functional dissonances. The main theme (Ex. 40-8b) starts right off on an appoggiatura to a diminished seventh chord. Like the augmented triad in the introduction, the chord thus introduced acquires a measure of stability by being made the object of a resolution. When the soprano resolution of E♭ to D arrives on the following downbeat, the bass shifts to another E♭, rendering the entire chord above it a dissonant suspension.

The key-defining tonic in root position does not appear in Example 40-8b until the middle of the fourth measure. On the way to it three more dissonant suspensions or appoggiaturas in the soprano intervene: F♯ resolving to F-natural as the third of the half-diminished ii₇ on the third downbeat, immediately followed by a dramatic skip of a seventh — itself a dissonance — to a dissonant E♭ that resolves as an appoggiatura to D, the chordal root. Such dissonant leaps to dissonant notes, a derivation from the "sighing" figuration common in operatic melodies, would remain a permanent, prominent, and very distinctive emotional signifier in the music of the Zukunftists and their heirs.

EX. 40-8B Franz Liszt, *Faust-Symphonie*, Allegro agitato ed appassionato (mm. 71–74)

Following the habit we have already observed in *Les préludes*, Liszt casts the exposition of the Faust movement over a tonal dichotomy involving a third rather than a fifth. This, too, was a permanent acquisition, derived from Schubert (though with roots in late Beethoven), and a step toward the general replacement of the circle of fifths by circles of thirds as the prime navigational compass for tonal plans. Needless to say, the third in this case is major rather than minor, which would have merely reproduced the normal or classical harmonic trajectory of a minor-mode exposition, requiring no new key signature. Instead of the customary E♭, the triumphant closing theme (*grandioso*, m. 225) comes in an untrammeled diatonic blaze of E major (Ex. 40-8c). The extra half step, seemingly so near at hand, is in fact equivalent to seven progressions along the circle of fifths. The melding of the proximate and the remote palpably bends one's sense of musical space.

EX. 40-8C   Franz Liszt, *Faust-Symphonie*, Grandioso (mm. 223–28)

The emergence of diatonic simplicity out of chromatic complication is another way of signaling resolution, of course—and in its likeness to a synthesis an especially Hegelian one (as well as an increasingly necessary one as tonal trajectories became cluttered with thirds and half steps). And yet, almost needless to say, Ex. 40-8c is eventually recapitulated in C major, thus fulfilling the Beethovenian Struggle-and-Victory scenario and betokening the composer's place in the legitimate dynastic succession.

But given the suggestion, tacit but implicit in the Hegelian scenario, that the virtually deified Beethoven was being not merely emulated but in effect surpassed, the charge of virtual blasphemy had to be met and deflected. Scarcely any discussion of Liszt's achievement could avoid an accusatory or a defensive tone, depending on the attitude of the writer. Here is how one defender, a Russian, handled the problem:

> If anyone should take it into his head to dampen my rapture at Liszt's music, for example, with this question: "If Liszt writes an orchestral fantasia of unheard-of perfection, does that mean that, in your opinion, Liszt as a symphonist is better and higher than Beethoven?"—I would answer thus: "Our [Russian painter, Alexander] Ivanov, naturally, has not put Raphael or Titian or Rubens in the shade, yet people in the know have every right to say about a picture by Ivanov that *in its own way* it is a miracle of art and an unprecedented miracle at that.[21]

But there was a problem that the theory failed to address: with closed circles of thirds and long stretches of tonally indeterminate chromatic writing competing with the diatonic fifth relations that had long driven tonal music to its climaxes, it was increasingly difficult to project tonal drama with a force commensurate with the startling new rhetoric of passionate local dissonance and orchestral splendor. In particular, it was difficult to plot a distinctive FOP (harmonic far-out point) that traditionally gave symphonic forms their overall there-and-back structure.

All became fantasia, beginning (and often ending) in medias res, which certainly accorded with the stated aims of the music of the future, but which nevertheless led to a certain arbitrary flattening of the tonal trajectory that could make the music seem paradoxically uneventful and disjointed. What was delightful when experienced within the confines of a small work like a Chopin prelude — or in Liszt's own exquisite *Bagatelle ohne Tonart* ("Bagatelle in no key"), which appeared a little ahead of schedule in the previous chapter (Ex. 39-10) — could seem bewildering and (many thought) even boring when stretched out at full symphonic length.

Another paradox was the sameness, the apparent uniformity, that often seemed to be the result of sui generis forms that followed content. This unexpected outcome may have been due to psychological principles that experiments in the realm of cognitive science have only recently confirmed: small differences with respect to a known model — tweaking, as it is sometimes called — often register more tellingly than do global (overall) differences of an apparently arbitrary character. Freedom can thus come at the price of significance. Along with constraint, the jettisoning of conventions could sacrifice effective communication.

ART AND TRUTH

Difficulties like these, however real, were nevertheless tolerable within a value system that equated innovation with liberation, and that took as its objective the freeing of the artwork and its producers from dependence on social norms defined by

FIG. 40-7   Alexander Nikolayevich Serov, autographed photo.

consumers. Boring or annoying their contemporaries was not only considered by committed Zukunftists a fair price to pay, it was often taken in itself to be a mark of progress. Casting the New German or neo-Hegelian philosophy of art in terms borrowed from economics, moreover, was very much the fashion at the time, vividly illustrating the way in which the innovatory spirit in the arts reflected other modes of nineteenth-century Utopian thought. At a time of widespread Utopian theorizing, it was considered the very opposite of a defect to be ahead of one's time, in communion not with one's contemporaries but with one's progeny. The myth of the artist-prophet, to which Beethoven was at once assimilated, had its birth in these theories. It still lives.

A striking specimen of these ideological commitments was an article by Alexander Serov (1820 – 71), the most enthusiastic

Russian follower of the New German School (and author of the hypothetical question and answer quoted above). It appeared in Brendel's *Neue Zeitschrift für Musik* in 1857 in the guise of a review of *Beethoven, ses critiques et ses glossateurs* ("Beethoven, his critics and his explicators"), a book by the conservative critic and Mozart biographer Alexander Ulybyshev (1794–1858). It was already typical that a debate about contemporary musical values should have taken place behind a Beethovenian screen. Beethoven's authority, acknowledged by all sides, was the most desirable of trophies. All factions in the esthetic wars of the later nineteenth century claimed him as their founder, none more zealously than the New German School. And the debate between Ulybyshev (writing in French) and Serov (writing in German) was an indication of the role that Russians were lately playing on the main stage of European musical art.

Serov's article, published as "Ulibischeff gegen Beethoven" (Ulybyshev vs. Beethoven), came to a climax with the dogmatic assertion of two "laws" that between them summed up with breathtaking succinctness practically the whole Zukunftist position:

1. Wenn eine Theorie nicht mit der Praxis eines Weltgenies stimmt, da wird sie nie bestehen, denn die Kunst lebt ihr Leben nicht in Büchern, sondern im Kunstwerk. (If theory [that is, classroom music theory] does not accord with the practice of a world-genius, then it must always give way, for art lives its life not in books but in artworks.)
2. Das Criterium des musikalischen Gesetzes liegt nicht in den Ohren des Consumenten, es liegt in der Kunstidee des Producenten. (The basis of musical law lies not in the ear of the consumer but in the artistic inspiration [literally, the art-idea] of the producer.)[22]

Liszt himself pronounced a benediction on these precepts in a *Neue Zeitschrift* article of his own, "Ulibischeff und Seroff. Kritik der Kritik" ("Ulybyshev and Serov: A Critique Critiqued"). They were received with fury back home in Russia, where notions of social utility hung on with unusual tenacity in art criticism, partly because both the autocratic Tsarist regime and its revolutionary foes wanted to enlist the arts in their political struggles. But Serov and Liszt were also engaged in a political struggle. The frankly Hegelian concept of the *Weltgenie*, the world-genius — on the one hand free to abrogate the laws of ordinary mortals and, on the other, charged with the making of new and ever more binding laws — was nothing if not a site of political power.

Vladimir Stasov (1824–1906), another Russian critic and Serov's nemesis, saw in it a ploy for the establishment of a "despotism of artists,"[23] free to abuse their contemporaries in pursuit of vainglorious goals that violated the proper boundaries of art. Pyotr Ilyich Chaikovsky (1840–93), the most eminent and abundant Russian composer of the later nineteenth century, complained that "formerly, music strove to delight people — now they are tormented and exhausted."[24] The Nietzschian concept of the Übermensch, the superman who existed on a plane beyond good and evil, a figure modeled originally on the artist-prophet envisioned by the Zukunftists, was already strongly prefigured.

The role of the artist as a prophet and a lawgiver was a religious and political extension of the idea of the artist as philosopher, the idea that motivated the New

German School and opened up a new era to add to Brendel's historical categories. Where Brendel had seen the Age of Beauty succeed the Age of the Sublime, his contemporaries, in large part at his enthusiastic instigation, now proclaimed the Age of Truth. And where an earlier generation of Romantics could proclaim with Keats that "'Beauty is truth, truth beauty,' — that is all/Ye know on earth, and all ye need to know" ("Ode on a Grecian Urn," stanza 5), the New Germans, their disciples, and even some who thought of themselves as their enemies, turned savagely on beauty as on some sort of loathsome falsehood.

Reacting a decade later than Serov (but no less angrily) against Mozart's panegyrists, whom he likewise saw as thwarting the historical tide, Friedrich Nietzsche lambasted the self-styled guardians of the classics. "Let us but observe these patrons of art at close range, as they really are, indefatigably crying 'Beauty! beauty!'" the philosopher taunted. "Do they really bear the stamp of nature's darling children who are fostered and nourished at the breast of the beautiful, or are they not rather seeking a mendacious cloak for their own coarseness, an aesthetical pretext for their own insensitivity?"[25] In a phrase that acquired a chilling resonance in the twentieth century, Nietzsche condemned the devotees of beauty as the standard-bearers of an *entartete Kunst*, a degenerate art.

In a similar vein but to a different purpose, the Russian composer Modest Musorgsky (1839–81) inveighed against the hypocritical "religion of absolute beauty,"[26] a devotion that, he believed, masked an altogether worldly "aim of winning a name and some public acclaim." In his view, "the artistic representation of beauty alone is coarse childishness — art in its infancy." Instead, the "thinking artist of the present day" must aim higher, or rather deeper: "The subtlest aspects of human nature and of humanity as a whole, the persistent exploration of these uncharted regions and their conquest — *that* is the true mission of an artist."[27] There are many truths, of course. The New Germans, Serov and Nietzsche were after metaphysical truth, an ideal truth not of this world. They followed directly in the footsteps of German romantics like E. T. A. Hoffman, and shared his veneration of Beethoven as the *Quelle der wahren Glaube*, the "source of the true faith." Their favored medium was instrumental music, a language of ineffable expression. Their tendency culminated in what the German musicologist Rudolf Stephan dubbed *Weltanschauungsmusik* — roughly, "music expressive of a philosophy of life," a music of grandiose conceptions and gigantic forms, always impressive but rarely pleasant.

Musorgsky and many of his non-German contemporaries were after experiential truth, a realistic truth very much of this world. They followed in the footsteps of Berlioz, and shared his veneration of Beethoven (the composer of *Fidelio*) as the voice of oppressed humanity. Their favored medium was opera. Their work culminated in naturalism and verismo, attempts (often didactic) to show the world and its inhabitants as they really are, warts and all, often as a spur to social change.

Against both were the keepers of the old flame, who mounted a considerable counteroffensive against what they deemed the anti-artistic bluster of metaphysicians and realists alike. Chaikovsky derided the German music of his day in newspaper articles and letters, protesting its "detestable pretensions to profundity, strength, and power." In his view it was "all seriousness and nobility of purpose, but the chief thing—*beauty*—is missing."[28] For what he considered his own countryman Musorgsky's studied ugliness he had, if anything, even greater contempt: "there is something low about him, something base," he admonished; "he passes the bounds of the possible."[29]

ART FOR ART'S SAKE

As all these Russian quotes suggest, much of the opposition to the New German School came from outside the German-speaking lands, many foreign musicians suspecting nationalistic designs behind the School's universalist pretensions. And yet the opposition's most famous single salvo came from the Austrian critic and music historian Eduard Hanslick (1825–1904), who in 1854 authored a tract called "On the Musically Beautiful" (*Vom musikalisch-Schönen*) that went through many editions (ten within the author's lifetime) and is still in print. It is difficult today to appreciate the polemical force of the title; but at the time, for a German critic to insist on beauty looked to many like virtual treason.

Unsurprisingly, Hanslick located the beautiful in music not in its freight of meaning, but in its sheer patterning ("arabesques") of sound. The object of derisive caricature from the beginning, his views are often misunderstood. Contrary to what his critics have alleged, he did not deny the emotional effects of music, nor did he deny its power to embody and convey poetic subject matter. What he did deny was the essentially musical nature of such a task (that is, its relevance to the true aims and tasks of music as an art), and hence the ultimate musical value of those effects and that embodiment.

"The Representation of Feeling," reads the title of the crucial second chapter, "Is Not the Content of Music." Needless to say, everything hinges on how the word "content" is defined, and on whether it is to be distinguished from "form" (another protean concept). The New German position cast feeling and form in opposition; the Hanslickian stance melded them. Hanslick's very definition of musical content (which became a famous and notoriously untranslatable slogan) was *Tönend bewegte Form*—something like "form put in motion by sound" or "sounding form in motion."

Although his antagonists tried to brand him a reactionary, and while he himself (like any contender in a war of ideas) tried to portray his ideas as age-old verities, Hanslick's ideas were in fact new. By asserting that there were timeless musical values that took precedence over the *Kunstidee des Producenten* and the *Ohren des Consumenten* alike, Hanslick and his followers introduced a new faction to what was fast becoming a struggle over the right to inherit and define the elite literate tradition of European music. To the extreme romantic view that privileged the producer, and the old aristocratic view that privileged the consumer, was now added a "Classical" or classicizing view that privileged Art itself and its so-called inviolable laws over the designs or wishes of its ephemeral practitioners and patrons. The real privilege, of course, was enjoyed by whoever could successfully claim the right to assert the law. These were the true stakes of the game. It is arguable that Hanslick, one of whose biographers proclaimed him the "Dalai Lama of music," emerged the big winner.

And that is because more than any other nineteenth-century academic, Hanslick was a forerunner of today's musicology. His side, in other words, was the one that got to tell the story of nineteenth-century music in the twentieth century. Indeed, a more revealing and less tendentious name for his tendency would be *academic* rather than "classical," since the academy has been its main home and breeding ground. It is the very opposite of an accident that Hanslick, its chief early formulator, was hired two years after the publication of his famous treatise by the University of Vienna as an adjunct lecturer, later as a full-time professor.

He spent forty years at the university, lecturing on what we would now call music appreciation. He was the first musician ever to occupy a German university chair; hence he was the first academic musicologist in the modern sense of the word. His formalist esthetic is the one that has underwritten the concept of classical music ever since his time. His neo-Kantian "art for art's sake" views have been the (sometimes tacit) mainstay not only of music appreciation but of practically all university music study until at least the middle of the twentieth century.

By presuming to draw a hard and fast distinction between what was "musical" and what was not in the work of his contemporaries; by insisting that the musical must be identified with the beautiful (rather than the spiritual or the expressive or the sublime or the true); and by so effectively propagating his views in the teeth of formidable opposition, Hanslick set the terms of an unsettleable (perhaps misconceived) debate that continues into our own time. Its terms would probably have been altogether unintelligible to musicians of the early nineteenth century and before; so in this sense, too, the middle of the nineteenth century marks the beginning of the musical world we have inherited and inhabit today.

Slavs as Subjects and Citizens

SMETANA, GLINKA, AND BALAKIREV

PROGRESSIVE VS. POPULAR

If the New German School did not lack opponents at home, neither did its influence stop at the border. One of its most enthusiastic disciples was Bedřich Smetana (1824–84), who is now chiefly remembered (to quote the *New Grove Dictionary of Music and Musicians*) as "the first major nationalist composer of Bohemia" (or, in today's vocabulary, the Czech lands). How could a Czech nationalist also be a "New German"? There are some paradoxes to sort out.

The first is best savored through a letter Smetana wrote to his friend and former pupil Ludevit Prochazka, the conductor of a men's singing society (Männerchor) in Prague, on 11 March 1860, shortly after his thirty-sixth birthday:

> First of all I must ask you to excuse all my mistakes, both in spelling and grammar, of which you will certainly find plenty in this letter, for up to the present day I have not had the good fortune to be able to perfect myself in our mother tongue. Educated from my youth in German, both at school and in society, I took no care, while still a student, to learn anything but what I was forced to learn, and later divine music monopolized all my energy and my time so that to my shame, I must now confess that I cannot express myself adequately or write correctly in Czech.[1]

Indeed Smetana, the son of a prosperous brewer who serviced the local gentry (including Count Waldstein, one of Beethoven's patrons), was brought up to call himself Friedrich rather than Bedřich, and to aspire to a cosmopolitan career like any urban, educated, middle-class child of a loyal Bohemian subject of the kaiser (Austrian emperor). Indeed, his place of birth (Bohemia), his native language (German), and his early cultural orientation were all the same as Hanslick's, although (as his surname, which means sour cream in Czech, suggests) his ethnicity was different. At first that did not matter.

So in one important sense he did not come from beyond the borders of the German lands at all, since those borders (as drawn politically) extended far beyond the German-speaking nucleus. The fact that Smetana ultimately came to identify with his Slavic ethnicity, rather than with his original native language, his Teutonic cultural milieu, or his lifelong political allegiances, encapsulates more vividly than any other single musical-historical fact the metamorphosis that the idea of nation underwent over the course of the nineteenth century.

The divine music that claimed Smetana's time and energy from his early years was the music of German cultivated society — simply music to a German-speaking bourgeois

FIG. 41-1   Bedřich Smetana.

in Bohemia or anywhere else—rather than the music of the Czech countryside, which like the Czech language was regarded as the property of illiterate peasants, baggage that could only keep one down on the farm. He never did learn to speak the language flawlessly, nor did he ever get to know much authentic Czech folk music. (Instead, he eventually became quite good at manufacturing his own.) A piano prodigy, Smetana had a life-shattering experience in 1840, when at the age of sixteen he heard Liszt play in Prague. Against the wishes of his father, who refused to support him, Smetana renounced higher education in favor of the life of a professional musician. For three years he worked as live-in piano teacher to the children of a German nobleman in Prague, meanwhile taking lessons in harmony and counterpoint from the best local teacher, a blind pianist and composer named Josef Proksch who had studied in Berlin and set up a private conservatory in his home. Smetana looked forward to becoming "a Liszt in technique and a Mozart in composition."[2]

But when the children of the house he lived in grew up and left, their piano teacher had to face reality, which for him meant the prospect of desperate poverty. Early in 1848, not knowing where else to turn, Smetana impulsively sent Liszt, who knew his teacher, the manuscript of his *Six morceaux caractéristiques* (that is, *Charakterstücke*) for piano, op. 1. The pieces in this set, all individually titled in German despite the French title page, were far from the first he had written; but they were the first (or so Smetana thought) that reflected a contemporary composerly outlook worthy of Liszt's approval, since all six pieces were unified by an idée fixe à la Berlioz.

Together with the music went three requests: first, for permission to dedicate the pieces to Liszt; second, for Liszt's assistance in getting them published; and third, for a loan of money to help Smetana set up a music school of his own like Proksch's.[3] Liszt ignored the last request, but he lavishly praised the *Morceaux caractéristiques* by return mail and placed them with a publisher, winning Smetana's eternal gratitude. They spent three years in press, however, during which time Smetana took the risk of opening the music school anyway—he called it the Lehr-Institut im Pianoforte-Spiele (Teaching Institute for Piano Playing)—in August 1848. He lived practically hand to mouth, teaching at the institute and giving occasional concerts, for the next eight years.

The year 1848 was as politically eventful in Bohemia as elsewhere, and Smetana's early compositions reflected its turbulence. He wrote his share of patriotic marches and anthems during the Prague revolt in June, but a far less ephemeral token of his political allegiances were the works inspired not by the revolt itself but by the consequent abdication of the Austrian Emperor Ferdinand in favor of his eighteen-year-old nephew Franz Joseph, who would reign gloriously for almost seventy years, dying at the age of eighty-six in the midst of the First World War, thus mercifully spared his empire's defeat and dissolution.

Like most patriotic Bohemians of his social background, Smetana greeted Franz Joseph's accession with joy; for what they really wanted was not the full independence of their ethnic homeland (whose language they did not speak) but only its legislative and fiscal autonomy within a federalized empire. (Among Austrian territories, only Hungary would achieve this status, and not until 1867.) Franz Joseph was perceived as favoring this idea, which he was expected to implement by accepting the historic Bohemian throne, vacant since 1620.

In anticipation of this great event Smetana wrote his earliest orchestral works: a very old-fashioned *Jubel-Ouvertüre* ("Festive overture") in D major, op. 4; and a big, brassy, cumbersomely titled *Triumph-Symphonie mit Benützung der österreichischer Volkshymne* ("Triumphal Symphony Utilizing the Austrian National Hymn") in E major, op. 6. Even the patriotic marches of 1848 had quoted German songs (including a verse of Haydn's Austrian hymn), and Smetana gave further evidence of his loyalty to the house of Hapsburg by becoming a kind of court pianist to the deposed Emperor Ferdinand, who took up residence beginning in 1849 in the venerable Prague Castle.

Instead of constitutional reform and kingdom status, however, the Czech lands received stern treatment under Alexander Bach, Prince Metternich's successor as chief minister of state, whose repressive and ultimately counterproductive policy of "Centralization and Germanization," enforced by a ruthless secret police, created a stifling political atmosphere during the 1850s and did more to stimulate the growth of Czech cultural nationalism over the next few decades than liberalization could possibly have achieved.

Despite the effort to stamp it out, the use of the Czech language among the educated classes grew; as a result of its spread, and of some significant demographic changes that followed the industrial revolution, Prague was transformed over the second half of the nineteenth century from a German- to a Czech-speaking city. Smetana himself reflected this change in his own linguistic habits, as we have seen; but the more immediate result of political and financial discouragement was his decision, in 1856, to emigrate. The two changes coincided: Smetana's first attempts to communicate with his countrymen in Czech followed his move to Göteborg (Gothenburg), a seventeenth-century university town on the Kattegat strait, Sweden's main seaport and second largest city.

He was an instant success in Göteborg. During his first year he opened another music school which immediately became the most fashionable one in town; he was named the director of the city's leading choral society; and he inaugurated a prestigious series of chamber music concerts at which he regularly appeared as pianist. Perhaps most decisive of all in reshaping Smetana's career, though, was renewed contact with Liszt, whom he visited at Weimar in the summer of 1857. After this visit, Smetana became so committed a disciple that Liszt invited him (along with Serov and a few other favored foreigners) to attend the great 1859 convocation in Leipzig and become a member of the Allgemeiner Deutscher Musikverein.

Smetana became in effect the exemplary New German, in some ways the most advanced of all. As he wrote to Liszt after another year in Göteborg,

> Since I spent those unforgettable September days with you in Weimar . . . I conceived, not just the "notion" (for this I already had), but the *necessity* of the progress of art, as taught by you in so great, so true a manner, and made it my credo. Please regard me as one of the most zealous disciples of our artistic school of thought, one who will champion its sacred truth in word and deed. At present the means at my disposal are, it is true, scant, . . . but as far as my limited means go, I work for the liberation of our art from the chains which bind it, and in which incomprehension, incompetence and egoism have sought to have cast it for ever.[4]

The first fruit of his conversion was, of course, a series of symphonic poems, among the earliest to follow Liszt's example. The first was *Richard III* (1858) after Shakespeare, which had its counterpart in Liszt's *Hamlet*; next came *Wallensteins Lager* ("Wallenstein's camp," 1859) after Schiller, a "battle piece" that had its counterpart in Liszt's *Hunnenschlacht* ("Battle of the Huns"). Although the title character, Albrecht Wenzel Eusebius von Wallenstein (1583–1634), was nominally a Bohemian (the progenitor of the Waldsteins, in fact), he was (like Smetana) a loyal vassal of the Holy Roman Emperor, and actually laid waste to Bohemia during the Thirty Years' War.

Schiller's dramatic trilogy, on which Smetana based his symphonic poem, concerned Wallenstein's defeat by the Swedes and his later treasonable attempt to negotiate a separate peace with them; Smetana's symphonic poem was, in ironic effect, an attempt to reap the approval of his Swedish audience at the expense of Bohemian nationalism. Smetana's third symphonic poem, *Hakon Jarl* (1861), about a mythical Norwegian usurper and the victory of Christianity over paganism in Scandinavia, also catered to the nationalism of his audience rather than expressing his own. The music, however, displays no particular Scandinavian coloration; its themes (both musical and poetic) are universally heroic and religious.

Where Smetana actually went beyond his mentor in his commitment to the aims of the New German School was in *Macbeth* (1859), later retitled *Macbeth a čarodějnice* ("Macbeth and the witches") — a symphonic poem in every sense except medium, for it was composed for piano solo, possibly envisioned as a vehicle for a comeback on the recital stage. Even Liszt, as we have seen, held back from transferring the programmatic method to the keyboard, at least where major works (like the Sonata in B minor) were concerned. But Smetana was determined to take the musico-poetic principle into every instrumental genre.

In this sense Smetana could be fairly described as Europe's most progressive musician as of 1859, and so he remained, one could fairly argue, virtually to the end of his career, when he wrote a programmatic — indeed autobiographical — string quartet (*Z mého zivota*, *From My Life*, 1876) that culminates with fine contempt for beauty in a ghastly high violin harmonic mimicking the onset of the deafness that heralded the composer's eventual deterioration from syphilis. If Smetana is remembered differently, if he is slotted into conventional historiography not as a leading progressive but as a leading nationalist, we shall have to seek the explanation not only in his music, but also in the conventions of historiography.

Even without the additional information given later by retitling it, it would be obvious that Smetana's "piano poem" took its cue from Macbeth's encounters with the witches in Shakespeare's tragedy. The piece is constructed in two parts, of which the first, in G minor, pits chilling Lisztian cadenzas for the witches, all based on heavily (and dissonantly) embellished diminished triads and sevenths, against a triumphant march theme that must surely represent not only Macbeth but also the nature of the witches' prophecies to him. The second part, in the devilishly tritone-related key of C♯ minor, must surely represent the dramatic reversal of the plot, Macbeth's triumphant melody now being disfigured by a whole-tone scale, a device with a considerable history by 1859 (at least among progressive musicians), and one specifically associated with horror in several works (by Glinka, Vietinghoff [Scheel], and Tausig) well known to Lisztian adepts, and to us. The triumph music must now pertain to Macduff.

Like Liszt's *Bagatelle ohne Tonart,* Smetana's *Macbeth* was published only posthumously. That is one of the reasons why despite its astonishingly advanced style it does not figure more prominently in Smetana's historiographical image. The more important reason, of course, has to do with the composer's return to Prague and to a new calling as founder of a national school. What lured him home was no abstract or idealistic commitment but a career opportunity: the announcement in 1861 of a competition for a Czech opera to open a new national theater where Smetana eventually became the music director. After one last season in Göteborg, Smetana came home to stay in June 1862.

Ever since Weber's *Freischütz,* and especially since Glinka's triumph with *A Life for the Tsar,* it was assumed — especially among the Slavic peoples, but also among the other ethnic minorities within the Austrian empire — that the founding of a truly national musical life could be achieved only through an inspiring representation of the nation on the operatic stage, a purpose that could be served only by a "real opera" with big numbers and recitatives, not just a folksy singspiel. Chopin's teacher Józef Elsner was very disappointed at his pupil's failure to become that founder in Poland. The one who eventually did was Stanisław Moniuszko (1819–72), with *Halka,* an opera with a conventional plot about a peasant maiden (but here obviously standing for Poland) who is seduced and abandoned by a heartless feudal lord (just as obviously standing for the powers that had "raped" the motherland in 1795); it was first performed in concert in Vilna (now Vilnius, Lithuania) in the revolutionary year 1848, and was first staged in Warsaw in 1858.

The Hungarian founder was Ferenc Erkel (1810–93), with several historical operas beginning with *Hunyádi László* (1844), about a martyred fifteenth-century patriot, and culminating in *Bánk bán* (1861), which concerned a thirteenth-century revolt against foreign domination. The founder of Southern Slavic (Croatian and Slovenian) opera was Vatroslav Lisinsky (1819–54), with *Ljubav i zloba* ("Love and malice," 1846), much touted in its homeland as the first opera after Glinka with a libretto in a Slavic language. Smetana was determined to play that decisive role in the Czech lands, where as of 1861 the only vernacular operas (mainly by the Prague conductor František Škroup) were still singspiels about merry tinkers and cobblers.

Smetana's maiden opera — the first of seven that covered all genres and established Czech opera as a "world" repertoire — could not have been more different from its local predecessors. Written to a libretto by Karel Sabina (1813–77), a major patriotic writer (but also, it later turned out, a secret police informer), it was called *Braniboři v Čechách* (*The Brandenburgers in Bohemia*). Like Erkel's *Bánk bán* it concerned a medieval war of liberation; and it began with these lines, set to a forceful accompanied recitative in the most progressive operatic manner, which could just as easily be read as pertaining to the nineteenth-century Austrians as to the thirteenth-century Prussians (Ex. 41-1a):

Já ale pravim: Nelze déle	But I say to you we must no longer
tu trpěti cizácké sbory.	Suffer foreign troops in the country.
Už potřebí se chopit zbraně	Now is the time we must take to arms
a vyhnat z vlasti Branibory,	And expel the Brandenburgers,
již hubí zem, náš jazyk tupí,	Who ruin the land and blunt our language,
pod jejichž mečem národ úpí!	Under whose sword the people suffers!

A little later the same character, the venerable Bohemian knight Oldoich, gives vent to an even timelier complaint: "Lord Otto Brandenburg has also suppressed our language, that glorious Czech language, so that you wouldn't recognize Prague!" Yet for all the emphasis on language — not just declared but exemplified in Sabina's libretto (as John Tyrrell, a historian of Czech opera, has pointed out)[5] by the use of meters that faithfully reproduce the peculiar accentual pattern of the Czech vernacular — there is not the slightest hint of vernacular music in the score. On the contrary, Smetana (unlike Erkel, Glinka, Moniuszko, and the rest) actively resisted its influence, preferring to couch his national opera in the most advanced international musical style of the day, as a later recitative of Oldoich's (Ex. 41-1b) will show with its restless diminished harmonies, ending in a baldly displayed scale issuing directly out of the Lisztian technique of interpolating passing tones between the notes of a diminished-seventh chord. These are badges not of nationalism but of "progress-ism."

THE NATIONALIST COMPACT

Smetana was adamant that a true national opera need not and should not rely on folk songs, even in the case of comic operas where their use had always been traditional. The Czech writer Josef Srb-Debrnov, a close friend of Smetana's who later translated a libretto for him, recalled a heated debate between the composer of *The Brandenburgers in Bohemia* and František Rieger, the director of the theater where the opera was to be produced. Rieger maintained that a national style had to depend on folk songs if it was to be recognizable as such. Smetana flew into a rage and (in Tyrrell's paraphrase) told Rieger that an opera written to such a prescription "would be a mere collection of songs, a potpourri, and not a unified artistic whole."[6] Later he wrote that "imitating the melodic curves and rhythms of our folksongs will not create a national style, let alone any dramatic truth — at the most only a pale imitation of the songs themselves." Ironically enough, he might have been describing Liszt's Hungarian Rhapsodies, potpourris not of Hungarian folk songs but (mainly) of Gypsy cabaret tunes. Liszt composed them, in full awareness of their ethnic spuriosity, not to give his ostensible countrymen an icon of self-representation, but to give his Western European audiences an exotic treat. (That Hungarian audiences nevertheless accepted them joyfully as a national icon adds a typically ironic wrinkle to the story; but their joy in the music was conditioned partly, even primarily, by the "world" celebrity of the composer.)

There is an echo of New German ideology in Smetana's rejection of *Volkstümlichkeit* (folk-likeness), recalling Brendel's stipulation that national character is mere *Schmuck* (decoration) rather than substance, and can act only as a brake on musical progress. There is also an echo of the object lesson implicit in Glinka's achievement, to the effect that national musics had to be internationally respectable and competitive if they are even to prove nationally viable (that is, a dependable source of national pride and

EX. 41-1   Bedřich Smetana, *Braniboři v Čechách*, two recitatives for Oldoich

EX. 41-1 (continued)

prestige). What makes the matter seem paradoxical is the insistence of Czech musicians and music lovers, from Smetana's day to this, that his style is despite everything intensely and inherently national in character, instantly recognizable as such by any native listener.

In such an insistence there is always a pinch of mystique, a trusty and (some would say) indispensable component of all nationalistic or patriotic ideologies. The mystique is finely encapsulated in a much-quoted statement on Smetana's *českost* ("Czechness") by the writer Jan Branberger, dating from 1904, when Bohemian separatism, a sentiment Smetana never knew, had become rife:

> When he began to write Czech folk operas, Smetana could not rely on any theory of Czech song, for he did not know its characteristics. He was, however, a great genius, a musician in whose soul slumbered unconscious sources of melody delightfully and faithfully Czech. He had no need to develop his Czechness, and with his first operatic note, he at the same time created a Czech dramatic style. Smetana grew out of his Czech inner self, thereby solving at a stroke all questions of style: he wrote just as his enormous instinct led him.[7]

There may be less of paradox here than meets the eye. Branberger's theory of Smetana's instinctual Czechness, which imbued anything he wrote with national character simply because he wrote it, is more than an avowal of nationalism. It is also heavy with the Germanic (and specifically New German) concept of "world-genius," casting Smetana as a musical Prometheus who created *českost* out of nothing but his own *Kunstidee* (artistic inspiration, to recall some terminology encountered in the last chapter).

More modern treatments of the subject, like that of Michael Beckerman, the leading American authority on Czech music, counter the theory that Smetana's *českost* was the unalloyed *Kunstidee des Producenten* by making room for what New German theory specifically rejected as a source of artistic law, namely the *Ohren des Consumenten* (the "ears of the consumer"), in the construction of national character. In Beckerman's interpretation, *českost* (or Russianness, or Germanness, or any -ness at all) arises not directly out of style, whether a personal style or a collective vernacular, but out of "musical symbols rich in associative possibilities." The source of these possibilities may lie in the national history, or in stylistic resonances, or even in a strongly asserted *Kunstidee*. But for their actualization a compact or bargain is required between producer and consumer. "*Českost* comes about," Beckerman writes, "when, in the minds of composers and audiences, the Czech nation, in its many manifestations, becomes a subtextual program for musical works, and as such, it is that which animates the musical style, allowing us to make connections between the narrow confines of a given piece and a larger, dynamic context." It is this dynamic consensus that Smetana must have been trying to describe to Rieger. And although he sought first (and, in his own mind, foremost) to realize it in the realm of opera, we can also observe it within the Lisztian genre of the symphonic poem, which Smetana continued to cultivate, albeit less progressively and more popularly than before. During the 1870s, he created a monument of *českost* in this medium that many (especially outside the Czech lands, where the language of his opera librettos is not understood) have regarded as his masterpiece.

Between 1872 and 1879 Smetana composed a cycle of six symphonic poems to which he gave the collective title *Má vlast* ("My fatherland"). It is actually a rather heterogeneous collection of pieces, all separately premiered; it was not until the first four had been composed that the idea of performing them as a cycle even occurred to the composer. Three of the poems—including the first two, *Vyšehrad* ("The high castle," 1872–74) and *Vltava* ("The Moldau," 1874)—are descriptive of places or of nature. (The remaining nature piece is no. 4, "From Bohemian Fields and Groves," 1875.) One (no. 3, *Šarka*, 1875) is drawn from pre-Christian Slavic mythology. The last and longest pair (no. 5, *Tabór*, 1878; no. 6, *Blaník*, 1879) deal with episodes in the fifteenth-century religious wars led by Jan Hus, the pre-Reformation Protestant, whose achievements the Austrian authorities were just then bent on eradicating through a policy of "re-Catholicization."

Despite its poetic and stylistic heterogeneity, the cycle is unified by the use of recurring musico-poetic emblems of the kind that Beckerman describes. *Tabór* and *Blaník* are both shot through with a prefabricated symbol in the form of a Hussite hymn, *Ktož jsú Boži bojovníci* ("Ye warriors of God"), first printed in 1530, which all Czechs know by heart, but which non-Czechs can learn to recognize in the course of listening (Ex. 41-2). The technique is anything but new, of course; as embodied in the emblematic cantus-firmus Mass cycles of the fifteenth century, it could be traced all the way back to Jan Hus's time. It could also seem a throwback to the kind of reliance on found objects that Smetana made such a point of despising in the case of folk songs. (But of course noble hymns had a better social pedigree than folk songs.)

EX. 41-2   Hussite hymn: *Ktož jsú Boži bojovníci* ("Ye Warriors of God")

Smetana's use of the old Hussite hymn is in any case of less historical interest than another musico-poetic emblem in *Má vlast*: a *Kunstidee* of Smetana's own devising that frames the entire cycle like a Berliozian idée fixe or an operatic reminiscence motif. But where operatic reminiscence motives and Berliozian idées fixes derive their significance from within the work in which they figure, Smetana's emblem achieves the wider resonance that Beckerman describes. It is first heard as a harp solo at the very beginning of *Vyšehrad* (Ex. 41-3), where its evocative "bardic" timbre (previously employed in *Hakon Jarl* to evoke Scandinavian antiquity), coupled with the composer-poet's explanatory preface to the score, invests it with a sort of invented past. "At the sight of the venerable rock," Smetana writes, the poet's memory is carried back to the remote past by the sound of the harp of the bard Lumír. There rises the vision of the rock in its ancient splendor, its gleaming golden crown that was the proud dwelling place of the Přemysl kings and princes, the ancient dynasty of Bohemia. Here in the castle, knights would assemble at the joyous summons of trumpets and cymbals to engage in splendid tourneys; here the warriors would gather for combat, their arms clanging and glittering in the sunlight. Vyšehrad resounded with songs of praise and victory. Yearning for the long-perished glory of Vyšehrad, the poet now beholds its ruin. The devastation of furious battle has thrown down its lofty towers; fallen are its sanctuaries; and demolished the proud abodes of its princes. Instead of songs of triumph and victory, Vyšehrad quakes at the echo of savage war-cries. The tempests are stilled. Vyšehrad is hushed and bereft of all its glory. From its ruins there comes only the melancholy echo of Lumìr's song, so long forgotten and unheard.[8]

EX. 41-3 Harp solo at the outset of Smetana's *Vyšehrad*

EX. 41-3 (continued)

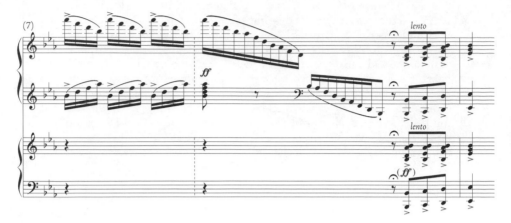

Of the motivic kernel of "Lumír's song," set off at the beginning of the score (like the opening *échappée* figure in *Les préludes*) with a fermata, Beckerman notes that its actual sounds, I – vi – V^6 – I in the key of E♭, are in no way "specifically Czech." And yet, he observes, "when Smetana juxtaposes these chords with the image of the great rock Vyšehrad, and that image is further abstracted into a symbol of the enduring quality of the Czech people, the chords become imbued with a sensibility, and the sensibility becomes tied to something concrete."[9] He calls the method, derived as it is from nothing more ancient than Liszt, an attempt "to recreate the past with the technique of the future." And just as the Vyšehrad motif acquires its national significance from a context and a calculated audience response, it then creates a context to lend national significance to other moments in the cycle, "redefining and enhancing," as Beckerman puts it, "the very sensibility that produced it." Two of its strategic returns are especially telling. One comes at the end of *Vltava* ("The Moldau"), the second poem in the cycle, which has established itself as a repertory item independent of the cycle.

FLUIDITY

Various reasons for its separate popularity, especially with non-Czech audiences, are not difficult to surmise. It makes virtuosic use of some very traditional, widely accepted representational devices; its program, or sequence of events, is represented in the music in an unusually straightforward, descriptive fashion; and its style, while never actually quoting a Czech folk song, is of a marked (and for Smetana, atypical) popular character that appeals to foreign audiences by virtue of its exoticism, the reverse side of the nationalist coin. Yet where patriotic symbolism is concerned, the famous main theme of *Vltava* is heavily fraught with irony, both on the producing and on the consuming ends.

By adding a few enumerations to the program as printed in the published score, one arrives at a serviceable list of its musical sections:

> 1: (E minor) The river springs from its two sources, splashing gaily over the rocks and glistening in the sunshine.

2: (E minor) As it broadens, the banks re-echo with the sound of:

3: (C major) hunting horns ["Forest hunt" in the score] and

4: (G major) country dances ["Peasant Wedding" in the score].

5: (A♭ major) Moonlight — gathering of nymphs.

[reprise of 2: (E minor)]

6: (modulatory [developmental?]) See now, the Rapids of St. John, on whose rocks the foaming waves are dashed in spray.

7: (E major [=2 in parallel key]) Again the stream broadens toward Prague, where it is welcomed by

8: (E major [=Ex. 41-3 in augmentation]) the old and venerable Vyšehrad.

The pictorial effects are as deft and effective as they are traditional. The undulating springs and rivulets in section 1 partake of a convention that we have observed as early as the madrigals of Monteverdi (and again in Vivaldi's "Seasons"). The hunt fanfares (section 3) go back just as far conceptually, and their orchestral realization derives from *Der Freischütz*. The country dance that represents the peasant wedding (section 4) is cast as a polka, a dance that Smetana treated very much the way Chopin treated the mazurka, with eighteen original polkas for piano (and another four in a larger set of *České tance* or "Czech Dances") composed over the course of his entire career and covering a whole spectrum of tempos and moods.

The name of the dance, incidentally, is evidence of a pre-nationalistic exchange among neighboring Slavic populations. It derives from *polska*, Czech for "Polish girl," and most scholars agree that this Bohemian national dance was originally appropriated from the Polish *krakowiak*, described in connection with Chopin in chapter 39. But in the heyday of Czech nationalism this etymology was widely denied in favor of derivations from *půlka* (Czech for "half," wishfully applied to the short heel-and-toe half steps of the dance) or *pole* (Czech for "field," i.e., peasant land). What was once a generalized Slavic affinity had narrowed to a specifically national one. To claim that the latter is incorrect or inauthentic merely because it is recent is to misread, from an outsider's position, the whole process by which music acquires — and keeps on acquiring — significance. As historical and cultural contexts change, so does musical signification.

The best possible illustration of this fluidity involves the recurrent broad theme representing section 2, the main stream of the river, the most famous melody Smetana ever wrote (Ex. 41-4a). Needless to say, as the emblem of the Czech national river, hence as a beloved emblem of nationhood in its own right, the theme has been presumptively identified, by Czechs and non-Czechs alike, as a folk song. And it *is* a folk song. But not a Czech one. It is a Swedish tune that Smetana heard in Göteborg as part of the incidental music to a folk pageant by a playwright whose sister-in-law was a pupil in Smetana's piano institute (Ex. 41-4b).

While it is unlikely that the composer remembered its provenance when appropriating it as an epitome of *českost* (probably accepting it when it came to him as the product of his own imagination), the fact that his memory could thus treacherously disguise itself as an invention—let alone one of such crucially fraught character—is all the evidence we need to refute the notion that *českost*, or any other kind of national character, is an immanent ("in-dwelling") or inherent property of a tune (invented or otherwise), or even of the *Kunstidee* of a *Weltgenie*. The Swedish origin of the melody that has represented Czech nationalism to the world for more than a hundred years is an eternally piquant reminder that art is artful rather than natural. Neither *českost* nor any other artistic character is an essence waiting to be tapped by genius. Like all the others, *českost* is a construction in which producer and consumer must collaborate.

E X. 41-4A   Bedřich Smetana, *Moldau* theme

E X. 41-4B   Swedish folk song: *Ack, Värmeland, du sköna*

E X. 41-4C   Zionist hymn, *Hatikvah* ("The Hope")

And the consumer is just as free as the producer to alter the terms of the bargain. A decade after Smetana's *Moldau* had become an international repertory standard, its big tune was co-opted by an arranger named Popovici for a collection of "Moldavian" (Eastern Romanian) songs, where it was given the title *Carul cu boi* ("Cart and oxen"), and where it was spotted in 1888 by Samuel Cohen, a Bohemian-born musician then living in Palestine, and fitted to the words of *Tikvatenu* ("Our hope"), verses published in Jerusalem two years earlier by the Polish-born Hebrew poet Naftali Herz Imber (1856–1909). The resulting hymn, *Hatikvah* ("The hope," Ex. 41-4c), was first published as such in 1895 in Breslau, a city in East Prussia (now Wrocław, Poland). Two years later it was adopted by the First Zionist Congress, meeting in Basel, Switzerland, as the official Zionist anthem, and as such became the national anthem of the State of Israel on its founding in May 1948.

The *Moldau* theme, in its Czech manifestation, can thus be looked upon as a stage in the history of a melody as it passed from its Swedish origins to its Israeli destination. But of course even this characterization is misleading. There are no origins and no destinations in such histories, only stages.

The only place in *Vltava* that retains the aggressively progressive approach of Smetana's earlier symphonic (and keyboard) poems is section 6, the portrayal of the rapids, where the violence of the imagery justifies the extravagant harmonic effect of a sudden stall on an augmented sixth chord in its most dissonant voicing (comparable to the 4/2 position of a dominant seventh), which then becomes the occasion for a swirling surface counterpoint of clashing scales figuring contending eddies and surges. When the harmony is adjusted (by the inflection of C to C♯) to a diminished seventh chord, the scales become near-octatonic for a spell, only their D-naturals holding them within the orbit of the chord's traditional function.

The other way in which the Lisztian precedent governs this symphonic poem is in its tonal plan, outlined within the program as set forth above. If item 4, the most overtly folkish component, is temporarily left out of the account, the scheme conforms to the same circle of major thirds found in Schubert's *Wanderer*-Fantasie (where Liszt first found it). Of course if item 4 is taken into account (as it must be in the actual listening experience), the circle of major thirds coexists somewhat uneasily with a diatonic arrangement of thirds around a C major triad (or, more pertinently, thirds above and below the tonic E).

The two-tiered scheme may in fact represent a programmatic set of tonal alternatives: the diatonic arrangement (leaving out A♭) omits the one fantastic or mythological element, while the symmetrically chromatic arrangement (leaving out G) omits the one folk — or even specifically human — element. The opposition of diatonics and symmetrically arranged chromatics to distinguish the human and magical spheres within a folk or mythological narrative was a convention, first established by Glinka in *Ruslan and Lyudmila* (1842), that turns up in many Slavic operas, and also (as we have seen) in Smetana's *Macbeth and the Witches*.

But Smetana wrote no operas with supernatural plots or characters, and it would be very rash to assume that Glinka's operas, epoch-makers though they were, were among his models. Smetana, a loyal Austrian subject who saw his country's best chance for national revival within the structure of a liberalized empire, remained cool throughout his career toward cultural emanations from the Slavic east, which (like Chopin) he associated with Russian (alias "Pan-Slavic") imperialism. His nationalism, though it occasionally found expression in vernacular terms, remained more a civic than an ethnic (let alone a racial) nationalism. And so he made scant common cause with Balakirev when the Russian composer came to Prague in January 1867 to conduct the first performances of Glinka's operas outside Russia.

As the newly named chief conductor of the Prague opera theater, Smetana was tangentially involved in these productions, and Balakirev blamed him for everything that went wrong with them, calling him a swine and accusing him of sabotage on behalf of what he called the "Polonophile" party, Slavs who had taken up the Polish cause

FIG. 41-2A   Poster announcing the premiere performance of Smetana's opera *The Bartered Bride*.

against Russia after the bloody events of 1830–31. A letter from Balakirev to Glinka's sister, Lyudmila Shestakova, suggests another dimension to the Russian's animosity toward his hosts: "When the curtain went up [on *A Life for the Tsar*]—oh, horror! What costumes!! The peasants were wearing some kind of peaked caps and overcoats with white buttons, and they had beards, but not Russian ones—Jewish ones!!!"[10]

Payback time came four years later, when Smetana's second (and best known) opera, a Figaro-ish comedy of peasants and landowners called *The Bartered Bride*, received its foreign premiere in St. Petersburg, where the chief conductor, Eduard Nápravník, was a naturalized Czech. César Cui, Balakirev's comrade-in-arms, was waiting. An excerpt from his review, published in the Russian capital's leading daily on the morning of 18 January 1871, will be enough to put to rest forever any notions of pan-Slavic solidarity among musical nationalists, or any idea of an ecumenical nationalist movement in music. "I frankly confess to my readers," Cui began,

FIG. 41-2B   *The Bartered Bride*, stage design for act III.

that it is much more pleasant to write about the Czech composer Smetana than about Beethoven. No matter what I write about Beethoven, I will always remain beneath my subject, while no matter what I write about Smetana, I will always be above it, so empty and nonsensical is this opera of his . . . . Mr. Smetana is obviously an experienced musician who has filled up a lot of music paper . . . . The best thing about *The Bartered Bride* is its slight whiff of Czech music, related to ours, which gives the opera a bit of color and makes it more bearable . . . . But as to quality, the music is simply a blank. Every sort of nothingness passes in review: sentimental nothingness, and pastoral nothingness, and poetic nothingness, and plain nothingness . . . . It's not a composition, it's the improvisation of a tolerably gifted fourteen-year-old.[11]

And on and on in this vein. Yet one must suspect that there was more at work here than just personal spite. The German music historian Carl Dahlhaus once speculated about

the possibility that the different manifestations of musical nationalism were affected by the types of political nationalism and the different stages in political evolution reached in each country: by the difference between those states where the transition from monarchy to democracy was successful (Great Britain, France) and unsuccessful (Russia), or between states formed by the unification of separate provinces (Germany, Italy) and those formed by the secession of new nation-states from an old empire (Hungary, Czechoslovakia, Poland, Norway, Finland).[12]

What may seem naive about this meditation are its universalist assumptions: that there is a single political evolution (toward democratic nation-states) in which all countries participate, successfully or unsuccessfully; that is a lingering legacy of Hegel. But if we look at things not from the perspective of political progress but from that of imperial powers vs. ethnic minorities, Dahlhaus's idea may bear more interesting fruit. It may suggest a more convincing way of accounting for the haughty tone a lordly Russian took toward the work of his ostensible brother Slav, who in his homeland was not master but vassal.

FOLK AND NATION

After these many digressions let us return to *Má vlast* and witness the outcome of its musico-poetic strategies by comparing the coda of *Vltava* (Ex. 41-5) with the peroration of *Blaník* (Ex. 41-6). The former brings the *Moldau* theme into sudden juxtaposition — or collision — with the explicitly labeled "Vyšehrad Motive," the theme on which the previous poem in the cycle had been built. The castle-rock theme is in a grandiose threefold rhythmic augmentation with respect to the rushing river music that continues beneath it, carrying echoes of the forest fanfares, and so the effect of climactic magnificence is inescapable, even to an audience unaware of the thematic recall. To an audience properly aware, of course, the effect is an ecstasy of *českost*.

But it pales beside the orgy of *českost* at the end of *Blaník* — the culmination of the whole cycle — when the "Vyšehrad Motive" is reprised in counterpoint with the Hussite hymn, first cited in Ex. 41-2. The thematic juxtaposition here has no express narrative or pictorial import. It is sheer nationalistic pomp, symbolic of a national glory that was

EX. 41-5   Bedřich Smetana, *Vltava*, mm. 359–62

EX. 41-6   Culmination of Bedřich Smetana's *Blaník* with its combination of emblematic themes

only a dream in 1880, when the cycle was first performed as a totality. Its counterpart is the final act of *Libuše* (first performed the next year), an opera based on the central founding myth of Bohemia, in which the title character, the legendary first queen of the land, has a prophetic vision in which all the heroic events of the national history (to her the national future) pass in review, culminating in a phantasmagoria of the Prague castle, magically illuminated, while the clairvoyant queen sings exultantly, "Můj drahý národ český neskoná!" ("My beloved Czech nation will not perish") (Ex. 41-7). During World War II, when the Czech lands were temporarily annexed to Nazi Germany, not only *Libuše* but also *Blaník* (and hence complete performances of *Ma vlast*) were banned as potentially seditious. The remarkable fact was that Smetana's Lisztian technique — in its day a trophy of rampant Germany — had made it possible to rouse an anti-German rabble wordlessly.

EX. 41-7   Bedřich Smetana, *Libuše*, Act III, "Můj drahý národ český neskoná!"

Except for the G-major episode in *Vltava*, moreover, the nation-building deed is done without any recourse to *Volkstümlichkeit*, conventional folksiness. The folk, the implication is clear, was for Smetana — as for the urban, educated, politically ambitious public that he served — only one part of the nation, and by no means necessarily the most significant one. The Nazis agreed. Smetana's comic operas, socially conservative works that celebrated the peasantry in idealized harmony with the gentry, and did it by an infusion of folksy charm (replete with pastoral drones and even a quoted peasant tune or two; see Ex. 41-8), were perfectly innocuous in the eyes of the occupiers.

Almost from the time of its premiere, moreover, and despite César Cui's sullen hostility, *The Bartered Bride* has proved a highly exportable commodity, affably representing the Czech nation to other nations, perhaps in its friendly exoticism reinforcing a reputation for bumpkinry that breeds condescension. Where *The Brandenburgers in Bohemia* was never produced during the nineteenth century except in the theater where it had its premiere, and *Libuše* only in the Czech lands, *The Bartered Bride* went around the world, playing by 1897 in fourteen cities in nine countries on two continents, and in eight languages. By now the Czechs themselves regard this most popular Czech opera as a national treasure, a compendium of folk life and character types expressed (quite Mozarteanly!) through a compendium of national dance rhythms. Originally, however, it was Smetana's monumental and progressive compositions, not his *volkstümlich* ones, that appealed most to Czech national sentiment.

Thus for a long time Smetana was honored at home as the composer of *Libuše* and *Má vlast*, and abroad as the composer of *The Bartered Bride* and *The Moldau*. That difference in perception embodies many hidden realities about nationalism in art, and highlights in particular the role of reception in defining both what is national, and its relationship to the exotic. Dahlhaus's dictum that "what does and does not count as national depends primarily on collective opinion,"[13] needs only one qualification: there can be more than one such opinion, representing different collectivities or interpretive communities, and they are always negotiable.

HOW THE ACORN TOOK ROOT

It was the Russians (or some Russians) who at midcentury put the most faith in traditional *Volkstümlichkeit* as the carrier of objective, non-negotiable national character even in instrumental music. There were two reasons. First, the Russians (or some

EX. 41-8A   Furiant: "Sedlák, sedlák," from K. J. Erben, *Napevy prostonarodnich pisni ceskych* ("The Tunes of Czech Peasant Songs"), no. 588

EX. 41-8B Bedřich Smetana, *The Bartered Bride*, II, Furiant, mm. 7–14

Russians) were particularly eager to form a national school in opposition to what they saw as the threat of German hegemony; and second, the arts in Russia were particularly inclined toward realism, or (in Glinka's phrase) toward the embodiment of "positive data,"[14] a truth-content that required no interpretation. As we shall see, the second ideal proved quixotic: artistic content, being a human product and a social one, always requires interpretation. But even the first was fraught with ironies.

The attempt to build a national Russian school on a foundation of folklore can be traced to Glinka, just as the New German School can be traced to Beethoven, although neither Glinka nor Beethoven ever had any premonition of such a project or historical role. For Glinka left a work that composers of the next generation took so zealously as a model that one of them, Chaikovsky, called it "the acorn from which the whole oak of Russian symphonic music grew."[15] But it was no spontaneous germination. The oak was very much a hothouse growth. Tracing the process through which composers of the post-Glinka generation tried to transform his legacy will offer a revealing insight into the difference between national and nationalist art.

Glinka, as we know, was by strong preference an operatic composer, not a symphonic one. But toward the end of his life he composed three *Fantaisies pittoresques* (picturesque fantasies) for orchestra under the spell of Berlioz, whom he met in Paris in 1845. Two of the three were based on Spanish themes; for Glinka (as for Berlioz) national character did not have to be native, just colorful. The third fantasia, originally called "A Wedding Song and a Dance Song" (1848), was based on two Russian folk themes. The title by which it is known today, *Kamarinskaya* (accent on the second syllable), is that of the second song, actually a well-known instrumental dance tune (*naigrïsh* in Russian) consisting of a single three-measure phrase that is repeated ad infinitum as the basis and framework for extemporized variations played by wedding bands, or else by a single

FIG. 41-3 The Kamarinskaya dance (anonymous nineteenth-century woodcut).

player on an accordionlike bayan, a concertina, or a strummed balalaika (as in Fig. 41-3), to accompany a strenuous and often competitive type of male dancing (performed *v prisyadku*, in a squat) well known in the West as typically Russian thanks to its exportation by professional folk-dance ensembles.

Glinka noticed an unexpected resemblance between the famous *Kamarinskaya* tune and the melody of a lyrical wedding song that was one of his personal favorites: the notes of the dance song marked with asterisks in Ex. 41-9, most of them in strong, conspicuous rhythmic positions, correspond with the first six notes of the wedding song. He based his brilliantly orchestrated fantasia on what thus amounts to a sort of abstract musical pun. The two themes are first given in stark contrast, as in a conventional symphonic first movement (Introduction and Allegro). But all at once, over a thirty-one measure passage in the midst of the Allegro, the fast theme is magically transformed into a reprise of the slow one, by means of the progressive revelation of their kinship.

It is a beautifully executed maneuver, but perhaps even more remarkable is the way Glinka derived the fantasia's introductory and transitional passages from the melody of

EX. 41-9   Folk themes in Glinka's *Kamarinskaya*

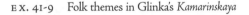

Iz - za gor, gor vï - so - kikh gor

EX. 41-9   (*continued*)

ad infinitum, with perpetual variation

the wedding song by extracting motives from it (labeled *x*, *y*, and *z* in Ex. 41-9). The very opening is built entirely on a sequential treatment of *y*, led to a surprising conclusion on B♭. This prepares, at short range, the first downbeat harmony of the wedding song. (At the long range, as we shall see, it is even more strategic.) The first transition from the wedding song to the dance song consists of a neat contrapuntal juxtaposition of motives *x* and *y* (Ex. 41-10a), and the second such transition makes similar use of motive *z* (Ex. 41-10b), meanwhile modulating with marvelous economy to the unexpected (but not unprepared) key of B♭, picking up the harmony left hanging at the end of the introduction.

Most striking of all is the final modulation. The reprise of the dance song having been made in the key of the flat submediant, the triumphant return to the D major tonic (Ex. 41-10c) is made by the same bass resolution as at the end of Ex. 41-10a, derived there from the incipit of the wedding song, motive *x*. The underlying tonal progression that lends contrast and a heightened structural unity to the dance song variations thus turns out to be a long-range projection of the opening motive of the wedding song. Such a thorough interpenetration of melodic and harmonic structures through the use of motives is the kind of thing one is used to finding (and therefore

EX. 41-10A   Motivic derivations in Glinka's *Kamarinskaya*, mm. 35–48

EX. 41-10B   Glinka, *Kamarinskaya*, mm. 155–169

EX. 41-10C   Glinka, *Kamarinskaya*, mm. 202–209

seeking) in Beethoven. It was precisely the reason for Beethoven's preeminence among symphonists. That Glinka managed to emulate the trick using nothing but folk songs as his melodic material was an astonishing tour de force. No wonder *Kamarinskaya* was so influential.

But note that what made it so was not its folkloric content per se, but the way in which it vied with the greatest protagonist of the German mainstream. That is the first irony we must contend with if we are to understand the nature of the Russian response to musical Germany, which had turned aggressive (or so it seemed to Glinka's nationalistic heirs) in the years after the great composer's death.

The protagonist of that aggression, where Russian nationalists were concerned, was Anton Rubinstein (1829–94), the indefatigable organizer of Russian musical life, who in 1859 founded the Russian Musical Society, the sponsoring organization behind the country's first full-time professional symphony orchestra, and who three years later founded the St. Petersburg Conservatory, the first school of its kind on Russian soil. A piano virtuoso of international fame and an incredibly prolific composer of German schooling, Rubinstein saw the future of Russian music in terms of its professionalization under the sponsorship of the aristocracy and the stewardship of imported master teachers. (It was a measure of his colossal energy and fame that he was able to gain such sponsorship despite his Jewish birth.) In 1855, Rubinstein had published an article in a Vienna arts journal called "Russian Composers," in which he outlined his Peter the Great–like program for Westernizing Russian music, and

FIG. 41-4 Anton (right) and Nikolai Rubinstein, in a photograph from the late 1860s, when both were directors of the conservatories.

also hinted that Russian musical nationalism was merely a sign of immaturity and dilettantism. Although even Rubinstein's worst enemies recognized that his motives were patriotic, and although everyone acknowledged that Rubinstein, both as lobbyist and as role model, deserved credit for creating the social and institutional means through which a professional musical life might flourish in Russia, his tactless words met with a chorus of righteous indignation. It could even be said that Russian musical nationalism, as a self-conscious artistic tendency, was touched off by this article from the pen of a musician for whom music was inherently and essentially "a *German* art," and in whose opinion "a deliberately national art cannot claim universal sympathy but awakens an ethnographical interest at best."[16]

The leaders of the nationalistic backlash were two figures whom we have already met: the arts publicist Vladimir Stasov, a librarian by profession, who inveighed lustily against the establishment of a conservatory system in Russia, and Miliy Balakirev, known to us thus far as a musical orientalist, who competed directly with Rubinstein as a public musician and educator. It was in this spirit of opposition to the German-dominated professionalization of St. Petersburg's musical life that Balakirev gathered around him his famous "mighty little band" (*moguchaya kuchka*) of talented musical mavericks and autodidacts.

They included the military fortifications expert César Cui (known to us as a journalist), the chemist Borodin (known to us as the composer of *Prince Igor*), the guards officer Modest Musorgsky (known to us as a musical realist), and the young naval cadet Nikolai Rimsky-Korsakov (1844–1908). The group's name was inadvertently invented by Stasov, in a journalistic puff about a concert of new Russian music conducted by Balakirev in 1867. It ended "with a wish: God grant that our audience never forget today's concert; God grant that they always remember how much poetry, feeling, talent, and skill there is in the small but already *mighty little band* of young Russian musicians."[17] The earliest truly "kuchkist" composition was Balakirev's *Overture on Russian Themes*, composed in 1857–58, about a decade before the group was named. It was at once a creative response to Glinka's *Kamarinskaya* and a calculated rejoinder to Rubinstein's slur, written as if on purpose to prove that Russian national instrumental music need not be immature or provincial. Unlike Glinka, Balakirev went looking for his themes. The determination to write a symphonic work on Russian folk songs preceded the specific embodiment (already a mark of the difference between "national" and "nationalist"). Unlike the themes in *Kamarinskaya*, the three songs Balakirev chose were all available in published anthologies, which was where he sought them out. They are set forth, both as Balakirev found them and as they are found in the Overture, in Ex. 41-11.

The criteria for their selection are obvious if one knows *Kamarinskaya*, and show how closely Balakirev sought to model his work on Glinka's. Like *Kamarinskaya*, the Overture is set out in a slow-fast Introduction and Allegro scheme; moreover, the pair of tunes that together make up the thematic content of the Allegro, although they are full-blown melodies rather than *naigrïshi*, are both built up out of three-measure phrases analogous to the single varied phrase in *Kamarinskaya*. This enabled Balakirev to achieve a headlong ostinato drive just as unremitting as Glinka's — in fact more so,

EX. 41-11 Folk songs in Miliy Balakirev's *Overture on Russian Themes* (1858)

EX. 41-11   (*continued*)

since there is no interrupting return to the slow theme. (Instead, the slow theme returns nostalgically at the very end.)

But Balakirev's piece makes use of three folk songs, not just two, and this turns out to be more than a mere quantitative difference. A glance at the two Allegro tunes reveals the reason for it: in B minor and D major respectively, they are the first and second themes in a bithematic sonata form exposition, with a conventional development section providing the pretext for an excursion to Glinka's flat submediant, here functioning as a traditional far-out point (FOP), and for a wealth of skillful contrapuntal juxtapositions of extracted motives.

Balakirev's *Overture on Russian Themes* can thus be viewed as a principled advance over Glinka's *Kamarinskaya* both as regards sheer dimensions, and also as regards symphonic character and procedure. Paradoxically, though, it is also a far more conventional composition. The advance was purchased at the price of a reconciliation with the standard operating procedure of German music, as Balakirev understood it — a seeming submission to the very hegemony Balakirev had made it his business to oppose. But the contradiction was in a sense built into the terms of the bargain: only a piece that could seem respectable by Germanic standards could counter Rubinstein's taunts. And unlike Glinka, Balakirev wanted more than just to write a piquantly impressive piece: he aimed at founding a school, and that meant establishing, observing, and handing down traditions (that is, conventions).

NATIONAL BECOMES NATIONALIST

Having established a type, Balakirev went on to develop it. Six years later, in 1864, he produced a second *Overture on Russian Themes* that marked as great an advance over his first in formal scope and symphonic procedure as the first had marked over *Kamarinskaya*. At the same time it exhibited a new determination on the composer's part to purify the national character of his style. In their symbiosis these two traits marked a new stage in the emergence of oak from acorn, because in conjunction they led to an unshakeable perception of programmatic content in the music.

In *Kamarinskaya* and in Balakirev's first Overture, the motivating impulse (hence the content) could be simply construed as entertaining song and dance. But the second Overture exhibited such a reweighting of priorities in favor of process — transition and development, departure and arrival — as to imply a narrative content, or what Balakirev later termed "instrumental drama." When such a piece is based upon characteristic material of any kind, the question immediately raised is not just "What is it?" but "What is it *about?*"

To use the more precise vocabulary of the music theorist Leonard B. Meyer, the "kinetic-syntactic" processes of Balakirev's Second Overture are so highly developed as inevitably to lend a "connotative" dimension to its musical material.[18] When that material is so obviously national, the piece no longer seems to be a *Fantaisie pittoresque* guided solely (as Glinka said he had been guided) by "innate musical feeling." It *means* something. It is in some sense — but *what* sense? — a statement about Russia. It is this programmatic element, brought about by the conjunction of a highly elaborated and kinetic structure with a highly characteristic thematic content, that made possible Balakirev's authentic and powerful musical nationalism.

In the years immediately following the composition of his first Overture, Balakirev had made a close study of Russian folk songs with an eye toward their creative exploitation. Dissatisfied with the quality of existing publications, he made his own collecting expedition along the Volga River, Russia's Mississippi, in the summer of 1860. The songs he collected in the Russian heartland were issued in an epoch-making volume of forty arrangements — Balakirev's *Sbornik russkikh narodnïkh pesen* ("Anthology of Russian folk songs") — in 1866.

The most significant aspect of the collection was the technique of harmonization that Balakirev worked out for it. The method preserved two aspects of the folk original that Balakirev particularly prized: first, the diatonic purity of the minor mode (both the natural minor and what Balakirev christened the "Russian minor," corresponding to what is otherwise known as the Dorian mode); and second, the quality of tonal mutability (*peremennost'* in Russian), whereby a tune can seem to oscillate between two equally stable points of rest, as if two tonics. These often coincided with the ordinary relationship of tonic to relative major or minor, but just as often the relationship involved the lower neighbor to the tonic in the minor mode, a degree for which there is not even an ordinary "Western" name. (Most often it is called the flat seventh since it lacks the sharpening it would receive in the harmonic or melodic minor.) In most previous collections of folk songs, and in most art music that quoted folk tunes, both of these features had been obscured by the use of the harmonic minor and of secondary dominants (or dominant embellishments). These devices Balakirev virtually banished from his harmonizations, as may be seen in Ex. 41-12, which reproduces from Balakirev's book a *protyazhnaya* or slow melismatic folk song cast in the Russian minor pitched on D. There is not a sharp or flat in sight, and the first cadence is made to C, the *peremennost'* tone. There is no chord that can be called a proper dominant. The cadences to D are introduced by the minor V, which lacks a leading tone, and in measure 6 the minor V and the major IV, precisely the chords the harmonic minor is designed to avoid, are placed side by side, lending the music a modality that contradicts and tries to neutralize conventional tonal expectations. In 1867, while in Prague for the production of Glinka's operas, Balakirev had the satisfaction of hearing a local conservatory professor pronounce his harmonizations *ganz falsch* (all wrong).

EX. 41-12   Protyazhnaya pesnya (melismatic folk song) from the Nizhny-Novgorod District, as harmonized in Miliy Balakirev, *Sbornik russkikh narodnïkh pesen* (St. Petersburg, 1866).

Ex. 41-13 shows the three songs Balakirev chose from his anthology (slightly in advance of its publication) for use in the second Overture, with the motives (*p, q, r*, and *s*) that will be extracted for development enclosed in brackets. For the slow introduction Balakirev picked a wedding song in the Russian minor ("There was no wind, then suddenly it blew . . ."), and for the Allegro he chose two *khorovod* or round-dance tunes: "I'm off to Constantinople," in the major, which will function as the first theme, and "Merry Kate, black-browed Kate," in the natural minor, for use as the second theme. (The Overture also contains a graceful theme of Balakirev's own invention, which functions as a close or codetta in the exposition and the recapitulation.)

EX. 41-13   Themes from Miliy Balakirev's second *Overture on Russian Themes* (1864), as printed in his anthology *Sbornik Russkikh narodnïkh pesen*

EX. 41-13   (*continued*)

It should be emphasized that the harmonic style of these settings, which colored not only Balakirev's Overture but any number of other compositions that came out of the school he founded, was Balakirev's personal invention. It is not a folk style at all; actual peasant harmonizations sound nothing like them, and Balakirev probably knew that as well as he knew that his "Georgian Song" (Ex. 39-19b) did not sound truly Georgian. But the style is instantly recognizable to connoisseurs of art music as generically Russian thanks to its thorough assimilation into the later compositional practice not only of Balakirev himself but that of his followers Rimsky-Korsakov, Musorgsky, and Borodin; and Rimsky-Korsakov, who became a great and famous teacher, passed it along in turn to his many pupils. So it may not be an authentically peasant or folk style, but it is indeed the authentic and distinctive style of the New Russian School, alias *moguchaya kuchka*.

And it not only governed local harmonizations like those in the folk song anthology, but when used in large-scale instrumental compositions also controlled the long-term tonal organization in a novel and original (hence identifiably "Russian") manner. The slow introduction of the second Overture (Ex. 41-14a) is a case in point. Like the wedding song in *Kamarinskaya*, the one in the second Overture begins with a unison statement, but the final pair of measures is fully harmonized. The whole gesture is then immediately repeated, forming parallel periods. The cadence of the first period is harmonized very much like the setting in the folk song anthology: a plagal cadence through a major IV, evoking Russian minor. The second period has a different termination, however: the pair of horns picks up the A♭ (the lower neighbor or *peremennost'* tone), and the continuation is transposed down a step so that the A♭ is tonicized in mm. 23–25, but again through a plagal — that is, dominantless — cadence.

Thus the tonal mutability of the original melody is reinforced through a tonal progression. Indeed, in keeping with his general avoidance of dominant harmony in the minor mode, Balakirev does not employ a single authentic cadence over the whole course of the introduction, only plagal ones. They are often deployed in chains suggesting the use of a term like "applied subdominant." At the very end of the introduction, for example, a progression along the circle of fourths (or fifths in reverse) leads back from the *peremennost'* tone (A♭) to the tonic for the final cadence: A♭–E♭–B♭. To a degree unprecedented in music Russian or otherwise, tonal properties of folk music, and techniques derived from them, have been allowed to invade and govern those of art music.

EX. 41-14A   Miliy Balakirev, second *Overture on Russian Themes*, mm. 5–25

EX. 41-14B   Miliy Balakirev, second *Overture on Russian Themes*, mm. 169–74

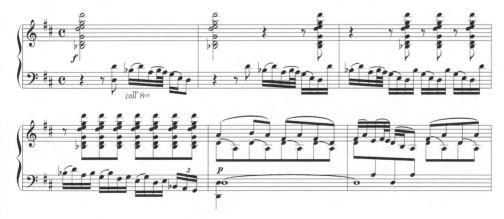

The second Overture is cast, like the first, in the form of a sonata allegro embedded within a larger ABA form created by a concluding reprise of the slow introduction in the form of a coda. Overall, the key relations are Lisztian, showing Balakirev to be, like Smetana (however profoundly they may otherwise have differed), a musical descendant not just of Germany but of New Germany. The sonata allegro, in D major, is sandwiched between slow outer sections in B♭ minor; and the development section, beginning in F♯ major, completes a full rotation around the Lisztian circle of major thirds. Not at all by accident, moreover, the main keys of the piece — D and B♭ — are the very ones on which the notable modulation in *Kamarinskaya* had turned, and Balakirev pays it further tribute by exactly modeling the transition into the first theme after the introduction on Glinka's striking modulation (compare Ex. 41-10c with Ex. 41-14b) — with one highly characteristic difference: Balakirev goes directly from ii_3^4 to I, eliding out the dominant harmony and (by touching G in the bass right before the first theme begins) turning the progression into what amounts to a plagal cadence.

In his second Overture on Russian Themes Balakirev really did what Rubinstein, for one, thought impossible: he constructed an extended, sustained symphonic composition almost wholly out of folkloric material with no loss of scale or gravity. Unlike *Kamarinskaya* or the first Overture, the piece is ample, even imposing in its dimensions and its complexity of design. All its themes are presented *Eroica*-fashion, with momentary departures leading back to climactic statements. Its tonal tensions, while not always classical, are urgently dynamic. Perhaps most conspicuously of all, Balakirev constructs marvelous mosaics and collages out of motives p, q, r, and s at transitional and developmental moments, of which there are so many.

THE POLITICS OF INTERPRETATION

So, it is high time to ask, what's it all about? What kind of a statement about Russia was Balakirev making? What kind of a story was he telling? As in all interpretative matters, there is room for alternatives and negotiations. Perhaps the most interesting fact about Balakirev's second Overture, and surely the most fascinating aspect of its history, is how many mutually exclusive alternatives and how much negotiation originated with the composer himself.

The period of truculent musical politics immediately preceding the founding of Rubinstein's Conservatory in 1862 had coincided with what was generally a turbulent moment in Russian history: the aftermath of the Crimean War and the multiple far-reaching reforms of the early reign of Tsar Alexander II. A typical incident of those years was a series of student demonstrations at the beginning of the 1861–62 academic year that led to a great number of arrests and the temporary closing of the three leading Russian universities, those at St. Petersburg, Moscow, and Kazan (where Balakirev had briefly studied).

From his London exile the radical democrat Alexander Herzen (1812–70) greeted this outbreak of political activism among the youth of Russia with an enthusiastic editorial in his journal *The Bell (Kolokol)*, entitled "The Giant Wakes!" It ended with an impassioned call to the students at the shut-down institutions:

In Russia the universities are closed, in Poland even the churches have been shut down, defiled by the police. There is neither light of reason nor light of faith! Where would they thus lead us in the dark? . . . So, where will you turn, brave youths, you who have been shut out from your studies? Where, indeed?

Listen, closely, since darkness does not prevent hearing: from all sides of our enormous fatherland, from the Don and from the Urals, from the Volga and the Dnepr, a moan is growing, a rumble is rising—it is the beginning of a tidal wave which is boiling up, attended by storms, after a horribly fatiguing calm. *To the people! With the people!*—That's where you belong.[19]

Stasov, whose library post gave him privileged access to censored and foreign literature, was a regular reader of Herzen's *Kolokol*. According to a letter from Stasov to Balakirev,[20] the conception of Balakirev's urgently dynamic second Overture was connected with their reading "The Giant Wakes!" together, and in particular with Herzen's image of the rising tidal wave. That interpretation of the piece naturally appealed to critics during the Soviet regime, which traced its ancestry back to Herzen and other pre-Marxist Russian radicals. On the basis of Stasov's letter, one such critic wrote that Balakirev's Overture was "a picture of Russia as seen through the eyes of one who has felt the powerful strength, the spiritual beauty, and the poetic gift of the 'awakening populace.'"[21]

But when the work was published in 1869, it was given the programmatic title *1,000 Years: A Musical Picture*, alluding to the recently celebrated millennium of the legendary founding of the Russian state by the Scandinavian Prince Rurik in 862. No evidence survives to suggest that Balakirev had any such idea in 1862, but there is a letter from Stasov to Balakirev, dated 17 December 1868, discussing a proposed design for the title page, which gives some idea of the program they then envisioned: "On the left there will be a drawing of 'primeval Russia'; in the middle, Moscow, or perhaps one of the autonomous princely cities; and finally, as if disappearing in the distance, 'modern times'—some city, a rushing locomotive, telegraphs, some new buildings."[22]

This is pretty far from a rising wave of popular discontent. It flies in the face of the previous conception, putting meliorism, the notion that things get better and better with time, in place of social criticism. In fact, the vicissitudes of the second Overture's program were just beginning. In the mid-1880s, having suffered a nervous breakdown and a prolonged interruption of his musical activities, Balakirev eased himself back into the swim of things by lightly revising a number of early compositions, *1,000 Years* among them. He retouched it in 1884 and published it in 1890 with a new designation—symphonic poem—and a new title: *Rus'*, the Old Slavonic name of his country, known in modern Russian as *Rossiya*. The preface now described the program in detail:

The unveiling in 1862 in Novgorod of a monument to the Russian millennium was the occasion for the composition of this symphonic poem. As its basis I selected the themes of three folk songs, by which I wished to characterize three elements in our ancient history: the pagan period, the Muscovite order, and the autonomous republican system, now reborn among the Cossacks. Strife among these elements, expressed in the symphonic development of these themes, has furnished the content of the instrumental drama.[23]

Far from either a social protest or a melioristic panorama, we are now faced with a glorification of Russian antiquity, particularly of those quasi-communal forms of social organization that were maintained by the Cossacks, for which they were admired by nationalist reactionaries, such as Balakirev had evidently become, and reviled by every progressive or liberal element. And he went even further. In the last edition of the score to come out within his lifetime, he amended the last sentence to read: "Their strife, culminating in the fatal blow dealt all Russian religious and national aspirations by the reforms of Peter I, has furnished the content of the instrumental drama."[24] In a letter to a fellow Pan-Slavist he actually maintained that his original intention in composing *Rus'* had been "to depict how Peter the Great killed our native Russian life."[25] What an anomaly this is: from its putative beginnings in Herzen, the ideological content of Balakirev's overture (or picture, or symphonic poem) had swung 180 degrees to the right, along with the composer's political and social outlook: from a progressive man of the sixties the composer had become a xenophobic reactionary. Without knowledge of the history of the piece, all three interpretations of its music might seem equally plausible. But all would be equally absurd if applied to *Kamarinskaya*. So the radical expansion of form Balakirev achieved in his second Overture can best be viewed as an effort to accommodate an ideological, not merely an evocative content — an effort demanded by a commitment to artistic nationalism that the aristocratic composer of *Kamarinskaya* not only lacked but despised.

Balakirev's nationalism, whether on the left or on the right, arose out of a self-imposed requirement, uniquely prevalent in Russia, that art be *engagé* — that it engage with civic and social issues. That need arose out of Russia's unique nineteenth-century status as the one remaining autocratic despotism in Europe, where censorship of public speech and public press was uniquely stringent, and where open debate about public policy was uniquely circumscribed by law. Under such circumstances, discussion of political and social issues had to go underground, into historiography and art (and, perhaps above all, into historiographically informed art). As Friedrich Nietzsche, in a typically brilliant aphorism, observed in 1880, "Music reaches its high-water mark only among men who have not the ability or the right to argue."[26] He was not talking about Russia at the time, but his astonishing sentence does more to encapsulate the peculiar history of music there, and explain its extraordinary sudden flowering in the late nineteenth century, than any other single sentence could ever hope to do.

Deeds of Music Made Visible (Class of 1813, I)

WAGNER

THE PROBLEM

A specter has been haunting the last six chapters of this narrative—the specter of Richard Wagner. We met him first as the pseudonymous author of a violent and rancorous tract, published in 1850, that heralded a new, aggressive phase of European nationalism. Next we saw him applying this new idea of nation, and the role of art within it, to the interpretation of Weber's *Freischütz*. We heard tell of him later still as a political revolutionary, temporarily exiled from Germany, and as an artistic revolutionary, the dread darling of Weimar, where Liszt's performance of Wagner's opera *Lohengrin* in 1850 was the very event that led to the christening of the music of the future. Now it is time to meet him as a composer and dramatist, and encounter at first hand the musico-poetic imagination in which these nationalistic, revolutionary, and artistic personas intersected—an imagination so powerful, backed up by a technique so novel and so impressive, that neither the music of his own day nor that of succeeding generations (even, some would say, down to the present) is conceivable without him.

So emblematic is Wagner of his time and his country, in their most glorious as well as their most horrible aspects, that he has become a figure of furious and apparently unendable debate. "Suffering and great as that nineteenth century whose complete expression he is, the mental image of Richard Wagner stands before my eyes," wrote the thoroughly haunted German novelist Thomas Mann in 1933 ("not, I confess, without misgivings"[1]), right before going into temporary exile from a Germany whose violent and rancorous new leaders saw themselves as Wagner's heirs. Yet Mann saw himself as Wagner's heir, too; and so, willy-nilly, have all twentieth-century Germans, and all European and Euro-American musicians regardless of nationality.

FIG. 42-1 Richard Wagner (1865) by August Friedrich Pecht.

And not only Germans, and not only musicians. Wagner's influence has been so great that the intellectual historian Jacques Barzun — in a once widely read book called *Darwin, Marx, Wagner* — cast him as one of the three pivotal figures of the mid- to late nineteenth century who ushered in the agonizing modern age, the age of the godless and materialistic twentieth century. The threat to Christianity posed by Darwinism, with its rival history of creation, and by Marxism, with its rival theory of social justice, is obvious. The nature of Wagnerism is more difficult to pin down, and not only because Wagner worked in a nonverbal medium (for he wrote words, too, well-nigh graphomaniacally). Clearly he was no materialist in the sense that Darwin and Marx were materialists. He even wrote a couple of ostensibly Christian dramas about knights of the Holy Grail: the already-mentioned *Lohengrin* (1848) and *Parsifal* (1882), his last work, whose title character was Lohengrin's father. Wagner was in an important sense a religious thinker in his own right. That is why Wagner's name — uniquely among artists — has become an "ism."

But his religion was not Christianity. *Lohengrin* and *Parsifal* were based on German legends that were only incidentally Christian, and it was German myth and legend that formed the basis of Wagner's mature work. The ecstatic and redemptive religion his works proclaimed was in effect a new paganism born of ethnic rather than political nation-worship, and anyone who knows the history of the twentieth century knows that ethnic nationalism has been an even more volatile force in that history than Darwinism or Marxism has been. Wagner's words and music, with their colossal power of suggestion and persuasion, played a crucial role in disseminating that baleful impulse.

Thus, even if we conclude that Wagner was no true intellectual bedfellow of Darwin or Marx, his comparable rank as a culture hero cannot be denied. Also undeniable is the fact that of all the artists of the nineteenth century, only Wagner demands (or deserves) to be placed in such company. To say this is not to say that he was the best or greatest of all nineteenth-century artists. (How could it be proved that he was better or greater than Beethoven — to pick the most obvious "rival" — except on specious Zukunftist grounds?) But the work of no other artist looms as large as Wagner's as a cultural and political watershed. And for a third undeniable thing, only a musician could have made such a list of nineteenth-century figures, and no such list could have been complete without a musician. Such was the stature of music among the nineteenth-century arts, and it was Wagner who preeminently embodied that stature.

Finally, like Darwin's and Marx's, Wagner's legacy has been one of quarrels and fanaticism. Alone among nineteenth-century composers, perhaps alone among composers, Wagner can still provoke a riot in the concert hall, especially in the state of Israel, where a strict if unofficial ban on the public performance of his works is occasionally breached and invariably enforced with loud spontaneous protests. Jacques Barzun's book was especially bound to include Wagner among the giants of the nineteenth century in view of its date of publication: 1941, when Europe (soon to be joined by the United States) was engaged in a war that had been provoked by the same self-designated and enthusiastic Wagnerians who had impelled Thomas Mann into voluntary exile eight years before.

Wagner, in short, is one difficult and problematical artist who has never stopped being a problem. That in its way is the supreme attestation of his genius: only an artist of the greatest and most unshakeable stature could have become so great and unshakeable a problem. Our task, then, will be an especially complicated one where Wagner is concerned. We cannot say it is done until we have grappled both with the greatness and with the problem.

ART AND REVOLUTION

In view of his eventual transformative stature in history, the most extraordinary fact in Wagner's biography is the ordinariness of his beginnings. No composer of comparable achievement — at least none up to then — had ever had a slower start. Wagner was no Mozartian or Mendelssohnian prodigy. He was no Lisztian virtuoso. A native Leipziger, he manifested no early signs of unusual talent for music. Like many late starters, he never developed perfect pitch, often taken as a measure of natural aptitude for music. His earliest artistic interest was, perhaps significantly, in Greek epic and drama. At school he made translations from the *Odyssey* and tried to compose an epic of his own. His first completed creative effort was a pseudo-Shakespearean tragedy, written in 1828, when he was fifteen. It was a wish to set the play to music that led Wagner to his first lessons in music theory and composition that year, with a local theater conductor. Later he studied violin and counterpoint at the Leipzig Thomasschule, where Bach had taught a century before.

By the time Wagner reached the age at which Schubert died, he had gained some experience as a conductor at a couple of provincial East Prussian opera houses, first in Königsberg (now Kaliningrad, Russia) and then in Riga (now the capital of Latvia, located in Wagner's time within the borders of the Russian empire). But as a composer he had accomplished practically nothing worth remembering. "I still remember, around my thirtieth year," the world-famous composer wrote in his fiftieth year, "asking myself whether I possessed the capacity to develop an artistic individuality of high rank; I could still detect in my work a tendency toward imitation, and contemplated only with great anxiety my chances of developing into an independent original creator."

This was a harsh judgment, perhaps (and in retrospect he could afford it), but it was not unfair. The work Wagner had produced up to 1842 had included three complete operas, several overtures (including one on "Rule, Britannia"), a hymn in honor of the Russian Emperor Nikolai I (required by the terms of his Riga contract), three piano sonatas, and some songs, but none of it survives in repertory with the exception of the occasionally exhumed overture to the third opera, *Rienzi*, a Meyerbeerian grand opera on a subject from Roman history. The two earlier operas were both comic works: *Die Feen* ("The fairies," never performed during Wagner's lifetime) after an old scenario by the Venetian playwright Carlo Gozzi, and *Das Liebesverbot* ("The ban on love," performed, once only, in 1836) after Shakespeare's *Measure for Measure*. The music, as Wagner admitted in retrospect, was completely derivative of the repertory current at the German theaters of the day, and bizarrely eclectic, mixing Weber with Bellini.

In 1839, having been fired from his post in Riga, Wagner made for Paris, where he fancied the as yet unfinished *Rienzi* might be staged, and remained there for two and one-half years. He utterly failed to establish himself as a composer, and kept from starving only by accepting low-paying work from music publishers making piano arrangements of popular operas, and by writing reviews and other articles (not all of them on music) for publication both in Paris and at home. When *Rienzi* was finally accepted for performance, it was in Dresden, not Paris. It became the occasion not for his success in the French capital, but for his leaving it. The lifelong resentment with which Wagner looked back on his three years in Paris had a considerable impact on the subsequent direction of his work.

But as of 1842, five years before the death of his contemporary Mendelssohn, seven years before the death of his contemporary Chopin, and fourteen years before the death of his contemporary Schumann, Wagner was still at square one, both creatively and in terms of his career. That is why one tends to forget that he was an only slightly younger member of the same generation as the three composers just named, and why he is associated even more firmly and exclusively than Liszt with the somewhat later period whose "complete expression" (to recall Mann) he unexpectedly became.

Wagner did receive one all-important musical impression in Paris, however — though he did his best in later life to cover it up. In the fall of 1839 Wagner heard Berlioz conduct his own dramatic symphony *Roméo et Juliette*, a work in the symphony-oratorio tradition of Beethoven's Ninth and David's *Le Désert*, in which vocal music alternated with instrumental — that is, texted music with absolute — in the delineation of Shakespeare's tragedy of ill-starred love. In Wagner's own recollection, it opened for him "a new world of possibilities which I had not then dreamed of,"[2] both in the handling of the orchestra and in the transmutation of drama into instrumental music — or, to put it the other way around, in the dramatic concretization of textless music.

Wagner never forgot this lesson from Berlioz, and acknowledged it a quarter of a century later in a presentation copy of the orchestral score to one of his own operas, inscribed "To the great and dear author of *Roméo et Juliette*, the grateful author of *Tristan und Isolde*." He also acknowledged it to Liszt, in a letter dating from the time of the *Lohengrin* premiere, when he averred that "there are only three of us who belong together nowadays, because only we are our own equals, and that's you — *he* [Berlioz] — and I."[3] At the very least, this was an enormous slight to Schumann, then the most eminent German composer by far. But Schumann had put himself at a distance from the New German School in reaction to Franz Brendel's critical excesses (see chapter 40), and (as we may remember from chapter 38) he had been somewhat chary in his praise of Berlioz's *Symphonie fantastique*. In light of the alliance Wagner now claimed with his French and Hungarian senior colleagues, the claims of the New German School to a bona fide national birthright seem more equivocal than ever.

But for public consumption Wagner told another story. In his autobiography *Mein Leben* ("My life"), written in the 1870s, when Wagner was widely if grudgingly recognized (in Carl Dahlhaus's words) as "the uncrowned king of German music,"[4] and after a newly powerful and united Germany had at last avenged itself in war against post-Napoleonic France, Berlioz's *Roméo et Juliette* was replaced in Wagner's account by a fictitious performance of Beethoven's Ninth Symphony as the shattering event of Wagner's Paris days, the purifying experience that ended "that whole period of deterioration in my musical taste" brought about by "my superficial theatrical activities," which "now sank away before me as if into an abyss of shame and remorse."[5]

Wagner now professed having been put off, in *Roméo et Juliette*, by "a great deal that was empty and shallow."[6] He performed something like a ritual of exorcism to purge his soul, and the souls of his readers, of any sense of kinship with French art, even Berlioz's: "While admiring this genius, absolutely unique in his methods," Wagner now admonished, "I could never quite shake off a certain peculiar feeling of anxiety; his works left me with a sensation as of something strange, something with which I felt I should never be able to be familiar, and I was often puzzled at the strange fact that, though ravished by his compositions, I was at the same time repelled and even wearied by them."[7] He was, in short, a *German*, to whose essential nature French culture was, by *its* essential nature, insuperably alien. This mystique of unanalyzable essences — "essentialism" as it is now usually called — was already on display twenty years before in his tract on Jewishness in music. A necessary component of racism (if not by itself a sufficient one), it was Wagner's signal contribution to music criticism.

The Dresden premiere of *Rienzi*, at the Royal Court Theater of Saxony on 20 October 1842, was a huge success, followed almost immediately by an incredible break: the sudden death of the Royal Court Kapellmeister, an Italian named Francesco Morlacchi (whose music, quoted in Ex. 38-3, may have had a chance influence on Schumann). Wagner, who until then had conducted only at Königsberg and Riga, and nowhere for the last three years, was offered the job. It was as if the former conductor of the Portland Junior Symphony were suddenly named director of the Metropolitan Opera. To cement the deal, Wagner supervised a production of his next opera — *Der fliegende Holländer* (*The Flying Dutchman*), his first on a German legendary subject and by common consent his first masterpiece — in February 1843.

The six-year tenure at Dresden thus so auspiciously inaugurated would reach its conclusion in the spring of 1849 on the city barricades, with the opera house in flames and Wagner so obviously delighted at the sight of the blaze that he was accused of having started it. A musician, spotting him in the crowd, yelled a merry parody of Schiller's and Beethoven's Ode to Joy: "Herr Kapellmeister, der Freude schöner Götterfunken hat gezündet!" ("Mr. Conductor, the divine spark of joy has ignited!"). A warrant for Wagner's arrest was issued on 16 May; eight days later, with Liszt's help, he escaped to Switzerland. He would not set foot on German soil for more than a decade.

By then Wagner had composed his grand romantic operas *Tannhäuser* and *Lohengrin*, which continued his series of German legends for the stage and marked him out as the white hope of the New German School. The combination of antiquarian romanticism in the work with revolutionary politics in the life is only a surface paradox: both the futuristic politics and the nostalgic esthetics were symptoms of a general utopianism that seized the European cultural avant-garde during the revolutionary decade. Moreover, the title characters of all three of Wagner's romantic operas — the

FIG. 42-2   *The Flying Dutchman*, final scene of the first production (1843).

Dutchman, Tannhäuser, Lohengrin — were heroic intruders whose advent irrevocably disrupts a corrupt or complacent social order: revolutionaries, in short, with whom Wagner, resentful parvenu that he was, identified intensely.

The Flying Dutchman (who should really be known as the Roaming or Wandering Dutchman) was a legendary symbol of uprooting and persecution akin to the Wandering Jew, condemned to roam unceasingly because he taunted (some say struck) Christ on the day of his crucifixion. In Wagner's version, borrowed from Heine, the title character, a phantom sea captain condemned to eternal maritime wandering in his phantom ship as penalty for the sin of pride, is redeemed by the sacrificial love of a pure maiden (Senta), daughter of a greedy merchant sailor who had plighted her to the Dutchman for the sake of material gain. To her father's despair she willingly perishes to free the stranger. The stormy D-minor Overture to *The Flying Dutchman*, Wagner's earliest palpable hit, is one of the most successful of the many emblematic nineteenth-century rewritings of the first movement of Beethoven's Ninth.

Tannhäuser was a historical figure. In fact we have met him, in chapter 4 of this book, as one of the thirteenth-century German knightly poet-musicians known as *Minnesänger*. In the opera, the full title of which is *Tannhäuser und der Sängerkrieg auf Wartburg* ("Tannhäuser and the singers' contest on the Wartburg"), he is a knight crusader who has dallied (both sacrilegiously and anachronistically) with Venus, the Roman love goddess, and has scandalized his peers with his lascivious songs, but is redeemed by the sacrificial love of Elisabeth, a pure maiden who inspires sincere remorse, by pilgrimage, and by divine forgiveness despite his sin (and despite the pope's obduracy).

The musical tour de force in Wagner's setting is the brilliant contrast between the impressive chorale-like solemnity of the pilgrimage music and the extraordinary sensuality of the music suggestive of the "Venusberg" (Mount of Venus or Mons Veneris, the goddess's abode). The Venusberg music certainly flaunts the lessons in timbre and orchestral texture that Wagner had learned from Berlioz. In the form in which it is performed today, however, the episode is an interpolation made for a (famously unsuccessful) Paris revival in 1861, after Wagner had broken through (in *Tristan und Isolde*) to a harmonic idiom unforeseen in 1845.

In retrospect, however, the most Wagnerian moment in *Tannhäuser* is the title character's long narrative monologue in the third and last act, in which the composer achieved what the Wagner scholar Barry Millington calls an unprecedented "musico-poetic synthesis,"[8] something inescapably reminiscent of earlier attempts to invent or re-invent opera along neoclassical lines. As in a recitative, say, by Monteverdi or by Gluck, Wagner's vocal line closely follows the contour and rhythm of the spoken language, while the form seems to follow no preconceived structure but responds instead, and with great flexibility, to the anecdotal and emotional sequence of the narrative. And following the unacknowledged example of more recent French composers, the orchestra supports the vocal line with a supple web of expressive and illustrative reminiscence motifs.

Later, however, another Wagner scholar, Carolyn Abbate, discerned a crucial additional element in the Wagnerian synthesis. She showed that underlying the apparently free form of the narrative is the traditionally strophic form of the narrative ballad, long associated (at least, in our experience, since the days of Goethe and Schubert) with Germanic imitation folklore. This was a particularly fertile insight since it bridged the modernistic (revolutionary) and the folkloric or archaic aspects of Wagner's legend-spinning technique.[9]

In *Lohengrin*, finally, the title character is a legendary knight of the Holy Grail. The opera follows no single literary prototype but is Wagner's own synthesis derived from anonymous medieval epics and from the romances of the Minnesinger Wolfram von Eschenbach (ca. 1170–ca. 1220), a contemporary of the historical Tannhäuser. In the plot the composer crafted from these sources, the pure knight comes out of nowhere in a boat drawn by a white swan, to aid a pure maiden (Elsa of Brabant) who has been falsely accused of murder by a scheming claimant to the throne to which her slain brother was heir. Lohengrin restores order to the troubled

FIG. 42-3   *Lohengrin*, costume design by Julius Schnorr von Carosfeld for the first production (Bibliothèque Nationale, Paris).

land, banishes the schemer and his sorceress wife, and prepares to marry Elsa. Because she could not contain her curiosity and demands to know his identity, he is forced to renounce her and she dies of grief, but not before her brother is miraculously released from the transmogrified swanlike state in which he had conveyed his sister's deliverer to his noble mission.

Like Tannhäuser, Lohengrin sings a self-revealing ballad-narrative in the third act, establishing it as the quintessential Wagnerian form. The other item in the opera that in retrospect assumes the character of a Wagnerian first is the Prelude (*Vorspiel*) to the first act. Instead of a conventional overture in several contrasting sections (or with several contrasting themes), a Wagnerian prelude aspires to complete formal unity, carried along as if on a single breath by what Wagner later termed *unendliche Melodie* ("endless" or "infinite melody"), a seamless stream in which every note is thematic. Many of Wagner's later preludes could be described as scene setters, but this one is something else. It is a summary of the opera's ideal content: the musically (that is, nonverbally) enunciated concepts and imagery of which the anecdotal plot that follows is to be a metaphor. Far from anticipating or preparing for the agitated opening scene, it contrasts with it in every way. Wagner called it a representation of a host of angels descending with the Holy Grail, and their return to heaven after delivering it. Lohengrin's serenely mysterious appearance and departure, and his powers of deliverance, are prefigured. The form of this seventy-five-bar composition is simplicity itself — a highly significant simplicity, in fact, since even here the strophic principle of the narrative ballad rules. The melody first heard in the ethereal timbre of divided violins immediately returns, reinforced by doubled woodwinds (and with a different continuation). Again, more richly yet, it returns in the horns and lower strings, yet again, powerfully, it returns in the massed brass, after which a composed diminuendo reverses the composed crescendo of perpetually strengthened instrumentation, until just four solo violins are left playing at the end.

Less audaciously simple in form, but more popular as a concert piece, is the boisterous prelude to act III with its brassy main theme sandwiching a quieter middle section for the winds in a conventional ABA form. It gives way, incidentally, to a number so popular as to have become folk music: Elsa's bridal song, known by many who are unaware of ever having heard any Wagner as "Here Comes the Bride." Even in the nineteenth century, the oral tradition remained as alert to emanations from the literate sphere as the other way around.

In keeping with his personal identification with his heroes — or, perhaps more to the point, with his wish to be identified *as* a hero — Wagner insisted on drawing links between his artistic output and his biography, many of which have been exposed as spurious. He claimed, for example, that *The Flying Dutchman* had been inspired by his own shipboard experience of storms off the Norwegian coast during a voyage to England in 1839. But examination of his manuscripts has revealed that the Norwegian setting was hastily substituted for a Scottish one only weeks before the Dresden premiere.

In a similar vein, Wagner claimed that the inspiration for *Tannhäuser* came when he caught a glimpse of the site of the eventual song contest, the famous castle at Wartburg in Thuringia (eastern Germany), on his way back from Paris to Dresden in 1842. As he put it in a famous passage from *Mein Leben*, the sight, "so rich in historical and mythical associations, so warmed my heart against wind and weather, against Jews and Leipzig commerce, that in the end I arrived hale and hearty."[10] A seemingly gratuitous dig, this; and yet, like all of Wagner's self-mythologizing, it points up the strong connections between art and myth, and between myth and contemporary politics, that guided Wagner's work from beginning to end, and that has always formed the context of its reception.

THE ARTWORK OF THE FUTURE, MODELED (AS ALWAYS) ON THE IMAGINED PAST

All the more ineluctable are these connections in view of Wagner's lifelong habit, which he made a point of enunciating not merely as practice but as principle, of writing his own librettos — or, as he put it, the "poems" for his "dramas." A playwright even before he was a musician, he found this a natural enough task. But he insisted that it was a necessary prerequisite for returning drama to its true estate as the supreme artwork in which all artistic media were united. Thus it is a mistake to regard the libretto of an opera, even one by Wagner, as providing in itself a *dramma per musica*, to quote the old Florentine slogan — a "drama for [i.e., to be realized through] music." Neither the words nor the music were privileged in Wagner's conception; the drama arose out of their union.

All of this theorizing became explicit during a momentous hiatus in Wagner's composing activity, one attributable in equal measure to factors internal and external. After the Weimar premiere of *Lohengrin* under Liszt in 1850 not another Wagnerian premiere would take place until 1865. And except for a single short and intensely frustrating bout in the summer of 1850, Wagner put hardly a note on paper between 1848 and 1853. This period of musical dormancy in Wagner's career has often been compared to the chrysalis or pupa phase in the life of an insect, during which the larva is passively — and, seemingly, miraculously — transformed into the imago, or fully developed organism. Wagner's was no passive transformation, however; no artist ever reflected more furiously or with a greater sense of purpose on his art. It was a willed self-transformation, an act of genuine renunciation and heroism that has scarcely a parallel in art history. Its results were equally unparalleled, and momentous.

To deal with the external factors first: *Tannhäuser's* poor reception in 1845, and the dismal failure of his repeated attempts to reform the administration of the court theater establishment, alienated Wagner from his job and inclined him toward increasingly open political agitation. In the big incendiary year 1848 he met the exiled Russian anarchist Mikhail Bakunin (1814–76), under whose spell he wrote a series of articles culminating in *Die Kunst und die Revolution* (*Art and Revolution*), written on a visit to Paris in the summer of 1849, at the beginning of his exile.

It is in this tract that we encounter for the first time, and in crude but highly concentrated (and quotable) form, the theory of music drama that Wagner would will himself into embodying over the next half-dozen years, and to which he gave most detailed expression in an extended pamphlet called *Das Kunstwerk der Zukunft* ("The artwork of the future," 1849) and a full-length book called *Oper und Drama* ("Opera and drama, 1851, rev. 1868). Like most of the reformist tracts in operatic history (think again of Monteverdi, or of Gluck), these writings purported to revive and renew the ritual theater of ancient Greece, and recapture its fabled ethos. Unlike earlier reformers, however, but very much in the spirit of his time, Wagner conceived of that ethos in social terms. The Greek tragedy, the union of Apollo and Dionysus, of strength of character and creative vitality, was in his view the mainstay of Athenian democracy.

This was the essential link—the essential allegory—binding art and the public weal. "Hand-in-hand with the dissolution of the Athenian State marched the downfall of Tragedy,"[11] Wagner vociferated in *Art and Revolution*. "As the spirit of community (*Gemeinschaft*) split itself along a thousand lines of egoistic cleavage, so was the great united work (*Gesamtkunstwerk*) of Tragedy disintegrated into its individual factors." Those disunited splinters, sad fruit of social degeneration, were the proud separate arts as practiced in modern times: poetry, music, painting, and the rest, each with its own canons of illusive isolated excellence, each with its own zealously guarded traditions of craft and technique. No wonder that the arts had degenerated into playthings of the wealthy and the titled, or—worst of all—sites of commercial ("Jewish") activity.

The spiritual condition the modern arts expressed, according to Wagner, was one of abjectness, "soft complacence," social alienation. Or rather, this fallen state expressed itself through the modern arts, for such debased artistic practices could not truly express anything, least of all the despairing state of the modern world. "Of such a condition Art could never be the true expression," Wagner sneered. "Its only possible expression was *Christianity*," which emphasized not the free actions of free men, but only "*Faith*—that is to say, the confession of mankind's miserable plight, and the giving up of all attempt to escape from out this misery."[12] Christianity, Wagner said here more explicitly than anywhere else, was the contemptible consolation of the weak. Here he came closest to the other pair of thinkers with whom Jacques Barzun linked him in infamy. (Compare Marx, for whom religion was "the opium of the people.")

But unlike Marx, Wagner did not oppose all religion. Art was his religion, as art (or so he conceived it) had been the religion of the Greeks. "To the Greeks," he wrote, "the production of a tragedy was a religious festival, where the gods bestirred themselves upon the stage and bestowed on men their wisdom."[13] The surest proof of the modern debasement of art and religion alike, for Wagner, was the fact that almost every government had censorship laws that prohibited the theatrical portrayal of religious sacraments: "our evil conscience has so lowered the theater in public estimation, that it is the duty of the police to prevent the stage from meddling in the slightest with religion," while all the while the stage should be religion's natural habitat. But what sort of religion, if not Christian? Here again the Greeks had the answer: "With the Greeks,"[14] Wagner wrote, the perfect work of art, the Drama, was the abstract and epitome of all that was expressible in the Grecian nature. It was the nation itself—in intimate connection with its own history—that stood mirrored in its artwork, that communed with itself and, within the span of a few hours, feasted its eyes upon its own noblest essence. All division of this enjoyment, all scattering of the forces concentrated on *one* point, all diversion of the elements into separate channels, must needs have been as hurtful to this unique and noble artwork as to the like-formed state itself.

Thus the result of that division was not just the debasement of the separate arts, but the downfall of the "public conscience" as well. The reuniting of the arts in the perfect Drama, then, will be a regeneration of society. And here is where the nexus of Art and Revolution becomes an explicit prescription.

> Each one of these dissevered arts, nursed and luxuriously tended for the entertainment of the rich, has filled the world to overflowing with its products; in each, great minds have brought forth marvels; but the one true Art has not been born again, either in or since the so-called Renaissance. The perfect Art-work, the great united utterance of a free and lovely public life, the *Drama, Tragedy,* — howsoever great the poets who have here and there indited tragedies — is not yet born again: for the reason that it cannot be *re-born,* but must be *born anew.*
>
> Only the great *Revolution of Mankind,* whose beginnings erstwhile shattered Grecian Tragedy, can win for us this Art-work. For only this Revolution can bring forth from its hidden depths, in the new beauty of a nobler Universalism, *that* which it once tore from the conservative spirit of a time of beautiful but narrow-meted culture — and tearing it, engulfed.[15]

That, of course, is the reconstituted social cohesion that only a reconstituted art-religion can vouchsafe. As Edward Gibbon presciently wrote in *The Decline and Fall of the Roman Empire* some sixty years before, "the exercise of public worship appears to be the only solid foundation of the religious sentiments of the people," adding pointedly that "the memory of theological opinions cannot long be preserved, without the artificial helps of priests, of temples, and of books."[16] Gibbon was reflecting on the death of the national pagan religion that had sustained Rome's glory days. It was the religion that Wagner — as artist-priest, author of books, and builder of temples — wanted to restore by providing the means for the renewed exercise of public worship.

As an ostensible follower of Bakunin, who preached the violent overthrow of all political states so as to restore mankind to its naturally virtuous and pacific nature, Wagner made a point, in his tract of 1849, of forswearing all political nationalism. "If the Grecian Art-work embraced the spirit of a fair and noble nation," he wrote, "the Art-work of the Future must embrace the spirit of a free mankind delivered from every shackle of hampering nationality; its racial imprint must be no more than an embellishment, the individual charm of manifold diversity, and not a cramping barrier."[17]

And yet he could not follow Bakunin all the way to the radical individualism that the Russian, a true anarchist, favored. Possibly in unwitting accord with his Lutheran upbringing, Wagner sought emancipation not in individual autonomy but in *Gemeinschaft* — community, or group spirit. Art's great task, as Wagner formulated it, was "to teach man's social impulse its noblest meaning, and guide it toward its true direction."[18] The envisioned brotherhood was that of *"the strong fair Man,"* as the composer put it, italicizing every word, "to whom *Revolution* shall give his *Strength,* and Art his *Beauty!"*

So the Art-work of the future celebrated and guided a cult of strength. "Only the *Strong* know *Love,"* Wagner continued, italics still lending his prose a fever pitch,

> only Love can fathom *Beauty;* only *Beauty* can fashion *Art.* The love of weaklings for each other can only manifest itself as the goad of lust; the love of the weak

for the strong is abasement and fear; the love of the strong for the weak is pity and forbearance; but the love of the strong for the strong is *Love*, for it is the free surrender to one who cannot compel us. Under every fold of heaven's canopy, in every race, shall men by real freedom grow up to equal strength; by strength to truest love; and by true love to beauty. But Art is Beauty energized and turned to Knowledge.

And as the Knowledge of all men will find at last its religious utterance in the one effective Knowledge of free united manhood: so will all these rich developments of Art find their profoundest focus in the Drama, in the glorious Tragedy of Man. The Tragedy will be the feast of all mankind; in it, — set free from each conventional etiquette, — free, strong, and beauteous man will celebrate the dolour and delight of all his love, and consecrate in lofty worth the great Love-offering of his Death.[19]

Needless to say, these ravings are of interest to us only because after a long, ruthlessly honest, and heroically self-disciplined quest, Wagner found the creative wherewithal to realize this dream in a fashion that many then and since have found overwhelmingly convincing. In themselves Utopian pronouncements matter little. They come as dependably from cranks, charlatans, and adolescents as from geniuses, and they usually possess nothing but historical interest (that is, as signs of the times). If Wagner's career had ended at this point he would be remembered today for his three romantic operas, and as a blustery "campus radical" in the enthusiastic but ineffectual spirit of '48. Not the theorizing but the creative work — not the intention, in other words, but the deed — has won Wagner his towering stature. The controversy that continues to surround his name is above all a controversy over the extent to which the deed necessarily embodied the intention. What it finally comes down to is a debate as to whether the identification of Wagner's creative achievement with his political and social purposes amounts to anything more than a particularly noisome and destructive instance of the genetic fallacy: the confusion of the actual nature or essence of a thing with the circumstances of its origin or its motivating premises.

FROM THEORY INTO PRACTICE: THE *RING*

To return now from the speculative to the historical plane and continue our narrative, the intentions implicit in *Art and Revolution* could hardly have been embodied more explicitly than they were in Wagner's next creative project. And equally obvious is the persistent identity of the Wagnerian cult of strength with a cult of nation after all — a nation conceived not in political but in ethnic (or "racial") terms. As Wagner put it shortly after returning from Paris to Zürich, his Swiss abode, exile had made him homesick — but not "merely for the modern homeland":

As though to get down to its root, I sank myself into the primal element of Home, that meets us in the legends of a Past which attracts us the more warmly as the Present repels us with its hostile chill. To all our wishes and warm impulses, which in truth transport us to the *Future*, we seek to give a physical token by means of pictures from the Past, and thus to win for them a form the modern Present never can provide.[20]

Thus was Utopia tinged by nostalgia. Under cover of a universalism that nevertheless drew exclusively on pre-Enlightened Germanic sources, nationalism had reentered through the back door.

The combination of futuristic utopianism by way of Bakunin and nostalgic utopianism by way of Nordic myth was a volatile one, to say the least. Wagner met

FIG. 42-4   Wagner, sketch for *Siegfrieds Tod* (1850), containing music that later went into *Die Walküre* and *Götterdämmerung* (Library of Congress, Gertrude Clarke Whittall Foundation).

Bakunin in the summer of 1848. He spent the fall of that year drafting the "poem" for a *grosse Heldenoper* ("great heroic opera") to be called *Siegfrieds Tod* ("The death of Siegfried"). Siegfried (or Sigurd) the Dragon-Slayer was the great folk hero of the early and medieval Germanic mythology in which Wagner was immersing himself. For Wagner, Siegfried was a revelation of "the fair young form of Man, in all the freshness of his force, the real naked Man, in whom I might spy each throbbing of his pulses, each stir within his mighty muscles, in uncramped, freest motion: the type of the true *human being.*"[21] Siegfried's legend looms especially large in the *Volsungasaga*, an Icelandic epic that recounts the mythic origins of the Nordic peoples, and in the *Nibelungenlied*, a thirteenth-century epic by an anonymous South German poet, which recounts many of Siegfried's exploits, including his brute seizure for his superior Volsung race of the great gold hoard of the Nibelungs (a race of dwarfs), his capture of Brynhild, the Icelandic queen, his death through her treachery, and her atonement through self-immolation, leading to the golden age of gods and Germans.

Wagner's enthusiasm for these old texts was not his alone. As the Wagnerian scholar Barry Millington has pointed out, by the 1840s the *Nibelungenlied* had become the object of a cult in Germany, where it had become "a potent symbol in the struggle for national unification."[22] None other than Franz Brendel, the force behind the New German School, had called for an operatic setting of the myth, no doubt already thinking of Wagner: "I believe the composer who could accomplish this task in an adequate manner would become the man of his era,"[23] he declared. But Wagner had his own reasons to be drawn to Siegfried. As George Bernard Shaw dryly observed in his lighthearted but instructive pamphlet *The Perfect Wagnerite* (1898), Wagner saw Siegfried as a sort of Norse "Bakoonin," a great (if thwarted) revolutionary figure.

Wagner first learned about the Volsungs and the Nibelungs by way of *Deutsche Mythologie* (1835), a best-seller by the great philologist Jacob Grimm of fairy tale fame, which contained alongside detailed synopses of the sagas a description of the Norse theogony (the genealogy and history of the gods), as preserved in the medieval Icelandic epics known as Eddas. The aim of *Siegfrieds Tod* was to link the personal tragedy of Siegfried, a traditional sort of operatic subject (and one already foreshadowed in the previous works of Wagner's early maturity), with the Edda myths, the history of the gods, and so elevate the drama to the level of a cosmogony (the story of the origins and destiny of the world). That would provide a suitably hallowed subject for his socially transforming "Art-work of the future." The libretto he came up with portrayed Siegfried's death as the end result and expiation of a curse on the Nibelung hoard, placed there long ago (according to the Eddas) by the dwarf Alberich from whom the gods had stolen it. In this blend of tragedy and epic (something, incidentally, that the Greeks said couldn't be done), the tragic element was to be portrayed through action, the epic through a wealth of ballad-narratives of a kind for which Wagner had already shown a strong predilection.

This time, however, it did not work. The biggest ballad-narrative in *Siegfrieds Tod* came right at the beginning, in a lengthy prologue that showed the three Norns, figures comparable to the three Fates of Greek mythology, who weave eternally the rope of destiny. As they weave, they tell the story of how the dwarf Alberich, of the Nibelung race, stole the gold hoard from the Rhine and fashioned from it a ring; how the gods contracted for themselves a magnificent castle and paid for it by stealing the ring from the Nibelungs, who cursed it, and by giving the cursed ring to the giants who built the castle; how Siegfried slew the surviving giant, who had assumed the form of a dragon; how the hero won the sleeping Brynhild (Brünnhilde in the opera), awakened and loved her (an archetypal Wagnerian "love of the strong for the strong") but failed to heed the portent of her treachery. This final section of the narrative brings the story to the point at which direct action can commence. A true ballad, it was even equipped with a refrain that is heard at the beginning and at every point where a semicolon occurred in the foregoing summary (Ex. 42-1).

Wagner sketched a setting of this narrative, and also began the next scene, a duet for Brünnhilde and Siegfried, before breaking off in despair. In a later tract, *Eine Mittheilung an meine Freunde* ("A communication to my friends"), published in 1851 as the hundred-page preface to a collected edition of the "poems" to his romantic operas, Wagner gave an account of his travails. "Just as I was setting Brünnhilde's first address to Siegfried," he wrote, "all my courage suddenly failed me since I could not refrain from asking myself which singer could bring such a heroine to life." Another reason for losing heart was the knowledge, as he put it, that "I should now be writing this music only for paper,"[24] that is, without any imminent prospect of a performance, exiled as he was from his homeland.

But as Carolyn Abbate has suggested, these were rationalizations, not reasons.[25] There was more to Wagner's impasse than practical concerns or temporary dejection. It peeps through the lines of his "Communication" where Wagner wrote—somewhat clumsily, at an uncharacteristic loss for words—of his "fear that my poetic purpose could not be conveyed in its full aspect to the only organ at which I aimed, namely the *Gefühlsverständnis* of any public whatsoever."[26] The best that Wagner's first English translator, William Ashton Ellis, could do with the crucial word, *Gefühlsverständnis*, was "feeling's-understanding." It would be fruitless to look for a better English phrase, since the German itself is murky. A gloss is required, an interpretation in the light of subsequent events. But first, back to Wagner. After some hemming and hawing, he continues his confession. If he continued setting the existing poem as it stood, he realized,

> I should have had willy-nilly to tax myself to *suggest* a host of huge connections in order to present the action in its full meaning. But these *suggestions*, naturally, could only be inlaid in *epic* [i.e., narrative] form into the drama; and here was the point that filled me with misgiving as to the efficacy of my drama, in its proper sense of a scenic exposition. But these connections were of such a nature that they could proclaim themselves only in actual plot situations, that is in situations that can only be intelligibly displayed *in Drama*. Only in this way could I have any chance of succeeding in *artistically conveying my purpose to the true emotional* (not just the critical) *understanding* of spectators who shall have gathered together expressly to learn it.[27]

Usually this passage, and the one before it, is interpreted to mean that Wagner wanted to convert the narrative component of the drama, which recounted all those "suggestions" of previous history, into directly portrayed action, which meant expanding

EX. 42-1 Norns' refrain and First Norn's first speech from Wagner's sketches for *Siegfrieds Tod*

EX. 42-I (*continued*)

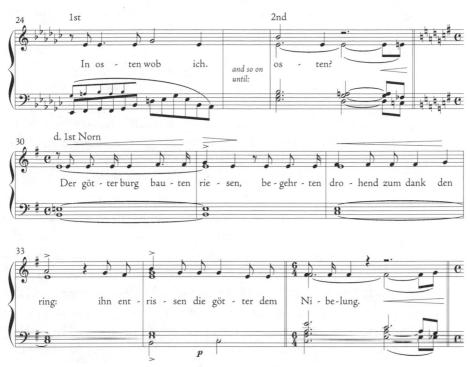

the conception of the dramatized myth into a whole trilogy of musical dramas plus a prologue: that is, the gigantic theatrical cycle that Wagner did in fact succeed in bringing forth (though it took him twenty-five years to do it) and that is now collectively known as *Der Ring des Nibelungen* ("The ring of the Nibelung," or "Alberich's ring").

But this explanation leaves us with a paradox: even after the remaining dramas were composed, the narratives in the last of them, which had been *Siegfrieds Tod* (now called *Götterdämmerung*, "Twilight of the Gods") not only remained in place but became even longer than before. And this applies especially to the narrative of the Norns, where all the trouble began. In the abortive version of 1850, its setting, a simple ballad with refrain, occupied 114 measures; its very complex successor in *Götterdämmerung*, even without counting the spate of orchestral music that precedes the singing, takes 277!

Thomas Mann had an inkling into what Wagner was really about when he wrote that in turning *Siegfrieds Tod* into the *Ring* Wagner was acting on "an overpowering need to bring that previous history within the sphere of his sense-appeal."[28] This begins to suggest that what Wagner felt was needed was a musically realized version of the past history of the drama that would give him the means of triggering through "sense" (that is, the sense of hearing) the kind of emotional response to the action — *whether directly portrayed or narrated* — that only music can elicit. That is what Wagner must have meant by "suggestions of connections"; and the emotional response to that sensory stimulus must be what he meant by "the feeling's-understanding." Put most simply, there had to be a preexisting *musical* reality with which the Norns' narrative, and everything else in the final drama, could suggestively connect.

Carolyn Abbate has built further on Mann's insight, casting Wagner's task as being one of creating "a past in music"[29] (rather than one merely described in words) that would be — precisely because it *was* in music — a truly mythic (or, to use Wagner's word, "engulfing") reality that the listener could be fully drawn into and could thus imaginatively inhabit for the duration of the performance. The purpose, then, of converting what was at first merely narrated by the Norns into directly portrayed action was to generate from it a fund of musical symbols with which to stock the audience's mind, so that when the same all-encompassing narration finally arrived at the beginning of what was the last in a colossal series of four operas, it would possess a palpable, engulfing, and, finally, irresistible emotional force.

By the time Wagner wrote his "Communication to My Friends," he had formulated this grand plan, had begun implementing it, and had even (in *Opera and Drama*) recast the whole history of music and drama from the Greeks to the present in order to justify it as the inevitable outcome of that history. No artist had ever exhibited such unmitigated arrogant ambition; but by the same token no artist had ever accepted so publicly the risk of risible failure. The eventual triumph of the *Ring* was what made Wagner for the last dozen years of his life the uncrowned king of German music. But these were also the first dozen years of the German Reich, the empire that finally united all the German princedoms and dukedoms under an actual single king. The prophecy of *Art and Revolution*, linking artistic regeneration with the regeneration of the body politic, could be seen, by those who wished, as having come true.

FORM AND CONTENT

The first step was to depict the events recounted by the last segment of the Norns' narrative: Siegfried's coming of age as a hero, his killing the dragon, and winning Brünnhilde. This was accomplished in a "poem" called *Der junge Siegfried* ("Young Siegfried"), composed in the spring of 1851 right after *Oper und Drama* was completed. Next, to explain how the sleeping Brünnhilde had got where she was (on a rocky peak surrounded by fire) when Siegfried

FIG. 42-5   *Die Walküre*, costume and stage designs by M. Ferdinandus. At left, Siegmund and Siglinde fall in love (Act I); at right, Wotan bids farewell to Brünnhilde (Act III).

penetrated her bastion and awakened her, and to clarify Siegfried's qualifications, so to speak, for his heroic calling (being the incestuous — thus purebred — offspring of two fine Volsung specimens), Wagner preceded *Der junge Siegfried* with another "poem," *Die Walküre* ("The Valkyrie," that is, Brünnhilde), composed between November 1851 and July 1852.

In the process of composing *Die Walküre*, Wagner completely reconceived the drama under the influence of Arthur Schopenhauer, the philosopher whose pessimistic worldview had converted Wagner from the optimistic ideas of the young Hegelians. He reconfigured the *Ring* around Wotan — the chief of the Gods and Brünnhilde's father — as central character, rather than Siegfried. Wotan's original sin, that of destroying the World Ash Tree by hacking his

FIG. 42-6   *Das Rheingold*, David Bispham (1857–1921) as Alberich.

invincible spear from it, now became the deed for which the whole history of the Ring was the expiation, an expiation that now ended tragically, not with the redemption of the gods (as in *Siegfrieds Tod*, which now had to be drastically revised), but with their violent destruction. Finally, to show the beginning of that history, namely the theft of the gold hoard and the forging of the ring by Alberich the Nibelung (as related in the first stanza of the original Norns' narrative), Wagner wrote one last poem to serve as prologue in the form of a single mighty (two-hour) act: *Das Rheingold* ("The Rhine gold"), completed in November 1852.

Only now could Wagner turn to the creation of his musical reality, beginning of course with *Das Rheingold* and ending with *Götterdämmerung*. Thus the composition of the poems and that of the music proceeded in opposite chronologies (see Table 42-1).

By the time Wagner returned to the Norns' scene at the beginning of what was now *Götterdämmerung* and composed its definitive version, nineteen years had passed during which he had written five "dramas" — for so he insisted on calling the works he wrote after *Opera and Drama*, in which he had pronounced conventional "opera" forever invalid. In the process he had completely transformed his methods and his style to conform with the precepts he had speculatively evolved. The big gap in the midst of *Siegfried* was due in the first instance to Wagner's despair at his prospects for

TABLE 42-1   Chronology of the *Ring*

POEMS	MUSIC
Siegfrieds Tod (1848–1849; revised 1852) ↓	*Götterdämmerung* (3 acts) (1869–1874) ↑
Der junge Siegfried (1851; rev. 1852)	*Siegfried* (3 acts) (acts I & II 1857; act II scored 1864–1865; act III 1869)
Die Walküre (1851–1852)	*Die Walküre* (3 acts) (1854–1856)
Das Rheingold (1852)	*Das Rheingold* (1 act) (1853–1854)

ever getting the *Ring* performed, but mainly by the composition of two other dramas, to which our discussion will eventually return: *Tristan und Isolde* (completed in 1859, performed in 1865), often cited as the supreme practical embodiment of his theories, followed by *Die Meistersinger von Nürnberg*, Wagner's one mature comedy (completed in 1867, performed in 1868).

The eventual return to the *Ring*, and its completion, were made possible by a godsend: the unsolicited intervention of Ludwig II, the newly crowned king of Bavaria (southern Germany). The infatuated eighteen-year-old monarch summoned Wagner to Munich, his capital, in 1864, paid off all of Wagner's mountainous debts, lifted all

FIG. 42-7   Festspielhaus at Bayreuth, 1875.

FIG. 42-8   Festspielhaus in longitudinal cross section. Onstage are the flats for *Parsifal*; the orchestra, famously, is below and under the stage in the "mystic abyss"; and the auditorium is, no less famously, without aristocratic boxes.

bans on his travel, commissioned the completion of the *Ring* for the unheard-of sum of thirty thousand florins, subsidized the construction of an opera house (or "festival playhouse," to use Wagner's somewhat righteous term) to the composer's specifications in the town of Bayreuth for the sole purpose of performing his works, and even made Wagner his unofficial yet very powerful political adviser. Needless to say, the king's munificence profoundly altered Wagner's political and social views, which quickly took a reactionary and loyally monarchist turn. It also brought Wagner's operatic "reform" historically into line with previous ones: like those of the Florentine Camerata or Gluck, Wagner's was now no revolutionary exploit but a neoclassical revival under the protection of a crown, about as socially conservative a concept as the history of music provides.

But even if their political underpinning had now swung 180 degrees to the right, Wagner's artistic precepts remained what they were. Here is how he summarized the elements of the "music drama" in a passage toward the end of "A Communication to My Friends" (with its sections numbered for reference in the ensuing discussion). The style of the prose itself suggests the leisurely, exhaustive, finally overpowering dramatic unfolding that Wagner now sought:

> [1: The shape of the drama as a Whole] I now saw that in making the music I must necessarily proceed to a gradual but complete upheaval of the traditional *operatic form*. This opera-form was never by nature a form embracing the whole of the drama, but was just an arbitrary conglomerate of separate smaller forms of song, whose fortuitous concatenation of Arias, Duets, Trios, etc., together with Choruses and so-called ensemble-pieces, comprised the actual edifice of Opera.

FIG. 42-9   Stage magic at Bayreuth: carriages that supported the swimming Rhine maidens in the first full production of the *Ring* in 1876.

In the poetic fashioning of my material, it was henceforth impossible for me to contemplate filling out these ready-made forms. Through my music I could only aim now at bringing the drama's inherent overall shape within the grasp of Feeling. In the whole course of the drama I saw no possibility of division or demarcation, other than the Acts themselves, in which the place or time is shifted, or the Scenes in which the *dramatis personae* change. Moreover, the pliant unity of the myth-material made it unnecessary to crowd the scenes with incident as modern playwrights do; the whole strength of my dramatic portrayal could now be concentrated in a few weighty and decisive moments of development. [. . .] The more I extricated myself from the influence of conventional form, the more definitely the Form of portrayal now required by the peculiarities of my material and its dramatic situations took shape in my mind.

[2: The musical form] This procedure, dictated by the nature of the poetic subject, exercised a quite specific influence on the *tissue* of my music, as regards the characteristic *combination and ramification of the Thematic Motives*. Just as the structure of the individual scenes excluded every alien and unnecessary detail and led all interest to the main all-governing mood of the whole, so did the whole construction of the drama join itself into one organic unity, whose easily-surveyed members were delineated by those few scenes and situations that determined the succession of moods. No mood could be struck in any of these scenes that did not stand in a significant relationship to the moods of all the other scenes, so that the development of the moods of each from the others, and the constant prominence of this development, should establish the unity of the drama in its very mode of expression.

Each of these chief moods, in keeping with the nature of the material, must also gain a definite musical expression, which should display itself to the sense of hearing as a definite musical Theme. Just as, in the progress of the drama, the intended climax of a decisive main mood was only to be reached through a development, continuously present to the Feeling, of the individual moods already roused, so must the musical expression, which directly influences the physical feeling, necessarily take a decisive share in this development to a climax. And this purpose was realized, as if all by itself, in the form of a *characteristic tissue of principal themes* that spread itself not over *one* scene only (as heretofore in separate operatic "numbers"), but *over the whole drama*, and did so *in intimate connection with the poetic aim*.

[3: The musical style] From the "absolute-music" period of my youth, I recall that I had often posed myself the question: How must I set about inventing thoroughly original melodies that should bear a stamp peculiar to myself alone? The more I approached the period when I based my musical construction upon the poetic material, the more completely this anxiety for a special style vanished, until (having gained my objective) I lost it altogether. In my earlier operas I was purely governed by traditional modern melody, whose character I imitated and, out of the concern just mentioned, I merely sought to trick out with rhythmic and harmonic idiosyncrasies that I might vainly call my own. I had always, moreover, a greater leaning to broad and longspun melodies than to the short, broken and contrapuntal *melismus* [this evidently means something like "short turns of phrase"] proper to instrumental chamber music.

In the *Flying Dutchman*, though, for the first time, I touched on the rhythmic melody of the Folk — but only where the poetic material brought me into contact with the folk-element *per se*, here taking on a more or less national character. Wherever I had to give utterance to the emotions of my dramatis personae, on the other hand, as displayed in their passionate exchanges, I was forced to abstain altogether from this rhythmic melody of the folk; or rather, it could not so much as occur to me to employ that method of expression. It was then my purpose that the dialogue itself, conforming to the emotional content, was to be rendered in such a fashion that *not the melodic expression per se but the expressed emotion* should arouse the interest of the hearer.

The melody, in other words, must spring, quite of itself, from the verse. It could not be permitted to attract attention in itself, as sheer melody, but only insofar as it was the most expressive vehicle for an emotion already plainly outlined in the words. Having arrived at this strict conception of the role of melody, I now completely left the usual operatic mode of composition. I no longer tried intentionally for customary melody — or, in a sense, for melody at all, but absolutely let it take its cue from the feeling-utterance of the words.

[4: The form and style of the poem] The only thing that stood in my way was *the imperfection of our modern verse*, in which I could find no perceptible trace of any natural melodic source, nor any standard of musical expression. The trouble was its *utter lack of genuine rhythm*. I could never have set my *Siegfried* [that is, *Siegfrieds Tod*] if I had to rely on such verse. Thus I needed to invent a Speech-melody of an altogether different kind. And yet, in truth, I did not have to give it much thought, but only take courage; for at the same primal mythic spring where I had found the fair young Siegfried [that is, in the *Nibelungenlied* itself] I also lit, led by his hand, upon the perfect mode of utterance wherein such a man could speak his feelings. This was the *alliterative* verse, bending itself in natural and lively rhythm to the actual accents of our speech, yielding itself so readily to every shade of expression — that very *Stabreim* which the Folk itself once sang, when *it* was still both poet and mythmaker![30]

In sum then, to paraphrase section 1, in order to invest his drama with the authentic attributes of epic, and create not in the spirit of a modern composer, but in that of a folk bard, Wagner envisioned a vast, sweeping structure in which a scene or even a whole hour-long act would be articulated not by means of the customary largish units or "numbers" of conventional opera, but by means of tiny musical particles in ever-changing combinations and amalgams. This building up of a great whole out of a uniformly deployed fund of tiny but intensely meaningful parts would both lend organic unity to an unprecedented temporal span and eliminate the need for a clutter of depicted action. The action of the music drama, like that of an epic, would unfold in a kind of rapt and ritualized stasis that evoked the timeless time of myth, taking its shape within the mind of the spectator under the influence of the particles streaming by, endlessly associated and re-associated by the events depicted or described.

For this purpose description is as good as depiction, and that is why Wagner left so much narrative in place in the fully elaborated *Ring*, and why the reason usually given for its elaboration — viz., to replace events narrated in *Siegfrieds Tod* (=*Götterdämmerung*) with events actually enacted and depicted in *Das Rheingold*, *Die Walküre*, and *Siegfried* — is so inadequate to the task of explaining its final shape. It was to gather up the fund (or "tissue") of musical particles that would give the events of the final epic-drama a true "past in music" or musical reality, and the possibility of the kind of thematic linkages Wagner now envisioned, that made the vast, slowly unfolding preliminary trio of epic-dramas necessary.

In section 2, Wagner named the particles *Hauptthemen*, "main themes," as had become the standard nomenclature (through the writings of the music theorist Adolph Bernhard Marx) for the constituent themes in the exposition of a symphony or sonata movement. Most of them are far shorter than what is usually meant by a full-fledged theme, though, and some are really atomic particles — a mere turn of phrase (*melismus*), a chord progression, even a single chord or (at their most minimal) a single interval, if played with a characteristic timbre. They are more like what music analysts call motives, the kind of elemental ideas from which themes are built up, or (more typically) into which they devolve when developed.

At its most characteristic, then, it makes more sense to regard the Wagnerian "tissue" not as a thematic exposition but rather as a vastly extended, tonally vagrant development section. In this way its kinship with (or more strongly, its actual origin in) what Wagner was the first to call "absolute music" — the transcendently and ineffably expressive instrumental music of German romanticism — is kept in view. In keeping with the deliberately unspecified (and therefore protean or multivalent) significance of "absolute music," Wagner never gave his themes or "particles" descriptive or programmatic designations, the way Berlioz, for example (in the *Symphonie fantastique*), designated and delimited the meaning of his idée fixe. Wagner evidently wished to let the meanings of his motives emerge by a wordless process of association with the unfolding action, as (on a much smaller scale) the use of "reminiscence motives" had worked in earlier operas all the way back to the eighteenth century.

In 1876, however, the year in which the complete four-day *Ring* cycle was first performed at Bayreuth, Wagner authorized Hans von Wolzogen (1848–1938), a young aristocratic disciple, to compile and publish what he called a *Thematischer Leitfaden durch die Musik zu Richard Wagners Festspiel 'Der Ring des Nibelungen'* ("Thematic guidebook through the music to Richard Wagner's festival play 'The Ring of the Nibelung'"), the first of countless such books, sold wherever Wagner is performed, in which the particles were isolated and listed, and given names for ready reference.

These particles, which Wagner (and following him, Wolzogen) simply called themes, had already been given another name by a number of other commentators. Its originator, ironically enough, was an old enemy of Wagner's named Heinrich Dorn (1804–92), an acquaintance from the early days in Riga, who had written a folksy opera of his own on the Nibelungen legend as early as 1854, and resented Wagner's arrogant pretensions to revolutionize the arts of music and drama. Seeking to make fun of Wagner's "particles," Dorn had dubbed them *Leitmotive* (singular, *Leitmotiv*), a term obviously related to "guidebook" (*Leitfaden*), which caricatured Wagner's thematic particles as "motives to guide you" (i.e., through this mess). Other writers immediately found the ill-meant designation useful, however, and it is now standard terminology in all languages. In English the word is usually spelled "leitmotif" (plural, "leitmotives").

Whether the labels that Wolzogen and many later writers have attached to Wagner's leitmotives are equally useful is another matter. Many writers have deplored them as simplistic or "inaccurate"—though by what measure their accuracy can be gauged is hard to guess, since Wagner never named them and so they are all inaccurate by definition—and have called for their rejection. Commentators have occasionally tried to make do with numbers. That Wolzogen's names have tended narrowly to limit their signification can hardly be denied, though, and that is indeed a drawback.

An even greater drawback is the implication that, once named, leitmotives operate as objective referents rather than (as Wagner wished) a stimulus to the listener's subjective involvement in the drama. Without knowing the non-Wagnerian origin of the labels, one could easily imagine that Wagner conceived his leitmotives abstractly or even prepared them in advance of composition, as raw material; whereas in fact they arose in the course of the compositional act in conventionally spontaneous response to the poem and functioned thereafter in a manner no different in kind from that of a reminiscence motif, albeit on a vastly greater scale, to the point where, in *Götterdämmerung*, they constituted practically the whole of the musical "tissue," just as Wagner intended from the outset. William Mann, a translator and a respected explicator of the *Ring* (and an eloquent advocate of numbers), has cautioned that "every listener must decide for himself what *The Ring* means to him, and he will do so reasonably and justly, not necessarily by mastering the labels assigned to the ninety-odd musical themes by Hans von Wolzogen or [others], but by observing at which significant moments the themes appear and what may, as a result, be deduced from this." To label them, Mann argues (echoing a sally by claude debussy), reduces leitmotives to the level of "musical visiting cards."[31]

And yet even the way Mann describes them shows why mere numbers will not do: the occurrence and recurrence of leitmotives, borne along in a compellingly directed temporal medium that Wagner called the "sea of harmony," are what *define* the "significant moments" in the drama. They have, in short, not only musical but dramatic significance, and do indeed evoke a conceptual as well as a sensory response; their whole intended magic, in short, lies in their capacity to link (and to *control* the link between) the sensory and conceptualizing faculties, thus producing a synergy that magnifies response (or what Wagner called the feeling's-understanding) far beyond what either music or poetry or spoken drama might individually elicit. They are the chief vehicle through which the artistic synthesis at the heart of the Wagnerian enterprise operates.

Therefore, in the discussion that follows, and in keeping with the idea behind Mann's suggestion, leitmotives will be treated not as abstract signifiers but, as far as possible, as reminiscence motives. That is, they will be identified not only with their convenient conventional labels, but also (and primarily) in terms of their first appearance in the drama. (In the case of *Götterdämmerung*, this means they will be traced to their appearances in the earlier operas in the cycle.) In this way their status as concrete references through which every moment in the unfolding drama is linked, both conceptually and sensorily, with other moments, can be savored the way Wagner meant it to be savored: that is, as the elements out of which a mythical world and its history — amounting to nothing less than a mythic or alternative reality — is assembled not only in the composer's imagination, but in the listener/spectator's as well. But it will not do to scorn the verbal labels in principle: as word-savers they are indispensable.

Before observing Wagner's tissue of leitmotives in action as the articulator of epic drama, there is one more idea to investigate, the very important but often overlooked point raised in sections 3 and 4 in the extract from Wagner's "Communication," where the matter of personal style comes into collision with that of "folk" (that is, common or communal) style. Wagner clearly hankered after a style that would be both personal and in some sense communal, because he wanted both the prestige of a romantic genius (who had to be original) and the social potency of a bard (who partook of the language of his community).

His early, artificial attempts at originality, he confesses, were futile, lacking in social potency. Later, in The *Flying Dutchman*, he attempted to write in a folk style, but that style limited his originality, and in any event was only available for use when the characters singing were plausible representatives of "the folk" (that is, for the most part, faceless peasants in chorus). What was needed was a communal language that not only his characters but Wagner himself could use and adapt into a modern personal style. What Wagner wanted, in short, was a folklore (or an archaic lore, which for him meant the same thing) that could be used not merely as an object of representation, but as a source of personal style.

This sort of folklorism was given a name — "neonationalism" — in the twentieth century, not by musicologists but by art historians, originally with reference not to German but to Russian art. It fits Wagner's ideals and methods perfectly, however: from the *Stabreim* of old bardic poetry (short for *Buchstabenreim*, "rhyming with letters," that is, with initials) he educed a highly rhythmic but unrhymed verbal idiom full of assonance and alliteration on heavily accented syllables, out of which arose a compelling rhythm that animated the music in turn. In his stylistic impersonation of an ancient bard Wagner paradoxically found the path to a modern, original, and instantly recognizable personal idiom. As Jean Cocteau, a theorist of twentieth-century modernism, once said, an original creator has only to copy something in order to demonstrate his originality.[32]

Wagner was in this sense perhaps the first modern artist. The community to which he gave voice was at first an imaginary community. But imaginary or no, he was its authentic voice, and around his work a real community of Wagnerian adepts did eventually form, a community unlike any other that ever arose around a composer. As the philosopher Bryan Magee has marveled, "the worship of Wagner by people of all kinds, including some who were themselves possessed of creative ability of the highest order, and in fields quite different from music, is something unique in the history of our culture."[33] To investigate the source and the mechanism of the Wagnerian magic will be to investigate simultaneous revolutions in art and in national ideology.

THE TEXTURE OF TENSELESS TIME

The obvious place to make contact with the mature Wagnerian magic is the Prologue to the first act of *Götterdämmerung*, which opens with the somber scene of the Norns and continues with the ecstatic morning-after duet of Siegfried and Brünnhilde. These, of course, are the very scenes with which Wagner had begun his abortive attempt to compose *Siegfrieds Tod* in 1850. He finished them around two decades later, in 1870, after having provided the past in music he had lacked the first time around. Because of these circumstances, and because the scene of the Norns at their weaving remained the most extended and "universal" narrative in the *Ring* cycle, this Prologue contains perhaps the most densely woven tissue of leitmotives Wagner ever produced. The Norns' colloquy, moreover, does not introduce a single new leitmotif; it is a ceaseless warp and woof of well-worn tunes.

EX. 42-2A   Richard Wagner, Prologue to *Götterdämmerung*, "Revival" leitmotif

EX. 42-2B   Richard Wagner, Prologue to *Götterdämmerung*, "Rhine" leitmotif

EX. 42-2C   Richard Wagner, Prologue to *Götterdämmerung*, "Erda" leitmotif

EX. 42-2D   Richard Wagner, Prologue to *Götterdämmerung*, "Fate" leitmotif

EX. 42-2E   Richard Wagner, Prologue to *Götterdämmerung*, "Death" leitmotif

EX. 42-2F   Richard Wagner, Prologue to *Götterdämmerung*, "Loge" leitmotif

EX. 42-2G   Richard Wagner, Prologue to *Götterdämmerung*, Norns' ballad refrain

EX. 42-2H   Richard Wagner, Prologue to *Götterdämmerung*, "Genesis" leitmotif

EX. 42-2I   Richard Wagner, Prologue to *Götterdämmerung*, "Valhalla" leitmotif

EX. 42-2J   Richard Wagner, Prologue to *Götterdämmerung*, "Treaty" leitmotif

EX. 42-2K   Richard Wagner, Prologue to *Götterdämmerung*, "Götterdämmerung" leitmotif

EX. 42-2L   Richard Wagner, Prologue to *Götterdämmerung*, "Ring" leitmotif

EX. 42-2M Richard Wagner, Prologue to *Götterdämmerung*, "Authority" leitmotif

EX. 42-2N Richard Wagner, Prologue to *Götterdämmerung*, "Omen" leitmotif

EX. 42-2O Richard Wagner, Prologue to *Götterdämmerung*, "Oblivion" leitmotif

EX. 42-2P Richard Wagner, Prologue to *Götterdämmerung*, "Grief" leitmotif

EX. 42-2Q Richard Wagner, Prologue to *Götterdämmerung*, "Liebe-Tragik" leitmotif

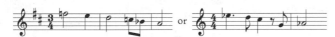

EX. 42-2R Richard Wagner, Prologue to *Götterdämmerung*, "Rhine gold" leitmotif

EX. 42-2S Richard Wagner, Prologue to *Götterdämmerung*, "Joy" leitmotif

EX. 42-2T Richard Wagner, Prologue to *Götterdämmerung*, "Gold's dominion" leitmotif

EX. 42-2U Richard Wagner, Prologue to *Götterdämmerung*, "Sword" leitmotif

EX. 42-2V   Richard Wagner, Prologue to *Götterdämmerung*, Siegfried's horn call leitmotif

EX. 42-2W   Richard Wagner, Prologue to *Götterdämmerung*, "Curse" leitmotif

EX. 42-3A   Richard Wagner, Prologue to *Götterdämmerung* in vocal score, leitmotives labeled (on first occurrence only) as in Ex. 42-2, mm. 105–111

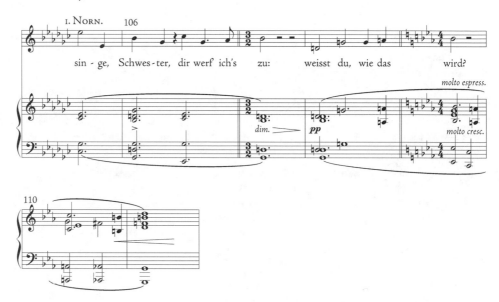

EX. 42-3B   Richard Wagner, Prologue to *Götterdämmerung* in vocal score, leitmotives labeled (on first occurrence only) as in Ex. 42-2, mm. 27–29

The denseness of the motivic weave is in itself an illustration of the poem, which (to recall the setting of 1850, sampled in Ex. 42-1) concerns the weaving of the rope of destiny. As Wagner put it in an exultant letter to a friend on finally finishing the scene where it had all started in May 1870, "I contemplated the Norns' scene with real horror, and for a long time I refused to get involved in it. But now, at last, I have woven this horror into the fabric of the rope, and I admit that it is a unique webbing."[34] And yet for all its complicated webbing the Norns' weaving song is still a ballad-narrative, just as it had been the first time around. Wagner, the epic bard, sings his tale in the manner of his medieval predecessors. Its refrain —

singe, Schwester,	Sing, my sister,
dir werf ich's zu:	I throw [the rope] your way:
weisst du, wie das wird?	Do you know what will be?

— is an excellent example of Wagnerian Stabreim incantation with its patterns of S's and, most obviously, W's (Ex. 42-3a). An even more striking example is the first line in the scene (Ex. 42-3b), sung by the Third Norn, which sets the tone for the whole opera: "Welch' Licht leuchtet dort?" ("What glow glimmers there?" in the translation by Rudolph Sabor,[35] who summons apt alliteration's artful aid). But Wagner's alliterations are not confined to initials. The combination -lch- at the end of Welch' is expanded first to Licht and then to leuchtet, while the new combination -cht at the end of Licht, also repeated in leuchtet, is echoed in the final t of leuchtet and dort. These combinations and recombinations correspond on the verbal plane to the tissue of combining and recombining leitmotives in the music.

The verses assembled out of the shifting alliterative patterns, together with the music that carries it aloft, serve to reconstitute the Wagner world in the mind of the spectator, and to recapitulate its history up to the point at which the action of the final opera will begin: that is, the point immediately preceding the catastrophic dénouement. The Norns' song in its final version does not correspond exactly to the story of the three preceding operas, since it begins at an earlier point in time. Rather, it is a summary of the all-encompassing world-epic that the four Ring dramas each partially enact. Here is a somewhat straightened-out and filled-in summary of the summary:

Long ago, as they worked, the Norns had slung their rope upon the world ash-tree, at the foot of which a spring whispering wisdom welled up. One day Wotan, king of the gods, came to drink from the spring and hacked himself a branch from the tree with which to make himself a shaft for his spear, upon which he inscribed the runes of binding treaties honorably respected, by virtue of which he made himself ruler of the world. Later, Wotan commissioned the giants Fasolt and Fafner to build him a stronghold, Valhalla, which was to be garrisoned with the souls of heroes fallen in battle. It was the duty of the Valkyrie maidens, daughters of Wotan and the earth-goddess Erda, to bring in these heroes from the battlefield. In payment of the giants' labors, Wotan promised Fasolt and Fafner Freia, the goddess of youth, which promise, however, trusting to the specious cunning of Loge, god of fire, he did not intend to honor. When called upon to do so, he tricked Alberich, lord of the dwarf Nibelung smiths, out of his hoard of gold, and with this he then bought off the giants. From this moment of Wotan's perfidy, the world ash-tree began to wither and the spring to dry up.

The Nibelung hoard contained a magic ring, the gold for which had been stolen from the daughters of the Rhine by Alberich, who had been able to fashion it only by forswearing love. Mastery of this ring would eventually lead its possessor to mastery of the world. When deprived of it by force, Alberich had laid a curse on it: death to whoever possessed it; a great deal of the story of the *Ring* is the story of the workings of this curse. Realizing that he had only escaped death himself by a technicality — that he had only briefly held Alberich's ring on its way to the giants (one of whom immediately kills the other for its sole possession) — Wotan has resolved that it be returned to the Rhine whence it was originally filched.

Because she attempted to execute her father's *secret* desire in defiance of his *expressed* wish (with respect to the outcome of a battle of heroes), Wotan was obliged to imprison his Valkyrie daughter Brünnhilde, locked in sleep, on a rock surrounded by Loge's fire. There she was to remain inviolate until such time as a hero who knew not the meaning of fear should come to wake her. Siegfried, son of the Volsung twins Siegmund and Sieglinde, appeared, set upon accomplishing this. Siegfried, however, was tainted by possession of the fateful ring, which he won by killing the surviving giant (in the guise of a dragon) at the behest of his foster father Mime, the brother of Alberich, who had raised Siegfried in hopes of gaining the ring for himself. With his spear, Wotan attempted to bar the young hero's passage to the flame-girt rock upon which Brünnhilde slumbered. The spear's might was shattered by the sword that Siegfried had inherited from his pure father Siegmund, after which the young superman continued on his way to Brünnhilde unopposed. Thwarted in his attempt to recover the gold for the Rhine maidens, foreseeing Siegfried's and Brünnhilde's deaths from the ring, and knowing that the world was doomed, Wotan dispatched heroes from Valhalla to hew the withered trunk and branches of the world ash-tree in pieces and pile them up around Valhalla so that they might catch fire, when the time came, from Siegfried's funeral pyre.

The spring of wisdom has dried up forever. Wotan sits in Valhalla surrounded by all the gods and heroes, awaiting the coming of the end. The Norns, deprived of their former abode, have moved to Brünnhilde's rock, where they have resumed their weaving, attaching the rope to the branch of a pine tree and to a promontory on the rock. The second Norn prophesies that Wotan will kill the cunning Loge, who led him fatally astray, with the shards of his shattered spear and will hurl it onto the pyre. These somber imaginings, coupled with the thought of the stolen gold still unreturned to its rightful guardians, trouble the minds of the Norns and cloud their vision. They fail to see that the rope is fraying against the rock until it is too late. Heaving on it to tighten its twist, they cause it to snap. Terrified, crying that eternal wisdom is ending and that they can speak to the world no more, the Norns sink down to their mother Erda, and vanish forever.[36]

The whole narrative is about the rupture of linear time and about the fatal necessity that interrelates and intermeshes past, present, and future, producing the tenseless time that myths inhabit. This, of course, was the very thing the tissue of leitmotives was devised to portray, and Wagner's music starts right out by proclaiming it. The majestic opening chords are a near replay of the music to which Brünnhilde greeted the sun after receiving the title character's awakening kiss in the third act of *Siegfried*, the finale of the previous drama ("Heil dir, Sonne," Ex. 42-2a). The allusion is no mere reminder of where the previous drama had left off, however, but a "transformation" (à la Liszt, it is fair to say) of the earlier passage.

Where at the end of *Siegfried* these chords made a gleaming progression from E minor to C major, at the beginning of *Götterdämmerung* (Ex. 42-4), the tonality is darkened considerably by transposition down a half step: E♭ minor and C♭ major. (In effect, it has been transposed to the key of Wagner's early sketch for *Siegfrieds Tod*, nor will this be the only instance of Wagner's uncanny recall of that twenty-year-old sketch which, scholars have determined, was no longer in his possession when he finally

EX. 42-4 Richard Wagner, Prologue to *Götterdämmerung* in vocal score, leitmotives labeled (on first occurrence only) as in Ex. 42-2, mm. 1–26

EX. 42-4 (*continued*)

returned to the scene.) In tone-color, too, the sound is muffled, and in an especially Wagnerian way. The trumpets and horns heard in *Siegfried* are replaced by horns and "Wagner tubas."

The latter—more formally, tenor tubas in B♭ and small bass tubas in F, each pitched an octave lower than the corresponding French horn—were first built to Wagner's specifications for the earliest performances of *Das Rheingold*, which took place in 1865, although the parts for them were composed in 1854. Adapted from the "saxhorn" (French band instruments manufactured beginning in the early 1850s by the Paris firm of Adolphe Sax, the inventor, somewhat earlier, of the saxophone), the Wagner tuba was meant to fill the gap between the horns and the standard contrabass tuba with the softened and covered timbre of conical-bore brass, rather than the thinner, more penetrating cylindrical-bore timbre of trombones.

Trumpets and trombones remained, of course; the Wagner orchestra, with its standard complement of seventeen brass instruments (from four to eight horns, up to four "tuben," four trumpets including the otherwise rare bass trumpet, four trombones, and standard tuba), complemented by fourteen woodwinds and a specified minimum of sixty-four strings, was the largest ever. But it was not large merely for the sake of volume. The "cushioned" sound of the Wagner orchestra, on its soft bed of brass—and especially when played, as Wagner further specified, in a covered pit such as the Bayreuth theater possessed—produces a sound of unprecedented pliant sensuality. The opening chords of *Götterdämmerung*, unlike their shining predecessors in *Siegfried*, are sublimely tranquilizing, trance-inducing. In this, they accomplish what countless accounts of actual bardic recitation describe as the function of the instrumental prelude that invariably preceded the singing of the tale.

But the most potent and (literally) telling part of the chords' transformation is what follows the first and accompanies the second; for here Wagner displays his mastery of what he called "the art of transition"—the bringing of musical entities into harmonious juxtaposition and the seamless passing from one to another. It is nothing less than the eternally rolling Rhine itself (Ex. 42-2b), as originally set forth in the Prelude to *Das Rheingold* at the very beginning of the *Ring* cycle (or even more primevally, in the accompaniment to the Norns in the early sketch as shown in Ex. 42-1), to which all will return at the end of *Götterdämmerung*.

This fluent commingling of primeval origins and eventual destiny with the moment at hand evokes what the Russian literary critic Mikhail Bakhtin (1895–1975) would later term the "epic chronotope" or epic time-mode, the "timeless past" or "time out of time" of myth.[37] As Bakhtin described it in his essay *Epic and Novel* (1941), the epic chronotope is a wholly alien, sealed-off quality of time that is understood to be an "absolute past" unfolding not as a linear development potentially leading to the present but as a completed, closed "circle" on which "all points are equidistant from the real, dynamic time of the present, as if the fullness of time were contained in a world in which we cannot participate," but in which we are easily absorbed. Bakhtin wrote with reference to Homer. Wagner's *Ring* is the supreme modern embodiment of this ancient time mode, and it is the musical texture that seals it off and makes it so perfectly and untouchably whole.

When the recall of Brünnhilde's awakening reaches its fourth chord (Db minor), the slower Rhine motif is transformed into the leitmotif associated with Erda, the Norns' mother, who is as primeval as the Rhine itself (Ex. 42-2c, quoted from its first appearance in *Das Rheingold*). In its original form, Brünnhilde's awakening motif circled back on itself with a repetition of the opening pair of chords. In *Götterdämmerung*, the second chord in this final pair is preempted, in a stunning example of "transition-art," by the weird progression that ever since the second act of *Die Walküre* has been associated with the concept of fate (Ex. 42-2d). It acquired this association from the original dramatic context: Brünnhilde appearing to Siegmund on the eve of battle to tell him that Wotan had been compelled to decree his death. And in its original context the motif was followed by another that is traditionally associated with the death itself, as decreed by fate (Ex. 42-2e). It first reappears in *Götterdämmerung* to provide the shuddering accompaniment to the beginning of the Norns' colloquy, already quoted in Ex. 42-3b.

The fate motif, it could be (and has been) fairly argued along lines noted above, has a wider relevance in the unfolding of the *Ring* drama than its facile label would allow. In the very next scene in *Die Walküre*, for example, it is heard when Siegmund recalls the apparition of Brünnhilde and the *comfort* that she brought him. In the next act, it accompanies Brünnhilde's reminder to Wotan that her outward defiance of his will (in trying to save Siegmund's life) was in fact her *obedience* to his secret wish. In the third act of *Siegfried*, it accompanies Erda's rebuke, on being awakened by the importunate Wotan, that he has only himself and his perfidy to blame for his predicament—a fixing of responsibility and just deserts that suggests the very opposite (or so one could maintain) of blind fate as controller of destiny. Indeed, most of the leitmotives in the *Ring*, if subjected to a similarly detailed census, would need to be interpreted in light of similar contradictions and paradoxes—all of which, it should be emphasized, only increases the yield of meaning (the way detailed study always does).

But to argue from such evidence that the famous label should be revoked would be to ignore the motif's wider relevance in the unfolding drama of modern music history. It was as the Fate motif—a widely recognized musical symbol with a potential range of relevance that far outstrips its original context in the *Ring*, vast as that may be—that the Soviet Russian composer Dmitry Shostakovich cited it at the outset of the somber finale of his Symphony no. 15 (1971), his last major orchestral work, and (by giving it a sequential treatment that hooked it up with the ancient *passus duriusculus*, the chromatically descending bass line of lamentation) helped give it that wider relevance (Ex. 42-5).

EX. 42-5   Dmitri Shostakovich, Symphony no. 15, beginning of fourth movement

As it functions in Shostakovich's symphony, the motif relates only indirectly, if at all, to the events of *Die Walküre* or *Götterdämmerung*. Indeed it could be argued that in its new context its relevance to the *Ring* no longer matters. The only reference that counts is to the oft-despised conventional label that Wagner himself never attached to the phrase. Only through the label could the motif now reflect so poignantly on the life of the symphony's composer, thence on the lives of all who were fated to live and work in the turbulent middle of the twentieth century, in a place where that turbulence had been focused through a lens of totalitarianism.

That "universal" message was something Wagner never anticipated, but it is no less real for that. Meaning is the product of history — in the case of art works, of a "reception history" — that in the case of the Fate motif includes at least two appropriations: first Wolzogen's, through which the label was attached in the first place, then Shostakovich's, through which the label was given a new association, unrelated (except through collateral descent) to its original context. Neither Wagner nor Wolzogen—nor Shostakovich for that matter—finally owns the motif's meaning. Like all symbols (like words, to pick the most obvious example), it responds to new conditions and contexts with new significance.

To return now to the *Götterdämmerung* Prologue, and proceed to the Norns' narrative: the leitmotif that accompanies their reaction to the dawn, and their decision to take up their spinning, is the one associated ever since *Das Rheingold* with Loge, the god of fire and light (and by extension, of intelligence), who, acting in a sense as Wotan's lawyer, tricked Alberich out of his hoard and set in motion the catastrophic sequence of events the outcome of which the Norns are about to foresee (Ex. 42-2f). The rocking chord progression that accompanies the Second Norn's "Wollen wir spinnen und singen" and launches the ballad-narrative on its way (Ex. 42-2g) is the only theme that is new to this scene (and therefore, very strictly speaking, not a leitmotif, especially since it will recur in no later scene). It is very important, however, since it comes back to accompany (hence identify) the refrains, and also because its ending "half-diminished" chord (F – A♭ – C♭ – E♭), already foreshadowed in the wake of the Fate motif (Ex. 42-4, m. 21), assumes such an independent significance in the course of the Prologue that it might even be thought of as a "Leitharmonie" in its own right.

When the first Norn begins to recount the tale of the World-Ash, the mother of all leitmotives is sounded, the "natural" horn signal that portrays the primeval Rhine at the very start of the cycle (Ex. 42-2h)—sometimes, in an aptly biblical figure, called the Genesis motif. Her ballad-narrative proceeds to its own theme as long as events preceding the beginning of *Das Rheingold* are its subject. But at the mention of Wotan, the motif associated with his fortress lodge Valhalla (Ex. 42-2i), the trophy of his greed and the cause of his fateful breach of contract, is sounded. And it is immediately followed, in a conjunction that goes all the way back to *Das Rheingold*, with the leitmotif associated with the broken treaty, or rather with the reminder Wotan receives from his wife Fricka "that contracts must be kept" (Ex. 42-2j). The consequences are hinted when the Norn recalls the death of the Ash: the motif that accompanies Erda's dire prediction, near the end of *Das Rheingold*, that Wotan's greed will bring about "a day of doom" is heard (Ex. 42-2k). Now usually (and somewhat confusingly) called the Götterdämmerung motif, it is obviously derived by inversion (and "crab"—reverse—motion) from the Genesis motif, as if undoing all that had in primeval times been wrought. Its mysterious Lydian character (with a sort of "raised fourth degree") arises from its invariable occurrence on a flat-sixth or Neapolitan harmony, the tonal remoteness of which cannily enhances its aura of uncanniness.

The cause of it all—the object of Wotan's greed and of Erda's warning, from which the whole colossal cycle takes its name—is finally adumbrated when the First Norn refers to the dark sadness of her song: the Ring motif (Ex. 42-2l), which consists always of a downward+upward arpeggio (sometimes outlining a triad, sometimes, as on its first appearance, a mere concatenation of thirds) that never manages to rise all the way back to its starting point. The end of the ballad refrain, which marks the transition to the Second Norn's narrative, is once again forebodingly accompanied by the Death motif.

To the skein of leitmotives already woven by the First Norn, the Second adds only one new item: the pompously dotted motif originally associated in the first act of *Siegfried* with Wotan's proud reference to the power of his spear, on which the laws of the world are engraved (Ex. 42-2m; compare Ex. 42-2j). It is usually called the Authority motif, and accompanies the Second Norn's reference to the sacred runes that, once transgressed, could no longer ward off Siegfried's conquest of Brünnhilde.

The Third Norn, again taking up the rope to the ominous strains of the Death motif, weaves the longest and densest motivic skein by far, full of ingenious juxtapositions in both the melodic ("horizontal") and harmonic or contrapuntal ("vertical") dimensions. So, for example, when she foretells the disastrous end of the drama, when flames shall in predestined retribution engulf Valhalla and consume the once-eternal gods, the orchestra sounds the Treaty, Valhalla, Götterdämmerung, and Fate themes in close succession, their progress punctuated by a timpani tattoo (Ex. 42-2n) of which the rhythm, ever since the entr'acte following the first scene of *Das Rheingold*, had played the role of a bad omen (Ex. 42-6). Among the grisly events it had helped accompany or foretell were Fafner's murder of his brother Fasolt in fulfillment of Alberich's curse on the Ring (in *Das Rheingold*), Siegmund's death on the battlefield (in *Die Walküre*), and Siegfried's slaying of Mime, his Nibelung stepfather (in *Siegfried*). Later in *Götterdämmerung* it will bear witness to the murder of Siegfried himself.

When she resumes her prophecies after some anxious discussion with her sisters, the Third Norn invokes a few more motivic recollections, putting the future in direct

EX. 42-6   Richard Wagner, Prologue to *Götterdämmerung* in vocal score, leitmotives labeled as in Ex. 42-2, mm. 175–83

EX. 42-6 *(continued)*

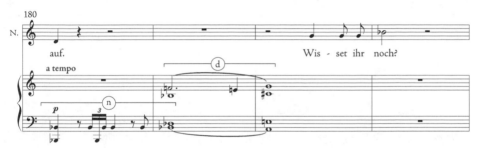

contact with the musicalized past and giving it the kind of musical reality that will ensure its accomplishment. Most balefully, the chord progression first associated in the third act of *Die Walküre* with Brünnhilde's entrancement (*Zauberschlafe* or "Magic sleep" according to Wolzogen) and associated thereafter with oblivion (Ex. 42-20) follows the news that the logs from the World-Ash are piled up around Valhalla, and is itself followed by the Fate motif. A wonderful example of Wagner's "art of transition" is the interpolation of the Oblivion motif between the strains of the final ballad refrain (Ex. 42-7): their common element, the falling semitone, is of course an ancient symbol of grief. As such it had actually been commandeered by Wagner to symbolize Alberich's grief (thence grief in general) in the first scene of *Das Rheingold* (Ex. 42-2p), which adds another resonance both to the Norns' refrain and to the Oblivion motif. Ultimately, as is becoming clear, hard and fast distinctions between Wagner's "particles" inevitably break down. All interpenetrates all, which is precisely the point.

EX. 42-7   Richard Wagner, Prologue to *Götterdämmerung* in vocal score, leitmotives labeled as in Ex. 42-2, mm. 255–72

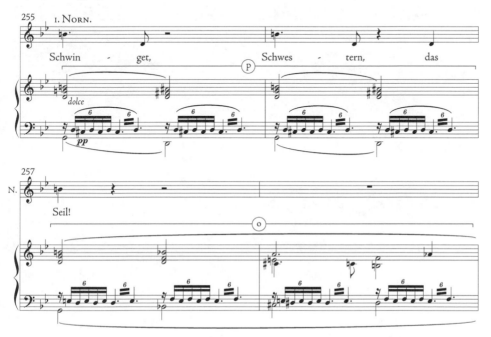

EX. 42-7 (continued)

EX. 42-7 (*continued*)

The interpenetration of Grief and Oblivion with the final Norns' refrain is almost too dramaturgically apt, for it is precisely here, at the end of Ex. 42-7, that the First Norn chimes in, aghast, with the news that the rope of destiny is fraying. Impending ruin puts the First Norn dimly in mind of Alberich's curse, as we are warned by a quick fourfold concatenation of motives. First there is the Ring itself. Next there is the motif somewhat cryptically but evocatively christened *Liebe-Tragik* ("Tragedy of love") by Wolzogen (Ex. 42-2q; he claimed that this one label actually stemmed from Wagner himself), which first appears in *Das Rheingold* when the ugly Alberich is rebuffed by the Rhine maidens. Next to be alluded to is the Rhine gold that Alberich then stole (Ex. 42-2r), a motif first associated in *Das Rheingold*, by specific indication, with a lighting effect that transfixes Alberich and inspires his deed. And finally, in ironic commentary, there is the motif first associated with the Rhine Maidens' joy in possessing the gold, and then with Alberich's at stealing it (Ex. 42-2s). In effect we have been given a wordless four-measure précis of the whole first scene of *Das Rheingold*.

When the Second Norn notices that Brünnhilde's rock, on which the rope is hung, is cutting through its threads, the leitmotives begin associating Siegfried, the unwitting avenger of Wotan's ancient misdeed, with the invincible power of the gold. As the Norn watches her rope unravel, the orchestra combines a motif (*Goldherrschaft* or "Gold's dominion" according to Wolzogen; Ex. 42-2t) first heard in the third scene of *Das Rheingold* as Alberich commands his enslaved fellow-Nibelungs, with that of Siegfried's sword, his legacy from his father Siegmund, with which he had shattered Wotan's spear (Ex. 42-2u). As the Third Norn misguidedly pulls on the rope to tighten its weave, Siegfried's horn call, the accompaniment to all his heroic deeds in the preceding opera, is heard with fell irony (Ex. 42-2v).

(The sword motif, it is worth noting, has had an especially telling interpretive history. Associated with the sword beginning with the first act of *Die Walküre*, it had actually been heard originally near the end of *Das Rheingold*, as Wotan joyfully contemplated Valhalla. It has been left to exegetes to reconcile these contradictory associations through a sort of Christianizing commentary, which though now an integral part of the *Ring* tradition (as the nonbiblical Talmud, a commentary on the Torah, is now an integral part of the tradition of Jewish law) nevertheless did not originate with Wagner. As one commentator, Rudolph Sabor, explains, the first occurrence of the Sword motif establishes the moment "when Wotan resolves to create a free hero: someone who is not tainted by the god's pragmatic dealings and who therefore carries neither guilt nor responsibility. To him will Wotan bequeath a conquering sword. This hero shall, of his own accord, right Wotan's wrongs."[38] (Wotan's resolve is Sabor's contribution to *Ring* lore, not Wagner's.) Finally, to the searing strains of the title character's curse, the most dissonant motif in all of *Der Ring des Nibelungen* (Ex. 42-2w), the rope of destiny snaps, to the Norns' ineffable horror. They sink into the earth to join their mother Erda to a concatenation of Curse, Oblivion, Fate, and, of course, Götterdämmerung motives.

THE SEA OF HARMONY

Impressively detailed though it may seem, this account of the musical texture of the Norns' scene, far from complete, has not even begun to broach what for Wagner was the main issue. Simply as a medley of twenty-three themes the scene would not even begin to be, in Wagnerian terms, "dramatic." For it would engage only the listener/spectator's cognitive faculties—that is, the faculties of mind that perform the task of recognizing symbols, which is to say the part of the dramatic impression that depends on representation. The purely (or merely) cognitive aspect of Wagner's tissue has often lent itself to satire or outright ridicule. The Russian composer Nikolai Rimsky-Korsakov, for example, writing almost a decade after Wagner's death, tried to discredit what he considered the tiresome hypercomplexity of Wagner's "polyphonic fabric" as a "colossal abuse of symbolism":

> The listener cannot derive any immediate impression from all these leitmotives as they steal in and out of the contrapuntal web. And in point of fact, if character A,

finding himself in a certain mood, were to speak with character B about character C, and if in the accompanying music we hear the contrapuntally interwoven motives A, B and C, perhaps with the addition of a fourth denoting their mood, can one then clearly distinguish such a situation from the reverse: i.e., where C speaks to A about B, or B and C discuss A?[39]

Rimsky-Korsakov also mocked Wagner's avoidance of set pieces in favor of *unendliche Melodie* (infinite melody) — the seamless, ceaselessly thematic or "developmental" orchestral continuity that swept through entire acts — by comparing the structure of a *Ring* opera to that of an enormous edifice "consisting entirely of a staircase leading from the entrance to the exit."[40]

Such dogged literalism, common in the anti-Wagnerian criticism of the time, can be read as a defense against the aspect of Wagner's music that works not through simple, easily parodied mechanisms of representation, but, far more potently, through direct presentation, bypassing the cognitive and addressing itself directly to the elemental life-driving appetites. That part is the part played by harmonic and tonal progressions — Wagner's "sea of harmony." For a preliminary excursion on the Wagnerian sea we can go briefly back over the Norns' scene, trace its tonal design, and proceed from there into a tonal/thematic overview of the rest of the *Götterdämmerung* Prologue. Putting ourselves in the position of one who has heard no more recent music — in the position, that is, of Wagner's original audience — we will be struck, above all, by the unprecedented range (or "freedom") of modulation, and on occasion by its blinding rapidity. (We will notice long stretches of unaccountably static, "becalmed" harmony as well.) We will be struck by the extreme rarity of full authentic cadences, which occur only at the most decisive moments (in theory, only once per scene); and by the reverse of that coin, the extraordinary abundance and variety of deceptive cadences, some of them prepared by really insistent dominant pedals. And we will be struck by the way these tonal and harmonic effects are geared to the scenic action.

That articulation of the drama through harmony is of course another aspect of the same interpenetration of the musical and the scenic that gave rise to the leitmotif technique. We might be inclined to call the music, in both of these dimensions, the metaphorical parallel to the unfolding drama, a substratum of sound that enriches or intensifies the emotional and cognitive effect of what is seen. Wagner, influenced by the philosophy of Schopenhauer, actually put it just the other way around. In an essay of 1872, "On the Term 'Music Drama,'" he defined this most central concept as consisting of "deeds of music made visible."[41] The *primary* bearer of meaning is the music, and it is the plot or dramatic action that provides the metaphorical parallel, giving cognitive specificity to what is heard. How Wagner could justify such a seemingly paradoxical view will become clearer as we investigate his harmonic procedures and their effects.

The reliance Wagner placed on harmony as the primary shaper of the drama should alert us that however limber and impulsive the modulatory plan may seem in its moment-by-moment ("local") vagaries, it is always under firm "global" control. That tandem of unpredictable flexibility at the short range and unerring long-range direction is perhaps the most impressive evidence of Wagner the harmonist's navigational skills.

FIG. 42-10 Alois Burgstaller (1871–1945) as Siegfried at Bayreuth, 1900.

The *Götterdämmerung* Prologue provides one of the best examples. The opening pair of chords — E♭ and C♭, derived from the leitmotif of Brünnhilde's awakening — function in tandem not only as a local succession, but also as a bipolar opposition that gives shape to the whole Norns' scene (or more pertinently, that delineates its entropy, its degeneration into chaos). At a higher level yet, the tonalities of which the two chords are the tonics — conceived, like Schubert's tonalities (see chapter 34), as freely encompassing the parallel major and minor — serve to close the Prologue (in E♭ major) and to open the dark scene of plotting that follows (in B [=C♭] minor; see Ex. 42-8). In between stretches the lengthy orchestral entr'acte known as *Siegfrieds Rheinfahrt* ("Siegfried's Rhine journey") when it is performed as a concert piece. The character's navigation of the great waterway here serves quite explicitly as the conceptual metaphor for a musical process.

The three great strophes of the Norns' ballad-narrative enact in harmony the fatal entropy that Wotan's sin has brought upon the world. The first strophe, sung by the First Norn, begins in a firmly established E♭ major/minor, and ends quite "classically" in the same key. In between, C♭, cadentially established and then enharmonically transformed to B, provides (again "classically") a contrasting middle section that meanders back via an enharmonic reversal involving the transformation of E major (next after B on

EX. 42-8A Richard Wagner, Prologue to *Götterdämmerung* in vocal score, leitmotives labeled as in Ex. 42-2, mm. 635–39

the circle of fifths) to F♭, coinciding with the Götterdämmerung leitmotif (Ex. 42-2k), which always expresses the Neapolitan ♭II.

The Second Norn begins her strophe with a cadence to C minor, preparing the perfectly conventional key of the relative minor. The harmonic motion is brusquely interrupted to illustrate Siegfried's destruction of Wotan's spear, but again the Götterdämmerung leitmotif appears as a Neapolitan to guide the strophe back to a conventional close.

It is the Third Norn, who sees the future, who plays havoc with harmonic closure, opening up the sluices and letting in the sea. With her the Götterdämmerung leitmotif serves not to guide the harmony back but to lead it astray, for its D♭ tonality functions this time not as ♭II but as I, and the C-minor cadence that it prepares is trumped by the baleful half-diminished F – A♭ – C♭ – E♭ harmony that had previously closed the Norns' refrain. That harmony, of course, can function as II₇ in E♭ minor, and so it might seem to promise return to the ballad narrative's original key.

EX. 42-8B   Richard Wagner, *Götterdämmerung*, Act I, scene 1, mm. 1–11

Instead, however, it is put through a threefold sequence by ascending minor thirds (compare mm. 161, 163, and 165), that lands it a tritone away from its starting point, on a B that no longer functions as a stable substitute for C♭ but points ahead (as II₇) to an A minor that never comes, even though its dominant is prominently displayed in m. 175. Instead, the expected A minor is preempted by a magniloquent cadential gesture toward C♯ (m. 177, coinciding with the Valhalla leitmotif), which is itself preempted in the next measure by a Neapolitan (the Götterdämmerung motif once more), which is likewise preempted in m. 180 by the Omen tattoo on B♭, functioning here (or so it seems) as a deceptive cadence in D minor. All of these progressions may be traced by analyzing Ex. 42-9, which then hooks up with Ex. 42-6.

Now B♭, the key that is reached at the end of Ex. 42-6, is of course the dominant of E♭, and it might seem that we are close to home after all. (Schubert would surely not have missed the opportunity of resolving it to everyone's delighted surprise!) But after all these feints the thread (to put it as the Norns might) is broken. There will be no return

EX. 42-9   Richard Wagner, Prologue to *Götterdämmerung* in vocal score, leitmotives labeled as in Ex. 42-2, mm. 158–175

EX. 42-9 (continued)

to E♭, at least not while the Norns are onstage, despite some very elaborate preparations. Where Wotan's last resolute act (the casting of Brünnhilde into flame-encircled sleep) is described, for example, a cadential $^6_4$ gives way to V in a way that promises E♭ with virtual certainty; but over a continuing B♭ pedal in the timpani, the Oblivion motif liquidates the impending cadence with a circle of minor thirds, so that when E♭ finally appears as a root (m. 252), it has been drained of its stability, the more so as the chord above it has the character of a dominant seventh that seeks (in vain!) a resolution of its own (Ex. 42-10).

EX. 42-10 Richard Wagner, Prologue to *Götterdämmerung* in vocal score, leitmotives labeled (on first occurrence only) as in Ex. 42-2, mm. 245–54

Or again, the appearance of the Rhine Gold motif near the end of Ex. 42-7 strongly expresses the dominant of E♭ (the key, incidentally, that witnessed the birth of the Rhine itself at the very beginning of the cycle); but again delaying measures (involving other leitmotives) rob the cadence of its urgency, and by the time E♭ arrives in the bass, the chord it supports has the character of a dominant, not a tonic. The one succession that could be read as containing immediate progression of dominant to tonic in E♭ (see the fifth measure of Ex. 42-7) happens in the middle of a harmonic sequence, again involving the Oblivion motif, in which E♭ is only an incident in a continuing circle of descending major thirds (G – E♭ – C♭).

The next long pedal — the F♯ that so dissonantly accompanies the Curse motif when the rope of fate comes undone — turns out (most unexpectedly or even incoherently in the short run, most logically in the long) to be the effective dominant. It picks up the full dominant-seventh harmony at the very moment of the Norns' disappearance (Dawn) and it is resumed at the end of Siegfried's Rhine Journey, where it is finally resolved, at the beginning of the first scene of act I proper (Ex. 42-8b), to the B minor that has been so long and so threateningly prefigured—so threateningly as to rupture the Norns' skein of destiny! Thus the F♯ of Alberich's curse, in the form of a functional dominant pedal, encloses the Prologue's entire second scene, which depicts the awakening of Siegfried and Brünnhilde after their night of bliss, and their ardent farewells as Siegfried embarks on his ill-fated quest "Zu neuen Thaten" ("On to new deeds!"), to quote Brünnhilde's famous first line. The whole ecstatic scene is played against the curse-pedal's implicitly continuous rumble—a constant baneful subtext to the outwardly ebullient action.

To introduce that ebullient action the pedal is temporarily liquidated by reinterpreting its harmony as an augmented (German) sixth chord—signaled or symbolized in the notation by respelling it as a G♭ (m. 318)—and resolved downward to the dominant of B♭ major, in which key one of the most important leitmotives in *Götterdämmerung* makes its first appearance (m. 327): a mellow but mighty brass chorale, first given out by a choir of eight horns, obviously derived from the tune of the young Siegfried's horn call (Ex. 42-2v), which now denotes Siegfried the Hero, or (per Wolzogen) "Siegfried, transformed by love." It is answered immediately by a pair of clarinets (one a gorgeously throaty bass clarinet), sounding the leitmotif denoting Brünnhilde, similarly transformed (Ex. 42-11). A surging orchestral crescendo, carried by a rising sequence of Brünnhilde motifs, and accompanying a light show that depicts the sunrise, leads to a great blaze of a seemingly recovered E♭ major to greet the lovers' appearance onstage.

EX. 42-11   Richard Wagner, Prologue to *Götterdämmerung* in vocal score, mm. 315–34

This, of course, is the key the Norns "lost" in the Prologue's first scene. Its restitution takes place, however, in a harmonic environment that has been fatally compromised by feints and deceptions of all kinds. In Wagner's ripest style, any dominant seventh can resolve as an augmented sixth (and vice versa); any major triad in first inversion can resolve as a Neapolitan, and chords prepared as Neapolitans can resolve as primary functions. Any tone can act as a common tone to create instant — if illusory, temporary — links between chords that are remotely placed along the circle of fifths, the traditional arbiter of harmonic relatedness.

A strategically placed $^6_4$ chord or a tremulous pedal can cause a key to heave up before the contemplating ear like an iceberg in the path of the Titanic; and the key so drastically prefigured can be "liquidated" (to use a term Arnold Schoenberg invented for the process a generation later) before any of its primary functions have been asserted. Indeed, there is a whole category of leitmotives (Fate and Oblivion, to recall two) that seem to have no other purpose than the securing of these effects — effects that resonate insidiously with their dramatic import.

So by now, a great flare-up of a long-awaited tonality like the present E♭ can be accepted as no more than provisionally decisive or conclusive. We can no longer trust harmonic functions to deliver, as once in Beethoven's time they did, on their *promesse du bonheur*, the "promise of happiness" that the French novelist Stendhal named as the most essential aspect of artistic beauty and the reason why art is cherished.[42] We feel ourselves buffeted by that loss of certainty more deeply than a theory of representation can ever explain, for here we come to the nub of what makes the Wagnerian "sea of harmony" so much more than a metaphor or a representation.

Not that Wagnerian harmonies no longer have representational or symbolic value. They have that, too, as we have certainly seen. Not only chords and chord progressions but actual keys can be symbols: witness all-important E♭ itself, the key of the river Rhine, and by extension the harbinger of the bliss of primeval nature whence all has sprung and whither all is fated to return. Its dissolution (through modulatory progressions) in the Norns' scene is obviously a representation of entropy's onset. The half-diminished F – A♭ – C♭ – E♭ harmony (the single most potent modulatory agent) is emblematic of destruction. And so on. But there is more.

DESIRE AND HOW TO CHANNEL IT

That "more" was first broached in this book as early as chapter 16, in connection with a music — that of the Counter Reformation, and Palestrina's in particular — that sought to induce a sort of esthetic ecstasy in listeners and save their souls from the snares of rationalism. Noted there were the effects of "strategic harmonic delays," as they were named in the vocabulary of that chapter. What was delayed was "closure" — that is, functional resolution. The heightened expressivity thus connoted did not arise out of cognitive symbolism or "extroversive" reference (as it was called in chapter 16), the representational mode of which Wagnerian leitmotives would be the supreme example. Rather, that expressivity arose out of "introversive" reference whereby the music, by forecasting closure and then delaying it, calls attention to its own need for cadential resolution.

"Its" need is actually the listener's psychological need, of course. The fluctuating musical tension analogizes the fluctuating tensions—psychological, emotional, sexual—of our lives as we live them. And here is where the process leaves the realm of representation altogether. Harmonic forecasts and delays play directly upon the listener's expectation, or, to put it more strongly, on the *desires* that the music induces in the listener. And so the musical events, relative to listener expectations, are translated directly into the intensified emotion that the fulfillment or frustration of desire produces in any context.

Although it became an "issue" in this book only with the sixteenth-century Counter Reformation, this aspect of music's effect on the listener—this uncanny directness—has been recognized (as the *ethos* of music) from ancient times. As early as Plato, it has led to calls for police action. The enhancement and ultimate perfection of this emotional potency had long been touted as the primary achievement of the "functional" harmonic practices that began with the composers of Palestrina's generation and reached fullest elaboration with Beethoven (or so it was thought until Wagner's time).

As Karol Berger, a musicologist who has branched out into general esthetics, reminds us, this power of "tonal" music goes much deeper than rational cognition into the wellsprings of our conscious experience as temporal. While it could be argued that what music evokes is a representation of that deep experience, it is a representation that is uniquely concerned with our mental and spiritual innards rather than with the world outside. "What I actually experience," Berger writes in a discussion that is crucial for understanding Wagner,

> when I experience the tonal tendency of a sound is the dynamics of my own desire, its arousal, its satisfaction, its frustration. It is my own desire for the leading tone to move up, the satisfaction of my own desire when it so moves, the frustration thereof when it refuses to budge or when it moves elsewhere, that I feel . . . . Thus, the precondition of my being able to hear an imaginary pattern of lines of directed motion in a tonal work is that I first experience the desires, satisfactions, and frustrations of this sort. In tonal music, the direct experience of the dynamics of my own desire precedes any recognition of the represented object, of lines of directed motion, and is the necessary precondition of such a recognition. I must first experience the desire that the leading tone move up, before I can recognize the representation of an imaginary ascending line when it so moves.

Therefore, Berger concludes,

> It follows that tonal music, like a visual medium, may represent an imaginary object different from myself, an imaginary world, albeit a highly abstract one, consisting of lines of directed motion. But, unlike a visual medium, tonal music also makes me experience directly the dynamics of my own desiring, my own inner world, and it is this latter experience that is the more primordial one, since any representation depends on it. While visual media allow us to grasp, represent, and explore an outer, visual world, music makes it possible for me to grasp, experience, and explore an inner world of desiring. While visual media show us objects we might want without making us aware of what it would feel like to want anything, music makes us aware of how it feels to want something without showing us the

objects we want. In a brief formula, visual media are the instruments of knowing the object of desire but not the desire itself, tonal music is the instrument of knowing the desire but not its object.[43]

Berger purports to write about all tonal music, but his remarks have special relevance to Wagner, who (precisely because of his ideological commitments, it could be argued) was more explicitly conscious of these aspects of the musical experience, and more determined to exploit them, than any other composer before or since. With Wagner, moreover, we are in an unusually favored position to investigate his aims, since he wrote so prolifically about them, and because, aspiring to their intellectual status, he read widely among his philosopher contemporaries in search of corroboration for his intuitions and theories.

Berger, in fact, builds his case about music on precisely those philosophers who most closely paralleled Wagner's thinking and eventual practice. One of them was the Danish religious thinker Søren Kierkegaard (1813–55), who argued that our most elemental knowledge of "the sensuous-erotic"[44] comes to us from music, the only art that can present desire to our minds "in all its immediacy." Even more fundamentally "Wagnerian" were the views of Arthur Schopenhauer (1788–1860), already mentioned as an influence on the composer's thinking, who was so impressed with the influence of music on his feelings that he promoted music to a status beyond any of the other arts, where it directly embodied the experience of "striving" that not only constitutes our life but also embodies the "Will," or essential axiomatic basis of all reality. "Music," Schopenhauer famously wrote, "gives the innermost kernel preceding all form, or the heart of things."[45] What better precept for a composer who wants to create worlds in music, and what better motivation or justification for the "formlessness"—a formlessness that goes to the very heart of things—that leitmotif technique enables.

FIG. 42-11 Arthur Schopenhauer, photographed in 1858.

That technique was the mechanism by which the channeling of desire took place, providing the thematic medium for a ceaseless process of harmonic movement that continually forecasts goals, and just as continually subverts them, subjecting us who listen to a constant manipulation of "the dynamics of our own desire," to use Berger's term. More than any other music, Wagner's plays on these basic sensations, magnifying the direct impact all music has on our nerves and bodies. Moreover, the leitmotives—which supply exactly that which, in Berger's formulation, music does not inherently possess—complement presentation or embodiment (Schopenhauer's "will") with representation, thus in Schopenhauer's terms completing a "world." By combining precognitive musical process with cognitive symbolism, in other words, Wagner had it both ways: the music through which he constructed his mythic dramas was the instrument of *both* "desire itself" *and* of "knowing the object of desire." It was frighteningly powerful, as Hanslick, the high priest of the Wagnerian opposition, knew best of all. The whole reason for writing his book in opposition to the current that produced the New German School, which immediately adopted Wagner as its standard-bearer, was Hanslick's acknowledgment that "music works more rapidly and intensely upon the mind than any other art," and, more strongly yet, that "while the other arts persuade, music invades us."[46] That is why music needed, in Hanslick's view, to be contained—and Wagner's above all. Hanslick's theory of musical beauty was above all an instrument of containment.

The act of freely submitting to such music turned one temporarily into a solipsist, for whom there is no external reality, only the inner reality of the psyche. Succumbing to its hypnosis—a hypnosis that differed from the music trance of Schubert's time because it was so actively manipulated and directed by the composer-operator—was valued as religious experience, as erotic experience, as narcotic experience, in any combination or all at once. Music that could produce such experiences and such states of consciousness was thought by its devotees to be the most sanctifying and exalting art in the world. Which is precisely why such music—for Hanslick, for Rimsky-Korsakov, and for so many since—could seem the ultimate in dangerous, degenerate art.

With these weighty thoughts in mind let us return now to the second scene of the *Götterdämmerung* Prologue, where Siegfried and Brünnhilde have just achieved their ecstasy of false consciousness in E♭ major. Where the Norns' scene, as befit its recapitulatory role, was built entirely out of existing leitmotives, the scene of the hero and heroine is a forging ground for new ones. Besides the two characters' own themes, there is an arching cadential phrase that first accompanies Brünnhilde's ejaculation, "dir zu wenig mein Wert gewann!" ("in winning me your reward was too small," Ex. 42-12), is immediately thrice repeated for emphasis before subsiding on the baleful F-A♭-C♭-E♭ chord, and thereafter underscores references to their union.

Apart from transient specific allusions of a kind that would have made Rimsky-Korsakov snicker, the three new leitmotives make up the whole thematic content of the scene, giving it the character of a purposeful thematic development. And its harmonic content, apart from brief departures the more forcefully to return, is similarly straightforward and stable. It is simply a reiterated approach, signaled both harmonically and by the use of the Union motif, to the key of E♭, the false "promise of happiness." In effect, Wagner replays and replays again the tense and finally triumphant "retransition" in the first movement of Beethoven's "heroic" Third Symphony. But where Beethoven's avowals were indubitably (that is, psychologically) "true," here the successive reiterations of arrival, each capping a longer temporal span than the last and controlling a greater modulatory range, further the cause of the Big Lie, the desire for the tonic analogizing both Siegfried and Brünnhilde's ill-fated desire for triumph over Alberich's curse and their henceforth-to-be-frustrated desire for each other.

What might be called the coda of the scene — beginning with the last approach to E♭, its seemingly ultimate confirmation, and its loss — is worth tracing in some thematic and harmonic detail (Ex. 42-13). The triumph of E♭ major at its outset is made all the sweeter by its proximity to the half-diminished harmony that played such a baleful role in the Norns' scene, functioning here in its most ordinary cadential capacity (as ii₇ of the parallel minor). Siegfried and Brünnhilde are singing of their oneness. The two of them now launch together into a little set piece in which the orchestra harps on a tune the young Siegfried sang in the opera named after him, all about the joy of freedom from fear. That Brünnhilde sings first to its accompaniment is a testimony to the merger of their identities. The irony of their fearlessness in the face of imminent destruction is all the more poignant because of their perfect subjective oblivion, symbolized by page after page with hardly a sharp or a flat to disturb the ecstatic stability of the soon-to-be-subverted key.

At the other end of the coda, the height of rapture, with both characters now reduced to a single word ("Heil! Heil! Heil! Heil!"), a theme from Brünnhilde's carefree youth (first heard in *Die Walküre*, the opera named after *her*) likewise insinuates itself into the texture, at first in counterpoint with the Union motif. An arpeggio in dotted triplet rhythms, it dates back to the early sketches of 1850, where (as a glance back at Ex. 42-1 will confirm) its contour informed the Norns' refrain. Later the same year Wagner recast it as a song for the Valkyries, Wotan's warrior daughters, as they sweep through the skies on winged horseback (Ex. 42-14).

EX. 42-12   Richard Wagner, Prologue to *Götterdämmerung* in vocal score, mm. 375 – 381

EX. 42-13   Richard Wagner, Prologue to *Gotterdammerung* in vocal score, leitmotives labeled as in Ex. 42-2, mm. 588–635

EX. 42-13 (continued)

EX. 42-13 (continued)

EX. 42-13   (*continued*)

By the time he actually composed *Die Walküre* the song had given way to an orchestral fantasy ("The Ride of the Valkyries"), which functioned in context as the prelude to act III, but is more often heard (in slightly different form) as a concert showpiece. It brings the duet at the end of the *Götterdämmerung* Prologue to a wild conclusion: set over the plagal harmony of Siegfried's freedom song, it even gives the soprano a chance to end with a traditional high C (albeit over the subdominant rather than the tonic harmony, which forces the singers to fall silent at the true cadence).

That cadence is the last we will hear of E♭ major for some time (and never again in so unclouded a form). It disappears along with Siegfried himself at m. 649, liquidated by a series of "common-tone" progressions — the key's leading tone (D) re-identified as the fifth of a G major triad and the seventh of a dominant seventh on E — into what sounds like a looming A major, an antipodal tritone away from E♭ along the circle of fifths. But after prolonging the dominant of A with a pedal lasting twenty bars, Wagner evades the promised key with a deceptive cadence borrowed from the parallel minor, when Siegfried's horn call is heard from offstage, accompanied by another dominant pedal promising F.

The apparition of F major lasts a good while. After a transitional passage played entirely over the dominant pedal, in which a leitmotif as old as *Das Rheingold* (labeled *"Liebesnot"* — "Love's distress" — by Wolzogen) gives way to the main theme from the Siegfried/Brünnhilde duet in the last act of *Siegfried* (*Liebesbund* — "Bond of love" — according to Wolzogen), the curtain falls, the dominant resolves, and we seem to be at the beginning of a jaunty orchestral piece reflective of Siegfried's euphoria and full of his themes, sometimes in counterpoint with the themes of others (e.g., Loge, one of whose attributes is god of fun, appearing at one point against the horn call in the bass).

A deceptive cadence tosses us suddenly into the key of A major as Siegfried's boat rounds the bend to meet the main current of the Rhine (identifiable by its leitmotif;

EX. 42-14   Richard Wagner, The Valkyries' Song as sketched in 1850

compare the analogous spot in Smetana's almost exactly contemporaneous *Moldau*, described in chapter 41). This is harmonic "navigation" at its most literal. The key seems altogether unprepared until we remember its very elaborate unconsummated preparation (twenty bars over a dominant pedal), that set the Rhine journey in motion. Again we must acknowledge the long-range design that gives harmonic coherence to the seemingly random vagaries of the Wagnerian surface. And yet we are not really in the key of A: it is just another apparition. While it confirms retrospectively the dominant sounded minutes ago, on this appearance it remains unconfirmed by a cadence. That makes it a prime target for liquidation; and sure enough, before any cadence in A has a chance to be heard, another bend is metaphorically rounded and the key of E♭ seems to return after all, in just as sudden and unprepared a fashion as its predecessor.

But wait: the E♭ harmony returns in the first inversion, and the descending scale, with its seemingly Lydian fourth degree (A-natural), identifies the chord as Neapolitan and the leitmotif as one of those (Götterdämmerung, Liebe-Tragik) portending doom. So even when the harmony settles down (through a plagal cadence) into root position for another bout of Rhine music, it has been destabilized both musically and dramatically. Memories of Brünnhilde (the Ride motif in the cylindrical brass) bring both a rush of joy (motif in the woodwinds) and an attempt to stabilize the key with an authentic cadence.

But liquidation has already been as if preordained, and we are not surprised to hear the bright subdominant replaced by its functional equivalent (but dramatic antipode), the half-diminished F–A♭–C♭–E♭ that recalls the debacle of the Norns forcibly to mind. After this baneful substitution, in which the noisome harmony supports the Ring motif redolent of Alberich and his curse, recapture of E♭ is impossible. The next attempt at resolution of the dominant produces only the Liebe-Tragik motif over an inverted C♭ major triad (another recollection of the Norns), in which the bass E♭ is roundly contradicted and rebuked by everything it is trying to support. Its loss of control is complete by m. 876, when the half-diminished harmony (in extraordinary third inversion) usurps the place of the tonic triad altogether (Ex. 42-15).

EX. 42-15   Richard Wagner, Prologue to *Götterdämmerung* in vocal score, mm. 876–92

Respelled enharmonically, with sharps in place of flats, the half-diminished chord is rerouted toward the key of the scene about to open, in which Siegfried's doom is plotted. That key, as already shown in Ex. 42-8b, is B minor ($=$C♭, similarly respelled), strongly prefigured but unconfirmed at the end of the Norns' scene. Its recuperation here brackets the confident euphoria of the immediately preceding scene and exposes its false consciousness. When next Siegfried and Brünnhilde meet, it will be as enemies whose misguided quarrel makes the final crisis of the drama inevitable.

THE ULTIMATE EXPERIENCE

The articulation of the drama through musical analogues — Wagner, of course, would have called it the articulation of the music through dramatic analogues — and its uncanny psychological potency are perhaps sufficiently illustrated by the *Götterdämmerung* Prologue. We will not have room for another musico-dramatic exploration so detailed. But one more Wagnerian experience needs to be sampled if we are to have an idea of the composer's accomplishment adequate to its historical resonance, because its repercussions will be felt on virtually every subsequent page of this book. Though *Götterdämmerung*, the culminating work in the *Ring* cycle, could be fairly described as Wagner's crowning achievement, bringing to consummation as it did the largest musical entity ever conceived within the European literate tradition, it is not his emblematic work. That distinction belongs to *Tristan und Isolde*, completed (between the second and third acts of *Siegfried*, as it were) in 1859.

What makes *Tristan* the extreme or limiting case, and a touchstone for all subsequent musicmaking and music-thinking, has to do with its subject matter — a tragic love story adapted from a famous medieval poem and treated on a typically monumental, archetypal scale — but even more with the relationship between its "deeds of music" and the responses they have elicited. If, as the British philosopher Bryan Magee suggests, Wagner's music "is both loved and hated more immoderately than that of any other composer,"[47] the same is true *a fortiori* of *Tristan* among his works.

FIG. 42-12   Lillian Nordica (1857–1914) as Isolde, ca. 1900.

The balance we have observed in *Götterdämmerung* between its cognitive symbolism and its precognitive or subliminal modes of signifying—between the *representational* as embodied in the leitmotives and the directly *presentational* as embodied in the sea of harmony—is drastically skewed in *Tristan* in favor of the latter. Where *Götterdämmerung* powerfully narrates a complex story, *Tristan* powerfully projects a sustained feeling. But in fact they are not equally powerful. If *Tristan* shows anything it shows that, unless protected, our minds (or the rational part of our minds, at any rate, the part that understands and interprets stories) must give way before our feelings, and that music—"tonal" music, Wagner's music—is their most powerful catalyst on earth.

The story is negligible: a man and a woman are seized with a forbidden love (act I); they attempt to act upon it but are forcibly separated, the man being mortally wounded in the process (act II); the man dies and the bereft woman, overwhelmed at the sight of his corpse, dies in sympathy (act III). In a program note he published around 1860, meant to elucidate the content of the work as embodied in its Prelude five years before the first performance of the whole opera, Wagner reduced the story quite graphically to the feeling it symbolized, a feeling to which only music—his music—could do full artistic justice: "Suddenly aflame," he wrote,

> they must confess they belong only to each other. No end, now, to the yearning, the desire, the bliss, the suffering of love: world, power, fame, splendor, honor, knighthood, loyalty, friendship—all scattered like an empty dream; one thing alone still living: yearning, yearning, unquenchable, ever-regenerated longing—languishing, thirsting; the only redemption—death, extinction, eternal sleep![48]

And here is the musical equivalent of the condition Wagner describes—or rather, the "deed of music" to which not only Wagner's description but the entire opera forms a "visible" outer garment (Ex. 42-16). The first three measures of the *Tristan* Prelude constitute perhaps the most famous, surely the most commented-on, single phrase of music ever written.

Long singled out for extensive glossing in its own right is the dissonant first harmony, so distinctive and seemingly unprecedented that it has been christened the

EX. 42-16   Richard Wagner, Prelude to *Tristan und Isolde*, mm. 1–11

"*Tristan*-chord." Its quality as sheer aural sensation is much enhanced by the mixture of orchestral colors in which it is clothed; and this in turn is the result of its being the point of confluence between two leitmotives that later function independently: the rising sixth with conjunct chromatic "recovery" in the cellos, and the rising chromatic tetrachord in the oboe, accompanied by (predominantly) other double reeds.

A closer look, however, shows the *Tristan*-chord (as sheer sound, anyway) to be nothing new. In fact it is a harmony that has already figured prominently in this very chapter, albeit spelled F – A♭ – C♭ – E♭ and functioning as the supertonic of E♭. In that guise it was the Norns' horror chord. In its new tonal context, that of A minor, it is famed as the chord of love's unquenchable desire. In musical semiosis (or "signing"), as in real estate, location is everything.

But what is its function in A minor, and how do we even know that A minor is the key in which it is functioning? True, the first note is *A*, but there are no A minor triads in the vicinity. Indeed, there is no simple triad of any kind until m. 17, and the triad that finally appears there is F major. The blank key signature, given the chromatic (or in any case "chromaticized") context, could merely be the absence of a key signature. If a key must be named, why not C major?

And yet if our experience with Wagner's sea of harmony has taught us anything, it has taught us to expect keys not to assert themselves explicitly but to loom. And what makes a key loom is not the tonic, which cannot identify itself as such without a cadence, but the dominant, which carries the implicit promise of that cadence within it. The end of the first phrase of the *Tristan* prelude is not only in terms of its intervallic structure (its "sound quality"), but also in terms of its preparation, the unambiguous dominant of A minor. The chord that fills the ensuing silence in the listeners' inner ear, assuming that they have any experience at all with tonal harmony, is the unstated — indeed, never to be stated, and ultimately needless to be stated — tonic of that key.

So the *Tristan*-chord, which so clearly (though only in retrospect) performs the function of a "pre-dominant" in A minor, must be interpreted as having F as its root — but an F that seeks resolution not along the circle of fifths (as it would — and has! — in E♭) but by semitonal descent to the dominant, since its degree function is VI. The spelling of the chord, in which F and D♯ coexist, is thus revealed to be quite traditional, since it is on the minor sixth degree that augmented-sixth chords have been occurring in our experience since the time of Bach. What makes the *Tristan*-chord unusual, then, and deserving of a name after all, is the fact that its "half-diminished" quality is the result of its containing a long, accented appoggiatura (G♯), which on its resolution to A clarifies the nature and function of the chord as a French sixth in A minor, resolving normally to the dominant.

This, too, is something that Wagner fastidiously prepares us to observe, if only in retrospect. The F on the first downbeat is a retrospectively recognizable appoggiatura to E, and the nature of the A♯ in m. 3 as a chromatic passing tone is self-evident. (Nobody, it seems, has ever heard the downbeat sonority of m. 3, which could be read as another French sixth, as another sort of *Tristan*-chord.) Thus all three downbeats are dominated melodically by accented nonharmonic tones. Their restlessness contributes tellingly to the affect of unfulfilled desire that Wagner described in his program note, but that we surely need no program note to detect. That restlessness, it should be emphasized, occurs within a fully operational (and fully "normal") tonal context, one that Wagner shared, say, with Mozart (compare Ex. 42-17, offered with apologies, with Ex. 30-7). Only against a background of normality, after all, with its implied promise of repose, could such a restlessness be evoked.

EX. 42-17   *Tristan*-chord conflated with Mozart Fantasia theme

The affect is palpable—and *immanent*, rather than merely symbolized—in the unresolved dominant seventh in m. 3. And it is made even more oppressively palpable in the sequential repetitions of the opening phrase (as given in the full text of the Prelude). Each phrase of the continuation begins with cello notes drawn from the dominant harmony previously left hanging, and proceeds through a *Tristan*-chord to a new dominant to be similarly left ringing, unconsummated, in the air. The affect of the third phrase is intensified and prolonged, in fact, in a manner that may be fairly described as sadistic: its harmonized portion is repeated after a fermata that extends the agony of incompletion, and after another similarly agonizing fermata the last two melody notes are repeated—and repeated again at the octave to rub it in—then reharmonized with the hanging dominant from m. 3, only to resolve, appallingly, in a deceptive cadence supporting yet another accented appoggiatura.

Any listener who by now is not feeling "yearning, yearning, unquenchable, ever-regenerated longing—languishing, thirsting," et cetera, has simply never learned to respond to the syntax of tonal music. For such a listener a program note will be of no assistance. For those capable of responding, explanation is superfluous.

So it is quite misleading to say that it is merely the first phrase of *Tristan und Isolde* that has excited so much comment, even if it is usually quoted (as in Ex. 42-16) and analyzed all by itself. To understand its fascination one must observe it in context, a context of unresolved dominant tension that lasts throughout the Prelude, sustained by Wagner's unprecedented skill in the arts of transition and feint, and that is revived and intensified at various points in the opera until it is at last cataclysmically discharged at the very end of the final act. These are the aspects of *Tristan und Isolde* that have made it a technical tour de force, an esthetic watershed, and even a moral touchstone, and that urgently demand our attention.

HOW FAR CAN YOU STRETCH A DOMINANT?

But before making closer inspection of Wagner's mechanisms of arousal, a general comment will be in order. As the most influential composer of the later nineteenth century, Wagner had an effect on his progeny similar to Beethoven's. Just as a multitude of nineteenth-century composers in the "post-Beethoven period" claimed Beethoven as a father however antagonistic their positions, so did a multitude of turn-of-the-century and early twentieth-century composers in the period post-Wagner claim descent from him. And just as Beethoven's contesting heirs made of him what they would, so did Wagner's. On the basis of the chromaticized harmony and the fluid modulatory schemes that we have observed in *Götterdämmerung* and will observe in *Tristan*, Wagner has been cast by many of his followers as the subverter or saboteur of tonal harmony.

He was anything but that. On the contrary, Wagner brought many aspects of traditional tonal practice to their technical and expressive zenith, always by working within the system. To put this proviso in more rigorous technical terms, Wagner's most important innovations had the effect, as we have already observed, of prolonging and intensifying the traditional dominant function. The true revolutionizers and subverters of tonal practice were those composers, beginning with Liszt in his New German phase, who sought to attenuate or even eliminate the dominant function from their music by replacing the structural functions of the circle of fifths, of which the dominant function is the most potent, with circles of major or minor thirds (see chapter 40).

It would be very easy to imagine a Lisztian variant of the *Tristan* Prelude. Liszt was very interested in the half-diminished seventh chord as a sonority, and may well have played a part in sparking Wagner's interest in the chord whose function he would so radically transform. We have seen how conspicuous the F – Ab – Cb – Eb harmony and its transpositions were in Liszt's symphonic poems and program symphonies, as a glance back at Ex. 40-8b will recall. The introduction to Liszt's song *Die Lorelei* ("The mermaid"), after Heine (Ex. 42-18a), has often been cited as a Wagnerian prototype, though the resemblance is more melodic than harmonic (the chord usually cited as the *Tristan* precedent is in fact not of half-diminished quality). There is an even closer precedent in Weber (Ex. 42-18b), where the harmony before the resolution of the appoggiatura has the same half-diminished quality as the *Tristan*-chord, even if resolution is made downward to a diminished seventh rather than upward to a French sixth.

But such examples are trivial; they can easily be multiplied, even in eighteenth-century music. The Wagnerian innovation, as we have seen, was not the *Tristan*-chord itself, but rather the deliberate failure to resolve the dominant seventh that follows it. But it is a false failure that achieves its awesome expressive power because the traditional resolution is insistently honored in the breach (that is, in our mind's ear).

EX. 42-18A Franz Liszt, *Die Lorelei*, mm. 1–7

EX. 42-18B *Tristan*-chord in Carl Maria von Weber, *Euryanthe* Overture

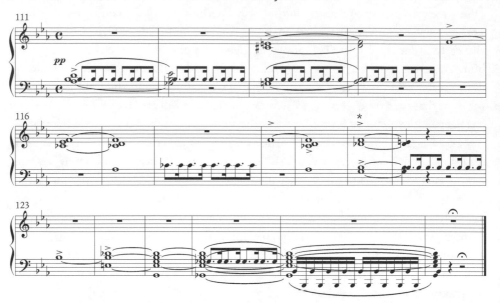

Ex. 42-18a already shows the fundamental difference between the Lisztian approach and the Wagnerian. Liszt's two phrases are in literal sequence, at a transposition of a minor third (expressed in the notation as a diminished seventh). The two finishing chords, therefore, are the same, since the diminished seventh chord, consisting of a stack of minor thirds, replicates itself when transposed by the interval of which it is exclusively composed. The passage neither accomplishes nor forecasts any harmonic motion and embodies little desire. The first sequential repetition in the *Tristan* Prelude is also at the minor third, making its "Lisztian" continuation easy to extrapolate (Ex. 42-19).

EX. 42-19 "Lisztian" variant of Richard Wagner's Prelude to *Tristan und Isolde* (opening)

This variant is much more "radical" than Wagner's, and much less effective. In fact it is trivial in its fatal predictability and harmonic stasis. By the third phrase all sense of desire for the dominant seventh resolution has been liquidated by the sequence, just as it is liquidated in the famous passage from the Prologue to Musorgsky's opera

Boris Godunov (1872) in which the tintinnabulation of coronation bells is simulated (Ex. 42-20) by two oscillating dominant sevenths with roots a tritone apart (and that consequently share a complementary tritone in common).

EX. 42-20   Modest Musorgsky, coronation bells in *Boris Godunov* (Prologue, scene 2)

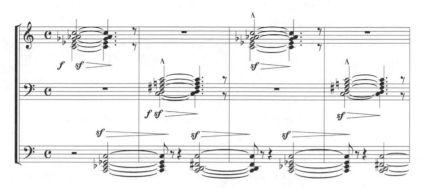

So despite the reputation of *Tristan und Isolde* as having instigated a "crisis of tonality" with its notorious freedom of chromatic modulation, Wagner (unlike Liszt and Musorgsky) exercised his freedom entirely within the established practice of functional harmony. Far from threatening it, he managed to wring from the common practice an unprecedented realization of its interdependent structural and expressive potentials, harnessing them together with unprecedented synergy. The paucity of cadences and the frequent changes of harmonic direction in no sense negate or dissolve the efficacy of the traditional harmonic functions (least of all the attraction of the dominant for the tonic). On the contrary, these functions operate in *Tristan und Isolde* with unexampled intensity. That overwhelming intensification of attraction and desire, as we have seen, is the whole poetic point.

The assumption that *Tristan* somehow started the process whereby functional harmony was fatally and inexorably weakened is an excellent example of historicist mythmaking. It embeds the opera in a progress narrative that justifies the radical departures of a later generation of German composers who did in fact attempt to attenuate, and finally eliminate, the role of functional harmony as a governor of musical structure. Their story, sometimes narrated as if it were about the collapse of tonality rather than about the changing techniques of a small group of composers, will be told in a later chapter. It is in no way implicit in this chapter's tale. It was worth foreshadowing here not only because the myth of Wagner, or of *Tristan*, as the instigator of the collapse has become so entrenched, but also because its entrenchment illustrates so well the historicist tendency to write history backward with an eye toward giving the present a justification, a desired past. Looking at the opera and listening to it, as far as possible, with contemporary eyes and ears (that is, the eyes and ears of *its* contemporaries), we will observe Wagner's reliance on the common practice at all levels from the most local to the most global, and will be all the better able to appreciate his expert manipulations of it. Putting the matter in terms of Wagner's manipulations of his materials — in terms, that is, of compositional technique — is to describe his achievement in "poietic" or "maker's" terms, to revive some terminology first used in chapter 20. But Wagner's manipulations of his materials translate directly into esthesic or experiential terms as well, as forcible manipulations of the listener's expectations and responses. Some find the manipulation of their consciousness and their appetites thrilling, others disconcerting, even frightening. It is another of the many factors that have made Wagner an incorrigibly controversial figure.

So we should not be surprised to find that Wagner's superb expressive efficacy depends on a relatively conservative approach to tonality. Comparison of Ex. 42-16, which contains the first eleven measures of the *Tristan* Prelude, and Ex. 42-19, its hypothetical Lisztian counterpart, tellingly illustrates that conservatism. The first difference between them comes at the beginning of the second phrase, which Wagner adjusts so that its first two notes are drawn directly from the preceding dominant harmony: the dominant function remains special for Wagner in a way that it does not for "Liszt," the author of our hypothetical example — or for the actual Liszt, to judge by the "Faust" or "Mountain" Symphonies sampled in chapter 40.

The differences between the respective third phrases are even more telling. Again Wagner adjusts the first note to retain a pitch from the preceding dominant-seventh chord. But then he interpolates an extra semitone both into the descending chromatic line in mm. 8–9 and into the ascending one in mm. 10–11, meanwhile inverting the *Tristan*-chord in m. 10 so that the tritone is on top and the perfect fourth below. The net result of these adjustments is the gaining of a semitone in the second transposition of the phrase. Instead of a simple Lisztian circle of minor thirds, Wagner has transposed the opening phrase first by a minor third and then by a major third. In this way the ending chords apply dominant functions in turn to the root, the third, and the fifth of the governing A-minor tonic triad. Thus the tonic also remains privileged in Wagner in a way that it no longer is in Liszt, whether the hypothetical "Liszt" of Ex. 42-19, or the actual historical Liszt of chapter 40.

As a result of these manipulations, the ending harmony in Ex. 42-16 is the tonally efficacious V of V rather than the tonally meaningless dominant of E♭ in Ex. 42-19 (or its further sequential extension, the dominant of G♭). A glance at the full text of the Prelude will reveal that Wagner's V of V is applied quite conventionally to V, which is then applied quite conventionally to I — except that the last connection is frustrated by the grating deceptive cadence on F. The frustration of the cadence becomes the listener's frustration in Wagner the way it no longer does, or even can, within Liszt's more "progressive" and experimental harmonic ambience.

Thereafter, the Prelude is a voyage on the sea of harmony that may be thought of as analogizing the voyage of the ship transporting Tristan and Isolde from Ireland to Cornwall, aboard which the performance of act I takes place. Schopenhauer, who glorified music as a direct sensuous copy of the Will, the primal or essential impulse to be and to become, had used navigational metaphors to describe both music and the Will itself. In its surges and swells, its climaxes on restless harmonies rather than on their resolutions, and its seemingly perpetual state of modulation, the Prelude to

Tristan und Isolde, which Wagner began sketching in 1856 after immersing himself in Schopenhauer's work, was an attempt conjointly to embody the motion of the sea, the very shape of desire, and (in its abstract, textless, "absolute" character) the pure reality of the Will, as only music could reflect them.

And then, when the curtain goes up on the first act to depict an actual ship at sea on which the flare-up of unquenchable passion will be enacted by a pair of actual lovers whose actions are explained by actually enunciated words, we have the most literal possible demonstration of Wagner's concept of musical drama as "deeds of music made visible." The entire drama, or at least its essential premise, is powerfully if abstractly enacted in the realm of the "real" before its visual and cognitive embodiment in the realm of "appearances" even begins.

The Prelude's tonal trajectory is in essence that of a single harmonic gesture, announced at the outset, and sustained through a wealth of surface variety to an appearance of climax, followed by a still unconsummated subsidence. Whatever else it may have been, it was a display of composerly virtuosity that no contemporary could deny (or equal), however grudging their acknowledgment. Wagner was surely the greatest master of dominant prolongation since Beethoven. That, far more than the devices of motivic development and thematic transformation that were already the common currency of the New German School, was the essence of Wagner's kinship with his great predecessor.

Far less often remarked is the fluidity of Wagnerian phrase structure, an aspect of rhythm that is every bit as original as the novel harmonic shadings, and every bit as important in achieving the seamless, uncanny transitions to which Wagner gave the name "infinite melody." Upbeats and downbeats can be as ambiguous as harmonic pivots. The main theme of the Prelude, which seems to grow out of the great harmonic balk where the cadence to A major is thwarted by F (and which will come back — once only — in act I, when the lovers have drained their potion and are reduced to the spellbound repetition of each other's name), is the prime case in point. It arises, and mainly recurs, on the upbeat (Ex. 42-21a), but is imperceptibly shifted to the downbeat

EX. 42-21A   Richard Wagner, Prelude to *Tristan und Isolde*, mm. 16–23

EX. 42-21B   Richard Wagner, Prelude to *Tristan und Isolde*, 55–63

in the turbulent middle of the piece — imperceptibly, that is, until its next entry cuts off its predecessor after seven beats (= $3\frac{1}{2}$ measures; see Ex. 42-21b). Effects like this are as disorienting to the listener, as consciousness-altering, as modulations. In the strictest (Kantian) sense they produce an intimation of the sublime — something uncountable and ungraspable, in the presence of which the Self is dwarfed.

WHEN RESOLUTION COMES...

The Prelude is thus the opera's essential deed of music, made immediately visible with the raising of the curtain. The resolution of the drama, as Wagner put it in his program note, cannot take place in the visible realm, but only in blissful extinction, which is transcendence of the Will:

> the rapture of dying, of being no more, of ultimate release into that wondrous realm from which we stray the furthest when we strive to penetrate it by the most impetuous force. Shall we call it death? Or is it not night's wonder-world, out of which, as the saga tells us, an ivy and a vine sprang up in locked embrace over Tristan's and Isolde's grave?[49]

The second act of the opera represents "night's wonder-world" on the level of sensuous appearance — the "phenomenal" level, to speak the language of philosophy. The third and final act portrays the attainment of the rapturous fulfillment in extinction: night's wonder-world on the level of the Will, of the truly real, or (as the German philosopher would put it) the "noumenal" plane. The musical relationship between the two acts — in particular, between their climaxes — will once again harness what the music theorist Heinrich Schenker would later call "der Tonwille" (the "tones' will"),[50] the essential structural functions of harmony and rhythm that undergird the visible action. In the Prelude, we have observed these forces in action on the local level, organizing a musical statement of some hundred measures. Now we shall see them functioning on the most global plane, organizing a pair of acts that between them last three hours.

Obviously we cannot encompass the entire two-act, three-hour span in a discussion like this. We shall have to settle on a *metonymy*: a part (or pair of parts) to represent the whole(s). But in doing so we will actually be following Wagner's own plan with optimal economy and focus.

The main event in act II is an extended nocturnal tryst, arranged with the reluctant compliance of Isolde's maidservant Brangäne, who stands watch over the lovers. The situation, as noted as long ago as chapter 4, is that of the *Tagelied*, a genre of medieval German song on which Wagner knowingly drew in order to invest his concept with the historical and national authenticity his theory of art demanded. The long central action of Wagner's act II is in effect an enacted or acted-out Tagelied. It is cast in three big sections. It is in the second of these that the music settles down for the first time in the act into a relatively stable key area (A♭ major); the lovers lose themselves in the higher reality of night's wonder-world; and the hugely protracted formal patterns of the medieval courtly song with refrains come to the fore.

The refrains are Brangäne's, and they consist of the warning—"Habet acht!" ("Beware!")—to which, locked in their love trance, the lovers pay no heed. Her alarms, though shouted urgently at close range, might as well be coming from another planet so far as Tristan and Isolde are concerned, and Wagner represents the situation with great subtlety. The onset of the trance coincides with a rare authentic cadence, to A♭, which establishes, as it were, the home-key of erotic bliss. Beginning with the words "O sink' hernieder, Nacht der Liebe" ("O descend upon us, night of love"), the music the lovers sing is a paraphrase of a song (*Traüme*, "Dreams"), one of five composed by Wagner in 1857 to words by Mathilde Wesendonck, a German poet whose wealthy husband, Otto Wesendonck, was the composer's chief benefactor during his exile in Switzerland. Their passionate though perhaps unconsummated affair (detected by Wagner's wife Minna, leading to divorce and a chaotic period of destitution and wandering) is assumed to have been, along with the discovery of Schopenhauer, one of the main stimuli toward the composition of this most spiritually erotic (or erotically spiritual) of operas.

FIG. 42-13   Mathilde Wesendonck (1828–1902), detail of a painting.

The whole section thus initiated, and ending with Brangäne's first intervention, is virtually quiescent in harmony. The tonic pedal initiated at the start holds uninterrupted for twenty-two measures, and is interrupted thereafter only for the briefest digressions, all of which, by circling right back to the pedal tone, may be regarded as embellishments or prolongations of the unchanging, transfixing harmony of night. In one case, excursions to the ♭VI in both the tonic and dominant regions, of a kind familiar since Schubert, are made; in another, the enharmonic transformation of the tonic pedal into a leading tone introduces a series of modulations by ascending chromatic degrees (to A, B♭, C♭, etc.) that goes exactly as far as the first primary function of the original key (D♭, the subdominant) before being redirected homeward; in a third, it is the *Tristan*-chord itself that briefly intrudes to press the harmony voluptuously toward the Neapolitan by way of its dominant.

Only Brangäne breaks the spell—or tries to. That her warnings fall on deaf ears is signaled by the fact that the lightly pulsing syncopations and the shimmering orchestration that together conjure up the lovers' state of ecstasy are unaffected by her entrance. (Wagner's care in marking the score *"Sehr ruhig/molto tranquillo"* at the very point where Brangäne begins to shout is in itself a pointed commentary on the action.) That her voice impinges from "out there," casting the action on a double plane of lower reality (hers—and possibly ours) and higher (theirs—also potentially ours!) is signaled by the harmonic modulation that her entrance initiates. By the time she actually enunciates her warning, the music is securely anchored in F♯ (minor, according to the key signature, but major according to the actual harmonies) on its way to a B major that is no sooner sounded than liquidated as the music gradually wends its way back to the lovers' key. The final section or coda of the love-duet-plus-Brangäne, a compressed and frenetic replay of the previous section as the lovers near their climax, begins with a new lyrical theme (Ex. 42-22). That the theme is a transformation of the opening measures of the Prelude (Ex. 42-16) is clear from its contour—an upward skip followed by a descent by chromatic degrees—and from its harmonic plan, consisting of sequential repetitions at the minor third corresponding to the first sequential repetition in the Prelude, only this time going a full Lisztian round (rising fourths respectively pitched E♭ → A♭, G♭ → C♭, A → D, and C → F).

Except for an abrupt but sumptuous detour to G major caused by Brangäne's second warning, this final section pursues a furious trajectory in which everything seems at once to rise and to accelerate toward liftoff over a dominant pedal that is prolonged even more spectacularly than the one in the Prelude. The dominant in

EX. 42-22   Richard Wagner, *Tristan und Isolde*, Act II, Love Duet ("Tagelied"), mm. 261–284

EX. 42-22 *(continued)*

question is the F♯ (=G♭), the dominant of B (=C♭). Its implied resolution corresponds to the second of the melodic fourths enumerated in the paragraph above, which itself corresponded with the first upward sequential swing in the Prelude. The whole body of the love scene, beginning in A♭ and now approaching a cadence on B, is thus a vast composing-out of this minor-third motion—the essential harmonic impulse, the "molecular" embodiment, as Schopenhauer would have grasped with joy, of the Will.

The F♯ pedal is sounded where the music is first notated with the key signature of B major. That key will always be announced by its dominant, never the tonic, for it is always represented, like the procreative impulse itself, in a state of perpetual becoming. As in the Prelude, there are various departures, but only to return. The first initiates a chromatic bass descent that gets as far as C♯, the dominant of the F♯ pedal, which is prolonged through a series of Neapolitan relationships and finally redirected to F♯ to coincide with the return of the B-major key signature. That is the first span of the pedal's prolongation.

The next span encloses a rhythmic compression of the previous acclamation to the night in a key area much closer to home. The combination of shorter note values, suggesting greater speed, and a more insistently goal-directed harmony produces the tremulously impending mood of a retransition. The sounding of the inexorably cadential tonic $^6_4$ initiates a hundred bars containing virtually nothing but sequences of ever-diminishing (that is, "accelerating") note values and unit durations. At first the singers' parts move in half notes and six-bar phrases. A dozen bars later they are trading two-measure units in four-measure phrases, the second unit in each phrase containing quarter notes. After ten more bars, eighth notes and even sixteenths are introduced (as embellishments) into the vocal parts. After another twenty they are trading phrases made up almost entirely of quarter notes.

In a final approach to the looming, inevitable cadence, the singers' by-now delirious sequences are accompanied by a steady chromatic descent in the bass that spans an entire octave, finally zeroing in on F♯ for what one feels sure is to be the long-awaited consummation. It *almost* happens. In m. 482 the subdominant is shunted in where the tonic was expected, and the tonic, when it finally comes a bar later, is in the irresolute first inversion — a classic Wagnerian feint. But now (Ex. 42-23) the process is repeated: the same melodic trade-offs in the vocal parts; the same chromatically descending bass. This time, however, another ingredient, even more insistently directed at the goal, is added in the form of a sequence in the orchestra of a single bar's unit duration, consisting of nothing other than endless reiterations of the four-note chromatic ascent first heard in the second measure of the Prelude, rising from the *Tristan*-chord.

Twenty-eight times in all this motive resounds. At irregularly contracting intervals it is extended by an extra note smuggled in via a triplet to jack the sequence up by a single chromatic degree in contrary motion against the chromatically descending bass. After another classic Wagnerian feint in the form of a shocking *piano subito*, the singers' parts are drawn into the irresistible soaring sequence. The bass, meanwhile, finally hits bottom on F♯ and stays there, grinding out twelve bars of dominant pedal intensified by a *molto crescendo*, at last pounding out the complete dominant seventh of B major in root position. At this point the rising sequence finally delivers Isolde's part to the leading tone. No composer had ever generated a comparable dominant-tension, for never before had a composer felt the need so to dramatize music's most basic business.

And then, disaster. Isolde's high B in m. 515, the long-promised triumph of the tonic, is harmonized instead as the seventh in a sadistically grating dominant-ninth chord couched in the most cacophonous voicing imaginable, as King Marke, Isolde's lawfully

EX. 42-23 Richard Wagner, *Tristan und Isolde*, Act II, climax of Love Duet ("Tagelied"), mm. 487–515

EX. 42-23 (*continued*)

intended husband, comes rushing onstage with his hunting party — shouting retainers, honking horners, barking dogs, and all. Another deed of music, this time perhaps the cruelest deceptive cadence ever perpetrated, is made visible as the lovers' rapture — not to mention the listeners' — is interrupted on the very point of consummation.

The remainder of the second act is the heart of what some have taken to be the tragedy, others the crisis of a religious drama. Tristan, after first securing Isolde's promise to follow him into "the land where dark night reigns, from which my mother sent me forth," allows himself to be fatally wounded in a duel of honor with one of King Marke's retainers. In the third act, Tristan dies in Isolde's arms and she, contemplating his corpse, undergoes what Wagner calls her *Verklärung* ("Transfiguration," here meaning a spiritual exaltation), as expressed in a final aria that has popularly become known as the *Liebestod* ("Death-by-Love"), the term Wagner actually meant to apply to the Prelude. At its climax she sinks dead into Brangäne's arms, and the curtain falls.

At a glance it is obvious that this climactic seventy-nine-measure solo aria is a truncated recapitulation, in diminished note values, of the 253-measure final section of the act II love duet. For sixty measures the correspondence between the two sections is virtually exact: splice mm. 261–282, 414–459, and 462–514 of the duet together and you get the *Verklärung* through m. 60. But at mm. 61–62 the bloodcurdling deceptive cadence that cut off the duet before its consummation is replaced by a cataclysmic authentic cadence (Ex. 42-24), the most strongly voiced cadence in the entire opera, in which the B-major triad in root position, ardently anticipated but thwarted in act II, is finally allowed to sound forth in glory. At this radiant moment, one may say, Isolde's soul passes irrevocably into "night's wonder-world" where it can join Tristan's, the lovers achieving in that transcendent space the union denied them on the terrestrial plane.

EX. 42-24   Richard Wagner, *Tristan und Isolde*, Isolde's *Verklärung*

EX. 42-24 (continued)

EX. 42-24 (*continued*)

Wagner consolidates the sense of long-postponed consummation by attending in the last five measures of the opera to a bit of unfinished business left over from the first three measures of the Prelude. He allows the original *Tristan*-chord to sound one last time along with its attendant leitmotif, the four-note chromatic ascent. Only this time he replaces the dominant seventh on E with an E-minor triad that can function as the subdominant of B major; and he extends the leitmotif in a pair of oboes, moving through C♯ to D♯, the third of the tonic triad. That D♯—the note that finally resolves the *Tristan*-chord, in the process becoming perhaps the most symbolically fraught single note in all of opera, if not all of music—is given an extraordinary spotlight when Wagner clears all of the surrounding harmony away (in some cases by notating actual rests, in others by the use of a staccato dot), allowing just the oboes to peep through for a brief instant, immediately before the final chord.

THE PROBLEM REVISITED

No matter what they thought of Wagner or how they valued his achievement, his contemporaries, and many listeners ever since, have been forced to acknowledge the unprecedented and perhaps never equaled rhetorical force of his music. Whether they loved the experience or hated it, all recognized that the experience of Wagner was emotionally draining and even physically exhausting in a way that no musical experience had ever been before. And all were aware that Wagner's force of expression was a force arising precisely out of his novel and audacious manipulations of the same age-old functional relationships that had governed musical structure and undergirded its coherence since the seventeenth century—since precisely the time, that is, when music's role as "the great persuader" (as we dubbed it in chapter 19) was upheld by the Florentine neo-Platonist academicians who midwifed the birth of opera out of the spirit of the ancient drama.

But as Plato himself was the first (at least in the European tradition) to recognize and warn, if music is the great persuader, then we have to ask what it is that music persuades us of, and we have to be wary of it. Clara Schumann, the aging widow of Robert Schumann, and (as the secret dedicatee of Schumann's *Phantasie*) a woman who knew a thing or two about love music but had ample reason to hate Wagner for snubbing her husband, was only one of many who saw in *Tristan und Isolde* an affront to moral decorum and, ultimately, a threat to social stability. After attending a performance in 1875, ten years after the opera's premiere, she wrote in her diary that it is the most repulsive thing I ever saw or heard in my life. To have to sit through a whole evening watching, listening to such love-lunacy till every feeling of decency was outraged, and to see not only the audience but the musicians delighted with it was — I may well say — the saddest experience of my whole artistic career . . . . It is not emotion that the opera portrays, it is a disease, and they tear their hearts out of their bodies, while the music expresses it all in the most nauseous manner.[51]

Indeed, anyone who, as Clara Schumann observed, takes delight in Isolde's orgiastic death by love (and delight is a mild word indeed to describe the reaction many listeners experience) has been momentarily persuaded that the resolution of the dominant-seventh chord on F♯ to the tonic triad of B major is the most important thing in the world — from which it follows that the visible embodiment of that deed of music, Isolde's mystic union with Tristan in death, was, as Shakespeare's Hamlet might have remarked, "a consummation devoutly to be wish'd."[52] Whether looked upon in Schopenhauerian terms as a transcendence of the world of appearances, or in terms more in keeping with our terrestrial experience as a symbolized (or simulated) sexual orgasm, the opera's all-conquering climax validates (and justifies?) a passion that defied every social norm and behavioral constraint of Tristan's and Isolde's world — and, by extension, if we revel in it, of our own.

Going beyond the more obvious question whether music, by virtue of its wordless-ness and its invisibility, was exempt from normal taboos on the explicit representation of sexual behavior, we are prompted to ask another. If we can be so easily persuaded of the superior claim of passion over propriety in the imaginary world of the opera, are we not susceptible to similar persuasion in the actual world that we inhabit? Wagner's contemporaries had to ask themselves that question when confronted not only by Tristan's and Isolde's licentious deeds but by Wagner's own flouting of moral law: first in his dalliance with his benefactor's wife in Zürich, in which the triangle of the composer and the two Wesendoncks vividly paralleled that of Tristan, Isolde, and King Marke; and second, even more notoriously, in his wooing of Liszt's own daughter Cosima, who deserted her husband, the pianist and conductor Hans von Bülow (a devoted Wagnerian, even afterward), to become Wagner's second wife in 1870.

Wagner was perhaps the most powerful advocate for the implied proposition that a great artist's private life, however scandalous, was to be condoned out of reverence for his artistic genius; that art, in Nietzsche's famous phrase, was "beyond good and evil";[53] and that artists were not subject to the same moral strictures as "ordinary mortals." Even more disquietingly, artworks like *Tristan und Isolde*, in their "liberatory" message, could seem to invite its audience to emulate the characters and their creator in their dangerously emancipated behavior. The questions that Wagner forced thus represented an encroachment of the Beethoven myth into dangerous territories that the original creators of the myth never foresaw.

As Brian Magee has put it, Wagner's art, unlike Beethoven's, is not only "aspira-tional": it does not seek only to express what is highest and best in us, but also what is forbidden. That is what gives his works their very special persuasive power, or in Magee's words their "special emotional impact which everyone, including people who do not like them, acknowledges."[54] The philosopher continues, "They give us a hotline to what has been most powerfully repressed in ourselves, and bring us consciousness-changing messages from the unconscious." This begins to suggest what many in the twentieth century have suggested: that the most appropriate context in which to appreciate Wagner's achievement is not the one into which Jacques Barzun inserted him in the book cited near the beginning of this chapter. Rather than with Darwin or with Marx, Wagner should perhaps be ranged as an artist with Sigmund Freud, another explorer of the unconscious desires that drive our conscious lives in directions we might be loath to acknowledge.

Nor are these the only parlous terrains toward which Wagner beckoned his listeners with his astounding persuasive skills. Here we circle back to the beginning of the chapter, where Wagner's relationship to his nation was broached. His tendency toward xenophobia and tribalism, expressed in bigotry—against the cosmopolitan Jews, against the "Enlightened" French, and by extension against internationalism and rationality themselves—was both symptomatic of the late nineteenth century's new exclusionary and aggressive brand of nationalism, and, to a much-debated extent, among its formative influences. His persuasive skills can look to those implicitly excluded like demagoguery. His appeal to the feeling's-understanding, implying a cerebral bypass, can look like the appeal of later German demagogues to "think with the blood"[55] rather than with the reasoning brain.

The ending of Wagner's single mature comic opera, *Die Meistersinger von Nürnberg* ("The master-singers of Nuremberg," composed 1861–67, performed 1868), is often cited as a case in point. The story, set in the sixteenth century, is an attractive one to say the least: proud young Walther von Stolzing, guided by the wise old master singer Hans Sachs (a real historical personage who has already figured in chapter 4 of this book), harnesses his native genius to his national traditions and produces the greatest artsong of the day, winning not only the singer's prize but also the hand of the maiden he loves. But Wagner could not resist the urge to give the final scene a didactically nationalistic turn, somewhat sinister even in its own contemporary context, when the German states under Prussia's leadership were preparing both for national unification and for a vindictive war on France, and increasingly sinister over the course of the twentieth century, with its two world wars largely caused by German aggression.

While the orchestra gives out the themes of the Master Singers, the Apprentices, and Walther's own *Preislied* (Prize Song), montaged in exquisitely wrought counterpoint, Sachs exhorts the assembled performers to

Habt Acht! Uns dräuen üble Streich':	Beware! Evil threatens us:
zerfällt erst deutsches Volk und Reich,	if the German land and folk should one day decay
in falscher welscher Majestät	under a false foreign rule
kein Fürst bald mehr sein Volk versteht;	soon no prince will understand his people any more;
und welschen Dunst mit welschem Tand	and foreign mists with foreign conceits
sie pflanzen uns in deutsches Land;	they will plant in our German land;
was deutsch und echt, wüßt' keiner mehr,	what is German and pure no one will know
lebt's nicht in deutscher Meister Ehr'.	if it does not live in our esteem for our German masters.
Drum sag ich Euch:	Therefore I say to you:
ehrt Eure deutschen Meister!	Honor your German masters!

FIG. 42-14   *Die Meistersinger*, Act II in the first production (Munich, 1868).

Dann bannt Ihr gute Geister;	Then you will have protection of the good spirits;
und gebt Ihr ihrem Wirken Gunst,	and if you remain true to their endeavors,
zerging' in Dunst	even if mists should dissolve
das heil'ge röm'sche Reich,	the Holy Roman Empire,
uns bliebe gleich	there would still endure
die heil'ge deutsche Kunst!	our holy German art!

Not only does the opera end on this note, but the music that accompanies the crowd's repetition of the last exhortation resounds with the leitmotif of ridicule for the old pedant Beckmesser, the comic baritone, whom many (and not only Jews) have recognized as a caricature of the impotent Jewish artist Wagner had already derided in his notorious essay of 1850. Beckmesser alone is unhappy at the end of the opera; indeed he has been banished from the happy people's midst. But the music is heavenly, all the better to persuade, and in its very heavenliness has confronted music lovers with a moral dilemma.

The first to face it were the *"welschen"* themselves. The word, translated (quite properly) as "foreign" in the extract just given from the libretto, has "Romance"—that is, Latinate—as its primary meaning. Often it simply means "French," and that usage gave Sachs's speech an inescapable subtext for the opera's original audiences, who in their everyday speech used the word *"Welschtum"* to mock "fancy Frenchy manners" or any pretension or foppishness. The French knew the word, too, and what the Germans meant by it. And no one greeted the humiliating outcome of the Franco-Prussian War in 1871 more gleefully than Wagner, who even wrote a malicious one-act farce called *Capitulation* to rub French noses in defeat.

The irony and the difficulty was that French musicians — fascinated by effects of harmony ever since the days of Rameau and very much aware of the power of symbolism in the work of their poet countrymen such as Charles Baudelaire (a hardened Wagnerolater) — were perhaps the most receptive of all to Wagner's musical innovations, and most susceptible to his spell. Their attempt to solve the dilemma by severing all consideration of Wagner's nationalism from appreciation of his music, and to declare "extramusical" considerations off-limits to any discussion of musical values, has set the tone for more than a century of still-raging controversy. Camille Saint-Saëns (1835–1921), already a famous composer by the time of the second *Ring* cycle at Bayreuth in 1876, covered it for a French newspaper. His aggressive intervention on Wagner's behalf was received by many as a breach of national honor. His arguments, however, were influential and are still relevant to the issue as it is debated today. "From the outset," he declared,

> let us avoid any confusion between nationalism and art. Richard Wagner hates France — but does that matter in considering the quality of his works? Those writers who have been insulting him in the crudest fashion for fifteen years now think him ungrateful — in this they may well be right, because nothing gave him greater publicity than their ceaseless attacks . . . . Let us, however, forget the author of this work and deal solely with the *Nibelungenring*. That poem was written out and published in 1863 and has nothing to do with the difficulties between France and Germany since that date . . . .
>
> I myself have studied the works of Richard Wagner for a long time. I have given myself completely to this study and all the performances I have attended have left me with a profound impression that all the theories in the world will never succeed in making me forget. Because of this I have been accused of being a Wagnerian. Indeed, for a while, I believed myself to be one. What a mistake and how far from the truth! I had only to meet some true Wagnerians to realize that I was not one of them and never could be! Because for the Wagnerian, music did not exist before Wagner, or rather it was still in embryo — Wagner raised it to the level of Art . . . .
>
> But what is there to be said about those who feel their sense of patriotism outraged at the very thought of Wagner having his operatic tetralogy performed in a small Bavarian town? Truly it is possible to impute much to this patriotism and it might be more sensible not to so misuse one of the finest of mankind's sentiments but to preserve it carefully as a weapon to be drawn only on special occasions. Others, true and proven Frenchmen, would gladly immolate themselves on their idol's altar if it took his fancy to ask for human sacrifices. I regret I am not able to share any of these feelings, I merely respect them.[56]

It seems clear that the anxieties surrounding Wagner have played a key role in inspiring the "estheticism" that came to dominance around the turn of the twentieth century and continues to infect discussions of art even now. Estheticism is the doctrine that the arts are concerned only with beauty and that beauty is an autonomous entity existing in a world apart from the "worldly" and the "historical," and (to re-borrow that useful phrase from Nietzsche) beyond good and evil. In uneasy alliance with the historicism encountered in the previous chapter — the belief that all history, including the history of art, is self-motivated and deterministic — estheticism has undergirded and safeguarded the autonomy of twentieth-century art and artists to the point where many have seen estheticism as a prerequisite for creative freedom, indeed for the continued possibility of artistic creativity itself.

And that is how an art conceived in politics and dedicated to social utopia has been resolutely depoliticized and desocialized even as (in the opinion of many) it has continued to have a momentous political and social influence in the sometimes horrible history of the twentieth century. Like historicism, estheticism has created a crux—a tangle, a knot, a quandary—in the history of modern art that will color every succeeding page of this book. Wagner—anything but an estheticist himself but unavoidably and tendentiously misunderstood—was its chief begetter.

Artist, Politician, Farmer (Class of 1813, II)

VERDI

The invisible orchestra! The idea is not mine, but Wagner's; and it is excellent. It is impossible today to tolerate horrible tailcoats and white ties against Egyptian, Assyrian, and Druid costumes; to set the orchestra, part of an imaginary world, so to speak, in the middle of the floor, right in the crowd as it claps or hisses. Add to all this the objectionableness of having harps, double basses, and the windmill arms of the conductor himself jutting into the air.[1]

Endless chatter about . . . how I don't know how to write for singers; how the few bearable things are all in the second and fourth acts (nothing in the third); and how on top of all that I am an imitator of Wagner!!! A fine outcome after thirty-five years to wind up as an imitator!!![2]

Our young Italian composers are not good patriots. If the Germans, proceeding from Bach, have come to Wagner, they do so as good Germans, and all is well. But when we, the descendants of Palestrina, imitate Wagner, we are committing a musical crime and are doing a useless, nay, harmful thing.[3]

You do well to honor your Maestro. He is one of the greatest geniuses. He has made people happy and presented them with treasures of immeasurable and immortal worth. You will understand that I, as an Italian, do not yet understand everything. That is due to our ignorance of German legend, the strangeness of Wagner's subject matter, its prevailing mysticism and the pagan world with its gods and Norns, its giants and dwarves. But I'm still young. I never cease exploring Wagner's sublime world of ideas. I owe him an enormous amount—hours of most wonderful exaltation. The work that always arouses my greatest admiration is Tristan! Before that gigantic work I stand in wonder and terror. I consider the second act, in its wealth of musical invention, its tenderness and sensuality of musical expression and its inspired orchestration, to be one of the finest creations that has ever issued from a human mind.[4]

SPOOKED

These remarks about Wagner, by turns admiring and impatient, generous and resentful, were made at various points during the latter part of his career by Giuseppe Verdi (1813–1901), Wagner's exact if longer-lived contemporary and the preeminent late nineteenth-century representative of what was by then the oldest and most distinguished living tradition in European music, that of Italian opera.

FIG. 43-1 Giuseppe Verdi, portrait by Giovanni Boldini.

The first of them is from a letter from Verdi to his publisher Giulio Ricordi, dated 10 July 1871, several months before the first Italian production of a Wagner opera (*Lohengrin* in Bologna) and five years before the Wagnerian "invisible orchestra" was actually realized at Bayreuth. It serves as a reminder about yet another Wagnerian watershed that has profoundly affected the world of music in which we now live: not the invisible orchestra, which has remained a rarity, but the practice of lowering the houselights, not only at operatic performances, but at symphony concerts and solo recitals as well.

Most of us now take the darkness for granted, for we have never known another way. In the case of opera performances it was a matter of enhancing the "stage illusion" (the illusion that what we are witnessing is really happening) by as far as possible shutting out distracting competition from everyday reality. In the case of "absolute music" the darkness abetted romantic "interiority" (the music trance, as we have been calling it since chapter 34). But while it favored esthetic reverie (not to mention the traditional use of the theater for amorous pursuits) it made reading librettos impossible (as well as card games), and was strongly opposed by many, especially aristocrats who sensed that lowering the houselights would diminish their traditional proprietary rights over the theater and its mores. It also fostered somnolence and made countervailing efforts, which could be quite burdensome, a part of everybody's musical experience.

In demanding such efforts, musical occasions became even more like church attendance. Many felt themselves oppressed. An exasperated Chaikovsky wrote to his brother in St. Petersburg after the first Bayreuth *Ring* (which like Saint-Saëns he covered for a newspaper so as to receive free tickets), that "before, music strove to delight people; now they are tormented and exhausted."[5] In addition to the usual complaints about the sheer length of the spectacles, the endless dialogues and narratives (which could no longer be followed with the eye), and Wagner's "conglomeration of the most complex and recherché harmonies," Chaikovsky railed bitterly at "the pitch-darkness in the theater." It was a symptom, in his eyes, of that dangerous shift in the balance of artistic power from the consumer to the producer that was being fostered by promoters of the New German School, to recall some pseudo-economic jargon from chapter 41.

Verdi's enthusiasm at the prospect of an invisible orchestra is interesting in view of the difference between his artistic world and Wagner's. Compared with Wagner, Verdi was very much a "realist." His subject matter was almost always of this world. He often used contemporary plays and even novels as source material. He was the first composer (in *La traviata*, 1853) to set an opera in the recognizable (near-)present. But he, too, favored a heightened stage illusion, which could serve to enhance any stage reality whatever its degree of proximity to the surrounding reality. And in seeking to abet the illusion he tacitly admitted that even a stage setting in the "here and now" required esthetic distancing from what was truly here and truly now if the stage action was to have any dramatic effect. (But terms are always slippery: Wagner, too, was often called a realist because of his hostility to conventional form and the so-called "musical prose" of his vocal parts, which, accompanied by a network of leitmotives, often had an irregular, seemingly ametrical phrase structure even at their most lyrical.)

The second epigraph is from another letter to Ricordi written about a year later than the first, when Verdi's grandest opera, *Aida*, was being rehearsed for its Italian premiere. The world premiere had been in Egypt, the opera having been commissioned as part of the festivities surrounding the opening of the Suez Canal, and performed in a new theater specially constructed for the occasion. No other composer, not even Wagner, had an international reputation at that moment that would have recommended him for such a commission (although, needing to make contingency plans, the commissioners listed Wagner after Verdi, and Gounod after Wagner). And yet to the extent that the new opera seemed stylistically up-to-date or in any way different from what Verdi's audience expected, the difference was automatically attributed to Wagner's influence despite the fact that Verdi was a world-famous master and Wagner's music was still practically unknown in Italy. (The Bologna *Lohengrin* had not yet been followed up by any other Italian theater.) This shows to what extent Wagner, with his voluminous theorizing and his genius for self-promotion, had managed to get himself accepted everywhere as the standard of musical "contemporaneity." Verdi's tone (exclamation points in threes!) betrays a private anxiety that practically everybody shared.

It made him fearful for the future of Italian opera, as he confessed to another correspondent a year later still, in 1873, after *Aida* had had a grandiose success that stilled murmurings about "Wagnerism."[6] He was strong enough and well enough established to withstand the pressure, he wrote, but imagine today, for example, a young man of the temper of Bellini: not very certain of himself, shaky because of his scanty training, guided by his instinct alone. And now imagine

FIG. 43-2   Emma Eames (1865–1952) as Aida, ca. 1900.

him attacked by the Wagnerites. He would finally lose confidence in himself, and he would be lost.

These were the fears that nudged Verdi over into pronouncements like the third epigraph above, from a letter written in 1889 (six years after Wagner's death) to a British impresario. Verdi's sentiments here offer Wagner's aggressive nationalism a riposte in kind, testifying to a generally heightened nationalistic tension all over Europe — even in Italy, which had gone through a national unification comparable to Germany's, and did so fully a decade earlier. But after the Franco-Prussian War, Germany was regarded everywhere as a ferocious nation, and Wagner as its bellwether. Not only did representatives of threatened traditions regard him thus; so did the Germans themselves, avidly. "Wagner's music was not only the best and most significant of its age," Arnold Schoenberg could still gloat half a century later, "but it was also the music of 1870 Germany, who conquered the world of her friends and enemies through all her achievements, not without arousing their envy and resistance."[7] Verdi in 1889 certainly gave evidence in support of Schoenberg's claim.

But by 1899, when, an eighty-six-year-old Titan, he was fawningly interviewed by a reporter for a German newspaper, Verdi relaxed his guard and issued the very diplomatic and (with regard to *Tristan*) even admiring assessment of Wagner that is cited as the fourth epigraph above. And yet there is sufficient evidence of leg-pulling ("I do not yet understand everything . . . but I'm still young") to justify a suspicion of irony, especially where Verdi writes (compare Chaikovsky!) about "making people happy," or about Wagner's "sublime world of ideas." Still, there comes a time when a survivor can afford generosity.

The question remains, why did Verdi feel the need so insistently to position himself and reposition himself vis-à-vis "Vanyer" (as he always pronounced the name)? He was a more famous composer than Wagner for most of his career. His works had formed the bedrock of the standard operatic repertory since the 1850s, and they continue to form it today. And his lineage, however you measure it, was far more ancient and distinguished. The tradition of German opera, where Wagner reigned supreme, was separated from the lifetime of Bach (the figurehead from which Verdi traced the German line in the third epigraph) by some decades at least. Its origins in the singspiel were lowly. The tradition of German symphonic music, where Wagner asserted a far more controversial claim to preeminence, was even younger. But the tradition that Verdi dominated went back almost a century before Bach's time, practically to the time of Palestrina himself, Verdi's equally artificial, equally mythologized Italian figurehead. In its Florentine humanistic origins Verdi's was the most aristocratic of traditions, whether one measured aristocracy in terms of patronage or in terms of culture.

By Verdi's time, Italians had gloried in musical preeminence for centuries. And thanks to the exportability of their product, so extensively documented in this book, Italian musicians had long come to see themselves as world conquerors, arbiters of "universal" taste. Since the rise of German instrumental music, with its heavy baggage of (to Italians) questionable philosophy, Italian musicians were happy to divide the musical world into spheres of influence: the vocal, where their superiority was unassailable (and which they regarded as the higher sphere because it was the one that the human organism could produce "naturally," without mediation), and the instrumental, which the Germans were welcome to if they wanted it. Any German (Mozart, say, or Handel) who wanted to excel in vocal music had to learn his trade from them, and practiced it on their terms, even when it came to language. Beethoven, with his one opera, and Weber, with his glorified singspiels, could be tolerated with condescension. They posed no threat.

But now, through Wagner, the parvenu German tradition had put the Italian on the defensive, and had begun to assert universalist claims not only at home but abroad. The nature of the Wagnerian music drama implied a dual claim to dominance, incorporating both vocal and instrumental supremacy. And it was winning converts even in Italy, where in the 1860s an increasingly vocal group of self-styled musical intellectuals called *scapigliati* ("shaggy folk," or "the long-hair set") began agitating for a "Wagnerian reform" of the local product.

Meanwhile, it is worth noting that Verdi's ambivalent but nervously intense interest in Wagner went completely unreciprocated. Wagner seems never to have uttered a single public word about Verdi, whether in writing or to an interviewer. The Italian goes almost unmentioned in Wagner's private correspondence. Even his wife Cosima's minute and worshipful diary that recorded his every word and deed for the duration of their marriage, a document that when published occupied some twenty-four hundred pages, deigns to notice the composer who now figures in history as Wagner's greatest rival only six times in passing. Wagner's remarks are usually quite noncommittal. It is only Cosima who registers active condescension or distaste. One evening in 1871, for example, in connection with the Bologna *Lohengrin*, the conversation turned toward things Italian. When a guest seated himself at the piano and tactlessly treated the Wagners to "a dreadful musical tour, Bellini, Donizetti, Rossini, Verdi, one after the other," Cosima reported, "feeling physically ill, I pick up and seek refuge in a volume of Goethe."[8]

The one-sidedness of the Wagner-Verdi relationship was not only a sign of the times, but also a portent; for Wagner was a "spook"—a crisis point, a phenomenon that nobody could ignore, and even more than that, a polarizing force, a phenomenon about which one had to take sides. Wagner's ironically counter-Hegelian legacy was the intensification of antitheses and the prevention of synthesis. The convergence often predicted in the nineteenth century—most explicitly, ironically enough, by the Italian revolutionary patriot Giuseppe Mazzini (1805 – 72) in an early essay on music—whereby Italian and German music would meet in the middle and bring forth a universal style that would combine their virtues, never took place. In Wagner's polarizing wake everything and everybody became "more so." Difference, celebrated since Herder's time, now became a fetish and a narcissistic obsession. Only because of Wagner (and the rampant "1870 Germany" he represented) did Italian and French musicians, whatever their level of patriotism, feel the need to become stylistic nationalists. Previously the style of Italian music had been the one European style virtually free of self-consciousness—a luxury enjoyed only by the self-confidently topmost, and a testimony to that happy state of security. But as we have just seen, by the end of his career even Verdi had been spooked. Even he needed to situate himself stylistically vis-à-vis the wizard of Bayreuth, and so have practically all composers ever since. Wagner's own style, as we have also seen, was probably the most self-conscious, self-willed, and deliberately assumed style in the history of European music. Unself-conscious style has not been an option for composers in the post-Wagnerian age, and that may be the post-Wagnerian age's best definition.

THE GALLEY YEARS

What made Verdi possible, first of all, was of course his talent. Why insist on such a truism? Because it is especially important to set Verdi's career in the context of his time and place. That will tell us what made Verdi not only possible but necessary.

The time and place were in a very volatile counterpoint just then. Pursuing an operatic career in that place still meant coping with the hectic factory conditions described in chapter 33, conditions that made adherence to manifold conventions — the old Code Rossini — a necessity. Verdi spent the first seventeen years of his career — from 1836, when he began his first opera, *Oberto*, to 1853, when *La traviata* was performed — as a *compositore scritturato*, a contract (or staff) composer, in constant negotiation with theaters and casts, writing frantically on commission, with only limited control of subjects and libretti, and then revising furiously during rehearsals. Verdi looked back on this period as his "years in the galley," comparing himself to the slaves who sweated over the oars in Roman ships of old.

During this time, between the ages of twenty-three and forty, Verdi produced nineteen of his twenty-eight operas in collaboration with seven librettists and nine theaters. At the height of his early fame, 1844–47, he managed to turn out eight operas in less than four years. None of this batch had permanent success, but one (*Macbeth*, 1847, after Shakespeare) was later reworked at leisure and has earned a place in the standard repertory. Signs of international recognition begin in 1847, with commissions from London (*I masnadieri*, after Schiller's play *The Robbers*) and Paris (*Jérusalem*, reworked from *I Lombardi alla prima crociata*, a historical drama set at the time of the Crusades). At the end of the galley period he produced a trio of masterpieces — *Rigoletto* (1851), *Il trovatore* (*The Troubadou*), and *La traviata* (*The Fallen Woman*, 1853) — that have remained the cornerstone of the Italian repertory in opera houses throughout the world. The triumph of this "popular trilogy," as it used to be called, bought Verdi's freedom from galley slavery.

One of the reasons for the traditional stylistic "unself-consciousness" of Italian opera was the galley system itself, the merciless conditions under which operas were produced. When writing under so many prescriptions and requirements one is not conscious of having a style, only a method. An opera, however, did have to have a style — a *tinta* (color/tone), as it was called — to make it effective and memorable. According to Abramo Basevi (1818–85), a famous music critic who in 1859 published the earliest full-length study of Verdi's operas and may have coined the term, it was his infallible capacity for endowing his operas with an effective *tinta* that made Verdi supreme.

It was something of an intangible, this *tinta* (or *colorito*, to use the word Verdi preferred). It might consist in one opera of recurrent tone colors or instrumental combinations, in another of recurrent harmonic effects. It could be the result of melodic turns, or of characteristic rhythms, or any combination of idiosyncrasies that provided a characteristic musical "substratum" below the level of theme or even leitmotif, and also below the level of whatever "local color" a libretto might require.

Julian Budden, the author of the most detailed published survey of Verdi's operas and a matchless connoisseur of their contents, speaks of "the upward thrust of so many melodies" in one opera, "the abundance of andantino in broken $\frac{6}{8}$ [i.e., with rests on beats two and five]" in another, "the bow-shaped melodic designs" in a third and "the minor-third figurations"[9] in a fourth as constituting their respective *tinte*. But Roger Parker, another Verdi expert, just as cogently cites the prevalence of syncopation as the decisive ingredient that tinctures *Ernani* (1844),[10] the first of Budden's four and Verdi's first international success. (It was based on a notorious blood-and-thunder melodrama by Victor Hugo.)

However difficult it may be to define, it is on the level of *tinta* that the influence of the times may be most strongly felt in Verdi's early work, setting it apart from that of his predecessors and contemporaries and giving it what, in historical hindsight anyway, may be called an individual manner. The time during which Verdi became the most famous and frequently performed Italian opera composer in Europe was a famously turbulent period in Italian history known as the Risorgimento (resurgence) — the name given by Count Vittorio Alfieri (1749–1803), an early nationalist poet, to Italy's struggle toward independence and national unity.

As Alfieri's noble rank implied, the Risorgimento was a revolutionary movement led "from above," by the aristocracy and the educated bourgeoisie, the art-consuming classes. The objective was to rid Italy of foreign rulers — Austria in the north, Napoleonic France in other areas including the environs of Rome — and to unite the independent Italian states under a single authority. The factions furthest to the left backed republican rule, those furthest to the right papal rule; the ultimately successful liberal middle favored a constitutional monarchy under Victor Emmanuel, king of Sardinia, scion of the house of Savoy, whose capital was the industrial city of Turin in the Piedmont region of northwestern Italy.

Independence and unification were won in stages, beginning with abortive uprisings organized in the 1820s in the wake of the Congress of Vienna; continuing through a series of more violent revolts (some briefly successful) in the revolutionary years 1848–49; a successful Sardinian campaign against Austria in 1859, after which Lombardy was joined to Victor Emmanuel's kingdom; a series of plebiscites in 1860; Garibaldi's conquest of Sicily later that year; and the proclamation of the kingdom in 1861 with its capital first at Turin, later at Florence. Venice and Rome were the last areas to be incorporated, the former as a diplomatic by-product of the Austro-Prussian war of 1866 (Victor Emmanuel having prudently allied himself with Prussia), and the latter as a similar by-product of the Franco-Prussian war of 1870. The Italian state as it exists today with Rome as its capital — the first political entity incorporating the entire Italian peninsula since the fall of the Western Roman Empire in the fifth century — was established in 1871.

The 1840s, the decade of Verdi's apprenticeship, was the period when the arts, led by the example of poets and novelists like Alessandro Manzoni (1785–1873) and

Giacomo Leopardi (1798–1837), began to be significantly affected by Risorgimento ideals, and to affect the movement in turn. It was, in Mazzini's words, a time of "social poetry." The romanticism it embodied, unlike the northern romanticism with which we are already very familiar, was hostile to morbid individualism. For Mazzini, a suffering Byronic hero was a thing of "wretchedness and impotence."[11] The proper role of romantic literature, he averred, using the very word (*risorgere*) that gave the great movement its name, was not to glorify or wallow in private pain but "to soothe the suffering soul by teaching it to *rise up* toward God through Humanity."

Part of the project was, simply, to teach the suffering Italian soul that it was suffering. As David Kimbell emphasizes in his study of Verdi, Austrian rule was not particularly burdensome to the northern Italians, and Milan, both the seat of the Austrian administration and the site of La Scala, Italy's most prestigious opera house, was a flourishing and contented city for most of Verdi's galley period.[12] It became the function of art to rouse not only the rabble but also the educated classes to action, to give the latter a political conscience despite their relative material well-being and the passivity to which contentment so easily gave rise. Morse Peckham, a prominent critic of romantic literature, has put the matter bluntly but memorably: "If the Austrian domination was to be overthrown, the level of aggression in enough Italians to make that possible had to be significantly raised."[13]

All national art became double-coded: an implicit model, even a manual of action that exemplified what could not be openly advocated by direct public exhortation. Peckham goes so far as to suggest that

> for the purposes of raising the level of aggression it made no moral difference if historical romances, paintings, and operas show Italians as brutal, bloody, and revengeful. They were Italians being highly aggressive. An Italian fictional or operatic villain was ambivalent and had a dual function—to raise awareness of oppression and to show an Italian as highly aggressive and capable of seizing and wielding power.

Italian romanticism of the Risorgimento period thus provided the impetus for perhaps the first self-conscious political vanguard—an avant-garde in the literal, quasi-military sense—to be actively promoted, and even led, by artists. And this vividly suggests the source of the special Verdi *tinta* that vouchsafed his early eminence. It was the *tinta* of cruelty, of strife, of force—in Peckham's word, of aggression—the *tinta* summed up by the epithet *il Verdi brutto* ("nasty Verdi") with which his more fastidious detractors tormented him in his galley years.

THE POPULAR STYLE

The most striking effect in the early Verdi operas, and the one most obviously allied to the mood of Risorgimento, was the big choral number sung—crudely or sublimely, according to the ear of the beholder—in unison. As a symbol of solidarity and of concerted action it could be read as political allegory no matter what the actual dramatic context. The prototype was "Va, pensiero, sull'ali dorate" ("Go, my thought, on golden wings"),

FIG. 43-3   Interior view of Teatro alla Scala, Milan, ca. 1830; painting by Ladislaus Rupp.

the chorus of Hebrew slaves in the third act of *Nabucco* (short for *Nabucodonosor*, "Neb-
uchadnezzar," 1842), Verdi's third opera and the one that first made him a national figure
(Ex. 43-1). Its text, by Temistocle Solera (1815–78), a poet and occasional composer
of herculean physique, already known for his booming verses, paraphrases the famous
137th Psalm ("By the waters of Babylon . . ."). It was an inspired interpolation, precisely
for the sake of *tinta*, into what was otherwise a love triangle — a prince of Jerusalem vs.
two rival princesses of Bablyon — set against a background of biblical warfare.

Rossini, struck by the originality of its conception, called "Va, pensiero" "a grand
aria sung by sopranos, contraltos, tenors and basses."[14] Indeed the melody was as
ornate as a Bellinian cantabile, the noble opening section of a bel canto aria, but its

EX. 43-1   Giuseppe Verdi, *Nabucco*, "Va, pensiero"

EX. 43-1 (continued)

Oh mia pa-tria sì bel-la e per-du-ta Oh mem-bran-za si ca-ra e fa-tal!

Go, my thought, on golden wings;
go, alight upon the slopes, the hills,
where, soft and warm, the sweet breezes
of our native land are fragrant!
Greet the hawks of the Jordan
and Zion's razed towers....
Oh, my homeland so lovely and lost!
Oh, remembrance so dear and ill-fated!

format was the one identified in chapter 33 with the concluding section, the square-cut cabaletta: four phrases cast as A A' B A', where A is "open" (ending on a half cadence) and A' is "closed" (ending on a full cadence). We have encountered variants of this scheme as early as the fixed forms of medieval danced poetry (see chapter 4), and it is still commonly used in popular songs and show tunes (the "32-bar chorus"). It was a "demotic" (common) or "vernacular" (indigenous) type that served folk and street music as well as opera. Arias cast in such a popular form all the more easily traveled back to the street and into the oral tradition, helped on its way by the ubiquitous organ-grinders and street singers who populated the thoroughfares of nineteenth-century Italian cities and disseminated theatrical hits just as radio and jukeboxes would later do.

"Va, pensiero" was certainly translated "back" into folklore in this way. It was sung by the throngs surrounding Verdi's horse-drawn hearse on the day of his burial, led by the augmented chorus of La Scala (the Milan opera house where *Nabucco* had its premiere almost sixty years before), under the baton of the young Arturo Toscanini (1867–1957), who though only a conductor rather than a composer inherited Verdi's mantle as national emblem and musical ambassador to the world. By then the chorus had become an emblem not only of Verdi (as Italy's "national" composer-laureate) but of the Italian *patria* itself.

Much of this significance was read back on the chorus from the perspective of the united Italy of the 1860s, in which Verdi had been honored with a personal seat in the new national parliament. Two legends in particular had sprung up around it: first, that the original audience of 1842, in a patriotic delirium, had compelled an "encore" (or *bis*) despite La Scala's normally rigid house rule against acknowledging requests for repetition; and second, that the cries of *Viva Verdi!* ("Long live Verdi") that rent the air on that occasion were a code for *Viva V. E. R. D. I.* — "Long live Vittorio Emmanuele, Re d'Italia" (Victor Emmanuel, King of Italy).

As to the first legend, Roger Parker has ascertained on the basis of contemporary documents that there was indeed an encore that night — but of another number, not "Va, pensiero"; and as to the second, the use of Verdi's name as an acronym for the king of united Italy only started up on the very eve of unification, when demonstrations in support of Victor Emmanuel's claim to the throne were no longer politically risky.[15] In

FIG. 43-4   *VIVA VERDI!* (engraving at Istituto di Studi Verdiani, Parma). During the war of 1859 between Sardinia and Austria over the northern Italian territories that included Milan and Venice, Verdi's name became a rallying cry as an acronym for Vittorio Emmanuele, Re d'Italia, who was supported by Italian patriots like Count Camillo Cavour (and Verdi). The defeat of Austria paved the way for the first united (northern) Italian state, proclaimed in 1861, in which Verdi was an honorary senator. (It took another decade for the whole Italian peninsula to be united under Victor Emmanuel.)

1842, when the Austrians ruled Milan, and when an acclamation there to an Italian king would have invited reprisals, nobody made them (at least not via Verdi). The growth of the Verdi myth proceeded in stages corresponding to those of the Risorgimento itself.

But while less dramatic, that correspondence in myth is still evidence of the connection between the composer and the cause, and still points to the Verdi *tinta* as a catalyst to political militancy and eventual action. In any case, the success of the patriotic unison chorus in *Nabucco* stimulated Verdi himself to further action. His next two operas (the first of them again to a libretto by Solera) also made a point of incorporating a similar choral set piece. Audiences were demanding them.

Ex. 43-1, since it shows only the first stanza of "Va, pensiero," stops short of the blazing middle section, in which the chorus suddenly opens out, rabble-rousingly, into chordal harmony, *fortissimo*. Also fairly subdued is Ex. 43-2a, which shows the first stanza of the chorus of pilgrims and crusaders, the analogous item in *I Lombardi alla prima crociata* (*The Lombards on the First Crusade*, 1843), in which the Lombards, medieval denizens of Milan and its environs, dying of thirst in the desert near Jerusalem, recall their beloved homeland (that is, the exact territory in which the opera, written for La Scala, was being performed at its premiere).

Not so gentle is the unison chorus in *Ernani* (1844), which bursts like a bombshell and leads directly to decisive stage action. Its parent play, Victor Hugo's *Hernani* (1830), a self-avowed manifesto of "liberalism," was politically risky, depicting as it did an attempt on the life of a future Holy Roman Emperor by a character (the Spanish bandit Hernani) who, as the romantic lead, is portrayed very sympathetically. The chorus, "Si ridesti il Leon di Castiglia" ("Let the Lion of Castile awake!"), is the conspirators' battle hymn, easily transferable to the patriots of Venice (also traditionally symbolized by a lion!), the site of the first performance, then struggling to free itself from the descendants of the same Holy Roman Emperor. This chorus was an especially clear instance of opera as a spur (or at least a testimonial) to aggression (Ex. 43-2b).

Its form, slightly more complex than those already in evidence, illustrates the way the basic "popular" AA′BA′ model could be expanded for the sake of enhanced dramatic scale. The "B" phrase is augmented into a full-fledged middle section in the dominant with an AA′BA(double prime) format of its own (here necessarily labeled BB′CB(double prime) because of the prior use of A), balanced at the end by a full reprise of the initial AA′, plus a concluding tag. The "C" strain, veering into G major (♭VI), provides a traditional harmonic far-out point that enhances scale in another dimension, so to speak. The result was at once popular and grand—grand in a sense that had formerly connoted regal pomp, not popular triumph. The combination, as much a political as a musical novelty, sounded a new note in European music, and a momentous one.

EX. 43-2A   Giuseppe Verdi, *I Lombardi*, "O signore, dal tetto natio"

O Lord, Thou didst call us
with holy promise from our native hearths;
We have hastened at the bidding of a holy man,
rejoicing on the rough road.
But the heads of thy bold and doughty servants
are bowed and humbled.
Ah! Let not thy faithful warriors,
O Christ, serve but as laughing stock to the world.

EX. 43-2B   Giuseppe Verdi, *Ernani*, "Si ridesti il Leon di Castiglia"

TRAGICOMEDY

The librettist of *Ernani* was Francesco Maria Piave (1810–76), with whom Verdi collaborated over the next eighteen years on more than a dozen projects, making Piave the composer's most faithful and prolific accomplice. Their partnership was by no means an equal one. The composer dominated the librettist mercilessly, reversing the traditional theatrical hierarchy and in so doing epitomizing the vastly heightened status of music — or, to put it more precisely, of musical originality ("genius") — in the later nineteenth-century scheme of things artistic, even in Italy.

The mature Verdi always had precise notions of what the dramatic situation required in terms of music. He demanded from his librettists both precisely tailored versification and an extreme economy of words that an ornate stylist like Solera (or any early nineteenth-century librettist) would have been loath to provide. Piave, verbally adept yet without any independent literary reputation or ambition, could afford to be accommodating. As a result, Verdi's mature operas were controlled—indeed, "micromanaged"—by the composer almost as completely as Wagner's, in which the words and music both actually issued from a single mind. But there the resemblance ceased. Where Wagner wanted to take opera back to its cultic or epic roots by impersonating Aeschylus or some other real or fancied Greek tragedian, Verdi wanted to become a Shakespeare.

What "being a Shakespeare" meant to a nineteenth-century dramatist was, in a word, dramatic "realism": the fusing of all existing dramatic genres into a single supple, pliant idiom known as "tragicomedy"—the true reflector of human character and experience. Fusion (and the implied overthrow of formal constraints) had been Victor Hugo's watchword, as expressed in the preface to *Hernani*, the very play on which Verdi modeled his fifth opera. Hugo, too, had invoked Shakespeare and the tragicomic, and so did Verdi's great contemporary, the novelist and fellow *risorgimentista* Alessandro Manzoni, when he remarked that "it was not any mere violation of rules that led Shakespeare to this mixture of the grave and the burlesque, the touching and the low; he had simply observed this mixture in reality and wished to convey the strong impression it made on him."[16] The literary scholar George Steiner deftly summed up the difference between the epic and the tragicomic—the Wagnerian and the Verdian—by noting that

> even in the blackest hours of a Shakespearean tragedy or a Verdi opera the morning light of human laughter, the feline energies of human rebound are close at hand.... The masters of the absolute—Aeschylus, Sophocles, [the French tragedian] Racine, Wagner—concentrate the sum of the world to a single immensity of encounter. Shakespeare and Verdi, on the contrary, know that the instant in which Agamemnon is murdered [in Aeschylus's tragedy] is also that in which a birthday party is being celebrated next door.[17]

The tragicomic vision, then, is one that projects drama in terms of foils and contrasts, not even excluding the contrast of poetry and prose. The most famous Shakespearean contrast of this sort is the famously farcical prose scene of the drunken porter at the gate (act II, sc. 3) that follows immediately on the horrific murder scene in *Macbeth*; and the most sustained example of Shakespearean tragicomedy is the character of the Fool or jester who shadows King Lear, the most pitiable of all Shakespearean tragic victims, in the play that bears the latter's name. Nothing was ever less a coincidence than the fact that Verdi's tenth opera (and third with Piave) was a *Macbeth* (1847); or that the phantom haunting Verdi's career from 1843 to the end of his days was his unrealized ambition to create an operatic *King Lear*.

True, Verdi's *Macbeth* has no porter. (The presence of supernatural characters—Shakespeare's witches—in a tragedy proved controversial enough). And (as the opera historian Piero Weiss has pointed out) the reason for his failure to produce *Il re Lear* was, in all likelihood, precisely the difficulty of imagining a musical technique for shadowing the tragic title character with the comic Fool, which would mean making the Fool a major character in a serious opera.[18] Yet despite his apparent failure or disinclination to emulate Shakespeare's most radical mixtures of genre, the fact remains that the double-edged Shakespearean ideal of fusion and contrast was Verdi's main objective in tweaking the conventions of Italian opera (with Piave's help) into new configurations that depended to an unprecedented extent on devices of irony.

The new Verdian manner reached its climax with that amazing trio of operas, composed all in a row between 1850 and 1853. Like *Ernani*, Verdi's *Rigoletto* was modeled on a politically "liberal" verse drama by Victor Hugo. That play, *Le roi s'amuse* ("The King amuses himself," 1832) had actually fallen afoul of the French censor because it portrays a French king (the early sixteenth-century monarch Francis I) as a philanderer. (In Piave's libretto, the royal rake is demoted to the level of a duke—and his duchy, Mantua, was by the nineteenth century no longer an independent city-state but a part of Lombardy then under Austrian rule, thus neutralizing any danger of affronting a sovereign.) Verdi immediately saw in Hugo's play an ideally "Shakespearean" subject for an opera, since the eventual libretto's title character, the hunchback Rigoletto (Triboulet in Hugo), was at once the tragic victim and a court jester by trade—Fool and Lear in one!

The whole plot of *Rigoletto* hinges on a single wrenching irony. As the Duke's court jester, Rigoletto mocks the father of a girl his master has seduced and abandoned, and receives a furious parental curse (act I). His own daughter, Gilda, is seduced by the Duke; Rigoletto contracts a professional hit man to avenge his paternal honor by murdering the Duke (act II). By a series of chilling mischances, Gilda is murdered in the Duke's place, devastating the poor jester and fulfilling the curse (act III). The two roles Rigoletto played in life—jester and father—thus fatally collide. The contrast, embodied starkly in act I, was made for music: Up until the moment of the curse, the first scene is purest comic opera; the second is purest tragedy (as reflected in its musical forms, which include an extended coloratura aria for Gilda). Act III, which we will examine in detail, is an unprecedented mixture throughout of the comic and the terrible.

Il trovatore was based on a fairly recent play (*Il trovador*, 1836) by the Spanish poet Antonio García Gutiérrez (1813–84), a follower of Hugo. The libretto was by Salvadore Cammarano (1801–52), one of Donizetti's chief collaborators (hence a poet of the "old school"). Although it was the last of the distinguished Cammarano's thirty-six librettos, it needed some doctoring (by Leone Emanuele Bardare) to suit Verdi's neo-Shakespearean needs. In an effort to get the venerable poet to modernize his style a little, Verdi came on to him for all the world like a Wagnerian (if an independent one, Verdi being as yet unacquainted with Wagner's theories):

> As for the distribution of the pieces [into "numbers"], let me tell you that when I'm presented with poetry to be set to music, any form, any distribution is good, and I'm all the happier if they are new and bizarre. If in operas there were no more cavatinas, duets, trios, choruses, finales, etc. etc., and if the entire opera were, let's say, a single piece, I would find it more reasonable and just.[19]

But Cammarano stuck to his habits, and of the three "middle Verdi" masterpieces *Il trovatore* is the most formally conventional. Its very conventionality can serve our analytical purposes, however, since it will provide us, when the time comes, with a lens through which to view the idiosyncratic departures in the last act of *Rigoletto*.

The plot of *Il trovatore*, complicated to the point of proverbial incoherence, is all but impossible to summarize. Here all we need to do is describe the main characters. The title character, the troubadour, whose given name is Manrico (tenor), is a nobleman (the son and heir of the Count di Luna), who was stolen as an infant by a gypsy woman, Azucena (mezzo-soprano or contralto) and brought up as a gypsy chieftain. All of this takes place before the action begins, and is revealed in narrative flashback. When the opera begins, Manrico and his unknowing half-brother, the present Count di Luna (baritone), are in love with the same woman, Leonora (soprano), the Duchess of Aragon. We learn from a conversation with her confidante Inez (soprano) that she loves an unknown knight whose troubadour has been serenading her.

What the main action of the opera accomplishes through a host of contrivances and coincidences is the progressive revelation of the truth despite many setbacks, the unmasking of Manrico's mistaken identity, and his union with Leonora. The plot's whole thrust and trajectory, in other words, was to get the prima donna out of the clutches of the baritone and into the arms of the true *primo uomo*, the tenor. Soprano and tenor were the new obligatory couple: their ardently romantic duet had to be vouchsafed come hell or high water. And thereby hangs a tale.

In the days of the *opera seria* the leading couple had been a soprano and a castrato—and then for a while (even more artificially) a soprano and a "musico" (woman in trousers and false whiskers). Only with the generation of Bellini and Donizetti had the romantic hero become a natural-voiced man—but only relatively speaking, since the conventions of bel canto demanded an extremely high tessitura for the tenor, a level of coloratura in his part comparable to that of the prima donna, and (for these reasons) a vocal delivery that depended on the free admixture of falsetto singing (or "head voice"), by definition soft and supple rather than forceful.

The great change in the distribution and definition of opera roles between Donizetti's time and Verdi's—hence the great change in the technical training of singers—was the institution of the *tenore di forza* (or *tenore robusto*), the "strength tenor," as romantic lead. Manrico was the quintessential, defining role for this urgently virile voice type, which had virtually no place in Italian opera before the 1840s. This, too, was a "realistic" innovation in its way, but the type of voice it demanded was as unnatural—and as arduously manufactured—as any other. Composers of the old school, notably Rossini (with whose nostalgia for bel canto we are familiar since chapter 33), found the noises made by *tenori di forza* intolerable. He compared the singing of Gilbert Duprez (1806–96), the first of the breed, who made a sensation in the role of Arnold in Rossini's *Guillaume Tell*, to "the squawk of a capon with its throat cut."[20] Receiving another famous *tenore di forza* late in life, Rossini asked him to kindly leave his high C♯ at the door.

For *tenori di forza* maintained their full (or "chest") voice over their entire range—even up to their highest notes, which assumed the vibrant, ringing (or, for those who hated it, the raucous, earsplitting) tone we now associate with Italian tenors. A tenor's ability to reach these notes in "chest" is now the most sought-after of all operatic skills. Those who have excelled at it—Enrico Caruso (1873–1921), Richard Tucker (1913–75), not to mention the "Three Tenors" (Placido Domingo, Luciano Pavarotti, and José Carreras) who in the 1990s became the highest-paid classical music act of all time—have been the emblematic opera stars of the twentieth century.

It goes without saying that they were all outstanding Manricos. Their line goes back to the relatively obscure Carlo Baucarde, who created the role, but in terms of enduring fame the line goes back to Enrico Tamberlik (1820–89), who sang Manrico for the first time in London in 1855, and virtually owned the role thereafter. (Tamberlik was the singer to whom Rossini made his cutting request; the C♯ Rossini so detested was one that Tamberlik was celebrated for interpolating into the bel canto role of Arnold in Rossini's *Guillaume Tell*.) The great defining moment for Manrico, hence for the *tenore di forza*, was "Di quella pira" ("Tremble, O tyrants, at my torch!"), a number with good Risorgimento credentials, that constituted the cabaletta to a big scene with Leonora and the chorus at the very end of act III (Ex. 43-3). As an act closer, it was designed to bring down the house.

Like many cabalettas in the past (including some we have witnessed ourselves in chapter 33), "Di quella pira" is cast in the meter and characteristic rhythm of a polonaise, the regal dance par excellence. (Here the "revolutionary" Manrico reveals his "nobility" after all.) Its form is the familiar AA′BA′ with a coda in which first Leonora, then the chorus, join in. Its high Gs, A♭s and As are all to be sung *forte*, from the chest, as Verdi still saw fit to remind the singer with the notation *con tutta forza*. The flourish on the final line of each stanza ("o teco a morir!") is notated up to the high A, but singers since Caruso have treated the composer's notation as a minimum expectation. Indeed, any singer who does not have a version of that final roulade up to Caruso's high C runs the risk of being hissed off the stage. (The matter became a scandal in December 2000, when the conductor Riccardo Muti, launching La Scala's Verdi centennial year with a new production of *Il trovatore*, based on a new critical edition of the score, treated the composer's notation as a limit and forbade his *tenor robusto* to sing the traditional high C, which one indignant journalist called "a gift to Verdi from the Italian people.")[21]

EX. 43-3   Giuseppe Verdi, *Il trovatore*, "Di quella pira"

EX. 43-3 (continued)

(B)
ᵖE - ra già fi - glio pri - ma d'a - mar - ti, non sa fre - nar - mi il tuo mar - tir...

(A)
ᶠMa - dre in - fe - li - ce, co - ro a sal - var - ti, o te - co al - me - no cor - ro a mo -

Coda
Più vivo
rir o te - co al - men cor - ro a mo - rir, o te - co al - men, o te - co a mo - rir!

FIG. 43-5 Cover of the first edition of *La traviata* in vocal score (Milan: Ricordi, 1853).

La traviata ("The fallen woman"), the most radically realistic opera of the three, was based *La dame aux camélias* ("The lady of the camelias") by Alexandre Dumas the younger (1824–95), a play (based on the author's own novel of 1848) that Piave adapted into a libretto during the first year of its run, 1852. Adapting a current theatrical hit with a contemporary setting into an opera was an unprecedented move. Even bolder was Verdi's determination to keep the time frame of the opera as contemporary as that of the drama. (Here he was overruled by the Venetian censors; the setting of the first production was pushed back to the eighteenth century.) Boldest of all was the choice of a drama centering on the life and loves of a courtesan — a euphemism for a high-class or "courtly" prostitute. But as Verdi wrote to a friend, it was "a subject of the times," and that justified all license. Only a composer who had been conditioned by the Risorgimento to associate art with "timeliness," or topical pertinence, could have reasoned so. Such a notion might seem the very antithesis of Romanticism.

And yet the character of Violetta, the fallen woman of the title, was perforce greatly idealized — that is, romanticized — by Dumas, and even more by Verdi. The Preludio to the opera seems a curious chip off the Prelude to Wagner's *Lohengrin*, and serves a similar purpose. Rather than setting the scene for the beginning of act I, which depicts a lively party in progress, it paints a spiritual or internal portrait of the heroine that contrasts utterly with her public facade. Where she is outwardly insouciant and flirtatious, the prelude shows her melancholy and sincerely amorous, and hints, by way of dissonant deceptive cadences and *tremolandi*, at her fatal malady.

The plot concerns the love of Violetta for Alfredo Germont, a young man "of good family," and its thwarting first by her unacceptability to Alfredo's father and finally by her early death. The whole story is narrated against the background of Parisian ballroom festivities, and the opera's *tinta*, unusually easy to discern and describe, is carried by its many actual, remembered, and etherealized waltz tunes. Both the cantabile ("Ah fors'è lui," "Ah, was it he?") and cabaletta ("Sempre libera," "Always free") in Violetta's scena at the end of act I are cast as waltzes in contrasting tempos. The cantabile reaches its climax in an expansively rounded melody in which Violetta recognizes true love, and which will function throughout the rest of the opera as a poignant reminiscence motif (Ex. 43-4a), while the cabaletta, in which she puts the thought aside with determined abandon, has become as much a showpiece for the Verdi soprano as "Di quella pira" is for the Verdi tenor (Ex. 43-4b).

EX. 43-4A   Giuseppe Verdi, *La traviata*, "Ah, fors'è lui"

EX. 43-4B   Giuseppe Verdi, *La traviata*, "Sempre libera"

At the other end of the opera, having been told by the doctor that death is imminent, Violetta takes leave of the world—her world—to the strains of another slow waltz-time cantabile (Ex. 43-4c); and when Alfredo arrives just in time to see her die, they sing a duet that functions as the corresponding fast-waltz cabaletta (Ex. 43-4d). Having at the last minute received the remorseful blessing of Alfredo's father, Violetta expires to a reprise of Ex. 43-4a, the opera's most full-blooded waltz number.

EX. 43-4C   Giuseppe Verdi, *La traviata*, "Addio del passato"

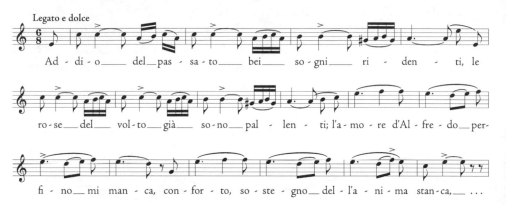

EX. 43-4D   Giuseppe Verdi, *La traviata*, "Parigi, o cara"

Throughout, but most conspicuously in the last scene, the tragic strains that accompany the sufferings of the protagonists are shadowed either downstage or offstage by the happy strains of revelry, underscoring the contradiction at the heart of Violetta's existence, but also providing that ironic mix of tragic and comic that, for Verdi as for Shakespeare, added up to "life." As Steiner puts it, "The joy of the Parisian revelers beats against the windows of the dying Violetta in *La traviata* not in contrapuntal mockery but simply because the varied pulse of life is more constant than any particular sorrow; Shakespeare and Verdi anchor their host of characters in history, in the local color of historical epoch and circumstance, distrusting that monotone of eternity so compelling to Wagner."[22] The thought rings true, but the word "simply" jars. It is no simple fact but profound insight and calculation that produces so potent a dramatic effect.

OPERA AS MODERN DRAMA

The third and final act of *Rigoletto* gives us Verdi's irony at fullest strength. It is perhaps the most "Shakespearean" scene in all of Verdi despite its source in Hugo, and Verdi knew it. "*Le Roi s'amuse*," he wrote to Piave,

> is the greatest subject and perhaps the greatest drama of modern times. Triboulet is a creation worthy of Shakespeare!! What is Ernani next to him?!! This is a subject that cannot fail. You know that six years ago, when *Ernani* was proposed to me, I exclaimed: Yes, by God, it can't miss. Now, going over several subjects, when *Le Roi* crossed my mind it was like a flash, an inspiration, and I said the same thing: Yes, by God, it can't miss.[23]

"There is such a ringing conviction to Verdi's words," Piero Weiss notes drily, "that one is apt to forget that what he was calling 'perhaps the greatest drama of modern times' was possibly the most notorious theatrical failure of the century." *Le roi s'amuse* had had one and only one performance in 1832, was condemned from all sides, political and artistic alike, and had been banned ever since. (The original play would see the footlights again only on its fiftieth anniversary, in 1882, by which time it was altogether overshadowed by Verdi's opera; it was received in virtual silence.) The reason for its continued failure was precisely the Shakespearean mixture of genres that so attracted Verdi. The critic in the *Journal des Débats*, where Berlioz wrote the music reviews, made no bones about this:

> Whenever the author rose to the heights of passion, whenever he thrust noble thoughts, true feelings of the human heart, into his dialogue, then all sympathies were awakened, and all literary factions even rallied to do him honor; but when he sank back into the buffoonish, the trivial, the popular, then inattention and disgust set in once more. *Le Roi s'amuse* embodied all the brilliant theories that bold innovators have been propounding for some time; only human life in this dramatic form seemed not truer, only uglier. The mixture of the buffoonish and the sublime threw the audience into a painful confusion.[24]

Far from pandering to current taste, then, Verdi was actually flying in its face by seizing on this ill-fated drama of Hugo's. But he knew, first of all, that music could do the job that the spoken theater had failed to accomplish; and, second, that (as he put it in the letter to Antonio Somma, a poet friend and future librettist),

> all the horrible plot vicissitudes arise from the frivolous, rakish personality of the Duke. Hence Rigoletto's fears, Gilda's passion, etc. etc., which make for many excellent dramatic moments, among others the scene of the quartet which as regards effect will remain one of the best our theater can boast.[25]

The quartet to which Verdi refers here is the centerpiece of the final act; and he achieved the "excellent dramatic moment" he predicted by tweaking the conventions of the genres he was fusing to cast the "frivolous, rakish personality of the Duke" in maximum relief. A virile *tenore di forza* role fashioned from the same cloth as the ardent Manrico, the Duke is the very opposite of the character type implied by his voice type. He uses his ringing tones not to affirm but to mock romantic love, most spectacularly in his heartily cynical act I *ballata* (dance song) "Questa o quella" ("This one or that"), in which he professes to love and value (that is, scorn and slight) all women equally. Sentiments formerly associated with buffo baritones like Don Giovanni — or even basses, like Leporello — are here enunciated through the mouth and vocal chords of a romantic tenor, a voice type created for the purpose of expressing ardent love in all its heartrending sincerity, as the late nineteenth century had come to value it. This drippingly, shockingly ironic item is the opera's very first set piece. By placing it at the outset, Verdi as much as announces that ironies and reversals, set off by the Duke's baleful frivolity (at first enthusiastically encouraged by his jester, Rigoletto) and communicated through the sign language (or "semiotics") of genre, will be the very stuff of this singular opera.

And this brings us to the last act, in which ironies and reversals are compounded and end in tragedy. The setting is a ramshackle inn to which the Duke has been lured,

FIG. 43-6   Cover of the first edition of *Rigoletto* (Milan: Ricordi, 1851), showing the quartet in act III.

there to be murdered by Sparafucile, the mercenary assassin or hit man with whom Rigoletto has made a contract, and whose sister Maddalena manages the inn. The whole act is played on a split set that depicts both the interior of the inn (both upstairs and downstairs) and the road outside. The all-pervading device that will lend irony to every number is the mutual isolation of the two halves of the stage and the characters inhabiting them. On the inside are the Duke, Sparafucile, and Maddalena. On the outside are Rigoletto and Gilda.

Rigoletto has brought Gilda to this brutal place not to witness the impending murder of which she has no inkling, but so that she can witness the lewd behavior of the man whose feigned love for her has awakened a sincere response that Rigoletto wants to quash. Through a chink in the wall the two outsiders observe the Duke's arrival, and hear him sing a carousing ditty over wine as he awaits Maddalena's services as prostitute. That song (canzone), the sublimely bumptious and hypocritical "La donna è mobile" ("Woman is fickle," Ex. 43-5), is another of the Duke's little pop tunes, like the act I ballata. Aware that despite its nauseating immorality (or because of it) the song would be the opera's great hit, Verdi had gone to unusual lengths to keep it under wraps until the first performance, so that the organ-grinders and sheet-music pirates would not leak it prematurely to the street. He held it back from orchestral rehearsals almost to the last minute, coaching the tenor (Raffaele Mirate) in private.

EX. 43-5   Giuseppe Verdi, *Rigoletto*, Act III , "La donna è mobile"

EX. 43-5 (continued)

Its eventual success was almost *too* great, since many who do not really know the opera ascribe to it, or even to Verdi, the song's trivial gaiety without realizing that its brashness was a calculated ironic foil. (A case in point is a *graffito* the author once saw in the New York subway: "Who Says Women Are Fickle?" read the billboard advertising some cheap lingerie or perfume, next to which someone had scrawled, "Verdi, that's who.") At first hearing, the irony is a mere matter of clash between jolly song and gloomy setting. But over the course of the act its range of reference, and consequently the range of its ironic resonance, will grow as it begins to function as a reminiscence motif, one of the most hair-raising in all of opera.

The next number is the quartet, *Bella figlia dell'amore* ("Comely daughter of love"), the most famous ensemble Verdi ever composed. The similarity of its opening tune to that of "Chi me frena?," the great sextet in Donizetti's *Lucia di Lammermoor* (Ex. 33-II), is often remarked, and Donizetti's work might well have served Verdi as a conscious or unconscious model. But the surface likeness only heightens the far more significant underlying contrasts. Besides the typically more popular cast of Verdi's melody, full of internal repetitions and "melodic rhymes" (in contrast to Donizetti's seemlessly long-limbed, "aristocratic" arc to climax), there is, again, the underlying dramaturgical irony. For this is not a traditional quartet in which four characters each reflect in lyric stop time on a change in the dramatic course. It is, rather, a double duet that takes place in real time, with two "insider" characters, the lascivious Duke and the beguiling Maddalena (dolled up for sex in a gypsy costume), and two "outsiders," the indignant Rigoletto and the heartbroken Gilda. The introduction, forty-eight bars of furious *parlante* of a sort that traditionally substituted for the even more traditional recitative, does not give way, as in earlier operas, to a single moment of shared reflection telescoped out into a collective aria, but prepares yet another cynical strophic song for the oblivious Duke, accompanied by three simultaneous commentaries from vastly differing perspectives. Action is not halted. It continues, but ironically, on multiple contradictory levels.

Thus the Duke's first stanza is answered first by Maddalena's flirtatious simpering, then by Gilda's restrained outcry and Rigoletto's admonition to keep her voice down. The bottled-up emotion of the two muffled outsiders, unable to find an outlet in sheer volume, seeks an alternative vent in harmony, coloring the music briefly with the chord of the flat mediant before returning to the original key so that the Duke can continue his song.

His second stanza (Ex. 43-6) is accompanied by the three other characters not in response but in actual counterpoint. Maddalena resumes her brittle flirting; Gilda resumes her long lyrical sighs descending in despair from ever higher, more piercing high notes; Rigoletto gives his daughter moral (and harmonic) support. At the coda, the two women's voices come into the foreground, again in ironic contrast: Gilda, her voice breaking with grief, begins to pant on pairs of sixteenth notes slurred into the beats, while Maddalena laughs merrily in staccato sixteenths that fill the gap between Gilda's, hocket-fashion.

At the repetition of the coda, the contrast between the insiders and outsiders becomes unbearably poignant: the former get ready to embrace, their voices mingling in the time-honored lovers' way, that is, with lyrical legato lines in well-lubricated parallel motion, while the latter, their spirits pulverized by the sight of the other pair, sing correspondingly broken melodies, alternating sixteenth notes and rests. At the end of the quartet the four characters are a study in contrasts: the Duke, as ever, oblivious to

EX. 43-6 Giuseppe Verdi, *Rigoletto*, Act III, Quartet, "Bella figlia dell'amore"

EX. 43-6 *(continued)*

all but his fleshly desires; Maddalena, as ever, mordantly detached (but aroused); Gilda crushed; Rigoletto bent on revenge.

Next comes a little clump of dialogue, played against a variety of picturesque musical backgrounds, to move the plot to the point from which the next dramatic ensemble is set to depart. Rigoletto, not wishing Gilda to witness the murder, sends her off to disguise herself in male traveling attire and await him in Verona. Against a background suggestive of a tolling clock, Rigoletto gives Sparafucile the down payment on the contract (Ex. 43-7).

This part of the scene, incidentally, is of special interest to the historian of "performance practice" because of Verdi's explicit admonition that "this recitative must

EX. 43-7   Giuseppe Verdi, *Rigoletto*, Act III, Rigoletto conspires with Sparafucile

be sung without the usual appoggiaturas," according to which the first note of the word "dieci" would be sung as a G, and the first note of the word "resto" in the next measure as an E. This is precious evidence, first, that unwritten ornaments were still routinely employed and expected in Italian recitative as late as the 1850s, whereas many performers beginning in the 1880s took to "weeding them out" even in Mozart, reflecting a new literalism that affected the way in which notation was interpreted as soon as unwritten ("oral") traditions lost their sway in pedagogy. What was mistakenly viewed as the removal of inauthentic accretions was in fact a modernization. (The same probably goes for Maestro Muti's "restoration" of Manrico's "original" cabaletta in *Il trovatore*.)

Verdi's performance direction is also evidence of when that modernization took place, and suggests that operatic "realism" was its original impetus. To give his scene a heightened sense of reality, Verdi purged it of conventions known to be operatic. Hearing bumpy thirds as notated where one expected the suave seconds that were usually interpolated effectively defamiliarized the music and gave it a refurbished dramatic immediacy.

The scene continues: against the background of a gathering storm, Sparafucile and the Duke make conflicting demands on Maddalena (the former to help with the murder, the latter to bed down with him), putting her in an unexpected quandary. (The appoggiaturas, by the way, have returned, but now — and henceforth — they have to be explicitly notated.) Sparafucile invites the Duke to spend the night and leads him to the bedchamber, where the Duke, expecting Maddalena in an hour's time, dozes off with *La donna è mobile* on his lips, planting in the ears of the audience a reminder of how it goes. The clock chimes again, signaling the start of what should be the last half hour of the Duke's life.

Unexpectedly, however, Gilda (disguised as a boy) returns to the scene against her father's instructions. Her entry signals the transition into another ensemble, one that will be even more peculiarly motivated than the preceding quartet. Still besotted by love, she is drawn back to the Duke, and from her wonted position on the outside overhears Sparafucile and Maddalena plotting inside the inn. As background to another introductory *parlante*, the storm continues to gather (Ex. 43-8) — a "Shakespearean" storm that, in the opinion of Verdi scholars, contains music that Verdi may originally have conceived in connection with his never-to-be-realized *King Lear* project.

EX. 43-8 Giuseppe Verdi, *Rigoletto*, Act III, beginning of storm

EX. 43-8 (continued)

Its most daring touch of realism is the use of a male chorus, humming closed-mouthed behind the scenes, to represent the voice of the howling wind. It may seem paradoxical to call such an artificial device realistic, but by now we have had many opportunities to absorb the lesson that artistic (especially dramatic) realism is not a matter of literal fidelity to nature, but of fidelity to the affective circumstances — to "human nature," so to speak. "Humanizing" the sound of the storm sends the same subliminal message as does the addition of a new orchestral effect — a staccato woodwind figure representing the start of heavy rain or hail — when Gilda takes action by knocking at the door, as if a rise in dramatic tension actually affected the course of nature. But of course we have seen storms (or musical reminiscences of them) functioning as external reflectors of inner agitation since the time of Handel. Stage murders rarely take place in good weather.

The storm music gives shape to the drama's dénouement and lends a gruesome *tinta* to the final act. The musical climax is a fleet yet resounding two-stanza *terzetto* for Sparafucile and Maddalena, bickering on the inside, and Gilda on the outside, beside herself at first with fear and then with frenzied resolve. Again, the ensemble follows not the Donizettian model of reflective stasis, but the older (Mozartean) one of evolving action *(strepitoso, strepitossisimo . . .)* that had its origin in comedy. In the first stanza Sparafucile and Maddalena compromise on a plan whereby if anyone should unexpectedly come knocking, that person shall be killed in the Duke's place; the disguised Gilda, overhearing this, immediately decides to sacrifice herself for her unworthy lover. Between the stanzas she screws up her courage and knocks, bringing on the heavy weather. During the second stanza the evil brother and sister get ready for murder and Gilda, steeling herself, prepares to die. At its conclusion she knocks again. The deed is quickly done, and the orchestral storm bursts forth in full fury, all piccolo scales and diminished seventh chords.

Two brief scenes remain. The first brings Rigoletto back onstage at the stroke of midnight to receive the promised body in the promised sack. Up to a point it is played entirely in recitative: Rigoletto natters in anticipation, Sparafucile hands over the sack, Rigoletto gloats. And then recitative suddenly gives way to song — "La donna è mobile," jaunty and insouciant as ever, as the unsuspecting Duke makes his merry way homeward at stage rear after his rendezvous with Maddalena. Irony compounded and recompounded! First the global irony: as Piero Weiss observes, for the Duke, unsuspecting instigator of it all, act III is "just a happy ending to an ordinary day."[26] But then there is far more bitter local irony — the irony, so to speak, of the masks. The merry song, giving evidence that the body in the sack cannot be the Duke's, now jars not only with the setting but with the plot itself. It no longer merely signifies the Duke's happy-go-lucky existence, but carries a horrifying double message to Rigoletto and the audience, who now must witness the terrible outcome of the curse.

"Comedy no longer alternates with tragedy but is superimposed on it," Weiss comments, underscoring Verdi's unprecedented Shakespearean achievement, "a drama in which a king (or duke) is a fool, a fool (or jester) a tragic hero, in which life, far from manifesting any intrinsic logic, produces unexpected results from dimly-percieved premises." Not everyone was ready to accept this bonfire of the traditional categories. But all agreed that they were witnessing a major innovation. Negative reviews of innovative works are often more illuminating than positive ones; the critic's resistance itself casts light on the specific nature of the novelty, and the threat that it implies. So here is one of the most resistant critiques *Rigoletto* received on the morrow of its Venice premiere, in the pages of the *Gazzetta ufficiale di Venezia*, the city's official newspaper:

> An opera of this sort cannot be judged in one evening. Yesterday we were overwhelmed by novelty; novelty, or rather strangeness in the subject; novelty in the music, in the style, in the very form of the pieces, and we did not grasp the work as a whole. It has something of the *opera semiseria*; it begins with a dancing song, its protagonist is a hunchback; it issues forth with a feast and concludes, none too edifyingly, in a nameless house where love is for sale and men's lives are contracted for: it is, in sum, Victor Hugo's *Le Roi s'amuse* plain and unadorned, with all its sins. The maestro, or the poet, succumbed to a posthumous affection for the Satanic school, by now antiquated and extinct; they sought ideal beauty in the misshapen, in the horrible; they aimed at effect not by the customary [Aristotelian] paths of pity and terror, but in the soul's distress and repugnance. In all conscience, we cannot praise such tastes.[27]

Yet another shock was the realistic end of the opera, with only two characters onstage, and only one of them alive. Again, what is likely to strike viewers of today as stylized or contrived — the stabbed and dying Gilda left with just enough energy to sing a final duet — could only have been read at the time as a bold departure from operatic norms (which would have demanded a full stage at the end) for the sake of the "truthful" portrayal of the specific human circumstances, the final reversal that leaves Rigoletto alone in the world and unloved.

But then the third act of *Rigoletto* honors convention almost entirely in the breach. As Julian Budden remarks at the end of the first volume of his massive study of Verdi's operas, "just after 1850 at the age of thirty-eight Verdi closed the door on a period of Italian opera with *Rigoletto*,"[28] and this after mastering all the difficult conventions of that period by the sweat of his brow. Instead, he placed his mastery on the side of realism and, as Budden goes on to observe, "the so-called *ottocento* in music was finished." There is shrewd irony in that remark, since *ottocento* simply means "the nineteenth century," which by the calendar was only half over. But before *Rigoletto* the term would have meant a period not only of time but also of style, a style created out of a recognizable common practice that (by definition) everybody followed, no matter how they tweaked it. After *Rigoletto* the nineteenth century was just a time period, during which Italian opera, no less than German, sailed out on uncharted seas. The *solita forma*, the "customary form" of cantabiles and cabalettas, was moribund. Over the 1860s and 1870s it would die out. Italian opera followed the general trend toward a form that strove to follow content as if spontaneously. In becoming "realistic," Italian opera inevitably lost its special identity, since the latter was a product or function of the conventions that were losing their grip. What it gained was immediacy of pathos — an immediacy Verdi learned from no musical contemporary (least of all Wagner), but rather from literary models like Hugo, and in back of him, the inevitable Shakespeare.

A JOB BECOMES A CALLING

It is absurd to look back on Wagner and Verdi as "progressive" and "conservative" poles (though that is how historians in the tradition of the New German School have tended to view them), just as it is absurd to attribute the special qualities of Verdi's late work, beginning in the 1870s, to Wagner's influence, even though that was the decade during which Wagner began to receive staged performances in Italy. Verdi's greater knowledge of Wagner's work translated not into imitation but into a fascinating dialectic; nor was acquaintance with Wagner the biggest or most telling change that took place in the composer's life during the decade in question.

The main event in Verdi's life during the 1870s was, quite simply, his retirement. The two decades following *La traviata* had been extremely lucrative ones for the composer. He followed the footsteps of Rossini and Donizetti to Paris for two grand operas — *Les vêpres siciliennes* ("The Sicilian vespers," 1855) and the especially grandiose *Don Carlos*, after a historical play by Schiller (1867). In between these came a commission from the tsar's own imperial Italian opera house in St. Petersburg, partly because of its remote location the highest-paying opera theater in Europe for star singers and star composers alike. For *La forza del destino* ("The power of fate," 1862), his last collaboration with Piave, Verdi received 60,000 French francs from the Russian treasury, more than twenty times the stipulated maximum payment a Russian composer could receive for an opera in the local language, in addition to an expense account of 5,000 rubles (approximately 10,000 francs) and a per-performance honorarium of 806 rubles and 45 kopeks. Widely regarded as a scandal, this extravagant outlay to the visiting foreigner did a great deal to foment nationalist sentiment among Russian musicians.

Rossini's death in 1868 left Verdi the richest composer-entrepreneur in Europe, another quintessential self-made man of art. Twice already he had been tempted to do as Rossini had done and use his earnings to escape from the hectic, exhausting world of opera, the more so as he was genuinely interested in farming the land on an estate called Sant'Agata near his north Italian birthplace of Busseto, which he had purchased in 1851. After *Aida*, the grandest of the grand, Verdi called it quits. Composing for him — in keeping with his hard apprenticeship and the unsentimental attitudes of the professional theater — was a job, not a "calling" from above, and he regarded the opportunity to renounce it in favor of gentleman farming as a promotion. This was the greatest, most telling measure of his cultural distance from Wagner, a distance that applied to their respective national traditions as much as it did to them as individuals.

FIG. 43-7   Verdi in St. Petersburg for the première of *La forza del destino* (1862).

Accordingly, Verdi's correspondence, the mother lode for biographers of any nineteenth-century figure, suddenly emptied itself of artistic or musical content (and political content too, Verdi having resigned his honorary seat in parliament) and began filling up with discussions of crops, livestock, soil, manure. He did not cease all musical activity. One of his most famous works, in fact, dates from the 1870s, but it was not an opera: it was a Requiem Mass composed in commemoration of the venerable Manzoni, like Verdi a symbol of the Risorgimento and an honorary senator, first performed on 22 May 1874, the first anniversary of Manzoni's death at the age of eighty-eight (the very age that Verdi would eventually reach). Even though it retains a vivid theatrical flair (especially in the Dies Irae), Verdi put it in a wholly different category from his operas — that of "serious music." To Camille du Locle, one of the librettists for *Don Carlos*, he declared that having written it he was "no longer a clown serving the audience, beating a huge drum and shouting 'Come on! Come on! Step right up!'"[29]

The irony here is delectable, because the most famous detail in the entire Requiem is the furious beating of the huge bass drum in the Dies Irae in counterpoint against the whole rest of the orchestra. But Verdi's double standard was understandable, and revealing. He wrote his operas as a hired hand, which in retrospect meant a servant and a clown; the Requiem he wrote on his own initiative, as a "free artist." Serious art was beginning, even in Italy, to mean art created not on commission but "for art's sake." Revising an opera "disinterestedly" — just to make it better, not because anyone asked—could also count as art for art's sake, and so Verdi lavished a great deal of time during his "retirement" on two of his weightier historical operas: *Simon Boccanegra* (1857, revised 1879–81) and *Don Carlos*, which virtually became a new opera in 1882–83 (usually performed in Italian as *Don Carlo*).

Finally, in 1884, thirteen years after *Aida*, Verdi allowed himself to be persuaded by his publisher Ricordi, and by his ardent would-be literary collaborator Arrigo Boito (1842–1918), to attempt an opera under these new, utterly unoperatic conditions of creative emancipation. The result was one of his greatest achievements. That outcome, and the esthetic attitudes that had conditioned it, added a new chapter to the ongoing postromantic debate about the nature and purposes of art.

The positions Verdi now espoused were those associated since Kant with German art (or at least with German art-theorizing), positions traditionally regarded by Italians (including the earlier Verdi) with some suspicion, lately renewed and enhanced by association with Wagner. Boito, who was a composer in his own right, had been one of the leading *scapigliati*—"scruffy" Wagnerians who thought the likes of Verdi outmoded—in the 1860s, and had a noble fiasco, an opera called *Mefistofele* to his own very metaphysical libretto after Goethe's *Faust*, under his belt to prove it. (Twice revised, *Mefistofele* had begun to make its way in the theater by the time Boito summoned the courage to approach Verdi.) Impressed with a libretto that Boito proffered him in 1879, Verdi tested him as a collaborator by having him supply a crucial scene for the revised *Simon Boccanegra*. Finally convinced of Boito's ability and his devoted respect, Verdi left off full-time farming and took up his old job, but this time as a calling.

As anyone might have guessed, the subject that lured Verdi out of retirement came from Shakespeare—a Shakespeare treated with unprecedented fidelity and (with one huge exception, the climactic *concertato* or ensemble finale in act III) an adventurous disregard of traditional libretto structure. That disregard was especially evident because the subject, *Othello* (or *Otello*, to use the Italian form to designate the opera rather than the play), had already been used some seventy years earlier by Rossini in a hugely successful, traditional *opera seria* that still maintained a toehold in repertory. The implied contrast or contest suggested bravado—a bravado that the aging Verdi, eager (probably for that very reason) to appear up-to-date, shared with his much younger, formerly scruffy accomplice.

Thus, at the very outset, the opera fairly screams its freedom from galley routines by opening not with an overture, nor even with a prelude, but at the very height of the

FIG. 43-8   *Illustrazione italiana*, cover of special issue, "Verdi and Otello" (1887).

tempest with which Shakespeare's second act begins (Ex. 43-9a). To take the audience literally "by storm," with a chord of such squalling dissonance, was a veritable act of modernist aggression, justified (as artistic aggression is always justified) by its "truth." And where many operas (especially comic ones) had begun with choruses, the one in *Otello* is reminiscent of the grisly trio in the third act of *Rigoletto*, also played against a storm: its "lyrical" content is pared down to thirty-three bars in the middle (Ex. 43-9b), preceded and followed by elaborate *parlante* passages in which choral and solo voices interact unpredictably over a surging orchestral tide.

Continuity and compression: these are the ruling criteria. They could be called "realist." At the time, many called them "Wagnerian." Yet it is possible, and desirable, to view the matter from a more elevated historical perspective that places both Wagner and Verdi in a single context (rather than Verdi in Wagner's). From that perspective,

EX. 43-9A   Giuseppe Verdi, *Otello*, Act I, scene 1, mm. 1–16

EX. 43-9A   *(continued)*

EX. 43-9B   Giuseppe Verdi, *Otello*, Act I, scene 1, Lyrical climax of chorus, mm. 1–8

EX. 43-9B (*continued*)

CHORUS: God, whose wrath has roused the waters,
At whose smile the whirlwind tarries!

both composers were striving to achieve what opera critics since the beginning of the century had called the "continuous finale": a flexible interaction of literary and musical devices modeled on the finales of the Mozart/Da Ponte comedies, now stretched over whole acts. The German claimed to be destroying the past and rebuilding from scratch; Italians tended to see the historical process as evolutionary or synthetic, the mutual adaptation of traditional categories. But for both the process had similar historical roots and a similar goal.

For the sake of continuity, both composers committed wholesale violations of traditional "form," though only Wagner boasted of it. For both composers, ultimately, the conscious objective became fidelity to artistic ideals, abstractly conceived, rather than to their audience's expectations. That was the cradle of what we now call modernism, shrewdly characterized by Leonard B. Meyer, an American music theorist, as "the late, late Romantic period."[30] And once Verdi could be viewed as a modernist, it became it possible for academic critics to view him as great.

These new virtues can certainly be explained without recourse to Wagner, but the esthetic parallel with Wagner need not be overlooked. The most essential parallel, to repeat, was the protomodernist conviction that artworks were not created only for the sake of enjoyment — that is, at any rate, for the audience's enjoyment. Artists wrote to please themselves. While working on *Falstaff*, the opera (also Shakespearean, also with Boito) that followed *Otello*, which he finished composing in his eightieth year, Verdi let it be known that "I am writing it in moments of absolute leisure, simply for my own amusement."[31] That made it respectable. And so did the assumption that underlay the composer's disinterested amusement: consciousness that his new manner of continuity and compression served the purposes of art.

COMPRESSION AND EXPANSION

That was the rhetoric. The reality, of course, was far more complicated and far more interesting. Take compression, to begin with. Fidelity itself demanded it: if Shakespeare was to be followed fully (even, as far as possible, at the level of actual dialogue), he would have to be radically condensed, since musical time moves so much more slowly than that of unmediated speech and action. Room had to be made for music, and that meant stripping away all nonessentials. In the case of *Otello*, Shakespeare's whole first act was famously treated as a nonessential, simply snipped. But to put it this way is obviously wrongheaded, for what is music if not the greatest "nonessential" of all; and what is supplying it unasked-for if not the most willful dramatic infidelity? Shakespeare's play, after all, had worked perfectly well all by itself for centuries.

Obviously, the music was thought to compensate in some way for whatever it crowded out. But in fact a great deal was added to the libretto for the sake of music that was not even in Shakespeare to begin with — and not just ballets or choruses, either, but the whole incandescent last scene in act I, with which our main musical discussion will begin. The opera was no mere condensation of the play, but a complex product of simultaneous compression and expansion. The result was manifestly *not* faithful to Shakespeare, or rather — to put it in a paradoxical way that has become popular with critics — it broke faith with the original (in literal or practical ways) so as all the better to keep faith with it (on a higher, "esthetic" plane).

The big departure from Shakespeare in act I is the love scene for Otello and his wife, Desdemona, whom he will eventually murder in a jealous rage. Boito cunningly extracted many of its words from Shakespeare's own text (lines spoken by each character about the other but not to each other, including a few from the otherwise omitted first act), but Shakespeare had provided no such scene. Neither, even, had Rossini. Verdi's (and Boito's) supplying one, which adds nothing to the plot but only (it seems) to the opera's musical range or at best to the lovers' characterization, might seem at first to be a throwback to the very conventions the composer and librettist now affected to despise, especially since the role of Otello is by all odds the most heroic *tenore di forza* role in all of Verdi, and what is a *tenore di forza* for, if not to sing a love duet with the prima donna?

Indeed, it is even possible to parse the duet, albeit somewhat disproportionately, into the four components of a traditional grand *scena*: introduction (mm. 1–50), characterized by the luscious sonority of a cello quartet; cantabile (mm. 51–96), beginning with a rounded sixteen-bar period for Desdemona and ending with a rapturously climactic melody sung by both lovers in succession ("set," Budden observes, "in an enchanted twilight between F major and minor");[32] *tempo di mezzo* (mm. 97–126) introduced by a *poco più mosso*, which introduces emotional agitation and physical palpitations; and finally a coda (or, to borrow a phrase from Budden, a "cabaletta-digest") in which the accumulated ardor is discharged in passionate kissing (mm. 127–156).

The concluding section (Ex. 43-10) is the least conventional, because (completely belying the nature and function of a cabaletta) the chief musical interest is transferred to the orchestra: first in the threefold arching melody that even without benefit of the disconnected words to which the libretto has descended ("a kiss . . . Othello! . . . a kiss . . . another kiss . . . ") obviously accompanies three separate osculations; afterward in the music that (following, yet transforming, longstanding customs of timbre, register, and contour) paints the starry sky; and finally in the reappearance of the cello quartet, a reminiscence of the scene's opening measures and a reassertion of its blissful opening mood. The sudden dominance of the orchestra — or, to put it

EX. 43-10   Giuseppe Verdi, *Otello*, Act I, scene 3, end

EX. 43-10 (continued)

more poetically, the sudden transfer of dramatic weight to the word-transcending medium of "pure music"—was widely read as the ultimate Wagnerization of Verdi's musico-dramatic technique.

And so it was, perhaps—but in a very special, very exact way. There is good reason to regard this scene not as a case of generalized Wagnerian "influence" but as Verdi's deliberate commentary on (or, if the word can be divested of its satirical connotation, his parody or remaking of) a specific work of Wagner's which we already know, and which we already know that Verdi admired: namely, *Tristan und Isolde*.

EX. 43-10 (continued)

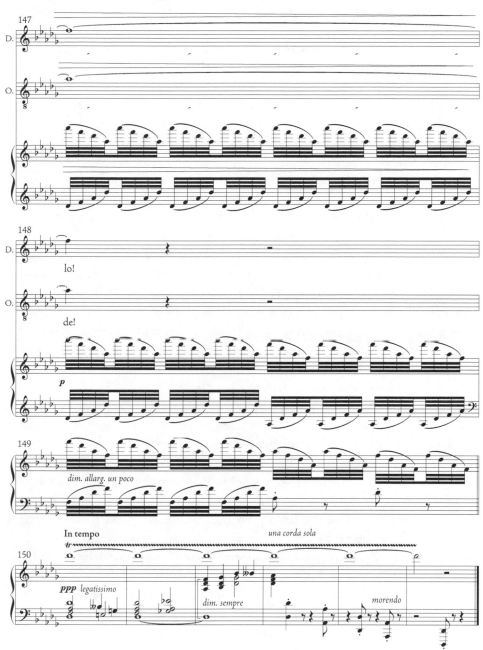

Imagine for a moment that Tristan and Isolde's world-transcending passion had been not tragically thwarted but had triumphed over its social obstacles, and that it had been able to evolve over time into mature wedded bliss. And now take a closer look at the "kiss" music in Ex. 43-10. Increasing harmonic tension tells us that each of the three kisses (that is, the three parallel two-bar phrases) is more ardent than the last. The first begins with a melodic appoggiatura (C♯) to the tonic triad. The second begins with the same melody note cast as appoggiatura to the dominant triad, producing a more complex, more dissonant harmony. And what harmony? None other than a *Tristan*-chord—a half-diminished seventh treated, just as Wagner treated it, as a chord containing an appoggiatura. Since the appoggiatura in this case resolves to a dominant seventh rather than a French sixth, the two chords—Wagner's and Verdi's—are functionally dissimilar. The tension of the one is never discharged (and that's the whole point of it), while the other is led smoothly back to cadential (and emotional) satisfaction.

The third kiss-phrase begins on a yet more restless harmony, a chord containing both the C♯ and the B, the note to which it nominally resolves. And this is another, yet more potent *Tristan*-chord, or rather another half-diminished sonority that is homonymous to the *Tristan*-chord, but whose constituent appoggiatura (F❌) resolves immediately to the third of the tonic triad, evoking not the torment of unconsummated passion but, once again (to quote a famous poem by William Blake), "the lineaments of gratified desire."[33] What could better delineate the difference between Wagner's lovers and Verdi's—but also, at the same time, their kinship? Once we have spotted the ersatz *Tristan*-chords at the climax of Verdi's love scene, many more will leap to our eyes and ears. Such harmonies were by no means common coin in Italian music, nor will we find them in any great profusion in Verdi's earlier music, however torrid. They lent this particular duet its special *tinta*, and their Wagnerian associations—surely deliberate!—added an element of typically Verdian (or should we say typically Shakespearean?) irony to the characterization. Tristan and Isolde as old marrieds! Stated baldly, as an oxymoron, the idea is merely amusing. Suggested by harmonic implication, its endorsement of uxorious "family values" over transcendent illicit desire is—how to put it?—morally seductive.

The first Tristanesque reference comes in m. 92, right after the lyrical peak of what earlier we called the duet's "cantabile" section. It maximizes harmonic tension (=ardor), but again, only so as to prepare its gentle resolution. The more agitated passage beginning there, which has already been compared to the *tempo di mezzo*, is riddled with Tristanesque harmonies. The most conspicuous ones (mm. 117, 119) again occur in a stingingly ironic position, supporting the "Amen" that follows the lovers' prayer that their bonds will last and grow with time.

The last Tristanesque reference (m. 137) introduces the final section of the duet, when the lovers contemplate the benignly shimmering sky. Again, the appoggiatura (A♯) resolves unproblematically to a member of the tonic triad, ironically reversing the chord's functional (=psychological) trajectory. No one ever demonstrated a greater understanding of *Tristan und Isolde* or its musical and dramatic implications than Verdi did in reversing them all. Ex. 43-11 summarizes all of these sightings of the *Tristan*-chord in the *Otello* love music, and compares their very different contexts and resolutions with the Wagnerian originals.

For a fuller appreciation of the love duet, its dramatic function, and the reason for its insertion into the libretto, we need to look to the other end of the opera, the fourth act, in which all the happy predictions that the lovers have made in act I come to grief on the shoals of Otello's misguided jealousy. This brief act, set in Desdemona's bedchamber, is fashioned out of Shakespeare (act IV, sc. 3; act V, sc. 2) almost without departure or digression although, inevitably, the action is much condensed. That very condensation, however, gives it an ideal shape for a memorable drama borne by music: a suspenseful stasis taken up with broad if heavily fraught lyricism, followed by a swift, terrifying denouement in which highly contrasted musical impressions come flying thick and fast.

It begins with Desdemona's lonely preparations for bed following her great humiliation at the act III curtain. As in Shakespeare, she vents her sad forebodings by singing a folksong to herself whose refrain, "O willow, willow willow," has caused it to be known as the Willow Song. Verdi captures its mood with yet another half-diminished harmony, set out as an arpeggio within the melody itself. The act opens with an anticipation of this phrase in the melancholy timbre of the English horn, answered by another phrase, even tinier (played by three flutes in unison), that will likewise prove to be a thematic anticipation (Ex. 43-12).

EX. 43-11   Giuseppe Verdi's *Tristan*-chords compared with Wagner's

EX. 43-12A   Giuseppe Verdi, *Otello*, Act IV, mm. 1–11

Since the half-diminished sonority here functions in its most ordinary diatonic usage, as ii$_7$ in the minor, there would be no reason to associate with its more exotic cousin in Wagner were it not for the love music in act I, which insists on that association. Since the whole fourth act is going to be an agonizing reversal or negation of that love scene, the opening harmony, as outlined by the English horn, can be seen as part of an all-encompassing web of ironic associations.

To prolong the suspense before Otello's sinister appearance, Verdi has Emilia (Desdemona's confidant as well as the wife of Iago, the villain) exit, leaving the victim alone onstage. To fill the time, Verdi and Boito make their one insertion into the Shakespearean action, borrowing an idea, as it happens, from the libretto to Rossini's old *Otello*, where it served a similar purpose: the good Desdemona prays, her *Ave Maria* beginning as a monotone "chant" recited by rote, but gradually taking on lyrical profile as the prayer becomes more personal and passionate.

At its dying away Otello appears among the shadows, his murky entrance — surely prompted by Shakespeare's "Put out the light, and then put out the light" — famously represented by a solo for the muted double basses extending from the very bottom of their compass to something like the very top (Ex. 43-12b). He raises the bed curtains and looks longingly at his sleeping wife, while the double basses' motive passes to Desdemona's plaintive English horn, in the parallel minor. Despite his murderous intent, he cannot forbear a kiss — or rather three kisses, accompanied by a reprise of the culminating music from act I. This reprise has the very same intent, and accomplishes the same dramatic work, as the first reprise of "La donna è mobile" in the third act of *Rigoletto*: it reminds the audience of an important musical association, and prepares them for the really crucial reprise that is yet to come.

She awakes. In fifty measures of gruesome *parlante* (recitative over a continuous orchestral motive), he accuses her; she denies it; he rebuts her denial with a lie; she protests; he smothers her. In one hundred measures more, the horrible truth is revealed to Otello and he embarks on his final aria, "Niun mi tema" ("Fear me not"), a mere seventy-four measures that can nevertheless be parsed into a full *scena*: introduction, cantabile (Adagio), *tempo di mezzo*, and cabaletta-digest. Except for the *tempo di mezzo*,

EX. 43-12B   Giuseppe Verdi, *Otello*, Act IV, scene 3 (Otello enters Desdemona's bedchamber)

where Otello suddenly stabs himself amid a general panic, each part of this painfully reflective aria is fraught with ironic reminiscences conveyed by lacerating musical recalls.

The first section reaches a bitter climax on the word "Gloria!" set in a manner that recalls Otello's first appearance in act I, as the victorious naval hero. *"Esultate!,"* he had sung then, *"L'orgoglio musulmano sepolto è in mar, nostra e del ciel è gloria!"*: "Rejoice! The pride of the Turks is entombed in the sea; Heavens be ours and the glory!" What had been the Turks' fate, to fall in consequence of their pride, is now Otello's.

The Adagio (Ex. 43-13a), in which Otello's utter loneliness is underscored by suddenly withholding the orchestral accompaniment, is largely based on the little flute refrain at the beginning of the act, associated there with Desdemona's melancholy (compare Ex. 43-12a). To that motive, a third descending through an accented passing tone, Otello describes Desdemona's aspect in death—*pallida, e stanca, e muta, e bella* ("pale and worn and still and lovely")—and, in another suddenly unaccompanied outburst at the end of the section, calls vainly on her name and grasps that she is dead. In a letter to his publisher, Verdi described the end of this burst (*"Ah!, morta! morta! morta!"*) as "sounds almost without key."[34] What makes it seem so is its conclusion, a descending phrase that implies tonic harmony (in C♯ minor) at its beginning but subdominant at the end. Its last four notes, of course, recapitulate the already fraught half-diminished harmony of Desdemona's Willow Song; far from being "without key," they are in precisely the key of the opening English horn solo.

The final section (Ex. 43-13b), which brings the opera to an end, is a setting of Othello's last line in Shakespeare, itself a heartbreaking reminiscence: "I kist thee, ere I kill'd thee; No way but this,/Killing my selfe, to dye upon a kisse." It recapitulates the

EX. 43-13A   Giuseppe Verdi, *Otello*, Act IV, scene 4 (Otello's remorse)

EX. 43-13A   (continued)

EX. 43-13B   Giuseppe Verdi, *Otello*, Act IV, scene 4 (Death of Otello)

EX. 43-13B *(continued)*

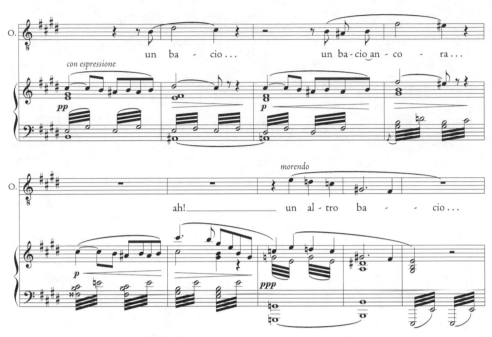

musical content of the moment in which, before killing her, Otello had gazed upon his sleeping wife and been overwhelmed with the grief of love lost. The last music heard before the curtain, then, is the kiss music from act I, in its final, crucial, reminiscence.

And now we know why the love scene in act I had to be written. It was not only to fulfill an operatic requirement. Nor was it merely to plant a motive for later reminiscence — or rather, to put it that way is to put the cart before the horse. What motivated the love scene was the dying Otello's last line, and the need to provide a "past in music" on which his concluding recollection could draw, thus justifying through music's word-transcending immediacy of feeling the whole project of turning what was already a great play into an opera.

Exactly this, we may recall, had been Wagner's motivation for expanding the *Ring* into a tetralogy — to provide the narrative of the Norns in *Götterdämmerung* with a past *in music* on which to draw. If we write off the *Otello* love duet off as a studied or cynical "plant," then we are bound likewise to regard the whole of *Das Rheingold*, *Die Walküre*, and *Siegfried*. If Wagner's operatic tetralogy is regarded, contrariwise, as a noble attempt to create a world in music, then so, in its far more humane and economical way, is *Otello*.

The feature that most decisively distinguishes Verdi, even at his most monumental, from Wagner is his insistence on a human scale. In this the two composers can truly be taken as opposites and as standard-bearers for opposing national traditions. Verdi's goes back to the humanism or man-centered philosophy of the Italian Renaissance, while Wagner's embodies centuries of accumulated antihumanistic German metaphysical thought, in which answers to fundamental human questions were automatically sought on a superhuman plane, a plane for which orchestral rather than vocal music was the ideal medium of representation. Only one of Verdi's operas, *Macbeth*, invokes a crucial supernatural or miraculous agency. Only one of Wagner's, *Die Meistersinger von Nürnberg*, fails to do so. At the emotional climax of *Otello*'s final scene ("Desdemona . . . Desdemona . . . Ah, morta! morta! morta!") the orchestra is silent. At the corresponding moment in *Tristan und Isolde*, the orchestra sweeps the singer away.

The dramatic tradition that leads to Verdi is at bottom the comic tradition, which is the one in which humankind is essentially responsible for its own fate. The specifically operatic tradition that leads to him is the one that proceeded through ever greater infusions of *buffa* styles, forms, and attitudes into the *opera seria*. The dramatic tradition that leads to Wagner is the tragic tradition, in which humans are the helpless playthings of the gods. The specifically operatic tradition that leads to him is the perpetually "reformist" or neoclassical tradition — the tradition of Metastasio and Gluck — that sought to enforce the purity of dramatic categories and in particular undertook periodic purgings from tragic opera of comedic admixtures and accretions.

Thus it is no surprise to find that Wagner's last opera, *Parsifal*, was an out-and-out religious drama, replete with actual sacred rituals enacted onstage, and ending with miraculous healings and redemptions — or that Verdi's last opera, *Falstaff* (fashioned by Boito after Shakespeare's *Merry Wives of Windsor*, with admixtures from the Henry IV plays), was a worldly-wise comedy, Verdi's first *"buffa"* in fifty years. It was an astonishing departure for a composer approaching eighty, the most astounding feat of artistic self-rejuvenation since Monteverdi, also a retired septuagenarian, came forth some 250 years before with *L'Incoronazione di Poppea* (see chapter 20). But with benefit of hindsight one could hardly imagine a more fitting consummation to Verdi's career, or a more logical outcome of its trajectory.

COMEDIZATION

The "comedization" of late-nineteenth-century opera was an unstoppable tide. The term should not be misunderstood. It does not necessarily have to do with humor, although the process it denotes did give humorous opera (among other things) a boost. It designates, rather, what is more often termed (or mistermed) "realism." Comedization works better than realism in this context because it suggests something concrete about forms and styles (namely, their shrinkage and "popularization") without making unwarranted claims about the nature of plots, which were often far from "realistic."

FIG. 43-9   *Illustrazione italiana*, cover of special issue, "Verdi and Falstaff" (1893).

As a case in point consider *The Stone Guest (Kamennïy gost')* by the Russian composer Alexander Dargomïzhsky — another member of the class of 1813, if a minor one. Left almost completely composed in vocal score at the time of its author's death in 1869, its holes were plugged by César Cui, its orchestration supplied by Rimsky-Korsakov, and it was first performed in St. Petersburg in 1872. Its literary source was a "little tragedy" by Alexander Pushkin that was inspired by Mozart's *Don Giovanni* — with its walking, talking statue (the title character in the Pushkin/Dargomïzhsky version) not the most realistic of plots. What made Dargomïzhsky's version a landmark of realism nevertheless was the composer's decision to base his work directly on Pushkin's dramatic poem without any mediating libretto — a demonstratively anti-operatic decision taken very self-consciously in the name of "truth."

Without a specially-fashioned libretto, there could be little or no provision for purely musical unfolding: no arias, no ensembles. There are two Spanish romances, interpolated by Dargomïzhsky where Pushkin merely indicated that a character sing a song. (The critic Hermann Laroche had fun with this, foreseeing a future when "truth" prevailed and composers would have to smuggle music into their operas by constantly having their characters invite one another to make some.)[35] For the rest, Dargomïzhsky treated Pushkin's verse drama as if it were the text of a gigantic through-composed art song, setting it not as recitative but quite lyrically, yet without formalizing repetition of lines (though continuous accompaniment figures often gather musical stretches up into perceptual units).

The most aria-like moment comes when Don Juan, seducing Donna Anna, reacts heatedly to her insinuation that he is mad. Here Pushkin used repetition as a rhetorical device, thus giving Dargomïzhsky permission to follow suit (Ex. 43-14): "If I were a madman," Don Juan remonstrates, in prose translation:

> I would wish to remain among the living; I would nurture hope of touching your heart with tender love.
> If I were a madman,
> I would spend my nights at your balcony, troubling your sleep with serenades; I would not hide myself; on the contrary, I would try to be noticed by you everywhere.
> If I were a madman,
> I would not suffer in silence.

[To which Donna Anna retorts, "You call this silence?"]

EX. 43-14 Alexander Dargomïzhsky, *The Stone Guest*: Act II, Don Juan's Arioso

EX. 43-14 (*continued*)

EX. 43-14 (continued)

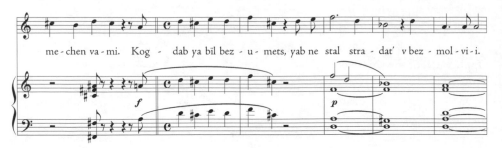

me - chen va - mi. Kog - dab ya bïl bez - u - mets, yab ne stal stra - dat' v bez - mol - vi - i.

EX. 43-15   Giuseppe Verdi, *Falstaff*, "Quand'ero paggio"

FAL.: Once when I served as the Duke of Norfolk's page,
I was a picture of elegant splendour;
I was perfection, gracefully, tenderly, splendidly, slender, so slender.

The repeated line is treated musically as a refrain, and is transposed up a step with every appearance. Between these markers, however, there is only minimal musical "rounding," chiefly a matter of short phrases set in sequence. And yet a minuscule "number" has been allowed to form in response to the structure of the text: a new application of the well-worn reformist plea (going all the way back to Monteverdi) that "poetry be the mistress of the music."

Needless to say, Dargomïzhsky's "formlessness" was derided in its day as Wagnerian; but what his procedures really resembled—by anticipation rather than by imitation—were Verdi's in *Otello* and, especially, *Falstaff*. We have already seen how the elevated lyrical style of the *Otello* love duet was achieved: it was a matter of allowing occasional climactic phrases to coalesce into repetitive sequences or fleeting rounded periods within an overall through-composed design. The same is even more typical of *Falstaff*, in which (as in *The Stone Guest*) only one tiny "number" emerges from the incessant lyric flux and flow: "Quand'ero paggio" ("When I was a page"), the bulky title character's brief reminiscence of his limber youth in the retinue of the Duke of Norfolk (Ex. 43-15).

The similarity of style, in particular the strictly syllabic declamation on short note values normally employed in recitative, may not have been a coincidence. Verdi, who (as we know) had visited Russia, and who had run into Dargomïzhsky, a high-society dilettante, at various salons and social functions, knew about *The Stone Guest* before it was performed or published, professed a collegial admiration for it, and owned a copy of the vocal score. But whether or not a direct line is traced from the one work to the other, *The Stone Guest* and *Falstaff* both exemplified the process of comedization that cut the imposing formal blocks of traditional opera down to size.

Cutting Things Down to Size

RUSSIAN REALISM (MUSORGSKY, CHAIKOVSKY); OPÉRA LYRIQUE; OPERETTA, VERISMO

GOING TOO FAR

To continue the argument of the previous chapter, the concept of "comedization" can accommodate without contradiction not only realism but also some other developments in European musical theater that on the face of it seem quite incompatible with realism. A defining moment for the concept, a sort of limiting case, was a creative crisis that unexpectedly intervened in the work of the century's most committed musical realist, altering the course of his career.

That composer was Modest Musorgsky, already mentioned in chapter 40 as a realist, and in chapter 41 as a member of the "mighty little bunch" of Russian nationalist composers who grouped themselves around Miliy Balakirev in the 1850s and 1860s. Musorgsky's nationalism, combined with his insecure nonprofessional status (having been trained not for a musical but for a military career), led him to adopt an extreme "outsider's" attitude toward the existing traditions and institutions of musical Europe. He rejected with equal fervor both the traditional curriculum of the German conservatory — counterpoint, mastery of "form," systematic theory, any manifestation of "braininess" — and the esthetic of Italian opera: bel canto, refined or ornate melody, all conventional canons of musical "beauty."

FIG. 44-1   Modest Musorgsky, painted by Ilya Repin in the hospital a week before the composer's death in February 1881.

Such a stance is easy enough to write off as a case of sour grapes. There was no Russian conservatory where Musorgsky might have studied until 1862, when he was already overage; and the Russian musical stage was dominated during his formative years by a state-supported Italian opera troupe from which the work of native composers was barred by official policy. Russian composers of Musorgsky's generation were effectively frozen out of the country's musical establishment — a situation comparable to that which existed in America, and lasted longer. Unless one went abroad for training, as Glinka and Gottschalk did, one had to content oneself with correspondence courses or self-education. And there were next to no performance outlets for one's creative labor unless one was a performing virtuoso, as Musorgsky (while a fine and much sought-after accompanist) was not.

What is left, though, after both brains and beauty have been renounced? Good character, obviously. That is where Musorgsky's high moral commitment to "truth" was born (a commitment he thought of as being particularly Russian, in opposition to the falsities of German and Italian routine) and hence his commitment to realism, with its contempt for fine manners and convention. He found a mentor in Dargomïzhsky (like him an aristocratic dilettante frozen out by the professional establishment), and a model in *The Stone Guest*, the opera mentioned at the end of the previous chapter. Dargomïzhsky had solved the problem of operatic "form" by dispensing with the libretto altogether, and that made him "the great teacher of musical truth," as Musorgsky put it in two separate dedications.

But Dargomïzhsky's solution was not complete, because the text of *The Stone Guest* consisted of artistic (that is, artificial) verse. In what may have been the most extreme "reformist" position ever adopted by an opera composer, Musorgsky proclaimed that the ultimate in musical truth could be achieved only if composers set librettos in conversational prose, with the music faithfully mirroring the tempo and contour of actual conversational speech. This was a particularly strict application to music of the old neoclassical (or "Renaissance") precept of *mimesis*, or "imitation of nature," the idea that art derives its power from the mimicking of reality. It was the same idea that had inspired the invention of opera in the humanist academies of Florence almost three centuries before (see chapter 19).

But music had always fit uneasily into the mimetic scheme of things because it had no obvious natural model. The old Florentine solution was similar to Musorgsky's: the idea that, if speech is taken to be the outward embodiment of emotion, then imitation of speech was tantamount to the imitation of emotion — that

FIG. 44-2   Alexander Dargomïzhsky, engraving from a photograph.

is, human psychological reality ("human nature"). The difference lay in the type of speech to be imitated. For the Florentines, living in the age of humanism, it was poetry composed in the style of Greek drama. For Musorgsky, living in an age of burgeoning scientific empiricism (or "positivism"), it would be the "natural" speech one observed in "real life."

This was unprecedented. Never had a composer envisioned the renunciation of verse, however terse, as the basis of musical setting. Outside the realm of functioning church liturgies in oral tradition (e.g., Gregorian chant), no one had ever seriously questioned the status of regular meter as a basic musical ingredient. In his quest for the ultimate musical embodiment of nature, Musorgsky did not shrink from questioning any assumption about "the nature of music." This was surely the most radical posture ever assumed by a nineteenth-century composer, and he gloried in it for a while because it turned all of his liabilities into advantages. Far from handicapped, he was *privileged* by his maverick, autodidact status to think the unthinkable. "On nature's scale," he wrote to a friend (typically imitating the language of science),

> man is the highest organism (at least on earth), and this highest organism possesses the gift of word and voice without equal among terrestrial organisms. If one admits the reproduction by artistic means of human speech in all its subtlest and most capricious shades —to depict it naturally, as life and human nature demand— would this not amount to the deification of the human gift of words? And if by this simplest of means, simply submitting strictly to artistic instinct in catching human vocal intonations, it becomes possible to capture the heart, then is it not a worthy enterprise? And if one could, along with that, catch the thinking faculties in a vise, then would it not be worthwhile to devote oneself to such an occupation?[1]

His conservatory would be the conservatory of life. To another correspondent he wrote, "whatever speech I hear, whoever is speaking (or, the main thing, no matter what he is saying), my brain is already churning out the musical embodiment of such speech."[2] These optimistic letters were written during the summer of 1868, when the twenty-nine-year-old Musorgsky was making his first attempt to realize these ideals in practice—or, to put it in the "scientific" terms he preferred, to carry out his first "experiment in dramatic music in prose."

The exercise in question was similar to *The Stone Guest* in concept: a verbatim setting of a preexisting play. The play in question, though, had to be a prose play, and that meant, according to the conventions of the nineteenth-century theater, that it had to be a comedy. Musorgsky chose *Marriage*, a farce by Nikolai Gogol about the vacillations of an unwilling bridegroom. The naturalistic dialogue in which it is cast must surely rank among the most unlyrical prose ever put on paper. For a sample of the unlyrical music with which Musorgsky clothed it, we can start right at the beginning with the main character's opening speech (Ex. 44-1).

As a Russian, Musorgsky had an actual advantage in writing naturalistic prose recitative, because the actual pattern of the spoken language imposes a sort of beat on most utterances that can be represented fairly accurately in ordinary musical notation. In ordinary Russian speech accents are distributed evenly, within a tempo that varies

EX. 44-1 Modest Musorgsky, *Marriage*, opening speech

Well, when you begin thus, alone, and at leisure to think about it, you see that you positively have to get married. What do you find? You live your life, but in the end, finally,
what a horror it becomes. Again I've let the winter go by, and all the while, it seems,
everything is ready: the matchmaker has been coming three months already. Really! You
get to feeling ashamed of yourself. Hey! Stepan!

according to affect. At the outset, Podkolyosin, the prospective bridegroom, is lying on a
divan, smoking his pipe. The accented syllables (*Vot, -nyosh', -din, -su-*, etc.) fall regularly
on a half-note tactus as befits his lethargic state. Unaccented syllables are arranged
in patterns of short equal values between the accented ones. An unaccented syllable
is never allowed to occupy the beginning of a beat, lest it introduce an un-Russian
secondary accent. (No matter how many syllables it may contain, a Russian word takes
only one accent: English-speaking students, who are used to introducing secondary
accents even in two-syllable words, often practice the word *dostiprimechátel'nosti*, which
means "points of interest," as in sightseeing.)

Where the notated beat is the quarter note and the accents fall on the half note, as
here, this means that the intervening quarter-note pulses will be occupied by rests, as is
uniformly the case in this example up to the words *nádo zhenít'sya*. The resultant strings
of little notes, evenly crowded into the space of one beat (entailing the very free use of
triplets and other *gruppetti*) and interrupted by a rest at the beginning of the next, are
instantly recognizable as "Musorgskian." Beginning with *nádo zhenít'sya*, ("you have to
get married"), the accents begin falling on the quarter notes in response to the anxiety
that the thought of marriage has aroused in a confirmed bachelor.

The other noteworthy feature is the fastidiousness with which note values are assigned. Musorgsky's ear for the tempo of Russian speech, as the quoted letter suggests, was practiced and marvelously refined. The rhythm of *na dosúge*, for example, decelerates (triplets followed by eighths), while the next word, *podúmïvat'*, reverses the order of note values and accelerates. These rhythms are not arbitrarily chosen; Musorgsky is indeed drawing faithfully and "scientifically" from life (from his own observed declamation, in all likelihood). Similarly, the lengths of upbeats vary according to the natural model. The first syllable of *odín* and the unaccented word *chto* are set as sixteenth notes, while the word *tak*, even when unaccented, is usually drawled in spoken Russian, and hence is entitled to an eighth note.

Yet the composer exercises a careful "artistic" control over the shape of the line, directing all tension to release on the explosive *nádo zhenít'sya*. This culminating phrase is the first since the initial word in which the first syllable is an accented one, hence unpreceded by an upbeat. It therefore gives the impression of being delayed, which heightens the sense of climax. Melodic contour is also handled naturalistically, but with artistic control. The climactic *nádo zhenít'sya* is exceeded, as melodic high point, only by *takáya skvérnost'* ("what a horror").

These emotional climaxes stand out all the more because they are surrounded with neutral utterances that reproduce the characteristic Russian monotone quite accurately. Podkolyosin's turbid deliberations at the outset are deftly transmitted by singsong oscillations between a "reciting tone" of sorts (E/E♭), which takes the strings of unaccented syllables, and a higher pitch area (A/A♭) that alternates with the lower pitch on accented syllables. Where irony is called for (*zhivyosh', zhivyosh'*), the contour of this oscillation is widened to a grotesque seventh. The intonational model is always provided by the spoken language, and melodic contour is dictated by the type of utterance — declarative, interrogative, exclamatory — that the music must reflect.

One of Musorgsky's most striking "antimusicalisms" is the harmonic ambience. In this musical prose, tonal motion is kept purposefully static and ambiguous for long stretches, since functional harmony tends to periodize phrase structure. There is no key signature anywhere in *Marriage*, and tonal ambiguity is maintained by means of an unprecedented reliance on augmented and diminished intervals, with chords of corresponding intervallic content in the accompaniment. These, of course, are the "unvocal" intervals shunned in lyrical melodies, hence all the more desirable if lyricism is to be renounced and the illusion of "ordinary speech" sustained despite the use of fixed pitch.

But needless to say, there is nothing ordinary about such music. It is a highly distinctive medium, and Musorgsky was certainly its master. Within his own domain he had evolved a very sophisticated and elegant technique. After setting a few scenes from *Marriage* (in Russian, *Zhenit'ba*) he was ready for a task that would put to a worthy test his conviction that his new style could produce a music of unprecedented moral and intellectual force, "capturing the heart and catching the thinking faculties in a vise." The worthiest task of all would surely be a historical drama with a national theme; and this, too, reflected conditions in Russia.

ART AND AUTOCRACY

Historical dramas were popular everywhere in the nineteenth century; the Parisian *grand opéra*, as we know, consisted of virtually nothing but. Artistic representations of history in all media had a special importance in Russia, however, and a special cachet. That was because by the latter half of the nineteenth century Russia was the only remaining autocratic state in Europe. Everywhere else monarchies had been at least to some degree constitutionalized, but in Russia the tsar's authority was absolute, neither fettered by law nor shared with a parliament. Public debate of social and political issues was more severely circumscribed than anywhere else, and liberal opinion usually had to be camouflaged in what was called "Aesopian" language. That is, it had to take place in the guise of scholarship or art, on the understanding that sophisticated readers would interpret such writings, objects, and performances metaphorically, alive to its potential contemporary relevance.

As a result, artists and scholars in Russia felt a greater obligation than anywhere else to invest their work with content "worthy of the attention of a thinking man,"[3] to quote the radical writer Nikolai Chernïshevsky (1828–89), an expert Aesopian (but not always a successful one: he spent many years of his life in prison or exile). Nowhere else was the content of art ever subjected to such scrutiny, both by official censors on the lookout for subversion, and by subversive thinkers on the lookout for ammunition. Nowhere was art so fraught with subtexts, nowhere was it invested with greater civic or social value, nowhere was it practiced with greater risk or greater zeal. Nowhere was there less interest in art's purely "decorative" role. Russian esthetics tended toward the ethical, even the "utilitarian." Art was valued to the extent that it was seen to do good. And so it was very difficult if not impossible to say whether the subtexts and the values that engaged "the thinking man" were drawn out of the artworks in which they were spotted, or were being read into them. Interpretation is always a two-way street. In Russia it became a teeming thoroughfare.

This set of values disrupted the nexus of "the Good, the True, and the Beautiful" on which romanticism was founded, and greatly magnified the general drift away from romanticism toward realism, which regarded beauty with skepticism. (To make things look beautiful was usually to lie; nothing good could come of that.) It gave "outsider" artists like Musorgsky, already predisposed toward a countercultural, "avant-garde" posture, a greatly empowering sense of mission. His artistic and esthetic coming-of-age, moreover, coincided with one of the most permissive moments in Russian intellectual history: the aftermath of the disastrous Crimean War, and the upheavals wrought by the emancipation of the serfs (Russian peasants bound by feudal law to work the estates of landowners as chattels; Musorgsky's own family was one of the many petty aristocratic clans that were ruined by the emancipation). To curb social unrest and maintain the good will of the educated classes, or intelligentsia, Russian censorship was significantly relaxed in the 1860s and 1870s.

Musorgsky's letters began filling up with memorable slogans. He became, as one critic eventually dubbed him, the "thinking realist of the Russian operatic stage."[4] To a friend he exclaimed, "the past in the present—there's my task!"[5] In so saying, he explicitly embraced the "Aesopian" cause and implicitly acknowledged that he had evolved his radical new style for its sake.

The recipient of this avowal, a history teacher named Vladimir Nikolsky, supplied Musorgsky with the ideal subject on which to exercise his skills: *Boris Godunov*, a fairly old (1825) but little-known play by Alexander Pushkin, composed in deliberate imitation of Shakespeare's "histories," and of *Henry IV* in particular. Like Shakespeare's King Henry, with his famous soliloquy, "Uneasy lies the head that wears a crown," Boris Godunov was a troubled ruler. According to widely accepted (but now refuted) tradition, Boris had ascended to the Russian throne in 1598 by having the legitimate heir, the nine-year-old Tsarevich Dmitry (youngest son of Ivan the Terrible), murdered. Tormented both by his conscience and by a pretender to the throne who claimed to be the risen Dmitry, Boris undergoes a steady decline, throughout the opera, to an early death, even as chaos tragically envelops Russia.

Immediately Pushkin's play became a covert treatise on kingship and legitimacy, dangerous subjects to raise within the borders of an absolute monarchy. If it was still little known in 1868, that was because until 1866 it had languished under the censor's ban, and was as yet unperformed. That did not faze Musorgsky in the slightest, even though censorship restrictions on operas were even more stringent than those on plays, and included one proviso that would seem to doom the project from the start: according to law, no Russian ruler could be portrayed in the servile act of singing before an audience.

The composer's antiprofessional attitude insulated him against such practical considerations, and this play had everything he needed: the same "Shakespearean" mixture of poetry and prose, tragedy and comedy, that had attracted Verdi; a wide range of character types from noble to beggar, to be characterized by distinctively musicalized speech; a large role for the crowd, which could (in unprecedented fashion) be treated as naturalistically as the soloists, thus advancing the realist program "toward new shores,"[6] to quote another Musorgskian slogan (for like any "scientist," Musorgsky was a firm believer in technological progress).

He never noticed, at first, that there were hardly any female characters, or that Pushkin had treated the one character who might have been suitable for a prima donna role in sketchy fashion and never provided her with a proper love scene. Indeed, Musorgsky cut her out of the opera altogether, because the one drawback Pushkin's play presented was its length. The composer intended to set it verbatim, as he had *Marriage* (or Dargomïzhsky *The Stone Guest*), but unlike those, Pushkin's was a full-evening's spectacle. If set to music as it stood, it would have rivaled Wagner's *Ring*. It had to be radically scaled down.

Musorgsky retained two scenes just as Pushkin had written them, and placed them side by side for maximum "Shakespearean" contrast. One took place in a monastery where the monk Grishka Otrepyev, egged on by Pimen, a chronicler who reveals to him Boris's criminal illegitimacy, hatches his plan to topple the tsar by becoming a pretender. It is cast in Shakespearean poetry: blank (that is, unrhymed) iambic pentameter, a new meter for the Russian language, and one that maintained a lofty cadence without sounding "artificial." The other scene set verbatim was one that took place in an inn near the Lithuanian border, where Grishka, posing as Dmitry and accompanied by a pair of roistering monks modeled on Shakespeare's Falstaff, barely escapes capture. It is a comic scene, cast in prose, and therefore a Musorgskian must. For the rest, as if cutting the Gordian knot, Musorgsky simply threw out every scene in which the title character failed to appear, then regrouped and conflated what remained. Almost every line of the opera's text came from Pushkin, but less than half of Pushkin was used: it was the truth and (pretty much) nothing but the truth, so to speak, but not the whole truth.

To give an idea of Musorgsky's *Boris* at its poetic and prosaic extremes, we can compare two starkly contrasting scenes in which Boris confronts the crowd. The first, the most famous in the opera, is the second scene of the prologue, the so-called Coronation Scene. Its text consists of a single speech for the title character, set off by one of Musorgsky's few additions to Pushkin's script: a choral procession, sung to the tune (and most of the words) of an old Russian folk song. The song is there, of course, to lend an authentic period flavor to a scene of public ritual, and also because more traditional theorists of realist esthetics (including Chernïshevsky, who wrote a treatise on the subject) cited folk song rather than speech as the "natural model" for music.[7] But Musorgsky's attitude toward this sort of verisimilitude was actually rather lax compared with his exacting standards of fidelity to the patterns of speech. On this level it was enough for him to conform to his audience's casual expectations rather than chart new ground.

FIG. 44-3 *Boris Godunov*, Act III, scene 2 ("Death of Boris"): Martti Talvela on the throne in the title role with set by Ming Cho Lee (Metropolitan Opera, New York, 1974).

The tune he used was famous — not least, ironically enough, because Beethoven had used it in a quartet dedicated to Count Razumovsky, the Russian ambassador in Vienna, who had given Beethoven a folk song anthology to mine for the purpose. The page from that collection (first published in 1790) to which both Beethoven and Musorgsky had recourse is shown in Ex. 44-2. The words — "As to thee, God in heaven, there is glory, let there be glory to the Tsar" — clearly recommended themselves as Coronation fodder. And yet anyone who really knew folklore (as Musorgsky, despite his reputation as a "nationalist," did not!) would have known from the heading in Ex. 44-2 that the song was a Yuletide song, not a coronation anthem, and would have known from the very word that caught Musorgsky's eye — *Slava* (Glory) — that it was a song meant to accompany a girls' fortune-telling game.

EX. 44-2   *Slava*, original folk melody (from Nikolai Lvov and Johann Pratsch, *Russkiye narodnïye pesni*, 1790)

It would be worse than pedantic to accuse Musorgsky of an error here. The knowledge that it takes to spot it is mere "book learning"; a more authentic original might well have been less "legible" to the audience as an emblem of Boris's power, representing the zenith from which he will spend the rest of the opera falling. Far more important to Musorgsky was the declamatory realism that informs the brief central monologue, for this was, according to his theory, the very crux of dramatic truth. The broad features of Podkolyosin's comic recitative, as we observed them in Ex. 44-1, are all in place. The range has been much widened, however; upbeats are sometimes lengthened to full-beat quarter notes; and the use of consonant melodic leaps in place of Podkolyosin's augmented and diminished intervals "lyricalize" the utterance. These departures from the conversational norm are admitted in order to elevate Boris's diction to the level of tragic eloquence; he assumes, as it were, the emotionally exalted tone that Russians actually adopt, even in casual or domestic surroundings, when they recite poetry.

The composer-critic César Cui, also a "kuchkist" (member of the *moguchaya kuchka*, or "mighty band," around Balakirev), christened this style "melodic recitative" in his newspaper reviews.[8] It is still classifiable as recitative because of its strict one-note-per-syllable declamation, its abundance of short repeated notes, its faithful mirroring of the intonational contour of the spoken language, and (beyond the two opening phrases) its absence of melodic repetitions, so that its shape is wholly dependent on that of the text. The poetry is the mistress, as Monteverdi would have said, the music the handmaiden. But each melodic phrase has "song potential"; one can easily imagine its development into an arioso.

The harmonization is deliberately archaic, "modal." Halfway through (Ex. 44-3) the key signature is "cleared," at 18, the tone centers become difficult to identify in terms of functional harmony. Is Boris's first line at 18 (*Teper' poklonimsya . . .*, "Now let us bow down") centered on A? Then why does it end on B? Is the mode "Aeolian," as the little progression before Boris's entry seems to suggest with its minor V chord? Then what is the status of the F♯? Part of an applied dominant to G? But what is the status of G? Or is the mode "Dorian"? Even within a tonal idiom as resolutely diatonic as this one it is possible to make radical departures from functional norms to evoke "otherness" (another time, another place), yet do it with "realistic" (albeit imaginary) specificity.

EX. 44-3   Modest Musorgsky, *Boris Godunov*, Coronation Scene, Boris's monologue

STALEMATE AND SUBVERSION

The most radically "realistic" harmonic effect of all is the one with which the scene opens, already quoted in Ex. 42-20 for comparison with Wagner's harmony. The stage direction specifies a "solemn peal of bells," and that is what the lengthy orchestral prelude depicts. It consists of just two chords, both of them describable in common-practice terms as dominant-sevenths with their roots on A♭ and D respectively. The common practice description is quite misleading, however, since neither of them ever resolves to the implied tonic (respectively D♭ and G). Nor, once their oscillation really gets going, do we even expect them to do so; for the oscillation emphasizes another relationship, namely their shared tritone (C and F♯/G♭). The two tritones, the one they share and the one their roots describe, arrest or neutralize their functional tendency.

It is not difficult to trace this progression, in concept, back to its source in Liszt's experiments with circles of major and minor thirds (see chapter 40). A tritone, after all, is equivalent to two minor thirds; Musorgsky's progression could be viewed as a sampling from the Lisztian one. As a matter of fact, Liszt's *Orpheus* (Symphonic Poem No. 4, 1854) begins with the very progression Musorgsky has borrowed: a dominant seventh on E♭, drawn out long by means of the "title character's" harp arpeggios, followed by one on A (Ex. 44-4). Liszt follows this opening pair, however, with another dominant seventh on C, as if splitting the difference between the opening pair, and maintaining a forward-moving harmonic drive.

EX. 44-4   Franz Liszt, *Orpheus*, opening

EX. 44-4 (continued)

Musorgsky's progression produces no motion forward, but a stalemate. He shapes the passage in which it occurs by rhythmic rather than harmonic means: at first by surface diminutions, then by doubling the harmonic rhythm, both of them devices actually copied from bell-ringing techniques. Then the whole thing is repeated with the position of the two chords reversed (but since they are functionally undifferentiated, their reversed positions make no difference to the character of the progression and can easily pass unnoticed by the listener). All he can do to bring the second passage to an end is drown it out with the heavy percussion. There is no possible functional cadence.

And that is why Musorgsky's progression, though much simpler in concept than the famous opening of *Tristan und Isolde*, was in fact far more subversive of tonal practice than Wagner's (just as Liszt's practice, as noted in chapter 42, was potentially more "radical" than his son-in-law's). However ingenious and sophisticated Wagner's usage (and there is no denying that Wagner gave his innovatory idea far more resourceful and sophisticated treatment than Musorgsky could hope to do), it remained within the system of functional relations. Musorgsky's was at the limits of the system, and perhaps beyond it. As we shall see in the chapters to come, younger Russian composers would build on Musorgsky's idea in such a way as to circumvent major/minor tonality altogether. In that way, Russia did succeed in "breaking free of Europe," and later exerting a satisfying counter-influence on "the West."

CRISIS

The complementary scene to the Coronation in *Boris Godunov* is the stark "Scene at St. Basil's Shrine" at the other end of the opera, in which Boris again confronts the crowd, but now a starving crowd that is no longer acclaiming him but cursing him and demanding bread. At the beginning of the scene they discuss the pretender's progress, and the anathema that is being pronounced on him inside the church on Red Square, where they have gathered. Then there is a bit of byplay for a group of boys tormenting a religious mendicant (called the *yurodivïy*, or Holy Fool), who croons a little song that degenerates into recitative as the accompanying harmony descends in a strange mudslide by semitones. The boys steal his penny. At this point Boris and his retinue come out of the church, and the *yurodivïy* confronts him, asking that he have the boys who vexed him killed, just like the tsarevich. When Boris has recoiled in horror and left the stage, the *yurodivïy* resumes his chaotic song, turning it into a lament for suffering Russia. The scene grinds to a baleful halt on an unprecedented unresolved dominant in the bass.

It is a searing moment, this scene of "speaking truth to power," and Musorgsky must surely have been counting on the audience to "read" it in terms of its subversive contemporary relevance. In its "thematization" of truth, the great cause for which realist art was prepared to sacrifice all beauty of form, the scene can be deemed an emblem of its moment in history, and Musorgsky did everything he could to accentuate its blunt primitiveness, which he regarded as the source of its power. Except for the *yurodivïy*'s song, which begins in the manner of a folk tune but dissolves into slime, and the choral song of supplication that greets the tsar, the whole scene is carried along in prose recitative, even the long choral "discussion" in which the various sections of the chorus confront and react to one another, and to the peasant Mityukha, whom they are questioning, like individual characters.

Boris's own role in the scene is very short but telling (Ex. 44-5). His manner of declamation has changed. All of his upbeats are now carried by eighth notes rather than quarters—a sure sign of prose setting, and a clue that the character's stature has been diminished. All in all, the Scene at St. Basil's Shrine, completed "during the night of May 21–22 1869" according to a note on the autograph vocal score, is the most extreme and concentrated dose of serious musical realism ever to be administered during the nineteenth century. But to say that is misleading, for the scene was never performed during Musorgsky's lifetime, nor published until 1926, two years before its public premiere. It was dropped in the course of revising the score in 1870–72, after the opera had been rejected for staging by the Russian imperial theaters.

The rejection might have been predicted, but it was not an ideological rejection. The review committee comprised musicians only, and the single reason given for turning the opera down was the lack of a prima donna role. It was easily supplied, since Pushkin had included some scenes showing the pretender's progress in Poland, where the Princess Marina Mniszek seduced him and co-opted his campaign at the behest of the Jesuits. Musorgsky expanded their "scene at the fountain" into the required love duet, and even added a scene in Marina's dressing room to give her a solo aria.

That made the opera more conventional, far less a "realist" manifesto. The legend has arisen that Musorgsky had to revise the opera against his will in order to make it palatable not only to musical but to political authorities. (It is a legend all the more readily believed in the twentieth century, when Russian artists were often forced to make highly publicized compromises with a totalitarian regime.) In fact, Musorgsky went so much further than required in his revisions that duress cannot account for them all. They went to the root of his dramatic and musical conception, something in which the bureaucrats vetting the libretto's content took little interest.

EX. 44-5 Modest Musorgsky, *Boris Godunov*, Scene at St. Basil's Shrine

In order to create the "Polish" scenes, Musorgsky had to add a great deal of his own to Pushkin's text. But then he went back and de-Pushkinized a great deal more. In particular he took out the Scene at St. Basil's Shrine, which followed Pushkin, and replaced it with another scene, with which he eventually ended the opera, in which the crowd is shown in active revolt against Boris—something far more potentially subversive than the deleted scene, and quite contrary to Pushkin's view of history. The only part of the original scene that survived was the episode of the *yurodivïy* and the boys, and the concluding song of woe, which now ends the entire opera (on the dominant!) to harrowing effect.

If the opera's revision is assumed to have been an ideological one, these facts are simply paradoxical. A more plausible explanation for the replacement is found in a letter the composer sent a friend in July 1870, while the opera was in limbo between submission and rejection. He had played it through for a select group of friends and sympathizers, and was disconcerted at its reception: "As regards the peasants in *Boris,*" he wrote, "some found them to be *bouffe*(!), while others saw tragedy." (The parenthetical exclamation point is the composer's.)[9]

In other words, the composer found that in the eyes—or rather, ears—of his audience, even a handpicked audience, prose recitative ineluctably spelled "comedy," its traditional medium, however tragic the actual content of the drama. Musorgsky's first impulse to revise his opera came not from the demands of the imperial theaters, but from his own private experience of communications-failure. It led him to reconsider his whole operatic technique, indeed his entire esthetic stance, with an eye toward clarifying the *genre* of the opera—that is, toward making decisive the contrast between what was "*bouffe*" and what was not, and generally toward elevating the tone of the opera to the level of tragedy, Shakespearean or otherwise. The lesson we may draw from his experience is that realism = comedy and comedy = realism, and that realism, like comedy, entails a lowering of tone. All of this, of course, is saying no more than what common sense already knows—that tragedy, like all beautiful or uplifting ("high") art, is a lie. Fully to disenchant or disillusion art in the name of literal or "scientific" truth risks destroying its power.

Thus the motivation for the most telling revision of all. In order to restore Tsar Boris to his full tragic dimension on the operatic stage, Musorgsky turned his back on all his prized theories and (as he put it in a letter to his best friend, the arts publicist Vladimir Stasov) "perpetrated" a traditional aria for the title character.[10] What in the original version had been a naturalistic recitative setting of Pushkin's counterpart to Shakespeare's great "Uneasy lies the head" soliloquy, cast amid a tissue of leitmotives, became after revision a lyrical outpouring in the grand manner, for which purpose Musorgsky borrowed a broad melody from an old abandoned opera project on the subject of Gustave Flaubert's "orientalist" novel *Salammbô,* and gave it a spacious development not only in the orchestra but in the voice as well.

CODES

Musorgsky's extremist realism was something that eventually had to be recoiled from because of its literalistic concept of truth—truth to empirical experience, to the conditions of daily life, without possibility of compromise. Art, the composer learned, lives in the compromise. It trades not in verbatim transcripts of existence but in metaphors. The Russian composer who understood this best was Chaikovsky. In *Eugene Onegin*, an opera based, like *Boris Godunov*, on a work by Pushkin, Chaikovsky created the other great monument of Russian realism in music.

But since the literary model in this case was not a Shakespearean historical drama but a novel of (almost) contemporary Russian society and mores, "monument" is not quite the right word. Its scale is small. Originally intended for performance by the Moscow Conservatory's opera workshop, it makes modest technical demands. Its remarkable emotional potency comes from its canny manipulation of symbols that interrelate genres of popular art with their associated social milieus. If Chaikovsky was the "great poet of everyday life," and "a genius of emotion," to quote two critical comments that have stuck to him, it was not because he alone found poetry in everyday life (every novelist does that) or because he was a genius at having emotions (we're all geniuses at that). It was because he knew how to channel life and emotion with great power and precision through coded conventional forms.

To describe him thus somewhat belies his reputation as a romantic artist, for romanticism distrusted conventions and sought to portray people (especially romantic artists) as uniquely free and spontaneous beings. Chaikovsky, as a realist, viewed people primarily in social contexts, as did Pushkin, and drew his power of expression from irony: that is, he took great delight in showing to what extent the emotions we subjectively experience as our own unique spontaneous experience are in fact mediated by social codes and standards of group behavior.

Pushkin's novel is famously short on plot. The title character, a dandy from the city, meets Tatyana, an openhearted country girl; she is smitten, he brushes her off; six years later he is smitten, she is married. There is also a subplot about the fop's friend, a country squire who dabbles in poetry and fancies himself a uniquely sensitive soul, and the country girl's sister, a shallow beauty with whom the poetaster is in love. Fop and friend fight a pointless duel over the sister and friend is (for no good reason) killed. It is the highpoint of the action in both novel and opera, but—another irony—it is only a distraction from the main concern, suggesting that the essence of life is not in dramatic events but in the small daily round, and that we learn to function happily in the social world not by giving our emotions free reign but by learning to sublimate them in conventional behavior. Once we have been successfully "socialized," our feelings are never entirely spontaneous but always mediated by the conventions and constraints, as often learned from literature as from "life," to which we have adapted. Therein lie both the tragedy (the constraints) and the salvation (the adaptation) of human society.

Chaikovsky embodied this worldly, unromantic but not unconsoling message in his opera by abstracting its musical idiom from the characteristic melodic and harmonic turns that identified the music of its time and place. In a book called *Musical*

Form as Process, the Russian musicologist Boris Asafyev coined the word "intonation" (*intonatsiya*) to denote these characteristic stylistic components. Linguists would call them "morphemes," minimal units that convey meaning within a conventional sign-system. Chaikovsky used these units to "sing" his opera in the musical language of its — *its*, not *his* — time. The period flavor that pervades the music becomes the carrier of Pushkin's novelistic irony.

The most conspicuous period "intonation" or morpheme in *Eugene Onegin* is the characteristic use of melodic sixths in shaping melodies, either as direct skips or as filled-in contours. The interval abounded in the so-called "household romance" (*bïtovoy romans*) of the 1830s and 1840s, songs composed not for the professional recital stage but for sale as sheet music for amateur performance at home. The outstanding composer of these sentimental popular songs at the time of *Eugene Onegin*'s action was Alexander Varlamov (1801–48). Ex. 44-6 contains two of his most famous melodies, one in the major, the other in the minor, with their constituent sixths bracketed for eventual comparison with Chaikovsky's music.

The first music sung in *Eugene Onegin* is an imitation Varlamov romance by Chaikovsky, sung offstage by Tatyana and her sister to an early lyric poem by Pushkin called "The Poet" (Ex. 44-7a). At the end of the verse it incorporates a reference to a tune already heard at the beginning of the opera's prelude (Ex. 44-7b), which will function throughout the drama as Tatyana's leitmotif. It, too, outlines a descending melodic sixth, showing the first stage of the interval's abstraction from its "natural habitat" in Varlamov (or imitation Varlamov) into the musical ambience that suffuses and symbolizes the lives of Chaikovsky's characters.

EX. 44-6A   Alexander Varlamov, *Krasnïy sarafan* (romance)

EX. 44-6B   Alexander Varlamov, *Na zarye ti eyo ne budi* (romance)

EX. 44-7A   Pyotr Ilyich Chaikovsky, *Eugene Onegin*, beginning of Act I (first verse of "Slikhal li vï" with sixths labeled)

EX. 44-7A (continued)

EX. 44-7A (continued)

TATIANA: Have you not heard the forest nightingale?
All through the night, he sang of love and sorrow;
when dawning light foretold a new tomorrow,
a shepherd's flute rehearsed his simple tale.
Have you not heard? Have you not heard?
Have you not heard? Have you not heard
the song that echoed in the dawn, the shepherd's tale?
Have you not heard? Have you not heard?
Have you not heard, have you not heard?

OLGA Have you not heard the forest nightingale?
He sang all night of love and sorrow;
when dawning light foretold a new tomorrow,
a shepherd's flute rehearsed his simple tale.
Have you not heard? Have you not heard?
Have you not heard? Have you not heard
the nightingale that sang his song
and in the dawn the shepherd's tale?
Have you not heard? Have you not heard?
Have you not heard, have you not heard?

EX. 44-7B Pyotr Ilyich Chaikovsky, *Eugene Onegin*, Tatyana's leitmotif

The full meaning of Chaikovsky's sixths is revealed when Tatyana has her most private and personal moment onstage, the so-called Letter Scene, in which she recklessly pours out her heart on paper to the object of her infatuation. One of the most extended arias in all of Russian opera, it is actually a string of four romances linked by recitatives:

1. *Puskai pogibnu ya* (Even if it means I perish): Allegro non troppo, D♭ major, $\frac{4}{4}$, da capo form (eighteen measures).

2. *Y ka vam pishu* (I'm writing you): Moderato assai quasi Andante, D minor, $\frac{4}{4}$, strophic form (fifty-six measures, including recits)

3. *Net, nikomu na svete ne otdala bĭ serdtse ya* (No, there is no one else on earth to whom I'd give my heart): Moderato, C major, $\frac{2}{4}$ (accompaniment in $\frac{6}{8}$), da capo form (eighty measures, including recits and transitions)

4. *Kto tĭ: moy angel-li khranitel'?* (Who art thou — my guardian angel?): Andante, D♭ major, $\frac{2}{4}$, da capo form (75 measures, 129 counting orchestral introduction and orchestral/vocal coda)

The resonances between the music of this scene and the duet-romance at the outset are many, conspicuous, and calculated: they are the resonances between Tatyana's inner and outer worlds. Both incorporate Tatyana's leitmotif (in the Letter Scene it comes in the middle of the last romance), but the leitmotif is already a bearer of a more generic resonance embodied in the melodic sixth. As Ex. 44-8 illustrates, the role of Tatyana (with that of Lensky, the doomed poetaster) is perhaps the "sixthiest" in all of opera.

In Ex. 44-8d, melodic sixths are nested within a harmonic idiom that displays a very telling "sixthiness" of its own: the constant use of the minor submediant (VI♭ or "flat sixth" in the major) as alternate harmonic root or tone center. As we have known since the time of Schubert, this alternation can take the form of an immediate local progression, as shown, or it can be projected in the form of a subsidiary key governing

EX. 44-8A   Pyotr Ilyich Chaikovsky, *Eugene Onegin*, sixths in Tatyana's letter scene, beginning of first romance

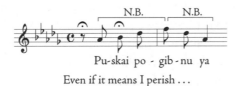

Pu-skai po - gib-nu ya

Even if it means I perish . . .

EX. 44-8B   Tatyana's letter scene, second romance, beginning of second strophe

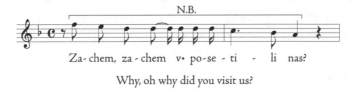

Za- chem, za - chem v• po-se - ti - li nas?

Why, oh why did you visit us?

EX. 44-8C   Tatyana's letter scene, beginning of third romance

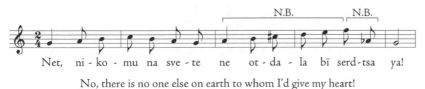

Net,   ni - ko - mu na sve-te   ne   ot - da - la bĭ serd-tsa   ya!

No, there is no one else on earth to whom I'd give my heart!

EX. 44-8D Tatyana's letter scene, introduction to fourth romance

large spans within the tonal structure. The orchestral prelude to act I of *Eugene Onegin* sets the precedent: its development section is all within the key of the submediant, which resolves to the dominant by way of "retransition" through a portentous descending semitone in the bass. In the Letter Scene, the whole vocal coda (*Konchayu! strashno perechest'*, "Finished! I dare not reread") is cast within the key of the starred chord in Ex. 44-8d, spelled enharmonically as A major.

The melodic-harmonic idiom is only one of many genre resonances that tie Tatyana's Letter Scene to the opening duet and thence to the whole sentimental world of the Russian romance. The harp-heavy orchestration of the first two sections is another. But the harp does more than evoke the sounds of domestic music-making. The harp chords that punctuate the woodwind phrases in Ex. 44-9, the actual letter-writing ritornello (at the ends of mm. 2, 4, 6, and 8), take their place within a marvelously detailed sound-portrait of the lovesick girl, in which Chaikovsky shows himself an adept practitioner of Mozart's methods of "body portraiture"—the realism of an earlier day—as outlined in the famous letter from Mozart to his father about *Die Entführung aus dem Serail*, quoted in chapter 28. As in the case of Mozart's Belmonte or Osmin, we "see" and "feel" Tatyana—her movements, her breathing, her heartbeat—in her music. This iconicity shows off music's advantages especially well: what the novelist or poet must describe, the composer (unlike the dramatist, who must depend on the director and the cast) can actually present.

And yet the use of the romance idiom signifies even more than we have noted up to now. It is more than just evocative. It also sets limits on scale—both the formal scale of the aria and the emotional scale of the character. However touching her portrait, Tatyana remains (like all the characters in the opera) the denizen of a realistic novel, not a historical spectacle or a "well-made" romantic drama. Compared with Chaikovsky's grander operas, or even with *Boris Godunov* in its revised form, *Eugene Onegin* exemplifies to excellent advantage the special late-nineteenth-century wedding of melancholy or poignant content and comic form.

EX. 44-9 Pyotr Ilyich Chaikovsky, *Eugene Onegin*, letter scene, "writing music"

LYRIC DRAMA

The closest parallels and antecedents to *Eugene Onegin* can be found in France, where a new genre — sometimes rather redundantly called *opéra lyrique* (or *drame lyrique*) after its bastion, the Paris Théâtre Lyrique (opened 1852) — had arisen in more or less conscious opposition to the bloated *grand opéra*, or at least as an alternative to the latter and a challenge to its proud status as the national opera of the French. The Théâtre Lyrique's showpieces were two operas by the prolific Charles-François Gounod (1818–93): *Faust* (1859), after Goethe's famous dramatic poem, and *Roméo et Juliette* (1867) after Shakespeare. As exemplified by Gounod, the genre could be described as a hybrid that retained the accompanied recitatives of the grand opera (albeit tuneful ones), but that cut the musical forms (and, consequently, the characters who express themselves through them) down to comic-opera size. The musical emphasis, like Chaikovsky's, is on characterization through attractive melody reminiscent of "domestic romances" and ballroom dances, rather than impressive musico-dramatic structures.

Thus unlike Boito, whose fame as Verdi's late literary collaborator has eclipsed his reputation as a composer, Gounod made little attempt to embody the metaphysical content of Goethe's poem in his Faust opera. Its character as a religious drama of

FIG. 44-4   The French bass Pol Plançon (1851–1914) as Méphistophélès in Gounod's *Faust*, a role with which he was particularly associated.

redemption through love is surely respected, but the accent is placed not on the "message" but rather on the emotional lives of the leading man and leading lady. There is no lofty Prologue in Heaven, and Gounod's very unsatanic Méphistophélès is for the most part reduced to a merry puppet master who sings in an appropriately swaggering opera buffa style: his strophic "Calf of Gold" aria in jig time, one of the opera's most popular numbers, is a drinking song in everything but name. The comedization or "lowering" of the role is entirely calculated, and a well-aimed slap at German pretension.

That has not prevented many critics, in thrall to German thinking in its "historicist" phase, from excoriating Gounod for "popularizing" (that is, trivializing) a great play. For Joseph Kerman, Gounod's opera was, "as Wagner observed, the classic case" illustrating the threat an unworthy opera can level at a literary masterpiece. "Goethe's play has given us an adjective, 'Faustian,'" he wrote, "but the world in which the Faustian spirit strives is entirely dissipated by Gounod's pastel timidities."[11] The suggestion that the dissipation in question was unintended surely misses the point of *opéra lyrique*.

Pastel shades will not be thought amiss in *Roméo et Juliette*, and the same expert muting of Goethe and Shakespeare can be observed in the work of Gounod's slightly older contemporary Ambroise Thomas (1811–96), whose most successful operas were *Mignon* (1866), after Goethe's romantic novel *Wilhelm Meisters Lehrjahre*, and *Hamlet* (1868), written in collaboration with the same team of librettists (Michel Carré and Jules Barbier) as Gounod's *Faust*. Thomas's *Hamlet* ends (timidly? audaciously?) not with the title character's death but with his victory and coronation.

Gounod's and Thomas's heir in the next generation was Jules Massenet (1842–1912), who combined the techniques of *drame lyrique* with the more contemporary and realistic subject matter favored by Bizet, Chaikovsky, and others of his generation. He, too, paid his respects to Goethe (*Werther*, 1892), but his most enduring contribution is *Manon* (1884), after an eighteenth-century novel about rapturous but ultimately disastrous illicit love, *L'histoire du chevalier des Grieux et de Manon Lescaut* (1731) by Antoine-François Prévost d'Exiles, known as Abbé Prévost. Under cover of a period setting, the opera treats its subject with a frankness that surpassed that of *La traviata*, prefiguring the naturalism (or verismo) that soon radiated from Italy throughout the world of opera. (In fact the same novel furnished the subject for the first significant opera by Giacomo Puccini, whose works will come into focus at the end of this chapter.)

Even more at seeming variance with its comic form was the stark horror at the core of Bizet's *Carmen* (1875), after a luridly naturalistic novella of seduction and murder by Prosper Mérimée (1803–70). It was composed, originally with spoken dialogue, for performance at the Théâtre National de l'Opéra Comique, a "family theater" whose codirector, Adolphe de Leuven, resigned rather than present an opera that culminated in a brutal "crime of passion" in which the tenor stabs the soprano in full view of the audience. Some comedy! Even the music gave offense to some, because the popular genres on which its music was based were not those of good French homes, but of vagabonds, gypsies, and others thought socially undesirable.

But of course what gave offense to some was powerfully alluring to others. As the title character's famous *couplets* or strophic song in the form of a Habanera shows (see Ex. 39-8), Bizet's opera drew the connection more strongly than ever between "orientalism"—the musical evocation of what from the audience's perspective were essentially alien or forbidden beings (in this case gypsy girls who worked in a cigarette factory, an only slightly camouflaged "house of ill repute")—and forthright sex appeal. The Habanera (literally, "Havana song") was a Cuban import of supposedly Negro origins. Bizet's was a "found object": a song (*El arreglito*) by Sebastián Yradier (1809–65), a Spanish composer who claimed to have collected it on location, leading Bizet to believe it was a folk song. As we may remember from chapter 39, its descending chromatic scale was a badge worn by "oriental" femmes fatales all over Europe. One could hardly spell things out more plainly than Carmen does in her refrain: "If I say I love you, watch out!"

In the end, of course, "morality" wins out (and so the opera, for all its brutality and sexuality, has become a family favorite after all). The seductress is killed by her prey, exacting society's revenge. The music powerfully endorses his act, even as it had formerly intensified her dangerous appeal. Nowadays it is as easy to question the justice of the plot's horrific resolution as it is difficult to resist the music's blandishments. As in *Manon* and *La traviata*, a woman whose allure has led a man astray pays with her

FIG. 44-5   Georges Bizet in 1874.

FIG. 44-6   Set and costume sketch by Émile Bertin for the last scene in the original production of Bizet's *Carmen*.

life. The difference lies in the unflinching portrayal of allure and vengeance alike. Unlike Verdi's Violetta or Manon, Carmen has no "heart of gold"; and she meets a much more violent end.

Bizet's achievement is almost universally regarded as greater than Massenet's. But here is a disquieting thought: does his greater achievement lie in the greater power of his music to subvert? And are there not two subversions: the one by which Don José, a good soldier, is degraded by a sexual obsession set in motion by the Habanera, and the one by which we spectators are finally led to cheer his crime? Both moments in the opera pose old questions — what is the relationship between esthetics and ethics? what should it be? — with new potency.

In all of these effects the music is aided by its colorful popular or "vernacular" base, and, paradoxically, by the comic style, which speeds action and objectifies moments of passion. The most insightful comment on the opera's power, and (implicitly) on the problems it raises, came from Friedrich Nietzsche, the German philosopher, who saw in its cleanly articulated forms and dance rhythms a liberation from the Wagnerian spell. It embodied in its pleasant forms a bitterly ironic truth (a "tragic joke"), which Nietzsche located with wonderful precision in the opera's very last line, in which the full horror of the situation is expressed in a beautifully lyrical phrase heavily redolent of popular song (Ex. 44-10):

This music seems perfect to me . . . . It is precise. It builds, organizes, finishes: thus it constitutes the opposite of the "infinite melody." Have more painful tragic accents ever been heard on the stage? How are they achieved? Without grimaces . . . . Love is translated back into nature. Love as fate, cynical, innocent, cruel, and at bottom the deadly hatred of the sexes! I know no case where the tragic joke that constitutes the essence of love is expressed so strictly, translated with equal terror into a formula, as in Don José's last cry, which concludes the work — *"Yes, I have killed her/my adored Carmen!"*[12]

EX. 44-10   Georges Bizet, *Carmen*, Don José's last line

DON JOSÉ: I have killed my own love!
I killed the one I love! She is dead!
Oh my Carmen, how I loved you!

SATYR PLAYS

Thus in Wagner's wake, as German opera became ever more apocalyptic (on the way to *Götterdämmerung*), and as grand opera became ever grander (on the way to *Don Carlos* and *Aida*), a contrarian strain began to appear: an opera that cut things down to size in pursuit of human (that is, personal) truth. The inevitable byproduct was a newly farcical and satiric breed of comic opera in which the symbolic butt of humor was opera itself. In a way this was a throwback to the very origins of comic opera, the intermezzi that had functioned as "satyr plays" between the acts of courtly extravaganzas. But the new genre consisted of full-length pieces (albeit modest ones) pitched at a bourgeois public that tended to find opera at once sublime and ridiculous. Giving an outlet to the tendency to mock the genre's ridiculous side — that is, its pretensions — the new genre actually protected the sublimity of the prototype.

The man who crystallized the new genre was Jacques (originally Jacob) Offenbach (1819–80), a German-born Jew whose father, a synagogue cantor, had brought him to Paris at the age of fourteen to perfect his technique as a virtuoso cellist. After some years spent conducting at various Paris theaters he began producing one-act farces, which he first called by the ordinary name *opéras comiques*. Beginning in 1855, he started dubbing them *opérettes*, a term that seems to have been coined by Louis August Joseph Florimond Ronger (1825–92), called Hervé, an organist and singer who in the early 1840s began producing one-act *vaudevilles-opérettes* and *parodies-opérettes* in little boulevard theaters. The term simply means "little opera," but it stuck to the Hervé-Offenbach genre and came to designate its special brand of frivolous buffoonery.

Offenbach himself reserved the term *opérette* for the one-act type. When he began writing full-evening works he called them *opéra bouffe* (a term that Musorgsky knew, as we have learned from his letter about the "peasants" in *Boris*). As the genre spread to central Europe (particularly Vienna) and England, however, the word operetta served to designate longer works as well. What they all had in common was the compulsion to josh opera, the genre on which operetta was parasitic.

FIG. 44-7　A caricature of Jacques Offenbach surrounded by characters from his three greatest hits: *Orpheus in the Underworld* (1858; revised 1874), *Fair Helen* (1864), and *The Grand Duchess of Gérolstein* (1867).

Out of the ninety-eight *opérettes* or *opéras bouffes* that Offenbach churned out in the course of his thirty-three-year career, one stands out as emblematic of the whole genre: *Orphée aux enfers* ("Orpheus in Hades"), his first two-act show, produced in 1858 at Offenbach's own theater, the *Bouffes-Parisiens*, and later (1874) expanded into a four-act extravaganza. Together with *La belle Hélène* ("Fair Helen of Troy"; 1864), it was his wildest success. The two of them, in their very titles, show to what an extent operetta relied on opera for its basic plots and situations, however twisted in the retelling.

Orpheus was present, we may recall, at the very creation of opera. Several of the earliest *favole in musica*, the "musical tales" that adorned north Italian court festivities in the early seventeenth century, were based on his myth, including Monteverdi's masterpiece (examined in detail in chapter 20). The Orpheus myth was a myth of music's ethical power, the supreme article of faith for all serious musicians. Since Monteverdi's time it had been revived, most famously by Gluck (see chapter 28), whenever the need was seen to reassert high musical ideals against frivolous entertainment values.

So there could scarcely have been a more calculated slap at sanctimony (or a more deliberate middle-class slap at aristocratic taste) than an Orpheus opera that was all frivolous excess, asserted in the teeth of high artistic ideals. In Offenbach's version, Orpheus is a hack violinist whose wife, Eurydice, cannot stand either his music or his dreary personality. She prefers a neighbor, the farmer Aristaeus. To remove his rival from the scene, Orpheus plants snakes in the farmer's field, but of course it is his wife who gets bitten. Aristaeus reveals himself to be Pluto in disguise. He takes Eurydice, now delighted to be dying, down with him to reign over the underworld. Good riddance, thinks Orpheus, until a character called Public Opinion (standing in for the Greek chorus) comes onstage to persuade him that for the sake of appearances he'd better try and rescue his wife.

In the middle acts there is a subplot involving Jupiter and his attempt, in the guise of a fly, to seduce Eurydice. The traditional story is resumed in the fourth act, which also contains the broadest musical satire. It opens on a Bacchanale, a feast in honor of the god of wine, in the midst of which Orpheus comes to claim Eurydice. Pluto, only too happy to be rid of her (for she has been behaving toward him just as shrewishly as she had toward Orpheus in act I) lets her go with the standard proviso (the reason for which Pluto says he has forgotten) that Orpheus not look around at her until they have reached the opposite shore of the river Styx. When it looks as though, egged on by Pluto, Orpheus will succeed, Jupiter hurls a thunderbolt at Orpheus's rear end, causing him involuntarily to turn around. Eurydice is lost to him — and to Pluto as well, as Jupiter transforms her (to her renewed delight) into a Bacchante, a priestess of Bacchus the wine god.

The end of the opera contains the most famous music. At the height of the Bacchanale, Jupiter calls for "a dainty minuet, as in the days of the Sun King." After a couple of minutes' minuetting, though, the ballroom explodes spontaneously into what the assembled gods call a "galop infernale," but which the audience could not help recognizing as a cancan. The fastest of all polka- or quadrille-type ballroom dances, it had come to France from North Africa in the 1830s and had by the 1850s migrated from the ballroom to the dance hall, where lines of girls entertained men with their high kicking and splits, both of them excuses for the display of frilly bloomers and bare legs.

After the cancan, Orpheus approaches, fiddling the familiar strains of Gluck's chaste aria of lament "Che farò senza Euridice," at the sound of which Eurydice runs for cover. The finale consists of Eurydice's glum submission to Public Opinion, who is heard giving Orpheus his final marching orders, a choral commiseration at the unhappy spouses' reunion, the thunderbolt in the rear (to — what else? — a Meyerbeerian diminished-seventh chord), and Eurydice's song of delight at her new status as Bacchante (and, it goes without saying, novice concubine to Jupiter). This last, preceded by a stunning roulade up to high E, is a reprise of the cancan in which all join in (Ex. 44-11). The curtain, as almost always in an operetta, falls on a general dance. It is that final dance frenzy — the predestined victory of mindless celebration — that validates operetta's claim as the ultimate escapist entertainment of its day. Like the earlier music trances of Schubert they envelop the audience — but in orgiastic exuberance rather than "inward" contemplation. The calculated licentiousness and feigned sacrilege, which successfully baited the stuffier critics, were recognized by all for what they were — a social palliative, the very opposite of social criticism. That is why, in an age when serious art was seriously policed (and nowhere more so than in the France of the despotic if affluent "Second Empire"), the cynical operetta could seemingly get away with anything. The spectacle of the Olympian gods doing the cancan threatened nobody's dignity; all it "said" was that as long as times were good, nobody cared who did what. That is hardly satire, as classically defined. It communicated tolerance, not resentment, of vice.

EX. 44-11 Jacques Offenbach, *Orphée aux enfers*, Finale

EX. 44-11   (*continued*)

rit. Au bon-heur sur terre, As-pire à toi, di_vin Bac-chus! Re-çois la prè-tres-se, Dont la voix sans ces-se Veut chan-ter l'i-vres-se A tes é-lus!

Even in Russia this was true. The only exception the tsarist autocracy ever made to its monopoly on theaters was for the sake of operetta, deemed a useful public diversion at a time of mounting civic strife. During the 1870s, two private establishments were set up to regale St. Petersburgers with the latest amusements from Paris. The larger of them, the *Teatr-buff* (that is, *Théâtre bouffe*) was able to import productions direct from Paris with the original casts. The protests came only from "thinking realists," puritanical radicals who were out to change society and did not want it to be diverted. Prince Pyotr Kropotkin, the utopian anarchist, recoiled in horror from what he called the "putrid Offenbachian current" that was "infecting all of Europe" and taking people's minds off social problems.[13] Musorgsky, surprisingly enough, was an enthusiastic attender — or maybe not so surprisingly: in the Russian context the *Teatr-buff*, as the only theater that was not state-supported, had an antiestablishment cachet that it did not have in Paris.

At any rate, operetta never took hold in Russia as a homegrown thing. Its next great arena was Vienna. And in keeping with its strong association with social dance, it was fitting that its main protagonist there should have been Johann Strauss II (1825–99), the so-called Waltz King, who as the "k.k. Hofballmusikdirektor" (music director of the royal court balls) had long led the city's foremost dance orchestra.

Just as Offenbach had a forerunner in Hervé, Strauss had one in Franz von Suppé (1819–95), who — in one of those multiethnic tours de force only possible in the polyglot Austro-Hungarian empire — was born in what is now Croatia to a Belgian father and a Czech-Polish mother, and grew up speaking Italian. Suppé was a theatrical professional: that is, he was hired by Vienna's Theater an der Wien at the age of twenty-five (after ten years of flute-playing in pit orchestras) both to conduct and to furnish overtures and arias on demand for singspiels and farces. (One of the overtures from this period, to a play called *Dichter und Bauer* — in English, Poet and Peasant — became a favorite concert curtain-raiser). In the 1850s he began imitating Offenbach's one-acters, and beginning in 1860 produced "true" Viennese operettas, in the sense that the libretti were not mere adaptations from the French. Again, one — *Leichte Kavallerie* ("Light cavalry"), 1866 — bequeathed its overture to the concert repertoire, and a couple of Suppé's later scores enjoyed good runs — especially *Die schöne Galathee* ("Beautiful Galatea"; 1865), an obvious knock-off from Offenbach's *La belle Hélène*.

But the Waltz King put him in the shade. Strauss's third "komische Operette," *Die Fledermaus* ("The bat", 1874), composed when he was almost fifty, established him as Offenbach's only viable rival. Its libretto was adapted from a play by the very team, Henri Meilhac and Ludovic Halévy, who were responsible for Offenbach's own *Belle Hélène* (and Bizet's *Carmen* besides). But *Die Fledermaus* does not even pay lip service to social satire. It is a domestic farce about a rich husband and wife who each try to deceive the other and who find each other out at the end. Minor hypocrisies and lighthearted marital infidelities, it is assumed, are simply the way of the world and the only thing to do is wink.

The only real lampoonery is directed, predictably, not at morals but at music. The wife's lover, a tenor, is mistaken for the husband and arrested on an old misdemeanor charge. At the beginning of act III, before all the characters converge on the jail where the plot's tangles are to be sorted out, the tenor's real misdemeanors are committed, when his voice is heard from offstage warbling snatches of his favorite arias (all in Italian, including the one by Wagner). The drunken jailer, overhearing, garbles them all ("La donna è mobile" comes out "Die Donau a Moperle," "The Danube at Moperle," etc.).

The second act, set at a ball given by Orlofsky, a Russian prince, contains more operatic spoofing. Casting the prince, a young rake hopelessly jaded by wealth, as a contralto in trousers was an in-joke for older operagoers who could remember the heroic "musico" roles in Rossini; but the *travesti* role is now more epicene than valiant, in keeping with more modern (that is, "realistic") gender stereotypes. This is the act that reaches its climax in the vertiginous dance without which no operetta was complete. Of course it is a waltz, which screamed "Vienna!" as loudly as the cancan yelled "Paris!" By this time Strauss was no longer writing actual ballroom waltzes, but this one is put together no differently from his famous dance hits such as *An der schönen, blauen Donau* ("The blue Danube"), op. 314 (1867), or *Geschichten aus dem Wienerwald* ("Tales from the Vienna woods"), op. 325 (1868), to name two of the most famous. (Strauss's opus numbers reached almost 500.) As the "Fledermaus Waltz" (arranged by others), the act II finale lived a life of its own in the dance hall, and was also the featured tune in the operetta's overture.

A "Strauss waltz" was actually a string or medley of waltzes (frequently equipped with an evocative slower introduction for concert purposes) in which the first often functions as a refrain. That format ideally suited the structure of the *Fledermaus* finale, in which a flirtation (between husband and disguised wife, it later turns out) is carried on during the episodes, against a background of general festivity represented by the main waltz tune and especially its second strain ("Ha, welch ein Fest"; "Oh, what a party"). The lines with which the guests react when the band strikes up the waltz could serve as the motto of the operetta genre: "Ja, ja, ein wirbelnder Tanz/Erhöht des Festes Glanz!" (Ah yes, a whirling dance, just the thing to bring diversion to its peak). As in Offenbach's infernal dance, the curtain music jacks things up even further with an abrupt transition from waltz to galop.

It is often claimed that operetta was an unimportant genre in music history (as opposed to social history) because it did not contribute to the evolution of musical style. The historicist bias implicit in that view (and the likely impoverishment of a music history that excludes social history) will be apparent to readers of this book, but in any case the work of Johann Strauss refutes it. There is one stylistic idiosyncrasy in particular that went from him into the general idiom of European (or European-style) music, and that is the freedom with which the sixth degree of the scale is harmonized, appearing as a functional consonance both within the dominant (where it adds a ninth to the chord) and against the tonic (where it is usually described simply as an "added sixth"). The familiar opening strain of the "Blue Danube" waltz supplies perhaps the classic illustration, one that many readers will be able to summon to memory without even looking at Ex. 44-12.

EX. 44-12   Johann Strauss, opening strain of the "Blue Danube" Waltz

The "Fledermaus Waltz" also contains many examples. The "V_9" occurs at the very first chord change (Ex. 44-13a), and the striking second phrase of the big choral refrain (on the highly charged line, "Liebe und Wein gibt uns Seligkeit!"; "Love and wine grant us bliss!") place dominant after tonic beneath a repeated sixth degree (Ex. 44-13b). That mild "liberated dissonance" gives a sense of the rush the text evokes; it is a musical stimulant. Most graphically of all, and proof of the composer's self-consciousness in its use, when the chiming clock briefly interrupts the festivities with a jolt, it is represented by that very sixth degree (Ex. 44-13c), acting as a modulatory pivot (which of course implies its functional consonance).

EX. 44-13A   Johann Strauss, *Die Fledermaus*, Act II Waltz Finale, ritornello

EX. 44-13B   Johann Strauss, *Die Fledermaus*, Act II Waltz Finale, "What a party!"

EX. 44-13B (*continued*)

EX. 44-13C   Johann Strauss, *Die Fledermaus*, Act II Waltz Finale (the chiming clock is heard)

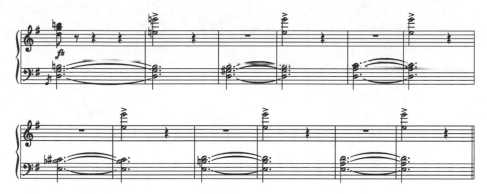

OPERETTA AND ITS DISCONTENTS

It was in order to make up a double bill with *La Périchole*, one of the later operettas of Offenbach, that a London theater manager, Richard D'Oyly Carte, commissioned a tiny one-acter from Arthur Sullivan (1842–1900), a graduate of the Leipzig Conservatory who was then serving as principal of a newly opened music academy called the National Training School (now the Royal College of Music). The libretto was by William S. Gilbert (1836–1911), then a staff writer for *Fun*, the Victorian equivalent of *Mad* magazine, who specialized in skits that burlesqued standard operas of the day.

Gilbert and Sullivan had already collaborated several years earlier, quite unmemorably, on an Offenbach-style comedy called *Thespis; or, the Gods Grown Old*, and had given no thought to future collaborations. *Trial by Jury* (1875), the result of their chance commission from D'Oyly Carte, marked the beginning of the most stable and successful operetta team in the history of the genre. Most unusually (and uniquely for Gilbert and Sullivan), this half-hour farce about a jilted bride's lawsuit, an outrageously biased jury, and an incompetent judge was a through-composed work, with recitatives instead of spoken dialogue, and was conceived frankly as a spoof of Italian opera. The most

FIG. 44-8   Poster for the New York premiere of Gilbert and Sullivan's *Pirates of Penzance*.

elaborate number, "A Nice Dilemma," is a very skillful caricature of a Donizettian *largo concertato*, the sort of showpiece ensemble described in chapter 33.

With *The Sorcerer* (1877) the pair hit their stride, producing the first of eleven two-act operettas (plus one in three) with spoken dialogue, and with *HMS Pinafore; or, The Lass That Loved a Sailor* they achieved an unprecedented hit for an English operetta — indeed for an English work of any kind since Handel's day. So successful was the steady stream of operettas they produced over the next dozen years that D'Oyly Carte built a special theater, the Savoy, to maintain the whole Gilbert and Sullivan canon in repertory. Its patent on the "Savoy operas" lasted until 1961, canonizing not only the repertory but also its traditions of performance in a fashion that Gilbert and Sullivan would no doubt have taken delight in spoofing had they lived to see it.

Both *The Sorcerer* and *HMS Pinafore* continued the manner established in *Trial by Jury* of aiming pointed barbs at specific operatic (and not only operatic) targets. The most conspicuous object of parody in the former, predictably enough, was Weber's *Freischütz*. In the latter, the basic premise — mistaken identity due to an exchange of babies by a befuddled nanny — was borrowed from the much-ridiculed libretto of Verdi's *Il trovatore*. The occasional accompanied recitatives in *Pinafore* exaggerated the mannerisms of Handel's oratorios, and the elopement scene alluded to in its subtitle took off on the one in Rossini's *Barber of Seville*.

Pinafore's popularity bridged the Atlantic Ocean, which actually made a problem for Gilbert and Sullivan when American companies began "pirating" it — that is, performing it without authorization from the publisher and without paying royalties.

They retaliated by mocking the marauders with an operetta called *The Pirates of Penzance* (the American equivalent might be *The Pirates of Coney Island*), and opened it in New York to establish copyright there. *The Pirates* contains Gilbert and Sullivan's most specifically directed operatic spoofing.

Il trovatore comes in for another round of friendly abuse, with a crashing parody of its "Anvil Chorus" sung as the pirates purportedly sneak noiselessly onstage ("With Catlike Tread"). The situation, too, joshes *Trovatore*, which contains an abduction scene in which a chorus of hidden warriors actually sing about their silence. The part of the tune that is actually closest to the Verdian model has become independently popular as "Hail, Hail, the Gang's All Here," a song that has long been propagated in oral tradition throughout the English-speaking world (Ex. 44-14a). In addition, the ingenue soprano, Mabel, sings a lilting waltz song modeled on those found in contemporary French "drames lyriques" like the famous ones in Gounod's *Faust* (Ex. 44-14b).

The pièce de résistance, however, is the so-called Chorus of Policemen, summoned by Mabel and her father the Major-General to capture the pirates. It is actually a

EX. 44-14A   Giuseppe Verdi, "Anvil Chorus" (*Il trovatore*, Act II) / Sir Arthur Sullivan, *The Pirates of Penzance*, "Come, friends who plow the sea"

EX. 44-14B   Charles Gounod, "Faites lui mes aveux" (*Faust*, Act II) / Sir Arthur Sullivan, *The Pirates of Penzance* "Poor wand'ring one"

more complicated number than its title would suggest. Besides sporting solos for three characters, it is the first Sullivanian "double chorus" of a kind that became a standard feature in the Savoy operas. (Its most relevant antecedent was a double aria for the two blind title characters in Offenbach's *Les deux aveugles*, but Offenbach himself had a famous precedent in Berlioz's "dramatic symphony," *The Damnation of Faust*, which Sullivan certainly knew.) First there is a chorus sung by one sex (in this case the policemen); then there is an ostensibly contrasting chorus sung by the opposite sex (in this case the Major-General's numerous daughters); and finally there is their unexpected (but of course eventually not only expected but eagerly anticipated) contrapuntal montage. The policemen confess their reluctance to expose themselves to danger; the maidens vainly seek to raise their morale with a promise of posthumous fame. The ensuing impasse produces a common operatic situation: the "extended exit" in which the action about which all are singing is impeded by the singing itself. (Again, the classic prototype is found in *Il trovatore*: Manrico's famous cabaletta "Di quella pira," in which an urgent mission of rescue is delayed for the sake of his high Cs.) The maidens sing, "Go!" The police sing "We go!" The Major-General, somehow standing outside the music and observing its contradiction of the action, sings "Yes, but you don't go!"

Ten years later, at the other end of Europe, César Cui—in an extended, quite humorless essay on the superiority of Russian opera, with its scrupulous realism, to the common run—pointed, among other things, to "choruses that shout *corriam, corriam* [let's run, let's run] but never budge an inch."[14] The difference was that only Cui seriously thought that such choruses could be dispensed with—or rather, that the distinction between "real" and "musical" time could be erased. Only Cui thought that renouncing the distinction between the "heard" and "unheard" music of an opera—the music the characters hear as music and the music only the audience hears as such—would be progress. By having his Major-General fail to make this distinction, Sullivan parodied not so much the failure of composers as the failure of obtuse listeners who cannot reconcile themselves to the most crucial of all operatic conventions.

Thus there are two ways (at least) to mock a convention. One can do it like Cui, with an eye toward its abolition; or one can do it like Sullivan, as a wry acknowledgement of its value. Cui's implication is that excessive indulgence of musical values can rob opera of its dramatic viability. Sullivan's is that excessively literalistic attention to dramatic values can rob opera of its raison d'être, its very reason for existence.

Finally it comes down to one's attitude toward the status quo, "the way things are"—a matter that goes far beyond the esthetic. In a startlingly rancorous critique of Gilbert and Sullivan, the English philosopher Michael Tanner, writing in 1991, protested the continuing popularity of their work after a century's heavy use, accusing them of practicing and perpetuating "that fatally English device of flattering an audience into a sense of complacency by presenting what they take to be satire but is actually no more than affectionate endorsement of the status quo, shown in all its lovable absurdity."[15] Their seeming mockery of the British class system, of nepotism, of gender inequality, or whatever else they seemed to oppose, in Tanner's view, was in fact a covert preservative.

There is no denying it. But it is not a peculiarly English vice. It is typical of art in any stable and affluent period of social history, when established authority and power are sufficiently secure to condone, and even encourage as a social steam valve, a certain amount of friendly caricature, which only encourages toleration of the inequities or abuses it exposes. Precisely the same was true of Offenbach and Strauss. In Offenbach's case the matter was a little poignant, in fact. There were always a few critics around who were sufficiently lacking in humor to take his cynicism for serious subversion, or at least for liberalism; he throve on their abuse. But as soon as the society he ostensibly mocked was overthrown (in the aftermath of the disastrous 1870 war with Prussia) and replaced by a more liberal régime, Offenbach's irreverence no longer seemed amusing. He declared bankruptcy in 1875, the very year in which defeated France accepted a republican constitution.

Victorian England underwent no such upheaval. Economically it went from strength to strength; the optimism of its social elite knew no bounds; and the popularity of Gilbert and Sullivan reflected that cheerful mood. Their work can seem, in its combination of surface reformism with underlying conformism, something like a classic expression of "Victorianism." Perhaps its most telling symbolic manifestation was the way in which Gilbert and Sullivan eventually began burlesquing not only the foibles of the upper classes (and of standard opera), but even their own mannerisms as endearingly absurd institutions to be teased indulgently.

Take the "patter song" for example, which the *New Grove Dictionary* aptly defines as "a comic song in which the humor derives from having the greatest number of words uttered in the shortest possible time."[16] It is usually sung in Savoy operas by the "comic baritone," a stereotyped role that is usually marked by pompous ineptitude and/or lechery. In *The Pirates of Penzance* that role is filled by the Major-General, whose patter song, "I Am the Very Model of a Modern Major-General," a list of all the superfluous intellectual baggage he carries around in place of military expertise, is the archetype of the genre. Its only rival is "When You're Lying Awake," the Lord Chancellor's virtuosically ridiculous recitation of a trivial nightmare in *Iolanthe* (1882).

Patter songs were in themselves parodies of a standard *opera buffa* technique that went all the way back to Pergolesi and his contemporaries, and that technique was itself a parody, translating the virtuosity of *opera seria* coloratura into the virtuosity of speedy enunciation, chiefly for bumbling basses at the opposite end of the spectrum, both in range and in moral character, from the male and female sopranos who sang the heroic leads. So when, in *Ruddigore* (1887), Gilbert and Sullivan parodied their own patter songs in a patter ensemble, it was a parody of a parody of a parody.

It takes the form of a trio in which the male lead, Robin Oakapple (or as he is also known, Sir Ruthven Murgatroyd), is encouraged by the comic baritone (Sir Despard Murgatroyd) and his sister the contralto (Mad Margaret, whose first entrance had already parodied the Mad Scene from *Lucia di Lammermoor*) to solve the dilemma on which the plot turns — and which we need not go into here, for reasons expressed by Sir Despard (and then the rest) at the end of the trio: "This particularly rapid unintelligible patter isn't generally heard, and if it is it doesn't matter"(Ex. 44-15).

EX. 44-15   Sir Arthur Sullivan, *Ruddigore*, Act II, "Matter" Trio ("My eyes are fully open")

It was a mark of the increasing specialization of composerly types and roles that set in during the latter half of the nineteenth century that there should have appeared specialist composers even for lightweight and "applied" genres like ballroom waltzes and operettas. Hardly any composer of the period could vie with, say, Mozart in versatility (or "universality"). Where Mozart was equally equipped, and equally valued, for writing operas (both comic and tragic), concertos, chamber music, and ballroom music, few of the great figures living a hundred years later could contribute to all of these genres.

The idea of symphonic music by Verdi or chamber music by Wagner is as bizarre as the idea of an opera by Bruckner or Brahms, two of the "symphonists" we shall meet in the coming chapters. And none of these composers ever wrote for the ballroom. The most universal composers of the period were probably Chaikovsky and Saint-Saëns. Both contributed operas and symphonies alike to the standard repertoire (although Saint-Saëns's contributions have somewhat faded from it in recent years), and they were the only ones unless one counts the youthful, once fairly popular Symphony in C Major by Georges Bizet, the composer of *Carmen*, written as a school exercise at the age of seventeen and performed only posthumously.

The nineteenth-century tendency toward specialization was much abetted by the widening gulf that set in between "high" and "low" genres in the twentieth, which increasingly entailed the segregation of performers and audiences as well as composers, and a rigid hierarchy of taste that reinforced social distinctions. That hierarchy is already evident in the case of operetta, not so much in the way in which the genre was valued by audiences as in the way in which it was valued by its own specialist composers. The three with whom we are acquainted—Offenbach, Strauss, and Sullivan—all eventually aspired to the higher status of the very genre they spoofed.

Offenbach almost succeeded. At the tail end of his shortish life he was working feverishly on *Les contes d'Hoffmann* ("Tales of Hoffmann"), an ambitious *opéra fantastique* in five acts based on the fantasy stories of E. T. A. Hoffmann, the German romantic writer whom we know best as a music critic (for his writings on Beethoven, quoted and interpreted in chapter 31). There is good reason to believe that his overwork on this project—which Offenbach saw as his last chance for rehabilitation after the failure of his own theater, and for recognition as a "contender" in the increasingly rarefied category of art—contributed to his premature death shortly before the opera would have been finished. It had to be given finishing touches by another composer, Ernest Guiraud, for its 1881 premiere, and it has undergone much additional modification over the years by a variety of hands. It has, and can have, no definitive version, but it has steadily gained in popularity owing to its attractive music, in particular the barcarolle ("Belle nuit, ô nuit d'amour"; "Gorgeous Night, O Night of Love") that suffuses the fourth act, set in Venice.

Sullivan's was a sadder story. As his career progressed he found himself under increasing pressure from many (including Queen Victoria herself) to live up to their expectations as the first great English composer in a hundred years. He chafed at the work that brought him success (and pleasure to a wide public) and doggedly applied himself, far less successfully, to the high prestige genres. The highest prestige in England then attached to oratorio, kept alive there since the time of Handel (and later, Mendelssohn) as a national tradition. For summer festivals at Birmingham, Worcester, and Leeds (the last of which he directed for a time), Sullivan wrote six oratorios, the most successful being *The Golden Legend* (1886), after Longfellow's reworking of a twelfth-century German *Minnelied* glorifying noble self-sacrifice and miraculous cures.

At the Queen's own urging, communicated at his knighting ceremony in 1883, Sullivan composed a clanking grand opera, *Ivanhoe* (1891), after the novel of medieval England by Sir Walter Scott. He declared his ambitions, and (perhaps unwittingly) the way they responded to the post-Wagnerian prejudices of the times, in a letter to a prospective operetta librettist:

> I think the whole tendency of stage music now is to get rid as much as possible of songs, duets and other *set pieces* and to become as *dramatic* as possible. In all the series with Gilbert, I found a dainty, pretty song was generally a drag and stopped the interest of the public in the action of the piece. It is on these lines that I am doing a *serious* opera now.

But he was not really thinking of the public. He was thinking of his reputation with "progressive" tastemakers. And they betrayed him. Despite a lavish staging by D'Oyly Carte at a new opera house in which he had invested, and although (unlike most of the operettas) it received performances abroad (including a production at the Berlin Court Opera in 1895), Sullivan's serious effort was a failure with the critics. George Bernard Shaw was especially cruel, dismissing *Ivanhoe* as "a good novel which has been turned into the very silliest sort of sham 'grand opera.'"[17] Having failed to establish himself as a contributor to the elite repertoire, Sullivan became embittered. His resentment at what he perceived to be his unfair banishment to the lighter genres—the result of "typecasting"—poisoned the well of his inspiration, and also soured relations with Gilbert. None of the operettas of his final (post-*Ivanhoe*) decade had any success, and the composer died—of bronchitis, not normally fatal—at the age of fifty-eight, feeling he had been mistreated and unjustly forgotten. In retrospect he might be fairly described as an early victim of historicism.

VERISMO

It was probably because his head, like those of most of his musical countrymen, was turned submissively toward Germany that Sullivan wrote an unwieldy historical opera like *Ivanhoe*. The true winds of operatic renewal were blowing again from Italy, and the tendency they furthered remained that of "comedization," cutting things down to size and making them pungent and "actual" (that is, related to the audience's experience) rather than impressive and remote. The Italian name for it was *verismo*, "truthism." It was under cover of this rigorously naturalistic idiom that Italian opera crossed into the twentieth century.

Verismo called (at least theoretically) for the eschewal of all traditional virtuosity in the name of forceful simplicity. It was originally a literary movement, led by Giovanni Verga (1840–1922), a writer and dramatist most famous for his short stories of life and strife amongst the peasants and fisher-folk of rural Sicily. Verga perfected a narrative style of blunt plainness and "objectivity," seemingly without any intrusion of an authorial point of view. But that impression of "letting the facts speak for themselves" was in fact a highly manipulative procedure, since the author gets to choose the facts. An impression of realism was created by the innovative use of local dialect (something akin to the time-honored technique of infusing operatic music with folkish idioms), but the basic tenor of veristic literature, unlike the literature of the risorgimento (or of Verdi's "Shakespearean" realism), was pessimistic. People fail in Verga because they are overmatched by implacable natural and social conditions, and the line between the natural and the social is deliberately blurred.

It could be said (with only minor exaggeration) that verismo opera was to Romantic opera as short stories were to novels. There was the same radical reduction in scale, the same lowering of tone and simplification of technique through which intensity took the place (or tried to take the place) of amplitude. All of these features are well displayed by the two most successful specimens of the genre: *Cavalleria rusticana*

FIG. 44-9   Ruggero Leoncavallo.

("Rustic chivalry;" 1890) by Pietro Mascagni (1863–1945) and *I pagliacci* ("The clowns;" 1892) by Ruggero Leoncavallo (1857–1919), both of them one-act operas that are now usually performed together on a double bill affectionately known by operagoers as "Cav and Pag." (To be scrupulously exact, "Pag" is nominally a two-act opera in which the

acts are connected by an intermezzo and played without an intermission.) "Cav" was based on a famous story by Verga himself, selected for setting in a prize competition by a canny publisher who wanted to capitalize on the new literary vogue. Thus in an unusually direct way, operatic verismo derived from its literary prototype.

Both Cav and Pag culminate in brutal crimes of passion — murders committed, in both cases, by jealous husbands. The bloody deeds are portrayed with an eye primarily on sensationalism or "shock value," and it was of little importance whose side the audience is on. Revealingly enough, the audience is manipulated in "Cav" to sympathize with the lover and in "Pag" to sympathize with the husband. But the main objective in both cases is the same: titillation, the administering of thrills to a comfortable and complacent

FIG. 44-10   Enrico Caruso as Canio in Leoncavallo's *I pagliacci* (Metropolitan Opera, New York), one of his most famous roles.

bourgeois audience, rather than the exposure of social problems and their amelioration (the objective of the realism of an earlier vintage), let alone a call to political action such as the art of the risorgimento had sought to inspire.

For by the 1890s the political goals of the risorgimento had been ostensibly achieved, and popular culture could now revert to a more innocently — or (depending on one's viewpoint) a more irresponsibly — entertaining role, as if confirming by negation Morse Peckham's theory (discussed in the previous chapter) of risorgimento art as stimulus to aggression. Verismo was widely viewed as a catalyst to voyeurism (a state of depraved moral passivity) or even, in view of its exceedingly violent content, as a moral narcotic.

Compounding the irony was the new concept of nationhood that arose in united Italy, a view that verismo both embodied and stimulated. Because of its preoccupation with the mores of the "southern" lower classes and their naturalistic depiction, often in dialect, verismo led to a new variety of "orientalism." In the theaters of affluent northern Italy these rustic *scene popolari* (scenes of life among the people) were picturesquely exotic, and nurtured assumptions of cultural as well as economic superiority. This, too, was regressive titillation of a sort, and one that reopened cultural divisions within the nation that the risorgimento had tried to heal, or at least to mask.

But while the late Shakespearean works of Verdi, written not for money but for love and full of snob appeal, are now considered the very cream of the Italian repertoire, and while the shabby little shockers of verismo, exploiting an unsophisticated taste for the sake of mercenary gain and increasingly written to formula by a new generation of hacks or "galley slaves," were immediately decried by the fastidious (as they still are), they both embodied, at aristocratic and demotic extremes, a common response to the demands of the contemporary theater. They can be viewed, even technically, as superficially contrasting siblings or cousins in a single line of descent from the Verdi of *Traviata*, *Trovatore*, and *Rigoletto*.

In both Cav and Pag, the lyric high points are brief ariosos for the *tenore di forza* (the lover in one, the husband in the other) in the voice's highest register. These powerful explosions of melody emerge out of ongoing dramatic continuities just as the lyric highpoints in Otello's role emerged in the parts of Verdi's penultimate opera that we have examined (or the way that Falstaff's not-yet-written "Quand'ero paggio" would emerge out of dialogue with Mistress Quickly in his last one), with their musical and dramaturgical properties diminished in scale but exaggerated by compression.

The so-called "Addio alla Mamma" (Farewell to Mother; see Ex. 44-16 for its conclusion), sung by Turiddu, the doomed lover, right before the grisly dénouement of Mascagni's opera, could almost be called a parody of *Otello* with its repeated calls for kisses ("un bacio . . . un altro bacio . . . ," etc.). It retains a vestige of strophic form, in which the melodic repetition is both set off and "motivated" (as strict realism demanded) by a little recitative exchange between the characters, and followed by a written-out cadenza that brings the singer up to high B♭ at the very roof of his range. A similarly deliberate crudity — verismo's greatest strength or its most glaring flaw depending on who is judging — marks the aria's harmonic idiom, with its bald juxtapositions of parallel major and minor.

EX. 44-16 Pietro Mascagni, *Cavalleria rusticana*, Turiddu's arioso

Turiddu: Oh pray that God forgive me!
Oh pray that God forgive me!
A kiss, one kiss, dear Mamma,
one more, dear Mamma, one kiss, dear Mamma.
Good bye!
Promise me, dear Mamma, you will help my Santuzza.
Now kiss me, Mamma, Goodbye!

"Vesti la giubba" ("Put on your costume"), which ends the nominal first act of Leoncavallo's opera, is possibly the most-parodied little number in all of opera, but the mockery it has attracted is fine testimony to its power. It is sung not by the victim of the crime but by the perpetrator, the enraged husband, who has just found out about his wife's perfidy, but who has to go out and perform anyway. On the page it looks like a more formal piece than Turiddu's. It is introduced by a recitative (famous for the "naturalistic" transformation of the tenor's high A into a bout of crazed laughter), and the arioso itself is formally labeled and accompanied at first by a typical "vamp." But on closer examination (see Ex. 44-17 for the voice part) the surprising realization dawns that this arioso contains no melodic repetitions at all. That absence of preconceived "form" — a musical "state of nature" — was a high realist cause.

And yet the arioso does not sound at all "formless," because it takes sly advantage of many conventions that render it fully comprehensible within the "ordinary operagoer's" experience. Its phrase structure is completely regular: a sixteen-bar period balanced by two of eight bars' length (the first of the pair extended by a melodic "stall" of a single measure's duration, a device we first observed as long ago as chapter 33, in Bellini). The modulatory scheme, reaching the relative major in m. 16, and proceeding from there to a harmonic Far Out Point in m. 19, telegraphs the da capo form, one of opera's most dependable. The expected return of the "A" section is avoided, but very "intelligibly": it is preempted by the climax, replete with high note, marked "with full voice, heart-rendingly." That is a sure-fire recipe, handled with mastery and aplomb: seemingly "free" and innovatory, but in fact giving listeners everything they are led to desire.

EX. 44-17   Ruggero Leoncavallo, *I pagliacci*, "Vesti la giubba"

EX. 44-17 (*continued*)

vo - la Co - lom - bi - na, ri - di, Pa - gliac - cio... e o - gnun ap - plau - di -

rà! Tra - mu - ta in laz - zi lo spa - smo ed il pian - to;

in u - na smor - fia il sin - ghioz - zo e'l do - lor... Ah!

Ri - di, Pa - gliac - cio, sul tuo a - mo - re in - fran - to! Ri - di del

duol che t'av - ve - le - na il cor!

Cynical? There were many who thought so, or at least who objected to such transparently manipulative methods. From the traditional Romantic perspective such art could look at once trivially sensational and reprehensibly "safe." Gabriele D'Annunzio, a romantic poet famous for his lofty transcendentalism, and who naturally detested verismo, published a practically libelous review of *Cavalleria rusticana* in which he dismissed Mascagni as an insignificant *capobanda* (bandmaster) and a "breakneck melodrama manufacturer"[18] whose success was due solely to his publisher's genius for publicity.

One who came quickly, if somewhat unexpectedly, to Mascagni's defense was Chaikovsky, a composer often but perhaps erroneously thought to be a model, even the epitome, of musical Romanticism. His "overture-fantasy" *Romeo and Juliet* (sampled in chapter 39) was nothing if not emotionally direct and "sincere" (a word that always needs to be placed in quotes, since we can only judge the appearance, never the reality, of anyone's sincerity but our own), but *Eugene Onegin*, while relatively restrained, can easily be seen as a forerunner of verismo in its calculated methods and its compression.

At any rate, with ten operas and three ballets to his credit Chaikovsky was the most successful Russian composer for the stage. Perhaps he took a certain pleasure in shocking his interviewer, a St. Petersburg reporter who probably expected a conventional recoil at the mention of the twenty-nine-year-old Italian upstart. Instead, he elicited a ringing endorsement, couched almost as an explicit refutation of D'Annunzio's charges:

> People are wrong to think that this young man's colossal, fabulous success is the result of clever publicity . . . . Mascagni, it's clear, is not only very gifted but also very smart. He realizes that nowadays the spirit of realism, the harmonization of art and the true-to-life, is everywhere in the air, that Wotans, Brünnhildes, and Fafners do not in fact excite any real sympathy on the part of the listener, that

human beings with their passions and woes are more intelligible and tangible to us than the gods and demigods of Valhalla.[19]

Playing the Wagner card may have been gratuitous, but Russian composers were even more sensitive than Italians to German claims of universality. Chaikovsky goes on to issue an even more fundamental challenge to romanticism, noting that Mascagni "operates *not by force of instinct* but *by force of an astute perception of the needs of the contemporary listener*" (the italics are his). D'Annunzio could not have put it better, but as the context makes clear, Chaikovsky intended the remark as praise. Was it praise of realism or praise of pandering?

TRUTH OR SADISM?

That was the question, all right. What really divided the musical world in the wake of romanticism was the relationship between the artist and "the contemporary listener" — that is, the paying public and its "needs." It is the issue that more than any other defined the terms within which the history of "art music" would unfold in the twentieth century, the first century that had need of such a category. (A preliminary teaser: What could be the reason for defining some — but only some — musical genres a priori as "art"? What is excluded from the definition? What should the excluded portion be called?)

The earliest focal point of twentieth-century controversy about art vs. commerce was the last great figure in the ancient and distinguished Italian operatic line: Giacomo Puccini (1858–1924), whose works remain a constituent of the core repertory at every opera house in the world today. From the very beginning of his career there were some who called him Verdi's legitimate heir and others who refused to take him seriously as a composer at all. What is remarkable is that the dispute remains heated even now, more than three-quarters of a century after his death, despite Puccini's long-since settled place in the active repertoire and in the hearts of opera lovers. Even more strangely, he is usually barely mentioned in books like this (that is, general histories of "art music"), even though his commanding stature within the world of opera has been a historical fact for more than one hundred years and thus would seem to constitute a robust claim to the composer's historical significance.

Since there is absolutely no chance of Puccini's being dislodged from his place in the operatic repertoire, no matter how much critical invective is heaped upon him, and no matter how little attention he receives from general historians, it is clear that something else is at stake. The critical invective identifies him as one of the twentieth century's emblematic figures. (By rights, of course, that should only quicken rather than dampen the interest of historians.) The phrase "shabby little shocker," applied above to the masterpieces of verismo, was borrowed from a famous harangue against Puccini that first appeared in 1956 in *Opera As Drama*, a widely read critical survey by Joseph Kerman, which was reissued in 1988 with all its invective in place. Kerman applied it to *Tosca* (1900), one of the most popular works in the repertoire, thought by most operagoers to be a masterpiece on a par with Verdi, far above the level of Mascagni or Leoncavallo.

FIG. 44-11 Giacomo Puccini (right) in New York for the premiere of his opera *La Fanciulla del West* (1910). The others are (left to right) Giulio Gatti-Casazza, general manager of the Metropolitan Opera; David Belasco, author of *The Girl of the Golden West*, the play on which the libretto was based; and Arturo Toscanini, the conductor of the premiere.

Puccini's treatment at the hands of historians is symptomatic of a general trend that merits study in its own right. That trend is the gradual divergence, over the course of the twentieth century, between the repertoire, the musical works actually performed for — and "consumed" by — "the contemporary listener," and what is often called the "canon," the body of works (or the pantheon of composers) that are considered worthy of critical respect and academic study. That divergence, in which the history of music becomes not the history of music performed but the history of, well, something else, is the result of "historicism," the intellectual trend first described in chapter 40, according to which history is conceived in terms not only of events but also of goals. In the case of music these goals have chiefly pertained to the "disinterested" advancement of style, a concept that depends on German esthetic philosophy (for the notion of "disinterestedness"), but also — quite circularly — on the narrative techniques of history itself (for the notion of advancement).

Accordingly, the historiography of music in the twentieth century has been fundamentally skewed, on the one hand, by the failure of actual events to conform to the purposes historicists have envisioned, and on the other, by the loyalty not only of many historians but also of many greatly talented and interesting composers to historicist principles. A great deal of music since the middle of the nineteenth century, much of it the music deemed most interesting and significant by historians, has been written not "for the repertoire" but "for the canon."

Puccini wrote for the repertoire (for "the needs of the contemporary listener"), as did most of the century's materially successful — that is, popular — composers. So despite his fame and his high historical profile, he has been slighted in the circularly conceived history of the historicist canon. And even though the present account is taking time out to "problematize" this state of affairs, there is no chance of solving it. A narrative history concentrates by nature on change, hence on innovation, and it has been one of the hallmarks of "repertoire" music, at least since the advent of historicism, that it tends to be far less innovative, stylistically, than "canon" music, which is written with the needs of the narrative in mind.

That does not lessen its value to the audience it serves, but it does lessen its "news value" to historians of style. A description of Puccini's style or technique will not add enormously to what we already know about the style and technique of Italian opera at the end of the nineteenth century. That is admittedly an invidious criterion of selection, and plays into the historicist purposes that more recent historiography (including this book, especially during its "time-outs") has sought to challenge. But historiographical genres have their limitations — one of the most fundamental being limitations of space — and impose constraints. They are lenses on the past, and inevitably distort even as they illuminate. A narrative history such as this one is not the best venue for assessing the value of twentieth-century "repertoire" music. For that purpose there are repertoire surveys, collective biographies, and critical studies.

We shall do best with Puccini, perhaps, to approach him from the standpoint of his popularity (that is, the pertinent "historical fact" as predicated above), considering the reasons for it, and weighing their implications. Puccini's career parallels Verdi's in one interesting regard: his three most famous and permanent works — recalling Verdi's *Rigoletto*, *Trovatore*, and *Traviata* — were written in a clump, one after the other, at the midpoint of his career. All, moreover, were written in collaboration with a single librettist — or rather a pair of librettists who collaborated with Puccini as a team: Luigi Illica (1857–1919) and Giuseppe Giacosa (1847–1906), both well-known playwrights (the former supplying the scenario and a sketch of dialogue, the latter supplying the actual verses).

La bohème (1896), the earliest, was based on *Scènes de la vie de bohème* ("Scenes of bohemian life"), a best-selling sentimental novel by the French writer Henri Murger that romanticized, and considerably prettified, the dire life circumstances of the struggling young writers and artists ("bohemians") inhabiting the garrets of Paris. The central plot line concerns the romance of Rodolfo, a starving poet, and Mimì, a consumptive seamstress: in act I they meet by chance; in act II they are happily in love; in act III they quarrel and are reconciled; in act IV she perishes.

This simple love story is portrayed in counterpoint with a busy backdrop of picturesque street and café life. Act II, with its café waltzes and songs, subsidiary flirtations, and anecdotal hubbub, is almost entirely given over to the "backdrop." There is no denying the theatrical effectiveness of the recipe. As in the case of verismo opera, however, objections are often raised against the opportunistic manipulativeness of the situation, particularly the device of inescapable doom contributed by Mimi's disease, a factor present from the outset and therefore "static." Is a plot governed by circumstances beyond the protagonists' control a truly dramatic plot? Must an opera have such a plot? Must an opera, in short, be "dramatic"? And if critics so decide, and if audiences go on enjoying the work anyway, then what is the force or value of the critique? Can critics be right and audiences wrong? What does it mean to say so? Who gets to define "quality"? By what criteria? With what consequences?

Tosca (1900), was based on a popular play by the French dramatist Victorien Sardou that was created as a star vehicle for the great actress Sarah Bernhardt: the title character is also a great actress, a fictional "diva" living at the time of the French Revolution. At the time Puccini decided to base an opera on it, the play, first staged in 1887, was still in current repertory. That became Puccini's standard procedure: of the seven operas that followed *Tosca*, four were based on current plays the composer happened to see in the theater, often in languages he did not understand. (Half in jest, he once said that his being able to follow a play despite ignorance of its language testified to its operatic potential.) Despite the historical setting, both the play and the opera are cast in the brutally naturalistic mode then fashionable, replete with an onstage murder, an offstage (but audible) scene of torture, an execution, and a concluding suicide.

More than in any other Puccini score (more, perhaps, than in any other standard Italian opera), the musical texture of *Tosca* is suffused with reminiscence motifs, sometimes treated in an abstract (though never "symphonic") manner that justifies the use of the Wagnerian term leitmotif. Possibly meant as an earnest of "seriousness," Puccini's appropriation of the device—or perhaps more to the point, the fact that (unlike Verdi) he never suffered accusations of capitulation to "Wagnerism" because of it—testifies to the increasing internationalism of procedures and techniques in turn-of-the-century opera.

Madama Butterfly, billed as a *tragedia giapponese*, went through four distinct versions between 1904 and 1906 before achieving lasting success. Its source was a very successful dramatization, by the American theatrical producer David Belasco, of a sob story from a popular magazine (supposedly based on a true incident related to the author by his sister, the wife of a missionary) about a Japanese geisha nicknamed Chô-san (Cio-cio-san in the opera), or Butterfly. She is seduced, "temporarily wedded" (according to then-existing Japanese law that cruelly discriminated against the rights of women), and then abandoned, by an insouciant American naval officer. Puccini followed Belasco in having the opera (unlike the story) end with the title character's suicide.

Like *La bohème*, *Madama Butterfly* relies a great deal upon local color, as operas with exotic settings (especially "oriental" ones) were prone to do. Puccini incorporated the characteristically pentatonic tunes of seven Japanese folk songs into the score. Interestingly, they appear mostly in the first act, which depicts Cio-cio-san's wedding to the officer, Lieutenant Pinkerton, who is also identified by a bit of local color (the opening phrases of "The Star-Spangled Banner," no less). It is, after all, only in the presence (that is, through the eyes) of the American that the Japanese milieu is exotic.

The vastly longer second act, played for the most part in Pinkerton's absence, and concerned mainly with Cio-cio-san's worsening fate, largely dispenses with Japanesery; it is cast, rather, in Puccini's own internationalized operatic style (the "universal language of feeling").

The disproportion between the lengths of the two acts was prompted by the excruciating silent scene of waiting that quickened Puccini's interest in turning Belasco's play into an opera. Representing the night that passes between Cio-cio-san's spying Pinkerton's ship in the harbor after three years' absence without communication, and her last tragic meeting with him, it consisted in Belasco's version of a theatrical tour de force: fully fifteen minutes of pantomime for the solitary leading actress, accompanied by harbor sounds, lighting effects, and, finally, birdsong to represent the dawn. As Puccini immediately recognized, that was already opera of a sort.

In the libretto, the waiting scene became an orchestral interlude between the two parts of act II. In the first part, Cio-cio-san displays her steadfast faith in her husband's return both by turning down an advantageous match with a rich suitor and by singing what has become probably the most famous aria in all of Puccini: "Un bel dí" ("One fine day"), in which she reproves her protective maidservant Suzuki for doubting, and imagines the joyful scene that awaits her. In the act's second part, Pinkerton does return—but with his American bride, and only to reclaim his son from Cio-cio-san. Puccini felt that the poignancy of the ironic contrast between the imagined outcome and the real one, and the musically enhanced scene of waiting that connected them, would carry the audience through an act of a colossal ninety minutes' duration, a demand that Wagner himself exceeded only once (in *Das Rheingold*).

He was wrong. One of the changes he was compelled to make in the opera after the disastrous opening night was to recast it in three acts so that the waiting scene follows the intermission and loses the suspenseful character that originally attracted Puccini to the subject. The by-product of the revision, however, was a second act that culminated in an orchestral reprise of "Un bel dí," as Cio-cio-san spies the ship. This provided a surefire curtain and vouchsafed the opera's lasting success. It does seem worth pointing out, however, in view of Puccini's reputation for pandering, that the surefire solution was not his first choice.

Be that as it may, a close-up on "Un bel dí" and its various reminiscences and reprises (Ex. 44-18) will afford us an ideal window on Puccini's style and methods, and the basis of his enduring success. Like the arias and ariosos we have been encountering in late Verdi and the *veristi*, "Un bel dí" is very terse. Its form could be described as da capo, since it begins and ends with a distinctive eight-bar melody that only has to be sung once to be memorable, since it descends gracefully through a slightly varied fourfold sequence of a single two-bar phrase (Ex. 44-18a). In between the two statements comes a disproportionately long middle section that begins with a balancing sequential idea (a four-measure phrase answered by its upwardly transposed repetition), but then devolves into what sounds like recitative, sung in "conversational" note-values with long strings of repeated pitches. Even though this is an aria, we are thus informed, it is being enacted in real time as Cio-cio-san narrates her fantasy of reconciliation to Suzuki.

The reprise of the opening phrase carries more emotional punch than the usual da capo return because it is sung triumphantly, at the opposite end of the dynamic scale from the gently wistful opening, casting the whole aria in retrospect as a single gathering crescendo to a climax. Once past the first phrase, moreover, the voice part again devolves into a recitative-like style, dividing the notes of the melody into short repeated note-values, while it continues to sound forth, intact, in the orchestra (Ex. 44-18b). Looking back at the beginning now, we notice that even there the singer followed the melody somewhat selectively. The tune as such, it turns out, belongs more to the orchestra than to the voice.

This point is driven home at the very end (Ex. 44-18c), where Puccini adopts a device that had been pioneered in *La gioconda* (1876), an opera (to a libretto by Boito) by Amilcare Ponchielli (1834–86), the leading member of the generation between Verdi's and Puccini's. As we find it in "Un bel dí," the singer's climactic statement of the main theme is immediately followed and trumped by a coda in which, after six measures' headlong ascent to a brilliant high B♭, the singer falls silent and the theme passes entirely into the orchestra for its peroration, as if achieving a transcendent emotional pitch that can only be represented wordlessly.

Within the very confines of the aria, in other words, the theme is already being treated as a reminiscence motif, producing at short range the emotional rush that the device of reminiscence had previously held in reserve. The aria's brevity, its climax driven structure and its pumped-up wordless coda conspire to deliver a sort of accelerated catharsis, an instant emotional gratification for the audience, who get to share Cio-cio-san's fantasy. From this point to the end of the act, the reminiscence theme from "Un

EX. 44-18A   Giacomo Puccini, *Madama Butterfly*, "Un bel di," mm. 1–8 bel dí" will serve as the emblem of Cio-cio-san's false belief in Pinkerton's return, the belief that sustains her and that, by her own avowal, gives her only reason to live. Like its Verdian antecedents it has been invested with an ironic double meaning; its every return will not only confirm her faith but also forecast her doom. The first of them accompanies Cio-cio-san's confident request that the American consul inform Pinkerton that he has a son, trusting that that will bring him back. The last (Ex. 44-18d) accompanies the arrival of Pinkerton's gunboat in the harbor, announced first by its cannon, next by the reminiscence motif as Cio-cio-san scans the harbor with her telescope.

She is being cruelly set up for a mortification that will be rubbed in over the whole duration of act III. The reminiscence motif plays its part in heightening the spectators' awareness of the impending catastrophe, and (let's face it) their (no, *our*) enjoyment of it. It can be argued, and of course it has been, that all tragedy is voyeurism; that by definition

EX. 44-18B   Giacomo Puccini, *Madama Butterfly*, "Un bel di," mm. 149–56

it contains or implies *Schadenfreude*, the enjoyment of another's misfortune; and that the noble concept of catharsis — tragedy's soul-cleansing function as immortally defined by Aristotle — is an idealizing mask for sentiments far less noble.

The particular tragic formula repeatedly employed by Puccini, in which the emblematic character is neither a robust *tenore di forza* nor an evil bass-baritone but rather a "soft, wilting heroine"[20] (in Julian Budden's apt phrase) who is victimized by an implacable situation (grinding poverty, fatal disease, the patriarchal order) and slowly tortured to death, brings the inherent hidden sadism of dramatic representation dangerously near the surface of consciousness. It can also be argued (and has been)

EX. 44-18C Giacomo Puccini, *Madama Butterfly*, "Un bel di," mm. 159–70

EX. 44-18D   Giacomo Puccini, *Madama Butterfly*, reminiscence of "Un bel di" at end of Act II

Suzuki: I believe it's a warship.

Butterfly: Big . . . white . . . with a U.S. flag; I see the Stars and Stripes.
I believe they are casting anchor!
Hold my trembling hand so that I may read the name . . . the name.

that watching a strong hero — Oedipus, Othello — brought low by fate in consequence of a moral flaw is edifying. It is harder to make such an argument in the case of a defenseless woman like Mimi or Cio-cio-san — or Manon Lescaut, the equally ill-fated title character of Puccini's first big hit (1894) on a subject that had already attracted Massenet.

Has Puccini's enduring popularity been due to his skill in administering sadistic gratification? If so, then shall we place the blame on Puccini, or on the ones who have made him popular, namely ourselves? Is an art that caters to "bad" instinct bad art? Does such catering promote social evil or (by giving our evil fantasies an acceptable outlet) social good? Is the fact that the art of the fin de siècle, or the "turn of the century," was so full of sadistic representations (as we will continue to observe) the result of "decadence" or degeneration, as some have charged, or the result of greater candor in dealing relatively openly with matters that had formerly been more heavily cloaked in hypocritical metaphor? A related question: Was the precipitate loss of scale in "realistic" or "naturalistic" art the result of lost faith or of greater honesty? And another: Was the habit of representing women in art as sacrificial victims the result of a new male brutality or was it an early reaction to the burgeoning social emancipation of women in "real life"?

These are the heady questions that underlie debate not only about Puccini but also about many popular (or "populist") artists. Is the postulate that popularity implies or actually requires a debased morality (to say nothing of a debased technique) a courageous refusal to compromise standards or a pusillanimous camouflage for snobbery?

Did Puccini's success at rendering "great sorrows in little souls"[21] (as he put it himself) magnify the souls or mock the sorrows? Budden writes that Puccini's true subject was *l'Italietta* — "little Italy."[22] Considering that fewer than half of his operas are actually set in Italy or derive from Italian sources, the remark is more a commentary about values (unheroic ones) than about subject matter. But is the assumption that great or good art necessarily embodies heroic aspirations an ethical improvement? Or is it a just another mask for social elitism? And hadn't Wagner shown that even heroism could acquire a bad name?

"Italietta" rings true in another way, though, because of the much-diminished place of Italy in the operatic scheme of things by the end of Puccini's life. His last opera, *Turandot*, after a dramatized fairy-tale by Carlo Gozzi, was first performed (posthumously) in 1926 with its final duet

FIG. 44-12   Cover of the first edition of the libretto to Puccini's *Turandot* (Milan: Ricordi, 1924).

673

completed by a younger composer named Franco Alfano. Another cruel oriental fantasy of feminine humiliation, it offered up two victims to the audience: the slave girl Liu, who fills the soft and wilting slot, is driven by torture to suicide; the title character, the haughty princess of China, is brought low by love, which compels her reluctant submission to her wooer Calaf, the *tenore di forza*.

Turandot was the very last Italian opera to enter the permanent international repertoire. As we shall see, there have since been only a handful of later additions to that repertoire, and they have been the work of French, Austrian, Russian, English, and (even) American composers, not Italians. In part, this drying up of the original fount of opera reflects the fate of opera in general: its status as primary medium of popular spectacular entertainment was usurped in the twentieth century by the movies, especially since the advent of "talkies," only three years after the premiere of *Turandot*.

And yet if films are to be regarded, in effect, as the operas of the twentieth century, then Italy has not ceded its place after all. Puccini's heirs have been the great Italian film directors, especially those like Roberto Rossellini, Vittorio De Sica, or Federico Fellini, who made up the so-called neorealist school of the 1940s and 1950s, which, arguably, inherited the mantle of verismo.

The Return of the Symphony

BRAHMS

THE DRY DECADES

W
e have not taken a close look at an old-fashioned "nonprogrammatic" multimovement symphony since the end of chapter 34, when our subject was Schubert's "Unfinished" (1822), nor have we even given the genre a passing glance since chapter 35, when Mendelssohn's subtitled but nonprogrammatic "Reformation" Symphony (1832) briefly served us as a foil to his oratorio *St. Paul*. Had we not been sidetracked by what seemed at the time to be more pressing "historical" concerns, we might have spared a moment for Schumann's four symphonies, composed between 1841 and 1850, all of them now staples of the orchestral repertoire. The fact that we did not take the time is only another illustration of the problem broached in the previous chapter: the ease with which the historian's attention is captured by novelty.

But even if we had been telling the story in the guise of a repertoire survey rather than a narrative, the "classic" symphony would have fallen out of the picture in the second half of the nineteenth century, despite its Beethovenian prestige. For two decades beginning around 1850, it was no longer viewed as a site of potential creative energy. It was seen, rather, as an illustrious but outmoded genre. Its meteoric career had carried it in the course of little more than a century from the status of aristocratic party music to that of momentous public oration, but its place had been decisively preempted by the programmatic genres pioneered by Liszt and the "New Germans." Wagner, going even further, made bold to declare (in *The Artwork of the Future*) that Beethoven's Ninth Symphony had made all purely instrumental music obsolete.[1]

Not a single symphony composed in the 1850s or 1860s has survived in the repertoire. It became a "conservatory" or "professor's" genre — a graduation exercise to demonstrate formal mastery — and its practitioners were for the most part academics. Perhaps the most prolific symphonist of the period, Anton Rubinstein (1829–94), a fire-breathing piano virtuoso but a conservative composer, was in fact the founder and director of the St. Petersburg Conservatory, and its head of composition. His counterparts in Germany — Julius Rietz (1812–77), Carl Reinecke (1824–1910), Salomon Jadassohn (1831–1902), and the Danish-born Niels Gade (1817–90) in Leipzig; the renegade Lisztian Joachim Raff (1822–82) in Frankfurt; Robert Volkmann (1815–83) in Vienna and Budapest; Karl Reinthaler (1822–96) and Schumann's brother-in-law Woldemar

Bargiel (1828 – 97) in Cologne; and Carl Grädener (1812 – 83) in Hamburg — maintained the genre through its fallow period, but made no lasting contribution to it.

No composer could graduate from the Paris Conservatory at this time without a "classical" symphony under his belt, and that is how the student symphonies by the sixteen-year-old Saint-Saëns (1852) and the seventeen-year-old Bizet (1855) got written. Gounod's two symphonies (1855, 1856) were the by-product of his meeting with Fanny Hensel in Rome (described in chapter 35), as a result of which he met her brother, Felix Mendelssohn, and heard him conduct the Leipzig Gewandhaus Orchestra. "On his return to Paris," the English critic Martin Cooper wryly noted, "Gounod was almost certainly unique among French musicians of his generation in his knowledge and understanding of music, past and present, that had nothing to do with the opera house and no place in the French tradition."[2]

But by then the symphony was considered an anomaly practically everywhere. Its continued cultivation, except as a didactic genre, was taken as evidence that music had entered "the age of the Epigones,"[3] or lesser descendents, to quote the most popular music history text of the 1880s, the *Illustrated History of Music* by Emil Naumann (1827 – 88), a Dresden professor who was himself a former pupil and "epigone" of Mendelssohn. Renewed vitality in this or any other "classical" genre was considered a historical (or "dialectical") impossibility, so ingrained had the historicist viewpoint become.

And yet, as Naumann's textbook illustrates, the inherent optimism of the historicist progress-myth was producing a pessimistic backlash. Wagner and Liszt, the great figures venerated by the "New German School," were at the time of Naumann's writing both recently deceased. It seemed to most observers that they had brought all the historicist prophecies to fulfillment. "Reflecting now on the achievements of the past," Naumann concluded, "we observe in the tonal art an organic whole. It is complete and finished. What is to come one cannot divine."[4] There seemed to be nothing left to do.

MUSEUM CULTURE

The last thing Naumann expected was the "symphonic revival" that was by then already well under way, although (like anyone committed to a theory of history) he failed to notice what was going on all around him. The reasons for this massive infusion of new creative energy into what had been considered a moribund genre are notoriously complex. Of course they include the appearance of a new generation of highly capable musicians; but that has to be considered not so much a cause as a contingency. Without "new symphonists," to be sure, there could never have been a "new symphony." But the talent and renewed dynamism that went into the symphony beginning in the 1870s could have gone elsewhere. Something had to revive the genre's prestige and renew its prospects in order to attract the talent. That something was a volatile compound of contradictory historical and social factors that transformed concert life, producing the powerful notion of a "classical tradition" in music that is still with us today.

With the swelling of urban populations in the wake of industrialization came a broadening out of the musical audience into what could be truly thought of as a "public": a cross-section of society — or, at least, a cross-section of "affluent society," people with "disposable income," uncommitted money to spend. The concert hall began to rival the opera house as a potential source of profits, and toward the middle of the nineteenth century halls of a size comparable to opera theaters but specifically designed for orchestral concerts — the kind of concert hall familiar to us all — began to proliferate.

The Leipzig Gewandhaus (drapers' hall), built in 1781, was for a long time an isolated badge of commercial prosperity and the appetite for concert music that it stimulated. It had no rival until 1831, a round half-century later, when the Vienna Gesellschaft der Musikfreunde (Society of Friends of Music), a "voluntary association" or private club supported by a paying membership, built a hall for the propagation of orchestral music. The "Gesellschaft" or "Society" (as it was known for short) was a very important organization, always at the forefront of public concert life in the Viennese capital. As the city grew in size and wealth, so did the Society, reflecting the city's burgeoning commercial prosperity and channeling it into musical ventures; as the Society grew, so did the concert life it managed. It is to that process that we must look if we want to understand the rebirth of the symphony.

Founded in 1812 as an amateur orchestra, the Society endowed the first Viennese conservatory in 1817, with an enormous library attached containing many autograph manuscripts by the giants of the "classical" repertoire, purchased for the Society by its wealthier members. The concert hall, Vienna's first, was erected three years after Beethoven's death and two years after Schubert's. Their symphonies had been played during their lifetimes in theaters, dance halls, and aristocratic palaces, not in specially designed spaces for which there was as yet no perceived social need.

Once the first public halls were in place, others followed, ever bigger; and as halls grew, so did orchestras. In 1860, public music-making in Vienna was rather belatedly professionalized on the Leipzig model with the establishment of the Künstlerverein (Artists' Club) orchestra, now called the Vienna Philharmonic. A hall was built for it ten years later by the Vienna Musikverein (Music Society); known as the Grosser Saal (Large Hall), and familiarly as the "Goldener Saal" (Golden Hall) because of its lavish appointments and superb acoustics, it had a previously unheard-of seating capacity of almost 2,000, larger than many opera houses. It was joined later the same year, 1870, by the Gewerbehaussaal (Chamber of Commerce Hall) in Dresden, with comparable dimensions and a fully professional Philharmonic Orchestra. Both the Vienna and the Dresden orchestras began offering full season subscriptions like those of the precocious Gewandhaus, and like all "major" big-city professional orchestras today. From 1870, then, one may say that such subscription series were "normal" in European concert life, and so they have remained, both in Europe and in its cultural colonies.

Shorter orchestral subscriptions had been a fixture of Paris music life since 1828, when the Société des Concerts du Conservatoire was founded by the Opéra concertmaster François Antoine Habeneck. It gave its concerts, as its name suggests, in the conservatory's Grande Salle. In 1853, a rival concert organization, the Société des Jeunes Artistes du Conservatoire, began giving concerts under Jules-Étienne Pasdeloup

FIG. 45-1   Interior of the Grosser Saal of the Musikverein (Great Hall of the Musical Society; now the Vienna Philharmonic), built by Theophil Hansen in 1870.

(1819–87), who went on, beginning in 1861, to offer a series called Concerts Populaires de Musique Classique in the mammoth Cirque Napoléon. The hall held 5,000, and the orchestra numbered 110. After the war of 1870, the Concerts Pasdeloup, as they had come to be called, faced competition from a pair of rival organizations, popularly named after their enterprising virtuoso conductors: the Concerts Colonne (after Edouard Colonne, 1838–1910) from 1873, and the Concerts Lamoureux (after Charles Lamoureux, 1834–99) from 1881.

London was the only other European city that, like Leipzig, had boasted a full-fledged concert hall (the Hanover Square Rooms, where Haydn appeared) before the end of the eighteenth century. The postindustrial burgeoning was especially spectacular there, as befitted the city that continued to be the nineteenth century's largest commercial center. St. James's Hall went up in 1858, with a gargantuan seating capacity of 2,127. It was the site of the series known as Popular Concerts, more familiarly as the "Pops." Nothing could compare, though, with the Royal Albert Hall, still London's premiere concert space, which opened in 1871 with an audience capacity of 6,500 when the parquet seating is removed, as it now is for the summer "Promenade" (or Proms) concerts at which the ground-floor audience stands (and circulates). Those concerts had actually started at the Queen's Hall (capacity 2,492), erected in 1893 but destroyed by a German bombing raid during World War II.

Russia's first professional orchestra was founded at St. Petersburg in 1859 by the aristocratic Russian Musical Society, the same organization that sponsored Rubinstein's conservatory. Its concerts were given in what was formerly known as the *Zal dvoryanskogo sobraniya* (Assembly Hall of the Nobility), built in the 1830s for fashionable balls. As converted to concert use it seats a mere 1,318. Mammoth halls on the order of the ones that went up in Western Europe in the heyday of bourgeois concert life had no real counterparts in imperial Russia, which maintained a quasi-feudal society until the 1860s, and where the growth of an entrepreneurial bourgeoisie was stunted by reactionary laws. Somewhat paradoxically, a burgeoning public concert life in Russia on the bourgeois model had to await the Communist (that is, antibourgeois) revolution of 1917.

The most prestigious nineteenth-century concert hall in America was New York's Music Hall (now known as Carnegie Hall after Andrew Carnegie, the steel magnate who financed it), with a seating capacity of 2,784. It opened its doors in 1891 (with the Russian composer Chaikovsky as the guest star of the inaugural gala) as a home for the orchestra of the New York Philharmonic Society (founded 1842; now the New York Philharmonic Orchestra). Carnegie Hall's only serious rival was Boston's Symphony Hall (capacity 2,645), built for the Boston Symphony Orchestra (founded 1881), in use since 1900.

The audience for "symphony concerts" reached a new plateau, then, around 1870, and only seemed to keep growing for the rest of the century. Up to a point, large halls and large audiences were symbiotic: big capacities meant lower prices, which meant more people, which necessitated bigger capacities. The Leipzig Gewandhaus, the original "symphony hall" had to be completely rebuilt in 1882–84, after about a century of use, at twice its original capacity in order to accommodate the socially diverse ("mass") audiences that now flocked to symphony concerts. Although the new building was never used as a textile trade center, it was still called the "draper's hall," since that name was now ineluctably and honorably associated with the history of orchestral music, now more popular and prestigious than ever before.

But we are facing a potentially grim paradox; for "symphonic" music began growing toward its new plateau of popularity and prestige exactly as its production was falling off. What were all those excellent new professional orchestras playing in their immense new concert halls?

The answer is implied in the statement of aims with which Pasdeloup launched his Société des Jeunes Artistes du Conservatoire in 1852: "to present recognized masterpieces alongside music by young composers." Pasdeloup's repertoire consisted of the "Viennese classics" — Haydn, Mozart, and Beethoven — plus Mendelssohn and Schumann (shortly destined to join the rest in the ranks of dead composers), with the works of "young composers" admitted only insofar as they were composed in "classical" forms. The early symphonies of Saint-Saëns and Gounod, mentioned above as conservatory produce, were all that Pasdeloup was at first prepared to admit alongside the masterpieces of the Teutonic dead. These were (in the words of David Charlton, a historian of French music) "among the earliest works in 'classical' forms by Frenchmen."[5] Audiences found them delightful, especially Gounod's. But from the historicist standpoint Pasdeloup was providing a counterhistorical incentive to "epigonism." By historicist lights, "works in 'classical' forms by Frenchmen" had no call or right to exist, at least not at that late date.

Pasdeloup's proclivities were matched by all the other enterprises that popularized symphonic music. In its first year, 1858, the London "Pops" at St. James's Hall presented (in descending order of frequency) works of Beethoven, Haydn, Mozart, Mendelssohn, and Weber. The next season the repertoire was broadened to encompass Handel and Bach—even older music!—and a single program of British music that "epigonally" imitated the composers already named. In other words, the symphonic repertoire as purveyed in the latter half of the nineteenth century—with increasing frequency, in ever improving performances, and to an ever widening public—had been frozen at the century's midpoint.

A startling statistic established by William Weber, a social historian who has made a specialty of the sociology of musical taste, reveals that around the turn of the nineteenth century about 80 percent of all the music performed in Vienna, Leipzig, Paris, and London (the cities mainly surveyed above) was the work of living composers, while after 1850, and especially by 1870, the ratio of living to dead authors performed had been almost exactly reversed.[6] Eighty percent of the music offered was by the ancient dead, and the composers of the remaining 20 percent now had a powerful "counterhistorical" incentive to become their elders' epigones. The concert hall had effectively become a museum, and so it has remained to the present day. As the music historian J. Peter Burkholder put it, commenting on Weber's findings, "a young composer [as of the 1850s] had not only living models but also dead and deified ones."[7] The newly professionalized, newly democratized, and newly profitable concert world of the late nineteenth century seemed willy-nilly to be aping and universalizing the aristocratic antiquarian taste of London's quaint old Concert of Antient Music. That society, founded in 1776 by the earl of Sandwich and some other noblemen, and unique for its time, had stipulated that no work should be performed at its concerts that was less than twenty years old. By the turn of the century it had become something of a laughing stock, owing to the "want of variety" in its programs, as one critic complained, and its "total discouragement of living genius." But it held on until 1848, and only disbanded when concert programs everywhere began conforming to its strange rule, thus depriving it of a raison d'être.

"Historical concerts"—panoramic, canon-solidifying surveys of the musical past—became fashionable everywhere. Anton Rubinstein toured the world with a series of seven historical recitals that established the royal line of keyboard succession (somewhat nationalistically colored at the end) as follows:

> *First concert* (sixteenth to eighteenth centuries): Byrd, Bull, Couperin, Rameau, Scarlatti, J. S. Bach, Handel, C. P. E. Bach, Haydn, Mozart
> *Second concert:* Beethoven (eight sonatas!)
> *Third concert:* Schubert, Weber, Mendelssohn
> *Fourth concert:* Schumann

Fifth concert (virtuoso composers): Clementi, Field, Hummel, Moscheles, Henselt, Thalberg, Liszt
Sixth concert: Chopin
Seventh concert: Chopin, Glinka, Balakirev, Cui, Rimsky-Korsakov, Anatoly Lyadov, Chaikovsky, Anton Rubinstein, Nicholas Rubinstein (his brother)

And now the biggest paradox of all: The driving impulse behind this newly universalized, high-minded "classicism" was, perversely, a commercial one. Selling music to a mass public meant guaranteeing its quality by invoking the "test of time." Veneration of the masters, moreover, conferred a cachet not only on producers and purveyors, but on consumers, too. As Peter Gay, the leading historian of bourgeois mores and foibles, puts it, to attend such a concert was "to document one's membership in a coterie"—an irresistible blandishment, albeit an ironic one, to an ever enlarging audience of social climbers.

Finally, the very nature of a public concert (especially an orchestral or a choral one) as a social gathering furthered the ossification of the repertoire. Such concerts, in William Weber's words, satisfied the "desire to celebrate the emerging urban-industrial civilization with a grand thronging together in public places."[8] And what drew the throngs together was "the need of the new industrial society to manifest its economic and cultural potency through its own grand rites of secular religiosity." The music of the "classical masters" had become a kind of liturgy.

The newly widespread "discouragement of living genius" was not only demoralizing to composers. It was also in flat contradiction with the historicist esthetic by which most of them had come by then to swear, with its call for perpetual progress and renewal of artistic means. The esthetic of Romanticism, in one of its major late strains, had collided with the realities of musical life as actually lived, even (or especially) in Germany. No wonder, then, that symphonic production had fallen off. On the one hand, it had been declared obsolete by the lofty arbiters of musical "progress," and on the other it had to vie in the real world (the world of expenses, promotions, and remunerations) with works that had been declared timelessly enduring—hence unsurpassable—achievements.

This untenable situation was already implicit in the contradictions between the romantic cult of original genius and the new concept of the musical "work of art." Once musical quality had been identified with masterworks, and masterworks with a specified collection of indispensable scores, then curatorship—preservation and display—became the job of performing organizations. As the repertoire was conceived as "complete and finished" (to recall Emil Naumann), the objectives of performers and composers began to diverge. The latter wished to add to the repertoire, but their additions were only welcome insofar as they were seen as compatible with the existing collection, or complementary to it—which is to say, practically never. The symphonies of Rietz or Reinecke or Jadassohn or Gade might be shown once or twice, especially locally, but the need was rarely seen to add them to the permanent collection. And now we have at last defined "classical music" as the term is used today, and pinpointed its origin: "classical music" is the music in the "permanent collection," first defined around 1850.

Against the "permanent collection" or closed tradition of classicism was pitted in fine paradox the "permanent revolution" celebrated by historicism. The paradox led to the rifts that have yawned ever since between repertoire and canon, on the one hand, and between contemporary composition and the contemporary public, on the other. A strange but durable amalgam of esthetic idealism and crass commercialism had equated repertoire and canon, at least for the present, and thereby frozen both. Music of easy audience appeal was excluded and had to find other outlets, other venues. Thus not only was "classical" or "art" music born at that crucial nineteenth-century midpoint; so was "popular" or "entertainment" music (commercially purveyed music not meant for permanent display but for instantaneous, ephemeral success). The simultaneous origin of both these categories, eternally antithetical though they may appear to us by now, was only inevitable, since each was defined by the other's exclusion.

Composers were now really in a bind. The only way they could at once maintain self-respect in the face of historicism and at the same time have access to the newly defined "classical" repertoire and its prestigious venues was to create "instant classics"—compositions that in their high-minded and compelling seriousness could somehow simultaneously project both novelty and enduring value. They had at once to communicate, first, sufficient freshness and originality to stimulate interest; second, sufficient conformity to traditional values to warrant inclusion in the permanent collection; and third, sufficient intricacy of design to encourage a test of time.

Such a prescription, involving as it did the juggling of so many contradictory criteria, was indeed daunting. But it is the prescription under which composers of "classical music" have been laboring ever since the musical museum was established. Burkholder aptly sums it up in all its paradoxical majesty by observing that

> Once the concert hall became a museum, the only works appropriate to be performed there were *museum pieces*—either pieces that were already old and revered or pieces which served exactly the same function, as *musical works of lasting value which proclaimed a distinctive musical personality, which rewarded study, and which became loved as they became familiar.*[9]

It sounds like something that couldn't be done. But someone did it. And in the process, as Burkholder observes, he provided "the model for future generations of what a composer is, what a composer does, why a composer does it, what is of value in music, and how a composer is to succeed."[10] In this formulation, of course, "a composer" here stands for *modern* composers, namely, in Burkholder's neat definition, "composers obsessed with the musical past and with their place in music history."[11] The definition is neat because it encapsulates yet another paradox, the ultimate one: modernity in music has come to be chiefly defined by a relationship to the past, rather than (according to the old "Zukunftist" definition) a relationship to the future.

NEW PATHS

The one who did it, who broke the vicious circle or logjam and (among other things, but preeminently) revived the "classical" symphony as a living genre, was Johannes Brahms (1833–97), the first major composer who grew up within, and learned to cope with, our modern conception of "classical music."

A Hamburger by birth but from 1862 a Viennese by adoption, Brahms was just old enough to have had a personal link to the as-yet-unproclaimed "classical" tradition as a living thing. It could not have been a more distinguished link, in fact, since from the age of twenty he had been identified as a protégé of Schumann, the last representative of what would be later defined as the classical (rather than the "modern") symphonic line. By 1853, only three years

FIG. 45-2   Johannes Brahms as a young man, by Josef Ludwig Novak.

before his catastrophically premature death, Schumann was already seeing himself as an embattled classicist in opposition to the emergent New German School. In view of his earlier distinction as the quintessential Romanticist of the keyboard and the lied (see chapter 38), and his former championship, as critic, of Berlioz and Liszt, this was an ironic outcome. But had he lived longer, Schumann would certainly have continued in his new role as spearhead of the reaction against the historicist party, whose official organ, in compounded irony, was the *Neue Zeitschrift für Musik*, his own journal, now in the hands of Franz Brendel (see chapter 40).

As a courtesy to his predecessor, Brendel allowed Schumann space in the magazine for what would be his very last article: "Neue Bahnen" ("New paths"), an encomium to the young and as yet practically unknown Brahms, which appeared on the front page in the issue of 28 October 1853. Whether by accident or design, Schumann's valedictory closely paralleled his debut article, the famous welcome to Chopin ("Hats off, gentlemen, a genius"), which also trumpeted the arrival of a new genius on the scene. Readers of the *Neue*

FIG. 45-3   Brahms's birthplace in Hamburg.

683

Zeitschrift could be forgiven for receiving Schumann's tribute with some skepticism: Brahms was being named as the preeminent worthy among what New Germans by then regarded as an academic crowd of merely local significance — Bargiel, Gade, and the rest (as Schumann listed them in a footnote). Even as he proclaimed his advent in Messianic terms, Schumann described Brahms's virtues in terms that could seem downright bathetic, as if well-schooled respectability were a mark of heroism.

"After such a preparation," Schumann enthused, alluding once again to the Bargiels and the Gades,

> it has seemed to me that there would and must suddenly appear some day one man who would be singled out to make articulate in an ideal way the highest expression of our time, one man who would bring us mastery, not as the result of a gradual development, but as Minerva, springing fully armed from the head of Cronus. And he is come, a young creature over whose cradle graces and heroes stood guard. His name is *Johannes Brahms*, and he comes from Hamburg where he has been working in silent obscurity, trained in the most difficult theses of his art by an excellent teacher who sends me enthusiastic reports of him, recommended to me recently by a well-known and respected master.[12]

There was a lot of subtext here. The "well-known and respected master" who had put Brahms in touch with Schumann was the violinist Joseph Joachim, formerly the concertmaster of Liszt's orchestra at Weimar, the very crucible of the "music of the future," who (as we may remember from chapter 40) noisily defected from that position to lead the opposition to "New Germany." His letter of resignation is a remarkably articulate (and astonishingly frank) statement of principles, indispensable to an understanding of Brahms. "Your music," wrote Joachim to Liszt,

> is entirely antagonistic to me; it contradicts everything with which the spirits of our greats have nourished my mind from my earliest youth. If it were thinkable that I could ever be deprived of, that I should ever have to renounce, all that I learned to love and honor in their creations, all that I feel music to be, your works would not fill one corner of the vast waste of nothingness that I would feel. How, then, can I feel myself to be united in aim with those who, under the banner of your name and in the belief that they must join forces against the artists for the justification of their contemporaries, make it their life task to propagate your works by every means in their power?[13]

This could be read as a manifesto of a different sort of historicism, or rather an "antihistoricism": one that looked to the past for timeless (hence not — or not merely — historical) values rather than for justification of further progress. Brahms was nurtured in this faith — by his teachers, by Joachim, but above all by Schumann, whom he worshipped, virtually becoming a surrogate son to him. In the last miserable years of Schumann's life, when the composer was confined to a sanatorium for the mentally ill, Brahms actually took his place at the head of the Schumann household, and remained on intimate terms with Clara Schumann to the end of her long life, only a year before the end of his own. (Yes, of course tongues wagged about the relationship between the bachelor composer and the widowed pianist, fourteen years his senior.) His intense personal experiences of and with the Schumanns, and the loyalty it bred, bound Brahms ever more tightly to their position in German musical politics.

Only once did he take direct political action on their behalf, again at Joachim's urging. The violinist had drafted a response to Brendel's remarks at the 1859 conference (described in chapter 40) commemorating the founding of the *Neue Zeitschrift*, in which he lauded the achievements of the "post-Beethoven development" and proposed that it be christened the "New German School," despite its having been inspired by Berlioz and led by Liszt (both non-Germans), since its achievements had been universally recognized as the sole legitimate bearers of Beethoven's legacy.

Taking umbrage at Brendel's smug tone and his brazen snubbing of Schumann, Joachim's open letter decried the assumption that "seriously striving musicians"[14] were all in accord about the value of Liszt's music, or about the worthiness of the New Germans' historicist program. On the contrary, he wrote, serious musicians "can only deplore or condemn the productions of the leaders and disciples of the so-called 'New German School' as contrary to the most fundamental essence of music." He sent it to Brahms, among others, for further circulation and signatures, particularly among those who would be attending the Lower-Rhine Music Festival, still a bastion of "classical" conservatism, in the summer.

Unfortunately for Brahms and Joachim, somebody (as we now say) "leaked" the document to an unfriendly journalist who printed it prematurely (on 6 May 1860) in a Berlin newspaper, with only four signatures—Brahms's and Joachim's plus those of the assistant conductor at the court of Hanover and an equally obscure conductor from the university town of Göttingen. This feeble gang of four was widely satirized for fancying themselves a new Schumannesque "Davidsbund," but now a Davidsbund of the right. A parody of the letter appeared in the *Neue Zeitschrift* itself, signed "J. Geiger" (J. Fiddler [Joachim]) and "Hans Neubahn" (Johnny Newpath [Brahms]). Brendel, in a sanctimonious rebuttal, branded it a "pathological" phenomenon. Wounded, Brahms retreated thenceforth from public debate, preferring to follow the advice he received from the venerable Ferdinand Hiller, that "the best means of struggle would be to create good music."[15] Still and all, his abhorrence of Liszt's works and horror at his influence continued to seethe, and left many lively traces, unprintable in family newspapers, in Brahms's correspondence.

This story would be too trivial to relate, were it not for the fact that Brahms finally managed to draft the first movement of his First Symphony in its aftermath. Clara Schumann herself gave him a nudge in this direction, in a letter of consolation and encouragement she sent him in June. "*A fine stormy sky can pass into a symphony,*" she wrote, underlining the words suggestively; "who knows," she added, "perhaps this has already happened."[16]

As early as the 1853 "Neue Bahnen" piece, Robert Schumann had been after Brahms to write a big symphony—that is, a loud public proclamation of his status as Schumann's (and, it goes without saying, Beethoven's) legatee. Within the article itself he had referred to the young composer's three early piano sonatas as "veiled symphonies" (a phrase that well suits at least the grandiose Third Sonata, opus 5 in F minor — the "Appassionata" key). An actual Brahms symphony, Schumann predicted, would mark the rebirth of Romanticism at its highest and best and least contaminated by the stain of "realism" (by which he meant explicit programmaticism). "If he will wave with his magic wand to where massed forces, in the chorus and orchestra, lend their strength," Schumann promised, "there lie before us still more wondrous glimpses into the secrets of the spirit world." They would be a long time in coming. To Joachim, Schumann wrote early the next year, "Now where is Johannes? Is he not yet allowing timpani and drums to resound?"[17] He was not, and it was the very sense of heritage and obligation that Schumann had thrust upon him that seemed to hold him back, as it did increasing numbers of modern musicians — musicians obsessed (to recall Burkholder's formulation) with the past and with their place in history, and with a consequent sense of their own cursed belatedness. After many abortive attempts, exasperated by a sense of failure, Brahms came close to giving up. He declared to one of his friends that he would never compose a symphony, adding, "You have no idea how it feels to one of us when he continually hears behind him such a giant."[18]

The giant, of course, was Beethoven, the (by definition) unsurpassable model by which Brahms felt he had to be measured. But all the past was stalking him, and the problem was compounded by the situation sketched earlier in this chapter, namely the ineradicable monopolizing presence not only of Beethoven but of all the "classical masters" in the newly standardized and canonized contemporary repertoire. In such a daunting atmosphere, composing an "ordinary" symphony, rather than a Lisztian programmatic work that asked to be measured by another (and, as far as Brahms was concerned, a meretricious) standard, became a well-nigh impossible task. Brahms approached it with extreme circumspection over a period that lasted, all told, more than twenty years.

THREE "FIRSTS"

The first try came shortly after Schumann's call, in response to tragic events. On 27 February 1854, less than eight weeks after Schumann wrote to Joachim asking after the symphony Brahms owed him, the tormented older composer made his famous suicide attempt, jumping headlong into the Rhine, which resulted in his confinement for the rest of his life in a sanatorium. By July 27, Brahms had sketched three movements of a symphony in D minor for piano duet, and had orchestrated the first movement. He sent the score to Joachim, who later told one of Brahms's biographers, Max Kalbeck, that it began with a covert (that is, unannounced as a "program") visualization of Schumann's anguished leap.

Whether it was something Brahms had told Joachim or something the latter had imagined on the basis of the state of mind they shared, the story rings true. The stormy opening (Ex. 45-1), which indeed strikes the portentous drum-saturated note Schumann had called for, is surely meant to recall or evoke a state of extreme emotional duress, with its immediate contradiction of the putative tonic by the first chord sounded, by the grotesquely dissonant trills on A♭, a diabolical tritone away from that same insistently asserted tonic, and by the bizarrely disruptive change of

EX. 45-1   Johannes Brahms, Piano Concerto in D minor, Op. 15, beginning

direction that shatters the opening melodic arpeggio with a startling leap(!). (The fact that Brahms disguises his portrayal of Schumann's leap by reversing its direction does not lessen the probability of its reality; veiling the literal depiction so as to keep the originating imagery private and leave only the emotional effect on public display is very much in the spirit of romanticism as opposed to "realism.")

What is perhaps most noteworthy about this nasty, intensely personal music, though, is the surprising fact that it is constructed almost entirely out of "classical" allusions. The most immediate one is to Schumann's own D-minor symphony, composed in 1841 as his Second, but revised in 1851 and published posthumously as his Fourth. It, too, begins by "allowing the timpani and the drums to resound" in a lengthy roll (Ex. 45-2a), and its first Allegro theme (alluded to thereafter in all the other movements) is also marked by a surprising leap that lands on the very same notes as does Brahms's intensified version (Ex. 45-2b).

But of course Schumann's D-minor symphony had itself been beholden to *the* D-minor Symphony, Beethoven's Ninth, and so is Brahms's. The surprising B♭ harmony at the outset of Ex. 45-1 is a sort of digest of the whole first section of Beethoven's exposition, in which the submediant (rather than the mediant) emerges unconventionally as the key of the second theme. And Brahms's much more insistent drum roll (on the tonic, instead of Schumann's dominant) is surely a recollection of Beethoven's first-movement recapitulation, one of the noisiest and stormiest (and most commented-on) moments in the literature.

Brahms never finished the D-minor symphony. Its first two movements later went into his first piano concerto (op. 15, published 1861), from which Ex. 45-1 is taken; and the third, even more radically transformed, later found a home in a choral work to which we will return. But the observations we have made about it remained characteristic of Brahms, and crucial to understanding both his eventual success and his historical role. The high level of allusiveness, for one thing, would be a permanent fixture, not merely (as might well have been thought at first) a sign of apprenticeship — which is to say that they were for the most part true allusions, rather than unconscious citations or imitations. Brahms's allusions, often extremely wide-ranging composites, would always be reforged, often with great virtuosity, into new configurations that in their combination made for a heightened intensity.

And for a second (related) thing, despite the eschewal of public programmatic content, Brahms's music was often anything but "abstract" in its conception. It was as laden with symbolism as Beethoven's Ninth itself, but like its famous antecedent (and unlike the work of the "New Germans") it contained no built-in decoder key, no public aids to interpretation, and hence no single certifiable message. But that, too, was an original and precious attribute of romantic art going at least as far back in our musical experience as Mozart, and given explicit acknowledgement by Schiller when he wrote, as early as 1794, that "the real and express content that the poet puts in his work remains always finite; the possible content that he allows us to contribute is an infinite quality."[19] Artworks of which that can be said have a greater hold on the imagination (or so a romantic would contend) than artworks with a single, explicit, paraphrasable meaning.

The reasons for Brahms's failure to complete his D-minor symphony, and its eventual withdrawal or transformation into works in less exacting genres, are unknown. Yet one can surmise them in part, perhaps, from the composer's subsequent behavior. His "neoclassical" bent was powerfully reinforced by the first paying position he secured after receiving his impressive sendoff from Schumann. It amounted to a sort of neoclassical throwback in its own right, for it allowed Brahms to spend four months a

EX. 45-2A   Robert Schumann, Symphony no. 4, I, slow introduction, mm. 1–7

EX. 45-2B   Robert Schumann, Symphony no. 4, I, *Lebhaft* (Allegro) theme, mm. 1–11

year from 1857 to 1859 in virtually "eighteenth-century" conditions, as Kapellmeister to the minor princely court of Detmold, a small city in north-central Germany. Brahms was thus one of the very last composers to enjoy, even briefly and part-time, the security of aristocratic patronage. Occupying as he did a position similar to Haydn's a hundred years before, Brahms was stimulated to imagine himself a Haydn and experiment "serenely" (as he put it) and for his own edification with classical form, in a fashion no composer had lately done with comparable opportunity or seriousness.

With a forty-five-piece orchestra at his disposal, the young Kapellmeister turned out two Serenades in a frankly retrospective style. The very name was retrospective: a throwback to the outdoor party music with which his patrons' eighteenth-century ancestors would have been supplied by their staff musicians for entertaining. As Brahms was more acutely aware than his less historically minded contemporaries, that lightweight environment had been the symphony's crucible. It was almost as if he wanted the ontogeny of his own works to recapitulate the phylogeny of the genre he wished to master. Equally, though, it was a retreat from the task to which his friends were urgently calling him, a temporary (and temporizing) refuge in the nineteenth century's eighteenth century—a fairyland of material comfort and artistic health.

Accordingly, the more frankly retrospective of the two serenades—the First, in D major, op. 11 (1858)—was a riot of "salubrious" and witty allusions, all of a bright and sunny nature as befits its key, the neutralizing reverse mode of Beethoven's Ninth, Schumann's Fourth, and Brahms's own first symphonic attempt. D major was the key of Beethoven's Second Symphony, at the opposite emotional extreme from the tortured opening movement of the Ninth. The fact, probably as well known to Brahms as to any historian, that the Second Symphony was composed at the most woeful juncture of Beethoven's life (the period of his irreversible deafness and the "Heiligenstadt Testament," described in chapter 31), surely enhanced its attraction to Brahms at this particular juncture of *his* life; for it argued against the popular romantic (but in fact "realist") assumption that artworks directly reflected the creator's biographical circumstances, that art was by nature confessional. Art was something one could, if one wished, actually hide behind (as Beethoven himself—who knows?—might have been doing).

That the D-major Serenade was palpably a retreat from writing a symphony is confirmed by its creative history. It began as a four-movement work with the fence-straddling title *Sinfonie-Serenade*. What turned it into a serenade and only a serenade was the addition to it of two frank *pastiche* movements between the slow movement and the finale: a pair of minuets such as no one had written in decades, and a second scherzo in which Brahms cleverly juxtaposed quotations from the two composers with whom he was temporarily identifying. Whereas in the D-minor Symphony he had looked to Schumann and through Schumann back to late Beethoven, in the D-major Serenade he looked to early Beethoven and through him back to Haydn. Many have noted (as they were surely meant to do) the delightful counterpoint of quotations, the trio from the scherzo of Beethoven's Second in the horn against the finale of Haydn's last ("London") Symphony in the cellos (Ex. 45-3).

Some have tried to see a serious polemic in this gay piece. Brahms is known, after all, to have been spoiling for a fight with the Lisztians, and as Donald Francis Tovey has observed, a work like the D-major Serenade can be read as an implicit refutation of historicism, or at least as a protest against it. Indeed, Tovey saw it for that very reason as "an epoch-making work in a sense that is little realized," for "it sins against the first and most ephemeral canon [rule] of modern criticism, the canon which inculcates the artist's duty to assert his originality in terms so exclusively related to this week's news as to become unintelligible by the week after next."[20]

EX. 45-3A Johannes Brahms, D-major Serenade, V (second scherzo)

EX. 45-3B   Ludwig van Beethoven, Symphony no. 2, Trio of Scherzo

EX. 45-3C   Joseph Haydn, "London" Symphony, Finale, mm. 1–8

That is well put, but it is a point that could only have been made in retrospect, at a time when the premises of historicism, while by no means vanquished, had long been under strong attack. In 1858, the Serenade would hardly have been thought an effective protest against the militancy of "New Germany," let alone its refutation. Reliance on classical models could only have looked weak compared with Liszt's bold forays, and that is precisely why Brahms could not offer it as a symphony. As Brahms put it himself to a friend who inquired about the change of title, "if one wants to write symphonies after Beethoven, then they will have to look very different!" But one thing that would make Brahms's own symphonies look different is already conspicuous in Ex. 45-3, and that is Brahms's mastery of traditional counterpoint and his fondness for indulging it not only in specially designated fugues or fugatos, but as a way of habitually loading the texture of his music with significant, often motivic, detail.

It was the combination of this motivically-saturated, highly allusive, polyphonic texture with the high strung, intensely personal expressive tension of the early D-minor attempt that is preserved in the First Piano Concerto, that finally produced the mature Brahmsian symphonic idiom in the aftermath of the failed polemic with the New Germans. In June of 1862 Brahms was able to show his friends the first full-fledged symphonic movement of his to survive into a finished work, eventually (after some further revision) becoming the first movement of his First Symphony. Clara Schumann wrote of it with delight to Joachim, quoting its "rather audacious" opening phrase (an echo of the old polemics?), and commenting, as an insider, on just those features of the work that will best repay our detailed examination:

> The movement is full of wonderful beauties, with a mastery in the treatment of the motives that is indeed becoming more and more characteristic of him. Everything is so interestingly interwoven, yet as spirited as the first outburst; one is thrilled by it to the full, without being reminded of the craft. In the transition from the second part back to the first [i.e., in the "retransition" from development to recapitulation] he has once more succeeded splendidly.[21]

Ex. 45-4a shows the beginning of the movement as Clara Schumann knew and quoted it in her letter to Joachim, extended from her four-bar quotation to eight measures in order to emphasize the contrapuntal "interweaving" to which her letter refers. The "soprano" in mm. 1–4 becomes the bass in mm. 5–8 to support a new motif in the soprano (one that will be given an immediate sequential development and extension). The weaving and reweaving, according to time-honored principles of invertible counterpoint, will continue throughout the movement. The transition to the second theme, for example (Ex. 45-4b), begins by inverting the texture of mm. 5–8, and then reinverts it so that the chromatic descent (the "middle voice" at the beginning of Ex. 45-4a) gets its turn to be the bass. In the slow introduction (Ex. 45-4c), which (though heard first) was a derivation made years later from the Allegro rather than its source, the contrapuntal relationship between the rising and falling chromatic lines is skewed to produce even more portentously dissonant harmonies over a pedal bass. Finally, the closing theme from the exposition (Ex. 45-4d) pits an inversion of the leaping motif first heard as the "soprano" in mm. 5–8 against a complex derivation from the soprano of mm. 1–4, in which each of the three chromatically ascending tones alternates in turn with the diatonic descent that follows in m. 3. One could almost say

EX. 45-4A Motivic interweaving in Johannes Brahms, Symphony no. 1, I, beginning of Allegro

EX. 45-4B Johannes Brahms, Symphony no. 1, I, transition to second theme

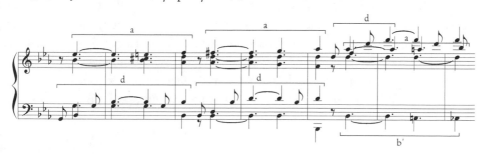

EX. 45-4C Johannes Brahms, Symphony no. 1, I, slow introduction

EX. 45-4D Johannes Brahms, Symphony no. 1, I, closing theme of exposition

that in place of the traditional thematic content of symphonic discourse Brahms has substituted a mosaic of motifs in an ever shifting contrapuntal design.

And what is more, virtually every "tessera," every stone in the mosaic, can be plausibly interpreted as an allusion. Of those already shown, perhaps the most obvious is the one labeled "d" in Ex. 45-4a. It belongs to a whole complex of Brahmsian themes that go back to the Schumann phrase shown in Ex. 45-2b; it was, evidently, a repeated tribute to Brahms's mentor that was finally internalized as a "stylistic trait." Other conspicuous allusions transcend the level of the individual motive. Most conspicuous of all is the one to which Brahms repeatedly made compulsive, nervously jocular references in his correspondence. "The symphony is long and difficult,"[22] he wrote to one. "My symphony is long and not exactly charming," he wrote to another. Finally, and most revealingly, he wrote to a third: "My symphony is long and in C minor."

STRUGGLE (WITH WHOM?)

In C minor. To anyone conversant with the tradition into which Brahms was trying, against the odds, to break, the words were enough to make the blood run cold. It meant that Brahms was taking on the model of models: Beethoven's Fifth. Vying with this symphony meant incurring a host of obligations that ranged far beyond the one with which we have already seen Brahms coping, namely the obligation to achieve a tight motivic construction. There was also the obligation to reenact (yet without merely repeating) Beethoven's archetypal "plot" or moral trajectory, embodied in the rhetoric of *Kampf und Sieg*, "Struggle and Victory" — a rhetoric that Beethoven himself had relinquished in the pessimistic post-Napoleon years, but that Brahms would now have to revive in a new historical and cultural context. Finally, though Brahms would put off reckoning with it for a while, there was the obligation to match Beethoven's signal achievement in the Fifth: the binding of the whole symphony together in a single thematic package through strategic recalls and returns.

The motif that eventually served this binding function is the first and shortest to appear: the three-note chromatic ascent, labeled "a" in Ex. 45-4, that is often presented in tandem with its descending complement ("b"). Its similarity to the unforgettably idiosyncratic opening (or answering) phrase in the Prelude to Wagner's *Tristan und Isolde*, while easily noticed, is often dismissed; Wagner, hero that he was to the New Germans, is an unlikely ally for a Brahms, let alone a mentor. He was a commanding, unignorable presence on the scene by 1862, though, and (although this is often forgotten) a contemporary of Schumann, hence old enough to be Brahms's father. And while *Tristan* would not be performed on stage until 1865, its vocal score had been published in 1860. So Brahms certainly had "access," as one says when adjudicating charges of plagiarism. But did he have "motive"?

Yes indeed, say musicologists aware of recent trends in literary criticism, particularly the theory of "anxiety of influence" put forth in the 1970s by the literary critic Harold Bloom. The very fact that Brahms was allegedly Wagner's antagonist has led some to suppose that the apparent (and pervasive!) allusions to *Tristan* in Brahms's First was an instance of unwitting mimicry and transformation—what Bloom calls "misreading"—caused by Brahms's fear of failure and his unconscious desire to overmaster it, an outcome that could only be achieved in contest with his strongest living elder and rival. In the early 1990s, a psychoanalytically oriented musicologist named Robert Fink even offered a reading of the symphony[23] (likewise predicated on the assumption that Brahms was unconscious of his debt to Wagner) that invested the proverbially erotic *Tristan* quote with the bachelor composer's repressed libido—that is, with sexual energies (and anxieties) that could find an acceptable outlet only in the semantically veiled medium of "absolute music."

One argument in favor of this reading is the fate of the *Tristan* motif in the second movement of the Symphony, the Andante sostenuto. It was not composed until 1876, when not only the first movement but also the finale was complete. Despite the long hiatus, or even because of it, Brahms took care to feature the *Tristan* motif prominently near the beginning of the movement, where it might promote the impression of a sponta-neous "organic" continuity that united the whole symphony in a single spiritual journey. That journey was also "microscopically" inscribed within the slow movement itself, thanks to the *Tristan* motif's recapitulation at the end. The two references, encircling the movement, contrast radically in affect: the first is chromatic and leads to an "open-ended" $\frac{6}{4}$ harmony (that is, a harmony in need of resolution), while the second is twofold: a repetition of the chromatic version followed by a diatonic one that leads to harmonic closure, thus replaying the transformation the original *Tristan* motif underwent at the tail end of Wagner's opera and wordlessly reevoking its symbolism (Ex. 45-5).

695

But there is really no reason to assume that Brahms could not have been conscious of his appropriations from Wagner. While he made no bones about despising Liszt's symphonic poems and program symphonies and deplored their influence (although he was as much in awe of the Hungarian's piano playing as anyone else), Brahms esteemed Wagner's music highly, and studied it (Fig. 45-4). To his friends he sometimes (half jestingly) called himself a "Wagnerianer," and treasured the autograph score of a scene from *Tannhäuser* among other manuscripts in a personal collection that included works of Haydn, Mozart, Schubert, and of course Schumann. (Wagner asked for it back on learning that Brahms was its owner; their letters make amusing reading.)

At any rate, if Brahms's was among the many imaginations stirred profoundly by the Prelude to *Tristan*, he could fairly claim his appropriation as "fair use," considering the striking reharmonization he gave the phrase in question, and the pointed way he directed it to a cadence on its first appearance, as if forestalling its Wagnerian (not to mention its erotic) consequences. Besides, the fact that Brahms's harmonic language had kept abreast of the latest in Wagner exempted him, to "New German" consternation, from the easy charge of epigonism. Indeed, the impressively "advanced" harmonic progression in which the supposed Wagner quote participates is the very one that gives rise to the movement's most impressive structural feature: the intermeshing of the most distinctive local harmonic progressions with the overall tonal design, as most

EX. 45-5A Johannes Brahms, Symphony no. 1, II, mm. 1–7

EX. 45-5B Johannes Brahms, Symphony no. 1, II, mm. 114–24

dramatically illustrated in the retransition passage to which Clara Schumann called attention. This was the profoundest lesson Brahms had learned from Beethoven.

Before tracing it, however, we need to trace the equally distinctive debt his harmonic idiom owed to Schubert, whose late symphonies, as we may recall, were posthumously retrieved from oblivion beginning in the 1840s, thus only since that decade available as an "influence" on younger composers. The "Unfinished," perhaps the greatest find of all, only saw the light of day in 1867, which is to say right in the midst of Brahms's lengthy symphonic gestation. He absorbed many lessons

FIG. 45-4   Brahms perusing the score of Wagner's *Siegfried*.

from it, as he did from the "Great" C-major symphony, which Schumann had rediscovered in 1840. Of all the composers of the nineteenth century, in fact, the only one whose mature idiom was even more heavily (if differently) indebted to Schubert's harmonic artifices was Liszt, who thus — and what could have been more ironic? — shared with Brahms, his most outspoken antagonist, a crucial common birthright.

These Schubertian "artifices," first described and illustrated in chapter 34, included, in the first place, the introduction of local progressions and modulations around circles of major and minor thirds alongside the "classical" circle of fifths. Another Schubertian innovation, strongly related to the first, was Schubert's reliance for purposes of harmonic multivalence (or "ambiguity") on what might be called "sonic homomorphism": the similarity in sound that can link chords with radically different structures and functions and allow their functions to be interchanged. The most potent of these homomorphisms — one could call them "puns," except that puns are jokes and these are not (necessarily) — was the one that obtained between the dominant seventh, the primary propeller of root motion along the circle of fifths, and the "German" augmented-sixth chord, which traditionally resolved by semitones in contrary motion to a dominant. (See the discussion of Schubert's Moment musical no. 6, Ex. 34-6.) These Schubertian devices play a decisive role in both the structure and the expressive rhetoric of Brahms's First.

In chapter 37 we already had occasion to cite Schubert's "Wanderer" Fantasy as a formative model for Liszt, providing a precedent for the "one-movement form" of Liszt's First Piano Concerto. Its status as a model for Brahms is even more specific: when the First Symphony was finally completed in 1876, its four movements exactly followed Schubert's path-breaking tonal trajectory along the circle of major thirds: C – E – A♭ – C. But even within the first movement, complete (except for the slow introduction) in 1862, Schubertian harmonies and tonal progressions rule.

The harmonization of the "Tristanesque" chromatic ascent, for example, first announced in Ex. 45-4a (and as of 1862 the movement's beginning), almost invariably involved an augmented sixth that functions locally as a "flat submediant," thus potentially subverting the dominance of fifth relations. The tension between fifths and thirds (in terms of root progressions), or between fifths and semitones (in terms of voice leading), pervades the movement, lending it a sense of taut tonal drama we have not encountered since . . . well, since Beethoven.

The drama is announced right along with the motifs and themes in Ex. 45-4a: the augmented sixth leads away from C minor to a D major that is marked as V of G. But the harmony is immediately forced back to the original tonic by adding a seventh to the G-major chord thus approached, turning D major retrospectively into V/V. The sense of constraint — of an impulse thwarted — is palpable. Clara Schumann's immediate reaction to its violence was keen. Having quoted it to Joachim, she added, "That is rather audacious, perhaps, but I have quickly become used to it."

At the very least, it is not the sort of comfortable music one associates with epigones. It is not just a pleasing play of tones but a *gesture*. We may interpret the thwarted chromatic impulse however we wish: as repressed libido, as counterthrust against "New Germany," as anything that may strike us as relevant or illuminating either with respect to Brahms or to ourselves as listeners. All such readings, however, can only be partial. They place limits on a meaning that, in its powerful inchoateness, precedes and subsumes all semantic paraphrases. And that, we may recall, was precisely the essence and purpose of "absolute music," lately rejected by the New Germans in the name of "union with poetry." Brahms rejected the union, and by the force of his example restored the viability of presemantic or "absolute" musical meaning, the sort of meaning that is indistinguishable from "structure" (that is, from the particularities of syntax that, by eliciting *affect*, produce a meaningful *effect*).

Tension between thirds and fifths, between fifths and semitones, continues. The whole movement's progress, at the "global" level, can be mapped according to its fluctuations. We can try to sum things up by describing the two main transitions.

The first, from the exposition into the development, takes off from a "Schubertian" modal mixture — E♭ minor following on its parallel major, the normal ("relative") key of the second theme in a C-minor symphonic movement. A more portentous model for the tonic-relative-parallel relationship, however, is the scherzo of Beethoven's Fifth, the specter evoked by Brahms's very choice of key. (For explicit confirmation that this was the model foremost in Brahms's mind one need only inspect the brass parts in Ex. 45-6.)

At the very moment where exposition gives way to development, however, Brahms takes an explicitly Schubertian plunge (Ex. 45-7a), reinterpreting the reiterated third and root of E♭ minor, the local tonic, as the third and fifth of C♭ major, the submediant, enharmonically respelled as B, with a consequent (and initially puzzling) metamorphosis in the key signature at the moment when the development arrives (that is, the downbeat of the exposition's "second ending"). Thus B, the leading tone — or, to use some archaic but suggestive terminology, the "subsemitonium" — is set in opposition to the tonic in place of the dominant: a semitone, in other words, assuming the traditional position (and doing the traditional work) of a fifth.

We may pick up the consequences of this pervading strain at the other end of the development, where the retransition is prepared in the traditional way, with "dominant tension" generated by a pedal point. The pedal on G is itself achieved through a reiteration of the motivically charged three-note chromatic ascent ("a"). Against the dominant pedal, this motive is given its lengthiest sequential development. The same chromatic motif that generated the pedal now threatens it, in a remarkable passage that combines the chromatic ascent in the bass with the equally motivic (Schumann-derived) octave leap, all pitted contrapuntally against the Beethoven-derived horn call in Ex. 45-6 and the motif labeled "c" in Ex. 45-4. The chromatic ascent is extended as far as D, enabling a reapproach, this time through the "classical" fifth relation, to the dominant pedal (now accompanying another sequence derived from "c").

The full dominant seventh on G is reached in m. 331 (Ex. 45-7b), and reiterated as a four-bar fanfare. There would seem to be nothing left to do but resolve it, with suitable panache, to the tonic. But at this point Brahms pulls off a superb Schubertian feint, resolving the chord not as a dominant seventh but as a German sixth, to the dominant of B, the opposing key. The lines of tonal conflict had not been so clearly or dramatically drawn in decades. And the conflict is played out to the inevitable dénouement through a Schubertian — or even a Lisztian! — circle of minor thirds, with German sixths cropping out of a chromatic sequence in contrary motion (an extension of the "a + b" complex first announced in Ex. 45-4a at the movement's very outset) on B♭ (m. 337) and D♭ (m. 339) before linking up with the original a + b complex and at last resolving, as the complex itself had first resolved, through two fifths (D natural and G) to the tonic and the "double return."

Liszt, of course, would have done it differently. The sequence of augmented sixths on G, B♭, and D♭ would have mandated, in one of his symphonic poems (say, the "Mountain Symphony" as discussed and illustrated in chapter 40) the completion of the sequence with a similar chord on F♭(E). A "New German" would no doubt call Brahms's modus operandi a pusillanimous retreat to the security of traditional "tonality." Brahms might well counter that the more radical Lisztian progression sacrifices all sense of conflict and drama to an inert (because functionally undifferentiated) sequence, colorful and superficially "progressive" but devoid of emotional significance. Brahms remained faithful to the German tradition — a tradition (as we have already observed, and as can scarcely be overemphasized) that included the Wagner of *Tristan* and the *Ring* — in staunch opposition to the new harmonic tradition that Liszt had been trying to establish.

So the lines were drawn at the end of the century. Each would find ample continuation in the music of the next generation, and beyond. But, to peek briefly at that future, there would be a significant difference in the work of the neo-Lisztians (mainly

EX. 45-6 Johannes Brahms, Symphony no. 1, I, mm. 243–52

EX. 45-6 (*continued*)

French and Russian composers) and the Germans who followed Wagner and Brahms. The former would use circles of major and minor thirds or their scalar derivatives (whole-tone and "tone-semitone" or octatonic scales) primarily for the depiction or exploration of nonhuman, subhuman, or superhuman imaginative terrains—natural, primitivistic, fantastic, occult—in which there would be a huge upsurge of interest at century's end. Pitch relations that preempted the forces of functional harmony were suited best to conjure up odd or alien worlds. German composers, meanwhile, would extend and intensify the exploration of the human inner world, that of emotions and desires, for which the dynamism of established tonal relations—the push of fifths, the pull of leading tones — would remain indispensable, as they had been for Wagner and Brahms alike.

The first movement of Brahms's First was a landmark in this extension; and yet the composer shelved it for more than a dozen years before providing it with its companion movements. Surely the demons of heritage and obligation were still plaguing the composer; but an equally important reason for this renewed delay was that in the mid-to-late 1860s Brahms embarked in earnest on his successful public career, a path that at first deflected him from his symphonic tasks.

EX. 45-7A Johannes Brahms, Symphony no. 1, I, mm. 185–91

EX. 45-7B Johannes Brahms, Symphony no. 1, I, mm. 331–43

A CHORAL (AND A NATIONALISTIC) INTERLUDE

It is one of the many ironies surrounding his career that Brahms, famous in history for shunning opera, for his faithfulness to the idea of "absolute music," and for his role in reviving it, should have gained his first real fame as a composer of choral music to romantic, religious, and patriotic texts. It was, however, a time-honored road to success for German composers in the older Romantic and nationalist tradition, with its many supporting institutions in the guise of singing societies and summer festivals. For a while it was the field in which Brahms was seen to specialize.

The first major appointment he was able to secure in Vienna was as director of the Singakademie, one of the city's two main choral societies. In pursuit of the post he unexpectedly embarked in the spring of 1863 on an elaborate cantata—*Rinaldo*, for tenor soloist, chorus, and orchestra—after a narrative poem by Goethe based on Torquato Tasso's epic of the crusades, *Jerusalem Delivered* (1581), which has already figured in this book (see chapter 20) as a popular source for Italian madrigals and early operas. The part Goethe had paraphrased had already been set as an opera by Lully (1686), Handel (1711), and Gluck (1777) by the time Brahms got a hold of it, and in its dramatic exchanges the work is as close as Brahms would ever come to writing an opera himself. (Indeed, had he found a suitable opera libretto in this ambitious phase of his career Brahms would not have hesitated to set it; his "principled" antioperatic stance was adopted later and was mostly a matter of image-building.)

By the time he had his first rehearsals at the Singakademie in the fall, Brahms realized that the organization's budget would not cover a performance of his work in progress, and it, too, was shelved for a while, not to be completed until 1868. For the time being Brahms concentrated as a conductor on *a cappella* and continuo-accompanied literature, and in the process discovered a wealth of sixteenth- to eighteenth-century music, particularly Heinrich Schütz and other early "German masters" from Henricus ("Heinrich") Isaac (then thought to be a German) to J. S. Bach, whose choral works were then only beginning to be published.

Brahms's stint with the Singakademie lasted only one year, but the impact of "early music" on his composing was decisive. He became an enthusiast, sought out the leading musical scholars of his generation—Gustav Nottebohm, Friedrich Chrysander, Philipp Spitta—as friends, and actually engaged in some amateur musicological work of his own, making many arrangements of early German choral music and participating in the preparation of "critical editions" (that is, editions faithful to original sources rather than arrangements) of music by Schubert and Schumann, and even a non-German, François Couperin.

"Even" a non-German, because musical antiquarianism, as an aspect of musical Romanticism, was ipso facto an aspect of musical nationalism as well, and it should not be assumed that his eventual stance in favor of "absolute music" put Brahms at odds with either the Romanticism or the nationalism of his time. The manner in which his antiquarian pursuits rubbed off on his composing only intensified its timeliness, so to speak, given the moment in which he lived, and the nation to which he belonged. Brahms's choral music, in fact, gives us an interesting new lens on an old question, namely the question of how the liberal German nationalism of the pre-1848 period metamorphosed into the more aggressive nationalism with which the world is now more familiar, and how music figured in the process.

Brahms's greatest choral work, *Ein deutsches Requiem* ("A German requiem," 1868), may be viewed as a sort of culmination of the older nationalist phase. It is not a liturgical work, but rather a setting, inspired by the death of Brahms's mother, of selected passages from the bible, in Luther's translation, that deal with consolation, acceptance of fate, and transcendence of suffering through love. As a work with "Lutheran" words (and a certain amount of chorale-like writing) but meant for performance throughout the German-speaking lands — including Catholic Austria, the composer's adopted home — it continued the ecumenical "Mendelssohnian" tradition of using music as a liberal uniter of the German-speaking peoples.

As hinted earlier, the Requiem contains one remnant salvaged from the aborted symphony in D minor: the second movement, "All of Flesh is Like the Grass," set as a funeral march in B♭ minor that in its original symphonic context would surely have recalled Beethoven's *Eroica*. But other sections of the Requiem give evidence of Brahms's profound assimilation of his nation's earlier legacy of sacred music. Fugues and fugatos abound, of course, but there are also many passages that bear traces of "musica antiqua" from archeological strata to which no previous composer had ever penetrated creatively.

The Requiem's very opening section, "Selig sind, die da Leid tragen" ("Blessed are those who bear their grief"), is a striking case in point. Its text is put together like the words of an old motet. That is, it is a patchwork of topically related lines from disparate biblical sources, in this case bridging the Old and New Testaments. After the first sentence, from the Gospel According to Matthew, the words come from Psalm 126, "Die mit Tränen säen" ("They who sow with tears"). This was a psalm that many old north-German composers had set. The most famous setting, perhaps, was the one by Johann Hermann Schein (1586 – 1630) in his collection *Israelis Brünlein* ("Fountain of Israel") of 1623.

Brahms surely knew it, and fashioned his own setting to reflect that knowledge, appropriating the contrapuntal and expressive techniques of Schein's day (or even those of Schein's actual setting) in order to achieve a similar marriage of "motet" style with "madrigalian" trappings (Ex. 45-8). Motet style means that successive lines are given individual musical treatment (or, to use the language of the nineteenth century, set to separate motifs), usually in imitative texture. The madrigalian element is the use of highly contrasting musical figures to point up the figures of speech employed in the text. The most sought-after figures were antitheses, the contrast of opposites, here "sowing with tears" and "reaping with joy."

Schein had set the former to a tortuous chromatic line in long note-values, the latter to an octave leap in short ones. Brahms does something similar, in nineteenth-century terms. The first phrase is set to drooping sigh-figures, with the quarter note as the shortest value. Except for the soprano, all the voices sing the same musical idea either in parallel harmony or in imitation. The soprano part intensifies expression through syncopation, chromaticism, and a final leap to a suspension at the top of its range. The

EX. 45-8A   Johann Hermann Schein, *Die mit Tränen säen*, the two opening points

EX. 45-8A   (*continued*)

EX. 45-8A (*continued*)

second phrase is set disjunctly, in halved note-values and (in seemingly direct reference to Schein's setting) in dancing dactylic rhythms that cover almost an octave's span in a single direction.

The harmony is fully up-to-date and highly expressive in Romantic terms, the orchestration likewise — and highly sophisticated, the violins being omitted for the sake of a "darker" sonority as Brahms had previously done in his second orchestral Serenade. The archaism is not so much stylistic (or "epigonal") as "procedural" — not an imitation or even an emulation (since there is no sense that Brahms was competing with Schein) but rather a reference or allusion, the rhetorical device of which Brahms is emerging as the supreme nineteenth-century musical master.

Allusion to early music also makes a significant contribution to the impact of the *Triumphlied* ("Song of victory"; 1871), Brahms's most grandiose choral work and during his lifetime his most popular one. (As in the case of Beethoven's *Der glorreiche Augenblick*, the reasons for its present near-total neglect have more to do with its tainted political content than its musical qualities.) It was composed in the aftermath of the

EX. 45-8B   Johannes Brahms, *Ein deutsches Requiem*, I ("Die mit Tränen säen...")

EX. 45-8B (continued)

EX. 45-8B (*continued*)

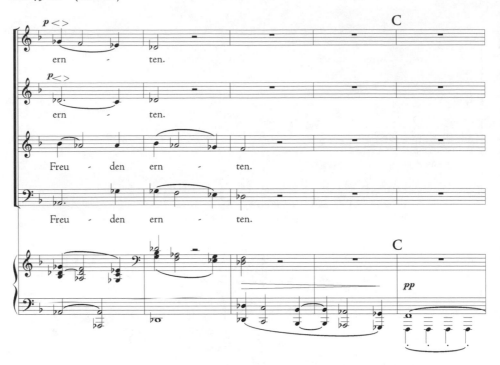

Franco-Prussian War, in expectation of the elevation of the king of Prussia to the exalted rank of *Kaiser*, emperor of the united German *Reich*.

Like the vast majority of his countrymen (including those who, like Brahms, lived under the rule of the other kaiser, Franz Josef of Austria) the composer enthusiastically supported the policies of Otto von Bismarck, the Prussian "Iron Chancellor," who engineered the long-awaited unification of Germany, and whose portrait, in the form of a bronze relief surrounded by a wreath, occupied a place of honor in Brahms's music room. The *Triumphlied*, a three-movement cantata for antiphonal mixed choirs (eight voice parts in all) in D major, accompanied by the largest orchestra Brahms ever employed, was published with a decorative flyleaf proclaiming it to be *Seiner Majestät dem Deutschen Kaiser Wilhelm I ehrfurchtsvoll zugeeignet vom Componisten*: "Reverently dedicated by the composer to his Majesty the German Emperor Wilhelm I."

Opportunistic? To be sure, but it was nevertheless an authentic expression of the German nationalism of its day, and this in two ways. In the first place it renders adoration to *Reich* and kaiser in explicitly religious terms, such as until then (within modern times) had been the exclusive province — and notoriously so — of the "backward" Russian Empire (as in Glinka's opera *A Life for the Tsar*, discussed in chapter 36). It is not just that the empire is declared to be the fulfillment of God's will. (That much had already been claimed, by Beethoven among others, for the post-Napoleonic imperial restorations.) In the *Triumphlied* the German *Reich* is implicitly compared, in a text drawn by Brahms himself from the biblical Book of Revelation, with the heavenly dominion (also a *Reich* in Luther's German), and the kaiser (blasphemously, as it might

FIG. 45-5 Brahms's music room in Vienna; the bas-relief portrait of Bismarck (with ribbon attached) is located between a reproduction of Raphael's *Sistine Madonna* and the huge bust of Beethoven at the upper right.

have seemed were it stated outright) with "the King of Kings and Lord of Lords" — that is, with God himself.

Brahms's musical antiquarianism was especially germane to this religious veneration of state and ruler, for the *Triumphlied* takes the form of a "polychoral motet," the most exalted form of early ritual music, pioneered in Venice by the Gabrielis but known to Brahms primarily through the work of Schütz, Giovanni Gabrieli's pupil. And the edge the *Triumphlied* orchestra has over all other Brahmsian ensembles consists in the use of three trumpets instead of two, which, in conjunction with the timpani, play fanfares antiphonally with the choruses' Hallelujahs in a manner that specifically apes the Baroque "festival" orchestra with its "Stadtpfeifer" (town piper) contingent, known best to Brahms and his contemporaries from Bach's D-major orchestral suite, some of the large cantatas recently published in the *Bachgesellschaft* (Bach Society) edition of J. S. Bach's complete works, which began appearing in 1850 — and especially from Bach's exuberant D-major setting of the *Magnificat* ("Mary's song of praise"), the most immediate model, which echoes and reechoes through the first movement of the *Triumphlied*.

The trumpet fanfares inevitably lend a military cast to the proceedings; and this is the second way in which the nationalism expressed by the *Triumphlied* is of the newer, hawkish type. The work celebrates not only a political event but (as its title proclaims) a military triumph as well, and the latter is asserted aggressively, with *Schadenfreude* — roughly "gloating," more exactly "malicious pleasure in another's misfortune," something for which, perhaps significantly, only the German language possesses a word.

The "other" in this case, of course, was France, and fallen Paris in particular. Brahms shared the general German contempt for Offenbach's city and found an ingenious way of expressing it in the *Triumphlied*, literally "between the lines." The text of the cantata's first movement consists of a portion of the heavenly shout transcribed in Revelations, 19:1–2: "Hallelujah! Victory and glory and power belong to our God, for true and just are his judgments!" The rest of the verse runs as follows: "He has condemned the great whore who corrupted the earth with her fornication, and has avenged upon her the blood of his servants."

Brahms never set these abusive words. But at one point, immediately following the last line that he did set, he inserted an orchestral theme, blared *all'unisono* by almost the full orchestra, that never returns in the voice parts, and that exactly fits the rhythm of the next line in German: *daß er die große Hure verurteilt hat* (Ex. 45-9). No one who remembered the bible could miss it; and just in case anyone did, Brahms "painted" the unsung word *Hure* (whore) with an outlandish diminished third. There can be no mistaking his intention, however reluctant we may be to acknowledge it: Brahms penciled the offensive lines into his own copy of the full score.

And another bit of "painting" depicts, for all with ears to hear, the Prussian advance upon the French capital. At what ought to be the climax of the first movement, Brahms inexplicably (as it seems) scales the dynamics down to pianissimo right where the choirs enter with "Victory and glory and power" for the last time. Over the next twelve bars, a crescendo carries the words through to fortissimo, while the brass instruments and drums begin beating a tattoo, and finally an imitation of hoof beats. At the crescendo's peak, a German sixth on B♭ is harrowingly suspended over a pedal A for two full measures. Bloodier battle music would have to await the twentieth century.

So with the *Triumphlied* we encounter a nationalism that projects itself with the force of religious dogma, and that not only loves but also hates. It would be an impertinence to credit Brahms with the innovation. He did give it an unusually vivid musical expression, however, and one that links up interestingly with other aspects of his musical profile. Particularly telling is the use of "Bach" trumpets in such a context. The canonization of Bach had been linked with German nationalism since the appearance of Forkel's biography at the beginning of the century. Associated since Mendelssohn's time with choral genres, a tradition that Brahms brought to its peak in the *Triumphlied*, the Bachian style (and related "baroque" devices) would soon be carried by Brahms into the "symphonic mainstream" — the domain of absolute music — as well. It was Brahms, in other words, whose music forged the link between Bach and the "Viennese classics" that has since been spuriously read back into the historical narrative, at first by German ("insider") scholars, and that has quite recently come under intense skeptical scrutiny, chiefly by Americans, the quintessential musicological outsiders.

EX. 45-9   Johannes Brahms, *Triumphlied*, 1

For in righteousness and truth,
for in righteousness and truth,
the Lord, yea, the Lord giveth judgment,
for He judgeth, He judgeth
in righteousness and truth, in truth.

As we redirect our own narrative now toward the "absolute" genres with which Brahms is now chiefly, and with every good reason, associated, one more work from his "choral period" will repay a sidelong glance: the *Schicksalslied* ("Song of fate"), completed in 1871, the same year as the *Triumphlied*, but of very different character. It is a setting of a poem by Friedrich Hölderlin (1770–1843), one of the great German romantic visionary poets, whose romantically unlucky fate (ending with his confinement in an insane asylum for the last thirty-four years of his life) paralleled Schumann's, quickening Brahms's interest in him.

The poem, originally titled "Hyperion's Song of Fate" after the Titan of Greek mythology, angrily contrasts the perfect, timeless bliss of the gods' abode, whose "fateless" denizens exist in utter serenity and obliviousness to pain, with the miserable lot of "suffering humanity," buffeted by the flux of time, "falling haphazardly from hour to hour like water dashed from crag to crag." Like any poem based on an antithesis, it is made to order for musical treatment. The first section of Brahms's setting, comprising the opening stanzas of the poem, is a soft and gentle "Elysian" song in E♭ major, in a leisurely common time, set off by gleaming flutes and by pizzicato strings doing their best to imitate harps. Bachian resonances abound. The first choral tutti, for example, is accompanied by a quotation from the pizzicato bass in the famously idyllic *Aria* from Bach's orchestral Suite in D major (the louder movements of which had already found echo in the *Triumphlied*). The tempo marking, *Langsam und sehnsuchtsvoll* (slowly and longingly), shows that heavenly bliss is being described from the earthly point of view, as an object of desire.

FIG. 45-6 Autograph score page from the middle section of Brahms's *Schicksalslied* (1871).

And then comes the last stanza of the poem, set in stark and sudden contrast as a stormy Allegro in C minor, the dark "relative" of the original tonic, moving in an agitated triple time, accompanied by tremolando strings and baleful rolls of the kettledrum.

But afterward, Brahms does something no one following the chorus from Hölderlin's text could have anticipated. He allows the storm and stress gradually to die away, and then appends a return to the opening section, but in the key of C major, the parallel rather than relative key of the stormy middle. Thus the *Schicksalslied*, uniquely in the work of Brahms (and with scant precedent anywhere but in opera), ends in a key other than the one in which it began. Brahms explained the anomaly, in a letter

FIG. 45-7   Friedrich Hölderlin, the poet of the *Schicksals-lied*, in a pastel portrait by F. K. Hiemer (1792).

to a prospective conductor of the piece, as a deliberate critique of the poem, asserting that "I am saying something that the poet does not say," and adding that "it would have certainly been better if what is missing had been the most important thing for him," that is for Hölderlin.[24] Elsewhere, he complained that Hölderlin "doesn't say the most important thing."

Yet, however we interpret Brahms's beatific coda, whether as a consoling foretaste of immortality or a Christian rebuke to pagan heartlessness or a contrasting portrayal of heaven "from the inside," or more simply as supreme emotional exaltation, the fact remains that neither Hölderlin nor any other poet could have said this "most important thing," since it is said without words. In one of the most pointed affirmations that the idea of "absolute music" ever received, the final consolation, or insiders' view of heaven, or what you will, is reserved for the instruments to disclose. It is the very removal of the verbal element that allows the sense of transcendence—what Hanslick, in an ecstatic review, called the "transfiguring power of music"—to supervene over what might otherwise appear a merely dutiful "rounding" of the musical form.

Absorbed in the act of composing the *Schicksalslied*, Brahms may or may not have been aware that he was precisely reversing and thus negating the trajectory, and the implicit "argument," of Beethoven's Ninth. Having finished the piece he experienced doubts. "A silly idea," he called it in another letter, "perhaps a failed experiment."[25] Audiences found the piece moving, however; its success gave Brahms courage. Eventually the reversal and its implications must have dawned on him and shown him a way out of the bind that had been paralyzing his work on the First Symphony.

INVENTING TRADITION

Still, he went on postponing it. He made his return to "absolute" orchestral music via a shorter work, a set of Variations for Orchestra on a Theme by Joseph Haydn, composed in the summer of 1873, just after turning forty. The theme may not in fact have been Haydn's. Its source is a very obscure composition indeed: the second movement in the last of a set of six wind octets or "Feldparthien"—suites to be played by *Feldmusiker* or military musicians (wind players)—that Haydn wrote, presumably for members of Prince Eszterházy's retinue, at some undetermined point during his employment at Eisenstadt. It cannot be dated because it exists only in late copies, one of which happened to belong to the library of Vienna's Gesellschaft der Musikfreunde (Society of Friends of Music), one of Brahms's favorite haunts. (It would remain unpublished until 1932, the bicentennial of Haydn's birth.) In the manuscript the theme Brahms chose is headed "Chorale St. Antoni" ("St. Anthony's Hymn"). It was probably a religious folk song for which Haydn merely provided a harmonization. Brahms's "theme" is actually Haydn's whole movement, first presented in Haydn's original scoring for oboes, horns, and bassoons (Ex. 45-10a). What probably attracted Brahms's ear to the piece was the unusual five-bar phrase structure (the result, very likely, of the now-forgotten words), but its reconditeness was surely another factor, testifying to the antiquarian, "musicological" tastes that distinguished him from most of his composing contemporaries. The Haydn Variations, in fact, was the first purely instrumental work by Brahms in which resonances not only from the "classical" but also the "preclassical" repertoire are conspicuous. The way in which Brahms combined them, thus forging a link that is now assumed to be a "historical" fact, was his signal achievement.

And rarely was the scholarly side of the equation more obvious. As a fortieth birthday present, the pioneer music historian Philipp Spitta gave Brahms the first volume of his landmark biography of J. S. Bach, then hot off the press. It included a long preliminary study of German keyboard and choral music in the century leading up to Bach's birth, in which Brahms found the discussion of ground-bass forms (chaconne, passacaglia, etc.) particularly interesting—and inspiring. He corresponded with Spitta about them, asked for more examples, and finished off the Haydn Variations with a giant set of ostinato variations based on a five-bar ground bass derived from a combination of melody and bass notes from the St. Anthony tune's first phrase (Ex. 45-10b). From the way in which the ground bass is suddenly transposed to the highest voice after thirteen variations, it is clear that the model Brahms had chiefly in mind was Bach's famous organ Passacaglia in C minor.

By making Haydn shake hands with Bach, by treating Haydn's theme in a manner no longer practiced in Haydn's time but of even more ancient and honorable pedigree, by giving a "classic" theme a "preclassic" development, Brahms consciously sought an ecumenical synthesis that connected the German present to a generalized German past, a synthesis that identified him in the eyes of many as the preeminent German master of the present. Over the five-year period between the premieres of the German Requiem and the Haydn Variations, Brahms achieved real celebrity, not to mention a secure income from royalties that made him financially independent.

Both his fame and his finances were helped by a couple of frankly popular opuses that he issued during the same period for domestic consumption: two books of Hungarian Dances for piano duet (1869) and a set of sentimental waltzes, also published in 1869 under the title *Liebeslieder* ("Love songs") for piano duet with optional vocal quartet singing words by a fashionable poet, Georg Friedrich Daumer, who wrote under the pen name "Eusebius Emmeran." Like his eighteenth-century forebears, he was trying for an ecumenical social reach, writing both "classical works" for the concert hall (the "temple of art") and "popular works" for the home.

EX. 45-10A   Johannes Brahms, "Haydn Variations," mm. 1–10

EX. 45-10A (continued)

EX. 45-10B Johannes Brahms, "Haydn Variations," beginning of Finale ("St. Anthony's Hymn")

By the time of his fortieth birthday, then, Brahms had become a big success, with a following that bridged all the strata of the music-loving and music-buying public from scholars to household pianists. It was a success that roundly contradicted the dogmas of the New Germans, refuting their claims much more effectively than that lame polemical fizzle, the open letter of 1860. They did not like it, or him. Remarkably, Wagner came to regard Brahms — young enough to be his son, and an admirer to boot — as a threat. The mudslinging began anew.

In an essay of 1869, *Über das Dirigiren* ("About conducting"), Wagner took note of what he called Brahms's "wooden, prim"[26] performance style as an excuse to lash out at "Saint Johannes," the "Musical Temperance Union" he represented and its various hypocrisies, the chief one being a secret yearning to write (what else?) an opera. The only thing that united the Brahms faction, Wagner hinted, was their constant failure to satisfy this wish, "and Opera, never happily wooed and won, can figure again and again as mere symbol of a lure to be resisted finally; so that the authors of operatic failures may rank as Saints par excellence."

From the New Germans' or at least the Wagnerian point of view, with opera (or "music drama") the uncontested and incontestable peak of musical achievement, this persiflage made a sort of sense. But Brahms really turned the tables on it when he finally came forth with the First Symphony in 1876, at least fifteen and perhaps as many as twenty years after making his first sketches for it. The year may be significant; 1876 was also the year in which the completed *Ring des Nibelungen* finally had its Bayreuth premiere. Raymond Knapp, the author of a study of Brahms's symphonies, has suggested that the "final push to complete his First Symphony"[27] in the year of the *Ring*, "which finally allowed him to overcome whatever dissatisfactions had beleaguered the project, was motivated in part by his desire to offer an alternative monument to the spirit of German nationalism recently revitalized by the Franco-Prussian War." The way in which the Symphony's finale picked up the thread of the development — as much an ideological as a musical development — that we have been tracing, not only in the Symphony's first movement but also in the *Schicksalslied* and the Haydn Variations, lends credence to Knapp's conjecture.

VICTORY THROUGH CRITIQUE

One of the most contentious points at issue between the New Germans and their opponents was the historical status of Beethoven's Ninth Symphony. Wagner had notoriously cast it, in suitably religious terms, as the "redemption of Music from out of her own peculiar element into the realm of *universal art*," and "the human evangel of the art of the future."[28] In other words, the mixture of vocal and symphonic media in the last movement closed the door on the further development of abstract instrumental music, making Lisztian programmatics and Wagnerian "synthesis" (or *Gesamtkunstwerk*, as it was misnamed) not only necessary but inevitable. To "revoke" the Ninth Symphony and its supposed mandate would be to revoke the New German charter, or so their opponents imagined, and with it the whole historicist creed. It would be a victory for Germany as well, paradoxical as that may sound, for it would rescue German art from its Wagnerian preoccupation with German "thematics" and return Germany to its place at the forefront (to borrow Wagner's own arrogant term) of "universal art." Brahms realized that the only way to accomplish the necessary reinterpretation would be to recompose the finale of the Ninth as a nonprogrammatic instrumental work. Encouraged by the response to the Haydn Variations, he finally returned to the First Symphony in the summer of 1874, resuming work not with the next movement in order of performance, but with the finale. It was only when the outer movements were in place — the dynamic C-minor "allegro" transfiguring Beethoven's Fifth and the monumental finale transfiguring the Ninth — that Brahms saw the work's trajectory whole, and was able quickly to fill in the middle movements.

Like the finale of the Ninth, Brahms's finale is in a hybrid form, the "true" identity of which has long been a subject of pointless debate. Rather than trying to decide whether it is a sonata, a rondo, a set of variations, a rondo-sonata, or what, it would be better (as in the case of Beethoven) to take stock at the outset of its highly diverse and even disparate ingredients and then trace their interaction.

Prominent among them, just as in Beethoven, are pastoral and religious emblems. The pastoral emblem is an "Alphorn theme" that first appears among Brahms's papers in the form of a birthday card he sent from Switzerland to Clara Schumann in 1868. It is replete with archaic rhythms (a "Lombard" snap in the second measure, a "double dot" in the fourth), a rustic "raised" fourth degree (the F♯ in m. 6), and words that parody old German folk songs: "High in the mountains, deep in the valley, I greet you a thousandfold!"[29] (Ex. 45-11a). There is little doubt that this is no transcription from life but an "ersatz" — an imitation folk song, more folky than the folk. The religious emblem is another ersatz: a chorale-like passage intoned on its first appearance by a choir of trombones, horns, and bassoons (Ex. 45-11b).

These two emblematic items serve to introduce what appears to be the movement's main theme. As in Beethoven's Ninth it takes the form of a great, though wordless,

EX. 45-11A   Johannes Brahms, Symphony No. 1, IV, alphorn theme

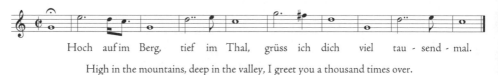

Hoch auf im Berg,   tief im Thal,   grüss ich dich   viel   tau - send - mal.

High in the mountains, deep in the valley, I greet you a thousand times over.

EX. 45-11B   Johannes Brahms, Symphony No. 1, IV, chorale theme

hymn. The resemblance to the choral theme from the Ninth is so pronounced and was so widely noted as to have become a standing joke, the best known version of which had Brahms answering someone who had pointed it out to him by saying, "Yes indeed, and what is really remarkable is that every jackass notices it at once."[30] Sometimes the squelch is interpreted to mean that Brahms found the suggestion that he lacked originality irritating. More likely, if he actually said it, he meant that the mere resemblance is uninteresting. The implications were what counted.

EX. 45-12A   Johannes Brahms, Symphony No. 1, IV, main theme

EX. 45-12B   Ludwig van Beethoven, Symphony No. 9, IV, choral theme (transposed)

For there can hardly be a doubt that Brahms intended his theme as a paraphrase of Beethoven's. If the two are written out in the same key, they even have a measure in common, and Brahms, by developing the phrase in which that measure occurs, all but insists that we notice (Ex. 45-12). Far less immediately noticeable is the equally strong resemblance of the opening phrase of the melody (which, in the parallel minor, had already served as the portentous opening phrase of the Finale's slow introduction) to a C-minor ground bass by Bach (Ex. 45-13). As the Brahms scholar David Brodbeck has plausibly suggested, if one of the references is a deliberate allusion, then in all likelihood both of them are.[31] And if so, then we have another attempt at forging a factitious link between Bach and the Viennese classics.

The fact that Brahms chose to make so obvious a reference to Beethoven's choral theme, and also the fact that his own theme actually makes a double allusion (first to Bach and only then to Beethoven), both take on increasing significance as the movement progresses. The most obviously significant aspect of the Beethoven reference was the simple fact that it was entirely—and pointedly—instrumental. By alluding to the choral theme but withholding (or suppressing) the chorus, Brahms seemed to be correcting the wrong turn Beethoven had—with laudable intentions but dire results—taken half a century before.

His friend, the musicologist Chrysander, got the point and publicized it. Far from the "weak and impotent imitation"[32] the New Germans were calling it, Brahms had created "a counterpart to the last sections of the Ninth Symphony that achieve the same effect in nature and intensity without calling on the assistance of song." This alone was enough to show that Brahms's attitude toward tradition was not merely reverential or epigonal, but active, participatory, and anything but uncritical. By not merely attaching himself to the Beethoven tradition but critiquing it, Brahms had brought about (or hoped to bring about) a change of course. In Chrysander's words, he had "led the way back from the symphony that mixes playing and singing to the purely instrumental sympho ny," ending the eclipse of the latter genre and restoring its historical validity. As we shall see (and go on seeing, far into the twentieth century), the subsequent history of the genre confirmed his success.

EX. 45-13A   J. S. Bach, ground bass from Cantata no. 106, "Gottes Zeit ist die allerbeste Zeit"

EX. 45-13B   Johannes Brahms, Symphony no. 1, IV, beginning of main finale theme

EX. 45-13C   Johannes Brahms, Symphony no. 1, slow introduction of finale, mm. 1–15

But there was even more than that to Brahms's critique of "Wagner's Beethoven." The difficulty critics and analysts have had in identifying the form of Brahms's finale arises from the unexpected behavior — or, perhaps, the unexpected fate — of the main theme. The manner in which it is introduced, establishing a new and faster tempo after a slow introduction that had ended on the dominant, identifies it as a symphonic "first theme" — that is, a theme that will be contrasted with another (in the dominant), will experience tonal vagaries and motivic development, and finally achieve a decisive or even triumphant restatement in the tonic to signal the movement's impending closure.

Up to a point that is just what happens. After its initial statement by the strings, the theme is repeated by the winds, as if replaying the strategy whereby Beethoven's choral theme had spread its brotherly contagion. A third repetition gives way to a preliminary motivic development of the opening Bach-derived phrase, opening onto a modulatory bridge that leads to the expected "second theme" (Ex. 45-14). It arrives at m. 118, and turns out to be another "typically Brahmsian" backward glance — a set of tiny variations over a four-note "descending tetrachord" ground that (as we have known since chapter 17) had a particularly distinguished historical pedigree.

EX. 45-14 Johannes Brahms, Symphony no. 1, IV, mm. 118 – 124 (strings only)

But the dialectics of "sonata form" (unknown, of course, in the seventeenth century) lend a delicious ambiguity to Brahms's revival of the ancient ground. Such grounds normally descended from the tonic to the dominant — and so does this one, except that at this point in the movement's tonal progress, the dominant has been "tonicized" (that is, made to function locally as tonic). The actual impression conveyed, therefore, is of a descent from subdominant to tonic. Thus Brahms again manages to have it both ways: a deliberate allusion to an outmoded style becomes the vehicle for an ingenious novelty.

To use one's knowledge of the past to create something fresh and original is more than an evasion of "epigonism." It is in its way a political statement about the nature of tradition. Tradition, in this view, is not a brake on innovation. On the contrary, tradition is the sole enabler of innovation that is meaningful rather than destructive, because it is mediated by social agreement (in this case, the recognition of a convention, permitting its intelligible transformation). That is classic "liberalism," anathema to radicals and reactionaries alike.

Brahms's sonata "exposition" continues to satisfy expectations with a rousing "closing theme" (Ex. 45-15), its move into exuberant triplets multiplying the Beethovenian resonances by alluding to the analogous moment in the finale of Beethoven's Fifth. The development, too, arrives right on time, although it begins with a feint that would long remain a Brahmsian trademark (compare, for example the first movement of his Fourth Symphony): an apparent "premature recapitulation" of the main theme in the tonic key, which unexpectedly modulates to a distant one before it is through. The modulation takes place at the last moment, as an extension of the final cadence, landing the music

EX. 45-15   Johannes Brahms, Symphony no. 1, IV, mm. 156–159

EX. 45-15 (continued)

in E♭ major, from which (as anyone listening must surely expect) a circuitous path back to the tonic will be traced for the recapitulation.

But that recapitulation never comes. Instead, the theme is "liquidated," to use a term coined many years later by a later Viennese, Arnold Schoenberg, who claimed to have learned the technique it denotes from Brahms. That is, it never recurs as a whole, but only in its various motifs, which gradually recede into the music's general motivic play and eventually lose their identity. So thorough is its receding that the dramatic moment of "retransition" comes and goes without any reference to the main theme. Instead the "Alphorn theme" from the Introduction, also in C major, is recalled to stand in for it. That this is in fact the "official" tonal return but without a thematic recapitulation (or, at any rate, without the expected one) is clear from the way in which the "second theme" follows the Alphorn theme in the tonic, with closing theme in tow. So there is recapitulation after all; it is just that the main theme has been deliberately, if enigmatically excluded from it.

It returns to initiate a Beethovenesque "development-coda," in a passage that alludes to the ascending chromatic sequence that begins the development section in the first movement of Beethoven's Third (*Eroica*) as clearly as previous allusions had invoked the Fifth and the Ninth. But once again, it is only the Bach-derived head-motif that gets to make an appearance. The part of Brahms's theme that so strikingly recalled Beethoven's choral Ode to Joy remains in eclipse — along with the whole idea of a choral symphony. It is as if Brahms had anticipated the argument made by the New Germans, and revived more recently by German critics and musicologists, that any reference to Beethoven's choral theme, even without a chorus, is in effect a submission to its authority. The act of "alluding to the vocal collectivity,"[33] as the musicologist Reinhold Brinkmann has put it, honors its necessity all the more strongly (as Hamlet might have said) in the breach than in the observance. But Brahms's methodical liquidation of the choral theme suggests otherwise. Beethoven's vocal collectivity had been conjured up only to be dispelled.

Yet not every vocal collectivity is dispelled. The fanfare-like last coda or *stretta* (*Più allegro*) begins (Ex. 45-16a) with one last motivic allusion to the head-motif (pared down by now to three notes) and makes what is obviously a headlong dash to peroration or rhetorical climax. When the climax comes, however, the main theme is once again preempted, this time (most unexpectedly) by the "chorale" unheard since the slow Introduction (Ex. 45-16b). That, too, evokes a vocal collectivity, but an older one than Beethoven's. Beethoven is not dethroned, merely subsumed along with the other Viennese classics into a larger view of German musical tradition that begins with Bach — or not even with Bach, perhaps, but with Luther.

And so the newness of the renewed symphony, as proclaimed and practiced by Brahms, was confirmed by reference to what was unexpectedly old. It was not a return to the past, which is always impossible, but a synthesis. Brahms's view of the symphony was classically "dialectical" and his achievement, in Chrysander's words, "signaled an expansion of those effects that can be created through instrumental means alone."[34] Brahms had encompassed within his symphonic purview much that had formerly been foreign to the symphonic tradition. Besides the evocation of "vocal collectivities," the new elements included the contrapuntal practices of ancient organists and the overarching thematic reminiscences and mutations of the most modern opera composers. All of it, however, was as thoroughly transformed by its inclusion in the symphony as the symphony, by including it, had been transformed.

RECONCILIATION AND BACKLASH

That is the meaning of dialectics: mutual transformation through mutual accommodation. And that, for liberals, is the meaning of tradition: a past that enables the present, but that in the process is itself transformed. Yet whatever is transformed also maintains recognizable (and legitimating) ties with its former guise. Ultimately, going against the

New German insistence on historical progress and directed evolution, Brahms believed in the "timelessness" of artistic problems and artistic greatness. That is what Bach symbolized (and has continued ever since to symbolize within the post-Brahms tradition of "classical music"). And beyond Bach, that is what nature (the Alphorn theme) and

EX. 45-16A Johannes Brahms, Symphony no. 1, IV, mm. 391–395

religion (the chorale theme) have always symbolized: everything that is "beyond history, unchanging, constant, essentially at rest,"[35] in Brinkmann's apt summary, and yet ever adaptable to new conditions and needs. That, too, is classic liberalism ("We hold these truths to be self-evident . . .").

EX. 45-16B   Johannes Brahms, Symphony no. 1, IV, mm. 407–416

The signal moment in the early history of Brahms's First was its ecstatic acceptance by the pianist and conductor Hans von Bülow, likened by some to a religious conversion. Bülow, we may remember from chapter 40, was a charter member of the New German School. The personal disciple of Liszt at Weimar and a close associate of Wagner, Bülow had married the former's daughter and lost her to the latter, in the meantime conducting the premieres of both *Tristan und Isolde* and *Die Meistersinger*. He made a specialty of Beethoven's Ninth, which he conducted twice on one occasion to demonstrate his faith in its peerlessness, that is, the unworthiness of any other work to share billing with it.

But after hearing Brahms's First, played to him in advance of publication by the composer at a summer resort in 1877, Bülow rushed into print with an article hailing it as "the Tenth Symphony." The article ended with an avowal — "Bach, Beethoven, and Brahms do not alliterate with one another by chance"[36] — that has lived on ever since in the catchphrase "the Three B's," proclaiming a new holy trinity and granting lasting victory to Brahms's (and the musicologists') campaign to locate the true spiritual beginnings of the German "universal" tradition of "absolute" music not in the older Viennese trinity of Haydn-Mozart-Beethoven but in the resurrected Leipzig cantor.

This was too much for Wagner. After Brahms was awarded an honorary doctorate in 1879 by the University of Breslau with a diploma proclaiming him "the leader in the art of serious music in Germany today," the dread image of Bayreuth struck back. In "Über das Dichten und Komponieren" ("On Poetry and Composition"), an essay composed in fury amid the publicity surrounding Brahms's degree, Wagner let his pen run wild. "I know of some famous composers," he wrote, "who in their concert masquerades don the disguise of a street singer one day, the hallelujah periwig of Handel the next, the dress of a Jewish Csardas-fiddler another time, and then again the guise of a highly respectable symphony dressed up as Number Ten."[37]

What brought on this enraged response was Wagner's evident realization that the New German School could no longer assert exclusive rights to the interpretation of German musical history. Wagner's claim to Beethoven's mantle, implicit in his works and explicit in his writings, was now irrevocably in dispute. There would henceforth be two interpretations of the great tradition: the radical historicist one, which cast it as a kind of permanent revolution, and the liberal evolutionist one, which cast it as an incremental and consensual growth.

At the very least, Brahms had made the "classical"-style symphony a viable option once again, one that could be freely chosen without the stigma of epigonism. The chances of inclusion in the "permanent collection" were as slim as ever, but the effort to make room for oneself was newly respectable and attractive. Brahms himself, once he had broken the logjam, followed up his first symphony with three more in less than a decade. The Fourth and last, in E minor, first performed under Bülow in 1885, ends (symbolically, it could seem) with a monumental chaconne over a ground bass adapted directly from the concluding chorus (marked *ciacona*) in Bach's Cantata *Nach dich, Herr, verlanget mich* ("Lord, I long for thee"; BWV 150), one of Bach's earliest and most traditional works. To base the latest link in the tradition on the earliest of models was a token of the timelessness of values.

BRAHMINISM

But the symphony was only the most public arena in which Brahms forged a revitalizing link with the tradition of "absolute" instrumental music. It was an arena that could not be evaded if one wished to refute the premises of "New Germany," which by virtue of the genres it promoted and its highly active press, had claimed the public sphere as its exclusive preserve. And yet the very publicness of symphonic music, increasing exponentially with the growth of urban ("mass") culture and the proliferation of orchestras, inspired a backlash among connoisseurs, who (out of disinterested artistic commitment, nostalgia for preindustrial ways, or social snobbery, depending on one's vantage point) placed a new premium on chamber music, the "aristocratic" genre par excellence.

By the late nineteenth century, of course, the nature of aristocracy and its relationship to music had changed. Rather than a noble aristocracy of birth and breeding, we are dealing now with a middle-class aristocracy of *Bildung* or education, of taste and "culture"—breeding of another sort. Like the older aristocracy, the newer one sought from music patronage a way of experiencing and expressing their elite status, and valued music whose performance would create elite occasions. They preferred music of a subtlety and reconditeness that would exclude listeners beneath their cultural station.

One of Brahms's best friends, the famous surgeon (and amateur violist) Theodor Billroth, gave a superb illustration of this attitude in a letter congratulating the composer after a performance of the First Symphony. Its music, he implied, was possibly too good for its genre:

> I wished I could hear it all by myself, in the dark, and began to understand [the Bavarian] King Ludwig's private concerts. All the silly, everyday people who surround you in the concert hall and of whom in the best case maybe fifty have enough intellect and artistic feeling to grasp the essence of such a work at the first hearing—not to speak of understanding; all that upsets me in advance. I hope, however, that the musical masses here have enough musical instinct to understand that something great is happening there in the orchestra.[38]

FIG. 45-8 Brahms in his graybearded maturity, seated with friends at Der Rote Igel ("The Red Hedgehog") in Vienna.

Chamber music, still often performed before invited audiences in well-to-do homes like Billroth's rather than in concert halls (but, in the case of difficult contemporary works and especially those of Brahms, usually by hired professionals rather than convivial amateurs) fit the bill. This was the audience, an audience of professed idealists who worshipped the same "timeless" values as did Brahms, that made up his most enthusiastic constituency, and so it will not surprise us to learn that Brahms wrote far more chamber music than symphonic: three string quartets, five piano trios (including one with horn in place of cello and one with clarinet in place of violin), three piano quartets, one piano quintet, two string quintets, two string sextets, a quintet for clarinet and strings, three sonatas for violin and piano, two sonatas for cello and piano, and two sonatas for clarinet (or viola) and piano — twenty-four works in all, more than any other major composer since Beethoven. And he produced them over the entire length of his career, from op. 8 (the first piano trio) in 1854 to op. 120 (the clarinet sonatas), forty years later.

Here too, though, there had been a hiatus. Just as in the case of the symphony, the last important composer of "classical" chamber music had been Schumann, with about twenty works composed over an eleven-year span. The "New German" attitude toward chamber music, frankly disdainful, was tactlessly enunciated by Liszt one evening when, as Schumann's house guest, he heard a performance of his host's Piano Quintet and mortified the composer by calling it "Leipziger Musik" — Leipzig music — that is, provincial and academic.

The only really prolific composer of chamber music whose birth date fell between those of Schumann and Brahms was Joachim Raff, described earlier in this chapter as a "renegade Lisztian." Raff was still Lisztian enough to try his hand at programmatic chamber works, however, including *Volker* (1876), a big "cyclic tone poem" for violin and piano. Another "Lisztian" chamber work was the First Quartet (1876) by Smetana, subtitled "From My Life," one of only four chamber works in the output of this prolific composer of operas, symphonic poems, and piano music. It concludes with an emotionally wrenching portrayal (via a long-sustained natural harmonic stridently attacked by the first violin) of the onset of the composer's deafness. It has survived in the repertoire, but its autobiographical program identifies it as an anomalous work in a genre widely perceived to be out of joint with the times.

Brahms made no effort to adapt chamber genres to the taste — that is, the "mass" taste — of the times. Instead, he deliberately cultivated an esoteric style founded on Viennese domestic traditions, particularly that of the "Schubertiade," the legendary gatherings of Schubert's friends who alone during the composer's lifetime were privileged to hear his most advanced chamber works and songs. Another powerful precedent, of course, was Beethoven — the deaf Beethoven of the late quartets, long a symbol of consummate genius, of artistic idealism and social alienation, and of cultural exclusivity.

The one chamber genre, then, that gave Brahms as much pause as the symphony was — inevitably — the string quartet. Again he felt the presence of the giant dogging his footsteps. Again there were many false starts — Brahms claimed as many as twenty — and there was another endlessly protracted gestation, that of the First

Quartet, in the key of (what else?) C minor. Brahms is known to have worked on it off and on for at least eight years; and when it was finally published, in 1873, as the first of a pair given the opus number 51, it bore a dedication to Billroth. It was in every way an emblematic work.

Especially in the outer movements, it wears its difficulty on its sleeve, self-consciously cultivating what the unimpressed French called "le style chef-d'oeuvre" (masterpiece style). The aristocracy of *Bildung* differed from the aristocracy of birth in its appreciation of (to quote Nietzsche) "music that sweats." The taste on the part of "lay" listeners for complexity and elaboration of texture may have been a reflection of the bourgeois work ethic, or it may have been another way of confirming their status as educated connoisseurs. Musicians themselves, of course, are drawn to such music by their intensive "ear training." As we shall see in chapters to come, the intense fascination Brahms's chamber music exercised on other composers would be a powerful stimulus to stylistic innovation in the twentieth century. The novelty was the "lay" liking, however much a minority taste (and however short-lived in the case of new works), for the sort of "musicians' music" the superbly equipped and resourceful Brahms could best purvey.

What is often questioned is how many of the details we are about to examine — especially the extraordinarily fine-grained motivic structure — were "heard" (that is, noticed and actively followed as relationships, the way a musician might) by the audience that patronized this music. At what point, to quote Carl Dahlhaus's version of the question, is such attention to detail perceived as a distraction, to be "repressed so as not to endanger the 'esthetic mood'"?[39] The question may be unnecessarily condescending, and it may posit a needless or groundless opposition. It must have been just this quality of attention, though, that Billroth had in mind when he wrote of having "enough intellect and artistic feeling to grasp the essence of such a work" as a Brahms symphony or, *a fortiori*, a Brahms quartet. While one cannot listen today with the ears of a nineteenth-century connoisseur, one can certainly detect efforts on the part of the composer to make the details of his *thematische Arbeit* or "thematic process" salient.

For a foretaste, compare the first ten measures of the quartet's first movement (Ex. 45-17a) with the last five measures of the last movement (Ex. 45-17b). The melodic and harmonic near-identity is hardly arcane; but what is most remarkable is the way the finale's concluding chords provide a closure to the first phrase that is very conspicuously withheld at the beginning. The whole quartet (like the whole of *Tristan und Isolde*, one can scarcely resist pointing out) is somehow subsumed within that contrasting parallelism, a phrase presented first open then shut. If one looks now at the beginning of the fourth movement (Ex. 45-17c), with its unharmonized, truncated, transposed, and therefore slightly ambiguous reference to the quartet's beginning, one will view the movement's end in a new light, as the explicit realization of an implication. Such implicit references and parallels are prevalent throughout the quartet: the end of the last movement discharges an account that had been accumulating over the course of all four movements.

For the rest, we had better limit the present account of the quartet's motivic structure to just the first movement's exposition and a few of its repercussions later on. (A full accounting would require a book, and a tedious one at that: better to compile one's own book through repeated, attentive, "Billrothian" listening.) For a last preliminary, however, compare the first movement's opening "period" as given in Ex. 45-17a with the beginning of the development — or starting, for an even fuller effect, with the "second ending" (Ex. 45-17d). Never have we seen a development as melodically indistinct from the exposition as this one.

Not that it will come as news to us at this stage of the game that the hard-and-fast textbook opposition of an exposition that "presents" material and a development that

EX. 45-17A   Johannes Brahms, Quartet no. 1 in C minor, Op. 51, no. 1, I, mm. 1–10

EX. 45-17B   Johannes Brahms, Quartet no. 1 in C minor, Op. 51, no. 1, IV, end

EX. 45-17C   Johannes Brahms, Quartet no. 1 in C minor, Op. 51, no. 1, IV, beginning

EX. 45-17D   Johannes Brahms, Quartet no. 1 in C minor, Op. 51, no. 1, I, beginning of development section

"breaks it down" had long been contrary to actual practice. By the late nineteenth century, sophisticated motivic elaborations and transformations no longer await the "official" development section but are present from the outset. Larger and larger musical entities are constructed out of smaller and smaller particles. But wait — isn't that just what, three chapters back, we identified as the great "revolution" of Wagner's *Ring* with its kaleidoscopic texture of leitmotifs?

DEVELOPING VARIATION

Indeed it is. One of Dahlhaus's most fertile insights was the observation that by the late nineteenth century all "serious" composers (as he put it; perhaps we'd better say all German composers) had become "miniaturists." That is, all did their thematic thinking-in-music in terms of motifs rather than full-blown melodies — whether their field was opera or chamber music — and the crucial composerly problem of the latter part of the century became the fundamental tension between "the brevity of the musical ideas and the monumentality of the formal designs."[40] To drive the point home, Dahlhaus proclaimed the two seminal practitioners of the new motivic "miniaturism" to have been the Wagner of the *Ring* and the Brahms of the chamber music. And while there was surely an element of calculated shock in the unexpected coupling, it is very liberating so to view them: it frees us from the polemics of contemporaneous musical politicking and allows us to view the supposed adversaries from a historical vantage point that subsumes (or as Hegel would have said, "sublates") their differences.

In any case, the real functional distinction between Brahms's exposition and his development is what it had always been in the works of sonata composers: a harmonic ("tonal") rather than a thematic distinction. The music in Ex. 45-17d is appropriately "far out" from the tonic. But melodically it is if anything more regular than the exposition. The process of motivic "breakdown" begins at the very beginning of Ex. 45-17a, and it is truly pulverizing. The opening idea, an old-fashioned "rocket" such as Mozart or even Stamitz (the Mannheim composer — see chapter 29) might have started with, is stated only once at its full eight-note, five-beat length and is then progressively truncated. First the last five notes (three beats) are extracted and subjected to a chromatically rising sequence. Then the first three notes of the foreshortened motif are extracted and augmented by a fourth to extend the arpeggio — or are they notes 3–6 of the original phrase? — and put through a fourfold sequence to the peak of the phrase.

Phrases and motifs are primarily identifiable through contour — their rise and fall — and rhythm. In terms of contour, the downbeats of mm. 2, 3, and 4 of Ex. 45-17a are all motivically equivalent, even though the intervals are different: a diminished seventh, a perfect fifth, and a minor sixth respectively. And thus by contour and placement at the end of the longest upward sweep of all, the descending semitone in m. 7 can also be construed as "motivic," even though it introduces an interval as yet practically unused. Needless to say, once marked in this way as thematically significant, the semitone will now perform its many important harmonic tasks with vastly enhanced significance.

And yet, however important the transformation of intervals may be to Brahms's technique of "developing variation" (as Arnold Schoenberg, its most zealous emulator in the Vienna of the future, would call it), intervallic constancy plays a role of equal if not greater importance. It, too, gives rise to characteristic devices. The second violin part in mm. 1–3, for example, is entirely confined to reinforcing at the octave the C–E♭ third in the first-violin arpeggios and linking it up with the filled-in third in the same register with which the first violin part begins. This, too, is a technique of motivic "extraction," amply confirmed by the role that the interval of a third — both as a skip and as a "filled-in" scale segment — will play throughout the quartet. Call the first three notes in the first violin "a" and the first two notes in the second violin "a′" and we are prepared to trace an astounding number of connections, some obvious, others arcane (but where to draw the line between the two? and who shall draw it?).

EX. 45-18   Johannes Brahms, Quartet no. 1 in C minor, Op. 51, no. 1, II, beginning

The introductory phrase in the second violin at the beginning of the second movement, to take one example, is clearly an "a" in a sort of stuttering variant (Ex. 45-18); and the main melody in the first violin, having been thus prefigured, is just as clearly built up out of an inverted "a" preceded by an upbeat, and followed by an "a'." And if the first two beats of the melody in the second movement's second measure are described as an inverted "a," then the first two beats of m. 3 can be similarly described. And if so, then the last beat of m. 3 consists of an extension of the inverted "a" to encompass a fourth rather than a third. And if the last beat of m. 3 is part of "a," then so are the last beat of m. 4, the last beat of m. 5, and the second and third notes of m. 6, preceded by an overlapping inverted "a'." Having taken note of this much, we are now prepared to find that almost every note in the accompanying parts up to the point that we have traced is similarly derived (or at least derivable) from "a" or "a'."

Admittedly, at some point arguments like this can begin to seem farfetched. But at what point, exactly? Nor have we even broached the question of "intentions," or distinguished between varieties of intention: Did Brahms consciously calculate these things? Did he have to? Did he want us to hear them? Did he want us to trace them? What do we accomplish by tracing them? To what purpose? The head swims. And perhaps in saying this we have at last found a means of distinguishing "serious" music (the kind of which his Breslau diploma declared Brahms the preeminent master) from . . . what?

Leaving the answers to these questions to the "Brahmins" (to use the joshing term that quickly attached itself to the self-declared Brahms enthusiasts who regarded themselves as an elite "caste"), let us press on to the third movement (Ex. 45-19a). Like the second, it is a relatively lightweight, entertaining, divertimento-like affair (the way middle movements in Brahms usually tend to be), but still "serious" enough to set our heads spinning again if we like the way that feels. Identifying "a" in at the beginning of the viola part is child's play, and so is noticing the way the melody (or should we call it the countermelody?) in the first violin and viola at mm. 11 ff. is constructed out of a sequence based on "a'."

But having accounted for the falling seconds in the second movement as an extension of "a," we are justified (or are we?) in similarly deriving the first violin's opening tune in its entirety. And if we can keep ourselves from becoming entranced by the harmony in Ex. 45-19b, where a sudden circle of fifths unexpectedly plunges us deep into the realm of flats, we will notice that the "charming" (*lusingando*) melody (as Brahms quietly boasts) played in playful canon by the same first violin and viola is entirely made up of repetitions of "a" and its inversion. When the two melodies are combined in counterpoint (Ex. 45-19c), we have what amounts to two variations of a single motif pitted one against the other.

Now that the matter of harmony has been broached, it is worth noting the elusiveness of the F-minor tonic in that seemingly lightweight third movement, so coyly marked *comodo* (cozy) and *semplice* (simple) by the composer. True enough, the very first harmony in Ex. 45-19c seems to be a tonic triad — that is, if we are willing to call the first violin's D♭ an (unprepared) appoggiatura. But the second harmony, with its B and D naturals, flatly contradicts the first. The only "tonal" way of hearing their relationship is to interpret the harmony on the upbeat not as a tonic triad at all, but as a D♭-major triad in first inversion, cast as a Neapolitan to the dominant of C. Sure enough, C arrives "on schedule" in m. 8, sounding very much like the result of an authentic cadence, even if according to the signature it is only a half-cadence.

Will m. 16 deliver the tonic at last? Don't bet on it. Measure 16 finds us on C once again, and as far as the phrase structure is concerned, quite in the midst of things. Looking for an F in the bass and finding one at the end of m. 22, we note with dismay that the harmony has not rid itself of that pesky D♭, nor has the continuation changed. We are still dealing, so far as aural effect is concerned, with functions of C, not F.

EX. 45-19A   Johannes Brahms, Quartet no. 1 in C minor, Op. 51, no. 1, III, beginning

Where does the cadence on F finally happen? Only at the very end, of course. (But wasn't that supposed to happen only in Wagner?) On the way to that cadence, there are some stunning feints. One, again, is that "charming" interlude (Ex. 45-19b) — and it reminds us that another possible translation of *lusingando* is "teasing." The reason why

EX. 45-19B   Johannes Brahms, Quartet no. 1 in C minor, Op. 51, no. 1, III, "charming" melody

it is such a tease is that the harmonic digression it embodies is a "composing-out" of the already teasingly reiterated Neapolitan progression with which the movement opened (further reinforced at mm. 22–23). Its jumping-off point is the D♭-major harmony of the opening, this time expressed as a dominant seventh and pushed further flatward.

And when the whole teasing passage is repeated, at m. 46 ff., the jumping-off point is the G-major harmony to which the original Neapolitan was applied, again treated as the dominant of C, but this time pushed beyond C to the long-awaited F, which arrives in m. 48, only dressed up (and this is the biggest tease of all) as another dominant-seventh chord on the way to B♭. That B♭ triad, while it frustrates our immediate expectation of a tonic cadence, nevertheless has its own strategic purpose. It manages at last, by providing a subdominant, to identify the C-major harmony at m. 51 as a dominant rather than a tonic, thus pointing in the long range to the long-deferred goal. (It is in fact the first such unambiguous pointer in the movement.) This little glimpse at the third movement already conveys something of the manner in which the quartet's motivic and harmonic contents interact. A final glance at the first movement's exposition will give us a close-up view of the process. Ex. 45-20 picks up right where Ex. 45-17a broke off.

A new motif appears at the outset (m. 11) in the first violin — or rather appears to appear, because we know by now that nothing past the first measure of a movement like this is going to be totally "new." Accordingly, the first interval, the descending third, takes its place among the many inversions of "a'" that we have already noted. The further descent by a second also has precedent, indeed a very conspicuous one: namely, the climax of the first phrase in m. 7 (which also links up conspicuously, both

EX. 45-19C Johannes Brahms, Quartet no. 1 in C minor, Op. 51, no. 1, III, contrapuntal montage

EX. 45-20   Johannes Brahms, Quartet no. 1 in C minor, Op. 51, no. 1, I, mm. 11–27

melodically and harmonically, with the opening of the third movement). If precedent is sought for a direct progression of descending third and descending second, it can be found (inverted) in the second violin, as the original version of motif "a'" progresses across the third bar line to F. And if a direct link with the motif in m. 11 is sought, it can be found in mm. 15 and 17, when the one motif (in the second violin) is accompanied by the other (in the viola, echoed by the cello).

Having established its legitimacy, so to speak, let us now trace the new motif's progress, from first violin in m. 11 (descending from F) to second violin in m. 15 (descending from C, a fourth lower), to viola and cello in m. 22, descending from G, another fourth lower, to link up with the tonic in m. 23. Of course we have omitted from this neat sequential account the altogether anomalous transposition of the motif in mm. 19–20 (second violin followed by viola at the octave), which pitches the motif on B natural, the leading tone, so that it ends on F♯.

The note is not unprecedented. Preceded by E♭ in the second measure of Ex. 45-17a, F♯ had played the role of dramatic appoggiatura, "dissonating" against a tonic pedal and crying out for resolution. This time, however, the note is harmonized consonantly on both of its occurrences, against a rising scale in the cello, whose rhythm identifies it as a sequential expansion of the original "a" motif. These consonant intervals in support of the F♯ — perfect fifth against B in m. 19 and an altogether disorienting unison in m. 20 — are tonally disruptive, to say the least. They neutralize the need to resolve, and as such imply an impasse. Has the music in effect modulated through a process of motivic transposition to the key of B minor? Is that any proper place to go, or have we in effect lost our way?

Brahms implies that we have done exactly that by breaking off the two lines in m. 20 after their improbable unison closure, and in the next measure rubs it in by repeating the wayward note (arrived at with perfect thematic logic and total harmonic lunacy) with rests on either side. The music has come to an eerie standstill. Walter Frisch, in a detailed study of Brahms's "developing variation" technique, captures well the uncanny feeling it inspires: "In bars 19–21," he writes, "Brahms leads us to the edge of an abyss, and, indeed, makes us lean far over."[41] It is a moment to make one shudder; and the more attentive and "Billrothian" our listening has been, the keener our sense of vertigo will be.

But then, Frisch continues, Brahms "pulls us suddenly back onto the *terra firma* of C minor," and restarts the main theme (in the bass) as if nothing had happened. We are relieved, if somewhat bewildered. But something has happened, and it will have consequences. Compare m. 9 in Ex. 45-17a with the analogous spot in the recapitulation (Ex. 45-21). In the former, the F♯ (disguised as a G♭) appears as a chromatic passing tone (with an associated "Neapolitan-style" harmonization), inflecting G toward F. In Ex. 45-21, the F♯ is the goal of the progression, approached directly from the uninflected G, and finally resolved as the dominant it had always seemed to be. The chickens have come home to roost, or, as Frisch puts it, "in the recapitulation Brahms actually does plunge us briefly into the chasm" from which he had previously pulled us back. But having faced up to the threat of B minor, Brahms (and we) are empowered at last to defeat it.

EX. 45-21   Johannes Brahms, Quartet no. 1 in C minor, Op. 51, no. 1, I, mm. 143–50

As Frisch explains, the B-minor triad in Ex. 45-21 "leads logically back to the tonic through D major and G⁷; thus the 'sore' F♯ and the B minor that once seemed so frighteningly remote are reintegrated into the familiar context of C minor." Brahms did not invent this ploy. We have seen it in Beethoven, in the way the notorious C♯ in m. 7 of the Symphony in E♭ (the "Eroica") returned at the other end of the movement (disguised as D♭) as unfinished business that required an extra development section to work through. And even earlier we saw it in Mozart, in the slow movement of another Symphony in E♭ (no. 39, K. 543), where a troublingly persistent chromatic note (B natural, come to think of it!) finally forced a radically disruptive modulation to its home key as if in an act of exorcism (see chapters 30 and 31).

Brahms knew these precedents, of course. The difference between them and his own tonal psychodrama lay in the difference of media. Beethoven's and Mozart's, being symphonic, were dramatic manifestations, bordering indeed on the melodramatic. And so was Brahms's own public skirmish with B minor in the opening movement of his First Symphony, described earlier in this very chapter. In the quartet movement the effect turns on tinycraft, on minute motivic relations. Its far greater concentration requires far more in the way of active engagement and response from the listener. Active engagement, the ability to respond to subtle signals, requires the possession of actual skills—aural discrimination, aural memory, mental agility. The rewards and satisfactions are commensurate with the exertion: the exhilaration that follows exercise; the gratification that comes with understanding; the fellow-feeling that successful receipt of an urgent communication inspires.

But there is also the self-satisfaction of belonging to a self-defined elite—an emotion that is gratified through exclusion. And that is where esoteric, "difficult" art inevitably becomes controversial in a postaristocratic, "democratic" age. The question is generally posed in terms of means and ends. Is the difficulty inherent in the message and essential to it—the price, so to speak, of full communication? Or is it, rather, a difficulty that is mandated for the sake of the exclusions that it affords, or what might be termed "elite solidarity"? If the latter, does it foster social division? Is that social division a threat to social harmony? Is the protection of social harmony something societies, and their institutions of enforcement and control (from critics all the way, in extreme cases, to censors and police), have an obligation to promote?

These questions became explosive in the twentieth century. Their origin goes back to the great fissure that opened up between the "mass" culture made possible by the demographics and technologies of the late nineteenth century and the traditional notion of "high" culture. The division bred conflicts and backlashes. And while Brahms himself was not much implicated in the social debates, we may be tempted to judge his attitudes by those of his "Brahmin" friends, like Billroth. As we shall see, those who led the debates to their explosive stage in the early twentieth century often sought their legitimacy, and their authority, in Brahms's example, just as some of the worst politics of the twentieth century sought its legitimacy in Wagner's.

So there is a "Brahms problem" as well as a "Wagner problem." From this perspective, too, these perceived antipodes were equally — and similarly — representative of their time and its social problematics. And that is yet another reason why "Brahms and Wagner" have remained a dynamic duo. The problems, however we choose to define their relationship to the figures whose names they bear, are stubborn historical facts.

The Symphony Goes (Inter)National

Bruckner, Dvořák, Beach, Franck, Saint-Saëns, Borodin, Chaikovsky

GERMANY RECEDES

Reviewing Brahms's Fourth Symphony at its Vienna premiere in 1886, Eduard Hanslick marveled that the city had witnessed nineteen symphonic premieres by as many composers over the previous twelve-month period. "It looks as though Brahms's successes have stimulated production, following the long silence which set in after Mendelssohn and Schumann,"[1] he concluded. Hanslick exaggerated Brahms's personal responsibility for the phenomenon — little things like wars also played a part, as we shall see — but he was certainly right to marvel. By the mid-1880s "symphonists" were no longer quite as rare as hens' teeth, nor were they all professors and pupils.

The revival's most impressive aspect, however, was its geographical reach. Of the seven composers surveyed in this chapter, only one was a native speaker of German. The others hailed from France, Russia, Bohemia (now called "the Czech lands"), and the United States. If we were aiming at a complete survey, we would surely have included some Scandinavian composers as well, who by the end of the century had established an important symphonic "school." (Its most important representatives, however, would produce their chief works after the turn of the twentieth century.)

We might even have dropped the names of some Italian symphonists (since the eighteenth century a veritable contradiction in terms) — for example, Giovanni Sgambati (1841–1914) or Giuseppe Martucci (1856–1909), whom one later Italian composer gratefully dubbed "the starting point of the renaissance of non-operatic Italian music."[2] Their work stimulated national pride by declining to conform to what high-minded Italians considered a demeaning national stereotype — in other words, they advanced their nation's musical cause precisely by not "sounding Italian." At the same time, however, increasing cosmopolitanism brought out a compensatory "nationalist" or regionalist strain in the work of some other contributors to the newly refurbished symphonic genre.

SYMPHONY AS SACRAMENT

Brahms's main Viennese rival as a symphonist was Anton Bruckner (1824–96), a slightly older composer who had an even later start than Brahms as a composer of symphonies.

He was trained as an organist and church choirmaster, and quietly plied that trade at St. Florian's, a seventeenth-century monastery near the Austrian port city of Linz, where he became kapellmeister in 1858. Ten years later he moved to Vienna to take a post as professor of harmony and counterpoint, and also worked as "provisional organist" in the Imperial Chapel until his spreading fame as a virtuoso and improviser procured his elevation to the post of court organist in 1878.

By that time he had had three symphonies performed (out of six composed). His switch from church to concert hall as main theater of operations had come about

FIG. 46-1   Anton Bruckner, painted in 1888.

in the wake of his belated exposure to Wagner's music, unplayed in provincial Linz until 1863. It was Wagner's musical style, pure and simple, with its luxuriant orchestra, its harmonic daring, and its complex motivic textures, that captivated Bruckner, who had no inclination at all for dramatic composition and paid no attention to Wagner's theories. (Or to the actual content of the operas, if a famous anecdote is to be believed: After listening enraptured to most of *Die Walküre* during the first Bayreuth *Ring*, Bruckner opened his eyes at last during the "Magic Fire" music and asked his companions, "But why are they burning that girl?")

And yet he proclaimed himself Wagner's disciple and became known as the "Wagnerian symphonist," another seeming contradiction in terms that brought him a degree of ridicule at first, and also the enmity of Hanslick, Vienna's most powerful critic, which considerably retarded his progress as a concert composer. It was in an effort to secure easier access to performance that some of his pupils began making simplified versions of his works and publishing them with their teacher's reluctant approval, thereby creating a nightmare of "versions" through which performers today have to chart their course.

Bruckner's work was often compared invidiously with Brahms's, especially by Hanslick, and the two composers regarded one another with suspicion and disparagement, Brahms referring to him as "that bumpkin" who wrote "symphonic boa constrictors"[3] and Bruckner declaring for his part that he'd rather hear a Strauss waltz any day than a Brahms symphony.[4] But Bruckner's music shares with Brahms's the crucial element of synthesis. The antithesis transcended in Bruckner's case was that between Wagner on the one hand, and on the other, the ancient sacred styles in which Bruckner had been trained to a point past mastery.

Thus Bruckner's music, too, resounds with evocations of "vocal collectivities." It, too, employs preclassical structural devices. And it bears unmistakable traces of organ improvisation: extremely slow, sustained adagios, and a heavy reliance on sequences and rhythmic ostinatos in the allegros that brought listeners either to a state of ecstasy or one of utter exasperation. Bruckner's lengthy rhythmic processes made for monumental — yes, Wagnerian; but also Schubertian — length. One of his ostinato patterns, a pair of quarter notes either followed or preceded by a quarter-note triplet (♩ ♩ ⌐♩³♩⌐ or ⌐♩³♩⌐ ♩ ♩), was so characteristic and so frequently employed as to become a trademark: musicians know it informally as the "Bruckner rhythm."

Bruckner, too, instrumentally rewrote Beethoven's Ninth, not once but repeatedly — and, it could be alleged, uncritically, or at least far less ironically than Brahms — in a fashion that, especially at first, invited the dreaded charge of epigonism. As Deryck Cooke, one of Bruckner's main twentieth-century advocates, has pointed out, Beethoven's last symphony provided Bruckner with "his four main movement types — the far-ranging first movement, the big adagio built from the varied alternation of two themes, the sonata-form scherzo, and the huge cumulative finale — as well as the tendency to begin a symphony with a faint background sound, emerging almost imperceptibly out of silence."[5] Bruckner's Third Symphony in D minor (the key of the Ninth), of which the first performance, on 16 December 1877 (Beethoven's birthday), was a legendary disaster, is the most heavily charged of all with specific appropriations from Beethoven's last symphony. Its beginning quite obviously replays Beethoven's opening gambit: preparatory arpeggios prolonging the tonic, a theme formed out of a root-fifth-root descent, a climactic unison. And the resemblances do not end there: a chromatically descending basso ostinato haunts its coda just as it did Beethoven's. And yet the Third Symphony was also the symphony that most demonstratively declared its composer's fealty to Wagner through its effusive dedication — a dedication that Wagner just as demonstratively accepted as a mark of his esteem. And well he might: in its ceremonious linkage of Beethoven and Wagner, Bruckner's symphony was telling Wagner's story, ratifying precisely the view of German musical history that Brahms had challenged.

Bruckner did not break into repertoire status alongside Brahms or achieve real public impact until he was sixty. The turning point was the triumphant Leipzig premiere (under Arthur Nikisch, one of the earliest "virtuoso conductors") of Bruckner's Seventh Symphony at a Wagner memorial concert on 30 December 1884. The symphony had become a Wagner memorial in its own right halfway through the process of its composition. Bruckner had written two movements, the first and the third (scherzo), when he had a dark presentiment. "One day I returned home feeling very sad,"[6] he wrote to Felix Mottl, a conductor and fellow Wagnerian. "The thought had crossed my mind that the Master would not live much longer, and then the C♯-minor theme of the Adagio came to me." He began writing the Adagio on 22 January 1883, only nineteen days before his forebodings were confirmed, and finished it in April.

Thus, because of its slow movement, the Seventh Symphony can also be considered a specially designated "Wagner Symphony," but a more mature and representative one than the Third, making this virtually unprecedented twenty-minute Adagio (probably Bruckner's most widely played single movement despite its length, owing to its frequent ceremonial use) an ideal vantage point for surveying his achievement. The very fact that the slow movement is the symphony's center of gravity is an aspect of that achievement: it salvages and develops an aspect of the Beethoven legacy to which other nineteenth-century composers did not respond. (In Brahms, most conspicuously, slow movements tend to have the character of intermezzi, considerably lighter in tone than the outer ones.)

Except for the absence of harps (which would be abundantly present in his next and longest symphony, the Eighth), Bruckner's orchestra for the Adagio (and the finale, which he composed afterward) is a somewhat more compact version of the *Götterdämmerung* orchestra, without piccolo, English horn, or bass clarinet, but replete with "Wagner tubas" plus contrabass tuba to furnish the burnished or "cushioned" Wagnerian sonority, and cymbals and triangle to accentuate the shattering C-major climax. The Wagnerian orchestra is deployed in a manner strikingly different from

EX. 46-1 Anton Bruckner, Symphony no. 7, II (Adagio), mm. 1–9

EX. 46-1 (*continued*)

Wagner's, however. Bruckner's use of the instrumental sections (strings, winds, brass) as separately functioning, often antiphonal choirs is widely thought to be a transfer from his organ technique, in which a "registration" is set so that the different keyboards will activate contrasting ranks of pipes that can be played off one against another or combined by "octave coupling" for tuttis. Bruckner's frequent homorhythmic textures of course evoke choirs of actual voices in the manner of chorales, or (within Bruckner's Catholic world) of antiphonal psalmody.

In form, the movement derives, as usual, from the slow movement of Beethoven's Ninth, with its alternation of two sections: A-B-A-B-A, with the As growing progressively more ornate (or, in Bruckner's case, more heavily laden with counterpoints and further extended through modulations and motivic development) and the Bs having the character of serene interludes, moving at a more measured pace and a slightly faster tempo (*andante* for Beethoven, *moderato* for Bruckner). In this movement the resemblance of the B section to its counterpart in the Ninth is too close to be anything other than a deliberate allusion.

The opening section begins with a striking contrast between two ideas that will each be given broad development. The first, a lyrical lament or threnody sung by the choir of tubas (the "C♯-minor theme" as Bruckner called it in his letter), will bring the movement to a close in a coda that Bruckner called his "funeral music for the Master." The other is the forceful chorale for the strings that answers the tubas, a melody later incorporated into an actual choral Te Deum to set the final words, *non confundar in aeternum* (let me never be confounded).

In the Adagio's opening section these ideas take four and six measures respectively (standing in a proportion of 2:3); the rest is given over to a concluding hymn that is developed sequentially to a climax. In the first return of "A," the two ideas are expanded by sequences into massive formal blocks in roughly the opposite proportion: about thirty and twenty measures respectively in a proportion of 3:2. The tonal progression between the sequence repetitions most frequently ascends by semitones, so that each seems to function as the leading tone to the next (or alternatively, so that each progression consists of a deceptive cadence to ♭VI).

In the passage shown in Ex. 46-2, for instance, the chorale motif is heard first in E♭ (a semitone higher than the root of the immediately preceding dominant-seventh chord on D) and then proceeds once by authentic cadence to A♭, next by a "Lisztian" descent down a major third to E (= F♭, also understandable as ♭VI, approached from the tonic rather than the dominant), and thence—in a manner that "Brahmins" thought unspeakably crude, though certainly effective—through four ascending half steps until the A♭ is regained at m. 133 to begin the second *moderato* section.

EX. 46-2   Anton Bruckner, Symphony no. 7, II, mm. 114–33

EX. 46-2   *(continued)*

Moderato

In the last and longest "A" section, the texture is augmented by a constant sextolet in the violins, borrowed directly from Beethoven's figuration at the analogous spot in the Ninth Symphony. Once past the opening gambit, the order of presentation is reversed. The chorale is put through a variety of extensions and sequential repetitions on the way to the climax, pitched on C natural so that the return to the tonic C♯ can sound like another deceptive ♭VI resolution; at which point the tubas return for the last extended reference to their opening threnody.

Both the dynamic, climax-driven shaping of the movement's vast expanse and its consistent saturation with ♭VI relationships testify to the composer's concern with "organic form," in which everything (following Wagner's conception of "endless melody") is thematic. It could go without saying that the main themes of the symphony's outer movements will likewise be variants of a single idea, an upward-sweeping tonic arpeggio following an initial descent from first degree to fifth (Ex. 46-3). It was a rare late-century symphony that did not display the sort of thematic interconnections and reminiscences taken for granted in the symphonic poem, suggestive not only of organic form but also of dramaturgy. This, too, has to be regarded as a dialectical synthesis in which formal principles initially thought incompatible gradually converged.

A BOHEMIAN PRESCRIPTION FOR AMERICA

Unsurprisingly, "cyclic" form (as it came to be called in the case of multimovement works) is most prevalent and systematically applied in the work of composers whose

EX. 46-3A   Anton Bruckner, Symphony no. 7, I, mm. 1–5

EX. 46-3B   Anton Bruckner, Symphony no. 7, IV, mm. 1–2

output contained both symphonies and symphonic poems or even operas, a versatility as unthinkable for a Liszt as it was for a Brahms. Brahms's own single-movement symphonic pieces, both composed in 1880, retained the old-fashioned designation "overture" and like Beethoven's overtures adhered to standard "first movement" form. While sporting "characteristic" titles — "Academic Festival" (composed on the themes of student songs as a thank-you for his Breslau degree) and "Tragic" — they were neither overtly programmatic nor conceived as narratives.

FIG. 46-2A   Antonín Dvořák, painting (1993) by A. Studnikow, after a portrait photo ca. 1879.

Far less fastidious about such distinctions was Antonín Dvořák (1841–1904), often regarded as a Brahms protégé. His first big break came in 1874 when, as a country-born Bohemian provincial working as an orchestral violist and church organist (and who unlike his older countryman Smetana spoke Czech as his native language), Dvořák submitted several of his compositions to a committee that included both Brahms and Hanslick in hopes of winning a stipend from the Austrian government. He won not only that year but in 1876 and 1877 as well, and through the good offices of Hanslick and Brahms found a publisher.

His first publications were of popular "national" fare, the exotic route being the easiest way for a young composer from the non-German provinces to promote himself. It is, however, a fair measure of the double standard that informs a lot of musical historiography to note that these early publications of Dvořák's—two books of "Moravian Duets" for mixed voices and piano, and a book of "Slavonic Dances" for piano four-hands—typecast him as a nationalist in a way that Brahms's almost exactly analogous early publications—the *Liebeslieder-Walzer* and the "Hungarian Dances"—did not.

Moreover, while no one ever thought of Brahms's Hungarian Dances as the expression of the composer's essential personality (because he was not a Hungarian), the opposite assumption was made in the case of Dvořák—even though, as scholars have demonstrated many times over, he did not use authentic melodies even when he could have, and the "Czech" style he presented to the world at large was altogether

FIG. 46-2B Dvořák's house in New York City, during his time as director of the National Conservatory, 1892–1895.

unlike the Czech style that Czechs recognize as Czech. To revive some terminology first applied to Chopin in chapter 39, Dvořák's early nationalism was almost entirely an opportunistic "tourist nationalism." Nevertheless, he found himself trapped in it at times, as if in a ghetto. It led inevitably to biased expectations and, in some cases, to invidious reviews when he failed to conform to German (or French, or American) listeners' ideas of properly Czech behavior.

Meanwhile, despite his location in Prague (not exactly a small town, but provincial in Viennese eyes), Dvořák was a musician of wide and eclectic background. As a teenager he had played in the Prague conservatory orchestra when it needed to be augmented for big works like *Tannhäuser* and *Lohengrin*, and he began his musical career a fervent Wagnerian. (In 1863 he played under Wagner himself in a concert that, among other things, introduced the preludes to *Tristan* and *Die Meistersinger* to Prague.) By 1871, his thirtieth year, he had two operas of his own to his credit.

The first, *Alfred*, was a grand historical opera in German that portrayed Anglo-Saxon resistance to the conquering Danes in the ninth century. The second, *The King and the Charcoal Burner*, was a comedy in Czech to a libretto reminiscent of Albert Lortzing's *Zar und Zimmermann* ("The Tsar and the carpenter," 1837), a folksy singspiel about mistaken identity and benevolent friendship across class lines that was very popular all over Europe. Dvořák's opera was no folksy singspiel, however; it was so full of Wagnerian adventurousness and ambition that it had to be sent back for radical surgery by the Prague Provisional Theater, the Czech-language house to which he had submitted it. (The simplified version was performed in the same year that Dvořák won his stipend.) Clearly, the composer of these works was no "Brahmin"; but neither was he a down-on-the-farm "nationalist."

Very much in contrast to such pigeonholes, Dvořák was arguably the most versatile ("universal"?) composer of his time. His output eventually included eight more operas, including one (*Dmitrij*, 1882; revised 1894–95) that updated the plot of Musorgsky's *Boris Godunov*, and another (*Rusalka*, 1900) that treated the famous legend of the water nymph who loves a mortal, widespread in the folklore of many European nations, in an unregenerately Wagnerian fashion. (The first act, for example, replays the opening scene of *Das Rheingold*, with Alberich and the Rhine Maidens dressed in Czech folk costume.) *Rusalka* alone has become an international repertoire item, but Dvořák's operas, with Smetana's, are the foundation of the operatic repertoire in his homeland.

Yet alongside this steady production of operas, and almost uniquely, Dvořák produced an equally steady stream of symphonic and chamber works. Here his indebtedness to Brahms as a model was as apparent as was his indebtedness to Wagner in the realm of opera. But in certain ways Dvořák managed to outstrip Brahms. He was, for one thing, far more prolific. His series of fourteen string quartets (composed between 1862 and 1895) was the most impressive such achievement since Beethoven. And he cultivated the other main chamber genres of his time with almost equal assiduity: five piano trios, two piano quintets, a piano quartet, two string quintets, a string sextet, and many more, including an octet (never published and now lost) for mixed strings and winds comparable to Schubert's except that it included a part for piano.

During their lifetimes, Dvořák's chamber music was (and probably would be found to remain, if statistics were available) more frequently performed than Brahms's. It owed its greater popularity (if not quite the same level of esteem from critics and connoisseurs) to its broader, more lyrical melodic content. Thus Dvořák could be viewed as standing in a line with Schubert as a chamber composer where Brahms, the "motivic miniaturist," claimed direct descent from Beethoven. It is a cliché born of biased expectations to describe Dvořák's greater lyricism in terms of his national origin. Only in the "scherzo" slot, formerly occupied by the minuet, did Dvořák habitually write in a folkish style, substituting characteristic Czech dances like the polka and the *furiant* (an exuberant dance full of hemiola — $\frac{3}{2} : \frac{6}{4}$ — rhythms) for what had often been in Haydn's day the "peasant" movement.

Dvořák's nine symphonies, though they came to a Beethovenian number in the aggregate, are individually quite motley in style. Again, the model that most frequently comes to mind is Schubert. There was one great difference between Dvořák's symphonic procedures and Schubert's, however, and that was his predilection for "cyclic" form, strictly a late-nineteenth-century phenomenon (though with a single colossal precedent in Beethoven). Both in his symphonies and in his concertos — especially late ones like the Ninth Symphony, op. 95 (1893), and the Cello Concerto, op. 104 (1895) — Dvořák occasionally recycled themes from movement to movement to a degree that lent his works a tinge of secret "programmaticism."

Not that that suspicion would faze a symphonist who (unlike Brahms) had no qualms about composing symphonic poems as well. In fact, Dvořák's last orchestral works (composed 1896–97) were a cycle of symphonic poems comparable to Smetana's *Má vlast*, based on the ballads of Karel Jaromir Erben (1811–70), famous as a folklore collector ("the Czech Grimm") but also a poet in his own right, who collected folk tales and worked them into narrative poems. Also Lisztian, both in title and content, were Dvořák's three Slavonic Rhapsodies for orchestra (1878). And yet Dvořák also wrote his share of fastidiously formed and titled concert overtures on the Mendelssohnian-Brahmsian model: *My Home* (1882), *Carnival* (1891), *Othello* (1892). And he even turned out a set of *Symphonic Variations*, a genre for which Brahms provided practically the only model, in 1877.

Dvořák's cyclic forms in symphonies and concertos are evidence not only of latent "poetic content" but also of virtuosically developed traditional skills, quite belying his cliché image as a "primitive." It was not as a folksy primitive but as a world-class master of European music in the broadest sense that Jeannette M. Thurber, an American philanthropist, invited Dvořák to New York to become the director of the National Conservatory of Music, an institution she was endowing (very much in the same spirit that had motivated Anton Rubinstein in Russia thirty years before) to allow the spread of European art music to new shores, and its cultivation there — or, to put it another way, to further the musical colonization of the New World by the Old.

Dvořák's last symphony was composed during his American sojourn, which lasted from 1892 to 1895. Subtitled "Z nového světa" ("From the new world"), it received its first performance in Carnegie Hall on Beethoven's birthday, 16 December 1893, under the baton of the Hungarian-born Anton Seidl (1850–98), an eminent Wagnerian conductor who was then at the helm of both the Metropolitan Opera and the New York Philharmonic. While immediately successful, and an enduring repertoire item ever since, the symphony has occasioned much debate. Its subtitle could be read in various ways. Did it simply mean a symphony written in the New World — "Impressions and Greetings"[7] (as the composer once put it) to those back home? Or did it imply that the thematic content — or perhaps even the "poetic" content — was in some sense (but what sense?) inherently American?

We will return to these questions, but only after taking a look at the music that gave rise to them. As in the case of Bruckner's Seventh, the slow second movement, which has become independently famous, is the obvious choice for a representative sample. Compared with its counterparts in Brahms, it is a curiously sectional, episodic piece, and in this, too, it seems to hark back to Schubert. Its thematic content is given out in fully rounded periods that later yield up motifs for development and recall, rather than proceeding the other way around (as Dahlhaus describes the Brahmsian manner) by starting with "an inconspicuous motive, which does not even appear as a theme at first, but only attains the function of a theme gradually, by virtue of the consequences drawn from it."[8] The following description can (and should) be matched up with the score for full comprehensibility.

The movement begins on a patently "Lisztian" note, with a sort of prefatory chorale in which the root progressions (except for the final plagal one) are entirely by thirds and "multiple thirds" (e.g., the initial tritone, representing two stages along the circle of minor thirds). The main theme, given out as a famous solo for the English horn (always an "exotic" timbre), could hardly be a more "finished" melody: twelve bars arranged by fours, ABA'. Following another invocation of the chromatic "chorale," the opening section continues with another contrasting phrase and another "A'."

At 2 a "middle section" in the parallel minor, at a slightly faster tempo, and in contrasting triplet rhythms ensues. It too consists of an alternation of rounded tunes (more obviously contrasting this time) in a format that can be summarized ABABA. The "B" section has a walking bass that (it is fair to say) inescapably evokes a procession. At 4 the mode shifts back to major for a much faster tune, notated in short note-values within a single bar but obviously a "four-measure" construction. Presented ostinato-fashion, it serves as the medium of a crescendo to a surging climax, after which (at 5) a return is made to the opening music, presented haltingly, with fermatas that interrupt the "singing" in a manner that recalls the muted end of the *Marcia funebre* in Beethoven's *Eroica* Symphony. The coda, almost needless to add, is based on the introductory chorale. If the material at 4 is regarded as transitional, the whole movement recapitulates (or amplifies) the ABA' structure of the opening section.

Not even the simplest formal description of the movement like the one just attempted can omit the "extroversive semiotics," the signs pointing beyond its boundaries to other pieces and images, in this case funereal. But there is a large component of "introversive" signing as well. The climax at 5 measures before 5 (Ex. 46-4), throughout which the harmony remains frozen on the fraught — Schubertianly fraught! — chord of the flat submediant (♭VI), is shot through with reminiscences of the first movement. As comparison with Ex. 46-5 will corroborate, the trombones refer to the arpeggiating main theme of the earlier movement; the trumpets, violins, and woodwinds divide up motifs from the same movement's second theme; and the French horns play reverberations (employing rustic "horn fifths") of the opening phrase from the second movement's English horn solo. The whole passage reverberates and repercusses over a diminuendo: a very apt way of representing the onset and fading of a sudden memory.

Even more evocative (and even more contrapuntally resourceful) is the coda of the finale — that is, the coda to the entire symphony (Ex. 46-6). It "montages" motifs from all four movements (motifs that have already been sounding at various points throughout the finale) into new and striking configurations. (For corroboration, Ex. 46-7 displays the main theme of the scherzo.) Immediately before the start of Ex. 46-6, the Largo's introductory chorale had returned in glory at the peak of a crescendo. At its subsidence the opening phrase of the English horn solo is played against a reminiscence of the scherzo that passes dramatically down by octaves from the piccolo through the string section and into the timpani, where its reverberations accompany the softly-beginning last recall of the finale's main theme. Last is immediately juxtaposed with first at the climax, where the trumpets blare the finale theme, very dissonantly harmonized against the first movement's arpeggio theme.

EX. 46-4   Antonín Dvořák, "New World" Symphony, II, 5 measures before fig. [5]

EX. 46-4 *(continued)*

We have previously encountered a concatenation of motifs like this only once, and that was in the Norns' scene from *Götterdämmerung* (see chapter 42). There, of course, the motifs had extroversive as well as introversive significance: they referred not only to other parts of the *Ring*, but to events, characters, and feelings. But as we have already had occasion to note in the case of the funereal slow movement, the "New World" Symphony abounds in extroversive reference (albeit of a conventional and generalized kind) and "intertextual" reference as well, as where Dvořák evokes Beethoven's Third Symphony, known presumably (or at least potentially) to most members of his original audience. Even without a program, moreover, thematic reminiscences, especially at such a level of concentration and climactic display, ineluctably suggest what the New Germans called "poetic content." A symphony that appropriates so many devices of signification, not only from the symphonic poem but even from opera, becomes something of an opera for orchestra. But an opera about what?

EX. 46-5A   Antonín Dvořák, "New World" Symphony, I, first theme

EX. 46-5B   Antonín Dvořák, "New World" Symphony, I, second theme

EX. 46-6   Antonín Dvořák, "New World" Symphony, IV, coda (motivic montage)

As Michael Beckerman, the leading American specialist in Czech music, has pointed out most recently (and in greatest detail), an answer to this question can be deduced by juxtaposing a comment Dvořák made to a New York reporter on the day of the premiere with the contents of a letter to Dvořák from Mrs. Thurber, his American employer. Dvořák himself pointed out that the symphony's Largo (then designated Adagio) was unusual in content and structure, "different from the classic works in this form."[9] As he felt he had to explain, "it is in reality a study or a sketch for a longer work, whether a cantata or an opera which I propose writing, and which will be based upon Longfellow's *Hiawatha*." Anything can be said for the sake of publicity, of course, but in this case Dvořák's correspondence corroborates his avowal. One of Mrs. Thurber's provisos in hiring Dvořák to head the National Conservatory was that he foster an American national opera by providing an example for native-born composers. She even specified *The Song of Hiawatha* as the basis for the libretto.

It was an almost inevitable choice. Operas on national myths had played an important role in establishing many national "schools," and (as detailed in chapter 36)

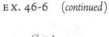

EX. 46-6   (*continued*)

EX. 46-6 (continued)

EX. 46-6 (continued)

EX. 46-7 Antonín Dvořák, "New World" Symphony, III, mm. 13–21 (woodwinds)

in some countries — Germany with its *Freischütz*, Russia with its *Life for the Tsar* — the opera in question served not only as a musical cornerstone but as a cornerstone of the nation's sense of nationhood. From the first, Longfellow's poem (published in 1855) had sought to serve this purpose, providing the United States with an ersatz national epic, something of which the nation's youth and modernity had deprived it.

The poem's heavy, frequently parodied trochaic meter ("BY the SHORES of GItchee GUmee . . .") was copied from the *Kalevala*, the national epic of the Finns, first published in 1822 and given its definitive literary form by Elias Lönnrot in 1849, only half a dozen years before Longfellow imitated it. It, too, was something of an ersatz: Originally assumed to date as a unit from around the first millennium B.C.E., it was later shown to be a patchwork of oral poetry of which parts had originated as comparatively recently as the sixteenth century, and of which other parts had actually been created by Lönnrot in the process of its literary adaptation. The trochaic meter, however, was endemic to Finnish, one of the European languages (Hungarian and Dvořák's own Czech being others) in which all words are stressed on their first syllables.

In the case of *Hiawatha*, of course, the trochaic meter achieved its atmospheric purpose precisely because it was not endemic to English, but rather conjured up an

FIG. 46-3 *Hiawatha's Departure*, after Longfellow.

air of nonspecific mythical exoticism and pseudoantiquity. The poem's protagonist, the legendary Mohawk or Onondaga chief Haionhwat'ha, actually lived in what is now upstate New York in the sixteenth century. He was credited in oral tradition with the founding, around 1570, of the Iroquois League, a mutual-defense confederation of five nations under an unwritten constitution, which became (with the assistance of Dutch arms) the foremost indigenous military power north of Mexico.

Except for one member nation, the League backed the British rather than the colonists in the American Revolutionary War; the ensuing hostility between the new United States government and the tribes was disastrous for the League's autonomy and led eventually to its destruction. Nevertheless, there is some evidence that the structure of the Iroquois League was among the models considered by the Continental Congress in drafting the Articles of Confederation, the provisional American constitution that was drawn up in 1776 and in force from 1781 to 1789, and that defined the United States of America as a "league of friendship" for common defense.

Thus despite the actual hostility of the United States to its Indian population, a policy that in its late-nineteenth-century excesses went as far as genocide, the Iroquois League, and the figure of its legendary founder, could play the role of indigenous progenitor in romantic national mythology. The musicalization of that mythology is what Mrs. Thurber had asked of Dvořák. He never completed the opera for want of an actual libretto; but the music he sketched for it suffuses at least two of the movements of the "New World" Symphony, and probably all four.

The scherzo, by Dvořák's specific acknowledgment, "was suggested by the scene at the feast in *Hiawatha* where the Indians dance."[10] Beckerman has suggested that it was a representation of the Dance of Pau-Puk-Keewis, the great athlete, described by Longfellow at the beginning of chapter 11 of the poem, "Hiawatha's Wedding Feast." Dvořák was less specific about the Largo, but to the critic Henry Krehbiel he confided that it was based on chapter 10, "Hiawatha's Wooing." Because of its pastoral tone, Beckerman has suggested that the opening section, featuring the famous English horn solo, depicts Hiawatha's journey homeward with his bride Minnehaha ("Laughing Water"): "Short it seemed to Hiawatha,/Though they journeyed very slowly,/Though his pace he checked and slackened/To the steps of Laughing Water."

The middle section, with all its funereal imagery (evident even without knowledge of a literary source), must correspond with the death and burial of Minnehaha in chapter 20. The grand concatenations of themes and motifs from all the movements in the finale are surely an indication that Dvořák envisioned his American mythic opera much along the lines of Wagner's German mythos in the *Ring*, with each of its acts (or movements in the corresponding symphony) drawing ever more extensively on a preexisting musical cosmos or past-in-music that gives ever increasing resonance to the unfolding narrative's events and reflections.

The remaining question, especially relevant in the case of a composer who often gave his music a national tinge, is whether the themes and motifs conceived originally in connection with *Hiawatha* or the "New World" Symphony were intended to be indicatively "American"; and if so, then on what stylistic basis? The only direct testimony is Dvořák's deliberate teaser: "the influence of America can be felt by anyone who has a 'nose.'"[11] Beyond that we must fall back on educated (which may mean biased) sniffing.

Dvořák is known to have been very much drawn to Negro spirituals and their professional arrangements called "plantation songs." In an article published in *Harper's Magazine* (February 1895), he called them "the most striking and appealing melodies that have yet been found on this side of the water." One of the students at the National Conservatory during Dvořák's tenure (though never his composition pupil, as has occasionally been claimed) was Harry T. Burleigh (1866–1949), an African-American singer and choral conductor, who over the course of his career made almost two hundred arrangements of spirituals for chorus, and who recalled singing dozens of them to Dvořák during the period of the "New World" Symphony's gestation.

There are numerous pentatonic melodies in the symphony that seem to resonate stylistically with spirituals. The Largo's English horn theme (or rather its "A" section) is one. Another, the second theme from the first movement (quoted in Ex. 46-5b), can be interpreted as incorporating a brief quotation from the spiritual "Swing Low, Sweet Chariot": its opening phrases correspond to the note sequence and (roughly) the rhythm to which the words "chariot,/comin' for to carry me home" are set in the spiritual (compare Ex. 46-8).

EX. 46-8   Spiritual, *Swing Low, Sweet Chariot*

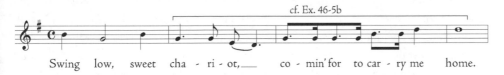

But of course many Bohemian folk tunes share the pentatonic structure of spirituals and plantation songs, as do the folk songs of many nations. And given the front-stressed accent patterns of the Czech language, many Bohemian folk tunes also exhibit the "lombard" short-long rhythm that Dvořák's theme and "Swing Low" have in common. Both traits can be found, for example, in themes from Dvořák's Eighth Symphony (1889), composed before he ever had a thought of setting foot in the New World (Ex. 46-9).

And yet Dvořák did not hesitate to give fatherly advice to American composers to do as the Bohemians had done, and (in Krehbiel's paraphrase) submit the indigenous musics of their country, namely Indian melodies and Negro spirituals, "to beautiful treatment in the higher forms of art."[12] There is every reason to suppose that in his *Hiawatha* opera, and in the symphony that had spun off from it, he intended to provide them with an object lesson. Whether or not this can ever be proved, the fact remains that his melodies were taken as "American"—particularly the Largo's English horn theme, which may not have been a spiritual to begin with, but which *became* one. Many who do not know its source in Dvořák know it as "Goin' Home"—and in view of Michael Beckerman's explanation of its basis in Longfellow, it seems possible that the

765

EX. 46-9A   Antonín Dvořák, Symphony no. 8 in G, I, flute solo, mm. 18–22 (pentatonic)

EX. 46-9B   Antonín Dvořák, Symphony no. 8 in G, II, eight measures after fig. [F] (woodwinds)

"back-transfer" of this composed theme into the oral tradition may have been facilitated by someone who knew of Dvořák's original intentions.

But still, what are "plantation songs" doing in a work that sought America's mythic past in Indian lore? Not that the symphony lacks conventional Indian lore. Dvořák called the scherzo "an essay I made in the direction of imparting the local color of Indian character to music,"[13] though no one has ever identified that character with quoted artifacts, or even with the style of the music except trivially — for example, in the use of insistent pedal basses (or "open fifths") expressed in pulses like drumbeats or tom-toms. A similarly accompanied themelet in the first movement, from which the bridge to the second theme is then constructed, has also been suppositionally identified as "Indian" (Ex. 46-10).

EX. 46-10   Antonín Dvořák, "New World" Symphony, I, "Indian" theme

AN AMERICAN RESPONSE

But the question regarding the appropriateness of "plantation songs" remains. His use of them implies that for Dvořák, coming as he did from the outside, Native-American and African-American folklore were interchangeably "American" in connotation. For Americans, the great majority of whom were by then of European immigrant stock, it was not so. For Americans interested in cultivating the European art music tradition — meaning, in the first instance, German immigrants, in the second, cultivated

Anglo-Saxons — it was even less so, for such an interest marked one off as even more "Eurocentric" than the average.

For such musicians, the unmarked native tongue for music was (like it or not) the same as it was for Dvořák — that is, German. That Dvořák never paused to consider that the national identities he was encouraging Americans to adopt belonged to separate, distinguishable (and, often, stigmatized) minority cultures, and that he never expected that this circumstance would bother Americans, shows to what an extent he remained an outsider to American history and culture. And it also shows that he valued his own Bohemianness (that is, valued it musically) as an element of exoticism — a manner of presenting the self as other. His fundamental loyalty — as a musician no less than as a citizen — was to the multinational empire in which he lived.

So while Dvořák could give his music an authentic "national" (that is, local or regional) coloring that represented within the multinational context an ethnically homogeneous, single, and separate "other," there was no such coloring available to Euro-Americans. For them, "American" described not an ethnic but a geographical and political identity. To put it in Dvořákian terms, "American" connoted something far closer to "Austro-Hungarian" than to "Czech." To claim to be "ethnically Austro-Hungarian" was an absurd contradiction in terms — but so was any claim by a white person to be "ethnically American."

So Dvořák's advice to his American pupils, while well meant, was unworkable — and deeply resented by his native-born peers, that is those few American composers, chiefly white Anglo-Saxons from affluent families, who had received their professional training in the conservatories of Europe and shared Dvořák's basic loyalty to the unmarked, "universal" Germanic style. His object lesson, though emulated for a while by a short-lived school of "Indianists," did not have a lasting impact on American composition. For most composers trained in "the higher forms of art," an African-American or Native-American style could only be adopted in whiteface — hardly a condition calculated to impart a sense of cultural authenticity.

That is easily enough seen even without taking racial prejudice into account. But of course prejudice, too, played a part in dismantling Dvořák's naive prescription. Edward MacDowell (1860–1908), a New York–born composer who had learned his trade from Joachim Raff in Frankfurt, and who was living in Boston during Dvořák's tenure in New York, felt the pressure to conform to the prestigious Bohemian master's ideas on musical Americanism, completing

FIG. 46-4   Edward MacDowell.

767

an "Indian Suite" (based on published field transcriptions) for orchestra, rather against his will, in 1895. Embarrassed by this concession to the vogue for vulgar "national trademarks," as he put it, he nevertheless managed to justify his choice of trademark by insisting that "the stern but at least manly and free rudeness of the North American Indian" was in any case preferable to "the badge of whilom [i.e., former] slavery" worn by blacks.[14]

His temporary residence in Boston made MacDowell the most eminent representative for a while of the first self-styled and recognized "school" of American composers in the European art-music tradition. Besides being the first American composer since Gottschalk to establish a strong European reputation (partly through the efforts of Liszt, his mentor's mentor), MacDowell was like Gottschalk a virtuoso pianist who toured the cities of Europe with his own concertos and concert transcriptions as his vehicles, and he produced four monumental "characteristic" sonatas — "Tragica," op. 45 (1892), "Eroica," op. 50 (1895), "Norse," op. 57 (1899), "Keltic," op. 59 (1900) — in the Lisztian mold. His many character-pieces for piano, issued in sets with evocative titles like *Woodland Sketches* (which opened with the once very popular "To a Wild Rose"), *Sea Pieces*, *Fireside Tales*, and *New England Idyls*, maintained the Schumannesque line past the turn of the century.

MacDowell had actually been Mrs. Thurber's first choice to lead the National Conservatory, a job that she felt by rights should have gone to a native-born composer, but he shunned the administrative duties that the job would have entailed, and there was no other American at the time who could have matched his prestige. Yet shortly after Dvořák's departure from New York, in 1896, MacDowell took his place there as a leading cultural figure in the nation's biggest city when he accepted appointment as head of the newly founded music department at Columbia University. Just as he had feared, the heavy pressures of his job, made more difficult by quarrels with the university administration, took a severe toll on his creative energies and his mental health. The last seven years of his life were barren, and he eventually became a "charity case" before dying of the combined effects of injuries sustained in a traffic accident and what was then diagnosed as "paresis" or general paralysis, a euphemism for the terminal effects of venereal disease.

Just what you'd expect from New York, his former Boston colleagues may well have muttered. Boston, the great museum and university city, defined itself in the nineteenth century (as to a degree it still does) in opposition to New York. New York, the commercial capital of the nation and perhaps the world, was in the eyes of Bostonians, and for that very reason, the capital of baseness and vulgarity. Boston was the capital of culture. Where New York symbolized the teeming immigrant "melting pot" to which Dvořák could appeal in urging an American style drawn from an amalgam of minority cultures, Boston was then the Anglo-Saxon stronghold. Despite the presence of a growing Irish immigrant minority, affluent Bostonians considered theirs to be a purebred city, the birthplace of the United States and the hub of "real" America. Its genteel mores nurtured the cultivation of the European fine arts, in contrast to the low mercenary culture of the big city to the southwest. These conditions made Boston the place where one might have expected the first school of professional Euro-American composers to appear, and also determined to a large extent the values that their music would embody.

The "Boston School" — sometimes called the "Second Yankee School" to distinguish it from the New England hymn writers of the colonial period — was a proudly academic establishment. Its first major representative, John Knowles Paine (1839–1906), was also the first professor of music at Harvard, which made him the first professor of music at any American university. Having composers teach at universities rather than conservatories was the British rather than the German tradition; the early music professors at German universities (of whom Hanslick was the first) lectured on music history and esthetics as adjuncts to philosophy departments. But Paine's training was solidly German, obtained at the Berlin conservatory (known as the *Hochschule für Musik*, the "High School of Music") between 1858 and 1861. He spent the rest of his life imparting a similar training to his pupils at Harvard.

The other major figures in the first Boston generation — that is, the generation trained in Europe rather than Boston — were George Whitefield Chadwick (1854–1931), who studied in Leipzig and Munich (with Josef Rheinberger, a famous organist and prestigious composer) and taught at Boston's New England Conservatory, where he became the director in 1897; and Horatio Parker (1863–1919), who after preliminary studies in Boston was sent by Chadwick to Rheinberger, and who taught at Yale, where he was dean of the School of Music from 1904 until his death.

The "Boston School's" second and third generations consisted of pupils of Paine, Chadwick, and Parker: Arthur William Foote (1853–1937), Frederick Shepherd Converse (1871–1940), Edward Burlingame Hill (1872–1960), Daniel Gregory Mason (1873–1953), John Alden Carpenter (1876–1951), David Stanley Smith (1877–1949). Like their teachers, they were all New Englanders by birth or education, were uniformly of Anglo-Saxon stock, and (with the exception of Carpenter, who went into business) earned their living as academics or organists.

The group had one other important member, however, who studied neither in Europe nor with any of the founders, but whose achievements realized the Boston School's aspirations in a particularly distinguished way: Amy Marcy Beach (née Cheney, 1867–1944), perhaps the nineteenth century's most successful woman composer of "large-scale art music" (to quote her biographer, Adrienne Fried Block). In

FIG. 46-5   Amy Marcy Cheney Beach.

keeping with a pattern we have noted at several earlier points in this book, her gender kept her, despite evidence of highly precocious talent, from the pursuit of a professional career.

Her wealthy parents thought it unsuitable for a well-bred girl to study at a European conservatory. Instead they engaged private teachers for her, but mainly in piano-playing, a proper social grace. Her training in composition was confined to some informal study of scores with Wilhelm Gericke, an Austrian conductor then leading the Boston Symphony Orchestra, and a single year of harmony and counterpoint with a local instructor, Junius W. Hill. Orchestration and fugue she taught herself by translating and working through the Paris conservatory textbooks in those subjects.

As a pianist, meanwhile, she flourished, making her first appearance with orchestra at the age of sixteen, and a formal, highly successful, Boston Symphony debut in 1885 with Chopin's F-minor Concerto. Later that year, she married Henry Harris Aubrey Beach, a socially prominent Boston surgeon, twenty-four years her senior, who lectured on anatomy at Harvard. Her married state precluded any more concertizing, and it appeared that her talent would go the way of Clara Wieck's and Fanny Mendelssohn's — that is, wither on the vine.

But the childless marriage between the eighteen-year-old musical prodigy and the forty-two-year-old society doctor turned out to be fortunate for her work. Her husband's wealth gave her unlimited leisure, indeed forced it upon her, and he had no objection either to her avocational composing or to her publishing her work. She was free to compose in the larger forms, and she had a ready and admiring public in Boston society. Whatever drawback her sex might have afforded under less ideal conditions were offset by her social prominence, by her conformity with social convention, and (in apparent — but only apparent — paradox) by the marginalism, in those days, of American composers generally. Indulged at first as a local favorite, "Mrs. H. H. A. Beach" (as, in accordance with domestic custom, she always signed her work) eventually acquired a national reputation. Anton Seidl, the New York conductor, is reported to have considered her music superior to Brahms's. (But he said it of Chadwick's music, too, and as a card-carrying Wagnerian may have had his reasons.) Beach embarked on her first and only symphony almost immediately after hearing the Boston premiere of Dvořák's "New World" in January 1894. It was obviously her model. The two symphonies are in the same key, the relatively rarely used E minor. While her symphony does not employ cyclic returns, at least not to anything like the extent that Dvořák's does, its complex and broadly constructed outer movements, as was increasingly the fashion, were developed out of a single fund of motifs. To compound the tour de force, they came from one of her many art songs, "Dark Is the Night," first published in 1890. Beach did not reveal this fact, but she fairly trumpeted the information that the middle movements (and the "closing theme" in the first) were based on the melodies of what she called "Irish-Gaelic" folk songs, for which reason the whole symphony bears the title, "Gaelic."

Thus Beach's symphony was an ambitious and advanced work not only from the standpoint of its proportions and its craftsmanship — though these were impressive enough to earn an accolade from Chadwick, who wrote the composer that her work was "full of fine things, melodically, harmonically, and orchestrally, and mighty well built besides," and that from now on she was, as far as he was concerned, "one of the boys." Beyond this, the symphony sought to engage directly in the esthetic debates of the day as they intersected with social ones.

Her use of Irish folklore was a response to Dvořák comparable to Brahms's response to Beethoven in the last movement of his First Symphony. It was both a declaration of affiliation and a corrective—in Beach's case, a characteristically Bostonian corrective. Like Dvořák, she sought a melodic content that advertised a specific national origin, in large part owing (as did his) to the use of pentatonic scales. But that national origin was "American" in a sense that only Boston, perhaps, would have fully endorsed or understood. "We of the north," Beach wrote in a letter to the *Boston Herald* in which she took explicit issue with Dvořák's prescriptions, "should be far more likely to be influenced by old English, Scotch or Irish songs, inherited with our literature from our ancestors." Like the composers of Europe, then, Beach defined the national not merely in terms of soil (as the Bohemian Dvořák had benignly, but condescendingly, urged Americans to do) but in terms of blood as well. She identified herself musically, as did most Bostonians (or Bohemians, for that matter), not with the country of which she happened to be a citizen, which had neither a uniform ethnicity nor a long history, but with the country from which she descended ethnically, assuming that that "Celtic" blood descent identified her as a sort of Ur-American, an American aristocrat.

For just back of the notion of the "Boston American" lay that of the "Mayflower American" or, in Mrs. Beach's case, the notion of nationality upheld by the Daughters of the American Revolution, to recall by name a politically conservative and, it must be added, a socially intolerant organization of which Mrs. Beach was not only a member but a leader. (The D.A.R.'s closest brush with music history came in 1939, when it denied the use of Constitution Hall, its public auditorium in Washington, D.C., to Marian Anderson, a famous black American contralto, for a recital that would have included a group of songs of the kind on which Dvořák naively proposed the founding of an authentically American art music.)

These socially divisive and hierarchical assumptions are among the subtexts that underlie Amy Beach's "Gaelic" Symphony, alongside more progressive ones like the artistic emancipation of women (of which, after her death, her career became a symbol for a new generation of feminist musicians and musicologists). Its finale, the most impressive testimony to her mastery of "the higher forms of art" and a most decisive rebuke to those who look for stereotyped expressions of "femininity" in music by women, contained "only themes of my own devising," Beach wrote. But, she went on, she intended it to convey the same impression as the movements drawn from actual folk artifacts. Just as the tunes in the middle movements, "like the folk music of every race, sprang from the common joys, sorrows, adventures and struggles of a primitive people," so the finale expressed "the rough, primitive character of the Celtic people, their sturdy daily life, their passions and battles, and the elemental nature of their processes of thought and its resulting action."

The emphasis on archaism was significant. It distinguished the ancient Celts, with whom the composer and her audience identified in solidarity, from the contemporary Irish — the newly arrived, working-class immigrant minority that was then just beginning to threaten Yankee hegemony in Boston — with whom they certainly did not. The same distinction was drawn in the case of Jews, between the contemporary diaspora "yids" encountered in daily life and the manly race of biblical "Hebrews" or "Israelites," another heroic warrior race celebrated musically since the days of Handel, who continued to be the object of much admiring attention from European and Euro-American composers who were otherwise conventionally, if not enthusiastically, anti-Semitic: both Chadwick in Boston and Alexander Serov in St. Petersburg, for example, wrote operas based on the Apocryphal book of Judith, which celebrates the Hebrew victory over the Assyrians.

Beach's finale is cast in "three-part sonata form" as taught in late-nineteenth-century textbooks and conservatory curricula. The composer's own analysis breaks it down into an exposition and recapitulation, linked by a "free fantasia" (that is, development) section. The thematic material consists of two themes, of which the first is drawn from a $\frac{2}{2}$ *alla breve* phrase that conspicuously intrudes (in a manner probably recollected from the scherzo in Beethoven's *Eroica* Symphony) on the first movement's coda, otherwise cast like the rest of the movement in $\frac{6}{8}$ time. (The first three movements of the symphony are all written in compound meters; that was evidently a part of the "Gaelic" characterization.) The lyrical second theme, while not derived from a folk tune, is nevertheless pentatonic in the folk manner.

Both themes are "fully worked out," as the composer put it, in the exposition, so that "the free fantasia is comparatively short, owing to the extensive development of the themes when first presented." That, as we have seen, was a characteristic of Brahmsian construction: a demonstratively advanced style of composing. In the development section (Ex. 46-11a), the initial motif of the first theme is extended into a syncopation that transforms it into a near twin of the very first phrase played (by the cellos) at the outset of Dvořák's "New World" Symphony (Ex. 46-11b) — too close and conspicuous to be anything but a deliberate reference — and given a chromatically ascending sequential treatment over the next forty bars that again evokes memories of Beethoven's *Eroica*. The coda, in which the lyrical second theme is finally recapitulated amid huzzahs from the heavy brass, in the tonic major and in augmented note-values, is the very essence of valiant affirmation.

These resonances were not lost on critics. Reviews of the Boston Symphony premiere repeatedly resorted to the epithet "heroic" to describe the symphony, or else (to quote one) conjured up images of "Ossianic heroes . . . gathering in spite of whirlwind and storm."[17] (Ossian was the legendary Celtic bard whose poems, published in 1762, were subsequently exposed as a forgery.) The ethical quality the image evoked was itself an expression of the Puritan ideals espoused by the composers of the Boston School, and dependably found by like-minded critics in their work.

Their collusion in what modern critics call "redemptive culture" represented (in the words of Macdonald Smith Moore, a historian of the Boston School) "a dual mission":[18]

on the one hand, "an errand into the wilderness of the impending twentieth century to manifest New England's right to speak for America"; and on the other, a campaign for what the English poet and critic Matthew Arnold (another enthusiastic student of Celtic lore) famously dubbed the culture of Sweetness and Light—"a secular religious force capable of formulating principles of individual and social value." Mrs. H. H. A. Beach's "Gaelic" Symphony was a monument to these once-powerful ideals.

EX. 46-11A   Mrs. H. H. A. Beach, "Gaelic" Symphony, IV, one measure before [F]

EX. 46-11B   Antonín Dvořák, "New World" Symphony, I, mm. 1–4

WAR BRINGS IT TO FRANCE

For composers of the Boston School, an even more influential symphonic model than Dvořák's "New World" Symphony, because it preached less a national than a spiritual sensibility, was the Symphony in D minor by César Franck (1822–90). Despite his Germanic surname, Franck was a Walloon (French-speaking Belgian) composer who plied his trade in Paris, and whose career paralleled Bruckner's in many ways.

Like Bruckner, he hailed from the cultural provinces; he was born in Liège, a medium-sized Belgian town, and received his early education there before coming to Paris with his family. Like Bruckner he earned his living for the greater part of his career as a church organist. (Unlike Bruckner, however, Franck composed some important music for his instrument that exploited the resources of the huge organs built by the French firm of Cavaillé-Coll, whose paid "artistic representative" he became.) Like Bruckner, Franck was an outsider to the musical establishment who eventually secured a teaching post at a prestigious institution (in his case, the Paris Conservatory), but not in composition (in his case, it was in organ playing). Finally, like Bruckner's, Franck's class quickly became an unofficial composition seminar that attracted a circle of eventually eminent composers who venerated him despite (or perhaps in part because of) his maverick status.

Franck composed his single symphony, one of his last works, in 1886–88, when he was already in his middle sixties. Its first performance (17 February 1889), by the Paris Conservatory orchestra, had an equivocal success, but its American premiere by the Boston Symphony under Gericke less than two months later was a triumph. The work long remained a beacon for the English-speaking music world, which was looking for "ideas," as Matthew Arnold put it, "that criticize life." This was the "aspirational" or affirmational view of art that more modern writers (like Bryan Magee, quoted near the end of chapter 42) have declared bankrupt in the wake of Wagner. But it outlasted Wagner, and (as we shall see) even saw itself, rightly or wrongly, as continuing the Wagnerian tradition.

Edward Burlingame Hill, John Knowles Paine's star pupil and one of his successors as head of the Harvard music department, pronounced Franck a musician "unique in the selflessness of his life, and the concentration of his efforts to reveal the luminous truth of Art."[19] As for the Symphony, it was the "ripest expression" of a "new creed of instrumental music."[20] In a remarkable passage, the Bostonian composer-critic extolled Franck's ascetic virtues in the unmistakable terms of Matthew Arnold's Anglo-Saxon artistic evangelism:

FIG. 46-6   César Franck at the organ, ca. 1890, portrait by Jeanne Rougier.

Franck's outlook upon Art may be accurately summarized as a *gospel* instead of a *métier* [profession]. Franck's ascendancy over his pupils springs from the spiritual reaction exercised upon them through his character. He taught the moral obligations of the artist, the need for elevated standards, the consideration of quality rather than quantity in the students' tasks, emotional sincerity as an absolute prerequisite in all artistic expression, and above all faith as a primary ingredient. Moreover, Franck steadily inculcated a disdain for immediate success, and a disregard of the public as a prerequisite for attaining durability in a work of art. But vital and constructive as were Franck's maxims for guidance in the artists' career, the fact that he bore out these principles in his own life made them the more compelling.[21]

And yet the most noteworthy aspect of Franck's status as preceptor and example remains the simple fact that he made his mark primarily as a composer — and inculcator — of "absolute" instrumental music. This was virtually unprecedented in a French composer. We have not associated the name of any French composer with instrumental music at all since the time of Berlioz. But a glance at the complete list of even Berlioz's works reveals a preponderance of vocal music, as it does for all French composers save the court instrumentalists (violinists, gambists, harpsichord specialists) of the seventeenth and eighteenth centuries.

Indeed, Berlioz's instrumental music, as we encountered it in chapter 38, was among the most powerful stimuli leading instrumental music into a *rapprochement* (as the French say) or reconciliation with opera, which from the time of the transplanted Parisian Rossini had been practically the sole focus of French composers. Even Hill agreed that Franck "showed an intellectual fervor and a sense of artistic responsibility as a rule uncharacteristic of the Gallic musician of the period."[22]

And yet his wide circle of pupils and disciples, who remained active and influential well into the twentieth century, put Franck forward as the spiritual guide of a new and resurgent French spirit in music, which they summed up in the always-capitalized slogan ARS GALLICA. All that the Latin phrase means is "French art." But when capitalized and applied to a certain school of composers, it meant a French art that arose in nationalistic response — a highly paradoxical nationalistic response — to the Franco-Prussian War of 1870–71.

On 25 February 1871, "a few days," as Carl Dahlhaus once tartly reminded his readers, "before the Prussian army marched down the Champs Elysées"[23] (the broad avenue that runs through the heart of Paris), a group of youngish French musicians headed by Camille Saint-Saëns founded an organization they called the Société Nationale de Musique: the National Musical Society. It was to be a concert-sponsoring association that would exclusively promote the work of living French composers, and that sought to assert through music the unique essence or spirit of France in a manner that would elevate and educate public taste. The preamble to the group's by-laws read:

> The proposed purpose of the Society is to aid the production and popularization of all serious works, whether published or not, by French composers. To encourage and bring to light, as far as lies within its power, all musical attempts, whatever their form, on condition that they give evidence of lofty artistic aspirations on the part of their author. Fraternally, with entire forgetfulness of self, with the

firm resolve to aid each other with all their capacity, the members will unite their efforts, each in his own sphere of action, to the study and performance of their countrymen's works which they shall be called upon to select and interpret.[24]

Yet despite these avowedly nationalistic aims, the Société Nationale, through its declared emphasis on "serious" music of "lofty artistic aspiration" and its practical emphasis on the larger instrumental forms, became in effect the vehicle for the unprecedented Germanization of French music. In retrospect it is clear that the motivation behind the founding of the Société Nationale was an aspect of the sense of national shame brought about by the outcome of the war with Prussia, and that the Society's aims implied a dual objective of repudiation and emulation: first, to restore high and respectable purpose to art after the Offenbachian bacchanale of the Second Empire; and second, to overtake and surpass the achievements of German "absolute" instrumental music, the highest and most respectable sphere of musical endeavor. Never was the music of any country so thoroughly transformed by an inferiority complex.

Franck served on the board of directors of the Society from the time of its founding. From 1886 to his death four years later at the age of sixty-eight he was its figurehead, during which time he composed, in addition to the Symphony, a violin sonata, a string quartet, and a neo-Bachian "Prelude, aria, et final" for piano. Other works he had composed since the founding of the Society included a Piano Quintet in F minor, the same key as Brahms's essay in the genre (1879), a set of "Symphonic Variations" for piano and orchestra (1885), and an even more neo-Bachian "Prelude, chorale, and fugue" for piano (1884). This was an output unprecedented for a French composer, even if Franck's four symphonic poems (including one, *Psyché*, with chorus) and vocal works from the period (one opera and two biblical oratorios) are reckoned in. The programmatic pieces and the oratorios were less successful than the essays in "absolute" music, and have fallen into relative neglect. The reception of Franck's music, no less than its production, was thus a sign of the times.

Not only in its general esthetic and stylistic orientation, but in all manner of specific details, Franck's Symphony announces its allegiance to Germanic rather than French tradition. To write a symphony in D minor was in itself such an announcement, and Beethoven's Ninth haunts the work no less pervasively than it had haunted Bruckner's Third Symphony, or the symphony that eventually became Brahms's First Piano Concerto. But Franck's invocation of Beethoven's reputedly hermetic and rarefied spiritual domain went beyond the Ninth to encompass the most emblematic and aura-surrounded works of all, the "late quartets." The symphony's thematic kernel was none other than the highly fraught *échappée* figure from the last movement of the last quartet (F major, op. 135; see Ex. 40-2), the movement jestingly titled "The Difficult Decision," in which a slow chromatic three-note motif mock-portentously labeled "Muss es sein?" (Must it be?) is hilariously answered by a quick diatonic inversion, "Es muss sein! Es muss sein!" (It must! It must!). Taken ultraseriously, as everything in late Beethoven was eventually taken, the phrase had haunted the whole nineteenth century. Among its progeny already familiar to us are the generative phrase in Liszt's *Les préludes* and the "Fate motif" that haunts Wagner's *Ring*, beginning with *Die Walküre* (see Ex. 42-2d).

Having suffused a quartet movement, a symphonic poem, and a trilogy of operas, with Franck the motif entered the domain of the traditional symphony. Not only did it furnish the first movement with its thematic mainspring; it was also incorporated into the main themes of the succeeding movements and returned in its original form in the coda to the finale (Ex. 46-12).

EX. 46-12   César Franck, Symphony in D minor, thematic conspectus

It was Franck (or rather his pupil Vincent d'Indy, in his biography of the master that came out in 1906) who officially dubbed this process of multimovement motivic unification "cyclic form."[25] No one ever claimed that Franck was its inventor—it all too obviously goes back through Liszt to Berlioz and beyond—but the dogmatic insistence on its spiritual necessity was distinctively Franck-school. To those who claimed that Franck derived his procedures from Liszt's "thematic transformations," the Franckists retorted (1) that their master had already recycled the themes of his Piano Trio in F-sharp Minor, op. 1, no. 1, composed in 1841 at the age of eighteen; (2) that Franck played the Trio for Liszt in 1842 and presented him with a copy; and (3) that therefore it was Franck who had influenced Liszt.

Both parties to the argument conveniently forgot that Schubert had recycled the slow movement theme in the finale of his Trio in E-flat major, op. 100, completed and published in 1828. But even Schubert had Beethoven's Fifth and Ninth as models. As usual Beethoven was the common progenitor; the heirs were merely squabbling in probate court, so to speak, over his estate. But though the point at issue may seem trivial in retrospect, the quarrel was not. Under the influence of historicist thinking matters of priority were becoming heavily fraught. In the twentieth century they would become obsessive and disastrous.

But we have only begun to explore the extent to which Franck's Symphony mined the legacy of the late Beethoven quartets. The unusual form of the first movement, in which the initial slow section (or Introduction, as it must at first appear) alternates with the ensuing allegro throughout the movement, emulates the opening movements of two of the late quartets: op. 127 in E-flat and op. 130 in B-flat. But where in Beethoven the alternation of tempos also involved an alternation of themes, in Franck both the portentous slow music and its frantic sequel are equally derived from the opening "Muss es sein" motto, differently continued.

Patently Lisztian after all is the key sequence, measured by the reappearances of the opening Lento. From D minor the first important modulation is to F minor. The F minor switches soon enough to F major to make way for a traditional "second theme" in the relative key. But the initial juxtaposition of minor keys pitched a third apart would commit a confirmed Lisztian to a complementary swing from D to B, and possibly an antipodal move to A♭/G♯ to complete the circle. These are supplied, in short order and not at all by coincidence, at the outset of the "free fantasia" or development section: A♭ minor (approached through a "classic" Lisztian sequence) at m. 199 and C♭/B major/minor at m. 206. At the recapitulation, moreover, which takes the form of a climactic, canonic Lento at m. 331, B minor is approached directly from D minor to mirror the opening ascent to F.

But if key relations tend toward the Lisztian (circles of thirds alongside traditional circles of fifths), the local harmonizations and progressions tend toward the Wagnerian—and not only the generally Wagnerian but the specifically Tristanesque. Franck and his generation (e.g., Brahms) were haunted by echoes of Wagner's Prelude as much as their fathers (e.g., Wagner) had been haunted by echoes of Beethoven—and of course they went on being haunted by Beethoven as well: the more "belated" a member of any tradition, the more haunted; and the more haunted, the more difficult it becomes to contribute. (Hence Franck's lone symphony as compared with Brahms's four, Beethoven's nine, Mozart's forty-one, and Haydn's hundred-plus.) To catch Franck in the act of being spooked, one can look for four-note chromatic ascents that come directly out of *Tristan*: a whole sequence of them goes from the first violin in mm. 17–21 into the viola at mm. 21–25 and back into the violins at mm. 25–28 (Ex. 46-13). Or one can look for the chromatically descending basses that combine resonances of the Tristan motif with those of the coda to the Ninth. They are pervasive. A short one accompanies the ascending sequence just described in contrary motion. Sometimes they are amazingly ample. At mm. 8–11 (repeated at mm. 55–59) the chromatic descent goes through eight degrees (ever so slightly disguised by octave transfers).

EX. 46-13   César Franck, Symphony in D minor, I, mm. 17–28

EX. 46-13 (continued)

The mother of them all occurs, as one would expect, in the development: it begins in m. 249 forward with the bass on A♭, makes an immediate descent through five chromatic degrees to E, where it is interrupted by a theme; it is resumed at 259 for another five degrees (through m. 261) where it stalls as a pedal before proceeding down one more degree to make eleven. Were it not for the whole step in the bass between m. 269 and 270, there would have been a full unfolding of the chromatic scale, the functional equivalent in this modulatory context of a full circle of fifths. For its ascending near-equal, nine progressions, see the bassoon in Ex. 46-14. The coda embeds an eight-degree progression within a motivic sequence: start tracking the bass at m. 485 to see E♭ descend to C♯; the next segment, C to B♭, follows in mm. 489–490, A to G in mm. 490–491.

EX. 46-14   César Franck, Symphony in D minor, I, mm. 298–304

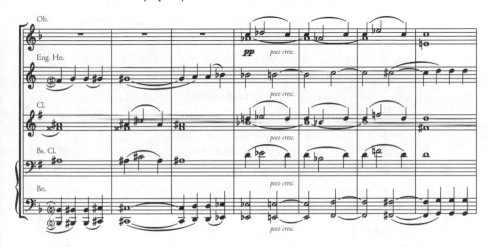

These slithery harmonies, directing myriad recombinations of charged motivic particles on their trajectory through musical space, produce an effect even more like that of a Wagnerian music drama than do Dvořák's contrapuntal montages. To compare the mumbled opening statement of the germinating motif with the ecstatic shout that closes the first movement, extending the same motif with an upward thrust to the third degree in the major, is to experience a rhetoric that vies in persuasion — but wordlessly — with Wagner's own. In their heavily fraught but semantically undefined character, Franck's chromatically and motivically saturated textures make metaphorical, metaphysical interpretation as irresistible as it is finally impossible, thus supremely realizing the objective of "absolute" music: to say what is unsayable, to speak the unspeakable, and make it seem (to quote Brahms's comment on his *Schicksalslied*) "the most important thing." All the more is this true since the germinating motif had been defined by longstanding "intertextual" tradition as a metaphysical question. Program annotations for the Franck Symphony, accordingly, assumed the character of religious commentary. Here is a sample, from an old handbook for American record collectors called the *Victor Book of the Symphony*. The author, an organist and conductor named Charles O'Connell (1900–62), had studied in Paris with Charles-Marie Widor (1844–1937), Franck's disciple and successor at the Conservatory, before becoming the head of "artists and repertoire" for the Victor Talking Machine Company, America's largest manufacturer of phonographs and records. O'Connell assures the reader that Franck, a "great and simple soul, is able to lead us to glimpses of a light beyond the world." The most "mystic" of all, according to this writer, comes in the second movement:

> There are flights toward that light as the movement progresses — flights of swift muted notes, like the beatings of thousands of invisible wings, coursing the misty upper airs in clouds of vibrant color and life. Incredibly we find that even this will-o'-the-wisp figure is remotely derived from the eternal question of the first movement — notwithstanding its soaring hopefulness. The meaning seems clear: out of eternal questioning, someday comes an answer; out of living, life.[26]

So was a piece of textless, "abstract" symphonic music promoted as moral instruction, as initiation into the ineffable, as indoctrination in faith. That was indeed the point of absolute music, as the tradition defined itself post-Beethoven. It was superbly ironic that it reached its zenith in the work of a French composer, a representative of the culture against which absolute music had traditionally defined itself. But it was dismally ironic that so lofty an esthetic so easily lent itself to commercial packaging, which is what O'Connell's book (primarily meant to sell records) amounted to.

Advocacy of "good music" as Arnoldian "criticism of life," and its promotion as an exercise in middle-class self-improvement, grew directly out of the ideology of the Société Nationale, and it is no coincidence that Matthew Arnold himself based his ideas about culture and society on the art and literature of chastened, post-1870 ("Third Republic") France. But of course it reached its commercial zenith in America, where recording companies, concert organizations, and schools all cooperated in a minor industry called "music appreciation": instruction in the passive consumption of "classical music" (with a nearly exclusive emphasis on the symphonic repertoire) as a part of liberal education.

Although it was a twentieth-century phenomenon, receiving its main commercial impetus in the mid-1920s when the market for phonograph recordings (thanks to hugely improved recording technology) expanded exponentially, music appreciation deserves mention here because it continued to reflect the values of the nineteenth-century symphony, and, as it were, to "freeze" the repertoire in its late-nineteenth-century tracks. It thus participated in the process of "reification" — turning artworks into things (most obviously in the case of physically tangible phonograph records) and treating the things thus created as marketable commodities.

And that made music appreciation, in its propagation of a frozen and reified repertoire, one of the factors contributing to the disastrous twentieth-century rift, within the literate or "art" tradition, between the interests of musical producers and those of consumers (a rift complicated, as we shall see, by the creation of two potentially competing or even antagonistic groups — composers on the one hand and manufacturers of records and sheet music on the other, each claiming the role of "producer"). Musical modernism, as we shall also see, threatened the equation of "serious" music with moral uplift; and so the marketing of classical music, which depended (or thought it depended) on that equation, turned all the more resolutely against the new. Only music that encouraged its listeners to identify themselves as a cultured ("Brahmin") and spiritual ("Franckist") elite was eligible for promotion under the banner of music appreciation.

Eventually the operation backfired, with dire consequences for the popularity of the music it purveyed. Even in its heyday, music appreciation received warnings from its own practitioners. Deems Taylor (1885–1966), a composer who was hired in the late 1930s to give inspirational intermission lectures during broadcasts by the New York Philharmonic, cautioned that "many a potential music lover is frightened away by the solemnity of music's devotees."[27] Association with self-defined elites put "good music" at risk, especially in America, of association with various kinds of social snobbery (and in the case of Mrs. H. H. A. Beach, we have seen that the concern was not unfounded).

Finally, to cast our eye ahead for a moment, when after World War II the esthetics of modernism finally gained the upper hand in American institutions of higher education, music appreciation was altered to accord with a new ideology—not of uplift but of "formalism" (the study of structure rather than meaning), reflecting the interests of composers rather than marketers. The older version of music appreciation had represented the survival of the older notion of absolute music (music as ineffable expression) into the twentieth century. By midcentury that notion had been done in by its votaries and exploiters, and it now inspires more suspicion than sympathy.

The grim history of the twentieth century—something Brahms or Franck could never have foreseen, to say nothing of Matthew Arnold or Charles O'Connell—played its part as well both in discrediting the idea of redemptive culture and in undermining the authority of its adherents. The literary critic George Steiner, one such adherent, after a lifetime devoted (in his words) to "the worship—the word is hardly exaggerated—of the classic,"[28] and to the propagation of the faith, found himself baffled by the example of the culture-loving Germans of the mid-twentieth century, "who sang Schubert in the evening and tortured in the morning." "I'm going to the end of my life," he confessed unhappily, "haunted more and more by the question, 'Why did the humanities not humanize?' I don't have an answer." But that is because the question—being the product of Arnoldian art religion—turned out to be wrong. It is all too obvious by now that teaching people that their love of Schubert makes them better people teaches them little more than self-regard. There are better reasons to cherish art.

SYMPHONIST AS VIRTUOSO

One time-honored, far less sentimental way of cherishing art is as an exercise of ingenuity and artifice that aims not at self-improvement but at euphoria. The late-nineteenth-century French symphonic repertoire boasts a work of that kind, too. Besides the high- minded symphonies of Franck and his pupils—they include Vincent d'Indy (1851–1931), who wrote five between 1870 and 1918, and the short-lived Ernest Chausson (1855–99), who completed one in 1890—there was also the flamboyantly virtuosic Third Symphony (1886) in C minor (but of course ending in a triumphant C major) by Camille Saint-Saëns, the original architect of the Société Nationale.

FIG. 46-7   Camille Saint-Saëns.

Its Beethovenian key and tonal trajectory notwithstanding, the symphony was an homage to Liszt—indeed, a veritable portrait of the "New German" icon, which became a memorial when its dedicatee died at Bayreuth, during the Wagner Festival there, while the symphony awaited its premiere. Its form is wholly indebted to Liszt's example: the main theme in each of its four movements, like the themes in a Liszt symphonic poem, is a different transformation of a single pitch sequence (Ex. 46-15). (Although obviously related to the Franckian "cyclic" idea, Saint-Saëns's method did not involve any recyclings of actual themes between movements.)

Another obvious Lisztianism, second nature to a composer who had already composed four symphonic poems, was the idea of consolidating the four movements into two by linking the ends of the first and third, by means of smooth transitions, into the beginnings of the second and fourth. Saint-Saëns claimed that the purpose of this dovetailing was to cut down on the need for recapitulations—"the interminable reprises and repetitions," as he put it in a note in the score, "that are leading to the disappearance of instrumental music"—but in fact the first movement's recapitulation is virtually complete. The transitions, like the thematic transformations (and the many third-related harmonic progressions and modulations), seem more a flourish of up-to-date composing technique than a formal innovation.

That display of composerly virtuosity evoked a Lisztian resonance of another sort, and the symphony follows through by including in its very ample orchestration two keyboard instruments associated with Liszt at different stages of his life (and with Saint-Saëns as well). The scherzo/finale pair features a scintillating part for the piano (solo in the scherzo, four-hands in the finale), and the slow movement (the second part of the first pair) features a very churchy sounding organ (representative of Liszt's last period, when he had taken minor clerical orders and had begun composing for the instrument).

The organ returns in the last movement, coinciding with the transformation of the symphony's theme into a hymn that alternates with elaborate cantus firmus textures and a full-blown fugue. This is a remarkable contrast with the Franck Symphony, which deployed only traditional symphonic (and, it could be argued, operatic) materials to produce an aura widely interpreted as profoundly, and sincerely, spiritual. Saint-Saëns deploys very concrete evocations of specific sacred genres and timbres to produce an aura of exhilarating virtuosity that no one seems ever to have taken seriously as religious expression. Nor has anyone ever been tempted, it seems, even to find a program in the work, despite the fact that it so conspicuously appropriated a constructive device ("thematic transformation") that had originally been developed in the context, and for the exclusive purposes, of program music.

In the heyday of music appreciation Saint-Saëns was given a rather indifferent reception. The *Victor Book of the Symphony* does not mention his Third Symphony at all (mainly, of course, because there was no Victor recording of it to sell — but that in itself is an eloquent comment in view of the symphony's one-time currency, initially far greater than Franck's). Its sophisticated play of genres and styles was ascribed to a fatal "eclecticism" by German writers who liked (and still like) to cite Saint-Saëns as evidence that despite everything the French were *au fond* (at bottom) irredeemable (or, as the familiar joke would have it, that deep down they were superficial).

Two years after the "Organ Symphony's" premiere, Emil Naumann wrote that "Saint-Saëns shows more intellectuality in his compositions than poetical inspiration, and more self-criticism in art-form than richness of invention."[29] Nearly a century later, Carl Dahlhaus was still mocking the "orchestral pomp that Saint-Saëns flaunts as a decorative façade," but that cannot conceal "the failure to which any eclecticism is condemned that seeks to unite the decorative monumentality of grand opera with a classicistic formal design and a transformation technique abstracted from program music."[30]

EX. 46-15   Camille Saint-Saëns, Symphony no. 3, thematic resume

In place of moral uplift, ran the nationalistic nineteenth-century cliché that music appreciation did its best to universalize in the twentieth, French music offered sensuous and intellectual gratification; in place of a redemptive scenario (German-surnamed Franck alone excepted), it offered a tempting menu. No wonder that for German artists and their disciples, "culinary"[31] became the squelch of all squelches. It stood for mindless — or worse, soulless — sensual gratification, the reputed house specialty of the French, chefs to the world. In the twentieth century, especially after the French had their chance to avenge themselves on the Germans in battle, this ordering of priorities was for a while decisively reversed.

THE EPIC STYLE

Russian symphonies in the nineteenth century came under two brand names. One was provided by the conservatories, founded in the 1860s by Anton Rubinstein in St. Petersburg and his brother Nikolai in Moscow. The other was provided by the last generation of aristocratic autodidacts, gathered around Miliy Balakirev in St. Petersburg beginning in the 1850s. Best known today as the *moguchaya kuchka*, the "Mighty Little Heap" (a sobriquet bestowed on them in 1867 by Vladimir Stasov, their publicist, but then monopolized for a while by their enemies), the Balakirev Circle preferred to call itself the New Russian School as a way of declaring solidarity with Liszt and the New Germans, as against the "old Germans" who manned the conservatories.

Each group produced one outstanding symphonist in the 1870s: from the Mighty Kuchka there was Alexander Borodin (1833–87), the remarkable chemist-composer whom we met in chapter 39 as an "orientalist;" and from the Conservatory side there was Pyotr Ilyich Chaikovsky (1840–93), an alumnus of the St. Petersburg institution's first graduating class (1866), who did his basic training with Anton Rubinstein. The surprising thing is that of the two, it was Chaikovsky, the conservatory product, who provided the most pointed challenge anywhere in Europe to German symphonic hegemony.

Because of their outsider, nonprofessional status, members of the Balakirev circle had no choice but to claim legitimacy on the strength of their ethnicity. They promoted a myth of Russian authenticity from which the conservatory was by definition excluded. The myth was exported to France by César Cui, a member of the circle who (like Schumann before him), wrote reams of press propaganda on behalf of the group, including a series of articles in French that appeared in 1878–79 in the *Revue et gazette musicale*, the leading Paris music magazine, and was published in book form a year later as *La musique en Russie*, the most influential tract of its kind ever to appear.

On its fairytale of radical opposition between a heroic school of honest nationalists (the *kuchka*) fighting the good ethnic fight against an entrenched band of aristocratically supported foreigners (the conservatory), practically the whole subsequent historiography of Russian music in "the West" has been based. In the early twentieth century, Sergei Diaghilev, the great impresario, exploited the French taste for exoticism in promoting his organization, the Ballets Russes, as purveyors of the authentic Russian soul. Their programs, brimming with folklore and orientalia, solidified the notion

FIG. 46-8   Fyodor Vasilyev, *Illumination of St. Petersburg at Night*. The large dome in the background is that of St. Isaac's Cathedral.

in the West that the authenticity of Russian music depended on its Russianness, which in turn depended on a heavily "Asiatic" component. Ever since, "how Russian is it?" has been the main critical question asked of Russian music by Western audiences and critics. And it had to be answered plainly enough for non-Russian ears to hear. As a result, Russian composers, more than any other comparable group, have been confined to an exotic ghetto that bears little resemblance to the country they actually inhabited.

Meanwhile, here is how the same César Cui described the early meetings of the Balakirev circle, in a memoir written not as foreign propaganda but for consumption at home:

> We formed a close-knit circle of young composers. And since there was nowhere to study (the conservatory didn't exist) our *self-education* began. It consisted of playing through everything that had been written by all the greatest composers, and all works were subjected to criticism and analysis in all their technical and creative aspects. We were young and our judgments were harsh. We were very disrespectful in our attitude toward Mozart and Mendelssohn; to the latter we

opposed Schumann, who was then ignored by everyone. We were very enthusiastic about Liszt and Berlioz. We worshiped Chopin and Glinka. We carried on heated debates (in the course of which we would down as many as four or five glasses of tea with jam), we discussed musical form, program music, vocal music, and especially operatic form.[32]

All the same issues, in other words, as were then being debated in the rest of Europe. For this was no band of narrow nationalists. What Cui was describing was a "Davids-bund," to borrow an appropriately Schumannesque word for it, a cabal of idealistic "progressives" opposing institutional authority on the one hand and "philistinism" on the other. Except for Glinka, all the objects of their veneration were located to the west of Russia—and how could it be otherwise? Glinka was at this point (the mid-to-late 1850s) the only Russian to venerate, precisely because he alone, among Russians, was then on a level with the Europeans. The autochthonous music of Russia, the tonal products of the soil and its peasant denizens, were not admired and not discussed.

And that is because Russian musicians in the European literate fine-art tradition, however alienated by temperament or by force of circumstance from the "mainstream" of local fashion or success, however dependent for their promotion upon their exotic appeal, and however inferior or superior they have felt in consequence, have always measured themselves by the only terms available—that is, the terms of the tradition within which they have chosen to pursue their careers. They have always construed their identities in a larger European context and drawn their "sentiment of being[33] (to cite Rousseau's romantic definition of authenticity) from that sense of relatedness to cultivated Europe, not peasant Russia.

When Balakirev himself, the one Russian composer (as we learned in chapter 41) who might fit anyone's narrowest definition of a "nationalist," was introduced in 1901 to the English writer Rosa Newmarch, who would become the Mighty Kuchka's most ardent propagandist in the West, he sat down at the piano to play her a kind of musical credo: Beethoven's F-minor sonata ("Appassionata"),[34] Chopin's B-minor, and Schumann's G-minor. Not a Russian note in the lot, but it characterizes Balakirev and his "kuchka" far better then their usual chauvinist label.

It was within the incubator described verbally by Cui and at the keyboard by Balakirev that Borodin received his "symphonic education." His First Symphony, laboriously composed over a five-year period (1862–67) with Balakirev at his elbow, was cast in the key of E-flat major. Knowing this, and knowing how Balakirev and his fellow-kuchkists worked, we would be far better advised to expect allusions or (perhaps unconscious) quotations from past symphonic masterpieces in the same key by Beethoven (no. 3, "Eroica") and Schumann (no. 3, "The Rhenish") than from Russian folk songs. There are also obvious references in the Symphony's scherzo to a scherzo by Berlioz ("Queen Mab" from his Dramatic Symphony *Romeo and Juliet*) and in the finale to a finale by Glinka (from *A Life for the Tsar*), practically exhausting the list, in Cui's description, of the "kuchka's" admired models.

Only in the slow movement, the last to be composed, did Borodin venture into terrain now identified as stylistically (because exotically) "Russian" (Ex. 46-16). Its highly embellished, repetitive lyricism, backed up by chromatically inflected harmony, may have evoked "Russia" to listeners in France and Germany, but to Russians it evoked "the East." There was no real contradiction: the Western view of Russia, like the Russian view of the Caucasian and Central Asian nations their empire was in the process of conquering, was an "Orientalist" view, at once fascinated and condescending.

EX. 46-16 Alexander Borodin, Symphony no. 1, III, cello theme

In Borodin's Second Symphony (1869–76, revised 1878), the national colorings are far more pronounced, for which reason the symphony was an instant international hit. It arose in the euphoric wake of the First Symphony's premiere, alongside the earliest sketches for *Prince Igor*, the orientalist opera supreme, which we sampled in chapter 39. When Borodin temporarily decided to abandon work on his operatic epic in the early 1870s, he transferred to the symphony music originally conceived to illustrate scenes of Russian heroic antiquity, on the one hand, and oriental voluptuousness on the other. Rather than segregate these images by movements, as the opera would have segregated them by scenes and acts, Borodin mixed them according to a traditional symphonic recipe, reserving the lionhearted warrior material for the assertive "first themes" in the outer movements and the main body of the Scherzo, and the yielding, serpentine, feminine tunes for the recessive "second themes" in the outer movements — and in the Scherzo, for a Trio section replete with belly-dancer's percussion (the triangle standing in for her finger cymbals).

This Scherzo — marked *Prestissimo*, in $\frac{1}{1}$ time, with the whole notes racing at 108 to the minute — is a tour de force of orchestration, and (when well played) of orchestral virtuosity, in which the heavy brass, negotiating the tricky syncopations and the difficult staccatos, are made to move with all the speed and precision of the smaller, less unwieldy instruments of the orchestra, just as the ancient Russian heroes or *bogatïry*, for all their legendary girth, performed their limber feats of derring-do (Ex. 46-17). Still, this was a symphony, and so the initial characterization of primeval Russian boldness and fortitude comes by way of Beethoven's Fifth, whose unisons and fermatas had made an inescapable impression on all European composers, however Asiatic their immediate intent (Ex. 46-18).

SYMPHONIES OF SUFFERING

Despite his resolutely European orientation and his conservatory education, Chaikovsky was just as acutely aware as the "kuchkists" of the condescension with which Western

EX. 46-17   Alexander Borodin, Symphony no. 2, II (Scherzo), mm. 370–77

EX. 46-18   Alexander Borodin, Symphony no. 2, I, mm. 1–7

Europeans regarded Russians, alien and "Asiatic" by virtue of their long-lasting "Mongolian captivity" (vassalhood to the descendents of Genghis Khan in medieval times), their geographical remoteness, their Eastern Orthodox religion, even their crazy alphabet. "You can read it in their eyes," he complained to his patroness, Nadezhda von Meck,

> "You're just a Russian, *but I am so kind and indulgent that I favor you with my attention.*" The hell with them! Last year [1876] I found myself against my will at Liszt's. He was nauseatingly deferential, but a smile that never left his lips spoke the sentence I underlined above with perfect clarity. It goes without saying that by now I am less disposed than ever to go to these gentlemen on bended knee.[35]

Chaikovsky wrote the letter while he was at work on his Fourth Symphony (secretly dedicated to Mme von Meck as "my best friend"), a work that seemed to break with the whole symphonic tradition as it was viewed in the nineteenth century. What it lacks almost completely is the highly atomized motivic texture that Brahms had educed out of Beethoven, or even the "thematic transformative" technique that "Lisztian" symphonists like Saint-Saëns or Borodin employed. Instead there was something approaching a suite of giant character pieces: a "symphonic waltz" for a first movement, explicitly marked *in movimento di valse*, "in waltz tempo"; an Andantino, marked *in modo di canzone* ("in the manner of a ballad"), with a very Italianate middle section, reminding us that the symphony was composed during a stay in Venice; an orchestrational tour de force of a scherzo, marked *pizzicato ostinato*, in which each orchestral choir has a distinctive theme, and then trades off fragments in breathtaking hockets; and a finale consisting of variations on a famous Russian folk song. The genres themselves, while somewhat unusual for a symphony, were not unprecedented. Although not explicitly marked as such, the first movement of Brahms's Third Symphony could be fairly

FIG. 46-9 Pyotr Ilyich Chaikovsky, photographed in 1890.

described as being in waltz time (albeit with lots of Schumannesque hemiolas), and plenty of orthodox German finales (including those to several of Brahms's concertos) sported folk-like themes. What did seem unprecedented was Chaikovsky's use of expansive melodies in place of tight motivic designs, and the constant conspicuous reference to song and dance.

The first movement's main waltz theme, for example, is twenty-five broad $\frac{9}{8}$ measures in length, consisting of a regular eight-bar phrase to a dominant half-cadence, and an expertly extended answering phrase that leads back, seemingly against all symphonic precedent, to a full cadence on the tonic. Even afterward the theme continues, in expansive phrases, toward a climactic restatement in the tonic that reaches another full close before embarking on a modulatory transition that finally reveals the movement to be a symphonic binary or "sonata-form" movement after all—but only, it seems, in a very broad sense.

As a result of these unusual or eccentric features, the German-dominated literatures of music history and music appreciation have tended to treat Chaikovsky's symphonies as debased specimens, appealing (perhaps unhealthily) to audiences but nevertheless revealing some innate deficiency in the composer. One recent English biographer has even claimed that Chaikovsky was biologically doomed to failure as a symphonist since "his was a Russian mind forced to find its expression through techniques and forms that had been evolved by generations of alien Western creators."[36] The best that could be said of him from this essentialist viewpoint was that "a composer who could show so much resourcefulness in modifying sonata structure so as to make it more compatible with the type of music *nature had decreed he would write* was no helpless bungler"[37] (italics added).

But symphonic styles are not racial endowments, and it unsurprisingly turns out that Chaikovsky chose his methods quite deliberately, with full knowledge of what he was rejecting. What he was rejecting, in a word, was Brahms, whose music (as Chaikovsky put it to Mme von Meck) was "made up of little fragments of something or other, artfully glued together,"[38] with the result that he "never expresses anything, or if he does, he fails to do it fully." Chaikovsky was painfully aware of a deficiency (as he saw it) in Brahms, one that came about in direct consequence of what is now generally considered his most valuable contribution.

For the Russian composer, the German's virtuosity in constructing large musical entities out of atomic particles represented no dialectical triumph but merely an unresolved, and therefore fatal, contradiction. "Aren't his pretensions to profundity, strength and power detestable,"[39] Chaikovsky wrote of Brahms to another correspondent, "when the content he pours into those Beethovenian forms of his is so pitiful and insignificant?" These comments strongly suggest that Chaikovsky's deviations from the Beethovenian, or at least the Brahmsian, straight-and-narrow were conditioned less by a lack of symphonic aptitude than by the wish to "express something fully."

But what? And how? The first movement of the Fourth Symphony contains two impressive clues. The first is its sheer stridency and violence, quite belying (or, at the very least, investing with heavy irony) the implications of its "waltz tempo." The stridency is proclaimed before the waltz even makes an appearance, in the earsplitting brass fanfares with which the symphony begins, and out of which the whole slow introduction is fashioned. The violence intrudes almost as early, in the peremptory diminished seventh chord that cuts the fanfares off—virtually decapitates them—in unlucky m. 13 (Ex. 46-19).

EX. 46-19   Pyotr Ilyich Chaikovsky, Symphony no. 4, I, beginning

That is operatic behavior; and the operatic impression is confirmed when the fanfares begin acting like a Berliozian *idée fixe*. The peak of violence, a real catastrophe, occurs in the development section, when the fanfares suddenly return and make three collisions with the waltz theme (Ex. 46-20), each more terrible than the last. (They also return in the fourth movement to disrupt the folksy festivities.) This is not merely "structure": this is dramaturgy. It bespeaks an encoding of events, a narrative—in short, a program. So, at any rate, Mme von Meck assumed, and wrote to Chaikovsky to inquire about it.

His answering letter has become a famous document. It is now often taken as the symphony's actual, explicit, or "official" program by those who have forgotten that Chaikovsky never published it or publicly alluded to it during his lifetime; who have not noticed (or have chosen to ignore) its obvious (convenient?) borrowings from the famous programs of Beethoven's Fifth and the *Symphonie fantastique*; and who have not weighed into the balance the fact that the composer furnished the symphony with its program at the specific request of the woman who paid his bills.

EX. 46-20   Pyotr Ilyich Chaikovsky, Symphony no. 4, I, the three collisions

EX. 46-20 (*continued*)

But even if we regard the "program" as a hasty verbal paraphrase of ideas best wordlessly expressed in "absolute" music, its congruence with the shape of the musical argument (at least of the first movement) is obvious, and makes its possible relevance to the movement's conception worth considering. The entire document is given in Weiss and Taruskin, *Music in the Western World*, no. 115; what follows is, as Chaikovsky put it, "roughly the program of the first movement":[40]

> The Introduction is the *kernel* of the whole symphony, without question its main idea: [here the fanfares are quoted]. This is Fate, the force of destiny, which ever prevents our pursuit of happiness from reaching its goal, which jealously stands watch lest our peace and well-being be full and cloudless, which hangs like the sword of Damocles over our heads and constantly, ceaselessly poisons our souls. It is invincible, inescapable. One can only resign oneself and lament fruitlessly: [Here the waltz theme is quoted].
>
> This disconsolate and despairing feeling grows ever stronger and more intense. Would it not be better to turn away from reality and immerse oneself in dreams? [Here the second theme is quoted.] O joy! A sweet tender dream has appeared. A bright, beneficent human form flits by and beckons us on: [Here the end of the exposition passage is quoted]. How wonderful! How distant now is the sound of the implacable introductory theme! Dreams little by little have taken over the soul. All that is dark and bleak is forgotten. There it is, there it is — happiness!
>
> But no! These are only dreams, and *Fate* awakens us from them: [Here the fanfares are quoted again as they appear at the beginning of the development section]. And thus, all life is the ceaseless alternation of bitter reality with evanescent visions and dreams of happiness. There is no refuge. We are buffeted about by this sea until it seizes us and pulls us down to the bottom.

Is it fair or relevant to *our* experience of the music to note that this deeply pessimistic document, and the symphony it describes, were written at what was arguably the low point of Chaikovsky's personal life, and in the aftermath of what was surely the most dramatic single episode in his biography? Despite the fact that he was homosexual (or rather, *because* of that fact, and his fear of exposure), Chaikovsky had impulsively accepted a proposal of marriage from Antonina Milyukova, a former pupil of his at the Moscow conservatory, who had developed a schoolgirl crush on her harmony professor.

What followed was a great fiasco of anguish, revulsion, flight, histrionic attempted suicide, legal separation, and moral convalescence abroad (which is how Chaikovsky happened to be writing the Fourth Symphony in Venice). Was the symphony, as Chaikovsky described his music in general to Mme von Meck, a "cleansing of the soul, which boils over with an accumulation that naturally seeks its outlet in tones, just as a lyric poet will express himself in verse"?[41] Should that matter to us? Does regarding the music as confessional enhance understanding of it? Must we know an artist's biography in order fully to appreciate the artist's output? Or is the meaning of the symphony sufficiently conveyed by the wordless sounds alone?

The alternatives suggested by these questions are neither exhaustive nor necessarily incompatible, but the existence of the letter to Mme von Meck has led to the reading of not just the Fourth Symphony but a great deal of Chaikovsky's music as autobiography — and reading it, inevitably, in light of that one great biographical event and the conditions that precipitated it. But what if we did not know that letter? What if all we had was the wordless sounds? What do (or can) they intrinsically express?

As soon as we are dealing with expression in any artistic medium, we are necessarily dealing with conventions of representation. Representation necessarily relies on similarities and associations. Where other arts can make reference directly to nature, music must work through mediating codes. We already know that one of the codes on which Chaikovsky relied in the Fourth Symphony was that of dance genres, since he expressly labeled one of his themes as a waltz. Recalling that a great deal of eighteenth-century music, particularly Mozart's, also relied on dance genres and their associations as mediators of musical representation, and knowing that of all composers Chaikovsky loved Mozart best (and expressly ranked him higher than Beethoven), we are equipped with some clues to interpret Chaikovsky's expressive strategies, and in the process to understand better his deliberate deviation from the structural principles that otherwise reigned in the world of the late-nineteenth-century symphony.

Although not explicitly marked, the fanfares that Chaikovsky interpreted as the Fate theme in his letter to Mme von Meck are cast just as recognizably in a dance meter as the expressly designated waltz theme. They are in the meter of a polonaise, a dance that had its origin in Polish court processionals, and that remained the most socially elevated of all the ballroom dances of the nineteenth century. By extension, the polonaise was often associated with military parades, that is with martial rhythms and brass bands, as a snatch from Chopin's "Military" Polonaise, op. 40, no. 1 (1838) will remind us (Ex. 46-21a). The stylistic giveaway is the triplet on the second half of the second beat, also found at the beginning of the Polonaise that opens the third act of Chaikovsky's opera *Eugene Onegin* — composed, as it happens, concurrently with the Fourth Symphony (Ex. 46-21b).

Just as in the Fourth Symphony, the Polonaise in *Eugene Onegin* is paired conceptually with a waltz that occupies the analogous position at the beginning of act 2. Between the two of them they define a social trajectory. The waltz is played at a name-day party for Tatyana, the country girl who (as recounted in chapter 44)

EX. 46-21A   Frédéric Chopin, beginning of Polonaise, Op. 40, no. 1

EX. 46-21B   Pyotr Ilyich Chaikovsky, *Eugene Onegin*, Act III, scene 1, Polonaise

has rashly declared her love for the title character, and to whom he feels disdainfully superior. The polonaise is played at a high society ball in St. Petersburg, where Onegin reencounters Tatyana six years later, and is smitten in his turn; she, however, now socially outranks him and turns him down. The moral: a polonaise will always trump a waltz!

And so it is in the Fourth Symphony. It is easy to see how the attributes of a polonaise could have attached themselves metonymically to Chaikovsky's Fate theme: first of all, the military associations, connoting bellicosity, hostility, implacability. Then, too, the idea of grandiosity and invincible power, derived from political or social awe. And finally, perhaps, the idea of impersonality, dwarfing individual concerns, as the unwritten laws of society frustrated Onegin's amorous designs, or as the idea of Fate frustrates the subject-persona of the Fourth Symphony (symbolized by the waltz theme) in pursuit of happiness. The submission of waltz to polonaise—of subject to fate—is palpably denoted in the coda (Ex. 46-22), when the waltz is reprised for the last time in triple augmentation: that is, at the speed of the polonaise, each beat of the waltz theme now stretched out to the length of one full measure, and therefore no longer a waltz at all. A moment like this expresses—*fully expresses*—a sublime "operatic" terror that was altogether outside Brahms's purposes to express, although Berlioz would surely have sympathized.

And so might Mozart. Not only have we already observed in chapter 28 (with the help of Wye J. Allanbrook's invaluable insight) the extent to which Mozart, like Chaikovsky, used dance meters and "characters" as mediators of human representation in his instrumental music as well as his operas; and not only have we observed in Mozart a comparable interest in representing subjective soul-states symphonically (see the discussion of Ex. 30-1); but we have also observed in Mozart's symphonies a sheer tunefulness akin to Chaikovsky's and alien to the later motivic preoccupations of Beethoven and his many nineteenth-century heirs, from Wagner to Brahms (both of whom, antipodes though they appeared to many, repelled Chaikovsky equally).

EX. 46-22   Pyotr Ilyich Chaikovsky, Symphony no. 4, I, m. 404

The main theme of the pathos-filled first movement in Mozart's G-minor Symphony (no. 40), for example, is a fully expressed melody of a kind we have not reencountered in symphonic works (at least not in first themes) until now. One begins to suspect the existence of a parallel tradition of the symphony that passed from Mozart to Chaikovsky without passing through Beethoven. Or perhaps it would be fairer to say that Chaikovsky was the recipient of, and participant in, a tradition that goes back to or passes through Mozart in a way that the nineteenth-century Germanic tradition, however reverently its aggressive claim of descent from the "classical masters" has been ratified in conventional historiography, does not.

It is the Franco-Italianate line, which passed from Mozart to Rossini, thence to Auber, Gounod, and Bizet. These were the composers whom Chaikovsky admired, particularly his French contemporaries, and especially the opera and ballet composer Léo Delibes (1836–91), who is no longer thought of as an important figure, but whom Chaikovsky venerated as the Mozart of his day. Today it is Chaikovsky himself, with Verdi, who seems the preeminent late-nineteenth-century representative of this tradition, especially since (like Mozart) he was equally drawn to the operatic and symphonic domains and made equally significant contributions to both. But his

Mozartean symphonic style had become so alien to the accepted practices of the late-nineteenth-century symphony that even one of his own former pupils, the composer Sergey Ivanovich Taneyev (1856–1915), reproached Chaikovsky in a famous letter for allowing his symphony occasionally to descend to the level of "ballet music."[42]

Not that Chaikovsky was unaware of the New Germans, or that he shut himself off from acquiring their most novel techniques. The first movement of the Fourth Symphony follows a thoroughgoingly Lisztian tonal plan, governed (like the one in Saint-Saëns's "Organ" Symphony) by a full circle of minor thirds: introduction and first theme in F minor (0); second theme in A♭ minor (3); close of exposition in B major (6); reprise of both main themes (beginning at m. 283) in D minor (9); coda in F minor (0 regained). (And now we know why the "recapitulation" does not begin in the tonic.) Nevertheless, Chaikovsky belonged to the line whose prime "theater of operation" remained literally the theater, and which therefore drew its musical imagery not from visions of transcendence but from the stock of daily life, human emotion and its vicissitudes.

But we are still left with our question: were the emotions Chaikovsky portrayed his own, and should that matter to us? In the case of the Fourth Symphony, his biography tends to confirm the idea. But beware: once the idea is accepted as a general rule, biographical fallacies are bound to follow. Consider the case of Chaikovsky's last symphony, the Sixth in B minor, op. 74, subtitled *Pathétique* ("A symphony of suffering"). The subtitle and its implications are mainly due to the last movement, which (like the last movement of Brahms's last symphony) is extremely unusual, perhaps unique, in form and character.

Chaikovsky's Pathétique was (apart from a few then-unknown early eccentricities by Haydn) the first symphony ever to put the slow movement last. Not only that, but the movement, suggestively marked "Adagio lamentoso," ends with a long, drawn-out decrescendo, unmistakably figuring "the dying of the light." The symphony ends, in other words, as if in polemical defiance of the Beethovenian prescription that symphonies enact and perpetually reenact narratives of triumph and transcendence. What to make of it? For the audience who heard Chaikovsky conduct it at its St. Petersburg premiere in October 1893, it was indeed a puzzle. The symphony was "not disliked,"[43] Chaikovsky wrote to his publisher in some bemusement, "but it has caused some bewilderment." The idea of adding the subtitle, to give the audience a clue to interpreting the piece, came from the composer's younger brother Modest, a playwright (later his elder brother's biographer). It was added the morning after the premiere.

Eight days later, Chaikovsky died suddenly, and most unexpectedly, of cholera, a disease that (because it was transmitted chiefly where sanitation was inadequate) mostly attacked the poor. The symphony was played again, *in memoriam*, subtitle in place. This time the audience was an audience of mourners, listening hard for portents. And that is how the symphony became a suicide note. Depression was the first diagnosis. "Homosexual tragedy" came later, in the aftermath of the trial of Oscar Wilde, the Irish writer and celebrated "aesthete," who in 1895 was convicted of "committing acts of gross indecency with other male persons" and sentenced to two years at hard labor.

Rumors about Chaikovsky's death that had been flying ever since it happened now coalesced on a story patently modeled on the Wilde affair. According to this account, which is still affirmed by many (even by some gullible scholars) although no evidence supports it, Chaikovsky had been discovered in a pederastic liaison with the scion of a noble family, had been denounced to the tsar (Alexander III, his personal friend), and had been sentenced by an honor court of fellow alumni from the Imperial School of Jurisprudence to commit suicide by drinking a poison (never identified) that would simulate the symptoms of cholera.

The story appeals chiefly to two constituencies: to homophobes, who like stories in which gay men meet bad ends in consequence of their vice; and to gay activists, who are glad to have a martyr to display. The lack of evidence is compensated by what is taken to be the transparent testimony of the "Pathetic Symphony's" finale. Even those who realize that the work was composed too early to have been the direct expression of Chaikovsky's "final tragedy" cite it as evidence of his generally miserable state of mind, which, they conclude, made him vulnerable to the honor court's decree. "I find it very difficult to believe that a man who produced something like the Sixth Symphony was totally at ease,"[44] one scholarly defender of the suicide rumor has written. "You have only to listen to the Sixth Symphony to hear a man in torment," writes another. "The finality of the testament of the Sixth Symphony almost makes it superfluous to indulge in any sort of speculation," writes a third.

Meanwhile, what documentary evidence there is as to Chaikovsky's state of mind near the end of his life flatly contradicts the "evidence" of the music. By the time in question, Chaikovsky had made a successful adjustment to his condition; with the help of loving family and friends, he had come to terms with his sexuality, found an acceptable *modus vivendi* within the moral constraints of the society in which he lived, and seems to have been a reasonably happy man. Indeed, the act of producing the Sixth Symphony filled his last summer with bliss. "I have never felt such self-satisfaction, such pride, such happiness," he wrote to his publisher, "as in the consciousness that I am really the creator of this beautiful work."[45]

After the first performance, he spent a cheerful week, his last, in St. Petersburg with Modest. During intermission at the theater one evening he went backstage to greet one of the leading actors, a friend of his brother's. Conversation turned to spiritualism, thence to death itself. The composer of the "Pathetic Symphony" waved the subject aside. "There is plenty of time before we need reckon with this horror; it will not come to snatch us off just yet!" he remarked to Modest, who entered it in his diary that very evening. Then he added, "I feel I shall live a long time."[46] In other words, the finale of Chaikovsky's Sixth Symphony, like the finale of Beethoven's Second, should stand as a warning, rather than an encouragement, to those who under the influence of "pop romanticism" would assume that art is by nature autobiographical. The cases are complementary: Beethoven's Second, one of his most cheerful (and in the finale, downright hilarious) works, was composed concurrently with the composer's despairing realization, attended by thoughts of suicide and expressed in his heart-rending "Heiligenstadt Testament" (see chapter 31), that his deafness was irrevocable.

The agonizing, heart-rending finale of Chaikovsky's Sixth Symphony, by contrast, was composed during as happy a period as the composer ever knew.

What does all of this prove? Only that art is . . . well, artful. And of no art is that truer than the romantic art of confession, of which Chaikovsky's "Pathétique" is an outstanding example. "Always be sincere," the comedy team of Flanders and Swann used to say, "whether you mean it or not." That might have been Chaikovsky's motto. His matchless ability to live up to it, to "do" sincerity with utter conviction, brought the romantic tradition in music — a thing of artifice, illusion, and manipulated codes — to its very climax.

Notes

CHAPTER 33: REAL WORLDS, AND BETTER ONES

1 Scott F. Balthazar, "Leonora," in *New Grove Dictionary of Opera*, Vol. II (London: Macmillan, 1992), p. 1150.

2 Arthur Schopenhauer, *The World as Will and Representation*, Vol. I, trans. E. F. J. Payne (New York: Dover, 1969), p. 263.

3 *Ersichtlich gewordene Thaten der Musik* (or, in W. Ashton Ellis's translation, "deeds of Music brought to sight"); R. Wagner, "On the Name 'Musikdrama'" (1872), in *Richard Wagner's Prose Works*, Vol. V (London: Kegan Paul, Trench, Trübner & Co., 1896), p. 303.

4 Gerald Abraham, "Introduction," in *New Oxford History of Music*, Vol. V (Oxford: Oxford University Press, 1982), p. v.

5 Philip Gossett, "Rossini," in *New Grove Dictionary of Music and Musicians*, Vol. XXI (2nd ed.; New York, Grove, 2001), p. 734.

6 Philip Gossett, "The Operas of Rossini: Problems of Textual Criticism in Nineteenth-Century Opera"(Ph.D. diss., Princeton University, 1970), p. 21.

7 Giuseppe Verdi to Camille Bellaigue, 2 May 1898; *Verdi: The Man in His Letters*, ed. F. Werfel and P. Stefan, trans. E. Downes (New York: Vienna House, 1973), p. 431.

8 Quoted in Richard Osborne, "Rossini," in *New Grove Dictionary of Opera*, Vol. IV (London: Macmillan, 1992), p. 57.

9 Rossini to Count Fay (1854); quoted in Carl Dahlhaus, *Nineteenth-Century Music*, trans. J. Bradford Robinson (Berkeley and Los Angeles: University of California Press, 1989), p. 58.

10 Pius X, *Motu proprio*, on sacred music; in Nicolas Slonimsky, *Music since 1900* (4th ed.; New York: Scribners, 1971), p. 1286.

11 "The Black List of Disapproved Music," in Slonimsky, *Music since 1900*, p. 1291.

12 Dahlhaus, *Nineteenth-Century Music*, pp. 58–59.

13 Julian Budden, *The Operas of Verdi*, Vol. I (New York: Praeger, 1971), p. 12.

14 Richard Osborne, "Rossini," in *New Grove Dictionary of Opera*, Vol. IV (London: Macmillan, 1992), p. 57.

15 Quoted (from Ross Wetzsteon) by John Updike in the Introduction to Vladimir Nabokov, *Lectures on Literature*, ed. Fredson Bowers (New York: Harcourt Brace Jovanovich, 1980), p. xxiii.

16 Budden, *The Operas of Verdi*, Vol. I p. 18.

17 Rossini to Tito Ricordi (1865); quoted in Gossett, "Rossini," in *New Grove Dictionary of Music and Musicians*, Vol. XXI (2nd ed.), p. 738.

18 See Philip Gossett, *The Tragic Finale of 'Tancredi'/Il finale tragico del Tancredi di Rossini* (Pesaro: Fondazione Gioacchino Rossini, 1977).

19 Stendhal, *Life of Rossini*, trans. Richard N. Coe (Seattle: University of Washington Press, 1972), p. 58.

20 Stendhal, *Life of Rossini*, p. 128.

21 Vladimir Odoyevsky, "Dni dosad" (Vexing Days, 1823), in T. Livanova and V. Protopopov, *Opernaya kritika v Rossii*, Vol. I (Moscow: Muzïka, 1966), pp. 312–13.

22 See M. Foucault, *The History of Sexuality: An Introduction* (New York: Vintage Books, 1990), p. 57ff.

23 Foucault, *The History of Sexuality*, p. 69.

24 Edmond Michotte, "An Evening Chez Rossini, 1858," trans. Herbert Weinstock, *Opera* XVIII (1967): 955–58, condensed.

25 Giuseppe Verdi to Camille Bellaigue, 2 May 1898; *Verdi: The Man in His Letters*, p. 431.

26 Michael Collins, "The Literary Background of Bellini's *I Capuleti ed i Montecchi*," *JAMS* XXXV (1982): 538.

27 Joseph Kerman, *Opera as Drama* (New York: Knopf, 1956), p. 146.

CHAPTER 34: THE MUSIC TRANCE

1 Immanuel Kant, *Critique of Practical Reason* (1788); in *The Philosophy of Kant* (New York: Modern Library, 1949), p. 261.

2 Jean-Jacques Rousseau, *The Social Contract*, trans. Henry J. Tozer (New York: Pocket Books, 1967), p. 22.

3 Title of a poem (1899) by Rudyard Kipling, which begins, "Take up the White Man's burden–/Send forth the best ye breed–/Go bind your sons to exile/To serve your captives' need."

4 From the concluding couplet in John Keats's *Ode on a Grecian Urn* (1820): "Beauty is truth, truth beauty — that is all/Ye know on earth, and all ye need to know."

5 See in particular Benedict Anderson, *Imagined Communities: Reflections on the Origin and Spread of Nationalism* (London: Verso, 1983).

6 William Hazlitt, "Observations on Mr. Wordsworth's poem, "The Excursion," in *The Round Table*" (1817).

7 Franz Liszt, "John Field and His Nocturnes"; for the full text (translated from L. Ramann [ed.], *Gesammelte Schriften von Franz Liszt*, Vol. IV [Leipzig, 1882]), see P. Weiss and R. Taruskin, *Music in the Western World: A History in Documents* (New York: Schirmer, 1984), pp. 367–69.

8 Quoted in Adrienne Simpson, "Tomášek," in *New Grove Dictionary of Music and Musicians*, Vol. XIX (London: Macmillan, 1980), p. 33.

9 Johann Georg Sulzer, *Allgemeine Theorie der schönen Künste* (2nd ed., Leipzig, 1792); quoted in M. H. Abrams, *The Mirror and the Lamp: Romantic Theory and the Critical Tradition* (Oxford: Oxford University Press, 1953), p. 89.

10 Johann Gottfried Herder, *Phantasien über die Kunst* (1799), quoted in Abrams, *The Mirror and the Lamp*, p. 93.

11 Ferdinand Hand, *Aesthetik der Tonkunst* (Jena, 1841), quoted in Jeffrey Kallberg, *Chopin at the Boundaries* (Cambridge: Harvard University Press, 1996), pp. 33–4.

12 Carl Kossmaly, *Allgemeine musikalische Zeitung* (17 January 1844); quoted in Kallberg, *Chopin at the Boundaries*, p. 34.

13 Frederick Niecks, quoted in James M. Huneker, *Chopin: The Man and His Music* (New York: Scribner's, 1921), p. 262.

14 Carl Dahlhaus, *Nineteenth-Century Music*, trans. J. Bradford Robinson (Berkeley and Los Angeles: University of California Press, 1989), p. 148.

15 Dahlhaus, *Nineteenth-Century Music*, p. 147.

16 Joseph von Spaun, notes prepared for Ferdinand Luib in 1858; quoted in Otto Erich Deutsch, ed., *Schubert: Memoirs by His Friends*, trans. Rosamond Ley and John Nowell (London: A & C Black, 1958), p. 128.

17 Robert Schumann, *On Music and Musicians*, ed. Konrad Wolff, trans. Paul Rosenfeld (New York: Norton, 1969), p. 110.

18 See Otto Biba, "'Schubert's Position in Viennese Musical Life," *Nineteenth-Century Music* III (1979–80): 106–13.

19 Moritz von Schwind to Franz Schober, 6 March 1824; Otto Erich Deutsch, *The Schubert Reader* (New York: Norton, 1947), p. 331.

20 Alex Ross, "Great Soul," *The New Yorker* (3 February 1997), p. 70.

21 Maurice J. E. Brown, "Schubert," in *New Grove Dictionary of Music and Musicians* Vol. XVI (London: Macmillan, 1980), p. 754.

22 Schubert to Bernhard Schott, 21 February 1828; *Franz Schubert's Letters and Other Writings*, ed. O. E. Deutch, trans. V. Savile (New York: Vienna House, 1974), p. 135.

23 Daniel Coren, "Ambiguity in Schubert's Recapitulations," *Musical Quarterly* LX (1974): 582.

24 Walter Pater, *Appreciations, with an Essay on Style* (1889; rpt. Evanston: Northwestern University Press, 1987), p. 246.

25 Vasiliy Vasiliyevich Yastrebtsev, *Nikolai Andreyevich Rimskiy-Korsakov: Vospominaniya, 1886–1908*, Vol. II (Leningrad, 1960), p. 374.

26 See Gerald Abraham, "Finishing the Unfinished," *Musical Times* CXII (1971): 547–8.

27 Deutsch, ed., *Schubert: Memoirs by His Friends*, p. 285; quoted in *The Cambridge Companion to Schubert*, ed. Christopher H. Gibbs (Cambridge: Cambridge University Press, 1997), p. 37.

28 Maynard Solomon, "Franz Schubert and the Peacocks of Benvenuto Cellini," *Nineteenth-Century Music* XII (1988–9): 193–206.

29 See Kristina Muxfeldt, "Schubert, Platen, and the Myth of Narcissus," *JAMS* XLIX (1996): 480–527.

30 Alexandre Oulibicheff, *Beethoven: Ses critiques et ses glossateurs* (Leipzig, 1857); quoted in Maynard Solomon, "Franz Schubert and the Peacocks of Benvenuto Cellini," *19th-Century Music* XII (1988–89): 193.

31 Susan McClary, "Constructions of Subjectivity in Schubert's Music," in *Queering the Pitch: The New Lesbian and Gay Musicology*, eds. P. Brett, E. Wood, and G. Thomas (New York: Routledge, 1994), p. 223.

32 Earl Jackson, Jr., "Scandalous Subjects: Robert Glück's Embodied Narratives," quoted in McClary, "Constructions of Subjectivity in Schubert's Music," p. 224.

33 Susan Kagan, *Fanfare* XIX, No. 2 (November/December 1995), p. 362.

34 See V. Kofi Agawu, "Schubert's Sexuality: A Prescription for Analysis?" *Nineteenth-Century Music* XVII (1993–94): 79–82.

CHAPTER 35: VOLKSTÜMLICHKEIT

1 Norbert Elias, *The History of Manners*, trans. E. Jephcott; quoted in Sanna Pederson, "On the Task of the Music Historian: The Myth of the Symphony after Beethoven," *Repercussions* II, no. 2 (Fall 1993): 13.

2 Quoted in Eugene Helm, "Reichardt," in *New Grove Dictionary of Music and Musicians*, Vol. XV (London: Macmillan, 1980), p. 704.

3 Goethe to Zelter, 21 December 1809; quoted in Eric Sams and Graham Johnson, "Lied (IV)," in *New Grove Dictionary of Music and Musicians*, Vol. XIV (2nd ed., New York: Grove, 2001), p. 672.

4 Joseph Kerman, "*An die ferne Geliebte*," in *Write All These Down: Essays on Music* (Berkeley and Los Angeles: University of California Press, 1994), p. 181.

5 William Wordsworth, *Prelude* (1805), XIII.

6 Heinrich Schenker, *Der Tonwille* (1921), quoted in Joseph Kerman, "A Romantic Detail in Schubert's *Schwanengesang*," *Musical Quarterly* XLVIII (1962): 36.

7 Kerman, "A Romantic Detail," p. 40.

8 *Richard Wagner's Prose Works*, Vol. III, trans. W. Ashton Ellis (London: Kegan Paul, Trench, Trübner, 1907), p. 96.

9 Felix Mendelssohn to Marc-André Souchay, 15 October 1842; Felix Mendelssohn, *Letters*, ed. G. Selden-Goth (New York: Vienna House, 1973), p. 314.

10 O. E. Deutsch, ed., *Franz Schubert's Letters and Other Writings*, trans. V. Savile (New York: Vienna House, 1974), p. 75.

11 W. H. Auden and Chester Kallman, "Introduction," *An Elizabethan Song Book*, ed. Noah Greenberg (Garden City, N.Y.: Doubleday, 1955), p. xvii.

12 Otto Erich Deutsch, *Schubert: A Documentary Biography* (London: J. M. Dent and Sons, Ltd., 1946), p. 906.

13 Charles Rosen, "Schubert's Inflections of Classical Form," in *The Cambridge Companion to Schubert*, ed. C. Gibbs (Cambridge: Cambridge University Press, 1997), p. 77.

14 Richard Kramer, *Distant Cycles: Schubert and the Conceiving of Song* (Chicago: University of Chicago Press, 1994), p. 126.

15 Hans Georg Nägeli, *Pestalozzische Gesangbilder*; quoted in Ulrich Asper, *Hans Georg Nägeli: Réflexions sur le choeur populaire, l'éducation artistique et la musique de l'église* (Baden-Baden & Bouxwiller: Éditions Valentin Koerner, 1994), p. 114.

16 "Gottschalk Wedel" (Anton Wilhelm Florentin von Zuccalmaglio), "Deutsches Volkslied," *Neue Zeitschrift für Musik*, 13 May 1842; quoted in Cecelia Hopkins Porter, *The Rhine as Musical Metaphor: Cultural Identity in German Romantic Music* (Boston: Northeastern University Press, 1996), p. 13.

17 Glenn Stanley, "Bach's *Erbe*: The Chorale in the German Oratorio of the Early Nineteenth Century," *Nineteenth-Century Music* XI (1987–88): 144 n6.

18 Stanley, "Bach's *Erbe*," p. 123.

19 Novalis, *Die Christenheit oder Europa* (1802); quoted in Stanley, "Bach's *Erbe*," p. 144 n10.

20 Ernst Moritz Arndt, *Von dem Worte und dem Kirchenliede* (Bonn, 1819), p. 23.

21 *Richard Wagner's Prose Works*, condensed, Vol. III, pp. 93–96.

22 Carl Dahlhaus, *Richard Wagner's Music Dramas*, trans. Mary Whittall (Cambridge: Cambridge University Press, 1979), p. 4.

23 Quoted in Nancy B. Reich, "The Power of Class: Fanny Hensel," in *Mendelssohn and His World*, ed. R. Larry Todd (Princeton: Princeton University Press, 1991), p. 91.

24 Goethe to Felix Mendelssohn, 18 June 1825; Felix Mendelssohn, *Letters*, p. 34.

25 Charles Gounod, *Autobiographical Reminiscences with Family Letters and Notes on Music*, trans. W. Hely Hutchinson (London: William Heinemann, 1896), p. 91.

CHAPTER 36: NATIONS, STATES, AND PEOPLES

1 Johann Gottfried Herder, *Essay on the Origin of Language*, trans. Alexander Gode (Chicago: University of Chicago Press, 1986), p. 135.

2 Wolfgang to Leopold Mozart, 18 December 1777; quoted in Margaret Grave, "Vogler, Georg Joseph," in *New Grove Dictionary of Music and Musicians*, Vol. XXVI (2nd ed., New York: Grove, 2001), p. 865.

3 Henry Edward Krehbiel, *A Book of Operas* (Garden City, N.Y.: Garden City Publishing, 1917), p. 207.

4 *Richard Wagner's Prose Works*, trans. W. Ashton Ellis, Vol. VII (London: Kegan Paul, Trench, Trübner, 1898), p. 183.

5 See Alexander Serov, letter to Vladimir Stasov, 18 August 1843, in A. A. Gozenpud and V. A. Obram, eds., "A. N. Serov. Pis'ma k V. V. i D. V. Stasovïm," *Muzïkal'noye nasledstvo*, Vol. I (Moscow: Muzgiz, 1962), p. 234.

6 Paul Bekker, *The Story of the Orchestra* (New York: Norton, 1936), Chap. 5.

7 See Anthony Newcomb, "New Light(s) on Weber's Wolf's Glen Scene," in *Opera and the Enlightenment*, eds. T. Bauman and M. P. McClymonds (Cambridge: Cambridge University Press, 1995), pp. 61–88.

8 Quoted in Newcomb, "New Light(s)," pp. 72–73.

9 Quoted in Newcomb, "New Light(s)," p. 74.

10 Quoted in Karin Pendle, *Eugène Scribe and French Opera of the Nineteenth Century* (Ann Arbor: UMI Research Press, 1979), p. 50.

11 *Richard Wagner's Prose Works*, trans. W. Ashton Ellis, Vol. V (London: Kegan Paul, Trench, Trübner, 896), p. 39.

12 Pendle, *Eugène Scribe and French Opera of the Nineteenth Century*, p. 397.

13 Jane Fulcher, *The Nation's Image: French Grand Opera as Politics and Politicized Art* (Cambridge: Cambridge University Press, 1987), pp. 40–41.

14 Quoted in Hugh Macdonald, "Juive, La," in *New Grove Dictionary of Opera*, Vol. II (London: Macmillan, 1992), p. 926.

15 Heinz Becker, "Meyerbeer," in *New Grove Dictionary of Music and Musicians*, Vol. XII (London: Macmillan, 1980), p. 253.

16 M. Elizabeth C. Bartlet, "Grand Opera," in *New Grove Dictionary of Opera*, Vol. II, p. 514.

17 Quoted in Pendle, *Eugène Scribe and French Opera*, p. 470.

18 Quoted in Pendle, p. 566 n20.

19 Ignaz von Seyfried, quoted in *Thayer's Life of Beethoven*, ed. Elliott Forbes (rev. ed., Princeton: Princeton University Press, 1967), p. 371.

20 Hugh Macdonald, "[G flat major, 9/8 time]," *Nineteenth-Century Music* XI (1987–8): 227.

21 *Richard Wagner's Prose Works*, Vol. III, p. 96.

22 Eduard Bernsdorf, "K. Freigedank und das Judenthum in der Musik," in *Neue Zeitschrift für Musik*, Vol. XXXIII (1850), p. 168; quoted in Sanna Pederson, "Enlightened and Romantic German Music Criticism, 1800–1850" (Ph.D. diss., University of Pennsylvania, 1995), p. 258.

23 Quoted in Paul Henry Lang, *Music in Western Civilization* (New York: Norton, 1941), p. 826.

24 Lang, *Music in Western Civilization*, pp. 830–32.

25 *Richard Wagner's Prose Works*, Vol. II, trans. W. Ashton Ellis (*Opera and Drama*) (London: Kegan Paul, Trench, Trübner, 1900), p. 94.

26 Robert Schumann, *On Music and Musicians*, ed. K. Wolff, trans. P. Rosenfeld (New York: Pantheon, 1946), p. 196.

27 Schumann, *On Music and Musicians*, p. 194.

28 Rudyard Kipling, *The English Flag* (1891).

29 Nikolai Gogol, "Peterburgskiye zapiski" (1836), in *Sochineniya i pis'ma N. V. Gogolya*, Vol. VII, ed. V. V. Kallash (St. Petersburg: Prosveshcheniye, 1896), p. 340.

30 Yanuariy Neverov, "O novoy opere g. Glinki 'Zhizn'za tsarya,'" quoted in David Brown, *Glinka* (London: Oxford University Press, 1974), pp. 112–13.

31 Neverov, "O novoy opere g. Glinki 'Zhizn'za tsarya,'" quoted in Tamara Livanova and Vladimir Protopopov, *Opernaya kritika v Rossii*, Vol. I (Moscow: Muzïka, 1966), part 1, p. 208 (italics original).

32 Mikhail I. Glinka, "Zapiski," in *Polnoye sobraniye sochineniy: Literaturnïye proizvedeniya i perepiska*, Vol. I (Moscow: Muzïka, 1973), p. 262.

33 "Tsirkulyarnoye predlozheniye G. Upravlyayushchego Ministerstvom Narodnogo Prosveshcheniya Nachalstvan Uchobnïkh Okrugov 'o vstuplenii v upravlenii Ministerstvom,'" quoted in Nicholas V. Riasanovsky, *Nicholas I and Official Nationality in Russia, 1825–1855* (Berkeley and Los Angeles: University of California Press, 1959), p. 73.

34 *Ibid.*, p. 74.

35 *Entsiklopedicheskiy slovar'* Vol. II (Moscow: Sovetskaya èntsiklopediya, 1964), p. 542.

36 Glinka, "Zapiski," p. 266.

37 Hubert F. Babinski, *The Mazeppa Legend in European Romanticism* (New York: Columbia University Press, 1974), p. 89.

38 Quoted in Alexander V. Ossovsky, "Dramaturgiya operï M. I. Glinki 'Ivan Susanin,'" in *Glinka: Issledovaniya i materialï*, ed. A. V. Ossovsky (Leningrad and Moscow: Muzgiz, 1950), p. 16.

39 V. F. Odoyevsky, "Pis'mo k lyubitelyu muzïki ob opere g. Glinki: Zhizn' za tsarya," in *Muzïkal'no-literaturnoye naslidiye*, ed. G. B. Bernandt (Moscow: Muzgiz, 1956), p. 11.

Chapter 37: Virtuosos

1 Boris Schwarz, "Paganini," in *New Grove Dictionary of Music and Musicians*, Vol. XIV (London: Macmillan, 1980), p. 86.

2 *Louis Spohr's Autobiography*, Vol. I (London: Longman, Green, Longman, Roberts and Green, 1865), p. 283.

3 O. E. Deutsch, ed., *Schubert: Die Erinnerungen seiner Freunde* (Leipzig: Breitkopf & Härtel, 1966), p. 261.

4 O. E. Deutsch, *The Schubert Reader* (New York: Norton, 1947), p. 773.

5 *Louis Spohr's Autobiography*, Vol. II, p. 168.

6 Alan Walker, *Franz Liszt*, Vol. I: "The Virtuoso Years, 1811–1847" (New York: Knopf, 1983), p. 118.

7 *Letters of Franz Liszt*, Vol. I, ed. La Mara, trans. Constance Bache (rpt. ed., New York: Haskell House Publishers, 1968), pp. 8–9.

8 *Letters of Franz Liszt*, Vol. I, p. 8.

9 Liszt, "Concerning the Situation of Artists and Their Condition in Society" (*Gazette musicale de Paris, 30 August 1835*), trans. Piero Weiss, in P. Weiss and R. Tauskin, *Music in the Western World: A History in Documents* (New York: Schirmer, 1984), pp. 366–67.

10 Charles Rosen, *The Romantic Generation* (Cambridge: Harvard University Press, 1995), p. 528.

11 Bernard Shaw, *Music in London 1890–94*, Vol. I (New York: Vienna House, 1973), p. 81.

12 Quoted in Walker, *Franz Liszt*, Vol. I, p. 365.

13 Vladimir Stasov, *Selected Essays on Music*, trans. Florence Jonas (New York: Frederick A. Praeger, 1968), p. 120.

14 Stasov, *Selected Essays*, p. 121.

15 See Owen Jander, "Beethoven's 'Orpheus' Concerto," in *Beethoven and the Musical Narrative* (Lincoln: University of Nebraska Press, forthcoming).

16 See Johann Wolfgang von Goethe, *Versuch die Metamorphose der Pflanzen zu erklären* (Gotha, 1790).

17 *Letters of Franz Liszt*, Vol. I, p. 330.

18 See Samuel Taylor Coleridge, *Biographia Literaria* (1817), Chap. 4: "That willing suspension of disbelief for the moment, which constituted poetic faith."

19 Felix Mendelssohn, *Letters*, ed. G. Selden-Goth (New York: Vienna House, 1973), p. 257.

20 Stasov, *Selected Essays*, p. 121.

CHAPTER 38: CRITICS

1   Robert Schumann, review of trios by Alexander Fesca, in Schumann, *Gesammelte Schriften*, Vol. III ed. Heinrich Simon (Leipzig, n.d.), p. 115.

2   Sanna Pederson, "Enlightened and Romantic German Music Criticism, 1800–1850" (Ph.D. diss., University of Pennsylvania, 1995), p. 81.

3   See Immanuel Kant, *Critique of Judgment*, trans. J. H. Bernard (New York: Hafner, 1951), pp. 170–71.

4   See John Daverio, *Robert Schumann: Herald of a "New Poetic Age"* (New York: Oxford University Press, 1997), Chap. 2.

5   Quoted in Edward Lippman, "Theory and Practice in Schumann's Aesthetics," *JAMS* XVII (1964): 329.

6   Schumann, *Gesammelte Schriften über Musik und Musiker*, Vol. I (Leipzig, 1854), p. 18.

7   Friedrich Schiller, review of Friedrich Mattheson's landscape poetry, quoted in Charles Rosen, *The Romantic Generation* (Cambridge: Harvard University Press, 1995), p. 93.

8   Schumann, *Gesammelte Schriften*, Vol. I, p. 39.

9   Lippman, "Theory and Practice in Schumann's Aesthetics," p. 314.

10 John Daverio. "Schumann's 'Im Legendenton' and Friedrich Schlegel's *Arabeske*," *19th-Century Music* XI (1987–88): 151.

11 See Anthony Newcomb, "Those Images That Yet Fresh Images Beget," *Journal of Musicology* II (1983): 227–45.

12 Clara Schumann, ed., *Jugendbriefe von Robert Schumann* (Leipzig, 1885), p. 278.

13 *Ibid.*, p. 302.

14 *Ibid.*, p. 303.

15 Rosen, *The Romantic Generation*, p. 101.

16 *Neue Zeitschrift für Musik*, 31 July 1835; trans. Paul Rosenfeld in Robert Schumann, *On Music and Musicians*, ed. Konrad Wolff (New York: Pantheon, 1946; rpt. Norton, 1969), p. 64.

17 F. von Schlegel, "Fragments" (1798), quoted in Rosen, *The Romantic Generation*, p. 50.

18 Schumann, *Gesammelte Schriften*, Vol. I, p. 43.

19 John Daverio, *Robert Schumann: Herald of a "New Poetic Age"* (New York: Oxford University Press, 1997), p. 301.

20 Hector Berlioz, *Correspondence générale*, Vol. I, ed. Pierre Citron (Paris, 1972), p. 182.

21 See Arthur O. Lovejoy, "On the Discrimination of Romanticisms," *Proceedings of the Modern Language Association of America* XXIX (1924); reprinted in *Essays on the History of Ideas* (New York: Columbia University Press, 1948).

22 Hugh Macdonald, "Berlioz," in *New Grove Dictionary of Music and Musicians*, Vol. III (rev. ed., New York, Grove, 2001), p. 386–87.

23 Hector Berlioz, *New Edition of the Complete Works*, Vol. XVI, trans. Piero Weiss (adapted) (Kassel: Bärenreiter, 1972), pp. 3–4.

24 Berlioz, "The Composer and the Symphony," in *Fantastic Symphony*, ed. Edward T. Cone (Norton Critical Scores; New York: Norton, 1971), p. 9.

25 Felix Mendelssohn-Bartholdy, *Briefe einer Reise durch Deutschland, Italien und die Schweiz* (Zürich, 1958), p. 124; quoted in David Cairns, *Berlioz: The Making of an Artist* (London: Allen Lane/The Penguin Press, 1989), p. 489.

26 D. Kern Holoman, *Berlioz* (Cambridge: Harvard University Press, 1989).

27 Berlioz, "De l'imitation musicale," in *Fantastic Symphony*, ed. Edward T. Cone, p. 41.

28 *Ibid.*, p. 38.

29 *Ibid.*, pp. 38–39.

30 Holoman, *Berlioz*, pp. 102–3.

31 Robert Schumann, "A Symphony by Berlioz," *Neue Zeitschrift für Musik*, 14 August 1835; trans. Edward T. Cone in Berlioz, *Fantastic Symphony* (Norton Critical Scores), pp. 246–47.

32 David Cairns, *Berlioz*, Vol. II: *Servitude and Greatness* (London: Allen Lane, The Penguin Press, 1999), p. 296.

CHAPTER 39: SELF AND OTHER

1 Robert Schumann, "An Opus 2," *Gesammelte Schriften über Musik und Musiker*, Vol. I (Leipzig, 1854), p. 3.

2 Robert Schumann, *On Music and Musicians*, trans. Paul Rosenfeld, ed. Konrad Wolff (New York: Pantheon, 1946), p. 132.

3 Schumann, "House-Rules and Maxims for Young Musicians," in *On Music and Musicians*, p. 35.

4 Schumann, *On Music and Musicians*, p. 132.

5 *Ibid.*, p. 131.

6 See Rosen, *The Romantic Generation*, p. 344ff.

7 *The Journal of Eugène Delacroix*, trans. Walter Pach; quoted in Karol Berger, "Chopin's Ballade, op. 23 and the Revolution of the Intellectuals," in *Chopin Studies 2*, eds. John Rink and Jim Samson (Cambridge: Cambridge University Press, 1994).

8 Don M. Randel, ed., *The New Harvard Dictionary of Music* (Cambridge: Harvard University Press, 1986), p. 653.

9 Oscar Wilde, *The Picture of Dorian Gray*, Chap. 6.

10 Rose R. Subotnik, "Romantic Music as Post-Kantian Critique," in *Developing Variations: Style and Ideology in Western Music* (Minneapolis: University of Minnesota Press, 1991), p. 134.

11 *Ibid.*, p. 130, 134.

12 George Sand, *Un hiver à Majorque* (rpt., Palma, 1968), p. 60; trans. Thomas Higgins in Chopin, *Preludes, Op. 28* (New York: Norton, 1973), p. 5.

13 George Sand, *Histoire de ma vie*, Vol. IV (Paris, 1902–04), p. 439; trans. Higgins, *Ibid.*, p. 94.

14 Hippolyte Barbedette, *Chopin: Essai de critique musicale* (Paris, 1861), p. 65; trans. Higgins, *Ibid.*, p. 92.

15 Wilhelm von Lenz, *Die grossen Pianoforte-Virtuosen* (1872); quoted in Richard Hudson, *Stolen Time: The History of Tempo Rubato* (Oxford: Clarendon Press, 1994), p. 191.

16 Felix Mendelssohn, *Briefe aus den Jahren 1830 bis 1847*, Vol. II, ed. Paul Mendelssohn Bartholdy (Leipzig: Hermann Mendelssohn, 1864), p. 41; quoted in Hudson, *Stolen Time*, p. 176.

17 Aristide Farrenc, *Le trésor des pianists*, Vol. I (Paris, 1861), p. 3; quoted in Hudson, *Stolen Time*, pp. 176–77.

18 Vittorio Rieti, "The Composer's Debt," in *Stravinsky in the Theatre*, ed. Minna Lederman (New York: Da Capo, 1975), p. 134.

19 *The Athenaeum*, no. 1079 (1 July 1848), quoted in Hudson, *Stolen Time*, p. 185.

20 *The Autobiography of Charles Hallé*, ed. Michael Kennedy (New York: Barnes and Noble, 1973), p. 54.

21 Schumann, *On Music and Musicians*, p. 140.

22 *Ibid.*, p. 142.

23 Parakilas, *Ballads Without Words*, p. 24.

24 Quoted in Parakilas, *Ballads Without Words*, p. 34.

25 Schumann, *On Music and Musicians*, p. 143.

26 George Sand, *Impressions et Souvenirs* (1873), quoted in Berger, "Chopin's *Ballade, op. 23*," p. 78.

27 Quoted in Robert Goldwater, *Symbolism* (New York: Harper & Row, 1979), p. 75.

28 Frederick Niecks, *Frederick Chopin as a Man and Musician* (London, 1988), quoted in Parakilas, *Ballads Without Words*, p. 57.

29 Berger, "Chopin's *Ballade, op. 23*," p. 76.

30 Sir Lewis Namier, *1848: The Revolution of the Intellectuals* (London, 1944), quoted in Berger, "Chopin's *Ballade, op. 23*," p. 74.

31 Chopin to Julian Fontana, 4 April 1848, quoted in Berger, "Chopin's *Ballade, op. 23*," p. 76.

32 Berger, "Chopin's *Ballade, op. 23*," pp. 76–77.

33 Namier, *1848*, quoted in Berger, "Chopin's *Ballade, op. 23*," p. 73.

34 Berger, "Chopin's *Ballade, op. 23*," p. 73.

35 Louis Moreau Gottschalk, *Notes of a Pianist* (Philadelphia: J. P. Lippincott, 1881), p. 33.

36 Gilbert Chase, *America's Music* (2nd ed., New York: McGraw-Hill, 1966), p. 315.

37 Quoted in Richard Jackson, "Gottschalk of Louisiana," introduction to *Piano Music of Louis Moreau Gottschalk* (New York: Dover, 1973), p. v.

38 Jeanne Behrend, editorial interpolation within Louis Moreau Gottschalk, *Notes of a Pianist* (New York: Knopf, 1964), p. 320.

39 Quoted in Jeanne Behrend, "Postlude," in L. M. Gottschalk, *Notes of a Pianist* (New York: Knopf, 1964), p. 403.

40 Gottschalk to his mother, undated fragment, ca. 1850; quoted in S. Frederick Starr, *Bamboula: The Life and Times of Louis Moreau Gottschalk* (New York: Oxford University Press, 1995), p. 50.

41 Lawrence W. Levine, *Highbrow/Lowbrow: The Emergence of Cultural Hierarchy in America* (Cambridge: Harvard University Press, 1988), p. 9.

42 Levine, *Highrow/Lowbrow*, p. 8.

43 Berlioz to his sister Adèle, 11 March 1858; quoted in Dorothy Veinus Hagan, *Félicien David 1810–1876: A Composer and a Cause* (Syracuse: Syracuse University Press, 1985), p. 147.

44 Edward W. Said, *Orientalism* (New York: Pantheon, 1978), p. 196.

45 Hermann Laroche (German Larosh), "'Der Thurm zu Babel' Rubinshteyna," in Larosh, *Muzïkal'no-kriticheskiye stat'I* (St. Petersburg: Bessel, 1894), p. 117.

46 François-René, Vicomte de Chateaubriand, *Itinéraire de Paris à Jérusalem, et de Jérusalem à Paris* (Paris: Le Normant, 1812).

47 See Peter Hopkirk, The Great Game: The Struggle for Empire in Central Asia (Tokyo: Kodansha International, 1992).

48 Vladimir Vasilievich Stasov, "Dvadtsat' pyat' let russkogo iskusstvo: Nasha muzïka, *Vestnik YEvropï* (1882–83), in V. V. Stasov, *Izbrannïye sochineniya v tryokh tomakh*, Vol. II (Moscow: Iskusstvo, 1952), p. 525.

49 *The Song of Igor's Campaign*, trans. Vladimir Nabokov (New York: Vintage, 1960), p. 70.

50 Ralph P. Locke, "Constructing the Oriental 'Other': Saint-Saëns's *Samson et Dalila*," *Cambridge Opera Journal* III (1991): 263.

51 Susan McClary, *George Bizet: Carmen* (Cambridge Opera Handbooks; Cambridge: Cambridge University Press, 1992), p. 110.

52 *Ibid.*

53 Miliy Balakirev to Pyotr Chaikovsky (13 December 1869), in *Perepiska M. A. Balakirevas P. I. Chaikovskim*, ed. Sergey Lyapunov (St. Petersburg: Zimmerman, 1912), pp. 49–50.

CHAPTER 40: MIDCENTURY

1 Franz Brendel, *Geschichte der Musik in Italien, und Deutschland Frankreich von den ersten christlichen Zeiten bis auf die Gegenwart* (5th ed., Leipzig: Verlag von Heinrich Matthes [F. C. Schilde], 1875), p. 594.

2 Karl Popper, *The Open Society and Its Enemies*, Vol. II (Princeton: Princeton University Press, 1966), p. 269. It is surely not without significance for readers of this book that, according to his autobiography, Popper's insights into the poverty of historicism originated in the context of the "progressivist" theory of music history traced in this very chapter: see Karl Popper, *Unended Quest: An Intellectual Autobiography* (LaSalle and London: Open Court, 1982), p. 68ff.

3 Brendel, *Geschichte der Musik* (4th ed., Leipzig, 1867), p. 623; quoted in Carl Dahlhaus, *Esthetics of Music*, trans. William Austin (Cambridge: Cambridge University Press, 1982), p. 57.

4 Dahlhaus, *Esthetics of Music*, p. 58.

5 F. Stade, "Vorwort zur fünften Auflage," in F. Brendel, *Geschichte der Musik* (5th ed., Leipzig: Verlag von Heinrich Matthes [F. C. Schilde], 1875), xx–xxi.

6 Paul Griffiths, "Zwilich in F-Sharp," *The New Yorker*, 15 March 1993, p. 116.

7 Brendel, *Geschichte der Musik* (4th ed.), p. 624; quoted in Dahlhaus, *Esthetics of Music*, p. 63.

8 Percy Bysshe Shelley, *A Defence of Poetry* (1821).

9 Quoted in Alan Walker, *Franz Liszt: The Weimar Years 1848–61* (Ithaca, N.Y.: Cornell University Press, 1993), p. 250.

10 Humphrey Searle, "Liszt," in *New Grove Dictionary of Music and Musicians*, Vol. XI (London: Macmillan, 1980), p. 31.

11 Franz Liszt to Freiherr Beaulieu-Marconnay, Intendant of the Court Theater at Weimar, 21 May 1855; *Letters of Franz Liszt*, Vol. I, ed. La Mara (New York: Haskell House, 1968), pp. 241–42.

12 Franz Liszt, General Preface to the symphonic poems; F. Liszt, *Sämtliche Werke*, Vol. I (Leipzig: Breitkopf und Härtel, 1901); quoted in Walker, *Franz Liszt: The Weimar Years*, p. 358.

13 The claim had previously been made in a more general context in Franz Brendel, *Die Aesthetik der Tonkunst*, Neue Zeitschrift für Musik, Vol. XLVI (1857), p. 186; trans. Martin Cooper in Bojan Bujic, ed., *Music in European Thought 1851–1912* (Cambridge: Cambridge University Press, 1988), p. 130.

14 Liszt, "Berlioz and His 'Harold' Symphony," *Neue Zeitschrift für Musik*, Vol. XLIII (1855); in Oliver Strunk, *Source Readings in Music History* (New York: Norton, 1950), pp. 859, 863.

15 Lina Ramann, *Franz Liszt als Künstler und Mensch*, Vol. III (Leipzig, 1894), p. 69; quoted in Alan Walker, *Franz Liszt: The Weimar Years*, p. 336; Ramann's evidence was an 1875 letter from Princess Sayn-Wittgenstein herself.

16 *Neue Zeitschrift für Musik*, Vol. L (1859), p. 272, trans. Piero Weiss in P. Weiss and R. Taruskin, *Music in the Western World: A History in Documents* (New York: Schirmer, 1984), p. 384.

17 Arnold Schoenberg, "National Music" (1931), trans. Leo Black, in *Style and Idea: Selected Writings of Arnold Schoenberg*, ed. Leonard Stein (Berkeley and Los Angeles: University of California Press, 1985), p. 170.

18 Andrew Bonner, "Liszt's *Les Préludes* and *Les Quatre Élémens*: A Reinvestigation," *19th-Century Music* X (1986–87): 107.

19 Richard Kaplan, "Sonata Form in the Orchestral Works of Liszt: The Revolutionary Reconsidered," *19th-Century Music* VIII (1984–85): 145.

20 Liszt to Ingeborg Stark, summer 1860, in *Letters of Franz Liszt*, ed. La Mara, Vol. I, pp. 436–37.

21 Alexander Serov, "Zagranichnïye pis'ma," *Teatral'nïy i muzïkal'nïy vestnik*, 21 June 1859; in A. N. Serov, *Stat'i o muzïke*, Vol. IV (Moscow: Muzïka, 1988), p. 110.

22 Quoted from Vladimir Vasilievich Stasov, "Ein Wort der Gegenwart gegen zwei Phrasen der Zukunftgilde," *Niederrheinische Musik-Zeitung* (1859); in V. V. Stasov, *Izbrannïye sochineniya v tryokh tomakh*, Vol. I (Moscow: Iskusstvo, 1952), p. 40.

23 Stasov, *Izbrannïye sochineniya*, Vol. I, p. 42.

24 Quoted in Alexander Poznansky, *Tchaikovsky: The Quest for the Inner Man* (New York: Schirmer, 1991), p. 181.

25 Friedrich Nietzsche, *The Birth of Tragedy out of the Spirit of Music* (1868), trans. Walter Kaufmann (New York: Vintage Books, 1967), p. 120.

26 Musorgsky to V. V. Stasov, 26 December 1872; M. P. Musorgsky, *Literaturnoye naslediye*, Vol. I, eds. A. A. Orlova and M. S. Pekelis (Moscow: Muzïka, 1971), p. 142.

27 Musorgsky to V. V. Stasov, 18 October 1872; *Ibid.*, p. 141.

28 Chaikovsky to Grand Duke Konstantin Konstantinovich, 2 October 1888; A. A. Orlova, ed., *P. I. Chaikovskiy o muzïke, o zhizni, o sebe* (Leningrad: Muzïka, 1976), p. 218.

29 Chaikovsky to Nadezhda von Meck, 5 January 1878; trans. Vera Lateiner, in *Letters of Composers through Six Centuries*, ed. Piero Weiss (Philadelphia: Chilton Books, 1967), p. 363.

CHAPTER 41: SLAVS AS SUBJECTS AND CITIZENS

1 František Bartoš ed., Bedřich *Smetana: Letters and Reminiscences*, trans. Daphne Rusbridge (Prague: Artaria, 1955), p. 59.

2 Diary entry, 23 January 1843; *Smetana: Letters and Reminiscences*, p. 5.

3 *Smetana: Letters and Reminiscences*, pp. 24–26.

4 *Smetana: Letters and Reminiscences*, pp. 47–48.

5 John Tyrrell, *Czech Opera* (Cambridge: Cambridge University Press, 1988), p. 258.

6 Tyrell, *Czech Opera*, p. 217.

7 Jan Branberger in Ças, 24 January 1904; quoted in Tyrrell, *Czech Opera*, p. 218.

8 Michael Beckerman, "In Search of Czechness in Music," *19th-Century Music* X (1986–7): 67, 73.

9 Beckerman, "In Search of Czechness," p. 73.

10 Quoted in Brian Large, *Smetana* (New York: Praeger, 1970), p. 209.

11 César Cui, "Muzïkal'nïye zametki: 'Prodannaya Nevesta', komicheskaya opera g. Smetanï," *Sankt-Peterburgskiye vedomosti*, 6 January 1871.

12 Carl Dahlhaus, *Between Romanticism and Modernism*, trans. Mary Whittall (Berkeley and Los Angeles: University of California Press, 1980), p. 89.

13 Dahlhaus, *Between Romanticism and Modernism*, pp. 87–88.

14 Glinka to Nestor Kukolnik, 18 April 1845, in M. I. Glinka, *Pis'ma i dokumentï* (Leningrad: Muzgiz, 1953), p. 276.

15 Diary entry, 27 June 1888; quoted in David Brown, *Mikhail Glinka: A Biographical and Critical Study* (London: Oxford University Press, 1974), p. 1.

16 Anton Rubinstein, *Muka i yeyo predstaviteli* (Moscow: P. Jurgenson, 1891), pp. 40, 83–84.

17 V. V. Stasov, "Slavyanskiy kontsert g. Balakireva," *Sankt-Peterburgskiye vedomosti*, 13 May 1867; in Stasov, *Izbrannïye sochineniya*, Vol. I (Moscow: Iskusstvo, 1952), p. 173.

18 Leonard B. Meyer, "Universalism and Relativism in the Study of Ethnic Music," *Ethnomusicology* IV, no. 2 (1960): 49–54.

19 "Ispolin prosïpayetsya," *Kolokol*, no 110 (1 November 1861); in Alexander Herzen, *Sochineniya*, Vol. VII (Moscow: Izdatel'stvo Akademii Nauk SSSR, 1958), p. 392.

20 See A. S. Lyapunova, ed., *M. A. Balakirev i V. V. Stasov: Perepiska*, Vol. I (Moscow: Muzïka, 1970), p. 27.

21 E. L. Frid, "Simfonicheskoye tvorchestvo," in *Miliy Alekseyevich Balakirev: Issledovaniya i stat'i* (Leningrad: Muzgiz, 1961), p. 136.

22 Lyapunova, ed., *M. A. Balakirev i V. V. Stasov: Perepiska*, Vol. I, p. 262.

23 Quoted in Lyapunova, ed., *M. A. Balakirev i V. V. Stasov: Perepiska*, Vol. II, 279.

24 Quoted in Frid, "Simfonicheskoye tvorchestvo," p. 132.

25 *Ibid.*

26 Friedrich Nietzsche, *The Wanderer and His Shadow* (1880), in *The Philosophy of Nietzsche*, ed. Geoffrey Clive (New York: New American Library, 1965), p. 303.

CHAPTER 42: DEEDS OF MUSIC MADE VISIBLE (CLASS OF 1813, I)

1 Thomas Mann, "Sufferings and Greatness of Richard Wagner"; in *The Thomas Mann Reader*, ed. J. W. Angell (New York: Knopf, 1950), p. 420.

2 Richard Wagner, *My Life* (New York: Dodd, Mead and Company, 1927), p. 234.

3 Wagner to Liszt, 5 July 1855; *Correspondence of Wagner and Liszt*, Vol. II, trans. Francis Hueffer (New York: Scribners, 1897), pp. 102–3.

4 Carl Dahlhaus, *Richard Wagner's Music Dramas*, trans. Mary Whittall (Cambridge: Cambridge University Press, 1979), p. 4.

5 Wagner, *My Life* (New York: Dodd, Mead and Company, 1927), pp. 214–15.

6 Wagner, *My Life*, p. 234.

7 *Ibid.*, p. 235.

8 Barry Millington, "Tannhäuser," in *New Grove Dictionary of Opera*, Vol. IV (London: Macmillan, 1992), p. 650.

9 Carolyn Abbate, *Unsung Voices: Opera and Musical Narrative in the Nineteenth Century* (Princeton: Princeton University Press, 1991), pp. 98–117.

10 Wagner, *My Life*, p. 266.

11 *Richard Wagner's Prose Works*, Vol. I, trans. William Ashton Ellis (London: K. Paul, Trench, Trübner, 1895), p. 35.

12 *Ibid.*, p. 37.

13 *Ibid.*, p. 47.

14 *Ibid.*, p. 52.

15 *Ibid.*, p. 53.

16 Edward Gibbon, *The Decline and Fall of the Roman Empire*, Vol. III, Chap. xxviii, Part 3.

17 *Richard Wagner's Prose Works*, Vol. I, pp. 53–54.

18 *Ibid.*, p. 56.

19 *Ibid.*, pp. 57–58.

20 Richard Wagner, "A Communication to My Friends," in *Richard Wagner's Prose Works*, Vol. I, p. 357.

21 *Ibid.*, pp. 375–58.

22 Barry Millington, "The Music: Operas," in *The Wagner Compendium: A Guide to Wagner's Life and Music*, ed. B. Millington (New York: Schirmer, 1992), p. 285.

23 Franz Brendel in the *Neue Zeitschrift für Musik*, 1845; quoted *ibid.*

24 *Richard Wagner's Prose Works*, Vol. I, p. 380.

25 Abbate, *Unsung Voices*, p. 158.

26 *Richard Wagner's Prose Works*, Vol. I, pp. 389–90.

27 *Ibid.*, p. 390.

28 Mann, "Sufferings and Greatness," p. 423.

29 Carolyn Abbate, classroom lecture overheard at Princeton University, November 1993.

30 *Richard Wagner's Prose Works*, Vol. I, pp. 367–76, condensed.

31 William Mann, "Down with Visiting Cards" (1965), in *Penetrating Wagner's Ring*, ed. John L. DiGaetani (New York: Da Capo Press, 1978), p. 303.

32 Jean Cocteau, "Cock and Harlequin," in *A Call to Order*, trans. Rollo Myers (London: Faber and Gwyer, 1926), p. 32.

33 Bryan Magee, *Aspects of Wagner* (New York: Stein and Day, 1969), p. 57.

34 Wagner to King Ludwig II of Bavaria, 5 May 1870, quoted in Richard Wagner, *Götterdämmerung*, translation and commentary by Rudolph Sabor (London: Phaidon, 1997), p. 23.

35 *Ibid.*

36 Adapted from the synopsis of *Götterdämmerung* by Peggy Cochrane in booklet accompanying the London/Decca recording under Georg Solti (1965).

37 See Gary Saul Morson and Caryl Emerson, *Mikhail Bakhtin: Creation of a Prosaics* (Stanford: Stanford University Press, 1990), pp. 419–23.

38 Richard Wagner, *Das Rheingold*, translation and commentary by Rudolph Sabor (London: Phaidon, 1997), p. 169.

39 Nikolai Rimsky-Korsakov, "Wagner: Sovokupnoye proizvedeniye dvukh iskusstv; ili, Muzïkaľnaya drama," *Polnoye sobraniy sochineniy Literaturnïye proizvedeniya i perepiska* (Moscow: Muzgiz, 1963), p. 54.

40 *Ibid.*, p. 57.

41 *Richard Wagner's Prose Works*, Vol. V, trans. W. Ashton Ellis (London: Kegan Paul, Trench, Trübner and Co., 1896), p. 303.

42 Marie Henri Beyle (pseudo. Stendhal), "De l'amour" (1822), Bk. I, Chap. 23.

43 Karol Berger, *A Theory of Art* (New York: Oxford University Press, 1999), pp. 33–34.

44 Søren Kierkegaard, *Either/Or* (1843), Vol. I, trans. Howard V. Hong and Edna H. Hong (Princeton: Princeton University Press, 1987), p. 64.

45 Arthur Schopenhauer, *The World as Will and Representation*, Vol. I (1819), trans. E. F. J. Payne (New York: Dover, 1969), p. 263.

46 Eduard Hanslick, *On the Musically Beautiful* (1854), trans. Geoffrey Payzant (Indianapolis: Hackett, 1986), p. 50.

47 Bryan Magee, *Confessions of a Philosopher* (New York: Random House, 1997), p. 270.

48 Richard Wagner, *Nachgelassene Schriften und Dichtungen* (Leipzig, 1895), pp. 163–64; trans. Piero Weiss in P. Weiss and R. Taruskin, *Music in the Western World: A History in Documents* (New York: Schirmer, 1984), pp. 376–77.

49 *Ibid.* p. 377.

50 See Heinrich Schenker, *Der Tonwille: Pamphlets in Witness of the Immutable Laws of Music* (1921–1923), trans. and ed. William Drabkin (New York: Oxford University Press, 2004).

51 Clara Schumann, diary entry (Munich, 8 September 1875); in Irving Kolodin, ed., *The Composer as Listener* (New York: Collier, 1962), pp. 206–7.

52 Shakespeare, *Hamlet*, Act III, sc. 1, lines 63–64.

53 Cf. Friedrich Nietzsche, *Beyond Good & Evil: Prelude to a Philosophy of the Future* (1886).

54 Magee, *Confessions of a Philosopher*, p. 269.

55 Slogan attributed (or misattributed) not only to Adolf Hitler but to a wide variety of English writers, including D. H. Lawrence and Rudyard Kipling.

56 Camille Saint-Saëns, *Harmonie et Mélodie* (1885); quoted in Robert Hartford, ed., *Bayreuth: The Early Years* (Cambridge: Cambridge University Press, 1980), pp. 57–58.

CHAPTER 43: ARTIST, POLITICIAN, FARMER (CLASS OF 1813, II)

1 Franz Werfel and Paul Stefan, eds., *Verdi: The Man in His Letters*, trans. Edward Downes (New York: Vienna House, 1973), p. 305.

2 *Ibid.*, p. 310.

3 Verdi to Franco Faccio, 14 July 1889; *Ibid.*, p. 392.

4 Felix Philippi, "Begegnung mit Verdi," *Berliner Tagblatt*, 13 July 1913; in Marcello Conati, ed., *Encounters with Verdi*, trans. Richard Stokes (Ithaca, N.Y.: Cornell University Press, 1984), pp. 328–29.

5 Pyotr Chaikovsky to Modest Chaikovsky, quoted in Alexander Poznansky, *Tchaikovsky: The Quest for the Inner Man* (New York: Schirmer, 1991), p. 181.

6 Verdi to Clarina Maffei, 9 April 1873; *Verdi: The Man in His Letters*, p. 322.

7 Arnold Schoenberg, "National Music," in *Style and Idea*, ed. Leonard Stein, trans. Leo Black (Berkeley and Los Angeles: University of California Press, 1984), p. 172.

8 Martin Gregor-Dellin and Dietrich Mack, eds., *Cosima Wagner's Diaries*, Vol. I (New York: Harcourt Brace Jovanovich, 1976), pp. 335–36.

9 Julian Budden, *The Operas of Verdi*, Vol. I (New York: Praeger, 1973), p. 40.

10 Roger Parker, "Ernani," in *New Grove Dictionary of Opera*, Vol. II (London: Macmillan, 1992), p. 71.

11 Giuseppe Mazzini, "Byron and Goethe," trans. A. Rutherford, quoted in David Kimbell, *Verdi in the Age of Italian Romanticism* (Cambridge: Cambridge University Press, 1981), p. 12.

12 Kimbell, *Verdi in the Age of Italian Romanticism*, p. 16ff.

13 Morse Peckham, *Romanticism and Ideology* (Hanover, N.H.: University Press of New England, 1995), p. 37.

14 Quoted in Carlo Gatti, *Verdi*, Vol. I (Milan: Alpes, 1931), p. 107.

15 R. Parker, *Leonora's Last Act: Essays in Verdian Discourse* (Princeton: Princeton University Press, 1997), p. 33.

16 Alessandro Manzoni, "Lettre à M. C***," quoted in Piero Weiss, "Verdi and the Fusion of Genres," *JAMS* XXXV (1982): 141.

17 George Steiner, "Maestro," *The New Yorker*, 19 April 1982, p. 171.

18 Weiss, "Verdi and the Fusion of Genres," p. 150ff.

19 Verdi to Cammarano, 4 April 1851; quoted in Budden, *The Operas of Verdi*, Vol. II (New York: Oxford University Press, 1979), p. 61.

20 John Warrack and Sandro Corti, "Duprez," in *New Grove Dictionary of Opera*, Vol. I, p. 1281.

21 Quoted in Philip Gossett, "Scandal and Scholarship," *The New Republic*, 2 July 2001, p. 30.

22 Steiner, "Maestro," p. 171.

23 Quoted in Weiss, "Verdi and the Fusion of Genres," p. 152.

24 Etienne Béquet, *Jounal des Débats*, 24 November 1832; quoted in Weiss, "Verdi and the Fusion of Genres," p. 153.

25 Verdi to Antonio Somma, 22 April 1953; quoted in Budden, *The Operas of Verdi*, Vol. I, pp. 483–84.

26 Weiss, "Verdi and the Fusion of Genres," p. 155.

27 Quoted in Weiss, "Verdi and the Fusion of Genres," pp. 155–56.

28 Budden, *The Operas of Verdi*, Vol. I, p. 510.

29 Verdi to Camille du Locle, 24 February 1874; Alessandro Luzio, ed, *Carteggi verdiani*, Vol. IV (Rome, 1947), 176n.

30 Leonard B. Meyer, "A Pride of Prejudices; or, Delight in Diversity," *Music Theory Spectrum* XIII (1991): 241.

31 Verdi to the mayor of Parma, 29 April 1891; *Verdi: The Man in His Letters*, p. 401.

32 Budden, *The Operas of Verdi*, Vol. III (New York: Oxford University Press, 1981), p. 354.

33 William Blake, "Several Questions Answered" (*Songs of Experience*, 1794).

34 Verdi to Giulio Ricordi, 21 January 1888; quoted in Budden, *The Operas of Verdi*, Vol. III, p. 398.

35 Hermann Laroche (German Larosh), review of *The Stone Guest*, in *Vestnik YEvropï*, no. 4 (1872), p. 895.

CHAPTER 44: CUTTING THINGS DOWN TO SIZE

1 Musorgsky to V. V. Nikolsky, 15 August 1868; in M. P. Musorgsky, *Literaturnoye naslediye*, Vol. I, eds. Mikhail Pekelis and Alexandra Orlova, (Moscow: Muzïka, 1971), pp. 102–103.

2 Musorgsky to N. A. Rimsky-Korsakov, 30 July 1868; Musorgsky, *Literaturnoye naslediye*, Vol. I, p. 102.

3 Nikolai G. Chernyshevsky, "The Aesthetic Relation of Art to Reality" (1855), in N. G. Chernyshevsky, *Selected Philosophical Essays* (Moscow: Foreign Languages Publishing House, 1953), p. 379.

4 Hermann Laroche (German Larosh), "Mïslyashchiy realist v russkoy opere," *Golos* (St. Petersburg), 13 February 1874.

5 Musorgsky to V. V. Stasov, 13 June 1872; Musorgsky, *Literaturnoye naslediye*, Vol. I, p. 132.

6 Musorgsky to V. V. Stasov, 18 October 1872; *Literaturnoye naslediye*, Vol. I, p. 141.

7 See R. Taruskin, "Realism as Preached and Practiced: The Russian *Opéra dialogué*," *Musical Quarterly* LVI (1970): 434–37.

8 See César Cui, "Opernïy sezon v Peterburge" (1864); in Cui, *Izbrannïye stat'i* (Leningrad: Muzgizm 1952), p. 36.

9 Musorgsky to Rimsky-Korsakov, 23 July 1870; *Literaturnoye naslediye*, Vol. I, p. 117.

10 Musorgsky to V. V. Stasov, 10 August 1871; *Literaturnoye naslediye*, Vol. I, p. 122.

11 Joseph Kerman, *Opera as Drama* (rev. ed.; Berkeley and Los Angeles: University of California Press, 1988), p. 226.

12 Friedrich Nietzsche, *The Case of Wagner* (condensed), trans. Walter Kaufmann (New York: Vintage Books, 1967), pp. 157–59.

13 Peter Kropotkin, *Memoirs of a Revolutionist* (Boston: Houghton Mifflin, 1899), p. 209.

14 César Cui, "Neskol'ko slov o sovremmenïkh opernïkh formakh" (1889), *Izbrannïye stat'i*, p. 408.

15 Michael Tanner, "Singing the Status Quo," *Times Literary Supplement*, 12 April 1991, p. 15.

16 *New Grove Dictionary of Opera*, Vol. III (London: Macmillan, 1992), p. 719.

17 G. B. Shaw in *The World*; quoted in Arthur Jacobs, *Arthur Sullivan: A Victorian Musician* (2nd ed., Portland: Amadeus Press, 1992), p. 335.

18 Gabriele D'Annunzio, "Il capobanda," *Il Mattino* (Naples), 2 September 1892.

19 "G. B.," "Beseda s Chaikovskim," *Peterburgskaya zhizn'*, no. 2 (1892); in P. I. Chaikovsky, *Muzïkal'no-kriticheskiye stat'i*, (4th ed., Leningrad: Muzïka, 1986), p. 319.

20 Julian Budden, "Puccini," in *New Grove Dictionary of Opera*, Vol. III (London: Macmillan, 1992), p. 1171.

21 *Ibid.*

22 *Ibid.*

CHAPTER 45: THE RETURN OF THE SYMPHONY

1 *Richard Wagner's Prose Works*, Vol. I, trans. W. Ashton Ellis (London: Kegan Paul, Trench, Trübner, 1895), p. 126.

2 Martin Cooper, *French Music from the Death of Berlioz to the Death of Fauré* (London: Oxford University Press, 1951), p. 11.

3 Emil Naumann, *The History of Music*, Vol. V, trans. F. Praeger (London: Cassell & Co., n.d.), p. 1193.

4 Naumann, *The History of Music*, p. 1194.

5 D. Charlton, "Paris," in *New Grove Dictionary of Music and Musicians*, Vol. XIX (2nd ed., New York: Grove, 2001), p. 108.

6 See Willaim Weber, "Mass Culture and the Reshaping of European Musical Taste, 1770–1870," *International Journal of the Aesthetics and Sociology of Music* VIII (1977): 5–21.

7 J. Peter Burkholder, "Museum Pieces: the Historicist Mainstream in Music of the Last Hundred Years," *Journal of Musicology* II (1983): 120.

8 William Weber, "Mass Culture and the Reshaping of Musical Taste, 1770–1870," *International Review of the Aesthetics and Sociology of Music* VIII (1977): 15.

9 Burkholder, "Museum Pieces," p. 119.

10 J. Peter Burkholder, "Brahms and Twentieth-Century Classical Music," *19th-Century Music* VIII (1984–5): 81.

11 *Ibid.*, p. 76.

12 Schumann, "Neue Bahnen," in Oliver Strunk, *Source Readings in Music History* (New York: Norton, 1950), p. 844.

13 Joseph Joachim to Franz Liszt, 27 August 1857; quoted in Alan Walker, *Franz Liszt: The Weimar Years 1848–1861* (Ithaca, N.Y.: Cornell University Press, 1993), p. 347.

14 Quoted in Walter Niemann, *Brahms*, trans. C. A. Phillips (New York: Tudor, 1929), p. 77.

15 Bernhard Scholz, *Verklungene Weisen* (Mainz, 1911), p. 142; quoted in David Brodbeck, *Brahms: Symphony No. 1* (Cambridge: Cambridge University Press, 1997), p. 96n28.

16 Clara Schumann to Brahms, 21 June 1860; quoted in Brodbeck, *Brahms: Symphony No. 1*, p. 9.

17 Robert Schumann to Joseph Joachim, 6 January 1854; quoted in Brodbeck, *Brahms: Symphony No. 1*, p. 2.

18 Remark to Hermann Levi, October 1871, reported in Max Kalbeck, *Brahms*, Vol. I (Berlin, 1915), p. 165; quoted in Brodbeck, *Brahms: Symphony No. 1*, p. 15.

19 Quoted in Rosen, *The Romantic Generation*, p. 93.

20 Donald Francis Tovey, *Essays in Musical Analysis*, Vol. I (London: Oxford University Press, 1935), p. 123.

21 Clara Schumann to Joseph Joachim, 1 July 1862; quoted in Brodbeck, *Brahms: Symphony No. 1*, p. 10.

22 Quoted in Brodbeck, *Brahms: Symphony No. 1*, pp. 16, 98n1.

23 See Robert W. Fink, "Desire, Repression, and Brahms's First Symphony," *Repercussions* 2 (1993), pp. 75–103.

24 Brahms to Karl Reinthaler, October 1871; quoted in John Daverio, "The *Wechsel der Töne*" in Brahms's "*Schicksalslied*," *JAMS* XLVI (1993): 90.

25 Brahms to Reinthaler, quoted in Daverio, "*Wechsel der Töne*," p. 86.

26 *Richard Wagner's Prose Works*, Vol. IV (London: Kegan Paul, Trench, Trübner, 1895), pp. 348–50.

27 Raymond Knapp, review of Johannes Brahms, *Symphonie Nr. 1, C-moll, opus 68*, ed. Robert Pascall, *MLA Notes* LIV (1997–98): 554.

28 *Richard Wagner's Prose Works*, Vol. I, p. 126.

29 The postcard is reproduced in facsimile in Brodbeck, *Brahms: Symphony No. 1*, p. 15.

30 Quoted in Kalbeck, *Brahms*, Vol. III (rpt. Tutzing, 1976), p. 109n.

31 David Brodbeck, *Brahms: Symphony No. 1*, pp. 67–68.

32 Friedrich Chrysander, performance review, *Allgemeine musikalische Zeitung*, Vol. XIII (1878), col. 94; quoted in Brodbeck, *Brahms: Symphony No. 1*, p. 86.

33 Reinhold Brinkmann, *Late Idyll: The Second Symphony of Johannes Brahms*, trans. Peter Palmer (Cambridge: Harvard University Press, 1995), p. 41.

34 Chrysander, quoted in Brodbeck, *Brahms: Symphony No. 1*, p. 86.

35 Brinkmann, *Late Idyll*, p. 45.

36 Quoted in Brodbeck, *Brahms: Symphony No. 1*, p. 85.

37 *Richard Wagner's Prose Works*, Vol. VI (London: Kegan Paul, Trench, Trübner, 1897), p. 148.

38 Theodor Billroth to Brahms, 10 December 1876; *Johannes Brahms and Theodor Billroth: Letters from a Musical Friendship*, trans. Hans Barkan (Norman: University of Oklahoma Press, 1957), p. 41.

39 Carl Dahlhaus, *Nineteenth-Century Music*, trans. J. Bradford Robinson (Berkeley and Los Angeles: University of California Press, 1989), p. 260.

40 Carl Dahlhaus, *Between Romanticism and Modernism*, trans. Mary Whittall (Berkeley and Los Angeles: University of California Press, 1980), p. 41.

41 Walter Frisch, *Brahms and the Principle of Developing Variation* (Berkeley and Los Angeles: University of California Press, 1984), p. 114.

CHAPTER 46: THE SYMPHONY GOES (INTER)NATIONAL

1 Eduard Hanslick, *Music Criticisms 1846–99*, trans. Henry Pleasants (Baltimore: Peregrine Books, 1963), p. 243.

2 Gian Francesco Malipiero, quoted in John C. G. Waterhouse, "Martucci," in *New Grove Dictionary of Music and Musicians*, Vol. XVI (2nd ed., New York: Grove, 2001), p. 10.

3 Quoted in Carl Dahlhaus, *Nineteenth-Century Music*, trans. J. Bradford Robinson (Berkeley and Los Angeles: University of California Press, 1989), p. 271.

4 Hans-Hubert Schönzeler, *Bruckner* (New York: Vienna House, 1978), p. 65.

5 Deryck Cooke, "Bruckner," in *New Grove Dictionary of Music and Musicians*, Vol. III (London: Macmillan, 1980), p. 364.

6 Quoted in Schönzeler, *Bruckner*, p. 80.

7 Josef Jan Kovařík to Otakar Šourek; quoted in Michael Beckerman, "The Master's Little Joke: Antonín Dvořák and the Mask of Nation," in *Dvořák* and *His World*, ed. Michael Beckerman (Princeton: Princeton University Press, 1993), p. 135.

8 Dahlhaus, *Nineteenth-Century Music*, p. 154.

9 *New York Herald*, 15 December 1893; quoted in Michael Beckerman, "Dvořák's 'New World' Largo and *The Song of Hiawatha*," *19th-Century Music* XVI (1992–93): 36.

10 *Ibid.*

11 Dvořák to Emil Kozanek, 12 April 1893; Otakar Šourek, *Dvorak in Letters and Reminiscences* (Prague: Artia, 1954), p. 158.

12 *New York Daily Tribune*, 17 December 1893, p. 7; quoted in Michael Beckerman, "Henry Krehbiel, Antonín Dvořák, and the Symphony 'From the New World,'" *MLA Notes* XLIX (1992–93): 471.

13 *New York Herald*, 15 December 1893; quoted in Beckerman, "Dvořák's 'New World' Largo and *The Song of Hiawatha*," p. 36.

14 Quoted in Lawrence Gilman, *Edward MacDowell* (New York: John Lane, 1908), p. 84.

15 Quoted in Adrienne Fried Block, *Amy Beach: Passionate Victorian* (New York: Oxford University Press, 1998), p. 103.

16 *Boston Herald*, 28 May 1893; quoted in Block, *Amy Beach*, p. 87.

17 *The Boston Courier*; quoted in Walter S. Jenkins, *The Remarkable Mrs. Beach, American Composer* (Warren, Mich.: Harmonie Park Press, 1994), p. 38.

18 Macdonald Smith Moore, *Yankee Blues: Musical Culture and American Identity* (Bloomington: Indiana University Press, 1985), p. 3.

19 Edward Burlingame Hill, *Modern French Music* (Boston: Houghton Mifflin, 1924), p. 35.

20 *Ibid.*, p. 38.

21 *Ibid.*, p. 36.

22 *Ibid.*, p. 35.

23 Dahlhaus, *Nineteenth-Century Music*, p. 283.

24 Quoted in Brian Rees, *Camille Saint-Saëns: A Life* (London: Chatto and Windus, 1999), p. 161.

25 See Vincent D'Indy, *César Franck*, trans. Rosa Newmarch (London: John Lane, 1910), pp. 91, 171.

26 Charles O'Connell, *The Victor Book of the Symphony* (New York: Simon and Schuster, 1941), p. 235.

27 Deems Taylor, *Of Men and Music* (New York: Simon and Schuster, 1937), p. xviii.

28 Peter Applebome, "A Humanist and Elitist? Perhaps," *New York Times*, 18 April 1998, p. A15.

29 Emil Naumann, *The History of Music*, Vol. V, trans. F. Praeger (London: Cassell & Co., n.d.), p. 1245.

30 Dahlhaus, *Nineteenth-Century Music*, p. 290.

31 Bertolt Brecht, "On the Use of Music in an Epic Theater," in *Brecht on Theater*, ed. J. Willet (New York: Hill and Wang, 1964), p. 89.

32 César Cui, "Pervïye kompozitorskiye shagi Ts. A. Kyui," in Cui, *Izbrannïye stat'i* (Leningrad: Muzgiz, 1952), p. 544.

33 Jean-Jacques Rousseau, *Second Discourse*, quoted in Lionel Trilling, *Sincerity and Authenticity* (Cambridge: Harvard University Press, 1972), p. 62.

34 Rosa Newmarch, *The Russian Opera* (New York: E. P. Dutton, n.d. [1914]), p. 200.

35 Chaikovsky to Nadezhda von Meck, 27 November 1877, P. I. Chaikovsky, *Perepiska s N. F. fon-Mekk*, Vol. I (Moscow: Academia, 1934), pp. 100–101.

36 David Brown, *Tchaikovsky*, Vol. IV (New York: Norton, 1991), p. 10.

37 Brown, *Tchaikovsky*, Vol. I (New York: Norton, 1978), p. 108.

38 Chaikovsky to Nadezhda von Meck, 18 February 1880; Chaikovsky, *Polnoye sobraniye sochineniy: Literaturnïye proizvedeniya i perepiska*, Vol. IX (Moscow: Muzgiz, 1962), p. 56.

39 Chaikovsky to Grand Duke Konstantin Konstantinovich, 21 September 1888; Chaikovsky, *Polnoye sobraniye sochineniy: Literaturnïye proizvedeniya i perepiska*, Vol. XIV (Moscow: Muzïka, 1974), p. 542.

40 Chaikovsky to Nadezhda von Meck, 17 February 1878; Chaikovsky, *Polnoye sobraniye sochineniy: Literaturnïye proizvedeniya i perepiska*, Vol. VII (Moscow: Muzgiz, 1962), pp. 126–27.

41 *Ibid.*, p. 124.

42 Sergey Taneyev to P. I. Chaikovsky, 18 March 1878; quoted in Modest Chaikovsky, *Life and Letters of Tchaikovsky*, Vol. I (New York: Vienna House, 1973), p. 292.

43 Chaikovsky to P. I. Jurgenson, 18 October 1893; *Life and Letters of Tchaikovsky*, Vol. II, p. 722.

44 David Brown, John Purdie, Alan Kendall, all quoted in R. Taruskin, "Pathetic Symphonist: Chaikovsky, Russia, Sexuality and the Study of Music," *The New Republic*, 6 February 1995, p. 40.

45 Chaikovsky to P. I. Jurgenson, 12 August 1893; *Life and Letters of Tchaikovsky*, Vol. II, p. 715.

46 *Life and Letters of Tchaikovsky*, Vol. II, p. 722.

Art Credits

35-1   Mortiz von Schwind, Bayerische Staatsgemaldesammlungen, Schack-Galerie Munich.

35-2   Ludwig Erk, *Deutscher Liederschatz* (Leipzig: C. F. Peters, c. 1882), Vol. 1, pp. 150–51.

35-3   Johann Joseph Schmeller, 1830, © Bildarchiv Preussischer Kulturbesitz, Berlin, 2003.

35-4   General Research Division, New York Public Library, Astor, Lenox, and Tilden Foundations.

35-5   Sketch by Felix Mendelssohn, 1837, © Bildarchiv Preussischer Kulturbesitz, Berlin, 2003.

35-6   Werner Stein, 1892, © Bildarchiv Preussischer Kulturbesitz, Berlin, 2003.

35-7   Wilhelm Hensel, 1829, © Bildarchiv Preussischer Kulturbesitz, Berlin, 2003.

36-1   Engraving by C. A. Schwerdgeburth, 1823, after a portrait by Carl Christian Vogel von Vogelstein, The Metropolitan Museum of Art, The Crosby Brown Collection of Musical Instruments (01.2.541).

36-2   Jean-Jacques Rousseau, *Dictionnaire de musique*, 1768. Music Division, The New York Public Library for the Performing Arts, Astor, Lenox and Tilden Foundations.

36-3   Lithograph by Adam et Hostein, after Johann Heinrich Ramberg, Bibliothèque de L'Opera, Paris, Joseph Martin / www.bridgeman.co.uk.

36-4   Lithograph by Lemercier after a drawing by Achille Deveria, Music Division, The New York Public Library for the Performing Arts, Astor, Lenox and Tilden Foundations.

36-5   Félix Nadar, ca. 1855, Coursaget Collection, © Réunion des Musées Nationaux / Art Resource, NY.

36-6   Edgar Degas, 1871, The Metropolitan Museum of Art, H. O. Havemeyer Collection, Bequest of Mrs. H. O. Havemeyer, 1929 (29.100.552).

36-7   Meyerbeer Archive, Staatliches Institut für Musikforschung Preussischer Kulturbesitz, Berlin. Reproduced from Stanley Sadie, ed., *The New Grove Dictionary of Music and Musicians*, Vol. 12, p. 248.

36-8   Drawing by V. Tauber, Society for Co-operation in Russian and Soviet Studies, London.

36-9   Reproduced from Mikhail Ivanovich Glinka, *Memoirs*, trans. Richard B. Mudge (Norman: University of Oklahoma Press, 1963), p. 101.

37-1   Jean-Pierre Dantan, 1832, © Photothèque des Musées de La Ville de Paris / Andréani.

37-2   Johann Peter Lyser, 1819, General Research Division, New York Public Library, Astor, Lenox, and Tilden Foundations.

37-3   Library of Congress, Paganiniana collection.

37-4   Culver Pictures.

37-5   Franz-Liszt-Museum der Stadt Bayreuth.

37-6   Museum für Hamburgische Geschichte.

38-1   Drawing by Eduard Bendemann after daguerreotype by Johann
        Anton Völlner, March 1850, Hamburg, Robert-Schumann-Haus
        Zwickau; Archiv-Nr.: 6024-B2.

38-2   Daguerreotype by Johann Anton Völlner, March 1850, Hamburg,
        Musée d'Orsay, Paris, © Réunion des Musées Nationaux / Art
        Resource, NY.

38-3   Wilhelm Hensel, 1829, Kupferstichkabinett, Staatliche Museen zu
        Berlin, Bildarchiv Preussischer Kulturbesitz / Art Resource, NY.

38-4   Robert-Schumann-Haus Zwickau; Archive-Nr.: 10463-C3/A3/A4;
        Programmsammlung Clara Schumanns, Nr. 290.

38-5   Philipp Veit, ca. 1805, © Bildarchiv Preussischer Kulturbesitz,
        Berlin, 2003.

38-6   Robert-Schumann-Haus Zwickau; o. Archiv-Nr.

38-7   Engraving by E. Metzmacher after photograph by Félix Nadar, 1857,
        Metropolitan Museum of Art, Crosby Brown Collection of Musical
        Instruments, 1901 (01.2.17).

38-8   Woodcut by Dumont, 1856, after drawing by Gustav Doré,
        akg-images.

38-9   Victoria and Albert Picture Library.

38-10   Sebastian Erard, ca. 1860, Metropolitan Museum of Art, Gift of
        Lyon and Healy, 1949 (49.31).

38-11   Anonymous, 18th century, Museé de la Ville de Paris, Museé
        Carnavalet, Paris, © Giraudon / Art Resource, NY.

39-1   Jan Styka, cliché Bibliothèque nationale de France.

39-2   Hendrik Siemirdzki, 1887, cliché Bibliothèque nationale de France.

39-3   Drawing by E. Radziwill at the Chopin Society, Warsaw, cliché
        Bibliothèque nationale de France.

39-4   Maurice Dudevant, 1844, akg-images.

39-5   Eugène Delacroix, Louvre, Paris, © Erich Lessing / Art
        Resource, NY.

39-6   Frédéric Chopin, *Quatre mazurkas pour le pianoforte*,Op. 6 (Leipzig: Fr.
        Kistner, 1832). Special Collections, Rare Books, University of
        Chicago Library.

39-7   Henry Louis Stephens, copy after Louis Moreau Gottschalk,
        engraving by Bobbett & Hooper Wood Engraving Company, ©
        National Portrait Gallery, Smithsonian Institution / Art
        Resource, NY.

39-8   Thomas Hicks, ca. 1850, © National Portrait Gallery, Smithsonian
        Institution / Art Resource, NY.

39-9   cliché Bibliothèque nationale de France.

39-10	© Snark / Art Resource, NY.
40-1	National Archives of the Richard Wagner Foundation, Bayreuth.
40-2	Lithograph by Julius Ludwig Sebbers, © Bildarchiv Preussischer Kulturbesitz, Berlin, 2003.
40-3	Lithograph by C. Fischer after painting by Casanova, © Bildarchiv Preussischer Kulturbesitz, Berlin, 2003.
40-4a	General Research Division, New York Public Library, Astor, Lenox, and Tilden Foundations.
40-4b	General Research Division, New York Public Library, Astor, Lenox, and Tilden Foundations.
40-5	Henri Decaisne, Musée Municipal, Macon, © Giraudon / Art Resource, NY.
40-6	Collection of the author.
40-7	Collection of the author.
41-1	Photograph ca. 1886, Czech Museum of Music, Bedřich Smetana Museum, Prague, S 217/17411.
41-2a	National Museum, Prague. AKG Images.
41-2b	Design by Brioschi, Burghardt, Kautsky. Czech Museum of Music, Bedřich Smetana Museum, Prague, č.př. 17/2003.
41-3	Reproduced from Victor Tsukkerman, *"Kamarinskaya" Glinki i eë traditsii v russkoi muzyke* (Moscow, 1957), p. 353.
41-4	Collection of the author.
42-1	August Friedrich Pecht, The Metropolitan Museum of Art, Gift of Frederick Loeser, 1889 (89.8).
42-2	© Bildarchiv Preussischer Kulturbesitz, Berlin, 2003.
42-3	Julius Schnorr von Carosfeld, Bibliothèque Nationale.
42-4	Library of Congress, Gertrude Clarke Whittall Foundation.
42-5	M. Ferdinandus, cliché Bibliothèque nationale de France.
42-6	Gustav Kobbé, *Opera Singers: A Pictorial Souvenir, with Biographies of Some of the Most Famous Singers of the Day.* New York: R. H. Russell, 1901, 1913.
42-7	National Archives of the Richard Wagner Foundation, Bayreuth.
42-8	National Archives of the Richard Wagner Foundation, Bayreuth.
42-9	National Archives of the Richard Wagner Foundation, Bayreuth.
42-10	Gustav Kobbé, *Opera Singers: A Pictorial Souvenir, with Biographies of Some of the Most Famous Singers of the Day.* New York: R. H. Russell, 1901, 1913.
42-11	© Bildarchiv Preussischer Kulturbesitz, Berlin, 2003.
42-12	Gustav Kobbé, *Opera Singers: A Pictorial Souvenir, with Biographies of Some of the Most Famous Singers of the Day.* New York: R. H. Russell, 1901, 1913.
42-13	© Bildarchiv Preussischer Kulturbesitz, Berlin, 2003.
42-14	© Bildarchiv Preussischer Kulturbesitz, Berlin, 2003.

43-1   Giovanni Boldini, Galleria Nazionale d'Arte Moderna, Rome, ©
       Scala / Art Resource, NY.

43-2   Gustav Kobbé, *Opera Singers: A Pictorial Souvenir, with Biographies of
       Some of the Most Famous Singers of the Day*. New York: R. H. Russell,
       1901, 1913.

43-3   Ladislaus Rupp, Museo Teatrale alla Scala, Milan, © Scala / Art
       Resource, NY.

43-4   Parma, Istituto Nazionale di Studi Verdiani.

43-5   Milan: Ricordi, 1853, Museo Teatrale alla Scala, Milan, © Scala / Art
       Resource, NY.

43-6   Milan: Ricordi, 1851, Library of Congress.

43-7   Parma, Istituto Nazionale di Studi Verdiani.

43-8   Raccolta Bertarelli, Milan, © David Lees/CORBIS.

43-9   Raccolta Bertarelli, Milan, © David Lees/CORBIS.

44-1   Ilya Repin, Tretyakov Gallery, Moscow, © Scala / Art
       Resource, NY.

44-2   Collection of the author.

44-3   Metropolitan Opera photo.

44-4   Gustav Kobbé, *Opera Singers: A Pictorial Souvenir, with Biographies of
       Some of the Most Famous Singers of the Day*. New York: R. H. Russell,
       1901, 1913.

44-5   Time Life Pictures/Getty Images.

44-6   Émile Bertin, cliché Bibliothèque nationale de France.

44-7   cliché Bibliothèque nationale de France.

44-8   The Gilbert and Sullivan Collection. © The Pierpont Morgan
       Library / Art Resource, NY.

44-9   Museo Teatrale alla Scala, Milan, © Scala / Art Resource, NY.

44-10 Metropolitan Opera Archives.

44-11 Metropolitan Opera Archives.

44-12 Milan: Ricordi, 1924, Museo Teatrale alla Scala, Milan, © Scala /
       Art Resource, NY.

45-1   Historisches Museum der Stadt Wien, Vienna, © by Direktion der
       Museen der Stadt Wien.

45-2   Josef Ludwig Novak, Historisches Museum der Stadt Wien,
       Vienna, © Erich Lessing / Art Resource, NY.

45-3   Bildarchiv d. ÖNB, Wien.

45-4   Reproduced from Robert Haven Schauffler, *The Unknown Brahms*
       (New York: Dodd, Mead, 1933). Original photography courtesy of
       Eugen von Miller zu Aichholz.

45-5   Historisches Museum der Stadt Wien, Vienna, © by Direktion der
       Museen der Stadt Wien.

45-6   Library of Congress.